Contents

In memory of Dr Hugh Brendan Davies
3 August 1948-11 October 2000

Hugh was born in 1948 in Edinburgh; his parents were teachers. He became a prize-winning student of Economics at Edinburgh University and went on to do a PhD at the University of Pennsylvania, being one of Robert Pollak's "brightest students". In 1974 he was recruited as a lecturer in the young Economics Department at Birkbeck College, London. For most of the past quarter of a century he continued to be a mainstay of the Birkbeck Economics Department, an inspiring and respected teacher, and a provider of pastoral guidance and advice. He was a Visiting Lecturer at Princeton University in 1977, and was seconded to the Department of Health and Social Security for a couple of years from 1978, where he helped to develop a Policy Simulation Model still in use. His boss remembered him as, "That nice Scotsman with a Welsh name".

His major contribution has been the building and re-building of a model of lifetime incomes, where the long-term consequences of various scenarios can be compared. Perhaps the most famous of these comparisons is that of Mrs Typical having two children rather than none, and thereby halving her lifetime earnings. The estimates for Mrs Typical were updated and elaborated in two major funded projects over the last five years. New parameters were produced with the help of Romana Peronaci. A new lifetime model was constructed (with the help of Randa Alami) for the Women's Unit of the Cabinet Office. The report on Women's Lifetime Incomes was published in 2000. It dealt with the gender pay gap and the consequences of caring for children, exploring their implications for poverty in childhood and old age. It has already informed the government's response to these issues and was cited at the Labour Party conference. This model alone would be an impressive monument, and it could not have been done without Hugh.

In recent years, building on this spate of research, Hugh also worked with pensions groups at Birkbeck, and taught a new course on the Economics of the Family. He was Course Director for the Postgraduate Certificate in Economics, Chair of the Library Policy Committee, and a member of many others. He was promoted to Senior Lecturer this year and was a Visiting fellow at the Centre for Longitudinal Studies, Institute of Education, University of London. He held a weekly econometric clinic at the London School of Economics and Political Science.

We hope to speak for all of us in remembering and mourning Hugh's kindness, good humour and wisdom. The love and affection of so many people for Hugh will truly outlast his leave-taking. If we can let the memory of his life inspire, his deeds of kindness and consideration, his goodness will live on.

Foreword

We have entered an era of rising inequalities. The Gini coefficient for market incomes has risen in just about all OECD countries. Only a handful of welfare states have managed to stem this tide via more redistribution – basically Scandinavia, together with France and the Netherlands. The new inegalitarian thrust is worrisome because it coincides with a sharp shift in the distribution of social risks across citizens' lifecourse, from the old to the young and, most problematic of all, to families with children.

Postindustrial society seems to play havoc with Rowntree's classical model of life cycle poverty, a model that depicted huge concentrations of poverty among older people (because of lack of work income) and among families with children (because they were very large). Older people are generally no longer at risk and, as we know, contemporary families with children are not exactly numerous. So why this novel appearance of child poverty in the advanced nations? Many point to the ominous threat of globalisation but, in reality, the causes are endogenous to our society. Families with children face growing risks in part because the new labour market is unkind to young workers and, in part, because families are less stable and often economically vulnerable. Increasingly, two earners are needed to ensure against poverty and want.

The great policy challenge we face is not simply that latter-day children are vulnerable to deprivation, but that the second-order consequences of poverty and need in childhood are ever more severe. As several chapters in this book show, economic hardship in childhood can have very troublesome ripple-effects throughout life, affecting school completion, earnings and career prospects later in life and, ultimately, well-being in retirement. Poverty and insecurity in childhood can overdetermine life chances. Research from the US shows that child poverty is associated with, perhaps, two years less education, with sharply lower wages as an adult and, worst of all, with a substantial likelihood of becoming a poor parent – thus reproducing the poverty syndrome from one generation to the next. Gregg and Machin's chapter find similar, if less devastating, effects for Britain.

It is important, however, to remember that money is only one of several catalysts of problematic life chances. Research shows that family instability, unemployment or alcoholism among parents yield similarly negative consequences. In any case, the life-chance penalty of a problematic childhood is probably rising for one simple reason, namely that knowledge-intensive economies 'up the ante' in terms of the human capital resources needed for a good life. Inadequate cognitive skills and educational qualifications will increasingly doom a citizen to a life of precarious employment, low wages, and spells of unemployment. In other words, the seeds of social exclusion are planted in early childhood. Hence, if we seriously want to avoid a two thirds society tomorrow we need to invest in children today. It is very well established that remedial programmes later in life are ineffective and costly, far more costly than it would be to eradicate child poverty here and now.

I use the term *investing in children* deliberately. For policy makers it is vital to recognise that public expenditures are investments – and not simply current consumption – when they yield an identifiable positive return, not just to the individuals concerned, but also to the collectivity. The well-being of today's children will have positive externalities decades hence, in part because the main competitive base of advanced economies lies in their human capital, in part because the coming cohorts will be small indeed. I, as one of the many baby-boomers, will retire in the coming decades and must therefore put my faith in the productivity and resourcefulness of tomorrow's workers (who happen to be today's children). In many OECD countries, 20 or 25% of youth fail to complete the equivalent of secondary education, and a sometimes alarming percentage possess insufficient cognitive abilities. This population, some decades down the line, is very likely to produce little, but will consume many welfare benefits.

The case in favour of public policy is usually made with reference to market failures. The presence of identifiable positive or negative externalities related to child well-being is therefore a very sound basis for concerted policy to combat poverty and need in childhood. Much of the evidence that is presented in this book points to the urgency of also considering widespread 'family failure'. Most contemporary welfare states, the Anglo Saxon and the Continental European in particular, continue to assume a family model that is, for all purposes, becoming extinct. We can no longer assume stable, lifelong partnerships; the male breadwinner can no longer guarantee adequate welfare for his kin; the full-time housewife is rapidly disappearing; and ever fewer children will grow up with both their parents throughout childhood. Yet, welfare policy continues to assume that families will internalise most welfare responsibilities. We witness proliferating family failure because more and more families lack the resources to internalise such responsibilities.

In other words, family policy remains by and large a residual in many contemporary welfare states. Residual in the sense that income support is modest or even non-existing; residual in the sense that it is too often assistential in nature, targeted to abject failures; and residual in the sense that the welfare state refrains from filling the caring gap that ensues when mothers are employed. It may appear paradoxical, but at this very historical moment, when families are small and children all the time fewer, we need more than ever an active and concerted family policy. Children may be a private good, but healthy and resourceful children are also a public good, without which our future economy will perform sub-optimally, and without which my future pension cheque will be miserably small.

The case in favour of an active investment strategy for children is easy to make on efficiency and welfare grounds. It should be obvious that it can also be made on equity grounds. If today's children are tomorrow's collective good, all will benefit from the investment. But the childless will benefit as free-riders on those who were parents. A just policy must, in other words, subsidise the cost of children by redistributing from the childless to families with children.

Children are obviously also becoming a very scarce good. The European Union, South East Asia, and Eastern Europe are all sliding towards a low-fertility equilibrium. This is not because latter-day adults embrace some kind of post-modern values that disfavour children. On the contrary, we have substantial evidence that adults in all countries desire, on average, 2.2-2.4 children. In Southern and Eastern Europe, they obtain roughly half of the desired number; in some regions, barely a third. Parenthood seems to be increasingly a utopia and I propose that we interpret contemporary fertility gaps as manifest welfare deficits. We pretty well know the underlying causes: delayed first births, the incompatibilities that women face, the lack of affordable day care. In large measure, the common denominator has to do with the changing cost-calculus of having children. Both the direct, and also the more indirect opportunity costs associated with parenthood are rising from the point of view of prospective parents. Societal welfare requires that we resolve the low-fertility equilibrium and, once again, this inevitably means that the collectivity must socialise part of the cost of children.

Social scientists have, in recent years, awakened to the disturbing trends that families with children now face. The book that Koen Vleminckx and Timothy Smeeding have put together here constitutes a scholarly climax, not only because it gives us the most exhaustive and systematic evidence so far presented, but also because it compels us to think quite radically about which kind of family policy and what kind of welfare state we will need if we seriously desire to live in a good society.

Gøsta Esping-Andersen
Barcelona, April 2003

Acknowledgements

The editors wish to thank a number of people who played a large role in this book and in the conference held in October 1999, which was organised by the Luxembourg Income Study, a division of CEPS/INSTEAD, a non-profit research centre in Differdange, Luxembourg. The editors and conference organisers were first aided by a planning committee, which helped sort through the large number of submissions, to design the conference and find some authors to fill missing holes. These included John Ditch of the University of York; Janet Gornick of Baruch College, City University of New York; Magda Mercader of the Autonomous University of Barcelona; John Micklewright, Research Director at the UNICEF Innocenti Research Centre in Florence; Lee Rainwater of Harvard University, Research Director of the Luxembourg Income Study (LIS); and Holly Sutherland of the University of Cambridge.

Others who helped with specific contributions of time and money were Gaston Schaber, President of CEPS/INSTEAD in Luxembourg; Larry Aber of the National Center for Child Poverty, Columbia University; Patricia Ruggles of the Office of the Assistant Secretary for Planning and Evaluation, Department of Health and Human Services, Washington, DC; Nancy Folbre and Robert Pollak of the MacArthur Research Network on the Family and the Economy; and Melvin Oliver, Vice President of the Ford Foundation.

The conference was run with great efficiency and in good humour by LIS administrative assistants, Caroline de Tombeur and Kati Foley, with the assistance of the LIS staff, particularly Paul Alkemade.

At The Policy Press Dawn Rushen organised the contracts, pushed us to improve the book (along with the advice of two outside referees) and generally shortened the publication lag enormously.

Finally we want to thank our own families and children: Ann, Mary Ann, Ryan, Erin, Patrick and Joseph, who paid the 'opportunity cost' of our time as we organised and managed this volume.

List of contributors

Bruce Bradbury is Senior Research Fellow at the Social Policy Research Centre, University of New South Wales, Australia. His current research includes work on inequality and poverty, income support policy design, labour supply, consumer equivalence scales and intra-household allocation behaviour.

Felix Büchel is Senior Research Scientist at the Max Planck Institute for Human Development and is affiliated to the Department of Economics at Technical University, both in Berlin, Germany. His main research interests include the economics of education, labour economics, and social policy research.

Karen Christopher is Assistant Professor at the University of Pittsburgh, USA. Her research examines the effects of the family, market and welfare state on mothers' and single mothers' poverty across Western nations. She also conducts research on US welfare reform and its effects on low-income women and their families.

John Coder is Technical Director of the Luxembourg Income Study, a division of CEPS/INSTEAD, Differdange, Luxembourg.

Candace Currie is a Reader at the University of Edinburgh, UK, based at the Child and Adolescent Health Research Unit in the Faculty of Education. She is the International Coordinator of the Health Behaviour in School-Aged Children (HBSC): WHO Cross-National Study and Principal Investigator for HBSC in Scotland.

Thai-Thanh Dang is Junior Economist in the Resource Allocation Division at the Economics Department of the Organisation for Economic Co-operation and Development (OECD). Her research interests are longitudinal poverty, income distribution, ageing and social policy issues in OECD countries.

The late **Hugh Davies** was Senior Lecturer in Economics, Birkbeck College, University of London and Visiting Fellow at the Centre for Longitudinal Studies, Institute of Education, University of London, UK. His interests included family economics, income distribution and pensions.

Paula England is Professor of Sociology at the University of Pennsylvania, USA, where she is also associated with the Population Studies Center and is Director of the Women's Studies Program. She is interested in gender inequality in labour markets and the family. She is also interested in the public benefits of paid and unpaid caring labour and how societies can support those who do this work.

Jane Falkingham is Reader in Social Policy and Population Studies in the Department of Social Policy at the London School of Economics, UK. Her main research focus concerns the social and economic implications of population ageing, and social security in later life. Publications include *Ageing and economic welfare* (Sage Publications, 1992) and *The dynamic of welfare* (Harvester Wheatsheaf, 1996). Over the last five years her attention has, however, been 'diverted' away from Britain and Europe towards Central Asia and the human costs of economic transition. She has worked in Kyrgyzstan, Azerbaijan and, most recently, Tajikistan.

Michael F. Förster is an Economist at the OECD Directorate for Education, Employment, Labour and Social Affairs (Paris), and a Research Fellow at the European Centre for Social Welfare Policy and Research (Vienna). His research and publications focus on poverty and income inequalities in OECD countries and in transitional economies.

Joachim R. Frick is Senior Research Economist and Data Operations Manager, German Socio-Economic Panel Study (GSOEP) at DIW, Berlin, Germany. His main research interests include income distribution, immigration and social policy research.

Frank F. Furstenberg Jr is Zellerbach Family Professor of Sociology at the University of Pennsylvania, USA. His interest in the American family began at Columbia University where he received his PhD in 1967. His recent book is *Managing to make it: Urban families in high-risk neighbourhoods* (University of Chicago Press, 1999) with Thomas Cook, Jacquelynne Eccles, Glen Elder and Arnold Sameroff. His current research projects focus on the family in the context of disadvantaged urban neighbourhoods, cross-national research on children's well-being, urban education and the transition from adolescence to adulthood.

Irwin Garfinkel is Mitchell I Ginsberg Professor of Contemporary Urban Problems and Chair of the Social Indicators Survey Center at the Columbia University School of Social Work, USA. He has authored or co-authored over 100 scientific articles and 11 books on poverty, income transfers, program evaluation, and child support. His most recent book is entitled *Fathers under fire: The revolution in child support enforcement* (Russell Sage Foundation, 1998). His research on child support influenced legislation in Wisconsin and other American states, the US Congress, Great Britain, Australia and Sweden.

Anne H. Gauthier is Associate Professor in the Department of Sociology at the University of Calgary, Canada. She specialises in cross-national family research. She has published in the field of family policies, children's well-being and time use.

Janet C. Gornick is Associate Professor of Political Science at Baruch College, City University of New York, USA. Her research is primarily cross-national, and focuses on the effects of social and labour market policies on women's economic outcomes. Her recent articles have appeared in *American Sociological Review*; *Work, Employment, and Society*; *Journal of European Social Policy*; and *Social Science Quarterly*.

Paul Gregg is Senior Research Fellow at the Centre for Management and Public Organisation at the University of Bristol, UK. He is also a member of the Council of Economic Advisers at HM Treasury. Research topics include unemployment, workless households, low pay and poverty.

Ann Harding is inaugural Director of the National Centre for Social and Economic Modelling and Professor of Applied Economics and Social Policy at the University of Canberra, Australia. She has previously worked in government on social policy and tax issues.

Herwig Immervoll is Research Associate at the Microsimulation Unit, Department of Applied Economics, University of Cambridge, UK. Research interests include: microsimulation, public finance, social policy and related issues of European integration.

Markus Jäntti has been a Senior Research Fellow with the Academy of Finland since 1996. Major research interests are income inequality, mobility and poverty in comparative perspective, applied labour economics and statistical inference for income distribution analysis.

Heather Joshi is Professor of Economic Demography and Deputy Director of the Centre for Longitudinal Studies, Institute of Education, University of London, UK. Her work is mainly concerned with gender and social inequality over the life course.

Alfred J. Kahn is Professor Emeritus, Senior Lecturer, and Co-Director of the Cross-National Studies Research Program at the Columbia University School of Social Work, USA. His research interests include comparative child and family policy, income transfers, personal social services and social expenditures.

Sheila B. Kamerman is Compton Foundation Centennial Professor for the Prevention of Child and Youth Problems and Co-Director of the Cross-National Studies Research Program at the Columbia University School of Social Work, USA. She is also Director of the University-wide Columbia Institute for Child and Family Policy. Her research interests include comparative child, youth, and family policy, and comparative welfare state developments.

Peter Krause is Senior Research Fellow, German Socio-Economic Panel Study (GSOEP) at DIW, Berlin, Germany. His major reserch interests are poverty, subjective indicators, inequality and income dynamics.

James Kunz is Assistant Professor at Columbia University, USA. His research interests include the effects of child support on child well-being, the economic and psychosocial consequences of teenage and non-marital childbearing, and the impact of poverty across the life span, with a particular interest in adolescence.

Amanda J. Lockshin, a recent honors graduate of Harvard University, now works at the Urban Institute's Health Policy Centre (Washington, DC) and is particularly interested in policies affecting people with disabilities or chronic illness. Her recent projects have included study of a Medicaid capitated long-term care programme in New York and research on Medicare reimbursement of skilled nursing facilities for people with AIDS.

Sara McLanahan is Professor of Sociology and Public Affairs at Princeton University, USA. She is Vice President of the Population Association of America and a member of the National Academy of Science's Board on Families, Youth, and Children. Her major research interests are poverty and family demography. She has published over 100 articles and is co-author of *Fathers under fire* (Russell Sage Foundation, 1998), *Social policies for children* (Brookings Institution, 1996), *Growing up with a single parent* (Harvard University Press, 1994), *Child support and child well-being* (Urban Institute, 1986), and *Single mothers and their children* (Urban Institute, 1986).

Stephen Machin is Professor of Economics at University College London and Director of the Centre for the Economics of Education, UK. He is also leader of the education programme at the Centre for Economic Performance at the London School of Economics and Political Science and a Research Associate of the the Institute for Fiscal Studies. He is currently an Editor of the *Economic Journal*. His research interests are determining factors of adult economic success or failure, the structure of wages, skills changes in international labour markets and income inequality.

Marcia K. Meyers is Associate Professor of Social Work and Public Affairs at Columbia University and Associate Director of the New York City Social Indicators Survey Center, USA. Dr Meyers' research focuses on public policies and programs for vulnerable populations, including public welfare services, child welfare programs, and childcare services. Her papers have appeared recently in the *Journal of Public Policy and Management*, the *European Journal of Social Policy*, *Social Services Review* and *Social Science Quarterly*.

John Micklewright is Head of Research at UNICEF Innocenti Research Centre, Florence, Italy. He was previously Professor of Economics at Queen Mary and Westfield College, University of London, and at the European University Institute. He is a Research Fellow of the Centre for Economic Policy Research, London, UK.

Brian Nolan is Research Professor at the Economic and Social Research Institute, Dublin, Ireland. He has a doctorate in economics from the London School of Economics, and has published widely on income inequality, poverty, public economics, social policy, health economics and health inequalities. He is currently studying poverty and inequality in the European Community Household Panel Survey.

Howard Oxley is Senior Economist in the Resource Allocation Division of the Economics Department at the OECD. His research interests are social spending in the public sector, poverty and income distribution, and ageing in OECD countries.

Laura R. Peck is a PhD candidate at the Robert F. Wagner Graduate School of Public Service, New York University and a Research Associate at the Columbia University School of Social Work, USA. Her research focuses on the effects of US social policy and on program evaluation methodology.

Michele Pellizzari is a graduate student at the London School of Economics and Political Science, London, UK. He has worked as a consultant for the OECD Directorate of Education, Employment, Labour and Social Affairs (Paris) and as a researcher for the Fondazione Rodolfo Debenedetti (Milan). His research interests focus on labour and welfare economics.

Richard Percival is Senior Research Fellow at the National Centre for Social and Economic Modelling, University of Canberra, Australia. His particular interests are the application of modelling techniques to government policy processes and aspects of inequality changes in Australia. He is currently undertaking research in the areas of child costs, aged care and the implications of an ageing population.

Shelley Phipps is Maxwell Professor of Economics at Dalhousie University, Nova Scotia, Canada. Her current research focuses on the health and wellbeing of Canadian children, international comparisons of social and family policy, poverty and inequality, and decision making within families.

Lee Rainwater is Professor Emeritus of the Department of Sociology, Harvard University, USA, and Research Director of the LIS, a Division of CEPS/INSTEAD, Differdange, Luxembourg.

Katherin Ross works for the Income and Benefits Policy Division of the Urban Institute in Washington, DC, USA.

Timothy M. Smeeding is Maxwell Professor of Public Policy and Professor of Economics and Public Administration at the Maxwell School,

Syracuse University, USA. He is Director of the Center for Policy Research and the LIS.

Cristina Solera is currently a researcher at the European University Institute in Florence, Italy. She graduated in Sociology at the University ofTrento with a thesis on child poverty and family policies. Her doctoral research concerns longitudinal analysis of women's labour market participation and how this is affected by institutional arrangements, in particular by labour market regulation.

Kitty Stewart is Research Fellow at the London School of Economics and Political Science, UK. She worked previously at the UNICEF Innocenti Research Centre, Florence, Italy, and has a doctorate in economics from the European University Institute, also in Florence.

Holly Sutherland is Director of the Microsimulation Unit in the Department of Applied Economics at the University of Cambridge, UK. Her particular interests include the incorporation of gender effects in microsimulation analysis, making microsimulation models as widely accessible and understood as possible and the development of comparable methods across countries. She currently coordinates a project to build a Europe-wide tax-benefit model, EUROMOD.

Patrick Villeneuve is Adjunct Faculty Member and PhD candidate at the Columbia University School of Social Work, USA. He specialises in the areas of social welfare policy, poverty, child support, welfare reform and comparative social policy.

Koen Vleminckx is Senior Research Fellow at the Department of Sociology of the Catholic University of Leuven, Belgium. His research interests include comparative social policy and welfare state research, income inequality and poverty and self-employment.

Klaas de Vos is Senior Researcher at CentER Applied Research, Department of Economics, Tilburg University, the Netherlands. His main research interests include poverty and social policy, income and labour supply of older people, and microsimulation.

Gert G. Wagner is Professor of Economics at the European-University Viadrina (Frankfurt/Oder, Germany), Research Director at DIW, Berlin, Germany, Senior Research Fellow of CEPS/INSTEAD (Luxembourg), and Research Associate of the Centre for Policy Research (CEPR, London).

INTRODUCTION

Ending child poverty in industrialised nations

Koen Vleminckx and Timothy M. Smeeding

"Societies are judged by the way they treat their children."
(Olaf Carlson, Swedish Prime Minister, January 1993)

Introduction

Every second, about four children are brought into this world, and the lottery of birth will decide where they will be raised. Even for children who are lucky enough to begin their lives in the industrialised world, the financial circumstances of their families and the support that governments provide will decide what kind of diet, healthcare and education they will receive. Those who grow up in disadvantaged families are more likely to suffer unemployment, low pay, and poor health in adulthood and to transfer this poverty of opportunity to their own children. Thus, poverty can grind down generation after generation.

Breaking this cycle is one of the greatest challenges at the beginning of the 21st century. Despite high rates of economic growth and improvements in the standard of living in industrialised nations throughout the 20th century, a significant percentage of the children in these nations are still living in families that are so poor that normal health and growth are at risk. While the postwar welfare states have in most industrialised nations been hugely successful in reducing poverty among older people, this has not been the case for younger people. On the contrary, in recent decades we have seen the re-emergence of high levels of child poverty in several western countries such as the United Kingdom (UK) and the United States (US).

If high economic growth rates, staggering improvements in the average standard of living, and the development of comprehensive welfare state programmes in the past 50 years were not able to eradicate child poverty in industrialised nations, shouldn't we just accept the problem as being inevitable? Our findings lead us to say no. If industrialised nations had considered the problem of impoverishment in old age as being inevitable, so many wouldn't have been so successful in reducing it. A century ago previous generations of citizens, business leaders and politicians in these countries decided that impoverishment in old age was socially unacceptable and not economically sound. They decided to introduce old age insurance programmes for salaried workers and, in the vast majority of industrialised nations, similar social insurance programmes were implemented in order to cover other contingencies such as sickness, disability and unemployment, which posed similar risks to economic well-being. A century later poverty in old age is for a vast majority of citizens in industrialised nations a problem of the past.

There is no reason why the same could not happen for the problem of child poverty. Few would argue that the problem is socially acceptable and it seems economically sound to make sure future generations of workers grow up in conditions that allow them to become healthy, well educated citizens who can cope with the flexibility and lifelong learning required by the emerging knowledge societies of the 21st century.

Although welfare state programmes have not yet managed to completely eradicate child poverty, it is wrong to say that they have failed altogether. Previous studies (for example, Rainwater and Smeeding, 1995) have revealed remarkable varietion in child poverty rates in countries at broadly similar levels of economic development. Poverty rates are generally lower in countries with comprehensive welfare state programmes for families with children than in countries that lack such programmes, although it is true that there is even considerable variation in child poverty rates among nations with such programmes. One of the challenges of this volume is to establish why this is the case. While ready-made solutions that can successfully be copied by other societies are rare, it is by learning from the results produced by policy programmes, and often combinations of programmes, that have been successfully implemented in other nations that we will be able to find the ideas needed to fine-tune our own programmes. What we need is the continued commitment of governments, business leaders, academics and citizens to find the methods and the means to reduce, maintain and, one day, eradicate child poverty in industrialised nations.

A few years ago this might have seemed to be an illusive dream, but there are signs that some governments are really committing themselves to this cause. During his March 1999 Beveridge lecture, Britain's Prime Minister, Tony Blair, set out a mission to halve child poverty by 2010 and to end it by 2020. At first the reactions were mixed, as many activists had heard sweeping promises before and many feared that the deadline was an excuse for not doing more immediately. However, before the end of that year, the British government unveiled a package of measures aiming to reduce child poverty by a quarter by 2004. Although the relatively small falls revealed by the latest statistics are disappointing, significant increases in financial support for children have been made.

Other European governments have also committed themselves to fight poverty. In 1997, the Irish government adopted a new official poverty measure and a new National Anti-Poverty Action Strategy (1997), which set specific poverty reduction goals to be achieved by 2007. At the 2000 UN World Summit for Social Development in Geneva, Belgium's Minister for Social Integration, Johan Van de Lanotte, made a similar commitment by announcing that his government would aim to halve Belgium's poverty rate by 2010.

In March 2000, the Lisbon European Union (EU) Council called for steps to make "a decisive impact on the eradication of poverty by setting adequate targets to be agreed by the Council by the end of the year 2000". This set in motion a process that entails great promises for the fight against poverty in Europe in general, and for the fight against child poverty in particular, as the Lisbon Council singled children out as one of the specific groups "for concern". In December 2000, a similar Council organised in Nice decided that the EU member states should implement two-year action plans for combating poverty and social exclusion, similar to the National Action Plans on Employment, which played and continue to play an important role in the improvement of employment policies in Europe. The first National Action Plans on Social Inclusion were submitted to the European Commission by June 2001. In these reports, each government assessed both the level and characteristics of poverty and social exclusion in their country, described the policies they had implemented so far in order to deal with these problems, as well as their aspirations and policies for the future. Several National Action Plans on Social Inclusion submitted in 2001 addressed the issue of poverty and social exclusion among children. The National Action Plans served as a basis for the *Joint Report on Social Inclusion* of the Council and the Commission, submitted to the Laeken Council on 14 December 2001, which was the first policy document on poverty and social exclusion formally endorsed by the EU.

In the US, welfare reform in 1996 established strict work requirements for welfare recipients, with tough penalties for those who flouted the rules, and set a five-year lifetime limit on payment of federal welfare benefits to any family. As the 1996 welfare law encouraged people to find jobs, more parents became part of the workforce while welfare caseloads declined by 54%. At the same time, child poverty rates dropped considerably. However, these results were also influenced by a decade-long economic boom and the decrease in child poverty rates stagnated in 2001 while the overall poverty rate increased. Unemployment rates are currently up and if the current recession lasts a rise in child poverty rates is again at risk.

The US House has just passed a tougher welfare reform proposal requiring still more hours of work for aid recipients, even as the labour market weakens. The US Senate also faces renewal of two important family welfare programs and is not likely to expand benefits significantly. Meanwhile, US states are likely to cut back on social programs now that the recession has seriously strained their finances.

The rationale for this volume

In recent years, economists, sociologists and social policy analysts have accelerated their study of the extent and trends of child poverty and well-being, its consequences for children and the adequacy of public policy in preventing child poverty. The emergence of cross-nationally comparable data on the composition of incomes and household structure (eg, the Luxembourg Income Study) and on child outcomes has supported this literature. Given the emergence of child poverty as a key policy concern in most rich nations, it was felt that a gathering of information on the present state (levels and trends) of child poverty on a comparative basis was needed. This would illustrate the effects of poverty on child outcomes and child well-being more generally and the implications of the findings for child and family policies. To meet the need, this volume presents very recent facts and insights on child poverty and its effect on child well-being in the richest industrialised countries and in a selected subset of emerging or 'transition' nations.

This volume is the result of an October 1999 conference organised by the Luxembourg Income Study (LIS), a division of CEPS/INSTEAD, a non-profit research centre in Differdange, Luxembourg. A request for funding from the European Community was favourably received. And when the demand for the conference exceeded these resources, other sponsors were called in and contributed handsomely to the enterprise. In the end, the conference was financed by the Directorate of Social Policy and Social Action of the Commission of the European Communities; the government of the Grand-Duchy of Luxembourg; the

US Department of Health and the Human Services – Office of the Assistant Secretary for Planning and Evaluation; the US National Center for Children in Poverty (NCCP); the Ford Foundation; and the Macarthur Foundation Research Network on the Family and the Economy.

The aim of the conference was to access current knowledge, to identify future research and policy priorities and to launch a series of cross-national research collaborations on the subject of child well-being in industrialised countries. The approach of this conference was both multidisciplinary and international in scope. The organisers received a total of almost a hundred offers to present papers shortly after the call had been put forth. A total of 33 (groups of) authors were asked to finish their papers and present them during the October 1999 conference. Most of these authors were later asked to contribute a chapter to this volume (other papers given at the conference can be found on the LIS website at http://lisweb.ceps.lu/links/cpconf/conf.htm). The volume combines contributions from 45 North American, Australian and European authors.

Although we recognise that child poverty and well-being is a worldwide issue, this book focuses on child poverty and well-being in industrialised and transition countries. In our opinion, it is clear that the basic needs of children in developing countries are to be prioritised. But we also wish to draw attention to the problems faced by children in more affluent economies precisely because their governments can afford to improve the well-being of poor children directly. It is not a matter of budget, rather a matter of priority that faces these nations.

The contents of the volume

This volume is divided into four parts, each dedicated to a different topical area following a logical sequence.

The topics covered are:

- the extent of child poverty and child well-being;
- outcomes for children;
- country studies and emerging issues;
- child and family policies.

Hence, the problem of child poverty is first identified and measured; the issue of outcomes for children are then identified and measured and linked to child poverty as far as is currently possible; specific country studies further illuminate the major themes identified in the first two parts of the book; and finally, the effects of public policy on child poverty and well-being are estimated and discussed.

The first part of the volume contains some of the most recent cross-national results on the extent and trends of child poverty and child well-being in industrialised and transition nations that are currently available. It also looks within three large nations (US, Canada and Australia) to measure comparable poverty rates at sub-national levels for the first time. The results suggest that a wide range of child poverty outcomes are found within as well as between modern nations.

The second part of the volume analyses the relationship between childhood experiences and children's health, educational attainment and adult labour market performance. The chapters not only describe the consequences of poverty for children, but also present evidence of the long-term effects of childhood poverty for educational opportunity, for the labour market, for mothers, and for the economy as a whole.

The third part presents several innovative and national studies, which highlight country specific developments, data sources or methodological developments that are interesting for an international audience. As such they present results and analyses that can be copied by other researchers in a comparative context.

The fourth and final part of the volume describes the evolution of child and family policies in the last decade, their effects on children's well-being and the impact of recent policy reforms. These can be seen as roadmaps for nations that desire to reduce child poverty and enhance child well-being.

A concluding chapter assesses what we have learned and where we should go from here in terms of both research and policy.

References

Lisbon European Council (2000) 'Presidency conclusions', 23 and 24 March, SN 100/00 EN, available at the official site of the Portugese Presidency, www.portugal.ue-2000.pt/

National Anti-Poverty Action Strategy (1997) *Sharing in progress: National anti-poverty strategy*, Dublin: Stationery Office.

Piachaud, D. and Sutherland, H. (2000) *How effective is the British government's attempt to reduce child poverty?*, Innocenti Working Paper No 77, Florence: Innocenti Research Centre.

Rainwater, L. and Smeeding, T.M. (1995) *Doing poorly: The real income of children in a comparative perspective*, LIS Working Paper no 127, Luexmbourg: Luxembourg Income Study (available from www.lisweb.ceps.lu/publications/wpapers.htm).

PART 1

The extent and trend of child poverty in industrialised nations

Introduction

The first part of this volume presents an overview of the most recent facts on the extent and trends of child poverty in industrialised nations. Although poverty is often referred to as being a multidimensional phenomenon, both chapters focus on the financial dimension of poverty. In part this can be explained by the fact that the availability and comparability of income data has improved considerably in the last two decades, which allows a far more comprehensive study of the extent and trends in income poverty rates. In contrast, the cross-national measurement of non-monetary dimensions of poverty in industrialised countries is still in a prospective phase. The focus on poverty of income can also be explained by the geographical scope of this volume, as it is assumed that in modern nations, characterised by a highly monetarised economy, the disposability of a sufficiently high income is an important precondition for reaching certain levels of well-being and social participation deemed minimal in these societies.

The first chapter by Bruce Bradbury and Markus Jäntti describes the extent of child poverty in a wide range of industrialised and transition countries. Their analysis relies on the Luxembourg Income Study database, the most recent and largest collection of income survey data for OECD countries that is currently available. They use three different poverty lines: one 'absolute' and two 'relative' poverty lines. 'Absolute' or, more properly, fixed real price poverty lines, are thresholds which permit people living in specified family types to purchase the same bundle of goods and services in different countries or times. Families that fall below the common consumption threshold are therefore considered to be poor. Bradbury and Jäntti use the US official poverty line for a couple plus two children in 1995 (US$15,299). In order to apply this poverty line to the other countries included in the study, Bradbury and Jäntti convert national currencies to US dollars by using the Organisation for Economic Co-operation and Development's Purchasing Power Parities (PPPs) for 1995, and national inflation rates to deflate incomes over time. 'Relative' poverty lines are typically defined with reference to a measure of 'typical' consumption levels (for example, half median income). Furthermore, Bradbury and Jäntti use an 'overall' median poverty line and a 'child' median poverty line. The overall poverty line is the conventional relative poverty line. For each individual in the population Bradbury and Jäntti calculate the household equivalent income. The poverty line is defined as 50% of the median of this variable across the national population. The child median poverty line is based on the household incomes of children. In this case the median of household equivalent income is calculated over children only.

The results based on the child median poverty line reveal considerable variation in child poverty across the industrialised countries covered by this study. The lowest poverty rates are for children in the Nordic countries, while Australia, Canada and the UK are all fairly high up in the child poverty ranking. Extremely high child poverty rates are reported for the US. The picture is less clear for continental Europe. Relatively low child poverty rates – similar to levels found in the Nordic countries – are reported for Belgium and Luxembourg. Slightly higher child poverty rates are reported for France and the Netherlands, but the highest child poverty rates on the continent are found in Germany and, especially, Italy. As for the Central and Eastern European countries, relatively high child poverty rates are reported for Hungary and Poland, but the lowest child poverty rates in the study are reported for the Czech Republic and Slovakia. The highest child poverty rate is reported for Russia. Strikingly, the Russian child poverty rate is just a few percentage points higher than the child poverty rate reported for the US. While the ranking within the richer countries differs between the relative and 'absolute' approaches, the broad grouping is not all that different. The poverty ranking of most of the transition economies, on the other hand, depends very much on this distinction. However, Bradbury and Jäntti remain sceptical of the extent to which the PPP-adjusted exchange rates correctly reflect the real living standards in these countries.

Across the whole spectrum of industrial countries considered, Bradbury and Jäntti find that those with higher levels of national income do tend to have lower real poverty rates. Important deviants from this relationship are the US, which has a much higher level of child poverty than its national income would suggest, and Taiwan, which has a lower than expected child poverty rate. Children are generally more likely to be poor if living with a lone mother, but variations in rates of lone motherhood are not an important reason for the variations in child poverty across countries.

Another important finding by Bradbury and Jäntti is that market incomes play a larger role than state transfers in accounting for the cross-national diversity of outcomes for disadvantaged children. Whether this is because of different labour market and family support policies (such as childcare subsidies), because of the different incentive structures imposed by different targeting patterns, or because of other factors, remains to be seen. Bradbury and Jäntti conclude that policy makers who are seriously interested in the well-being of children need to think more closely about which features of labour markets best protect the living standards of children.

While Bradbury and Jäntti reported relative child poverty rates defined at a national level for each country included in their study, as the nation is the usual reference group for poverty measurement, this need not always be the case. Increasingly sub-national levels of government are being called upon to finance safety nets for otherwise poor families with children. The recent welfare reforms in the US are but one instance of this devolution of policy responsibility to lower levels of government.

In Chapter Two, Lee Rainwater, Timothy M. Smeeding and John Coder wonder whether relative poverty should be measured in relation to a national average or to the average in the local community or lower level of government. They argue that people might primarily compare their standard of living to those of important reference groups who are geographically, socially, and politically more similar. The issue of the property reference group has until now received little attention in most national and cross-national studies of poverty and social exclusion. The study by Rainwater, Smeeding and Coder mainly focuses on regional differences in child poverty rates within the US, although regional (provincial) differences in poverty rates within two other industrialised nations, Australia and Canada, are also analysed. Estimates for other countries are not included, because they would only be suggestive due to the small size of the surveys in these countries. However, their results for Italy and Spain can be found on the conference website (www.lis.ceps.lu).

Chapter Two shows that there is considerable variation in child poverty rates among the different US states. When a common US child poverty standard is applied to all the states, the highest child poverty rates are reported for New Mexico, Mississippi, Louisiana and West Virginia. The lowest child poverty rates are reported for the combined states of Colorado/Utah/Nevada, for Minnesota, for Alaska/Hawaii and the combined Maine/New Hampshire/Vermont areas. However, Rainwater, Smeeding and Coder find that the state ranking is quite different when separate-state child poverty standards are defined and applied for each state, indicating large differences in incomes and perhaps also costs of living, particularly housing costs, among these US states. The southern states in particular look less poor when state poverty standards are applied, and there is clearly more variation within this group of states often thought to be homogeneous. When state poverty standards are applied, the US states with the highest child poverty rates are New York, California, Massachusetts and Arizona. The lowest rates are reported for North Dakota/South Dakota, Iowa/Kansas/Nebraska, the Colorado/Utah/ Nevada group and the three small New England states. However, while the application of state poverty standards makes a big difference for the state child poverty ranking, it does not make a big difference on a national level. In the US the child poverty rate according to the national standard is 20.3% and according to the state standards is 20.1%.

In the case of Australia the study finds relatively little difference in the poverty rates according to the two standards. In most states the state poverty rate is about the same as the national standard poverty rate. There is more shifting around in the case of Canada, where fairly large decreases are found in Newfoundland, Nova Scotia and Prince Edward Island. The child poverty rate increases in Ontario, the only province in which there is a notable increase. Overall, the shifting in Canada is more like that of the US than is the case for Australia. What is notable in Canada is that the provincial poverty rates make Canada seem much more homogeneous than does the national standard. Only British Columbia, with a higher rate, and Quebec and Prince Edward Island, with lower rates, stand apart. This is in contrast to Australia where the differences among regions are about the same for both state standards and the national standard, with a range from around 10% to 16%.

Together these chapters chart the broad picture of child poverty and therefore frame the extent of the issue before us.

ONE

Child poverty across the industrialised world: evidence from the Luxembourg Income Study

Bruce Bradbury and Markus Jäntti[1]

Introduction

Recent comparative research has confirmed that there remain wide variations in the extent of cross-sectional child poverty across countries at otherwise similar stages of development. In this chapter we present the latest evidence on variations in child poverty across the industrialised world, and assess the contributions of family structure, state transfers and market incomes to this variation.

Our results are based on data from the Luxembourg Income Study (LIS)[2] which, at the time of writing, covers some 25 industrialised countries, many with information for several years. We utilise almost all these data in the results presented here. The countries examined include most of the OECD, several of the important non-OECD economies of Eastern Europe (including Russia) and one representative of the newly industrialising countries of East Asia (Taiwan).

The remainder of the chapter is structured as follows. In the next section, we briefly describe the methods we use to measure poverty. Then we show both the ordering of countries by child poverty in the latest available wave of LIS, as well as the poverty trends that can be estimated using all of the LIS data points for each of the countries. We discuss the role of the public sector in affecting poverty rates from a few different points of view and present in the final section some concluding remarks.

The measurement of child poverty

The sharing unit and equivalence scale

Two major decisions that must be made in any poverty study concern the choice of sharing unit (eg, within nuclear families or within households) and the equivalence scale (the needs of different types of sharing units). There is a very large literature that addresses these issues (see for example, Jenkins and Lambert, 1993; Gottschalk and Smeeding, 1997; Jäntti and Danziger, 1999). Our choices on these matters are fairly standard.

Our measure of resources is annual[3] disposable income. This includes market incomes and government cash transfers, and deducts income taxes and compulsory social insurance contributions. While this is not a comprehensive indicator of the resources available to the families of children (eg it excludes non-cash services) it remains the best available indicator of cross-national variations in living standards. These issues of the appropriate resource measure (and the role of non-cash benefits in particular) are discussed in more detail in a longer version of this chapter (Bradbury and Jäntti, 1999).

We assume resources are shared within *households* and define every person in the household to have the same poverty status. This definition is the one that is most commonly available across our countries. The exceptions to this are Sweden and Switzerland, where the source data are limited to tax units, corresponding to nuclear families of parents and their dependent children. In these two countries, adult children and lone parents living with their parents are treated as separate units.

In most of our results, we assume that needs differ according to both the number of adults and the number of children in the household according to the formula

$$needs = (adults + children \times 0.7)^{0.85}$$

People aged under 18 years are defined as children. This structure for the equivalence scale is used by Jenkins and Cowell (1994) and also recommended for use by the US National Science Foundation Poverty Commission (National Research Council, 1995). The particular numerical values chosen yield a scale that is very close to the widely used OECD scale.

The poverty threshold and counting methods

The literature on poverty measurement has typically used two types of poverty threshold: 'absolute' and 'relative' poverty lines. 'Absolute', or more properly, fixed real price poverty lines, are thresholds which permit people living in specified family types to purchase the same bundle of goods and services in different countries or times. Families that fall below the common consumption threshold are therefore considered to be poor. 'Relative' poverty lines, on the other hand, are more closely related to concepts of social exclusion. These poverty lines are typically defined with reference to a measure of 'typical' consumption levels (eg half median income).

Both relative and real provide important insights into the way the living conditions of the most disadvantaged children vary across countries. In this chapter, we employ three types of poverty lines:

- An *overall median* poverty line. This is the 'conventional' relative poverty line. For each individual in the population we calculate their household equivalent income. The poverty line is defined as 50% of the median of this variable across the national population.
- A *child median* poverty line based on the household incomes of children. In this case the median of household equivalent income is calculated for children only.
- The *US official* poverty line. This real poverty line is set equal to the US official poverty line for a couple plus two children in 1995 (US$15,299). National currencies are converted to US dollars by using OECD Purchasing Power Parities (PPPs) for 1995 and national inflation rates to deflate incomes over time. These price adjustments are likely to be less robust for the transition countries, not least because of the hyperinflation experienced in many of these after 1989 (the general limitations of PPP adjustments are discussed further in Bradbury and Jäntti, 1999).

We present results showing the proportion of children below all three of these poverty lines, although with an emphasis on the first (our 'base case') and the last. The child median line presents a different picture to the base case for only a small number of countries. In addition, we later present alternative indicators of deprivation based on the mean incomes of the poorest fifth of children.

Child income poverty across nations

Three measures of child poverty

Table 1.1 shows the level of child poverty for the latest available LIS years using the three poverty definitions. The countries are sorted by descending child poverty rate, using the half overall median poverty line. The first pair of columns in Table 1.1 show this poverty rate, the second the poverty rate relative to the child median and the third pair the proportion of children below the US poverty line[4].

There is great variation in measured rates of child poverty across countries. Taking first our base case, the poverty rate relative to the overall median, the likelihood that a randomly picked child will live in a poor family ranges from 1.8% in the Czech Republic to 26.6% in Russia. Northern European countries have fairly low poverty rates. The Nordic countries range between 3.4% (Finland) and 5.9% (Denmark). Central European countries follow, with Austria, Belgium, Luxembourg and the Netherlands having rates between 5.6% and 8.4%. Italy, Australia, Canada, Ireland and the UK are all fairly high up in the poverty ranking, while Spain, France and Germany fall towards the middle of the 25 countries.

As noted above, the five former socialist countries in the LIS database have the lowest average incomes and this is reflected in their poverty rates based on the US poverty line. However, in terms of relative poverty, these data show wide diversity in the experience of transition from socialism. Of the 25 countries, Russia has the highest (overall median) child poverty rate and the Czech Republic the lowest. Although the process of industrialisation is often associated with increased inequality, our single example of an East Asian economy, Taiwan, has a comparatively low child poverty rate – not that different from those found in Northern Europe.

For most countries, child poverty is about a third lower when measured against the child rather than the adult median. This is because the equivalent family income of the median child is somewhat lower than the equivalent family income of the median person. These relativities between children and others are sensitive to the equivalence scale, and so this particular result is of limited interest. More interesting is the fact that the overall ranking across countries on the two measures is very similar; and that there are three countries where the general tendency for child poverty to fall by about a third does not apply.

Table 1.1: Child poverty rates

		Poverty rate using different poverty lines					
		50% of the overall median		50% of the child median		US poverty line	
Country	**Year**	**Rate**	**Rank**	**Rate**	**Rank**	**Rate**	**Rank**
Russia	1995	26.6	(1)	25.4	(1)	98.0	(1)
United States	1994	26.3	(2)	18.6	(2)	18.5	(12)
United Kingdom	1995	21.3	(3)	11.0	(5)	28.6	(10)
Italy	1995	21.2	(4)	15.7	(3)	38.1	(9)
Australia	1994	17.1	(5)	11.0	(6)	20.7	(11)
Canada	1994	16.0	(6)	11.2	(4)	9.0	(16)
Ireland	1987	14.8	(7)	6.5	(13)	54.4	(6)
Israel	1992	14.7	(8)	10.3	(8)	45.3	(8)
Poland	1992	14.2	(9)	10.9	(7)	90.9	(3)
Spain	1990	13.1	(10)	9.7	(10)	47.3	(7)
Germany	1994	11.6	(11)	7.1	(11)	12.4	(14)
Hungary	1994	11.5	(12)	10.1	(9)	90.6	(4)
France	1989	9.8	(13)	6.8	(12)	17.3	(13)
Netherlands	1991	8.4	(14)	5.8	(14)	10.0	(15)
Switzerland	1982	6.3	(15)	3.9	(18)	1.6	(24)
Taiwan	1995	6.3	(16)	4.1	(17)	4.3	(20)
Luxembourg	1994	6.3	(17)	1.9	(23)	1.1	(25)
Belgium	1992	6.1	(18)	4.2	(16)	7.9	(17)
Denmark	1992	5.9	(19)	5.1	(15)	4.6	(19)
Austria	1987	5.6	(20)	3.3	(20)	5.4	(18)
Norway	1995	4.5	(21)	3.5	(19)	2.8	(22)
Sweden	1992	3.7	(22)	3.2	(21)	3.7	(21)
Finland	1991	3.4	(23)	2.5	(22)	2.6	(23)
Slovakia	1992	2.2	(24)	1.5	(25)	95.2	(2)
Czech Republic	1992	1.8	(25)	1.6	(24)	85.1	(5)
Rank correlation				(0.951)		(0.454)	
					(0.480)		

Note: Children are poor if their household has an equivalent disposable income less than 50% of the overall or child median or less than the official US poverty line. Countries are sorted by the overall median rate. Rank correlations are placed equidistant between the two columns of ranks to which they refer.

Source: Authors' calculations from LIS

In Russia there is little difference in the poverty rate, while in both the UK and Ireland, the drop in poverty is greater. This is because the median income of children compared to others is relatively high in Russia and relatively low in the UK and Ireland. It is this overall disadvantage which leads to the high poverty rate of children in the UK, according to the conventional overall median definition. If, on the other hand, we are concerned with those children who have living standards much lower than those of the average child (ie the child median poverty concept) then child poverty in the UK is of a similar magnitude to that in Australia and Canada.

We now turn to our third definition of poverty, that based on the US poverty line and PPP-adjusted incomes. The poverty ranking using this 'real' standard of living definition is quite different from the ones obtained using relative definitions. In particular, the transition economies now all have very high poverty rates. For instance, in the Czech and Slovak Republics (which had the lowest poverty rates using both relative definitions) almost all children are now counted among the poor. Although there is no doubt that absolute poverty rates are very high in these countries, we would not like to ascribe too much importance to the precise estimates shown in the table, as it is very difficult to estimate accurate PPPs for countries with widely different income levels.

Turning to the wealthier countries where we can better measure differences in prices between countries, we find that a large proportion – almost a fifth – of US children are poor, compared to the low of 1.1% in Luxembourg or 1.6% in Switzerland. The North European and Nordic countries with low levels of relative child poverty have also low levels of poverty measured against the US poverty line. For instance, in Sweden 3.7% and in Belgium 7.9% of all children are poor. Italy, Ireland and Spain all have very high levels of child poverty using this measure. In Australia and the UK, more than a fifth of all children have a standard of living that is lower than the US official poverty line.

In Figure 1.1 we compare these poverty estimates with the aggregate national incomes of each country (in the relevant years). As would be expected, countries with higher national income levels are able to ensure that fewer of their children live in families with incomes below the US poverty line.

The most important exception to this general relationship is the US itself. Despite having the highest national income after the small country of Luxembourg, it has a real child poverty rate that is in the middle of these 25 countries, and in the bottom half of the OECD countries included

Figure 1.1: National incomes and the proportion of children below the US poverty line

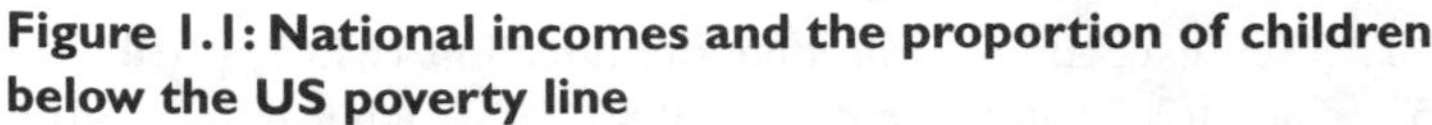

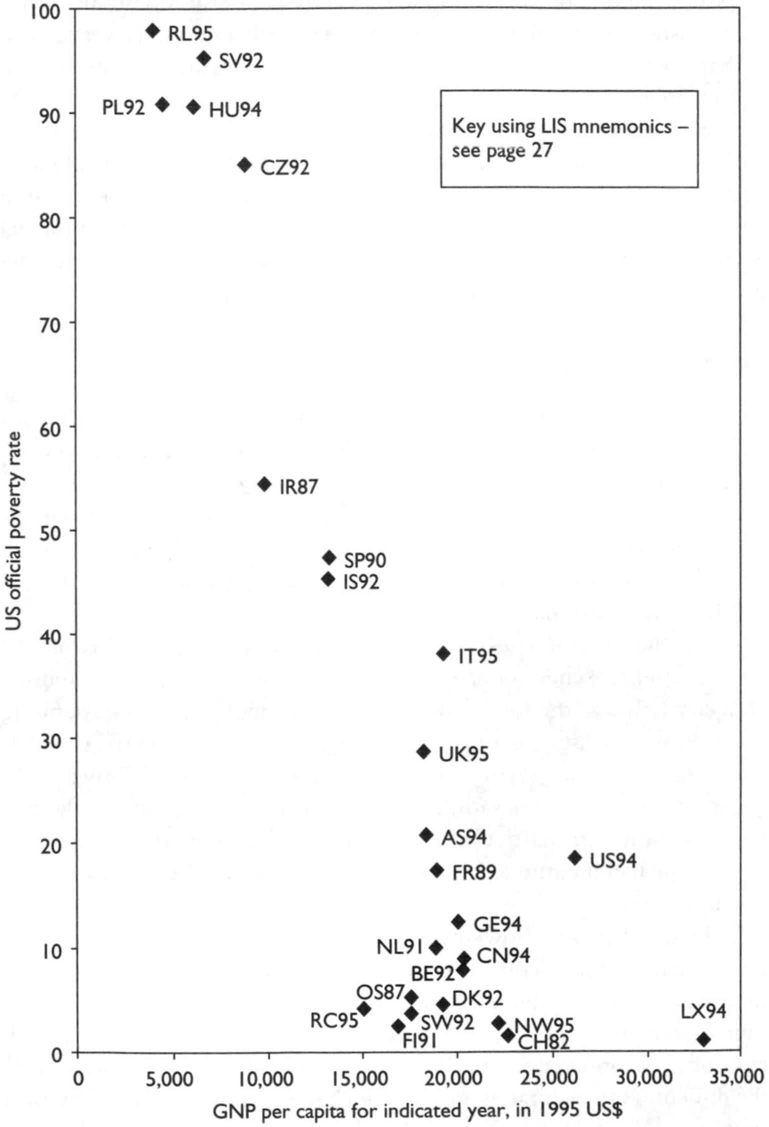

Sources: Child poverty rates, Table 1.1 GNP per capita, as for Table 3.1 in Bradbury and Jäntti (1999) (although here for the same year as the poverty estimate)

here. The key exception in the opposite direction is Taiwan (labelled RC95), which has a national income only slightly higher than in Spain and Israel but one of the lowest child poverty rates. Although not clearly distinguished in the figure, other countries with low poverty rates but with incomes only slightly higher than Taiwan are Finland, Sweden, Austria and Denmark.

The other two outliers, Luxembourg and Italy, are perhaps of less substantive interest. In the first case the poverty rate is close to negligible. The results for Italy, on the other hand, may be a reflection of the large informal economy in this country. While estimates of the informal economy are incorporated into the national accounts measures of income, this is more difficult to do at the household level.

Trends

To summarise the changes in child poverty observed in the LIS, we estimated for each country and each of the three poverty definitions the slope coefficient in a regression of poverty rate against year. When only two years are available, this is the same as the annualised percentage point difference in poverty rates. In Figure 1.2 we show these estimates for the two relative poverty measures, while Figure 1.3 shows results for the US official poverty estimates.

Across the 20 countries in Figure 1.2, the dominant trend is one of increasing relative child poverty, with the most dramatic increases in Russia, Hungary, Italy and the UK[5]. The Nordic countries figure strongly among those with decreases (or negligible increases) in child poverty, together with France, Canada, Spain, Israel and, most prominently, Taiwan. In general, poverty outcomes for the child median are more favourable than the overall median (particularly in the UK and Hungary). This implies that the median income of families with children has fallen relative to the overall median.

In Figure 1.3, we show the corresponding trends when poverty is measured using the US official poverty line. Growing average real incomes means a more favourable outcome in many cases. However, we exclude from this figure those countries that had experienced extremely high rates of inflation over the period (Russia, Poland and Israel) because of the difficulties in accurately measuring changes in purchasing value over time[6].

Increases in real poverty occurred in Italy, Germany and the UK (although note that Germany expanded its borders to include East Germany over

Figure 1.2: Poverty trends using the half median poverty lines

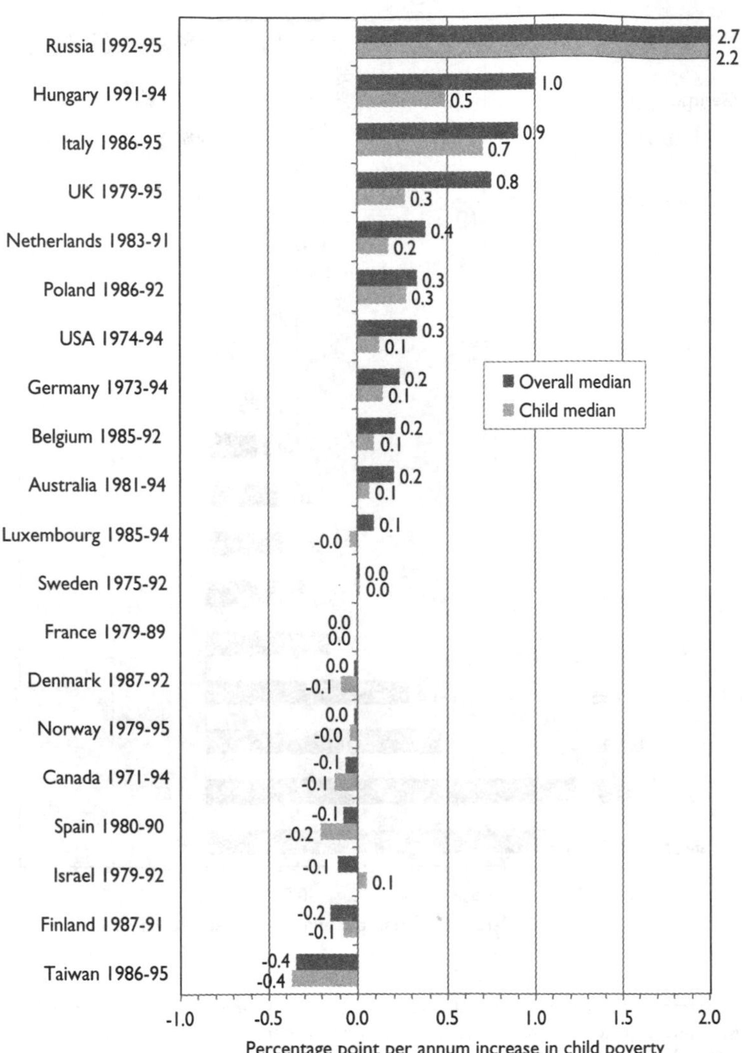

Note: Numbers shown are the slope coefficient of a regression of the poverty rate against time using all available LIS data points for a country. Countries are sorted by the rate of increase in the overall median child poverty rate. Russian bars are truncated.

Source: Authors' calculations from LIS

Figure 1.3: Poverty trends using the US official poverty line

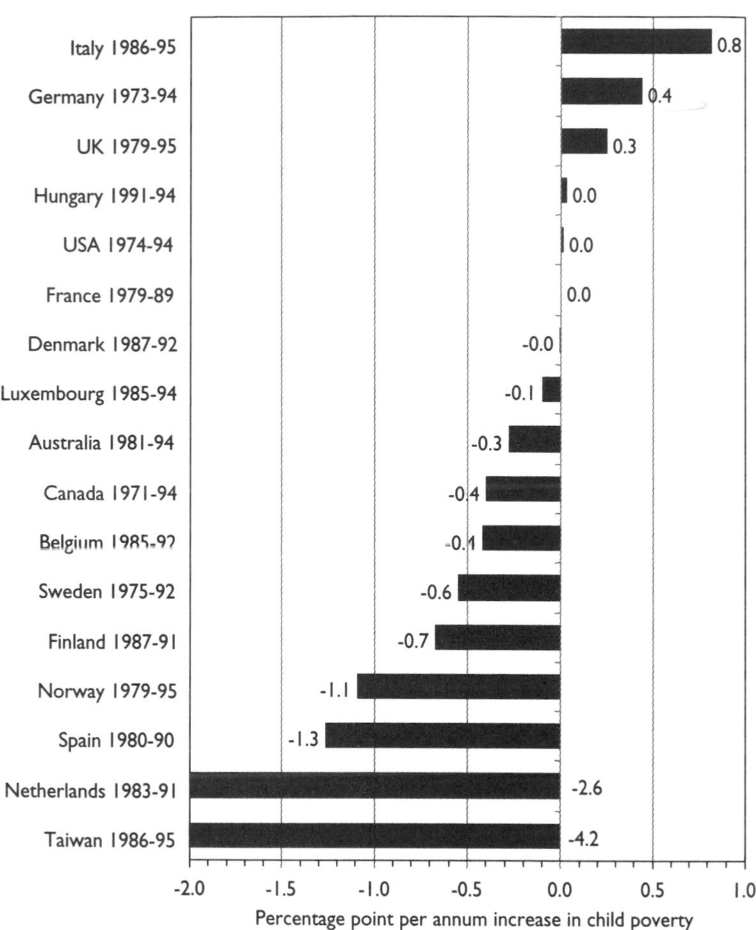

Note: Numbers shown are the slope coefficient of a regression of the poverty rate against time using all available LIS data points for a country. Countries are sorted by the rate of increase in the child poverty rate. Countries which have experienced hyperinflation over the period are not included. Bars are truncated for the Netherlands and Taiwan.

Source: Authors' calculations from LIS

the period, and that these percentage point changes need to be considered in the light of the widely differing levels of real poverty shown in Table 1.1). Falls in absolute poverty were found in countries with high rates of income growth such as Taiwan, the Netherlands, Spain and Norway.

For many countries, the direction of poverty change is uniform across all three poverty definitions. Child poverty *decreased* using all three definitions in Taiwan, Canada, Denmark, Finland, Norway and Spain. Poverty *increased* in Germany, Hungary, Italy, the UK and the US For the rest of the countries, the direction of change varied between the three definitions. The most common pattern, however, is that relative poverty increased – reflecting an increase in inequality – and poverty based on the US official line decreased – reflecting an increase in real disposable income. For instance, poverty in the Netherlands increased by 0.4 percentage points per annum by the overall median definition but decreased by 2.6 percentage points per annum using the US poverty line definition.

It is possible, however, that the average change in poverty over time shown in the figures could conceal as much as it reveals. For instance, a country with a U-shaped time series of poverty will be registered as having almost no change over time. For many of the LIS countries there are only one or two data points. However, an examination of the actual trend data for the countries whose data in LIS span the longest period tend to be well in line with the summary measures reported above (Bradbury and Jäntti, 1999, 2001).

The key conclusion to be drawn from the overall pattern of the levels and trends in child poverty is that there is wide diversity of outcomes for countries at similar states of development. This is, in itself, an important, although not entirely surprising, finding.

Clearly there are factors other than the overall level of development (as measured by, for example, Gross National Product [GNP] per capita) that affect the prevalence of low income among children in different countries. One such factor is the different demographic compositions of the different countries, in particular, the extent to which children live in two-parent or lone-parent families. Do these demographic factors explain any of the variation in poverty rates across countries?

Lone parenthood and child poverty

Learning what groups of children are poor or whether or not children face greater poverty risks than, say, older people, provides us with a richer picture of the nature of child poverty. Looking into the structure of child poverty is also one way to approach the question of what accounts for child poverty and its variations across countries.

We examine here the poverty rates of children in lone-mother, two-parent and 'other' households. For children in each of the three household types, we show in Table 1.2 the proportion of children and the poverty rate in each type using the base case definition of the poverty line. A lone-mother household is defined as a household with a female head with at least one child but no other adults present (adults are persons aged 18 or over). Our two-parent households are restricted to two-adult families, that is, there must be both a head and a spouse but no other adults present.

As noted earlier, the household definition is narrower in Sweden and Switzerland, which leads to few households of type 'other'. At the other extreme, there are some countries where high proportions of children live in these larger households. This is particularly the case in Taiwan, Spain, Russia and Hungary where between 41% and 28% of children live in households other than the lone-mother and two-parent types identified above. In many cases, these are households where lone mothers are living with their parents, although this category also includes many other common household types, such as those where adult children remain at home[7].

Across the 25 countries, the proportion of children living in lone-mother households varies widely. In many countries (eg Ireland, Italy, Israel, Spain and Taiwan) the proportion of children in lone-mother households is negligible. The highest proportions are found in the UK (19%), the US (15%), Sweden (15%), Norway (14%) and Denmark (13%). It is noteworthy that the first two of these are also the two countries, after Russia, which have the highest child poverty rates.

The right-hand panel of Table 1.2 provides information on the relationship between child poverty and lone parenthood. In almost all countries, lone-mother children have greater poverty risks than children in two-parent households. The two exceptions are Italy (where only 2% of children are in lone mother households) and Poland[8].

The poverty rate of US lone-mother children is the highest. At 59.6%, it exceeds by more than 15 percentage points the next highest rate, Canada (45.3%). In both countries, children in lone-mother households are around three-and-a-half times more likely to be below the poverty line than children in two-parent households. Australia, Germany and the UK have poverty rates for children in lone-mother families close to 40%. Sweden has the lowest (4.5%), followed by Poland and Finland.

Table 1.2: Child poverty rates by family type

Country		Population shares			Poverty rate (%)		
		Lone mother	Two parent	Other	Lone mother	Two parent	Other
Russia	1995	0.08	0.60	0.32	31.0	26.0	26.5
United States	1994	0.15	0.60	0.25	59.6	16.7	29.1
United Kingdom	1995	0.19	0.70	0.12	40.3	17.5	13.9
Italy	1995	0.02	0.73	0.25	20.2	20.9	22.3
Australia	1994	0.09	0.73	0.18	38.3	14.7	16.6
Canada	1994	0.11	0.69	0.20	45.3	12.3	13.4
Ireland	1987	0.03	0.73	0.24	29.8	16.7	7.1
Israel	1992	0.03	0.71	0.25	26.6	14.0	14.8
Poland	1992	0.05	0.72	0.24	4.9	13.7	17.5
Spain	1990	0.02	0.62	0.36	25.2	12.4	13.5
Germany	1994	0.09	0.77	0.14	43.3	8.5	7.3
Hungary	1994	0.06	0.66	0.28	12.0	10.9	12.9
France	1989	0.07	0.75	0.17	25.4	7.7	12.6
Netherlands	1991	0.08	0.82	0.10	29.6	6.8	4.2
Switzerland	1982	0.07	0.88	0.05	21.2	4.8	12.5
Taiwan	1995	0.02	0.57	0.41	15.2	5.1	7.5
Luxembourg	1994	0.06	0.76	0.19	30.1	4.4	6.8
Belgium	1992	0.07	0.78	0.14	11.8	6.1	3.0
Denmark	1992	0.13	0.76	0.10	10.5	5.5	2.8
Austria	1987	0.10	0.73	0.18	33.2	2.9	2.0
Norway	1995	0.14	0.73	0.14	10.4	3.4	4.4
Sweden	1992	0.15	0.82	0.03	4.5	3.6	2.6
Finland	1991	0.09	0.79	0.13	6.2	3.0	4.1
Slovakia	1992	0.05	0.73	0.22	7.6	2.1	1.4
Czech Republic	1992	0.07	0.75	0.19	8.9	1.3	1.4
Average (weighted by the number of children in 1996, see Table 3.1 in Bradbury and Jäntti, 1999)		0.10	0.66	0.24	37.9	15.5	19.8

Note: Sorted by the overall child poverty rate. Poverty defined with the half overall median poverty line.

Source: Authors' calculations from LIS

The association between lone motherhood and poverty is quite clear. Is this association responsible for any of the cross-national variations in child poverty rates? Some of the evidence presented above would suggest that lone motherhood might play an important role. The US and the UK, in particular, have both high rates of lone motherhood and also high child poverty.

One way to address this question is make some counter-factual estimates of the national poverty rates under either a counter-factual common family-type distribution (but country-specific family-type poverty rates) or common family-type poverty rates (but country-specific family type distributions). Bradbury and Jäntti (1999) calculate such counter-factual poverty rates, but conclude that lone motherhood explains only a negligible component of the child poverty 'league table'. Although the US and UK have high rates of child poverty and lone motherhood, this relationship does not hold generally. Norway and Sweden, in particular, have high rates of lone motherhood but low rates of child poverty. This is the case even though lone mothers in Norway, in particular, are still significantly worse off than couples and larger households.

Social transfers, market incomes and child poverty

Why is there so much variation in child poverty across nations? Since we define child poverty as low income relative to needs, the income sources of families of children provide the natural starting point for the answer to this question. Most research on patterns of poverty in rich nations has, not surprisingly, focused on public income transfers, as these are the policies which are most directly charged with providing incomes to disadvantaged families.

A common approach in the literature is to show the association of selected indicators of welfare effort with the (child) poverty rate. There is, in general, a qualitatively significant relationship between these – countries with a high share of GNP spent on social expenditure have lower relative poverty rates. Much of the social expenditure that is recorded, however, is spread more broadly across the population rather than only being targeted at those likely to be poor. In particular, most countries (the US being a prominent exception) spend substantial amounts on programmes that provide cash transfer support to all or most families with children (Bradshaw et al, 1993).

It would be reasonable to expect that the link with poverty would be stronger if we could identify income transfers going to families likely to fall into poverty. However, previous research on this issue has found the opposite. Atkinson et al (1995) compare poverty rates for the working-age population with the levels of transfers received by the population with below-median incomes. Although their ranking of poverty rates for all the non-elderly is similar to our ranking of child poverty rates, they find a much weaker relationship between poverty and below-median transfers. Norway, for example, has low poverty but also low transfers, while the UK and Ireland have high transfers but also relatively high poverty rates.

The reason for this weaker relationship must lie in the other sources of income available to households. In particular, even for the families of the most disadvantaged children, market incomes often comprise a major component of their 'income package'. What is the relative importance of market and transfer incomes for the living standards of poor children? Are social transfers or labour market policies likely to be more important for their living standards?

The simplest disaggregation of family incomes relevant to this question is the decomposition into (net) social transfers and market incomes. Which of these contributes the most to the observed variation in child poverty across nations?

A commonly used method for addressing this question is to compare poverty rates based on market incomes alone and rates based on disposable income. The difference between the two poverty rates is often used as an index of the effectiveness of the tax and transfer system in reducing poverty. Such comparisons do in general show that low poverty rates tend to be associated with tax/transfer systems that have large impacts on poverty rates (Bradbury and Jäntti, 2001). Such findings suggest that income transfers may be an important part of the reason why child poverty rates vary across countries.

However, one problem with this approach is that it is not symmetric; it shows the effect of excluding transfers, but does not show the complementary possibility of households living on transfers alone. Moreover, any counter-factual assumptions are just that – counter to fact. It is very likely that market incomes would change substantially in the total absence of public transfers, particularly since this counter-factual implies that large fractions of the population would have zero incomes. If there is substitution between social transfers and market incomes (eg via labour market or savings incentives or changes in labour demand), then this type of counter-factual over-estimates the redistributive impact of social transfers (Whiteford, 1997).

For these reasons we introduce an alternative way of looking at the relative contribution made by social transfers and market incomes to child poverty outcomes. Instead of the poverty rate, we examine the cross-national distribution of the disposable income of the bottom fifth of children measured in PPP-adjusted US dollars[9].

Rather than focus only on children below the poverty line, we therefore examine a closely related question: how do the one fifth of children who are most disadvantaged in each society fare? In particular, we are interested in the variation in the living standards of these different groups of children across nations. Does the variation in living standards stem from variations in social transfers or from different levels of market incomes?

For the poorest one fifth of children in each country, we calculate the elements of the identity

Average disposable income = Average market income + Average net social transfers

where all incomes are measured in equivalent PPP-adjusted constant US dollars[10]. These different income components are shown in Figure 1.4 for each of the 23 countries with recent LIS data (excluding Austria, where we cannot separately identify market incomes). The five transition countries have been separately identified with open diamonds[11].

Since market income and net social transfers are defined to add up to disposable income, the latter can also be read directly from this figure. The lines running from *top-left* to *bottom-right* indicate contours of *equal disposable income*. The further is the diagonal band from the origin, the higher is the living standard of the most disadvantaged children. Disadvantaged children in Luxembourg, the Nordic countries and Taiwan had the highest absolute living standard, followed by Canada and Belgium. The bottom fifth of children in France, Germany and the Netherlands had incomes between US \$4,000 and US \$5,000, while the other English-speaking countries fared somewhat worse, followed by children in the Southern European and transition economies.

The *rays from the origin* in Figure 1.4 indicate the *share* of income received from market incomes. This share varies widely, from around three quarters of disposable income (Taiwan, Italy, Finland, Spain, Germany) to as low as one quarter (the UK). In most countries, this market income is mainly wages and salaries. In Taiwan, Russia, Ireland and Finland, however, around one third of market income is from other sources (eg farm and

Figure 1.4: The income package of the poorest quintile of children

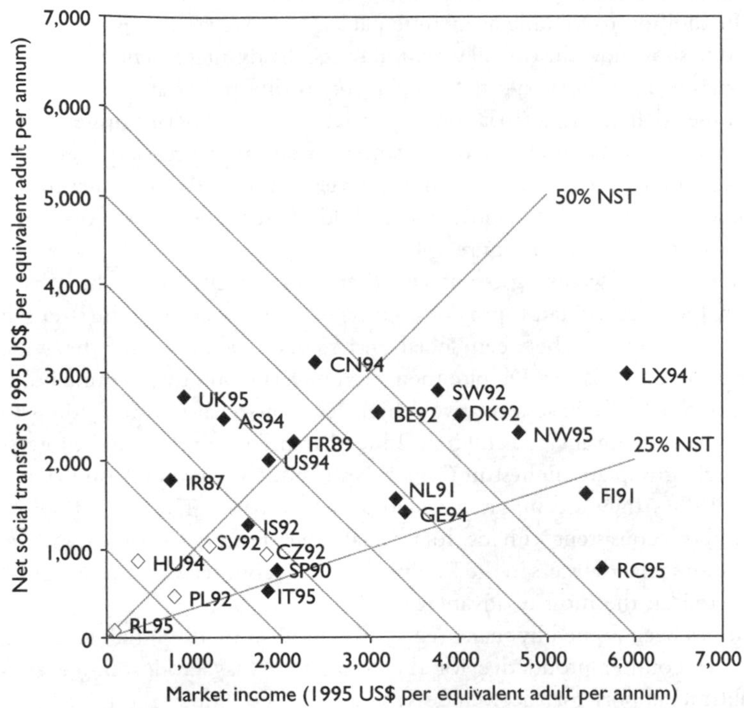

Key of LIS mnemonics

AS	–	Australia	LX	–	Luxembourg
BE	–	Belgium	NL	–	Netherlands
CH	–	Switzerland	NW	–	Norway
CN	–	Canada	OS	–	Austria
CZ	–	Czech Republic	PL	–	Poland
DK	–	Denmark	RC	–	Taiwan
FI	–	Finland	RL	–	Russia
FR	–	France	SP	–	Spain
GE	–	Germany	SV	–	Slovakia
HU	–	Hungary	SW	–	Sweden
IR	–	Ireland	UK	–	United Kingdom
IS	–	Israel	US	–	United States
IT	–	Italy			

other business income) and in a number of countries these sources contribute around one fifth of market income.

In addition to looking at income packages, however, the figure can be used to show how the overall variation in the disadvantage of poor children (variation from bottom-left to top-right) is due to variation in market incomes (left to right variation) or variation in net social transfers (up-down). Even though there is substantial variation in net social transfers, there is much greater variation in the levels of the market incomes in the households of the most disadvantaged children (ie there is more horizontal than vertical spread in Figure 1.4).

The English-speaking countries other than the US, all of which have fairly high poverty rates, provide an interesting illustration of the strength of the correlation between social and market incomes, and the wide variation in the latter. Despite their high poverty rates these countries, as a group, actually have a relatively high level of social transfers going to their most disadvantaged children. Indeed, transfers per child in the lowest quintile group are highest in Canada, and about as large in Australia and the UK as they are in, say, Sweden and Denmark. This high level of transfers is consistent with low total social expenditure on income transfers, because social transfers in the English-speaking countries are more closely targeted on the most disadvantaged.

It has been argued by many (eg, Korpi and Palme, 1998) that targeting can be counter-productive for the poor, as it may erode middle-class political support for the welfare state and hence reduce the total funds available for transfers. The higher level of poverty in the English-speaking countries could be seen as providing some support for this proposition. However, the data here also suggest a different interpretation. In the English-speaking countries, with the prominent exception of the US, social transfers to the families of the poorest one fifth of children are quite substantial. Instead, the reason for their high level of child poverty lies in the low levels of *market* incomes received by the most disadvantaged families.

An interpretation that is consistent with our data (but by no means the only one) is that the high degree of means-testing and the relative absence of universal and work-related transfers in the English-speaking countries, and the opposite in many European countries, may account for part of this pattern. Increased means-testing appears to be an attractive solution to the fiscal problems in many countries. If our findings are due to the different principles underlying transfer schemes, increased means-testing may ultimately prove to be less desirable for poor children.

Conclusions

Child poverty, whether measured in relative or real terms, varies widely across the industrialised countries. Our results, based on the latest available LIS data for early to mid-1990s are, in most cases, in line with earlier studies. Nordic and Northern European countries have low rates of child poverty, whereas Southern European and English-speaking countries tend to have high rates. While the ranking within the richer group countries differs between the relative and 'absolute' approaches, the broad grouping is not all that different. The poverty ranking of most of the transition economies in LIS, on the other hand, depends very much on this distinction. We remain sceptical, however, of the extent to which the PPP adjusted exchange rates correctly reflect the real living standards in these countries.

Across the whole spectrum of industrial countries considered here, those with higher levels of national income do tend to have lower real poverty rates. Important deviants from this relationship are the US, which has a much higher level of child poverty than its national income would suggest, and Taiwan, which has a lower than expected child poverty rate. Children are generally more likely to be poor if living with a lone mother, but variations in rates of lone motherhood are not an important reason for the variations in child poverty across countries.

Cash transfers to poor families are important for their living standards, but market incomes are also important. Indeed, we find that market incomes play a larger role than state transfers in accounting for the cross-national diversity of outcomes for disadvantaged children. Whether this is because of different labour market and family support policies (such as childcare subsidies), because of the different incentive structures imposed by different targeting patterns, or other factors, remains to be seen. It appears to us, in conclusion, that policy makers who are seriously interested in the well-being of children need to think more closely about which features of labour markets best protect the living standards of children.

Notes

[1] The authors are grateful to the UNICEF Innocenti Research Centre and the Australian Research Grants Council for financial support. They would also like to thank Jonathan Bradshaw, Stephen Jenkins, John Micklewright, Albert Motivans, Lee Rainwater, Timothy M. Smeeding and other seminar participants for comments on previous drafts. This chapter is a shortened version of a discussion

paper, prepared for UNICEF (Bradbury and Jäntti, 1999) and, in part, of Bradbury and Jäntti (2001).

Most importantly, we wish to acknowledge the central role of the Luxembourg Income Study, without which the analysis in this chapter would not be possible. Thanks, in particular, to Koen Vleminckx for providing technical advice. The UK data providers to LIS also require that we include the following statement: Material from the UK surveys is Crown Copyright; has been made available by the Office for National Statistics through the ESRC Data Archive; and has been used by permission. Neither the ONS nor the ESRC Data Archive bears any responsibility for the analysis or the interpretation of the data reported here.

The opinions expressed in this publication are those of the authors and do not necessarily reflect the policies or views of UNICEF.

[2] The Luxembourg Income Study comprises a database of household income survey information, adjusted to be as comparable as possible. For more information see http://lis.ceps.lu/.

[3] Except in the UK and Russia, where 'current' income is used.

[4] See Bradbury and Jäntti (1999, 2001) for details regarding the economic conditions of each country at the time of the LIS surveys.

[5] We are aware of changes to the survey methodologies of the Italian, Russian and Australian surveys over this period, but the direction of potential bias is not known.

[6] Other studies show absolute child poverty to have increased dramatically in Russia (see Klugman and Kolev, 1999).

[7] See Motivans (1999) for more information on the Russian family type distribution.

[8] It should be noted that in 1986, lone-mother households in Poland had a particularly high poverty rate. It is possible therefore that this result in 1992 represents sampling or data coding error.

[9] In Bradbury and Jäntti (1999) we also examine the corresponding relative measures (divided by the median income) and provide information on the relative contribution of transfers and taxes to net social transfers.

[10] This equation is used at the household level to calculate net social transfers as a function of market and disposable income, and so holds by definition. In the calculations of this section, we also make some adjustments to the raw income data of the LIS data files. The measurement of negative incomes and income taxation varies somewhat across the LIS data files, and because means are more sensitive than poverty headcounts to extreme values, we have adjusted the incomes of cases with negative incomes or apparently very high taxation. For most countries this means a negligible change. The most important exceptions are Australia and the Netherlands. See Bradbury and Jäntti (1999) for more details.

[11] For seven countries (France, Italy, Luxembourg, Spain, Hungary, Poland and Russia) only net incomes are available. This has little impact for the three transition countries, as income taxes were negligible or non-existent. For the others, if incomes in these countries were defined in the same way as for other countries, their data points in Figure 1.4 would be moved down and to the right. The bias is unlikely to be large, however, as taxes are likely to be a small component of net incomes for those in the poorest fifth.

References

Atkinson, A.B., Rainwater, L. and Smeeding, T.M. (1995) *Income distribution in OECD countries: Evidence from the Luxembourg Income Study*, Paris: OECD.

Bradbury, B. and Jäntti, M. (1999) *Child poverty across industrialized nations*, UNICEF Innocenti Occasional Papers Economic and Social Policy Studies, no 71, Florence: UNICEF International Child Development Centre.

Bradbury, B. and Jäntti, M. (2001) 'Child poverty across 25 countries', in B. Bradury, S.P. Jenkins and J. Micklewright (eds) *The dynamics of child poverty in industrialised countries*, Cambridge: Cambridge University Press.

Bradshaw, J., Ditch, J., Holmes, H. and Whiteford, P. (1993) *Support for children: A comparison of arrangements in fifteen countries*, DSS Research Report No 21, London: DSS.

Gottschalk, P. and Smeeding, T.M. (1997) 'Cross-national comparisons of earnings and income inequality', *Journal of Economic Literature*, vol 32, no 2, pp 633-86.

Jäntti, M. and Danziger, S. (1999) 'Income poverty in advanced countries', Working Paper 193, Luxembourg Income Study, Differdange. Forthcoming in A.B. Atkinson and F. Bourguignon, *Handbook of income distribution*, Amsterdam: North-Holland.

Jenkins, S.P. and Cowell, F.A. (1994) 'Parametric equivalence scales and scale relativities', *Economic Journal*, vol 104, no 425, pp 891-900.

Jenkins, S.P. and Lambert, P.J. (1993) 'Ranking income distribution when needs differ', *Review of Income and Wealth*, vol 39, no 4, pp 337-56.

Klugman, J. and Kolev, A. (1999) 'The welfare repercussions of single parenthood in Russia in transition', in J. Klugman and A. Motivans (eds) *Single parents and child welfare in the new Russia*, Basingstoke: Macmillan.

Korpi, W. and Palme, J. (1998) 'The paradox of redistribution and strategies of equality: welfare state institutions and poverty in western countries', *American Sociological Review*, vol 63, no 5, October, pp 661-97.

Motivans, A. (1999) 'Trends in family stability and structure', in J. Klugman and A. Motivans (eds) *Single parents and child welfare in the new Russia*, Basingstoke: Macmillan.

National Research Council (1995) *Measuring poverty: A new approach*, Washington, DC: National Academy Press.

Whiteford, P. (1997) 'Targeting welfare: a comment', *The Economic Record*, vol 73, no 3, pp 45-50.

TWO

Poverty across states, nations, and continents

Lee Rainwater, Timothy M. Smeeding and John Coder[1]

Introduction

This chapter examines issues concerning regional variations in poverty, in particular, child poverty. That is, what difference does it make for our understanding of the situation of poverty in a country if one focuses not on the nation as a whole but on particular communities or other reference groups within the nation? In our case we are concerned especially with possible variations in child poverty rates among the 50 United States (plus the District of Colombia) as compared to variations across the nation states of the European Union (EU), for instance. To provide a broader context for this discussion we also use Luxembourg Income Study (LIS) data to make comparisons with variations by regions in two other countries – Australia and Canada[2]. This chapter therefore moves beyond our own and others recent studies of child poverty based on LIS data and breaks new ground (eg, see Smeeding and Torrey, 1988; Rainwater, 1990; Smeeding et al, 1990; Förster, 1993; Smeeding et al, 1995; Smeeding, 1998; Bradbury and Jänttii, 1999).

Studies of poverty, particularly comparative studies, almost always take the nation as their prime focus and reference group, certainly with respect to the definition of the poverty line but also often more broadly than that. This focus on the nation is very much taken-for-granted in most countries. One would be hard put to find thorough examinations of whether the nation is the appropriate social reference group and physical unit for defining and then measuring the extent of poverty.

For example, while the definition of poverty adopted by the European Community (EC) in 1994 reflects a conception of poverty grounded in an understanding of the nature of social stratification in prosperous industrial societies, it adopts without discussion the nation as the unit for defining 'limited resources', 'exclusion', and 'minimum acceptable way of life'.

> The poor shall be taken to mean persons, families, and groups of persons whose resources (material, cultural, and social) are so limited as to exclude them from the minimum acceptable way of life in the member state in which they live. (Commission of the European Communities, 1994)

Yet, there could be important variations in different communities *within* a country in how these characteristics of the standard of living are defined. Alternatively, the question of who is poor could in the future move beyond national borders to groups of nation states and then even to continental levels, such as the EU broadly defined. Thus, the choice of social reference group for poverty comparisons and particularly for measuring social exclusion may be open to debate.

Differences in policy focuses

If the responsibility for fighting poverty lies at the national level, the nation is the natural unit of poverty measurement and anti-poverty effectiveness can be judged on a national basis. However, there are important exceptions to this rule both as they apply to nations and their subcomponents and supracomponents.

In the US, the recent devolution of the primary social assistance programme, formerly Aid to Families with Dependent Children (AFDC) and now called Temporary Assistance to Needy Families (TANF), to each of the 50 states marks a new era in federal/state relations. Increasingly, anti-poverty policy has been moving from the nation to state level since the 1970s when the Food Stamp and Supplementary Security Income (SSI) social assistance programme for the aged, blind and disabled offered nationwide guaranteed levels of benefits. A number of 'national' programmes, including SSI, have always had important interstate variations: different matching rates for federal support; different options for supplementation of benefits above the federal minimum; and even differences in state administration. These have been part of the history of the US safety net since 1935. Even health benefit programmes like Medicaid have always had significant interstate variations. However, the Personal Responsibility and Welfare Reform Act (PRWRA) of 1996 was unique in that it gave states a very liberal discretion in programme design, benefit structure and entitlement status within TANF. In fact, it turned AFDC into a capped state bloc grant and set a few overarching rules, but otherwise gave the states full latitude to determine who should be entitled to what and for how long.

This devolution has produced a myriad set of state differences in efforts to move persons off welfare, to help low-income mothers and children with supportive services, and to punish them (eg, sanctions from overstepping state-imposed rules). While the jury is still out regarding the successes and failures of this effort, there is considerable new interest in interstate differences in the poverty status of children and the anti-poverty effect of policy to reduce (or increase) child poverty. A number of studies of children's progress, children's budgets, and state-specific reports have begun to be produced by think tanks and other groups (eg, Flores et al, 1998; Loprest 1999). Hence, there is a renewed policy interest in US state estimates of child poverty, as the state has become the policy reference group.

Because the Canadian and Australian nations also have strong provincial (state) roles in poverty alleviation, there is similar interest in these countries. For instance, the Canadian 'Social Union', a set of political agreements between Canada and its provinces has taken the 'National Child Benefit' programme as its early test case for joint federal – provincial budgetary and programmatic support (Office of the Auditor General of Canada, 1999).

In contrast, as the EU becomes a more important political reality, there is interest to move beyond the nation/state and to develop measures of poverty for groups of nations. The European Community Household Panel (ECHP) project was begun to collect data on the lives, incomes and conditions within the original 13 EC member states. It has published reports on poverty and income distribution in these states using both "national" and "European" poverty lines (eg, Eurostat, 1998). And European-wide microsimulation models are being built to estimate the anti-poverty effects of adopting one or another social programme across the EC (eg, see Immervoll et al, 1999)[3].

Geographical and ethnic issues

Another reason for breaking down the US into its component parts is an interest in more precise comparisons of the nation/states of Europe and Scandinavia with America. Many analysts would like to compare Norway's four million people and Sweden's nine million people with the US states of Minnesota (five million) or Wisconsin (five million) which both have strong Scandinavian backgrounds and offer the opportunity for unique 'ethnic' comparisons (eg, Bjorklund and Freeman, 1994). Others may seek other specific comparisons not because of ethnicity, but because of immigration status (eg, Texas or California versus eastern Germany), policy similarities or differences, climate, geography, or other particular reasons. These reference group selection issues also come to bear in other nations as well. Considerations of the 'aboriginals' living in sparsely inhabited areas of central Australia present reference group issues in measuring poverty in Australia. In Canada, a nation of 30 million people, close to 90% of the population lives within 200 miles of the United States border. The remaining 10% are loosely scattered across the other 95% of the geographical area of Canada and its northern territories running to the Arctic Circle. Again, issues of proper reference group for poverty measurement must be addressed in such cases. And in fact, the Northwest Territories and Yukon Territory had to be excluded from our calculations due to small sample size.

'Local' versus 'national' concepts

One would think about this question of national versus sub-national regions and choice of reference groups as the proper focus for defining poverty differently depending on whether one adopts an absolute or relative approach to defining poverty. With respect to either approach, there are two kinds of possibilities in examining regional variations in poverty.

First, there can be variations in poverty rates in different regions even when the standard for defining poverty line is a national one because the measure of resources (eg, income) varies across regions and households. This kind of question is routinely dealt with in poverty studies in the US but less frequently in poverty studies in the European countries (but see Eurostat, 1998). And then there is also the possibility of variations in standards for defining poverty across the regions of a nation which produce variations in poverty across regions that are reflective of differences in resources across regions (and households) *and* differences in needs standards across region.

If one adopts the absolute approach, a shift of focus from the national to the local level would involve defining a market basket that is adjusted for local prices instead of the more common practice of applying the market basket and national prices across the whole country. Nevertheless, the content of the market basket would stay, and the same significant regional differences in costs would vary by regions. This is the recommendation of the recent report by the US National Academy of Sciences that recommended adjusting the national poverty line for differences in regional housing costs (Citro and Michael, 1995). It is also the approach used by Statistics Canada in defining its Low Income Cut-offs or LICOs (Grolet and Morrissette, 1999).

In the case of a relative standard, there is the more consequential choice to substitute a local relative standard for the national one. This is the approach that we take in this chapter. In previous studies done by a great many scholars using the LIS, the poverty line has been defined as one half of the national median equivalent income[4]. Shifting to an approach that takes regional standards seriously, one would define the poverty line as one half of the median equivalent income in the local area, however that local area might be defined. We believe this brings the definition of a poverty line closer to the social reality of the lives of the people being studied in that it approximates much better the community standards for social activities and participation, which define persons as of 'average' social standing or 'below average' or 'poor' (Rainwater, 1991, 1992). As such, it also comes close to a measure of social exclusion in that one's position is judged to be inadequate (or 'to be in poverty') based on a reference group within the community. Hence, one who is poor might be judged as having such a low income as to be excluded from participation in the local community[5].

Using a local relative standard to define a reference group for poverty measurement takes into account variations in the cost of living, differences in consumption bundles, *and* relevant differences in social understanding of what consumption possibilities mean for social participation and social activities. With this as our philosophical stance, we now move on to operationalise our concept.

Measurement issues

Economic well-being refers to the material resources available to households[6]. The concern with these resources is not with consumption per se but rather with the capabilities they give household members to participate in their communities and societies (Sen, 1992). These capabilities are inputs to social activities and participation in these activities produces a given level of well-being (Coleman and Rainwater, 1978; Rainwater, 1990).

All advanced industrial societies are highly stratified socially (and sometimes geographically, as noted here). Some individuals have more resources than others. The opportunities for social participation are vitally affected by the resources that the family disposes particularly in nations like the US where there is heavy reliance on the market to purchase such social goods as healthcare, education, and childcare services (Rainwater, 1974). Money income is the central resource in these societies. But there are still other important kinds of resources such as social capital (Coleman, 1988) and noncash benefits.

In this chapter, we are concerned only with disposable money income. Detailed comparable information exists on money income, on taxes paid (including state and local income taxes) and on certain kinds of transfers which have a cashlike character, for example housing allowances or fuel assistance or food stamps, for the five nations which we will investigate and for their subregions. Unfortunately, we cannot take into account the major in-kind benefits which are available in most countries – for example, healthcare, day care, and preschool, general subsidies to housing and the like. To the extent that the level and distribution of these resources is different in different countries, our analysis of money income must be treated with some caution. However, they would be unlikely to change the conclusions reached in this chapter. In fact, they may even exacerbate them. (See Smeeding et al, 1993, for an analysis that includes many of these benefits.)

Income and needs: equivalence scale issues

Families differ not only in terms of resources but also in terms of their needs. We take the differing needs because of household size and the head's stage in the life course into account by adjusting income for family size using an equivalence scale. The adjustment for household size is designed to account for the different requirements families of different sizes have for participating in society at a given level. Different equivalence scales will yield different distributions of well-being. Several studies in Europe, the US and Australia point to an equivalence scale which implies rather dramatic economies of scale in the conversion of money incomes to social participation among families with children (Buhmann et al, 1988; Bradbury, 1989; Rainwater, 1990). Analysis of some of these surveys also suggests that there are important variations in need as a function of the head of the household's age.

Drawing on these studies we have used an equivalence scale which defines need as the product of the cube root of family size multiplied by a factor which sees need as increasing roughly 1% per year for head's age up to the mid-40s and then decreasing at the same rate. Hence, we define equivalent income in the following way:

$$EI = Y / (S^{.33} .99^{|A-45|})$$

That is, equivalent income (*EI*) is defined as an individual's family disposable income (*Y*) divided by the product of the cube root of the family's size (*S*) and .99 compounded by the absolute value of the number of years difference between the head's age (*A*) and 45. The reader should keep in mind that all money income estimates in the chapter are based on adjusted or equivalent income calculated according to the above formula, including estimates for working age adults and for older people. (For more on this scale, see Rainwater and Smeeding, 2000, chapter 7.)

Having defined equivalent income in this way we determine the median of all individuals in each country (or state). We then examine the distribution of incomes of all population groups in relation to the median for all individuals. In this analysis, we tabulate the percentage of children who have given characteristics, not the percentage of families with children. In technical terms, our calculations are weighted by the number of children in each family. We do the same for working age adults (aged 18 to 64) and for older people (aged 65 and over). We also use a new set of state-specific child weights that are explained below.

The LIS United States state file 1995-97

Because our prime focus is on the US states, we have created a database which provides enough cases to produce reasonably stable estimates of state level poverty lines and poverty rates. This has been done by combining the three Current Population Surveys (CPS) for the years 1995, 1996 and 1997 yielding a total sample of 150,239 households (see Appendix I, The LIS United States 1995-97 state file). Because the populations of some states are rather small, even this number of households does not give us a good statistical base for all states. We are able to make analyses separately for 27 states; we have had to combine the other 24 states into nine multi-state regions of two to four units. In the tables that follow, these combined units are indicated by a name that compounds the standard abbreviations for the states (eg, MENHVT combines Maine, New Hampshire and Vermont).

We define a 'state' poverty line as the average of one half of the median equivalent incomes in that state in each year[7]. The US median equivalent disposable income in 1995 was $25,756, $26,801 in 1996, and $28,012 in 1997. The state poverty line is defined as half of the state median, just as the national poverty line is defined as half of the national median. In the analysis that follows, we express the state medians as a percentage of the national medians and the state poverty line is expressed as a percentage of the national poverty line[8].

For context, we have chosen two other countries that have quite different political and economic dynamics – Australia and Canada – to examine how much difference regional variations might make in other national contexts. We chose these nations because they are geographically large and have multi-levelled national and state/provincial governments. They also have important regional differences in political, ethnic or other groups within each nation[9]. The pattern of child poverty in each nation also differs with the US having high child poverty rates plateaued at about the 20% level and Australia and Canada having stable (flat) trends in child poverty at the 13% to 14% level. In addition, we provide national poverty rates for a group of other European and Scandinavian nations, again to emphasise the range in poverty rates that is found across our sub-national regions and nations compared to those found in European and Scandinavian nation states.

Child weights

One additional important step was undertaken in order to prepare our data. The population survey weights in the CPS database are set each year to produce accurate counts of the state population by age, race, ethnicity and gender, *but* only for the population aged 16 and over. The lack of weights for children has resulted in year-to-year fluctuations in the CPS estimates of the number of children within each of the 50 states. As a part of this project, LIS and the US Department of Health and Human Services contracted with Avenir Research to produce a set of accurate weights for the number of children by age, relationship to parent, gender, race and ethnicity. Further details are contained in Appendix I, Section B and Coder (1999). We have assumed that population weights are correct at the state level in the other LIS databases used in this chapter.

Results

In this section, we present a number of tables and charts that summarise our results. We concentrate mainly on the US, but other sub-national and sub-continental breakdowns are also presented.

To what extent do states differ in average incomes?

The first empirical issue that needs to concern us is the degree to which there is heterogeneity in average standards of living among regions. The second, discussed in the next section, is whether the amount of poverty differs among regions.

Table 2.1 gives state medians as a percentage of the US national median while Figure 2.1 charts the deviation from the national median of each of the state medians. In Figure 2.1, we see that in two states the state median is more than 20% greater than the national median. This is true of the combined Rhode Island and Connecticut region and in New Jersey. Interestingly it is not the case that New York, which people often think of as a very rich state, has a higher median. In fact, its median is 2% less than the national median, and comparable to North Carolina and Oregon, both 4% less than the national median.

The next most prosperous states appear to be Massachusetts at 15% above the national level and Washington at 12% above. Just as New York does not stand out, California's median is only 2% above the nation's median. Of course, these two large states (with 12% and 7% of the national population, respectively) have a very big impact on the national median, so one might not expect their medians to be very far from the nation's. The second largest state, Texas, however, has a state median which is 8% below the national median.

It is also not surprising that the South has the less prosperous states. From West Virginia to Texas, we find medians below average. West Virginia, Mississippi and Arkansas as well as New Mexico have medians at least 20% below the national standard. Overall, we find a range among the 51 American states from a high in New Jersey of 25% above the national median to a low in Arkansas of 25% below. While not quite half of the states have medians in the band of minus to plus 10%, there is still significant variation across the states.

We would therefore expect significant variations in the state poverty rates based on the national median. What is not clear is whether there would be similar variations based on the state medians. If the income

Table 2.1: Median incomes and poverty rates according to national and state standards[a] (%)

	Incomes	Poverty rates					
	State median as % of national median	Children, aged < 18		Working age adults, aged 18 to 64		Elders, aged 65 and over	
State		National standard	State standard	National standard	State standard	National standard	State standard
ME,NH,VT	102.6	12.7	13.7	10.2	11.0	21.2	22.3
Massachusetts	114.6	18.4	24.2	10.4	13.9	19.9	25.3
RI,CT	120.8	17.3	22.7	10.0	13.8	16.0	25.1
New York	98.3	26.9	26.3	16.2	15.9	23.1	22.4
New Jersey	125.3	13.6	21.8	8.3	13.9	18.6	29.3
Pennsylvania	102.7	17.6	18.4	12.7	13.3	20.8	21.9
Ohio	103.5	17.5	18.6	11.7	12.5	19.0	20.3
IN,MO	100.9	13.4	13.8	10.5	10.6	18.0	18.3
Illinois	108.1	18.8	21.7	10.7	12.5	18.4	22.3
Michigan	107.2	16.9	19.5	11.0	12.6	17.8	21.5
Wisconsin	107.9	13.1	15.1	3.9	10.4	18.5	21.6
Minnesota	110.1	12.3	15.8	12.3	11.3	19.1	17.2
ND,SD	93.0	14.9	12.3	8.7	10.7	24.8	28.9
IA,NE,KS	96.0	14.4	13.0	14.0	12.0	26.6	23.4
DE,MD,VA,DC	110.2	14.9	18.8	10.5	13.2	17.8	23.0
West Virginia	79.2	27.9	18.5	21.1	14.0	28.8	16.1
North Carolina	95.7	19.8	17.2	12.9	11.2	23.9	22.9
South Carolina	90.8	22.6	18.0	14.6	12.1	30.0	22.9
Georgia	95.3	20.9	18.8	14.1	12.8	25.1	23.3
Florida	95.0	23.0	21.2	15.2	13.8	20.2	18.2

Table 2.1: contd.../

State	Incomes	Poverty rates					
	State median as % of national median	Children, aged < 18		Working age adults, aged 18 to 64		Elders, aged 65 and over	
		National standard	State standard	National standard	State standard	National standard	State standard
Kentucky	90.9	25.1	20.5	17.5	14.6	25.3	19.9
Tennessee	91.1	22.4	18.2	16.7	13.3	27.0	23.3
Alabama	88.2	25.0	20.3	17.8	13.3	28.0	21.7
Mississippi	77.0	30.6	18.9	21.9	12.7	30.0	18.1
Arkansas	75.2	25.7	14.1	19.2	10.4	33.8	19.8
Louisiana	87.0	28.0	22.8	19.3	15.8	27.1	20.4
Oklahoma	83.9	24.2	17.6	17.7	13.2	26.0	17.8
Texas	92.1	24.7	20.7	16.9	14.3	25.9	22.2
New Mexico	76.3	33.3	21.6	24.6	15.8	26.3	16.5
Arizona	91.3	27.1	23.6	17.2	14.3	17.4	15.3
MT,ID,WY	87.7	20.3	13.9	16.0	11.5	19.4	13.6
CO,UT,NV	105.9	10.7	13.1	9.9	11.4	15.1	16.8
Washington	111.8	15.8	19.0	11.1	13.8	15.6	19.0
Oregon	95.9	17.7	16.2	11.9	10.9	15.3	12.3
California	102.3	24.6	25.7	15.5	16.1	18.1	18.8
AK,HI	108.5	12.6	16.1	9.8	11.7	15.3	17.0
United States	100.0	20.3	20.1	13.6	13.4	20.9	20.8

[a] Equivalent income is age-adjusted cube root of family size. National median income is calculated for each year (1995-97) and set at 100. State medians are percents of national median. Poverty line is one half of relevant median.

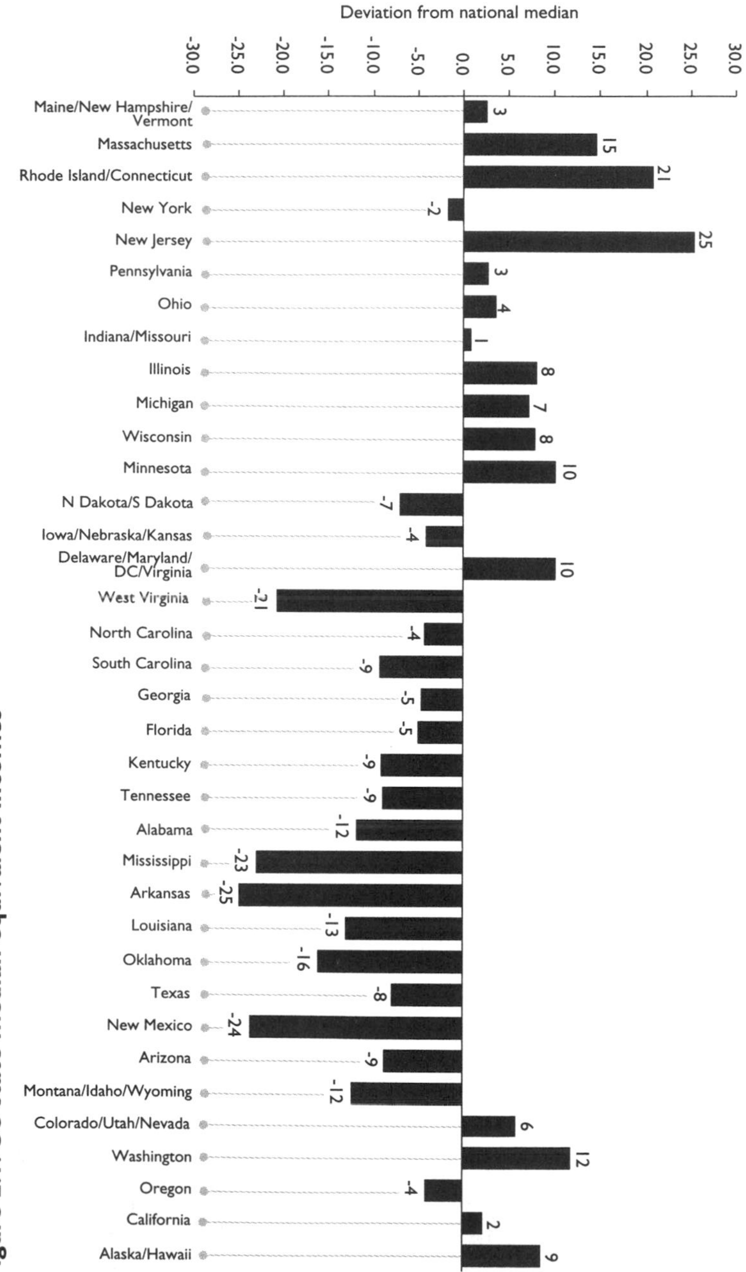

Figure 2.1: US state median equivalent incomes

inequalities, particularly the inequalities in the distributions below the median, were more or less the same in all of the states, then we might well find roughly the same poverty rates based on the state standards despite dramatic variations based on the national standard. Or indeed the relationship might go in the other direction if it turned out that the more prosperous states also were those with the greater degree of inequality in the distribution of income below to median. We might find rich states with high poverty and low-income states with low poverty.

In fact, we find a very low correlation between the median equivalent income in a state and its poverty rate based on the state standard – only 0.12. In contrast, the correlation between the median income of the state and its poverty rate based on the national standard is high – 0.77. As expected, the less affluent states have higher poverty rates by the national standard; but that is most definitely not the case with state standards. We return to these state-based poverty rates below.

The US state variations and those in some other countries

We have selected two countries to investigate variations in regional affluence to compare with our results for America's states. In Figure 2.2, we show state medians in these countries as a percentage of their respective national medians. Because the samples are rather small, these results may be unstable[10]. In some cases, we have combined regions in the LIS data to produce results that are somewhat more reliable. (See Appendix II for regional maps of both nations.)

We find that in Canada the provincial variations are not as dramatic as for states in the US. The range is from 9% above the national median for Ontario to 18% below in Newfoundland and 11% or 12% below in New Brunswick, Nova Scotia, Saskatchewan and Prince Edward Island. British Columbia also appears above average but only by 6 percentage points. In Australia, we find a similar pattern with a range from minus 7% in Tasmania to plus 14% in the Australian Capital Territory (ACT) and the Northern Territory (NT) combined. In the other five regions, the deviations from the national median are quite small. These other large nations and continents (Australia being both) thus have less variation in income within them than the US. One may argue that breaking an aggregate into 50 pieces as compared to seven (Australia) or ten (Canada) is bound to produce such a result. The nine US Census regions show that the West South Central and East South Central regions (the so-called 'Deep South') have median incomes 20% below the national median.

Figure 2.2: State median equivalent incomes in Canada and Australia

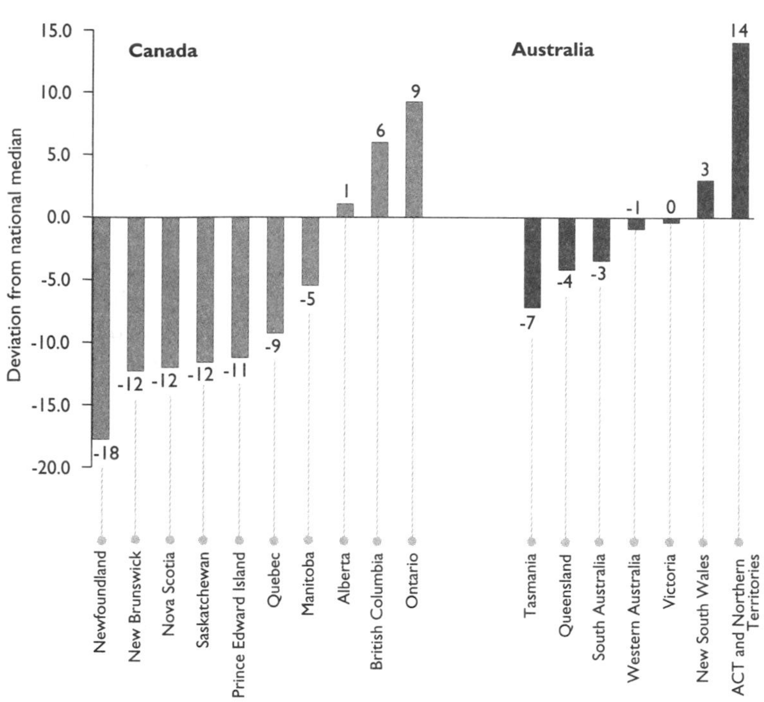

US and other nations' national and state standards

When we apply national and state or local standards to these five data sets, we find that the *national* poverty rate differs very little whether we use the national or the state standard. In the US the child poverty rate according to the national standard is 20.3% and according to the state standard 20.1%. The differences in the two rates are even smaller in Australia (13.5% versus 13.4%). In Canada, it is slightly larger but still not as large as 1% (Table 2.2). However, when we examine poverty rates by state or national standards *within* nations, there is a great deal of variance. We present US child poverty rates according to national and local standards for 27 states and 9 regional combinations of small states (see Table 2.1). For comparison, we have also given the poverty rates for working age adults and for elders.

Table 2.2: State poverty rates in the United States, Canada and Australia, and national rates in 14 European nations

Poverty rate	United States, 1995-97[a] State	Rate	Canada, 1994[a] Province	Rate	Australia, 1994[a] State	Rate	Europe Country	Rate
Total	United States	20.3	Canada	14.2	Australia	13.5		
Under 5%							**Sweden (1995)**	**2.4**
							Finland (1995)	**3.2**
							Denmark (1992)	**3.4**
							Norway (1995)	**3.9**
							Belgium (1992)	**3.9**
							Netherlands (1991)	**5.0**
							Luxembourg (1994)	**4.3**
Under 10%			Prince Edward Island	8.9			**Austria (1987)**	**5.3**
							France (1994)	**5.6**
							Germany (1994)	**8.7**
Under 15%	North Dakota, South Dakota	12.3	Quebec	12.4	South Australia	10.3	**Israel (1992)**	**10.6**
	Iowa, Nebraska, Kansas	13.0			ACT and NT	11.0	**Spain (1990)**	**12.4**
	Colorado, Utah, Nevada	13.1			Victoria	11.9		
	Maine, New Hampshire, Vermont	13.7			Queensland	12.6		
	Indiana, Missouri	13.8	Alberta	14.2	Western Australia	13.2		
	Montana, Idaho, Wyoming	13.9	Ontario	14.4	**Australia[b]**	**13.4**		
	Arkansas	14.1	**Canada[b]**	**14.7**	Tasmania	13.6		

Table 2.2: contd.../

Poverty	United States, 1995-97[a]		Canada, 1994[a]		Australia, 1994[a]		Europe	
rate	State	Rate	Province	Rate	State	Rate	Country	Rate
Total	United States	20.3	Canada	14.2	Australia	13.5		
Under 20%	Wisconsin	15.1	Nova Scotia	15.1				
	Minnesota	15.8	New Brunswick	15.2				
	Alaska, Hawaii	16.1	Saskatchewan	15.5				
	Oregon	16.2	Manitoba	15.6			**United Kingdom (1995)**	**16.2**
	North Carolina	17.2	Newfoundland	15.9	New South Wales	15.9		
	Oklahoma	17.6						
	South Carolina	18.0	British Columbia	18.0				
	Tennessee	18.2						
	Pennsylvania	18.4						
	West Virginia	18.5						
	Ohio	18.6						
	Deleware, Maryland, DC, Virginia	18.8						
	Georgia	18.8						
	Mississippi	18.9						
	Washington	19.0						
	Michigan	19.5					**Italy (1995)**	**19.5**

Table 2.2: contd.../

Poverty rate	United States, 1995-97[a] State	Rate	Canada, 1994[a] Province	Rate	Australia, 1994[a] State	Rate	Europe Country	Rate
Total	United States	20.3	Canada	14.2	Australia	13.5		
Over 20%	**United States[b]**	**20.1**						
	Alabama	20.3						
	Kentucky	20.5						
	Texas	20.7						
	Florida	21.2						
	New Mexico	21.6						
	Illinois	21.7						
	New Jersey	21.8						
	Rhode Island, Connecticut	22.7						
	Louisiana	22.8						
	Arizona	23.6						
	Massachusetts	24.2						
	California	25.7						
	New York	26.3						

[a] National rate using one half median national income. [b] National rate using one half median state incomes, or weighted average of state poverty rates.

Examination of the two child poverty rates within the US (Table 2.1) shows that there is not a very high correlation between them – only 0.534. Thus, we can expect a fair amount of reshuffling when we move from the national to the local standard. For example, the four states with the highest child poverty rate according to the national standard are New Mexico, Mississippi, Louisiana and West Virginia. The four states with the highest poverty rate according to the local standard are New York, California, Massachusetts and Arizona.

The four states with the lowest poverty rate according to the national standard are the combined Colorado/Utah/Nevada, Minnesota, Alaska/Hawaii and Maine/New Hampshire/ Vermont areas. Even by the state standard, these states have below average poverty; but the honours for the very lowest state standard poverty rates go to North Dakota/South Dakota, Iowa/Kansas/Nebraska, the Colorado/Utah/Nevada group and the three small New England states.

Figure 2.3 charts the relation of the state and national child poverty rates in a way that highlights the differences between them. Here we show the percentage increase or decrease the state poverty rate represents compared to the national standard poverty rate. We see very large increases of a quarter or more in the poverty rates for Massachusetts, Rhode Island/ Connecticut, New Jersey, Minnesota and Delaware/Maryland/District of Columbia/Virginia. On the West Coast also we find three states with very large percentage increases in the poverty rate – Colorado/Utah/ Nevada, Washington and Alaska/Hawaii. As might be expected given the fact that the state medians are about the same as the national median in New York and California we find very little change in their child poverty rates.

We note the local standard poverty rates are lower than the national rates in the southern states in general, beginning with West Virginia and moving on around the southern rim to Texas and the mountain states. We find the poverty rates in Massachusetts, Rhode Island/Connecticut and New Jersey increase by six to eight percentage points[11]. In contrast we find a nine percentage point decrease in the poverty rate of West Virginia, and even greater decreases for Mississippi (11.7 points), Arkansas (11.6 points), and New Mexico (11.7 points). There is also a decrease in the six percentage point range in Montana/Idaho/Wyoming.

It clearly matters whether the state or national standard is used in many of the states. If we use state standards, New York, California and Massachusetts are the poorest states. These states are also relatively large in population terms (and geographically in terms of California). They

Figure 2.3: Percentage increase or decrease of state child poverty rate over national child poverty rate[a]

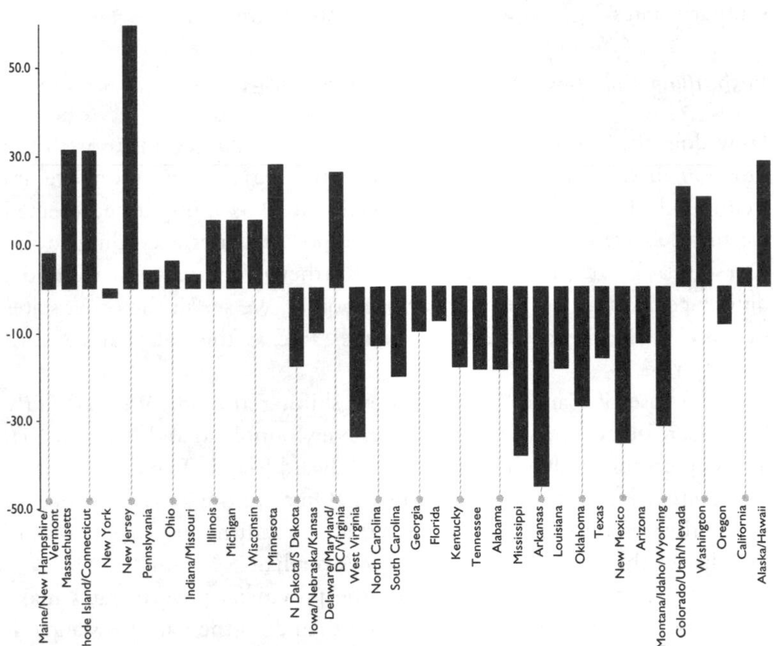

[a] Table presents comparison of state median income-based child poverty rates and national median income-based child poverty rates in each state from Table 2.1. Percentage point differences are not shown, only percent differences. See text for further explanation.

Source: Author's calculations from LIS

also contain relatively large shares of recent immigrants (southern California and New York City, in particular) and relatively large ethnic and racial minorities (in all three states).

Large differences in costs of living, particularly housing costs, make the southern states look much poorer in national versus state standards. New Mexico and Louisiana have above average poverty rates by either standard, while the state specific poverty rate in Arkansas (14.1%) is much closer to the lowest state median based rate of 13% (Iowa, Kansas, Nebraska) than to the average state rate (20.1%). In fact, when we move to state standards there is a very large variation within groups of states often thought to be homogeneous. The state specific poverty rate in Arkansas (14.1%) is very different from that of the contiguous states of Louisiana (22.8%), Mississippi (18.9%) and Tennessee (18.2%), all of which are considered 'high poverty southern states' by most observers (see also Figure 2.6).

Reshuffling child poverty rates in other countries

How does this shifting among the regions of the US compare with the situation in the four other countries whose regional variations we are examining? In the case of Australia (see Figure 2.4) as might be expected we find relatively little difference in the poverty rates according to the two standards. It is only in the ACT/Northern Territory that we find a difference greater than two percentage points. We see in the other states that the state poverty rate is about the same as the national standard poverty rate.

In the case of Canada, there is more shifting around. We find fairly large decreases, of the order of 20%, in Newfoundland and Nova Scotia. The decrease is about a third in Prince Edward Island. The child poverty rate increases by about one quarter in Ontario, the only province in which there is a notable increase. Overall, the shifting in Canada is more like that of the US than is the case for Australia.

What is notable in Canada is that the provincial poverty rates make Canada seem much more homogeneous than does the national standard. Thus, we find province standard child poverty rates converging from just below to just above 15% in Newfoundland, Manitoba, Saskatchewan, New Brunswick, Nova Scotia, Ontario and Alberta. Only British Columbia with a higher rate and Quebec and Prince Edward Island with lower rates stand apart. This is in contrast to Australia where the differences among regions are about the same for both state standards and the national standard with a range from around 10% to 16%.

We combine the national and state child poverty rates for the various regions in the five countries in Table 2.2. This tabulates child poverty rates according to state standards for the US, Canada and Australia, and national standard rates in Spain, Italy and 11 other European countries, all based on LIS data. Here we find the full range of child poverty rates from a rate of less than 3% in Sweden to a high of 26% in New York State.

We note that there is overlap between a number of Canadian provinces (those with higher poverty rates) and some American states (those with lower poverty rates). And there is some overlap between the very low poverty rate American states and Australian states. But still we find that

Figure 2.4: Child poverty rates in Australia and Canada according to state and national standards

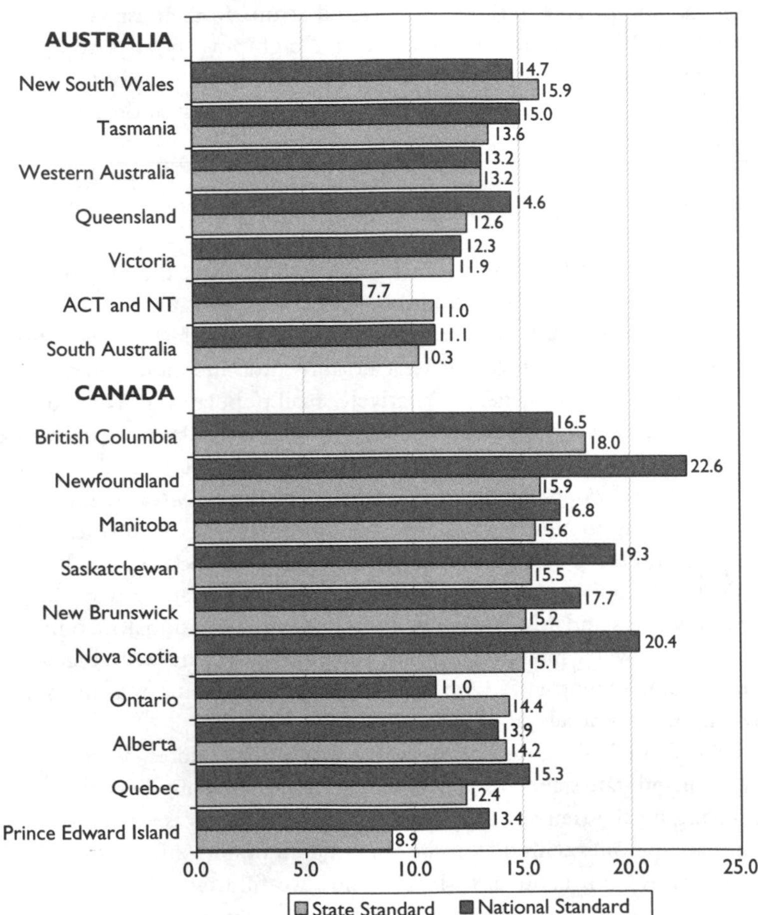

Source: Author's calculations from LIS

the highest poverty regions in Canada (British Columbia) and Australia (New South Wales) are experiencing levels of poverty (18.0% and 15.9%, respectively) weight below the median US state (Tennessee at 18.2%) and below the average of the US states (20.1%).

Clearly, the range of poverty rates across the US states (12.3% to 26.3%) is greater than the range in Canada (8.9% to 18.0%) or Australia (10.3%

to 15.9%) by a large margin. By state standards, many US states have poverty rates in the 10% to 15% range, below those found in the UK or Italy and comparable to those in Israel and Spain. In contrast, California, New York, Massachusetts and Illinois have high poverty rates compared to any national or subnational breakdown. And even the lowest US state has poverty rates well above all of the northern and central European and Scandinavian states.

US state variations in local child poverty rates

Figure 2.5 shows how the various states diverge from the average state poverty rate of 20.1% for all children in the nation, while Figure 2.6 maps the state standard poverty rates. We see a very clear pattern of the lowest rates in some states of the west, north, central and mountain regions. These are states with generally relatively small populations. We also find that they have a more equal distribution of income than is true of the other states (not shown). The high poverty rate regions make a band from California down across the southwest of the country to Louisiana and then jump to New York and the populous states of the northeast. We note again that the southern states are not uniformly poor states. In fact, aside from Louisiana they tend to have roughly average poverty rates. Thus, by the standards of state income rather than national income we see higher poverty rates are primarily the product of states with big cities, and to some extent states with large immigrant populations as measured by parents or household head being foreign born[12].

Table 2.3 takes account of the number of poor children according to national and state standards. There we see, in terms of numbers, the effect of changing the standard. We note that it is still the case that the large states are the ones with the most poor children despite effects of the shift of standards from national to local. Thus, we find over 2 million poor children by the state standard in California, and over 1 million in New York and Texas. Over one third of the 14.5 million poor children in the US live in one of these three states, and all three states have higher than average poverty rates by either standard. More than 500,000 poor children are found in each of the states of Pennsylvania, Ohio, Illinois, Michigan and Florida. When combined, these eight large states contain over one half of all poor American children.

These figures and charts raise a question as to the statistical significance of these estimates. The standard error for child poverty rates by both national and state standards is plotted in Figures 2.7a and 2.7b. These

Figure 2.5: US state child poverty rates: deviation from national poverty rate of 20.1%

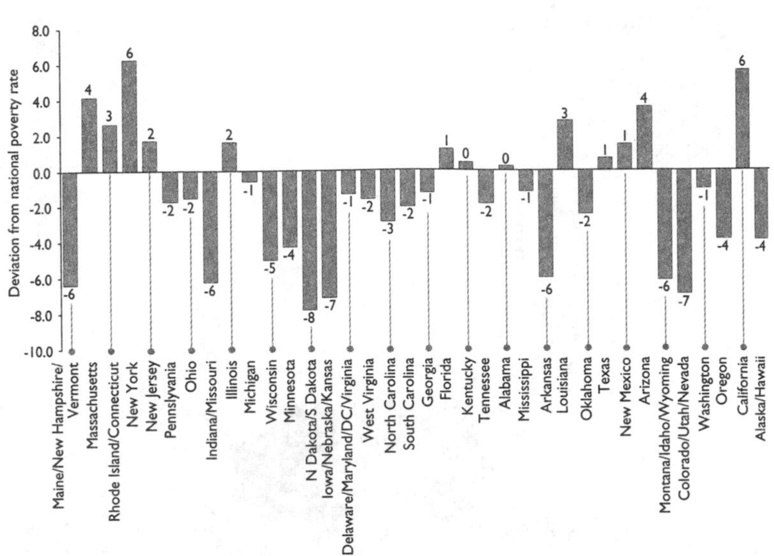

standard errors are calculated according to the US Census Bureau estimates (Statistical Abstract of the United States, 1999, Appendix C, pp C-6). Different analysts use different levels of significance to assess whether one estimate is different from another. Twice the standard error roughly corresponds to a 95% confidence interval. Using this rough rule of thumb, we can examine the differences in Figures 2.7a and 2.7b.

For the national standard, both the level and the variance in poverty rates are higher than for the state estimates (compare Figures 2.7a and 2.7b). There are, however, statistically significant differences at the 95% level in both figures. By the national standard, several states are significantly above and below the US poverty rate of 20.1%. Among the states with significantly higher poverty rates, we find California, New York and Texas, as well as several smaller states. For those significantly below the US average we find the Delaware, Maryland, Virginia, and District of Columbia grouping[13], Minnesota and several other largely midwestern states and groups of states.

Switching to the state standard, the variance among states is less at the extremes. But still California and New York are significantly poorer than average. Whereas a group of smaller New England states (New Hampshire,

Vermont, Maine) and midwestern states (eg, the Dakotas, Colorado, Utah, Nevada, Iowa, Nebraska, Indiana, Missouri) and Arkansas are significantly less poor than the average.

Figure 2.6: Child poverty rates according to state standards

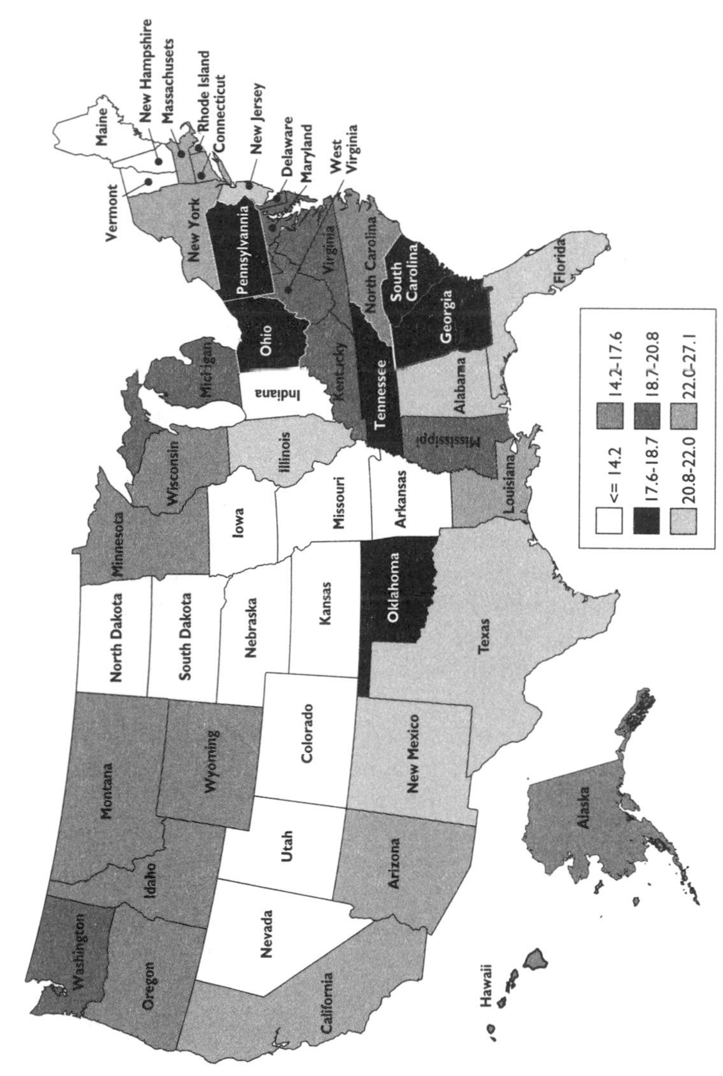

Table 2.3: Poverty rates and number of poor children according to national and state standards

State	State median as % of national median	% poor		Poor population (000s)		
		National standard	State standard	National standard	State standard	Difference
ME,NH,VT	102.6	12.7	13.7	1.14	1.23	0.09
Massachusetts	114.6	18.4	24.2	2.74	3.60	0.87
RI,CT	120.8	17.3	22.7	1.82	2.39	5.68
New York	98.3	26.9	26.3	12.57	12.32	-0.25
New Jersey	125.3	13.6	21.8	2.78	4.44	1.66
Pennsylvania	102.7	17.6	18.4	5.19	5.42	0.22
Ohio	103.5	17.5	18.6	5.11	5.43	0.32
IN,MO	100.9	13.4	13.8	3.99	4.12	0.12
Illinois	108.1	18.8	21.7	6.11	7.05	0.94
Michigan	107.2	16.9	19.5	4.36	5.02	0.67
Wisconsin	107.9	13.1	15.1	1.81	2.09	0.28
Minnesota	110.1	12.3	15.8	1.58	2.03	0.44
ND,SD	93.0	14.9	12.3	0.55	0.46	-0.09
IA,NE,KS	96.0	14.4	13.0	2.75	2.48	-0.28
DE,MD,VA	110.2	14.9	18.8	4.88	6.15	1.27
West Virginia	79.2	27.9	18.5	1.20	0.79	-0.41
North Carolina	95.7	19.8	17.2	3.77	3.27	-0.50
South Carolina	90.8	22.6	18.0	2.21	1.76	-0.45
Georgia	95.3	20.9	18.8	4.24	3.81	-0.43
Florida	95.0	23.0	21.2	8.09	7.46	-0.63

Table 2.3: contd.../

State	State median as % of national median	% poor		Poor population (000s)		
		National standard	State standard	National standard	State standard	Difference
Kentucky	90.9	25.1	20.5	2.49	2.03	-0.45
Tennessee	91.1	22.4	18.2	3.03	2.36	-0.57
Alabama	88.2	25.0	20.3	2.77	2.25	-0.52
Mississippi	77.0	30.6	18.9	2.38	1.47	-0.91
Arkansas	75.2	25.7	14.1	1.75	0.96	-0.79
Louisiana	87.0	28.0	22.8	3.47	2.83	-0.64
Oklahoma	83.9	24.2	17.6	2.18	1.59	-0.59
Texas	92.1	24.7	20.7	13.98	11.74	-2.24
New Mexico	76.3	33.3	21.6	1.71	1.11	-0.60
Arizona	91.3	27.1	23.6	3.46	3.03	-0.44
MT,ID,WY	87.7	20.3	13.9	1.49	1.02	-0.47
CO,UT,NV	105.9	10.7	13.1	2.18	2.67	0.49
Washington	111.8	15.8	19.0	2.35	2.82	0.48
Oregon	95.9	17.7	16.2	1.47	1.35	-0.13
California	102.3	24.6	25.7	22.58	23.52	0.94
AK,HI	108.5	12.6	16.1	0.64	0.82	0.18
United States	100.0	20.3	20.1	144.81	142.95	-1.87

Figure 2.7a: Estimated poverty levels and 95% confidence intervals for child poverty using national poverty standard[a]

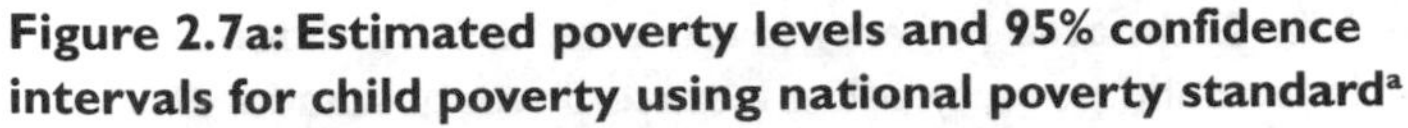

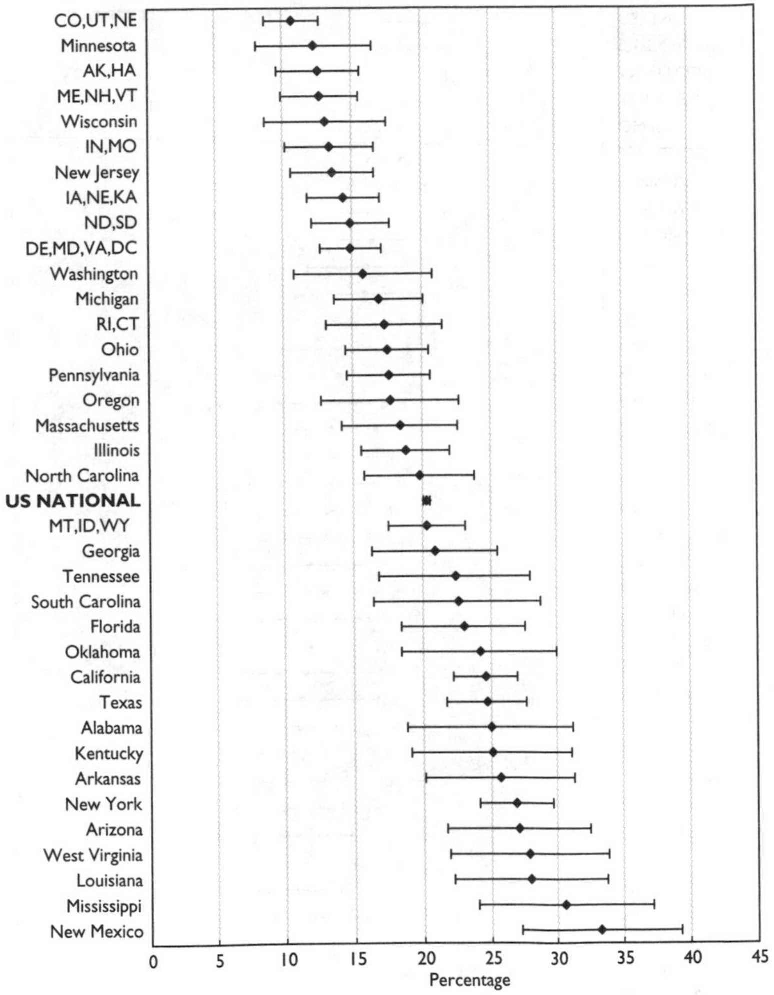

[a] Poverty rates calculated as in Table 2.1, second column.

Source: Author's calculations

Figure 2.7b: Estimated poverty levels and 95% Confidence Intervals for child poverty using a state poverty standard[a]

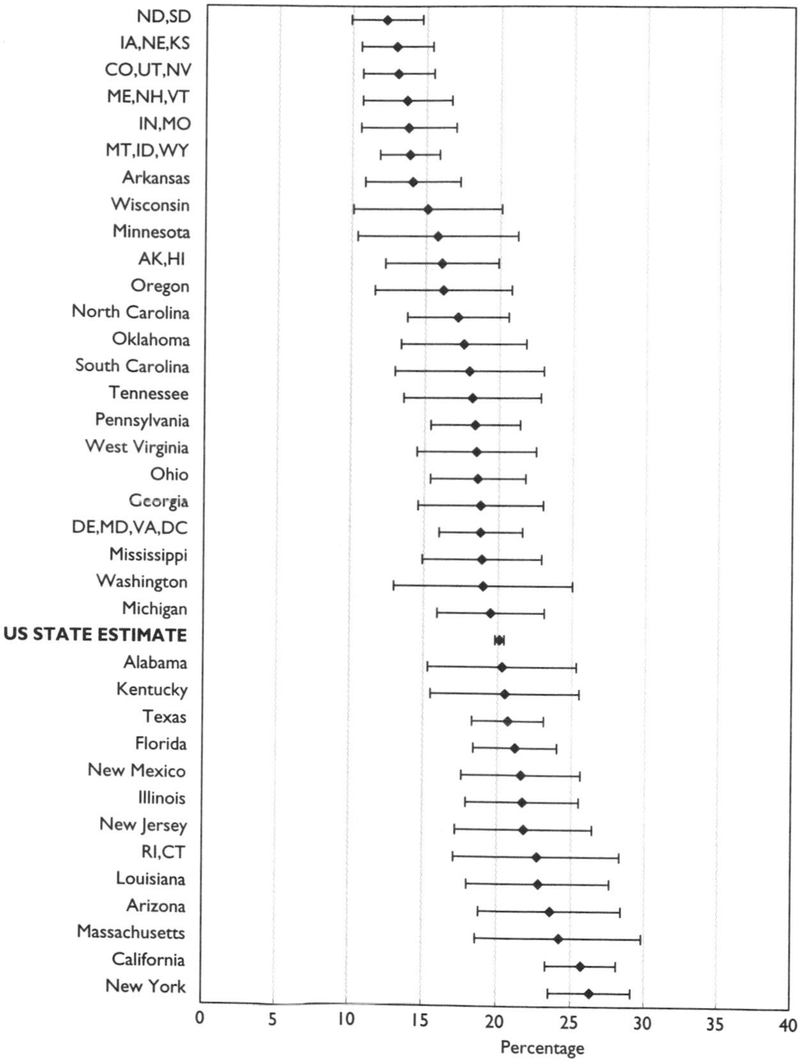

ND,SD
IA,NE,KS
CO,UT,NV
ME,NH,VT
IN,MO
MT,ID,WY
Arkansas
Wisconsin
Minnesota
AK,HI
Oregon
North Carolina
Oklahoma
South Carolina
Tennessee
Pennsylvania
West Virginia
Ohio
Georgia
DE,MD,VA,DC
Mississippi
Washington
Michigan
US STATE ESTIMATE
Alabama
Kentucky
Texas
Florida
New Mexico
Illinois
New Jersey
RI,CT
Louisiana
Arizona
Massachusetts
California
New York

0 5 10 15 20 25 30 35 40
Percentage

[a] Poverty rates calculated as in Table 2.1, third column.

Source: Author's calculations

Table 2.4: Poverty rates by family type and national and state standards (%)

State	All children		Solo mother's children		Couple's children		% distribution by family type for state standard			
	National standard[a]	State standard[b]	National standard	State standard	National standard	State standard	Solo mother	Couple	Solo father	All
ME,NH,VT	12.7	13.7	42.2	43.2	7.2	8.2	14.5	81.5	4.0	100.0
Massachusetts	18.4	24.2	50.1	59.1	8.1	12.9	23.6	72.6	3.9	100.0
RI,CT	17.3	22.7	47.9	59.2	6.7	10.3	23.5	73.1	3.4	100.0
New York	26.9	26.3	60.4	59.5	13.0	12.6	28.1	68.6	3.3	100.0
New Jersey	13.6	21.8	47.5	59.3	5.6	12.6	18.3	78.7	3.0	100.0
Pennsylvania	17.6	18.4	51.2	52.0	9.4	10.2	18.6	77.6	3.8	100.0
Ohio	17.5	18.6	47.4	50.2	8.7	9.3	21.9	74.8	3.3	100.0
IN,MO	13.4	13.8	37.2	37.6	7.5	7.9	18.6	77.8	3.6	100.0
Illinois	18.8	21.7	48.9	52.1	8.9	11.7	23.9	71.9	4.2	100.0
Michigan	16.9	19.5	49.2	55.4	6.5	7.9	22.9	72.6	4.5	100.0
Wisconsin	13.1	15.1	36.2	39.3	7.5	9.4	18.5	78.6	2.9	100.0
Minnesota	12.3	15.8	42.7	49.2	6.8	9.7	15.4	82.0	2.6	100.0
ND,SD	14.9	12.3	44.6	38.8	9.2	7.0	14.2	80.8	5.0	100.0
IA,NE,KS	14.4	13.0	39.1	36.7	9.2	7.9	16.6	79.4	4.1	100.0
DE,MD,VA	14.9	18.8	41.1	50.8	7.1	9.0	22.7	74.2	3.1	100.0
West Virginia	27.9	18.5	65.1	53.3	18.1	9.4	19.6	77.3	3.1	100.0
North Carolina	19.8	17.2	46.4	42.7	10.1	7.9	24.5	70.8	4.7	100.0
South Carolina	22.6	18.0	57.6	48.9	9.5	6.3	27.7	69.0	3.4	100.0
Georgia	20.9	18.8	50.0	45.4	9.1	8.1	26.7	68.9	4.4	100.0
Florida	23.0	21.2	52.5	48.9	12.5	11.3	25.3	70.1	4.6	100.0

Table 2.4: contd.../

State	All children		Solo mother's children		Couple's children		% distribution by family type for state standard			
	National standard[a]	State standard[b]	National standard	State standard	National standard	State standard	Solo mother	Couple	Solo father	All
Kentucky	25.1	20.5	54.2	47.7	18.7	14.8	16.8	79.1	4.2	100.0
Tennessee	22.4	18.2	55.0	45.1	9.6	7.8	27.9	69.4	2.7	100.0
Alabama	25.0	20.3	64.7	56.9	10.7	7.1	26.4	67.9	5.7	100.0
Mississippi	30.6	18.9	60.6	41.2	12.8	5.7	35.8	60.5	3.7	100.0
Arkansas	25.7	14.1	61.8	42.0	14.2	4.9	23.0	74.2	2.9	100.0
Louisiana	28.0	22.8	57.89	52.2	14.1	9.2	30.3	64.7	5.0	100.0
Oklahoma	24.2	17.6	56.6	45.4	13.5	8.6	23.0	73.5	3.5	100.0
Texas	24.7	20.7	51.0	45.4	17.6	14.1	20.3	76.2	3.5	100.0
New Mexico	33.3	21.6	56.3	42.2	24.9	14.3	24.5	72.2	3.3	100.0
Arizona	27.1	23.6	55.0	53.3	18.6	14.9	20.3	73.9	5.8	100.0
MT,ID,WY	20.3	13.9	54.5	43.1	13.8	8.2	14.0	81.7	4.3	100.0
CO,UT,NV	10.7	13.1	36.5	40.0	6.3	8.6	14.4	80.9	4.7	100.0
Washington	15.8	19.0	36.1	38.0	10.0	13.5	21.2	74.4	4.4	100.0
Oregon	17.7	16.2	46.6	42.5	10.1	9.1	19.7	75.4	4.9	100.0
California	24.6	25.7	50.1	51.0	18.2	19.3	19.3	76.0	4.7	100.0
AK,HI	12.6	16.1	40.0	46.7	6.6	9.6	16.4	80.3	3.3	100.0
United States	**20.3**	**20.1**	**50.0**	**49.3**	**11.6**	**11.5**	**21.7**	**74.3**	**4.0**	**100.0**

[a] Income less than one half national adjusted median. [b] Income less than one half state adjusted median.

Table 2.5: Poverty rates of children under age six according to national and state standards

State	Population under age 6 (in millions)	Poverty rate (%) National standard	Poverty rate (%) State standard	Poor population (000s) National standard	Poor population (000s) State standard	Poor population (000s) Difference
ME,NH,VT	0.294	13.3	14.1	0.39	0.42	0.25
Massachusetts	0.500	18.3	24.3	0.92	1.22	0.30
RI,CT	0.360	17.3	24.0	0.62	0.86	0.24
New York	1.667	28.6	28.2	4.77	4.70	-0.07
New Jersey	0.721	12.5	19.2	0.90	1.39	0.48
Pennsylvania	0.976	18.8	20.0	1.84	1.95	0.11
Ohio	0.959	20.0	20.9	1.91	2.00	0.09
IN,MO	0.983	13.6	13.7	1.33	1.35	0.01
Illinois	1.135	22.8	25.4	2.59	2.88	0.29
Michigan	0.840	19.9	22.7	1.67	1.90	0.23
Wisconsin	0.433	16.3	19.2	0.70	0.83	0.13
Minnesota	0.398	14.0	17.2	0.56	0.68	0.13
ND,SD	0.112	19.6	17.4	0.22	0.20	-0.02
IA,NE,KS	0.602	17.4	15.5	1.05	9.35	-0.11
DE,MD,VA	1.105	17.0	21.1	1.88	2.33	0.45
West Virginia	0.131	34.3	23.1	0.45	0.30	-0.15
North Carolina	0.654	22.0	19.5	1.44	1.28	-0.16
South Carolina	0.318	21.4	17.2	0.68	0.55	-0.13
Georgia	0.696	22.9	19.8	1.59	1.38	-0.21
Florida	1.195	27.0	25.4	3.23	3.04	-0.19

Table 2.5: contd.../

State	Population under age 6 (in millions)	Poverty rate (%) National standard	Poverty rate (%) State standard	Poor population (000s) National standard	Poor population (000s) State standard	Difference
Kentucky	0.329	24.2	18.2	0.80	0.60	-0.20
Tennessee	0.456	26.7	21.0	1.22	0.96	0.26
Alabama	0.366	27.9	22.7	1.02	0.83	-0.19
Mississippi	0.258	34.8	23.0	0.90	0.59	-0.31
Arkansas	0.224	29.3	16.6	0.66	0.37	-0.28
Louisiana	0.396	35.0	29.0	1.39	1.15	-0.24
Oklahoma	0.283	28.5	20.4	0.81	0.58	-0.23
Texas	1.983	26.6	22.7	5.28	4.50	-0.78
New Mexico	0.166	36.1	22.0	0.60	0.37	-0.23
Arizona	0.466	28.6	25.2	1.33	1.18	-0.16
MT,ID,WY	0.225	26.5	18.5	0.60	0.42	-0.18
CO,UT,NV	0.665	13.3	15.7	0.89	1.04	0.16
Washington	0.496	18.8	23.8	0.83	1.18	0.24
Oregon	0.264	23.1	21.3	0.61	0.56	-0.05
California	3.379	26.5	27.5	8.06	9.29	0.33
AK,HI	0.180	12.9	17.3	0.23	0.31	0.079
United States	**24.315**	**22.7**	**22.3**	**54.95**	**54.12**	**-0.84**

Poverty by state and family type

Examining child poverty rates by family type using the state standard, we find no particular shift from the national standard (see Table 2.4). The shift in standard seems to affect both of the family types tabulated separately. That is, the poverty rates of children in lone-mother and two-parent families respond to the shift in standards in about the same way (see Table 2.5). (We do not tabulate separately lone-father families because there are so few once broken down by state.)

Children in two-parent families do much better than children living with single mothers in every state. But even child poverty among couples is nearly 20% in California and above 15% in many states using either standard. Using state standards, child poverty in couple families is higher (19.3%) in California and is 14% or higher in Texas, New Mexico and Arizona, compared to a 11.5% national average rate.

Children in single-parent families do poorly (average poverty rates of 50%) by either state or national standards with rates in the 30% range in only a few states (Indiana, Missouri, Wisconsin, Colorado, Vermont, Nevada and Washington). Child poverty rates among single parents of almost 60% are found in New York, New Jersey, Rhode Island, Connecticut and Massachusetts by their own state standards. These are far above state-based single-parent rates in the south where only Alabama (56.9%) and Louisiana (52.2%) are above 50%. The national single-parent poverty rate is about 50% by either state or national measure.

Single-parent poverty (one minus couple poverty) varies from 18% to 40% of the poor depending on the state in question (Table 2.4, right side). Poor children living with single parents are the largest as a share of the poor in the deep south (eg, Mississippi, Alabama, Louisiana, Georgia, South Carolina) and in New York (31.4%). In contrast, poor children living with single parents are only about 24% of the poor in California, and even less in several other states (eg, 18% in Minnesota, Maine, New Hampshire and Vermont).

Conclusions

Measuring poverty requires that resources be compared to needs where needs and resources are relative to some reference group. The nation is the usual reference group for poverty measurement. But people might also compare themselves to the important reference groups which are geographically, socially and politically more similar. The issue of the proper reference group has until now received little attention in most national and cross-national studies of poverty and social exclusion.

We would argue that the state standards explored here come closer to the social standards that in fact operate when societies define some people as poor. It is in the local community that these evaluations and self-evaluations are made. It is a practical problem to carry out statistical studies that seek to approximate the living standards of the local community. Moving from the national level to the state level would seem to be a move in the right direction. And given the problems of small sample size as one moves toward the local community, it may be that the state as the unit for defining a poverty line is the most realistic choice available. In the US, it may also be the most policy-relevant grouping, considering the effects of efforts at fighting child poverty. We note that we can accomplish even this level of detail only by combining the large US current population survey March income supplement for three years. Because of the limited number of Canadian and Australian sub-regions, they too can be disaggregated But estimates for other countries can only be suggestive given the small size of the surveys.

Our next steps will be to further refine these first estimates and also to add several types of analyses, including selecting out children living with parents or adults who are foreign born and children living in large central cities in the largest states. Clearly, it is also important to investigate the determinants of state and regional child poverty and the extent to which market incomes (earnings and property income) as compared to state and local tax-transfer policy alleviate or exacerbate child poverty. We thus see this chapter as the first step in a series of analyses. In one sense, and considering the US alone, we have added 50 'new' databases to LIS. Indeed, many of our US states are far larger than are Scandinavian or the European nation/states. This opens great future possibilities for LIS analysis that use different levels of geographical and political aggregation. We hope that these possibilities will also be of interest to other researchers and policy analysts.

Notes

[1] The authors want to thank the LIS member countries for their support of LIS and hence this research. This research was sponsored in part by a grant from the MacArthur Network on the Family and the Economy, by the Ford Foundation, and by the US Department of Health and Human Services. The author would like to thank Bob Haveman, Frank Fürstenberg, Neil Bennett, Patricia Ruggles,

participants in the Conference on Child Well-Being and Child Poverty, and participants in the 1999 APPAM Conference Symposium on Poverty Measurement, for comments on an earlier draft of this chapter. The authors assume full responsibility for all conclusions and opinions contained here.

[2] We also have regional data for Italy, Spain, and the UK, which is not included here. We could prepare similar data for other LIS datasets, or combinations of datasets, eg, the Benelux nations. However, we have not included data on other population sub-groups in this paper.

[3] Unfortunately, LIS is not yet able to obtain the ECHP national datasets for all of the EC nations, particularly the Mediterranean nations (Portugal, Spain, Greece) and Ireland. Hence, we are unable to present 'supranational' poverty rates for the EC to contrast to Australia, Canada or the US.

[4] This convention is also adopted by OECD and by the EC (Townsend, 1979; Förster, 1993; Hagenaars et al, 1998; Eurostat, 1998).

[5] This shift to local standards as well as local prices is not as likely if one's conception of poverty involves an absolute standard. Conceivably a researcher might chose to define market baskets that take into account differences in consumption in different regions; but so far as we are aware this has not been done for poverty measurement nor is a rationale for it at all developed in the literature. Perhaps that is just as well.

[6] We use the terms household and family interchangeably. Our formal unit of aggregation is the household – all persons living together and sharing the same housing facilities – in almost all nations. In Canada, the 'household' refers to a more narrow definition of the economic 'family' unit. But given that few unrelated individuals live together in Canada, and that by and large children live with one or both of their parents, this is not a particular problem in this chapter.

[7] In what follows we use the term 'states' to apply to whatever regional breakdowns are available for each of the countries, ignoring whether these regions are formally named states or provinces or regions.

[8] We worked from the national (and state) medians in each survey year, not from a single year's median. If one wanted to use absolute poverty lines, they could do the same, or price every year's income to the median for the mid- or ending year, and use a single poverty line.

[9] In our original conference paper, we included both Italy and Spain. These tabulations are available from the authors, but were excluded here because of space constraints.

[10] Canada has only 30 million people, Australia 18 million California, at 32.2 million, has a larger population than Canada. The Australian population is slightly less than that of Texas (19.4 million) and about the same size as New York (18.1 million). All figures here are for 1997 and are taken from the United Nations (1999, Table 2.17, p. 197), and the *Statistical Abstract of the United States, 1998* (1998, Table 33, p 33).

[11] The 8.2 percentage point difference for New Jersey, ie, 21.8% of poor children by the state standard, versus 13.6% by the national standard translates to a 60.2% difference (ie, 8.2 divided by 13.6) in Figure 2.5.

[12] Indeed if we were not stretching the small state samples, they might want to make adjustments to states standards for the metropolitan and non-metropolitan areas within them as well.

[13] The poverty rate among this group is a bit misleading because the District of Columbia has a much higher poverty rate than do the others, which it is combined with.

References

Björklund, A. and Freeman, R. (1994) 'Generating inequality and reducing poverty the Swedish way', NBER Working Paper No 4945, Cambridge, MA: National Bureau of Economic Research, December.

Bradbury, B. (1989) 'Family size equivalence and survey evaluations of income and well-being', *Journal of Social Policy*, vol 11, no 3, pp 383-408.

Bradbury, B. and Jänttii, M. (1999) 'Child poverty across the industrialized world: evidence from the LIS', mimeo, Turku, Finland: Turku University, August.

Buhmann, B., Rainwater, L., Schmaus, G. and Smeeding, T.M. (1988) 'Equivalence scales, well-being, inequality and poverty', *Review of Income and Wealth*, June, pp 115-42.

Bureau of the Census (1999) 'Poverty in the United States: 1998', *Current Population Reports*, Washington, DC: US Government Printing Office, pp 60-207.

Citro, C. and Michael, R. (1995) *Measuring poverty: A new approach*, Washington, DC: US National Academy of Sciences Press.

Coder, J. (1999) 'Population weights for children in the CPS', Final Report to LIS and DHHS, Annapolis, MD: Avenir Research, September.

Coleman, J. (1988) 'Social capital in the creation of human capital', *American Journal of Sociology*, vol 94, pp S95-S120.

Coleman, J. and Rainwater, L. (1978) *Social standing in America*, New York, NY: Basic Books.

Commission of the European Communities (1994) 'The demographic situation of the European Union', Document No COM(94) 595 final, Luxembourg: Office for Official Publications of the European Communities, December.

Eurostat (1998) 'Analysis of income distribution in 13 EU member states', *Statistics in Focus*, no 11, Luxembourg: European Statistical Office, August.

Flores, K., Douglas, T. and Ellwood, D. (1998) 'The children's budget report: A detailed analysis of spending on low income children's programs in 13 states,' New Federalism Series Occasional Paper No 14, Washington, DC: Urban Institute, September.

Förster, M. (1993) 'Comparing poverty in 13 OECD countries: traditional and synthetic approaches', *Studies in Social Policy No 10*, Paris: OECD, October.

Grolet, M. and Morrissette, R. (1999) 'To what extent are Canadians exposed to low income?', Catalogue no 75Fao2MPE99001, Ottawa, Canada: Statistics Canada.

Hagenaars, A.J.M., de Vos, K. and Asghar Zaidi, M. (1998) 'Patterns of poverty in Europe', in S. Jenkins, A. Kapteyn, and B. Van Praag (eds) *The distribution of welfare and household production: International perspectives*, Cambridge: Cambridge University Press.

Immervoll, H., O'Donaghue, C. and Sutherland, H. (1999) 'An introduction to EUROMOD, EUROMOD Working Paper EMO/99, Cambridge: Department of Economics, University of Cambridge.

Loprest, P. (1999) 'How families that left welfare are doing: a national picture', New Federalism Series B, No B-1, Washington, DC: Urban Institute, August.

Office of the Auditor General of Canada (1999) *Report of the Auditor General of Canada: Human Resources Development Canada: Accountability for shared social programs: National Child Benefit and Employability Assistance for people with disabilities*, Ottawa, Canada: Minister of Public Works and Government Services Canada, April.

Rainwater, L. (1974) *What money buys*, New York, NY: Basic Books.

Rainwater, L. (1990) 'Poverty and equivalence as social constructions', LIS Working Paper No 91, Luxembourg: Luxembourg Income Study.

Rainwater, L. (1991) 'The problem of social exclusion', in *Human Resources in Europe at the Dawn of the 21st Century*, Luxembourg: Eurostat.

Rainwater, L. (1992) 'Social inequality in Europe and the challenge to social science', in M. Dierkes and B. Biervert (eds) *European social science in transition: Assessment and outlook*, Frankfurt am Main/Boulder, CO: Campus Verlag/Westview Press.

Rainwater, L. and Smeeding, T.M. (1995) 'US doing poorly-compared to others-policy point of view', *Child Poverty News & Issues*, vol 5, no 3, Fall.

Rainwater, L. and Smeeding, T.M. (2000) 'Establishing equivalent family income', mimeo, Centre for Policy Research, Syracuse University/LIS.

Sen, A. (1992) *Inequality reexamined*, Cambridge, MA: Harvard University Press.

Smeeding, T.M. (1992) 'US poverty and income security in a cross-national perspective: the war on poverty: what worked?', *Challenge* (January/ February), pp 16-23.

Smeeding, T.M. (1998) 'Reshuffling responsibilities in old age: the United States in a comparative perspective', in J. Gonyea (ed) *Re-securing social security and Medicare: Understanding privatization and risk*, Washington, DC: Gerontological Society of America.

Smeeding, T.M. and Torrey, B.B. (1988) 'Poor children in rich countries', *Science*, vol 242 (November), pp 873-7.

Smeeding, T.M., Rainwater, L. and O'Higgins, M. (eds) (1990) *Poverty, inequality and income distribution in comparative perspective: The Luxembourg Income Study*, London/Washington, DC: Harvester Wheatsheaf/Urban Institute Press.

Smeeding, T.M., Saunders, P., Coder, J., Jenkins, S., Fritzell, J., Hagenaars, A.J.M., Hauser, R. and Wolfson, M. (1993) 'Poverty, inequality and family living standards impacts across seven nations: the effect of noncash subsidies for health, education and housing', *Review of Income and Wealth*, vol 39, no 3, September, pp 229-56.

Smeeding T.M., Danziger, S. and Rainwater, L. (1995) 'The Western welfare state in the 1990s: toward a new model of anti-poverty policy for families and children', LIS Working Paper No 126, Luxembourg: Luxembourg Income Study.

Townsend, P. (1979) *Poverty in the United Kingdom*, Harmondsworth: Penguin Books.

Statistical Abstract of the United States, 1998 (1998) Washington, DC: US Bureau of Census, October.

United Nations (1999) *Human Development Report 1999*, United Nations Development Programs, New York, NY: Oxford University Press, July.

Appendix I

The LIS United States 1995-97 state file

In order to facilitate comparisons of countries in the LIS database with individual states, a special data set has been created and placed along with other LIS data sets. This data set was created by combining three separate March CPS files, those for March 1996, 1997 and 1998 (income in 1995, 1996 and 1997, respectively). These three data sets were combined in order to increase sample sizes and reduce sampling variances that would otherwise result from the use of data for a single year. Data from these files were 'lissified' (converted to the standard LIS format) and then concentrated. The survey weights on each file have been divided by three so that the results from the combined file sum to the average for the three-year period. Income amounts are stated in the prices of the income reference year (users may price adjust the files using the price deflator of their choice).

The data from some states have been combined because the sample size, even after combining the three surveys, was deemed too small to provide reliable estimates at a 5% confidence level. States that were combined and shown as groups include the following:

Maine/NewHampshire/Vermont;
Montana/Idaho/Wyoming;
Colorado/Utah/Nevada;
Indiana/Missouri;
Iowa/Nebraska/Kansas;
North Dakota/South Dakota;
Maryland/Virginia/Delaware;
Alaska/Hawaii.

All other states are identified separately. The resulting data set includes a total of 150,239 households, 301,771 adult, and 92,089 child records. This file can also be used to undertake research at the national level for population sub-groups whose sample sizes may be somewhat too small for any single year.

Adjusting the March CPS child survey weights

The survey weights provided by the Bureau of the Census on the public use data file sum to population controls by detailed age, race and gender at the national level. These controls are based on the Census Bureau's best estimates of the civilian non-institutional population as of the survey month and are adjusted for the estimated 1990 Census undercount. Unfortunately, the Census Bureau does not require that the sum of these survey weights correspond to its best estimates of the population at the state level. At the state level, control is maintained only for estimates of the population aged 16 and over. This lack of control at the state level for important population sub-groups, such as children under age 18, has resulted in year-to-year fluctuations in the estimates within states, which can make the data difficult to use.

The data used in this study have been adjusted ('reweighted') so that the sum of weights at the state level correspond to the Census state estimates of the number of persons aged, 'under 5' and '5 to 17'. A multivariate raking procedure was employed to derive weighting adjustment factors, which ensure that the sum of weights at both the national and state levels meet population controls. In this case, national level counts were controlled to the original survey estimates for the under-18 population by poverty status, relationship, gender and race/ethnicity.

Appendix II

A Regions of Australia
No states are combined

B Regions of Canada

No provinces are combined. Northwest territories and Yukon are excluded.

PART 2

Outcomes for children

Introduction

Ultimately we are interested in the effects of child poverty rates on children's physical and mental development, health and survival rates, educational achievement and job prospects, incomes and life expectancy. In Part 2 of this volume various authors try to answer the question of whether those that spend their childhood in poverty are at a marked disadvantage, as measured by various indicators.

In the first chapter Shelley Phipps explores connections that exist among values, policies and outcomes for young children in three nations: Canada, Norway and the United States. Phipps analyses three collections of microdata from the early to mid-1990s: the World Values Survey (1990); the Luxembourg Income Study (1994 and 1995 LIS); and three national surveys (the Canadian Longitudinal Survey of Children and Youth, the Norwegian Health Survey and the US National Longitudinal Survey of Youth – Mother/Child Survey). This is a ground-breaking study because of Phipps' ability to combine all three types of data in one study. It is among the first to address child poverty and outcomes in one cross-national study.

The results emphasise the importance of values in shaping social policies that affect the well-being of children, while existing social policies may help to shape the values of the people who experience them. The results also confirm that social policies available to households with young children have important associations with household poverty status as well as being indicators of children's well-being such as physical or emotional health or success at school. In addition the results provide evidence to support the underlying hypothesis of most of the chapters in this volume: child outcomes vary negatively and systematically across nations; more national child poverty is correlated with negative outcomes for children.

In Chapter Four John Micklewright and Kitty Stewart consider a set of measurable differences in the well-being of children between current

European Union member states and the ten Central and Eastern European countries. The authors adopt a broader view than is typically taken, which includes a comprehensive picture of the well-being of children similar to that of the UNDP's *Human Development Report* and the associated 'capability' approach of Amartya Sen. Three dimensions of well-being are analysed: economic welfare (child poverty), health (mortality among children and young people) and education (school enrolment and learning achievement).

The authors find, on the basis of several indicators, that some of the Central and Eastern European countries still, after the upheaval of social and economic transition, compete well with the EU member states and often perform better than other countries with similar levels of national income. Fourteen-year-olds in the Czech Republic, for example, performed better at standardised math tests than their peers in any other potential EU state, while the level of achievement in both Bulgaria and Hungary was well above the EU average. Romania and the Baltic States did relatively poorly on the standardised math tests, but no worse than Greece or Spain and much better than Portugal – all countries with substantially higher per capital GDP. Under-5 mortality rates are higher in all Central and Eastern European states, except Slovenia, than the EU average, but lower than in other countries with a similar per capita GDP. Micklewright and Stewart also suggest that the Czech Republic would emerge well from a comparison of child poverty rates with its Western neighbours, a fact that is confirmed by Bradbury and Jäntti in Part 1 of this volume. Despite the present situation, the prospects for the region seem less promising, as Micklewright and Stewart report rising child poverty rates in much of the Central and Eastern European region.

The third and the fourth chapters in this second part of the volume address whether low income in childhood leaves a lasting scar throughout life. Both studies focus on a particular country, as few countries have the data necessary to track children through to later life. Paul Gregg and Stephen Machin study the relationship between childhood experiences, subsequent educational attainment and adult labour market performance, and how these factors link with the somewhat larger body of work on the extent of intergenerational mobility. Their study draws on data from two British birth cohorts, born during a week in March 1958 (the National Child Development Study, NCDS) and during a week in April 1970 (the 1970 British Cohort Study, BCS70). These are unique data sources that follow cohort members from birth, through the childhood years and into adulthood, collecting an important amount of information along the way. The two surveys have similar structures and, for some of the analysis, therefore enabled the authors to compare the two birth cohorts. Their findings reveal that financial distress faced during childhood entails a persistent (negative) association with the subsequent economic success of individuals. An important aspect of this link is educational attainment, which is vastly inferior for disadvantaged children. Furthermore, Gregg and Machin found that children of parents who also grew up in socially disadvantaged situations have lower early-age cognitive abilities, suggesting a potentially important cross-generational link that may well spill over to affect the subsequent economic fortunes of children of disadvantaged individuals.

Felix Büchel, Joachim R. Frick, Peter Krause, and Gert G. Wagner also address the relationship between inequality and poverty as they affect educational attainment in West Germany. They use pooled data from a West German subsample of 14-year-old children included in the German Socio-economic Panel Study, collected from the mid-1980s to the mid-1990s. The contribution from Büchel et al shows that a socially oriented education policy plays an important role. They found that the parental attitude at the time of decision making about a specific kind of school to be attended by their child was more influential than their financial situation once the child had enrolled. The results also show that among the 'real' poor in Germany there is a substantial portion of households that are able to keep educational options open to their children and, in doing so, offer promising long-term perspectives to their children. The opportunities for poor children to attend *Gymnasium* are not significantly less than for children living in households with intermediate incomes. Büchel, Frick, Krause and Wagner consider this as an indication of the success of Germany's socially aware education policy.

Anne H. Gauthier and Frank F. Furstenberg Jr add a new dimension to the cross-national measurement of child well-being, the use of time. Here they analyse the patterns of time use of teenagers and young adults, aged 15 to 24 in Austria, Canada, Finland and Italy. Their aim is to document the inequalities among young people, both between and within countries, as revealed by their patterns of time use. This is a first exploration of 'time budgeting' data to approach the complex topic of inequalities and social exclusion. Time budgeting data provide an extremely rich window into the world of youth but are not completely adequate to reveal the important differences in the nature and quality of young people's experiences and daily activities. Nevertheless, Gauthier and Furstenberg's results suggest some relationships between young people's patterns of time use and levels of public spending and income inequality. Further inquiries using these data will yield important results in years to come.

The chapter by Karen Christopher, Paula England, Sara McLanahan, Katherin Ross and Timothy M. Smeeding analyses gender inequality in poverty in eight industrialised countries and its consequences for child poverty, with mothers' poverty as the vehicle that generates poverty. Using data from the LIS, the researchers try to establish why lone-mother households are poorer than lone-father ones and how welfare states and family demography affect gender inequality in poverty. Women have higher poverty rates than men in all the countries included in their study, except in Sweden where both rates are extremely low; but the researchers report considerable differences in the ratio of women's poverty to men's among non-older people in most other nations. This ratio is the highest in the US, followed by Australia. In both countries, and also in Canada, France and Germany, the welfare state seems to do little to reduce the gender inequality in poverty produced by single motherhood and labour market inequalities. In the UK, the welfare state considerably reduces gender inequality in poverty, but the nations whose welfare states do the most for women relative to men are the Netherlands and Sweden. In Sweden, both women and men experience the same poverty rates, even before taxes and transfers; but taxes and transfers further reduce gender inequality in poverty. As regards family demography, they find that all nations would have higher gender inequality in poverty if they had the US family demography.

The chapters in Part 2 suggest the broad outlines of important aspects of child well-being: heath, education, the use of time and mothers' well-being. The studies discussed in the chapters are among the first to assess the effects of poverty on the well-being of children.

THREE

Values, policies and the well-being of young children in Canada, Norway and the United States

Shelley Phipps[1]

Introduction

This chapter explores connections that exist among values, policies and outcomes for young children in Canada, Norway and the United States. For example, values are likely to be directly associated with the well-being of children by influencing parenting styles and the expectations which parents have for their children. Values may help to shape social policies that affect the well-being of children; existing social policies may help to shape the values of the people who experience them. Social policies available to families with young children might be expected to have important associations with family poverty status as well as indicators of children's well-being such as physical or emotional health or success at school; perceptions about problems/success of children will influence perceived social policy needs.

To examine some of these connections, use is made in this chapter of three different collections of microdata from the early to mid-1990s: The World Values Survey (1990); the Luxembourg Income Study (LIS) (1994 and 1995); and three microdata surveys which provide information about child health and well-being (the Canadian National Longitudinal Survey of Children and Youth (1994/95); the Norwegian Health Survey (1994) and the US National Longitudinal Survey of Youth – Mother/Child Survey (1994).

An obvious question to ask at this stage is why it makes sense to study Canada, Norway and the US? The US and Canada are obvious choices for comparison, given the proximity and policy similarities between the two. Norway makes an interesting third choice insofar as it is a country with policies that are very different from the other two. (Of course, a necessary condition was also that all countries have accessible microdata on child outcomes, which in practice was a very limiting condition.) While there are differences in policy between Canada and the US, they are less dramatic than the difference between what is available in Norway and what is available in either of the North American countries. This variation increases what can be learned from the cross-country comparisons.

While Canada, Norway and the US are all affluent, industrialised countries, it should be noted at the very beginning that the three countries studied do differ significantly in terms of geography and culture. Canada and the US are huge geographically, relatively 'young' and have more ethnically heterogeneous populations than Norway. Results should be interpreted with such differences in mind – it may not always be possible to straightforwardly transfer a particular policy from one country to another, given differences in history, culture and circumstance.

The remainder of the chapter is organised as follows: the next section discusses differences in values across the three countries studied, I then focus on differences in policies, followed by a discussion on child outcomes and, finally, a conclusion.

Values and children

This section of the chapter uses data from the World Values Survey (1990) to provide evidence of differences in values that exist across the three countries studied. (The World Values Survey is a set of microdata sets in which respondents in each included country were asked the same questions concerning their attitudes/values.) Three themes are explored. First, what do people perceive to be the reason for poverty? Second, how do people feel about income inequality? Third, what are social expectations about what children should learn at home?

Perceptions of the reason for poverty

Tables 3.1a and 3.1b take up the first values-related theme, and compare the three countries in terms of what people perceive to be the reason for poverty. Specifically, Table 3.1a compares answers to the question 'Why are there people who live in need?' Possible answers include: unlucky,

Table 3.1a: Attitudes about why people live in need

Question: Why are there people in this country who live in need? Which of these reasons do you consider most important?	Canada n=1,691		United States n=1,769		Norway n=1,200	
	Male	Female	Male	Female	Male	Female
Because they are unlucky	8.50	9.12	8.17	7.88	14.72	14.43
Because of laziness and lack of will power	34.68	29.04	40.13	38.03	14.72	7.39
Because there is injustice in our society	30.37	33.20	30.57	34.35	44.98	52.75
It's an inevitable part of modern progress	22.62	22.81	18.26	16.07	22.01	21.48
None of the above	3.83	5.83	2.87	3.68	3.56	3.95

Note: The sample is all respondents who answered this question regardless of age or child status.

Source: Author's calculations using the World Values Survey

Table 3.1b: Probit regression of the probability of answering that people live in need because they are lazy

Variable	Coefficient	Standard error
Dummy=1 if respondent is female	-0.184*	0.043
Dummy=1 if married	0.064	0.053
Dummy=1 if children	0.006	0.059
Age of respondent	-0.023*	0.008
Age squared	0.00026*	0.0001
Income	-0.021**	0.010
Dummy=1 if US	0.150*	0.048
Dummy=1 if NW	-0.747*	0.063
Intercept	0.125	0.161
Ordered Value =1 lazy most important	1,180	
=0 lazy not most important	2,832	

Significance: * = 99%, ** = 95%, *** = 90%.
Note: The sample size differs from Table 3.2 due to missing values for independent variables.
Source: Author's calculations using the World Values Survey

laziness, social injustice, part of progress, none of the above. As a quick glance at Table 3.1a reveals, there are striking differences across countries in answer to this question. While 52% of women in Norway perceive poverty to be the result of social injustice, only 33% of women in Canada and 34% of women in the US made this response. Men in all three countries are more likely than women to believe that people live in need because they are lazy and are less likely to feel that people live in need as a result of social injustice.

Probit analysis of the probability of believing people live in need because they are lazy, using the three countries pooled indicates that individuals living in the US are significantly more likely than Canadians to believe this is true, individuals living in Norway are significantly less likely to believe poverty is the result of laziness (see Table 3.1b). This pattern accords with much cross-country comparative research on social policy in general (eg, Ringen, 1987; Esping-Andersen, 1990; Gauthier, 1996) which groups Canada and the US together as 'liberal' countries very much focused on preserving efficiency through the maintenance of appropriate work incentives. That is, policy discussion in these countries is extremely concerned that 'too generous' transfers will lead people, naturally lazy, to take advantage of the programmes by working less for pay and 'enjoying' more time jobless. Such thinking goes back many years (eg, the British Poor Laws of the 17th century), but still characterises policy discussion today.

Attitudes toward income inequality

Figures 3.1a and 3.1b and Table 3.2 focus on attitudes toward income inequality. Survey respondents were asked 'On a scale of 1-10, what are your views about income distribution?' A response of '1' indicates that incomes should be more equal; a response of '10' indicates that there should be greater individual effort. Again, there are striking differences across the three countries. Focusing this time on men, over 50% of male respondents in both Canada and the US chose 8 or higher (ie, they are *not* egalitarians) versus only one third in Norway. Figures 3.1a and 3.1b also indicate interesting differences in the *pattern* of responses across countries. The Norwegian responses more closely resemble a normal distribution, with many responses in the middle, and relatively fewer at the tails (of being very concerned about income inequality or very unconcerned). The Canadian and US responses are skewed, with many

Figure 3.1: Attitudes about income inequality

a) Males

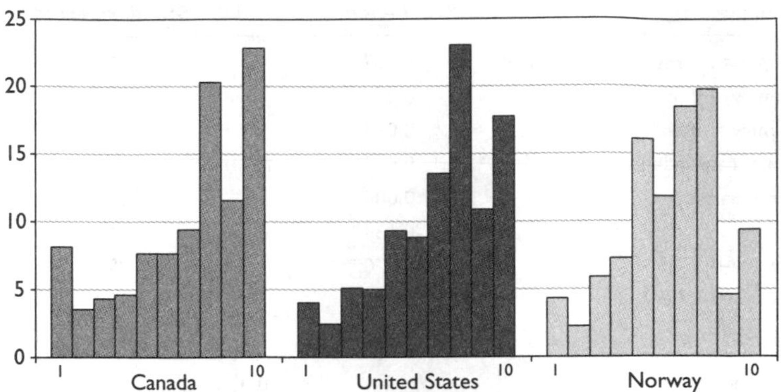

b) Females

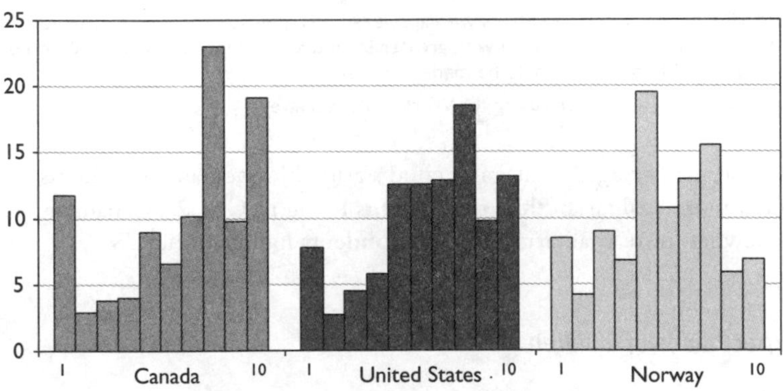

Note: '1' means the respondents agrees completely with the statement 'Incomes should be made more equal'; '10' means the respondent agrees completely with the statement 'There should be greater incentives for individual effort'.

more people expressing a lack of concern about income inequality. This is particularly true of men. One important Canada/US difference is that there is a small, but clearly evident spike at '1' for Canada, indicating the highest level of concern about income inequality that is less apparent for the US.

Results of ordinary least squares regressions reported in Table 3.2 indicate that the statistical differences across countries remain after controlling for

Table 3.2: Attitudes about income inequality ordinary least squares regression–dependent variable scale 1-10

Variable	Coefficient	Standard error
Dummy=1 if respondent is female	0.437*	0.083
Dummy=1 if married	0.061	0.104
Dummy=1 if children	-0.094	0.113
Age of respondent	-0.012	0.015
Age squared	0.0001	0.0002
Income	-0.134*	0.018
Dummy=1 if US	-0.170***	0.098
Dummy=1 if NW	0.680*	0.109
Intercept	5.223*	0.315
Adjusted R^2	0.035	
sample size	4,059	

Significance: * = 99%, ** = 95%, *** = 90%.

Note: The sample is all respondents who answered this question regardless of age or child status. (1: agree completely with greater incentives for individual effort, 10: agree completely with incomes should be made more equal)

Source: Author's calculations using the World Values Survey

income, gender, age, marital and child status. Norwegian respondents are much more egalitarian than respondents living in Canada; Canadians are somewhat more egalitarian than respondents living in the US.

Expectations of children

Finally, the third theme pursued in this section is that expectations of children may differ across countries, with associated differences in what they are taught or which pressures they face and this may have links with observed outcomes for children. Table 3.3 reports on qualities people feel children should learn at home in Canada, Norway and the US. Notice, first, that there are some broad similarities across countries. For example, a majority of respondents (male and female) in all three countries cite good manners, responsibility, and tolerance and respect for others as qualities children should learn at home. However, while there is some consensus about what children should learn at home, there are also striking differences across the countries. Respondents in Norway are more likely than Canadians to mention independence, good manners, responsibility

Table 3.3: Attitudes about qualities children should learn at home

Question: Here is a list of qualities children can be encouraged to learn at home. Which, if any, do you consider to be most important? (Choose up to five)

	Canada n=1,730		United States n=1,839		Norway n=1,239	
	Male	Female	Male	Female	Male	Female
Good manners	75.97	74.13	77.24	77.73	76.06	77.98
Independence	40.99	46.49	46.73	58.40	83.15	88.91
Hard work	40.08	30.29	55.41	41.50	8.35	4.80
Responsibility	71.67	78.29	68.78	73.18	87.87	91.56
Imagination	24.98	20.77	26.53	27.53	27.24	35.60
Tolerance and respect for others	79.62	80.37	70.10	73.89	58.58	69.04
Thrift/value of money and things	22.26	20.57	29.80	26.92	22.68	20.53
Determination	37.98	37.36	36.84	34.11	35.43	29.97
Religious faith	27.71	33.19	51.43	56.38	11.50	16.89
Unselfishness	43.48	41.05	35.51	38.46	12.13	6.79
Obedience	26.11	30.61	38.47	36.64	32.60	29.97

Note: The sample is all respondents who answered this question regardless of age or child status.

Source: Author's calculations using the World Values Survey

and imagination, and less likely to mention hard work, unselfishness, religious faith or tolerance/respect. Respondents in the US are more likely than Canadians to mention independence, hard work, imagination and religious faith; they are less likely to mention tolerance/respect[2]. An interesting question to ask is whether or not there are any observable differences in children's behaviour which reflect differences in emphasis across countries in what children are expected to learn (and correspondingly in pressures children face to learn/achieve).

Values and policy – a discussion of connections

This section of the chapter discusses differences in child-related policies across the three countries in the context of some of the differences in values outlined in the previous section. Many authors (eg, Baker, 1995; Gauthier, 1996; Kamerman and Kahn, 1997) have provided excellent cross-

Table 3.4: Taxes and transfers received by families with children and selected sociodemographic characteristics

	Canada 1994 n=17,005	United States 1994 n=28,097	Norway 1995 n=3,238
Lone mother households	16.0%	31.3%	32.4%
Mother with positive earnings – All	62.5%	62.5%	79.0%
Mother with positive earnings – Lone mother households	50.4%	61.2%	71.1%
Household received social transfers – All	92.2%	56.1%	99.7%
Household received social transfers – Lone mother households	99.8%	90.0%	99.6%
Average social transfers ($94 Cdn)[a] All	6,222	3,648	7,599
Households who receive Average social transfers	6,748	6,501	7,624
($94 Cdn)[a] – Lone mother households – All	10,465	7,249	11,856
Households who receive	10,482	8,052	11,906

[a] Converted to 1994 Canadian dollars using purchasing power parities (household consumption).

Note: The sample is all children aged 0-11 (each child is one observation; there can be more than one observation per household).

Source: Author's calculations using the LIS

country analyses of variations in family policy. What is provided here is illustrative material that enables the discussion of possible connections between values and policies rather than a comprehensive survey of policies for children in the three countries. Note also that since outcomes data for children were collected in 1994/95, policies in place at that time are those discussed.

Three themes, generally linked to those discussed in the values section of the chapter are developed here: (1) overall generosity of programmes available; (2) attitudes toward work incentives and the design of programmes for children; (3) public versus private responsibility for children.

Table 3.5: Relative poverty status of families with young children all households and lone-mother households

		Canada (1994)	United States (1994)	Norway (1995)
All households		n=17,005	n=28,097	n=3,238
Poor	Before taxes and transfers income	26.1%	32.2%	19.8%
	After taxes and transfers income	16.9%	29.3%	6.1%
Rich	Before taxes and transfers Income	20.0%	24.3%	16.0%
	After taxes and transfers income	9.0%	14.8%	4.9%
Lone-mother households		n=2,555	n=7,195	n=265
Poor	Before taxes and transfers income	66.8%	68.4%	64.6%
	After taxes and transfers income	42.5%	60.7%	12.2%
Rich	Before taxes and transfers income	3.8%	5.6%	3.4%
	After taxes and transfers income	1.3%	3.5%	1.7%

Notes: For these calculations, it is assumed that the child shares equally the parents' standard of living. 'Poor' means family equivalent income is less than 50% of the country equivalent income; 'Rich' means family income is greater than or equal to 1.5 times the country equivalent income. 'Equivalent income' adjusts for family size using the OECD equivalence scale. The aftertax measure is used to calculate the poverty line in all three cases.

The sample is all children aged 0-11 (each child is one observation; there can be more than one observation per household).

Overall generosity of programmes

A first important point to make is that Norway has, overall, the largest state sector of the three countries: levels of taxation and of spending on social security programmes, as a percentage of GDP, are higher than in the other countries, and this has been true since the late 1960s. The US has the lowest levels of taxation and the lowest level of social spending (OECD, 1996). Microdata from the LIS indicate that in 1994/95, 99.7% of families with children aged 0 to 11 received some social transfers in Norway; 92% received transfers in Canada; only 56% received transfers in the US (see Table 3.4). Not only do almost all families with children receive transfers, but the average level of transfers received is also highest in Norway. Children living in lone-mother households are particularly vulnerable in almost all countries and most single-mother households receive transfers in all three countries studied here (99.8% and 99.6% in Canada and Norway, respectively, and 90.0% in the US). However, the level of transfers received is higher in Norway ($11,906) than in Canada

($10,482) or particularly the US ($8,052 – all figures are in 1994 Canadian dollars[3]).

One reason Norwegian lone mothers fare relatively well is that a special set of benefits is available to lone parents in Norway. First, a 'transition benefit', intended to provide subsistence if a lone parent is unable to support himself/herself as a result of childcare responsibilities, is available. The transitional benefit is sizable (about Can$12,500) and can be received until the youngest child reaches the age of ten years. The transitional benefit can be received when the lone parent is in the labour force, but at a reduced amount. It can also be collected while a lone parent attends school. Special educational benefits also help to cover expenses. As well, lone parents may receive childcare benefits if they are either in the labour force or attending school. Finally, a woman on her own who gives birth to a child is entitled to a birth grant (about Can$2,000) which is in addition to other regular maternity benefits to which she may be entitled[4].

Table 3.5 also uses LIS data to make the point that the state more effectively re-distributes resources in Norway than in either of the North American countries. If we consider all children aged 0 to 11 years, the incidence of poverty[5] in Norway is reduced from 19.8% before taxes and transfers to 6.1% after taxes and transfers. In contrast, poverty is reduced from 32.2 to 29.3% after taxes and transfers in the US. The Canadian record is intermediate; poverty is reduced from 26.1% before taxes and transfers to 16.9% after. More children also live in relatively rich[6] families in the US (14.8%) compared to Canada (9.0%) or especially Norway (4.9%).

Differences across the countries are even more marked if we consider only children aged 0 to 11 years living in lone-mother families. While the before taxes and transfers incidence of poverty is very similar across the three countries (64.6% in Norway, 66.8% in Canada and 68.4% in the US), there are vast differences in poverty experiences after state intervention (12.2% in Norway, 42.5% in Canada and 60.7% in the US). Clearly, the Norwegian state is much more successful at alleviating poverty than that in Canada or especially in the US.

Whatever the direction of causality, it seems consistent that the country in which individuals expressed the most concern about income inequality is the country that most effectively redistributes income, while the country with the least concern about income inequality is the least effective.

Parental work incentives and programmes for children

Evidence from the World Values Study makes it quite clear that people living in Canada and especially the US are much more likely to believe that people live in need because they are lazy than are people living in Norway. Not surprisingly, then, many transfer programmes in the North American countries are designed to minimise negative work incentives. For example, social assistance payments, the principal source of transfers for many lone-mother families in Canada and the US (although not in Norway), are kept low to discourage anyone from choosing not to work in order to collect them. Or, in the US and Canada, the idea of 'making work pay' has recently become popular. Cash benefits are available to low-income parents who are working in the paid labour market. These benefits are thus not purely based on need – anyone who does not have a paid job is not entitled. They are not for all individuals who are 'working poor' because people without children are not eligible. They are not for all families with children who have low incomes. In Canada, the 'earned income supplement' is an 'add-on' to the child tax benefit (and so was discussed in the earlier section). In the US, the 'Earned Income Tax Credit (EITC), enacted in 1975 and enriched in the early 1990s is now one of the most important means of income support for low-income families with children. Again, eligibility depends upon both parenthood and labour force participation. Recipients receive higher benefits if they have two or more children (Kamerman and Kahn, 1997).

On the other hand, worries about negative work incentives seem less prevalent in the design of Norwegian policies, which is consistent with the fact that Norwegians are much less likely than North Americans to feel that poverty is the result of laziness. As outlined earlier in the chapter, extremely generous transfers are offered to all lone mothers in Norway, apparently without concern that this will diminish incentives to take paid employment. It is thus interesting that rates of labour-force participation by lone mothers are higher in Norway than in the other countries studied (71.1% in Norway versus 61.2% in the US and 50.4% in Canada – see Table 3.4). Paradoxically, higher rates of labour-force participation may be partially a result of the universal rather than the income-tested nature of many of the Norwegian benefits, which will not be lost as a result of labour-force participation. (Countries concerned about work incentives typically offer smaller, income-tested cash transfers – eg, social assistance in Canada or the US.) High labour-force participation by lone mothers in Norway is likely also partially a result of the other supportive policies in place (eg, generous parenting leave programmes, better, although not truly wonderful, childcare).

Public versus private responsibility for children

It has been argued in the social policy literature (eg, Kamerman, 1980) that in Europe children are more likely to be regarded as a public rather than exclusively as a private responsibility. Unfortunately, there is no question in the World Values Survey that directly addresses this issue. However, a survey of programmes available in each country offers some evidence of the validity of this claim. First, differences across the three countries in the availability and structure of child allowance programmes are consistent with the idea that children are most regarded as a social responsibility/resource in Norway and least in the US. Consider child allowance programmes first. No such programme is available in the US. Both Canada and Norway offer child allowances, but, using LIS data, the average level of child allowance benefits received by children in two-parent families in Canada was noticeably lower (4.7% of adjusted per person standard of living versus 8.8% for Norway in 1994/95).

There are also important structural differences in child allowances across the countries. In Norway, children receive the same benefit, regardless of family income level (although the first child in a lone-parent family receives double the basic amount). The family allowance benefit is regarded as a universal entitlement; a recognition of social responsibility for the well-being of all children. In Canada, poor children receive 44% of the basic Norwegian child allowance (although the Canadian benefit is taxable income while the Norwegian benefit is not). Rich children in Canada receive almost nothing. This is regarded as 'efficient' targeting of benefits to those who need them most without 'wasting' dollars on more affluent children[7].

As a second example, if a non-custodial parent does not pay child support in Norway, the state advances the payment to the lone parent and child. In this way, the cost of the default is shared socially rather than imposed exclusively on the child (and his/her custodial parent), as is the case in Canada or the US. As a result of this programme, a much higher fraction of children in lone-mother families receive child support in Norway (73%) than in the US (30%) or Canada (16%[8]). While the US has appeared a 'laggard' with respect to other benefits, it is interesting that in terms both of level and incidence of receipt, the US compares quite favourably with the other countries studied here. One possible reason for this may be that it is in keeping with the idea that children are a private responsibility of their parents to insist that absent parents should continue to make contributions to their children's incomes. In fact, the US has taken some effort to collect child support payments before allowing lone mothers to receive welfare payments. However, the state does not advance maintenance payments to children should fathers default – thus the child rather than the taxpayer suffers in this case. No social responsibility for preserving the child's standard of living is accepted.

Outcomes for children

This section of the chapter provides a three-country, microdata-based comparison of children's well-being. Canadian estimates are based on the National Longitudinal Survey of Children and Youth (NLSCY). The Statistics Norway Health Survey and the National Survey of Children for the US are reasonably comparable microdata sets obtained to conduct cross-national comparisons. In each case, the survey was conducted during a visit to the respondent's home. In locating data sets for the non-Canadian countries, a key condition was that the surveys contain reasonably similar information to that available in the NLSCY. For the US, this was not a problem, since content is extremely similar. The content of the Norwegian survey is more limited in focus to health-related issues, since the child-related questions that we use were a subset of the 1995 Statistics Norway Health Survey. Unlike the Canadian and US studies, there were no questions about problem behaviours, for example. (See Phipps, 1999b or 1999c for more detail about these data sets.)

Since the first wave of the Canadian NLSCY only contains information about children aged 0 to 11 years, and thus we only compare outcomes for children in this age range, the relative youthfulness of the US parents is not a serious problem for this analysis. Moreover, while the range of parental age is greater for Canada and Norway than for the US, mean age of mother is nearly identical. We choose to focus on the full samples for Canada and Norway since this gives the best information about child outcomes in these countries.

In the Canadian survey, the person answering the questions is the 'person most knowledgeable about the child' (PMK) – the mother in 97.7% of cases for the Child Questionnaire. For the US survey, only female respondents with children were asked about their children. Thus, the child sample consists of all children born to NLSCY female respondents who were living in their mother's household at the survey date (several

Table 3.6: Means of child outcomes (national level) (standard errors in parentheses)

	Asthma	Injured	Activity limitation	Anxious/ fearful	Disobedient at school	Success at school (top category)
	Ages 4-11	Ages 0-11	Ages 0-11	Ages 4-11	Ages 6-11	Ages 10-11
Canada	13.2 (0.298)	10.2 (0.209)	3.8 (0.132)	36.1 (0.423)	17.8 (0.392)	45.8 (0.836)
United States	n/a	10.7 (0.498)	3.5 (0.293)	31.6* (0.888)	20.7* (0.899)	37.1* (1.435)
Norway	8.2* (0.830)	7.9* (0.666)	2.0* (0.344)	11.2* (0.953)	n/a	n/a

* indicates significantly different than Canada at 90% level of confidence. Canada: 22,831 observations 0-11 years old. Norway: 1,646 observations 0-11 years old. United States: 3,961 observations 0-11 years old.

Note: The sample is all children in the age groupings (each child is one observation; there can be more than one observation per household).

surveys have been carried out – we use the 1995 survey). In Norway, the respondent to the health survey would answer the child-related questions, regardless of the sex of the respondent.

For each data set, a small number of individuals did not answer particular questions about children's well-being. These observations are excluded as appropriate for the reporting of levels of child outcomes. Sample size is much the largest for Canadian children, with 21,045 observations for children aged 0 to 11. In contrast, we have only 3,961 observations for the US and 1,644 observations for Norway. And, in fact, we most often analyse even fewer observations since many questions were only relevant for subsets of the population (eg, only children of school age can be 'disobedient at school').

While income may be an extremely important input to the well-being of children, in itself it is surely not the best measure of children's well-being. First, as a growing literature on the distribution of well-being within families points out, 'family income' is not the best measure of the well-being of any individual family member. Since young children, in particular, have so little direct access to income of their own, they may not always share equally in the benefits associated with family income. Second, household production activities (reading stories, helping with homework, cooking a healthy dinner) seem especially important for the well-being of young children whose lives are often very centred around home, yet household production is missing from a simple income proxy.

Sen's (1993) 'functionings' approach is useful for measuring the well-being of children. Examples of basic 'functionings' are: 'being adequately nourished'; 'being in good health', 'avoiding escapable morbidity/premature mortality'; 'having a good education'. While adults control income, which they may or may not use to the benefit of their children, children themselves directly experience outcomes such as 'health', and so on. (See Phipps, 1999a for a more complete development of these ideas.) Thus, the approach adopted in this chapter is to compare child well-being across the three countries in terms of child 'functionings'[9].

'Physical health' is a first key functioning studied. We consider three dimensions of physical health for which we have directly comparable information in the microdata: asthma; experience of accidents/injuries; activity limitations. As Table 3.6 indicates, 13.2% of children aged 4 to 11 are reported to experience asthma in Canada versus only 8.2% in Norway (and this is a statistically significant difference). (Data on the experience of asthma is not available for all children in the US data.)

Accidents or injuries requiring medical attention[10] are a second dimension of physical well-being about which we have information for all children (0 to 11 years) in Canada, Norway and the US. In the 12 months preceding the survey, 10.6% of children in the US experienced an accident; 10.2% of Canadian children had an accident or were injured; only 7.9% of Norwegian children had an accident/injury. The accident rates for young children in Canada and the US are not statistically different; Norwegian children are significantly less likely to have had accidents than children in Canada.

The final measure of physical functioning considered is whether the child has any long-term condition/health problem that limits his/her ability to participate at school, at play or in other activities normal for a child of the same age. This information is available for children aged 0 to 11 years. In Norway, 2.0% of children are reported to have an activity limitation versus 3.8% in Canada and 3.5% in the US. The Norwegian estimate is statistically different from the Canadian; the US estimate is not statistically different from the Canadian estimate.

Table 3.6 also reports the estimated experience of anxiety and/or fear among children aged 4 to 11 years. 'Being free of fear' seems a compelling dimension of child well-being. Norwegian children are much less likely to be anxious/frightened than are children in the other countries under study. Of 4- to 11-year-old children, 36.1% are 'sometimes or often' 'too anxious/frightened' in Canada; 31.6% are 'sometimes/often' 'too anxious frightened' in the US; but only 11.2% are 'a little/quite/extremely troubled' by 'constant anxiety or fear' in Norway. These results are all significantly different. Thus, reported levels of anxiety are significantly higher for young Canadian children than for young children living in the US, or, especially, in Norway.

The final two functionings considered relate to educational outcomes, but are only available for children living in the US and Canada. First, we have reports about 'disobedience at school' (for 6- to 11-year-old children). In Canada, 17.8% of children are reported by their parents to be sometimes/often/always disobedient at school; in the US, 20.8% are sometimes/often disobedient (at school). While this difference is not very large in percentage terms (16%), it is statistically significant. Finally, 45.8% of Canadian parents assess their 10- and 11-year-old children as performing 'very well' at school (the top category). This is versus 37.1% of US parents who rank their children in the top scholastic achievement category and this is again a statistically significant difference although perhaps not a particularly large one.

We are relying on parental reports for these measures of child functioning, and as noted earlier in this chapter, there are differences across countries in expectations of children which may be important directly (ie, in what parents teach their children or expect their children to achieve) and indirectly, insofar as it affects the parent's perception of how well the child actually fares. For example, there are striking differences between Norway and the North American countries in the emphasis placed on 'hard work,' which is mentioned by many more North American respondents (eg, 55.4% of US men versus 8.4% of Norwegian men). Being expected to 'work hard' might be anxiety producing for children in the US and Canada. Another example is that many more US respondents mention the importance of obedience than Canadian respondents (38.5% versus 26.1% for male respondents). If obedience is more highly prized in the US, parents may be more sensitive to any misdemeanours in the US than in Canada and this may help to explain the difference in reported outcomes for children. In summary, parental expectations may have real consequences for children's well-being; parental expectations may also influence parental perceptions of children's well-being/performance that will influence the answers they give.

Conclusions

It seems clear that values differ across the three countries studied and that these value differences are connected to differences in policies available. It is also clear that outcomes for children differ. For all of the outcomes for which comparable microdata were available, children in Norway are better off than children in Canada or the US. That is, Norwegian children have less asthma, they are less likely to have accidents, they are less likely to experience activity limitations and are less likely to be anxious or frightened.

A first observation to make about this evidence is that people in Norway care more about income distribution; they correspondingly spend much more on re-distribution. A second observation is that programmes in place in Norway acknowledge some social responsibility for all children; child-related programmes tend to be universal, for example. While no definitive conclusions can be drawn, the evidence provided here is consistent with the idea that both higher levels of spending and programmes with a more universal flavour are associated with better outcomes for children. A third observation is that people in Canada and the US are more likely to believe that people live in poverty because they are lazy. This is reflected in the design even of programmes for children, which, in North America, are more likely to attempt to minimise negative work incentives for parents. Yet, rates of labour-force participation are higher among lone mothers in Norway than in either Canada or the US. Paradoxically, this may be the result of the universal design of the very generous transfers available in Norway that do not fall as women's earnings increase. It may also be the result of additional programmes (eg, day care, time off for sick children, generous maternity/parental leaves), which help to support women's labour-force participation. The set of programmes available in Norway may at least partially explain the dramatically lower reported levels of anxiety for children. Stresses associated with labour-force participation may be lower; fewer children experience poverty; even stresses associated with the *risk* of poverty will be lower in Norway, given the excellent social safety net available for all.

Notes

[1] I would like to acknowledge the excellent research assistance of Lynn Lethbridge. This chapter is drawn from a larger project originally funded by Canadian Policy Research Networks and Human Resources Development Canada and I would like to thank these organisations for their financial support.

[2] Only descriptive evidence is provided here; however, these results have been confirmed through multivariate work not reported here due to space constraints. See Phipps (1999b).

[3] Conversions to Canadian dollars are made using purchasing power parities (OECD, 1996).

[4] Family allowance supplements and advance maintenance of child support payments are also available, but are discussed later in the chapter.

[5] Poverty is defined as having household income less than 50% of median after-tax income, using an OECD equivalence scale.

[6] Rich families have equivalent incomes more than 150% of median equivalent income.

[7] It is worth noting that there is no general tax credit or deduction for children in Canada. Such a benefit is available in both the US and Norway, although the Norwegian allowance is larger. See Phipps (1999b).

[8] While LIS data do not report child support payments separately, Galarneau (1992) reports that in 1988, 16% of lone mothers received child support or alimony. The median level of benefits received per child (adjusted to Can$1,994) was 11.7% of mean disposable equivalent income. While these figures reflect an earlier time period and a household-level analysis rather than a child-level analysis, they suggest that the Canadian record in terms of payment of child support is poor in an international comparative context.

[9] A limitation is that the Norwegian survey was conducted in Norwegian, and we are working with a translation. Moreover, of course, many Canadians would have been asked the question in French, while presumably some US respondents worked in Spanish. Thus, we cannot know whether questions that appear to

have the same content in translation have exactly the same nuances of meaning in the different languages.

[10] For the US and Canada, the parent is asked whether the accident was serious enough to 'require' medical attention. For Norway, the parent was asked about accidents or injuries for which the child 'received' medical attention. While this is an important distinction, we hope that universal medical coverage in Norway means that there is a very close correspondence between needing and receiving medical attention.

References

Baker, M. (1995) *Canadian family policies: Cross-national comparisons*, Toronto, Canada: University of Toronto Press.

de Tombeur, C. et al (1993) *Luxembourg Income Study (LIS): Information guide*, LIS Working Paper No 7, Luxembourg: LIS.

Esping-Andersen, G. (1990) *Three worlds of welfare capitalism*, Cambridge: Polity Press.

Galerneau, D. (1992) 'Alimony and child support', *Perspectives on Labour and Income*, vol 4, pp 8-21.

Gauthier, A.H. (1996) *The State and the family: A comparative analysis of family policies in industrialized countries*, Oxford: Clarendon Press.

Kamerman, S. (1980) 'Child care and family benefits: policies of six industrialized countries', *Monthly Labour Review*, vol 103, no 11, pp 23-8.

Kamerman, S. and Kahn, A. (1997) *Family change and family policies in Great Britain, Canada, New Zealand and the United States*, vol 1, Oxford: Clarendon Press.

OECD (Organisation for Economic Co-operation and Development) (1996) *OECD economics at a glance, structural indicators*, Paris: OECD.

Phipps, S.A. (1999a) 'Economics and the well-being of Canadian children', *The Canadian Journal of Economics*, vol 32, no 5, pp 1135-63.

Phipps, S.A. (1999b) *An international comparison of policies and outcomes for young children,* Canadian Policy Research Network Study No F05, Ottawa, Canada: Renouf Publishing.

Phipps, S.A. (1999c) 'The well-being of young Canadian children in international perspective', Working Paper No 99-01, Dalhousie University, Department of Economics.

Ringen, S. (1987) *The possibility of politics: A study in the political economy of the welfare state*, Oxford: Clarendon Press.

Sen, A.K. (1993) 'Capability and well-being', in M. Nussbaum and A.K. Sen (eds) *The quality of life*, Oxford: Clarendon Press, pp 30-53.

FOUR

Child well-being in the EU – and enlargement to the East

John Micklewright and Kitty Stewart

Introduction

The European Union (EU) is expanding – over the next decade as many as 13 new members may be admitted, ten of them transition countries in Central and Eastern Europe (CEE). In this chapter we consider measurable differences in the well-being of children between current club members, the EU member states, and the ten CEE applicants seeking admission[1].

Discussion of the suitability of applicants to join any club provides an opportunity to look in a mirror and consider the state of the existing membership. We therefore emphasise the differences among the current members as well as contrasting them as a group with the applicants. And we consider whether applicants have a comparative advantage over members in any dimension of well-being – a possibility that is completely overlooked in both media and academic focus on the relative economic strengths of the two groups of countries. To anticipate one result: Slovenia has an under-5 mortality rate that is below the EU average.

We first discuss (a) criteria for EU membership, emphasising the human rights dimension, and (b) the approach currently taken by the European Commission to measuring differences in living standards within the Union. In both cases we emphasise the need for a much broader view than is typically taken, and one that includes a comprehensive picture of the well-being of children – the 79 million in the current EU15 and the 25 million in the CEE applicants.

We then consider in turn three dimensions of well-being of European children; their economic welfare, their health, and their education. The account we give is far from complete, but this rough sketch provides a starting point for the full picture that we argue is needed.

EU membership, human rights and 'cohesion'

The best-known criteria on which applicants for EU membership are judged, and those which form the corner-stone of negotiations over accession, are the economic criteria. Applicants must have a functioning market economy in place and the capacity to cope with competitive pressures and market forces.

However, the 'Copenhagen Criteria', agreed in 1993 to govern EU entry, are in reality much wider than this. In addition to meeting the economic and financial conditions, "membership requires that the candidate country has achieved stability of institutions guaranteeing democracy, the rule of law, human rights and respect for and protection of minorities". As the former foreign affairs commissioner, Hans van den Broek, put it in an interview on enlargement in December 1998, "we are not merely a Union of economic benefits, but also a Union of shared values".

The non-economic aspects of the Copenhagen Criteria are taken seriously in relation to applicants. (We return below to the issue of human rights within existing member states.) In June 1997 all ten CEE countries with the exception of Slovakia were agreed to have met the political criteria, but a number of them were judged to have progress still to make with respect to democracy and the protection of human rights and minorities.

In the October 1999 Commission report on progress towards accession, all CEE candidate countries, and Slovakia in particular, were agreed to have made considerable advances in both these areas. But corruption, the judiciary and the treatment of minorities (in particular the Roma) were raised as ongoing concerns. In addition, Romania's chances of being granted membership were in effect declared conditional on action to improve the situation of the 100,000 children in institutionalised care. As the 1999 report on progress states: "The rights of these children to decent living conditions and basic health care is a human rights issue" (Composite Paper, Reports on Progress Towards Accession by Each of the Candidate Countries, October 1999)[2].

Human rights and EU enlargement

There is no doubt that conditions in Romania's orphanages are indeed a human rights issue. Human rights today are internationally recognised as encompassing much more than just political and civic freedoms. Both the Universal Declaration of Human Rights (1948), and, more recently, the UN Convention on the Rights of the Child (CRC) (1989) have been ratified by all EU and CEE countries. Both documents embody a wide range of rights, 'positive' as well as 'negative', implying the responsibility of the state not only to protect all individuals from violation by others, but also to provide them with certain conditions and opportunities for life. The CRC, for instance, includes articles on the right of all children to education, to 'the highest attainable standard of health' and to 'a standard of living adequate for physical, mental, spiritual, moral and social development'.

These rights receive little attention in the Progress Reports, beyond a confirmation that freedom of education, the right to a minimum subsistence level of income and (in some cases) the right to health are 'guaranteed' by national constitutions[3]. Poor living conditions for children in orphanages are mentioned in the original Opinion on Bulgaria, but only in the case of Romania do they receive extensive and repeated attention[4]. In addition to the emphasis on children in institutions, the Romanian report points to concerns about the economic well-being of the population, noting the deterioration in living standards caused by economic contraction and increased unemployment, and highlighting the fact that World Bank poverty data indicate that one third of the population live below the subsistence level. No other report refers to material living standards, although it is well known that these have deteriorated across the region[5].

Human rights within the existing member states also need to be considered. It is safe to say that in no EU country are the economic and social rights of all children fully respected in practice. The recent attention of the UK government (rightly placed as we will see later) to such issues as child poverty and social exclusion among the young is a reflection of this. Some might argue that the principle of 'subsidiarity' within the EU (the requirement that decisions be taken at the closest level to the citizen at which they can be effective), coupled with the existence of an official UN monitoring body for the CRC, implies that the EU itself should have little concern with human rights within member states[6]. But such a position is inconsistent with the treatment of the applicant countries and the Union's external policy in general, which takes a principled stand on human rights in dealings with other states. And it is also at variance with concern for greater 'economic and social cohesion' within the union.

Economic and social cohesion in the EU

The Treaty on Union emphasises that the strengthening of 'economic and social cohesion' among the member states is one of the EU's principal goals, essential to the Union's 'overall harmonious development' (Articles 2 and 130a). In the first of what is to be a series of regular reports on progress towards this goal, the Commission defined cohesion to imply "greater equality in economic and social opportunities", towards the ultimate end of "rais[ing] living standards and the quality of life" (European Commission 1996, p 15). However, this first report stuck to disappointingly traditional measures of opportunity, largely employment and average income – although it did also take a brief look at poverty[7].

We argue elsewhere for a much broader vision of cohesion, one that takes a wider view of development and of individual well-being, more similar, for example, to that of the UNDP's *Human Development Reports* and the associated 'capability' approach of Amartya Sen (Micklewright and Stewart, 1999, 2000). Such a view, with its attention to a wide range of different dimensions of individual well-being, leads naturally to attention to the position of children within the EU, both those in the current member states and those in the CEE applicants. Convergence in well-being across the Union means moving towards similar opportunities for European children wherever they are born – because children are European citizens too, and because the nature of their childhood helps determine the shape of Europe's future.

The importance of children's well-being to society's future is underlined by considering the socialist inheritance of the CEE countries in terms of human development. The comparative advantage of socialism over capitalism in the field of family policy is often exaggerated, as is the extent of 'cradle to grave' support provided under socialism (Ferge, 1991, Atkinson and Micklewright, 1992). Nethertheless, it is broadly the case that policy in socialist countries attached much greater emphasis to some aspects of children's development than was the case in other countries at similar levels of national income. The results in terms of healthcare and educational outcomes can still be seen today (as we show below), despite the upheavals of the past decade. It is partly *because of* the past investments in children in the CEE region that the EU is now able to contemplate applications from countries that in some cases are hugely adrift in terms of current levels of national income.

Similarly, it is important that attention is paid to current investments in children in CEE countries if the path taken by societies in the region is to result in greater cohesion in the long-term in an expanded Union. If some children miss out on key aspects of their development as a result of the economic and social pressures of transition, it will not be easy for them to recoup those deficits in later life. All children may suffer if public expenditure on education, for example, falls precipitously. And greater inequalities in health and educational opportunity, caused in part by a widening distribution of income, may lead to the exclusion of particular groups. None of this will aid economic and social cohesion in the future EU.

Measuring the well-being of Europe's children

Implementation of human rights or the strengthening of cohesion clearly involves change to policy. However, an inspection of the policies represented by the legislation and administrative frameworks of EU and CEE countries provides an insufficient guide to what actually happens in practice. The complete canvas, when painted, would involve the depiction of both polices and outcomes, with a full palette of colours employed. But here we attempt only an incomplete black and white sketch in which the policies do not feature explicitly[8].

We focus on a handful of outcome indicators of child well-being that reflect (although they do not precisely measure) how far some of the rights enshrined in the CRC are a reality for children in EU members and CEE applicants. They also relate to several dimensions of well-being that should enter a full assessment of cohesion in the Union. We look at the material welfare of children, their health and their educational attainment. In particular we focus on differences in:

- child poverty;
- mortality among children and young people; and
- school enrolment and learning achievement.

We concentrate on data for the most recent year available, but at times we also put the rankings that these provide in the context of recent trends. (The trends within the member states are the focus in our earlier work reported in Micklewright and Stewart, 1999, 2000.)

Space and data constraints rule out the analysis of several issues. Youth unemployment is conspicuous by its absence from our list. This is a subject of concern both as a measure of labour market opportunity for the young and because of its association with other problems. Youth unemployment rates in 1997 varied from 7% in Austria to 39% in Spain, with an EU15 figure of 21% (Eurostat, 1999a, p 143; ILO definition, 15-24 year olds). Rates among the CEE applicants in 1996/97 averaged exactly the same – 21% – and ranged from 8% in the Czech Republic to 36% in Bulgaria (Eurostat, 1999a, p 43). Both members and applicants clearly face a serious problem, but one that varies from country to country.

A further restriction is that our investigation is almost entirely at the national level – the 15 member states and the ten CEE applicants. This contrasts with the Commission's own analysis of cohesion that focuses in particular on the sub-national unit of the region (of which there are nearly 200 in the EU countries (NUTS-2 level regions) and around 90 in the CEE applicants). A major motivation for the Commission's approach is that a number of EU policies to encourage employment and income growth operate at the regional level (in the sense of eligibility for funding). While we are critical of the Commission's examination of cohesion as being too narrow in terms of subject matter, we should acknowledge that the combination of analysis at both the national and sub-national level clearly provides for a richer investigation.

This combination would still be possible with a broader approach to cohesion. Child-related indicators such as infant mortality and teenage fertility that are based on population and vital statistics are available at the sub-national level (as we illustrate below). And the use of these other indicators at the regional level would enrich the analysis of incomes and employment. For example, raising a region's GDP will not prevent social exclusion if a high rate of births to teenage mothers prevents greater employment opportunities being shared by all young women[9].

What sort of variation among members and applicants in any indicator might we consider large? Figure 4.1 presents the benchmark of differences in GDP per capita, the indicator that forms the popular approach to representing variation in living standards across the EU and CEE countries. The four lowest values among the EU15 are for the so-called 'Cohesion Four', where EU policy aims to promote catch-up growth (the tag emphasises the association in practice within the Commission of the concept of cohesion with income per head). When the figure for each

Figure 4.1: GDP per capita (purchasing power parity) in 1997 (EU 15=100)

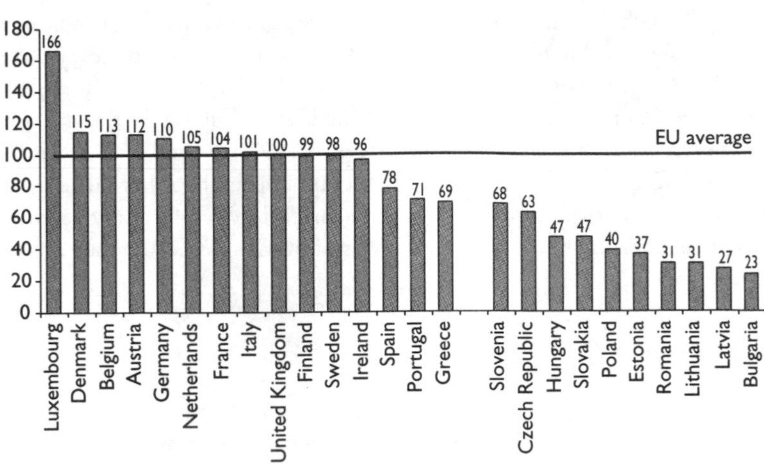

Source: Eurostat (1999a, p 232) and Eurostat (1999b, p 67)

country is weighted by population size, the differences within the EU15 have narrowed over time, with GDP per capita in the Cohesion Four rising from two thirds of the EU15 figure in 1983 to three quarters by 1996. With the exception of Luxembourg, all the other member states have GDP per capita within 15% of the average.

The experience of the CEE applicants in the 1990s has been very different, with marked falls in national income during the process of transition away from the socialist system. The economies in almost all cases have now been growing for several years (Bulgaria and Romania are exceptions with a rocky recent period), but there is clearly enormous catch-up growth to be made if typical levels of EU income are to be reached. Only Slovenia had income per head in 1997 as high as the bottom limit of the EU15 range – and only in Poland had GDP grown to exceed its 1989 level (several other Central European countries were nearly there but Bulgaria and the Baltics were still 25-45% down). In Romania, Lithuania, Latvia and Bulgaria, national income per head in 1997 was less than a third of the EU15 average. The differences within the CEE group are much larger than those among the EU members (the weighted coefficient of variation is nearly three times higher).

The effect on the comparison between members and applicants of moving away from a focus on national income per head can be summarised by a comparison of the ranking on GDP per capita with that on the UNDP's Human Development Index (HDI). Besides GDP per capita, the HDI includes life expectancy and a composite educational indicator combining enrolment and literacy. Both groups of countries are on average higher up the (world) ranking on the HDI than they are on GDP per capita alone (UNDP, 1999, Table 1). But while the average difference in the ranking was four places in 1997 for the EU15 it was as much as 13 places for the CEE-10, reflecting in part the inheritance from the socialist period of the investments in children referred to earlier. Allowance for the two other dimensions of human development starts to change the picture.

Child poverty

Imagine calculating the numbers of children in EU members and CEE applicants that live in poor households, defining poverty as income below a line common to all 25 countries – a line fixed everywhere as the same number of Euros. The differences in national income per head shown in Figure 4.1 would be reflected strongly in the ranking of national child poverty rates that would emerge from such a calculation. But Figure 4.1 would be a far from perfect guide to the variation in child poverty since the differences in the graph refer only to average incomes. The differences *within* each country, and where children come in those national income distributions, would also enter the equation. The ranking among the richer EU countries, in particular, would be far from a mirror reflection of the ranking of GDP per capita (as we will see).

Such a common poverty line, establishing a fixed threshold relevant for every household, whether it be in Sweden or Slovakia, is one way of thinking about poverty in Europe. In terms of solidarity or cohesion within the Union, a common threshold appears attractive, as it captures what convergence of incomes is about: poorer parts of Europe, and children with lower living standards, catching up with the others.

But 'poverty' should be a meaningful term within each country, relevant to national sentiment and policy making as well as to international comparison. What a person needs to participate in normal life clearly depends on what those around him or her have. It is this concept of living standards relative to the national norm that is found in the EU's broad definition of poverty as persons with "resources (material, cultural and social) that are so limited as to exclude them from the minimum acceptable way of life *in the Member States in which they live*" (Eurostat,

1997, p 3; emphasis added). Poverty, in terms of cash incomes, is assessed by comparison with a national yardstick, and not a common EU poverty line as in the calculation outlined above[10].

What measure of child poverty would a human rights approach lead one to? The CRC provides for the right to "a standard of living adequate for physical, mental, spiritual, moral and social development" (Article 27), which among other things underlines one reason why child poverty is such a cause for concern – its impact on an individual's future life. The wording in the CRC suggests a relative measure, given that what is adequate for full participation in society will be higher where average incomes are higher. When the European Commission's report on Romania's progress towards accession draws attention to the large numbers of people living below the subsistence level, that level is defined within the national context.

Figure 4.2 shows the proportion of children in EU and CEE countries living in households with incomes below 50% of the national median, a conventional definition of relative poverty. The data are drawn from the Luxembourg Income Study's collection of harmonised household surveys and the same adjustment for differences in household size and composition have been applied to the data for each country. The majority of member states are present in the graph, but there are data for only four applicant countries. In view of the changes in income inequality that have occurred in the CEE countries during the 1990s (which we return to below) we have indicated for these four the exact year to which the data relate.

The variation in child poverty across the EU countries is enormous, ranging from 3% in Finland to 21% in Italy and the UK. (Both the extent of the differences and the average level have risen somewhat since the mid-1980s; Micklewright and Stewart, 1999.) These figures underline how misleading national income per head may be as a guide to material living standards of children at the lower end of national income distributions. Figure 4.2 showed Finland and UK at the same level of GDP per capita but here they are at opposite ends of the spectrum. Since the UK is a much more unequal country, the child poverty rate there is much higher (the difference in the years to which the data in Figures 4.1 and 4.2 refer is not important in this case).

The four CEE countries also display considerable variation. Hungary and Poland had rates of child poverty in the early 1990s which were above the (unweighted) average for the EU of 10%, but the two parts of former Czechoslovakia had rates – in 1992 – that were below even that of the best performer among the EU member states.

Figure 4.2: Child poverty rates (%)

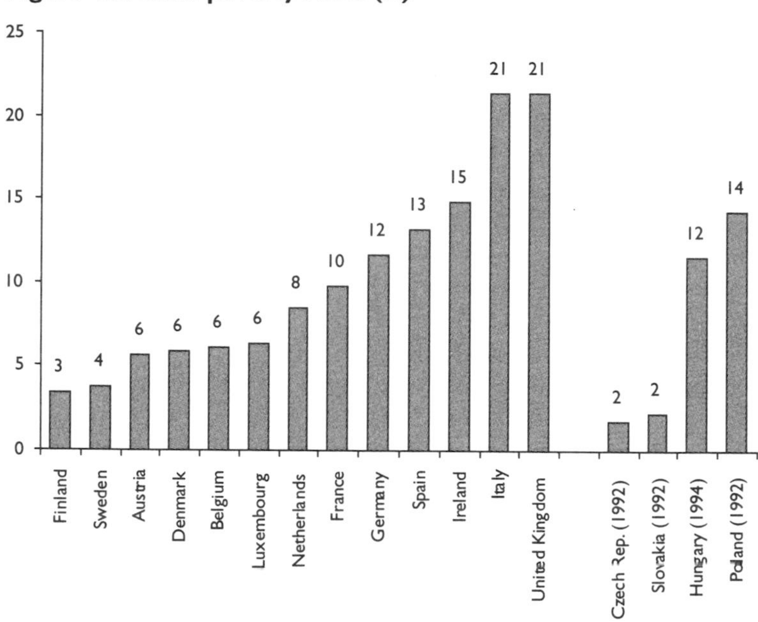

Notes: The EU figures typically relate to the early 1990s. The rates displayed are the percentage of children living in households with income below 50% of the national median. Household incomes are equivalised by the factor (adults +0.7*children)^0.85.
Source: Bradbury and Jäntti (1999, Table 3.3)

The position of Slovakia and the Czech Republic in Figure 4.2 reflects the low degree of income inequality that these countries inherited from the socialist period. Former Czechoslovakia was an extreme case but the broad picture found across the CEE countries at the start of the 1990s was one of less dispersion in household incomes than that generally found among EU members.

Figure 4.3 shows the picture of income inequality in the second half of the 1990s, giving the Gini coefficient for the distribution (among individuals) of household per capita incomes in the ten CEE countries (higher values of the Gini indicating higher levels of inequality). The average value for the distributions calculated on the same basis for 11 EU countries in the mid-1980s is also shown (the EU range at this time was from 0.22 in Finland to 0.36 in Ireland). (More recent EU figures on the per capita basis are not available.)

Seven of the applicant countries have levels of income inequality just

Figure 4.3: Income inequality in CEE countries (1997): Gini coefficient of per capita income

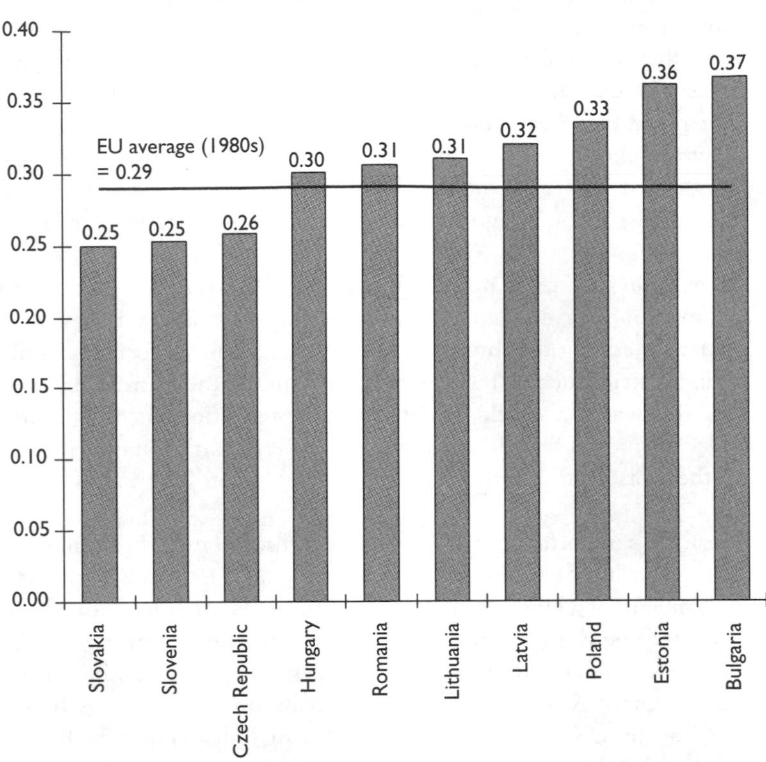

Source: CEE countries from UNICEF (1999, Table 10.13), except the Czech Republic (Vecernik, 1999, Table 2), Hungary (Galasi, 1998, Table 1) and Latvia (data supplied by Latvian Statistical Office). Data for the Czech Republic and Slovenia are for 1996; data for Hungary are for March-March 1995/96. The Hungarian figure is from the TARKI survey (also the source drawn on in Figure 4.2); the official budget survey gives a lower Gini coefficient (Flemming and Micklewright, 1999, Figure 11). The EU average (which relates to the mid-1980s) is from Flemming and Micklewright (1999, Table 3) drawing on Atkinson et al (1995, Table 4.10)

or well above the EU average, with only Slovakia, Slovenia and the Czech Republic clearly below. Estonia and Bulgaria are at the top end of the EU member range. It is notable that the richer countries (in per capita GDP terms) tend to have lower levels of inequality, and vice versa, implying that differences among the CEE countries, if poverty were assessed with a common Euro line, would be even larger than the differences in average incomes.

The 1990s have seen some significant increases in income inequality in the CEE countries. This means that the impact on living standards of the resumed economic growth in the second half of 1990s has been at least partly offset for children at the bottom of the distribution. If average incomes rise by a third but the distribution of incomes widens by the same amount then the incomes of those at the bottom of the distribution will remain unchanged. The problem has not been restricted to the CEE applicants. The experience of the UK over the 1980s was one in which rising average incomes and increased income inequality went hand in hand.

Were figures for child poverty available on the same basis for all ten CEE applicants for the late 1990s, they would most likely display wide variation, as among the four in Figure 4.2. The best performers would shame countries such as the UK and Italy among the current member states. (In fairness it should be noted that the reduction of child poverty has recently moved centre-stage in the UK government's domestic policy.) And the worst performers would threaten cohesion if admitted to the Union.

Finally, it is important not to lose sight of what life at the bottom of the income distribution really means for children. The careful statistical measurement of child poverty among both EU members and CEE applicants needs to be accompanied by an understanding of the consequences for children's daily lives. Analysis of cohesion in the current or future Union would benefit from drawing on such work as Roker (1998) for the UK and World Bank (1999) for Bulgaria, in which poor families and children are interviewed about their experiences. The plight of children in these studies highlights the question of whether the right provided by the CRC to an adequate standard of living given available national resources is being protected sufficiently.

Mortality among children and young people

Indicators of mortality and morbidity, or of health risk, are natural candidates for inclusion in any broad assessment of the EU's 'overall harmonious development' and hence of cohesion between current and future members. (We have already referred to the presence of life expectancy in the UNDP Human Development Index.) A rights-based approach to development also leads easily to the same indicators. For example, the CRC requires countries to take appropriate measures to diminish infant and child mortality, besides recognising the rights of children to "the highest attainable standard of health" (Article 24).

A number of indicators of health status among the young would be interesting choices to look at, both for comparison between the EU members and applicants taken as groups, and for comparison within each group. These include several relating to teenagers and other young people that reflect health-related behaviour, the leading cause of ill-health in industrialised countries for those in their teens and early-20s. Smoking and alcohol abuse, drug-taking and unsafe sex are in principle all candidates for inclusion, although in practice the availability of data certainly varies. For example, there were on average two cases of syphilis per 100,000 persons (of all ages) in the EU in 1997, and about the same in Central Europe, but around 85 in Bulgaria and Lithuania and over 120 in Latvia (UNICEF, 1999, p 71). And incidence is much higher among the young.

In this chapter, however, we restrict ourselves to measures of mortality. Sen (1998) gives three reasons for considering mortality in any appraisal of human development: first, there is the intrinsic importance attached to life itself; second, the fact that other 'capabilities' are contingent on being alive; and third, that mortality indicators provide rough proxies for a number of other values for which data are less readily available – most obviously morbidity.

We take one indicator relating to young men aged 15-24, deaths through accidents and injuries (including suicide and murder), a serious and under-recognised problem in the transition countries and one for which variation is surprisingly high within the EU. But we start by looking at deaths among the under-5s from all causes, the most widely-used measure of child mortality in developing countries.

Under-5 mortality

Figure 4.4 shows that under-5 mortality rates (U5MR) in several of the CEE applicants are not too out of line with those in the EU. The Czech Republic is within the EU range while Slovenia performs particularly well with a rate that is even below the EU15 average. If member states with a higher rate were to have had the Slovenian U5MR, there would have been 4,000 fewer deaths among children of this age in the EU15 in 1996.

On the other hand, the poorer countries of Bulgaria, Latvia and Romania stand out with U5MRs that are far higher. A child born in these countries has a probability of death before the age of five of 2% or

Figure 4.4: Under-5 mortality rates (1996)

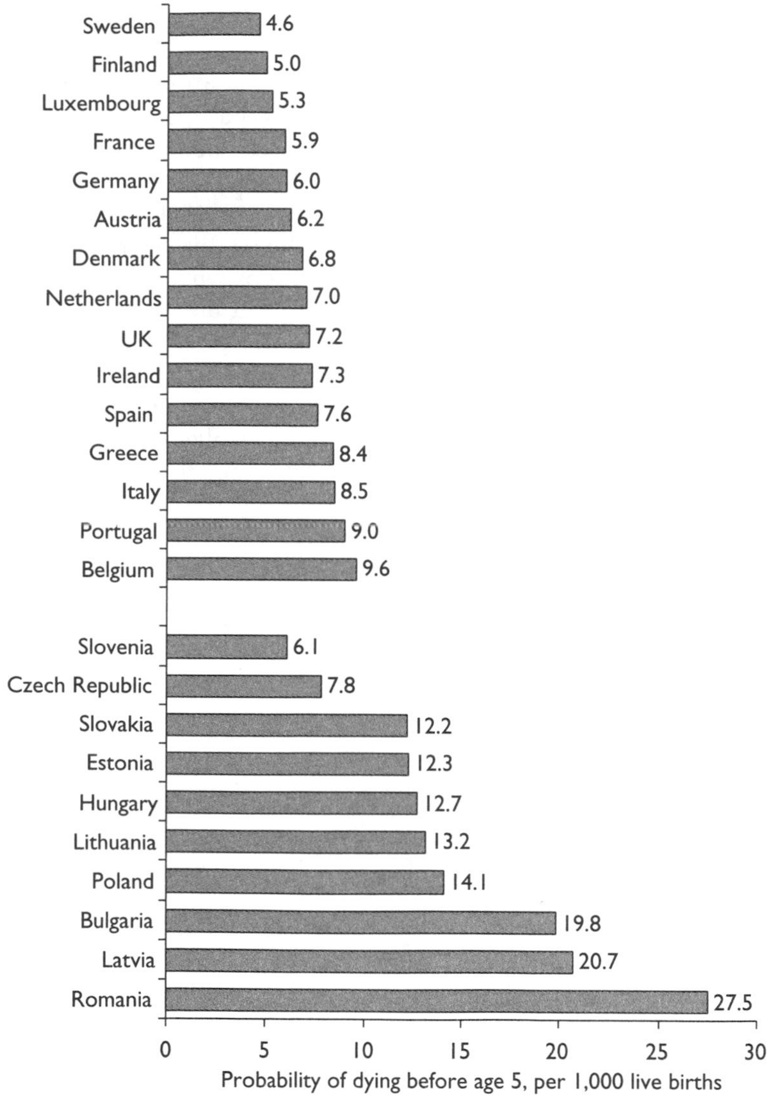

Note: Data are for 1992 for Belgium, 1993 for Ireland and Italy, 1994 for Spain and 1995 for Finland.

Source: WHO *Health for all* and UNICEF *TransMONEE* databases

more. And if all CEE applicants were to have had the same U5MR as the EU average, there would have been nearly 11,000 fewer deaths among the under-5s in the ten countries.

The rate shown for Romania is similar to that in Greece in the mid-1970s; and those in Latvia and Bulgaria are similar to the rates in Austria, Germany, Italy and Spain at the same time. This suggests that these CEE countries are currently about 20 years behind progress in the EU. That said, it is wrong of course to think of the EU15 as a homogeneous group. The variation today within the EU is such that 10,000 lives would have been saved in 1996 if all member states had had the U5MR of Sweden. Even among the richer countries already in the club there is clear room for improvement.

The case of Slovenia, with GDP at the lower limit of the EU range but with a better performance than the EU average in terms of child survival, illustrates a wider phenomenon. Although higher national income in general implies lower child mortality (the association is less clear cut if attention is restricted to just the EU members), the CEE applicants as a whole perform better than one would expect given their levels of GDP.

To show this we took the top 100 countries in the world ranked by 1995 GDP per capita (the poorest CEE applicant ranked number 100) and ran a regression of U5MR in 1996 on GDP per capita (in purchasing power parity terms) in 1995 (both in natural logs), including three dummy variables for the 15 EU members, the ten CEE applicants and the four other former socialist countries in the region (in the top 100 on GDP). The results imply that the CEE applicants (and the other socialist countries) had levels of U5MR that on average were nearly 60% less than would be predicted on the basis of just GDP per capita, and, when allowing for the differences in national income, 25% less than those of EU members[11].

Of course, national income declined sharply in all the CEE countries during the 1990s and in most has not yet recovered to 1989 levels. Did mortality among young children rise as a result? The answer in most cases is 'no' and one of the more welcome trends of the transition in terms of human welfare has been the continued decline in U5MR in many CEE applicants (Bulgaria is an exception). Most countries have therefore been living up to their responsibility under the CRC to 'diminish child mortality' despite severe economic setbacks.

We have noted that indicators based on population and vital statistics, such as mortality rates, are available for sub-national analysis. For the EU15 we have made some preliminary investigation of the infant mortality rate (IMR) at the level of the (NUTS-2) region and its association with

Figure 4.5: Injury death among 15- to 24-year-old males (1994)

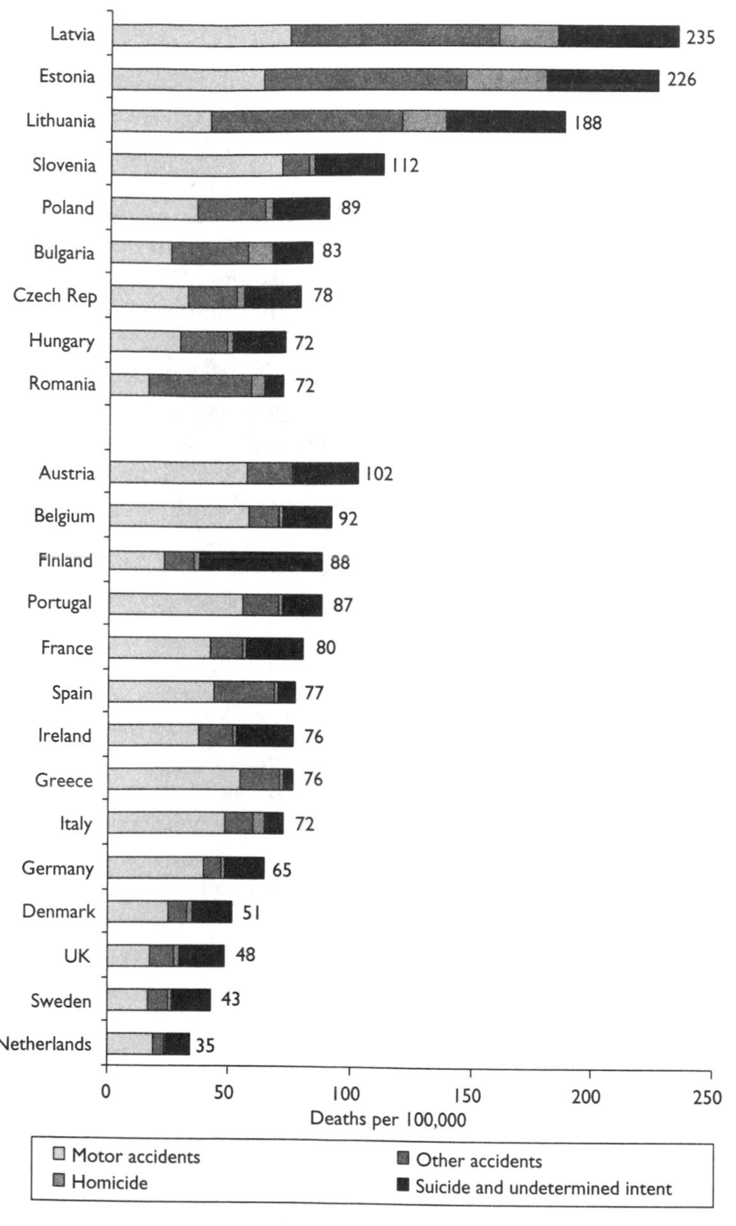

Source: WHO *World Health Statistics Annual* (various years) and UN *Demographic Yearbook*

regional GDP per capita. (Deaths among infants – children less than 12 months old – account for the bulk of under-5 mortality.) Taking average values for 1994-96 for regions in ten countries (data for the other five were not readily available), we found a correlation between the two variables of only –0.42. In some countries IMR varied little despite significant differences in GDP (eg, Germany) while in others IMR differed notably among regions with similar GDP (eg, Greece). The Greek rates varied from 4.5 deaths per thousand live births in Notio Aigaio (the richest region) to 10.6 in Dytiki Ellada (one of the poorer ones).

We have less information on the differences within the CEE countries but it is clear that as in the member states the size of the variation is not the same in each country. IMR in Hungary in 1997 ranged from 8.8 in Western Transdanubia to 11.7 in Southern Transdanubia. But in Bulgaria the extremes in the same year were 9.7 in the capital, Sofia, and as much as 27.4 in the region of Bourgas bordering on Turkey. (Our information is drawn from the 1997 Hungarian and 1998 Bulgarian statistical yearbooks.)

Injury death among young men

Death from injuries is one of the most important causes of mortality in Europe for children above the age of five. These are all, by definition, preventable deaths, and the same article of the CRC that refers to infant and child mortality explicitly mentions the prevention of accidents.

Figure 4.5 shows mortality rates from all forms of injury across EU members and applicants for males aged 15-24 in 1994. (The rates for females in all countries are much lower, proof that the variation across country cannot be due to some peculiarly national bad luck.) Four categories of cause of death are distinguished: deaths from motor vehicle accidents ('road deaths'), other injury death excluding those from violence (eg drownings, burns and poisonings), homicide and suicide (we include among suicides those deaths from violent causes undetermined whether deliberate or not – see the discussion in Micklewright and Stewart, 2000, chapter 4).

A word of comment is merited on the differences between the concepts measured in Figures 4.4 and 4.5 and on their orders of magnitude. A figure of 200 deaths per 100,000 persons aged 15-24 implies that *each year* everyone in this age group has an average probability of 0.2% of dying from injuries. Over the ten years an individual spends in this age range the probability is therefore 2% – a figure that is strikingly high (and how much greater must be the burden of non-fatal injuries alongside those that result in death). The rates in Figure 4.4, on the other hand, are already converted into probabilities over a numbers of years, five in this case. If U5MR is equal to 20 per 1,000 this implies that the average probability of death over five years is 2%.

Injury death rates vary enormously, differing by a factor of nearly 7 to 1 between the worst CEE performer, Latvia, and the best EU performer, the Netherlands. In Latvia and Estonia the probability of death from injury over ten years exceeds 2% (assuming an unchanged mortality rate) and in Lithuania it is only just short of this level. The Baltics stand out within the CEE countries, their average rate being some three times higher than that in the other applicants – the latter have rates that are at or above the EU average. But within the EU there is considerable variation too, with Austria three times higher than the Netherlands, and above five of the CEE countries. Several other member states have rates above those of Romania, Hungary, the Czech Republic and Bulgaria.

What types of injury cause these big differences? Homicides represent a negligible amount of injury death except in the Baltics (and to a lesser extent Bulgaria and Romania). The homicide rate alone in Estonia is equal to the total injury death rate in the Netherlands. These figures seem to accord with the general impression of a more violent society that has characterised the 1990s in some other parts of the former Soviet Union. Suicide is also notably high in the Baltics, but here a matching record is found in the EU in Finland. Elsewhere in the CEE region, similar suicide rates exist to those in various other EU members. Road deaths are not at an exceptionally high level in the Baltics by EU standards, although Estonia and Latvia are outside the EU15 range (they vary by a factor of about 3 to 1 within the Union), while in a number of other CEE countries they are below the EU average. But Latvia, Lithuania and Estonia again stand out as having a very poor record on 'other accidents' with rates around six times higher than the average across the EU15.

How have these figures changed over time? The broad pattern – all CEE countries above the EU average, with the Baltic states way out of line – does not depend on the year selected, at least for the early 1990s (LSHTM, 1998). Within the EU, Finland has emerged over the last 25 years as an outlier on suicides, although it is also the case that the EU suicide rate rose by 40% from 1970 to 1995 (Micklewright and Stewart, 2000). Some positive news on the Baltics is that injury death declined during the years 1994-97 in all three countries by between 10-35%

Figure 4.6: Education enrolment (1995) and maths achievement (1994/95)

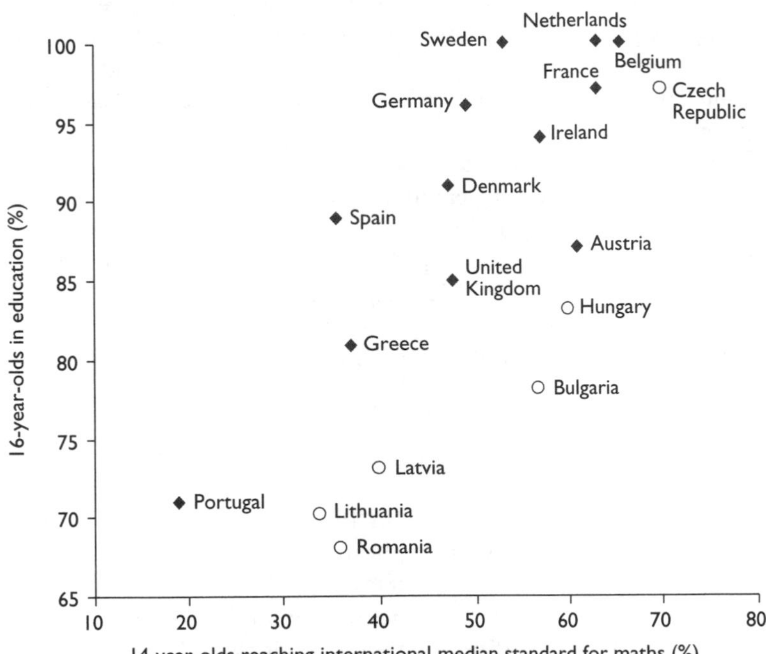

Notes: The correlation between the two series is 0.73. [b] Maths achievement score for the UK is a weighted average of scores for England and Scotland. The score for Belgium is a straight average of scores for the Flemish and French educational systems.

Source: Enrolment data from UNESCO website (http://unescostat.unesco.org/indicator/indframe.htm, Age-specific Enrolment Ratios). Maths scores from Beaton et al (1996, Tables 1.4 and 1.5)

(UNICEF, 1999, Annex Table 3.6; data for males aged 5-19, excluding suicide)[12].

Education – enrolment and achievement

The narrow view of economic and social cohesion within the EU as largely a matter of income and employment opportunities leads one quickly to consider differences in educational outcomes among both member and applicant countries. (The Commission's own work on cohesion draws attention to some of the differences.) But education has many effects beyond that of increasing material living standards. These enrich a person's life in various ways, giving him or her the capability to achieve a wider set of Sen's 'functionings'. For example, Haveman et al (1998) list (in the US context) "occupational prestige, health status, efficiency in consumption, marriage and fertility choices, and offspring quality" (p 346). All these effects of education are clearly relevant to the wider view of cohesion that we argue is needed.

An approach to child well-being based on human rights should also have education as a key element in the list of issues to be considered. The CRC emphasises the right to education, and to the development of the child's abilities to their fullest potential (Articles 28 and 29). And it underlines that countries should achieve educational rights "on the basis of equal opportunity"[13].

How then do educational opportunities vary across the member states and the CEE applicants? The different dimensions of education for children defy easy summary. One approach is to consider inputs, in particular public expenditure as a percentage of GDP. Here the member states certainly exhibit convergence since 1980, although the Cohesion Four still had the lowest spending in 1995 (Micklewright and Stewart, 2000, Figure 5.1). The CEE applicants have seen large falls in real expenditure per pupil on account of lower levels of national income. But broadly speaking they have maintained (or in some cases increased) education's expenditure share at typically about 5% of GDP, the level on which the EU member states are converging (Hungary and Bulgaria are two exceptions; UNICEF, 1999, Annex Table 7.6). However, moves to decentralise provision and financing of education in several of the former centrally planned economies raise the issue of within-country differences in funding (UNICEF, 1998).

One level of educational provision on which most of the CEE applicants still score well is pre-schooling, reflecting in part the former socialist system's commitment to child development and in part its need to mobilise female labour supply. Enrolment rates dipped in the early 1990s due to both supply- and demand-side factors but now seem in general to be recovering. The rates vary substantially (the Czech Republic and Hungary led the field in 1997 with rates of over 80% for 3- to 5-year-olds, while Latvia and Lithuania brought up the rear with rates of around 50% and 40% respectively of 3- to 6-year-olds).

There is increasing recognition in all industrialised countries of the value of pre-school investment in children, and the CEE countries' tradition in this area is an important inheritance. Tradition varies substantially in the EU members with countries such as Ireland and the UK recently initiating new policy to promote pre-schooling, or realising the need to do so.

Figure 4.6 shows two measures of national educational performance for older children, age-16 enrolment rates and age-14 achievement in standardised maths tests. Results for the latter are taken from the Third International Maths and Science Study (TIMSS), a rigorously conducted investigation of learning achievement in some 40 countries. The graph is restricted to those countries for which both indicators are available, 12 from the EU and 6 from CEE.

The vertical axis shows the enrolment rates. The EU15 have been converging strongly since the mid-1960s, with the average rate rising (Micklewright and Stewart, 1999, Figure 4). Nevertheless, in Greece and Portugal around 20% and 30% respectively of 16-year-olds were not in education in mid-1995. These are the two poorest EU members in terms of national income per head; but the UK, with GDP per capita at the EU average, is another laggard (and even more so in earlier years).

The enrolment rates in the CEE countries display substantial variation. Romania, Lithuania and Latvia, three of the poorest applicants, have rates similar to that for Portugal – although the fact that Portugal's measured GDP per capita is some two to three times higher should not be forgotten. The Czech Republic is up with the best of the EU members.

But total enrolment is only part of the story. The issue of what form of education the enrolment is in has come to be especially important in the CEE countries. The educational systems of the planned economies encouraged many children, especially boys, away from a general education at age 14 or 15 and into vocational and technical schools, some of them highly specialised. (Romania is an example of a country where there was extreme specialisation in schools.) It is the broader skills taught in general secondary schools that are in greater demand in the transition to a market economy, and these schools also provide the easier route into tertiary education, which is undergoing a big expansion. In fact the story here in the ten CEE applicants is typically a positive one, with falling enrolments in vocational and technical schooling and rising enrolments in general secondary schools.

Whether young people in CEE and EU countries are all on the same level playing field depends not just on the type of school and the curricula but also on what they actually manage to learn. The horizontal axis of Figure 4.6 gives the TIMSS results for maths at age 14, showing the percentage of children who scored at least as high as the median among all children in all 40 participating countries.

Among both members and applicants, countries with higher enrolment rates in general have the further advantage of children with higher maths scores too, emphasising the differences that exist between the educational systems in both sets of countries. The differences in maths achievement are indeed considerable, larger than those for enrolment. In Lithuania and Romania only half as many children reach the international median as in the Czech Republic. Portuguese children are hugely adrift of those in most of the rest of the EU.

It is also clear that the EU members do not dominate the CEE applicants regarding maths achievement. The Czech Republic out-performs *all* 12 EU members, and Hungary comes higher in the ranking than eight of them. Bulgaria, the poorest country, comes higher than such large EU countries as Germany and the UK. Even the two Baltic countries and Romania are on a par with Greece and Spain, as well as being well ahead of Portugal.

These data on learning achievement would repay more detailed analysis. They could be used to reveal much more about the extent of variation in achievement *within* countries. Our focus on the percentage of children reaching the international median can be likened to the application across EU members and applicants of a single poverty line, with the results affected by both differences between countries in average scores and the differences within them. One notable result in the published TIMSS report for maths is that the advantage in learning achievement associated with greater parental education seems just as large in the CEE countries (Beaton et al, 1996, p 103). This questions whether 'equal opportunity' is indeed the basis for educational progress in the transition countries – an issue of continued relevance in EU members as well.

How has learning achievement changed in the CEE during the transition years? Evidence suggests increasing inequality in what children have learned – in line with increasing income inequality (UNICEF, 1998; Micklewright, 1999). But investigation with comparable cross-country data will have to await the results of the TIMSS follow-up study conducted in 1999. Comparisons of all the EU members with both themselves and Poland, Hungary and the Czech Republic will also be possible for a wider assessment of 'functional literacy' among 15-year-olds being conducted by the OECD. Results for 16- to 25-year-olds from a more limited exercise in 1994 showed Poland to be far adrift of the six EU members included in the survey in terms of the ability to absorb the correct information from written documents. Ireland and the UK scored well below Sweden and the Netherlands (OECD, 1997, p 154)[14].

Conclusions

Many of the CEE states applying for EU membership bring an impressive inheritance with them. A long history of low-income inequality, combined with a tradition of investment in the social sectors in general and in children and the family in particular, has left a lasting mark. On several indicators of child well-being there are CEE countries that compete well with current EU members, despite much lower levels of national income, and even after the upheavals of the last decade.

Fourteen-year-olds in the Czech Republic, for example, performed better at standardised maths tests in 1995 than their peers in any other present or potential EU state, while the level of achievement in both Hungary and Bulgaria was well above the EU average. The limited data available also suggest that the former Czechoslovakia would emerge well from a comparison of child poverty rates with its Western neighbours: child poverty was just 2% at the start of the transition, and even by 1997 both the Czech Republic and Slovakia had income inequality below the 1980s EU average.

Not all applicants have so much to be proud of, but performance in several areas is still impressive given current levels of national income. Romania and the Baltic states did fairly poorly on the standardised maths tests, for instance, but no worse than Greece or Spain and much better than Portugal, all countries with substantially higher per capita GDP. Similarly, under-five mortality in all CEE states except Slovenia is above the EU average – but well below that of other countries with similar levels of national income.

In some ways, the comparison of EU and CEE performance shows up the gaps in EU achievement, or at least that in certain member states (there are of course wide disparities within the EU group). While the current membership ponders whether its eastern neighbours are fit to join the EU club, it should also note that the new members may bring important lessons with them. If admitted tomorrow, in some areas of child welfare some CEE countries would set new high standards for the rest of the Union to follow.

On the other hand, there are also large disparities in performance within the CEE group, and in several applicant countries there are matters for concern. As noted, the standard of living of children in Romania's child institutions has been raised as an issue by the EU's reports on progress towards accession, but attention should be paid to rising child poverty in much of the CEE region. We also described the disturbingly high level of violent death among teenagers and young adults in the Baltic states. This reveals a side to society not picked up by the standard economic indicators of progress in the Baltics, raising questions about whether these countries are ready to join a 'union of shared values'.

Our discussion has focused on just a few indicators of child well-being, and the chapter has not attempted to provide a comprehensive picture. We have sought to highlight dimensions of well-being that are not being studied under the current interpretation of the Copenhagen Criteria governing EU entry. Without diminishing the importance of the issues that are at present considered in EU progress reports, such as the treatment of minorities and the realisation of basic civic and political freedoms, we have aimed to draw attention to the fact that human rights extend beyond these boundaries. The accession criteria should not represent double-standards, however. The enlargement process offers a valuable opportunity for existing member states to hold up a mirror on their own performance. Few, if any, should be fully satisfied with what they see.

The indicators examined are also important from the perspective of the analysis of economic and social cohesion within the EU, which ought to be broader than the Commission's current focus on employment and incomes. While many aspects of well-being tend to correlate roughly with per capita GDP, the impact of other factors, including public services and the distribution of income, ensure that GDP is only ever the beginning of the story – a fact underlined by the superior performance of some CEE countries in some areas. A serious study of economic and social cohesion should cover a wide variety of aspects of life, and there would be no better place to start than with the very disparate opportunities currently faced by the 100 million children of the EU and CEE.

Notes

[1] The CEE applicants are the Czech Republic, Hungary, Poland, Slovenia, Estonia, Slovakia, Latvia, Lithuania, Bulgaria and Romania. (The first five were originally treated as being at the front of the queue.) The three other official applicants are Cyprus, Malta and, since December 1999, Turkey.

[2] The Commission concluded that Romania fulfils the Copenhagen political criteria,'on the assumption that the authorities continue to give priority to dealing with the crisis in their child care institutions'. The Commission's initial Opinions on Applications for Membership and subsequent Reports on Progress can be found at http://europa.eu.int/comm/enlargement.

[3] Commenting on the initial Opinions, Nowak (1999) notes that their analysis of human rights "seems rather superficial and relates more to the *de jure* than the *de facto* situation" (p 695).

[4] While the conditions in Romanian orphanages may be of particular concern, excessive institutionalisation and the factors associated with it are a region-wide problem in the CEE countries (UNICEF, 1997). Bulgaria, rather than Romania, had the highest rate of infants aged 0-3 in institutions in 1997 (over 1%) and the growth in institutionalisation among young children has been largest in Estonia, with a rise of 75% over 1989-97, followed by Latvia with a rise of two thirds (UNICEF, 1999, Annex Table 8.1).

[5] Other rights relating to children are mentioned in the reports, although again in haphazard fashion. Several reports refer to issues relating to juvenile justice. The 1999 report on Poland raises the need for policies to address violent and abusive treatment against children, while the Slovenian report notes that provisions on the rights of children are included in the Constitution. The original Opinion on Lithuania highlights the absence of appropriate legislation against child prostitution or the sexual abuse of children. Children also come up in discussion of minority rights (eg, with regard to discrimination against Roma and to the question of citizenship for ethnic Russians in the Baltic states).

[6] The periodic reports of EU and CEE countries to the UN Committee on the Rights of the Child, which monitors the CRC, can be found at http://www.unhchr.ch/html/menu2/6/crcs.htm. Issues of human rights within the EU are discussed at length in Alston (1999). (See in particular the introductory chapter by Alston and Weiler.) In extremis, the Treaty on Union permits the suspension of benefits of membership in the case of a member state committing a 'serious and persistent breach' of human rights.

[7] The Commission's *Sixth Periodic Report* on development of EU regions extends the first cohesion report's analysis to the CEE countries (European Commission, 1999).

[8] The convergence of polices affecting children within the EU member states is considered by a variety of authors, including Ruxton (1996) and Ditch et al (1998).

[9] Of course, greater employment opportunities may help reduce teenage motherhood, but the strength of the local labour market is far from being the only factor involved (the issues are reviewed in Micklewright and Stewart, 2000).

[10] We focus exclusively on cash incomes in this section but the EU definition is a reminder that 'poverty' can be the deprivation of things other than money. On the issue of a common EU line, see Atkinson (1998) who explores the idea of a weighted average of common and national thresholds.

[11] The difference between the coefficients on the CEE and EU dummies was significant at the 2.5% level. The data were drawn from the *Human Development Report*.

[12] The same source suggests that the rate for Slovenia in Figure 4.5 is much higher than for other years in the 1990s.

[13] Hammarberg (1998) discusses in detail the shape of educational policy based on the principles in the CRC.

[14] Results of the TIMSS follow-up and of the new OECD assessment are both expected to be available in 2001 (see http://timss.bc.edu and http://oecd.org/els/pisa).

References

Alston, P. (ed) (1999) *The EU and human rights*, Oxford: Oxford University Press.

Atkinson, A.B. (1998) *Poverty in Europe*, Oxford: Basil Blackwell.

Atkinson, A.B. and Micklewright, J. (1992) *Economic transformation in Eastern Europe and the distribution of income*, Cambridge: Cambridge University Press.

Atkinson, A.B., Rainwater, L. and Smeeding, T. (1995) *Income distribution in OECD countries*, Social Policy Studies No 18, Paris: OECD.

Beaton, A., Mullis, I., Martin, M., Gonzalez, E., Kelly, D. and Smith, T. (1996) *Mathematics achievement in the middle school years: IEA's Third International Mathematics and Science Study*, Chestnut Hill, MA: Centre for the Study of Testing, Evaluation and Educational Policy, Boston College.

Bradbury, B. and Jäntti, M. (1999) 'Child poverty across industrialized nations', Innocenti Occasional Paper no ESP 71, Florence: UNICEF Innocenti Research Centre.

Ditch, J., Barnes, H., Bradshaw, J. and Kilkey, M. (1998) *Developments in national family policies in 1996*, Brussels: The European Observatory on National Family Policies, Commission of the European Communities.

European Commission (1996) *First report on economic and social cohesion 1996*, Luxembourg: Office for Official Publications of the European Communities.

European Commission (1999) *Sixth periodic report on the social and economic situation and development of the regions of the European Union*, Luxembourg: Office for Official Publications of the European Communities.

Eurostat (1997) *Statistics in focus* (Population and Social Conditions), no 6.

Eurostat (1999a) *Eurostat yearbook 98/99*, Luxembourg: Office for Official Publications of the European Communities.

Eurostat (1999b) *Statistical yearbook on Central European countries 1998*, Luxembourg: Office for Official Publications of the European Communities.

Ferge, Z. (1991) 'Social security systems in the new democracies of Central and Eastern Europe; past legacies and possible futures', in G.A. Cornia and S. Sipos (eds) *Children and the transition to the market economy*, Aldershot: Avebury.

Flemming, J. and Micklewright, J. (1999) 'Income distribution, economic systems and transition', Innocenti Occasional Paper no ESP 70, Florence: UNICEF Innocenti Research Centre.

Galasi, P. (1998) 'Income inequality and mobility in Hungary, 1992-96', Innocenti Occasional Paper no ESP 64, Florence: UNICEF Innocenti Research Centre.

Hammarberg, T. (1998) 'A school for children with rights', Innocenti Lecture no 2, Florence: UNICEF Innocenti Research Centre.

Haveman, R., Wilson, K. and Wolfe, B. (1998) 'A structural model of the determinants of educational success', in S. Jenkins, A. Kapteyn, and B. van Praag (eds) *The distribution of welfare and household production: International perspectives*, Cambridge: Cambridge University Press.

LSHTM (London School of Hygiene and Tropical Medicine) (1998) 'Childhood injuries: A priority area for the transition countries of Central and Eastern Europe and the Newly Independent States', LSHTM: Final Report under contract 97/C/29 for UNICEF Regional Office for CEE/CIS/Baltics, Geneva, available at www.lshtm.ac.uk/centres/ecohost.

Micklewright, J. (1999) 'Education, inequality and transition', *Economics of Transition*, vol 7, no 2, pp 343-76.

Micklewright, J. and Stewart, K. (1999) 'Is the well-being of children converging in the European Union?', *Economic Journal*, vol 109, no 459, pp F692-F714.

Micklewright, J. and Stewart, K. (2000), *The welfare of Europe's children: Are EU member states converging?*, Bristol: The Policy Press.

Nowak, M. (1999) 'Human rights "conditionality" in relation to entry to, and full participation in, the EU', in P. Alston (ed) *The EU and human rights*, Oxford: Oxford University Press.

OECD (1997) *Literacy skills for the knowledge society*, Paris/Ottawa: OECD/Human Resources Development.

Roker, D. (1998) *Worth more than this: Young people growing up in family poverty*, London: The Children's Society.

Ruxton, S. (1996) *Children in Europe*, London: NCH Action for Children.

Sen, A. (1998) 'Mortality as an indicator of economic success and failure', *Economic Journal*, vol 108, no 446, pp 1-26.

UNDP (1999) *Human Development Report 1999*, New York, NY: Oxford University Press.

UNICEF (1997) *Children at risk in Central and Eastern Europe*, Regional Monitoring Report no 4, Florence: UNICEF Innocenti Research Centre.

UNICEF (1998) *Education for all?*, Regional Monitoring Report no 5, Florence: UNICEF Innocenti Research Centre.

UNICEF (1999) *Women in transition*, Regional Monitoring Report no 6, Florence: UNICEF Innocenti Research Centre.

Vecernik, J. (1999) 'Distribution of household income in the Czech Republic in 1988-1996: readjustment to the market', Luxembourg Income Study Working Paper no 198.

World Bank (1999) *Bulgaria: Consultations with the poor* (background paper for *WDR 2000*) available from http://www.worldbank.org/poverty/wdrpoverty.

FIVE

Childhood experiences, educational attainment and adult labour market performance

Paul Gregg and Stephen Machin[1]

Introduction

The relationship between childhood experiences and subsequent labour market performance as an adult is an important area of study for several reasons. First, we may be interested in looking empirically at the transmission mechanisms that underpin the extent of intergenerational mobility (or immobility) of economic status. It is clear that the association between childhood factors and adult earnings, employment and unemployment is likely to play a role as one such transmission mechanism (or intervening factor). Second, uncovering any links between childhood disadvantage and performance in the adult labour market is useful in shedding light on the way in which pre-labour market factors (other than education which has been widely studied, or early age test scores which have received some, although less, attention[2]) are connected to labour market success or failure. Third, uncovering such associations may be important in informing future policy related to child outcomes, especially if one can (as we do) study changes over time.

In this chapter we consider what can be said about these kinds of associations, drawing on data from two British birth cohorts, born during a week in March 1958 (the National Child Development Study, NCDS) and during a week in April 1970 (the 1970 British Cohort Study, BCS70). These are unique data sources that follow cohort members from birth, through the childhood years and into adulthood, collecting a huge amount of very rich information along the way. The two surveys have similar structures and, for the some of the analysis, comparisons can be made across the two birth cohorts.

The main findings are as follows:

- On the basis of studying quite large samples of parents and children, the extent of intergenerational mobility in Britain is limited in terms of earnings and education. If anything, mobility seems to have fallen for the 1970 cohort as compared to the earlier 1958 cohort.
- Childhood disadvantages (specific to the child and to its parents) are an important factor in maintaining and reinforcing patterns of immobility of economic status across generations.
- Educational attainment is an important transmission mechanism underpinning the extent of mobility, as it partially ameliorates the (negative) associations with disadvantage.
- One of the key factors of childhood disadvantage, child poverty, has risen massively in the last 30 years or so. In cross-cohort comparisons child poverty seems to have an important (negative) effect on success in the adult labour market. While the effect is dampened down once one controls for education, negative effects on adult wages and employment remain.
- Indicators of disadvantage have a cross-generation effect on the cognitive skills of children whose parents grew up in a disadvantaged environment.

The rest of the chapter is structured as follows. First we present a brief discussion of estimates of the extent of intergenerational mobility based on data from the two cohorts. We then present a summary of our earlier findings about the links between childhood factors and adult outcomes using the NCDS cohort data. The next section uses NCDS data and, as children of the cohort members have now been sampled, explores whether one can pin down any evidence of an intergenerational spillover by relating children's maths and reading test scores to measures of childhood disadvantage of their (NCDS cohort member) parent. Finally, we carry out some simple BCS70 comparisons with NCDS, focusing on associations with child poverty, before offering our conclusions.

Intergenerational mobility in Britain

This section sets the scene by considering the extent of mobility (or immobility) of economic and social status across generations using the 1958 and 1970 cohort data. The comparison undertaken here is to estimate the extent of mobility using the same kind of data and modelling specifications for the two cohorts.

There are two principal ways in which researchers have looked at intergenerational mobility. The first, the regression approach, simply runs a regression of a given economic or social outcome for children (as adults) on the same outcome of parents[3]. The second, the transition matrix approach, considers in more detail where children end up in their generation's distribution of a given economic or social outcome conditional on where their parents were in their own generation's distribution.

Regression estimates defined in a similar way in the NCDS and BCS70 show that, if anything, mobility seems to have fallen across the two cohorts. Data constraints (BCS70 does not contain parental labour market earnings) mean that, to ensure the same experiment is being undertaken, we are forced to look at associations between earnings of cohort members and the income of their parents[4]. The following two regressions are for 1,773 sons matched to parental income in NCDS and 2,717 sons matched to parental income in BCS70:

NCDS, 1,773 pairs: ln (son's earnings) = 0.115 ln (parental income)
(0.019)

BCS70, 2,717 pairs: ln (son's earnings) = 0.163 ln (parental income)
(0.015)

The correlation between a son's earnings and parental income rises over time, pointing to reduced intergenerational mobility between the 1958 and 1970 cohort. This is also borne out when one considers transition matrices. These are reported in Table 5.1 and show more mobility in the NCDS than in the later cohort. One summary statistic (of several possibilities) is to take the sum of the entries on the leading diagonal and adjacents. This rises from 2.77 in the 1958 cohort to 2.95 for the 1970 cohort[5]. It seems that mobility has, if anything, fallen. It certainly has not risen, and it appears the case that higher earning sons are more likely to be from rich families for the later cohort[6].

Table 5.1: Changes in the extent of intergenerational mobility in Britain

Sum leading diagonal and adjacents: NCDS 2.77; BCS70 2.95

NCDS	**Son's earnings quartile**			
Parental income quartile	Bottom	2nd	3rd	Top
Bottom	0.31	0.28	0.23	0.18
2nd	0.30	0.23	0.26	0.21
3rd	0.21	0.26	0.27	0.26
Top	0.18	0.23	0.24	0.36
BCS70	**Son's earnings quartile**			
Parental income quartile	Bottom	2nd	3rd	Top
Bottom	0.35	0.27	0.22	0.15
2nd	0.27	0.28	0.24	0.21
3rd	0.19	0.25	0.28	0.28
Top	0.17	0.20	0.24	0.39

Links between childhood factors and adult outcomes

We now turn to the transmission mechanisms underpinning intergenerational mobility, particularly the links between childhood factors and adult outcomes. The methodology we adopt is a sequential modelling approach following cohort members as they age. The NCDS has sampled cohort members at ages 0 (in 1958), 7, 11, 16, 23 and 33. This data collection process enables us to use the following modelling approach to address the questions of interest.

Modelling approach

We begin by trying to characterise disadvantage measures (family and child-based) derived from econometric models of age-16 outcomes that hold constant a number of age-7 childhood and parental outcomes. We estimate econometric models that we then use to pin down measures of disadvantage for the subsequent analysis. These econometric models hold constant a host of age-7 and parental variables to 'level the playing field' (or proxy individual specific fixed effects). When we then follow individuals through time, we are able to pick up who moves into a situation of childhood disadvantage and who does not.

The analysis then proceeds to later-age outcomes. The first is an important one for the interpretation of the effects we isolate in the empirical work. We look at links between educational attainment (by age 23) and child disadvantage, again holding constant the early age factors. This proves important as, probably not surprisingly, the disadvantaged are seen to have massively inferior levels of educational achievement. We are therefore interested in the extent to which those disadvantaged children are able to 'escape' poor adult labour market performance through reaching higher educational levels. We address this question in the discussion of the empirical work below.

The second part of the analysis of later-age outcomes is concerned with links between measures of economic and social success or failure (at ages 23 and 33) and the disadvantage measures (once again holding constant age-7 and age-16 variables). There are two strands to this. The first looks at the (conditional) correlations between the age-23 and age-33 outcomes and disadvantage. The second considers how much of the estimated effects can be explained by differences in measured educational attainment between those classified as disadvantaged and those who are not, thereby trying to pin down education's role as an intervening factor.

Age-16 outcomes

The analysis at age 16 looks at the associations between three outcomes and a range of child, family and environmental factors. The three outcomes of interest are:

- School attendance in the autumn (fall) term of the last year of school (aged 15-16). This comes from school records and is defined as the proportion of possible half days attended by the cohort member = (number of possible half days attendance – number of half days absences)/number of possible half days attendance.
- Contact with the police, elicited by the question, 'Has the child ever been in contact with the police or probation office?'
- Staying on at school after the compulsory school leaving age (age 16 in this cohort).

The child, the environmental and parental factors are a whole range of factors designed to in some sense 'level the playing field at age 7'. These are in (a), (b) and (c) as follows:

(a) age-7 individual-specific characteristics: ethnicity, age-7 cognitive skills measured by maths and reading test score), indicators of illness[7] and behavioural problems[8] and whether the child was classified as an educational special needs child;
(b) parental educational status;
(c) age-7 to age-16 variables: whether the child was living in a lone-mother family; whether the father figure was unemployed at the survey date; whether the family was in financial difficulties in the year prior to the survey date[9], and whether the child has ever been in care.

We prefer to think of the inclusion of the variables in (a) and (b) as fixing what we might call the 'initial conditions' (ie, standardising the characteristics of individuals at an early age) so that we can then follow a sequential modelling approach as individuals grow older. Put alternatively, we are interested in the relationship between our age-16 outcomes and the variables in (c) above in models that hold constant these initial conditions.

The key findings from the estimated econometric models are:

- staying on at school, better school attendance and reduced contact with the police are more likely for children with higher age-7 maths and reading ability, for children with more educated parents and for children who grew up in families that did not face financial difficulties in the years during which the children grew up;
- the impact of family financial difficulties is more important than family structure (whether the father was ever unemployed, or living in a lone-mother family);
- if children were ever placed in care during their childhood, this massively increased their chances of contact with the police.

Table 5.2 presents a summary of the age-16 results by defining a 'representative' cohort member with a given set of characteristics and then altering these characteristics to see what the econometric models predict in terms of school attendance, contact with the police and the likelihood of staying on at school. The table draws out the relative magnitudes of the associations, and also lets us combine together the effects of more than one variable (in the last two rows of the table). The largest positive effect on school attendance comes from higher age-7 reading ability and on staying-on rates from better reading and maths

Table 5.2: Summary of econometric estimates used to characterise disadvantage at age 16 for the NCDS cohort (marginal effects calculated as deviations from base)

	Males			Females		
	School attendance	**Contact with police/ probation**	**Stay on at school**	**School attendance**	**Contact with police/ probation**	**Stay on at school**
Base individual	**0.853**	**0.024**	**0.509**	**0.841**	**0.006**	**0.444**
Deviations from base:						
Non-white	–0.001	+0.001	+0.050	+0.010	–0.004	+0.114
Top quintile of maths test scores	–0.003	+0.018	+0.123	+0.002	–0.002	+0.208
Top quintile of reading test scores	+0.018	–0.015	+0.346	+0.025	+0.004	+0.310
Ever in care	–0.001	+0.098	–0.109	–0.006	+0.028	–0.027
Father left school aged 15 or less	–0.019	+0.018	–0.232	–0.013	+0.010	–0.184
Mother left school aged 15 or less	–0.012	+0.013	–0.239	–0.022	+0.001	–0.209
Lone-mother family at child age 7	–0.005	+0.003	–0.039	–0.001	+0.000	–0.057
Lone-mother family at child age 11 or 16	–0.010	+0.007	+0.003	–0.013	+0.001	–0.053
Father unemployed at child age 7	–0.024	+0.002	–0.086	–0.033	+0.001	+0.040
Father unemployed at child age 7	–0.013	+0.003	–0.032	–0.009	–0.001	–0.075
Family in financial difficulties at child age 7	–0.021	+0.020	–0.186	–0.033	+0.003	–0.129
Family in financial difficulties at child age 11 or 16	–0.023	+0.018	–0.092	–0.038	+0.006	–0.091
Top quintile of maths and reading test scores	+0.017	–0.007	+0.406	+0.026	+0.002	+0.444
Father and mother left school aged 15 or less, family in financial difficulties at child age 7, 11 or 16	–0.099	+0.134	–0.482	–0.136	+0.042	–0.409

Notes: Derived from Tobit models of school attendance and Probit models of staying on at school and police contact (estimated separately for males and fermales). Independent variables included in all models were: Non-white; dummies for 2nd, 3rd and top lowest quintile of maths test scores (age 7); dummies for 2nd , 3rd and top lowest quintile of reading test scores (age 7); Behavioural response 1, 2/3 and 4 (see footnote[8]); Ever educational special needs; Ever in care; Father left school aged 15 or less; Mother left school aged 15 or less; Lone-mother family at child age 7; Lone-mother family at child age 11 or 16; Father unemployed at child age 7; Father unemployed at child age 11 or 16.

The base individual is white, lowest quintiles of test scores; never in care; father and mother left school after15; never in lone mother family; Father never unemployed; Never in family with financial difficulties, not sick in last school.

Source: Reproduced from Gregg and Machin (1999a)

ability at age 7 for both males and females. For example, the second last row of the table combines the two effects showing that being in the highest quintile of both raises staying-on rates by a huge 0.41 higher than the base for males and 0.44 for females.

The most negative effects on school attendance are from growing up in a family facing financial hardship. The same is true for staying on rates, along with a strong negative effect from low parental education. The last row of the table highlights this pattern, showing that school attendance is 0.10 and 0.14 points lower than the base. The staying on rate is 0.48 and 0.41 points lower than the base for males and females who grew up in low parental education families that faced financial difficulties during the childhood years.

Contact with the police or probation services is much higher for children who have ever been in care at 0.10 higher than the 0.02 base for males and 0.03 higher than the 0.01 base for females. Children growing up in low parental education families with financial difficulties during the childhood years are also much more likely to have contact with the police for both males and females (with positive deviations of 0.13 and 0.04 for males and females respectively).

Characterising disadvantage

We use these age-16 findings to characterise the childhood years of cohort members with certain characteristics as disadvantaged. We utilise both family and child-based disadvantage measures. One should, of course, note that this distinction is somewhat hazy and, indeed, that we are somewhat selective in terms of what disadvantages we focus upon. Nevertheless, this results in the construction of two groups of disadvantage measures. The family-based measures are:

- whether the cohort member was ever placed in care during his/her childhood;
- whether the family was ever in financial difficulties;
- whether the cohort member ever lived in a lone-mother family, but did not report financial difficulties;
- whether the cohort member's father was unemployed at any of the age 7, 11 and 16 interview dates, but did not report financial difficulties.

We adopt these definitions, conditioning the lone-mother and father unemployed variables on not being in financial difficulties, because of the clear overlap between them and the family financial difficulties variable and the fact that the latter always dominated in the econometric estimates of the age-16 outcome specifications.

The child specific measures we consider are:

- low school attendance (<0.75);
- contact with police.

The extent of disadvantage

For our birth cohort of people born in March 1958, 16.7% of children in our sample experienced financial distress at any of the observed ages 7, 11 or 16[10]. In terms of the other disadvantage measures, 3.8% of children were ever placed in care during their childhood years, and 7.4% had a father unemployed at least once at ages 7, 11 or 16. Only 2.9% had an unemployed father without also reporting financial difficulties at some time. Ten point seven per cent were living in a lone-parent family at some point in time and 5.5% reported being in a lone-parent family without financial distress. In terms of the child-specific anti-social measures, around 10% had school attendance below .75 at age 15 (excluding sick individuals). Finally, 6.3% had contact with the police by age 16.

The subsequent analysis looks at the relationship between age-23 and age-33 economic and social outcomes and these measures of disadvantage, utilising the sequential modelling approach outlined above[11].

Educational attainment

The starting point of the analysis between adult outcomes and disadvantage concerns the association between educational achievement and childhood disadvantage. It is very clear that the educational attainment of the disadvantaged is considerably lower[12]. For example, only 1% of boys who had school attendance of less than 0.75 or who had been in contact with the police went on to get a degree (or higher) by age 23; this compares to 13% of the other NCDS boys. Figures for girls are 1% and 11% respectively. In terms of family disadvantage only 4% of boys (3% of girls) who were ever placed in care or lived in a family facing financial difficulties went on to degree level. This compared with 13% of boys (11% of girls) who were not in such a situation in their childhood years.

At the other end of the education spectrum, the disadvantaged are heavily over-represented in the part of the population that has no educational qualifications. For example, 53% of boys (62% of girls) with school attendance of less than 0.75 or who had been in contact with the police left school with no educational qualifications. This compares to 19% of boys and 25% of girls with better attendance and no police contact.

Because of this very strong association it seems likely that success in education is likely to be a potentially important transmission mechanism underpinning links between childhood disadvantage and adult economic and social outcomes, and therefore the extent of intergenerational mobility. As such it is important in the analysis of age-23 and age-33 economic and social outcomes, which is discussed next, to look at what happens when one does and does not net out the education differences between the disadvantaged and non-disadvantaged cohort members.

Age-23 and age-33 outcomes

At age 23 four economic and social outcomes were looked at, with the fourth one differing for male and female cohort members. For both sexes, we looked at age-23 hourly wages, employment status at the 1981-survey date and time spent unemployed (in months) since age 16. Then for male cohort members we looked at the probability of having experienced a prison or borstal spell since age 16, and for female cohort members we looked at the probability of having become a lone mother by age 23. At age 33 we look at wages and employment status for both sexes. These variables enable us to consider a relatively wide range of outcomes (from higher wages through to prison attendance for males and lone parenthood for females) in our search for factors that shape relative success or failure in the early years of adulthood.

Some simple descriptive statistics for the economic and social outcomes at ages 23 and 33 are reported in Table 5.3. In these raw data descriptions age-23 hourly wages and the probability of being employed are lower than average, and months spent unemployed since age 16 is higher than average for those characterised as disadvantaged in almost all cases. The probability of having had a prison/borstal spell for males, or being a lone parent for females is higher for the disadvantaged. There is some variation in the raw associations, with low school attendance being strongly associated with lower wages and employment. Also, ever being placed in care during the childhood years and being in contact with the police/probation between ages 10 and 16 are associated with a much higher

Table 5.3: NCDS age 23 and 33 outcomes by disadvantage status

Male cohort members	Hourly pay, age 23	Employment, age 23	Unemployment time (in months) since age 16, age 23	Prison spell since age 16, age 23	Hourly pay, age 33	Employment, age 33
All males	2.71	0.86	5	0.01	7.63	0.91
Low school attendance	2.50	0.72	11	0.04	5.80	0.81
Contact with police	2.61	0.77	9	0.05	6.43	0.82
Ever in care	2.56	0.72	11	0.07	6.36	0.75
Ever in financial difficulties	2.60	0.77	9	0.03	6.28	0.83
Ever in lone parent family (no financial difficulties)	2.71	0.86	6	0.01	7.73	0.91
Father ever unemployed (no financial difficulties)	2.65	0.78	6	0.02	7.19	0.91

Male cohort members	Hourly pay, age 23	Employment, age 23	Unemployment time (in months) since age 16, age 23	Lone mother by age 23, age 23	Hourly pay, age 33	Employment, age 33
All females	2.38	0.66	4	0.08	5.24	0.76
Low school attendance	2.05	0.47	7	0.20	3.95	0.62
Contact with police	2.02	0.44	6	0.19	4.49	0.63
Ever in care	2.22	0.51	6	0.17	4.78	0.62
Ever in financial difficulties	2.24	0.49	6	0.16	4.22	0.65
Ever in lone parent family (no financial difficulties)	2.42	0.68	3	0.08	5.94	0.70
Father ever unemployed (no financial difficulties)	2.16	0.62	5	0.08	4.75	0.69

incidence of prison/borstal spells for men. At age 33 hourly wages and employment rates are markedly lower in respect of the first four measures (low school attendance, police/probation, ever in care, ever in financial difficulties), although there is less difference for those from a lone-parent (in the absence of financial difficulties) background.

Results

We have estimated statistical models that build by age and do and do not take account of age-23 educational attainment. A summary of the main results is given in the flow diagrams in Figures 5.1 and 5.2 for male and female cohort members respectively. The flow diagrams report the association between childhood disadvantage and each outcome variable in column 1, after controlling for the age-7 attributes listed earlier. Column 2 introduces the age-16 anti-social measures and reports how much of the original association with family disadvantage is left after allowing for them. In a similar vein, in column 3 we introduce educational attainment at age 23 and in column 4 age-23 employment or wage outturns in the age-33 models.

Consider the relationship between male employment rates and family financial distress, given in row 3 of Figure 5.1. The employment rate of men at age 23 is 8.0 percentage points lower for those experiencing financial distress in their families as children. When we add in the age-16 anti-social behaviour variables, this falls to 6.4 percentage points. So one can think of poor school attendance and contact with the police accounting for 1.6 percentage points of the negative employment effect associated with childhood financial distress. Moving on, when one then includes educational attainment this is further reduced to 5.3 percentage points.

The overall picture emerging from the flow diagrams is that of a clearly marked (and negative) relationship between childhood disadvantage and adult economic and social outcomes. It is also clear that educational attainment acts as an important transmission mechanism as the magnitudes of the associations are usually considerably diminished by including the education variable. Nevertheless, an important and often sizeable fraction of the association with disadvantage remains intact. The main exception to this is the wage results at age 23, but we would argue that looking at wages at age 23 is probably too early in the life cycle to identify any important effects. For females, almost all outcomes are significantly worse for most of the disadvantage variables (except for the lone parent and father unemployed variables, whose effects are more mixed), and remain so (albeit smaller) once one controls for education.

Looking in a little more detail, the quantitatively most important effects in the age-23 models that control for educational attainment are as follows. Individuals growing up in a family facing financial difficulties have joblessness rates about 5% higher (men) and 9% higher (women). Being in contact with the police or probation services results in much lower employment probabilities (reduced by 5% for men, 13% for women) and significantly higher probabilities of a prison/borstal spell for men (by 1.6%) and lone parenthood for women (4.5%). By age 33 the effects of some of the disadvantage still persist. Most notably the childhood poverty measure (family financial difficulties) is significantly associated with worse economic outcomes (lower wages and employment probabilities) for men even after netting out education differences.

The educational attainment variable reduces the estimated coefficients by up to 50% (the 'typical' reduction is probably about one third). As these estimated models include the early age 'ability' related measures (what we earlier called the 'initial conditions' variables) this shows that education is indeed an important transmission mechanism that underpins the relationship between disadvantage and inferior economic and social outcomes.

Intergenerational links

Some of the NCDS cohort members now have their own children, and the data set contains information on test score outcomes from a battery of tests administered to the cohort members whose children were old enough in 1991. This data allows an intergenerational aspect to our study and lets us ask the very important question of whether social disadvantage faced by the NCDS cohort member in their formative childhood years has any clear relationship with their own children's cognitive abilities.

Table 5.4 reports information on two tests administered to the cohort members' children for those aged between 6 and 9 in 1991. The tests are the well-known Peabody Individual Achievement Tests (for maths and reading recognition) and are standardised for age differences (see Social Statistics Research Unit, undated, for more details). Children have been classified into percentiles of the test scores distribution, and we report the mean percentile broken down by parents' social disadvantage in the table. A clear and strong pattern emerges. For maths and reading tests children whose parents faced social disadvantages in their own childhood have

Figure 5.1: Summary of results, male cohort members

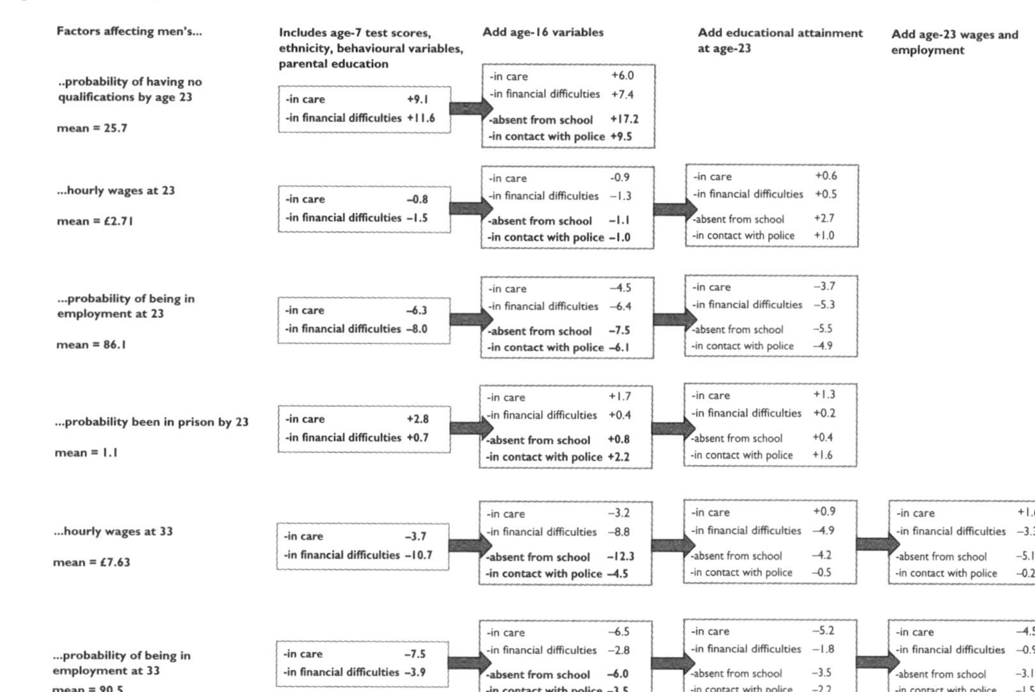

Note: **Figures in bold represent initial effects of factors,** figures in plain represent the effects once new factors have been taken into account

Figure 5.2: Summary of results, female cohort memebers

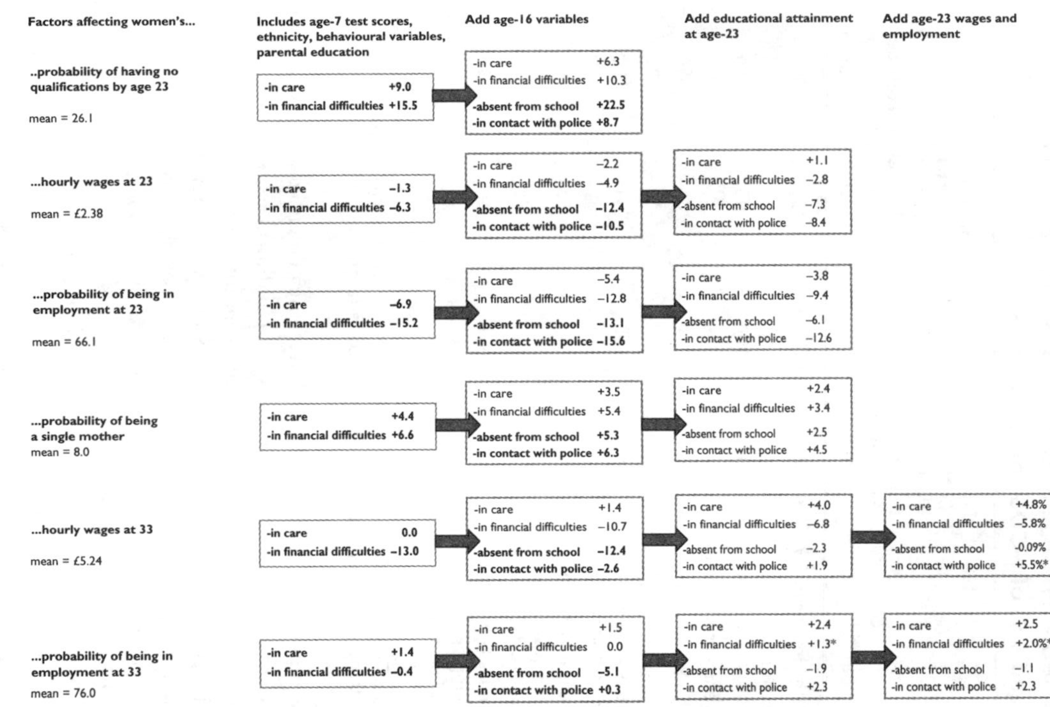

Note: **Figures in bold represent initial affects of factors,** figures in plain represent the effects once new factors have been taken into account

Table 5.4: Maths and reading test score percentiles for children (aged 6-9) of NCDS cohort members

	Percentile in Maths Peabody Individual Achievement Test	Number of children	Percentile in Maths Peabody Individual Achievement Test	Number of children
All children aged 6-9	52	1,007	51	1,008
Parent had low school attendance	48	104	45	105
Parent was in contact with police	41	56	36	56
Parent was ever in care	38	37	35	37
Parent grew up in family facing financial difficulties	45	182	44	183
Parent ever in lone-parent family (but not financial difficulties)	56	65	53	65
Parent's father ever unemployed (but not financial difficulties)	54	31	48	31

Notes: Taken from Gregg and Machin (1999b). Age range of children is from 6 years and 0 months to 9 years and 0 months inclusive (at the time of taking the tests).

lower percentile rankings. In particular, the percentile scores are extremely low for children whose parents' own childhood experiences included a spell in care (by a huge 14 percentile points for boys and 16 points for girls relative to the average) and for those with parents who had been in contact with the police/probation services as a youth (by 11 and 15 percentile points relative to the mean for boys and girls respectively).

These results demonstrate a further effect of social disadvantage when growing up, namely the existence of an intergenerational spillover[13]. The children of parents who grew up in socially disadvantaged situations are more likely to have lower scores in tests administered to them at an early age. As early-age maths and reading ability are important determinants of economic and social success or failure as an adult, this suggests that the negative economic and social effects of childhood disadvantage persist over more than one generation.

Figure 5.3: Trends in child poverty in Britain

Note: Based on Family Expenditure Survey data with a relative poverty line defined as half average equivalised income in year.

Source: Gregg et al (1999)

Cross-cohort comparisons

The motivating discussion and some of the findings on intergenerational mobility, reported on earlier, stressed the need to look at changes through time. The case for this is made all the more relevant when one notes that the time periods between early labour market years of the NCDS and BCS70 cohorts were characterised by rising wage and income inequality (Machin, 1996, 1998; Goodman et al, 1997), and by increased child poverty (Gregg et al, 1999). Figure 5.3 shows increasing child poverty rates, from about 1 in 10 in 1968 to just under 1 in 3 by 1995/96. As the figure shows, the proportion of children in poverty showed a moderate rise in the 1970s, but increased at a rapid rate thereafter.

As the designs of the NCDS ad BCS70 cohort surveys are similar (indeed some questions are identical), we have begun to look at the extent to which associations between economic and social outcomes and childhood experiences vary across cohorts. The age-16 data on staying on at school and contact with the police are the same across the two cohorts, so Table 5.5 reports the associations between these two outcomes and the childhood poverty measure (ie, the variable indicating that the family reported being in financial difficulties). The associations

Table 5.5: Cross-cohort comparisons of associations between age-16 outcomes and child poverty

	Staying on at school		Contact with police	
Male cohort members	NCDS	BCS70	NCDS	BCS70
Family faced financial difficulties: marginal effect (standard error)	–0.104 (0.023)	–0.088 (0.031)	0.073 (0.016)	0.067 (0.022)
Mean of financial difficulties	0.104	0.160	0.104	0.160
Female cohort members	NCDS	BCS70	NCDS	BCS70
Family faced financial difficulties: marginal effect (standard error)	–0.122 (0.022)	–0.154 (0.028)	0.038 (0.012)	0.022 (0.015)
Mean of financial difficulties	0.106	0.152	0.106	0.152

Notes: derived from Probit models of staying on at school and police contact estimated separately for male and female cohort members in each cohort. Other variables included in all models were: mother's and father's education; whether the father was living with the cohort member at ages 7 (NCDS), 5 (BCS70) and 16 (both cohorts); whether the father was unemployed at ages 7 (NCDS), 5 (BCS70) and 16 (both cohorts); whether the cohort member was ever placed in care.

are rather stable for both male and female cohort members. But childhood poverty rose between 1974 (when the NCDS cohort was 16) and 1986 (when the BCS70 cohort was 16), as shown by the rising mean of the financial difficulty variable in the table. This suggests a more important link between disadvantage and the age-16 outcomes for the older cohort. While this requires a lot more research, it seems likely that this type of link is a potentially important factor underpinning the earlier findings that intergenerational mobility has probably fallen over time in an era of rising labour market and income inequality.

Conclusions

This chapter surveys some of our recent work on connections between childhood experiences, subsequent educational attainment and adult labour market performance, and how these link with the somewhat larger body of work on the extent of intergenerational mobility. Our findings reveal that disadvantages faced during childhood display a persistent (negative) association with the subsequent economic success of individuals. An important transmission mechanism underpinning these links is educational attainment, which is vastly inferior for those we classify as disadvantaged. However, over and above this, factors such as poor school attendance and growing up in a family in financial distress matter in shaping adult labour market performance (in our work they matter more than lone parenthood, which seems to be dominated by family poverty). Further to this, the children of parents who grew up in a socially disadvantaged situation during their own childhood have lower early-age cognitive abilities suggesting a potentially important cross-generational link that may well spill over to affect the subsequent economic fortunes of children of disadvantaged individuals. As such, the fact that some of the measures of disadvantage we consider, such as child poverty, have increased in recent years means that careful empirical study of cross-cohort differences form an important future area of study. This is particularly true, given that the inequality of labour market outcomes has risen in Britain in recent years.

Notes

[1] This paper draws on some of our earlier work (Gregg and Machin, 1999a) that was funded by the Joseph Rowntree Foundation and part of the paper is taken from the JRF report *Child development and family income*. We would like to thank Susan Harkness for help with the NCDS data and Jo Blanden for help with the BCS70 data.

[2] See Card (1999) for a thorough survey of links between education and earnings.

[3] The best examples of this work in economics are the US studies of Solon (1992) and Zimmerman (1992) who carefully go through methodological issues to do with obtaining unbiased estimates of the extent of intergenerational mobility. Of course the regression based approach dates back at least as far as Galton's (1886) study of intergenerational correlations of height. For an up-to-date survey, see Solon (1999).

[4] The implications of this for modelling intergenerational correlations and how they have altered over time is discussed in more detail in Gregg and Machin (1999b). One thing to note here is that no correction is made for the fact that the parental income measure may not necessarily reflect permanent income. To the extent that there is a divergence this will result in the estimated intergenerational parameter being biased downwards (see Solon, 1992, and note that Dearden et al, 1997, do in fact report higher correlations for labour market earnings of NCDS cohort members and their fathers). As such one should not pay too much attention

to the size of the parameter but, as long as the bias is not changing through time, the cross time comparisons should be legitimate.

[5] Blanden (1999) reports very similar rises (from 2.75 to 2.93) in terms of income correlations between family income of cohort members and the income of their parents.

[6] For daughters some preliminary work reveals little change across cohorts. But the comparison here is much more complicated, due to rapidly changing female labour-force participation patterns.

[7] The illness variables correspond to the age 15/16 school year and are included in the school attendance and staying on models to ensure that we are not classifying children as low school attendance individuals or poor school performers if they are ill.

[8] The behavioural problems variables are defined from the following eight 'syndrome' scores given in NCDS: unforthcoming, withdrawal, depression, anxiety, hostility towards adults, anxiety for acceptance by children, restlessness and 'inconsequential' behaviour. They are entered into the empirical models as 0-1 dummies indicating positive scores on 1, 2/3 and 4 or more of the 8 measures (with no positive scores being the reference group).

[9] To be precise, the age-11 and age-16 questions on family financial difficulties related to the previous year but at age 7 it referred to the child's early years.

[10] There is in fact a strong mapping between the NCDS financial distress measure and child poverty rates computed from Family Expenditure Survey (FES) data. In NCDS 11.0% reported financial distress at age 11 (1969) and 10.5% at 16 (1975). In the FES data poverty rates were 12.0% (after housing costs) and 10.3% (before housing costs) in 1969 and were 12.2% and 10.0% respectively in 1975.

[11] See also some early work using the NCDS up to age 23 by Elias and Blanchflower (1987) and the more recent studies by Kiernan (1995) and Hobcraft (1998).

[12] Educational attainment is measured by a nine-fold ordered ranking of educational qualifications (academic and vocational) ranging from no educational qualifications to a degree or higher (see Gregg and Machin, 1999a).

[13] Econometric models in Gregg and Machin (1999a) show the pattern of significantly lower child test scores is preserved in a multivariate analysis.

References

Blanden, J. (1999) *Changes in the impact of childhood disadvantage on adult outcomes: Is there a relationship between cross-sectional inequality and intergenerational transmissions of economic status?*, Unpublished MSc dissertation, Department of Economics, University College London.

Card, D. (1999) 'The causal effect of education on earnings', in O. Ashenfleter and D. Card (eds) *Handbook of labor economics*, Volume 3A, North Holland.

Dearden, L., Machin, S. and Reed, H. (1997) 'Intergenerational mobility in Britain', *Economic Journal*, vol 107, pp 47-64.

Elias, P. and Blanchflower, D. (1987) *The occupations, earnings and work histories of young adults – Who gets the good jobs*, Department of Employment Research Paper No 68. Warwick: University of Warwick Institute of Employment Research.

Galton, F. (1886) 'Regression towards mediocrity in hereditary stature', *Journal of the Anthropological Institute of Great Britain and Ireland*, vol 15, pp 246-63.

Goodman, A., Johnson, P. and Webb, S. (1997) *Inequality in the UK*, London: Institute for Fiscal Studies.

Gregg, P., Harkness, S. and Machin, S. (1999) 'Poor kids: child poverty in Britain, 1966-96', *Fiscal Studies*, vol 20, pp 163-87.

Gregg, P. and Machin, S. (1999a) 'Childhood disadvantage and success or failure in the labour market', in D. Blanchflower and R. Freeman (eds) *Youth employment and joblessness in advanced countries*, Cambridge, MA: National Bureau of Economic Research.

Gregg, P. and Machin, S. (1999b) 'Intertemporal intergenerational mobility', Unfinished draft.

Hobcraft, J. (1998) *Intergenerational and life-course transmission of social exclusion: Influences and childhood poverty, family disruption and contact with the police*, CASE Paper 15, London: Centre for Analysis of Social Exclusion, London School of Economics.

Kiernan, K. (1995) *Transition to parenthood: Young mothers, young fathers – Associated factors and later life experiences*, Welfare State Programme Discussion Paper Number WSP/113, London: STICERD, London School of Economics.

Machin, S. (1996) 'Wage inequality in the UK', *Oxford Review of Economic Policy*, vol 7, no 1, pp 47-64.

Machin, S. (1998) 'Recent shifts in wage inequality and the wage returns to education in Britain', *National Institute Economic Review*, vol 166, pp 87-98.

Social Statistics Research Unit (undated) *NCDS5: Child assessments*, London: City University.

Solon, G. (1992) 'Intergenerational income mobility in the United States', *American Economic Review*, vol 82, pp 393-408.

Solon, G. (1999) 'Intergenerational mobility in the labor market', in O. Ashenfleter and D. Card (eds) *Handbook of labor economics*, Volume 3A, North Holland.

Zimmerman, D. (1992) 'Regression toward mediocrity in economic stature', *American Economic Review*, vol 82, pp 409-29.

SIX

The impact of poverty on children's school attendance – evidence from West Germany

Felix Büchel, Joachim R. Frick, Peter Krause and Gert G. Wagner

Introduction: childhood poverty and school attendance

Over the last decades most Western industrialised countries have experienced a considerable change concerning the economic situation and relative income position of the old and the young. While the situation of older people significantly improved in quite a few of those countries, the well-being of children appears to have got worse (Cornia, 1997; Habich and Krause, 1997; Burniaux et al, 1998; Bradbury and Jäntti, 1999; Bradshaw, 1999). On the other hand, educational opportunities for children in general have improved in most OECD countries (OECD, 1998). This leads to the expectation of increasing differences in educational prospects. The question of whether income inequality and poverty do affect educational attainment remains therefore a most crucial one in educational research.

> Attending school is important for two reasons. First and most obviously, school helps children to acquire learning skills and information on a wide range of subjects. Second, and in many ways just as important, formal schooling provides the forum through which children develop social skills, learning to be independent and to relate to non-family members in a group-based setting. This latter reason is particularly important for children who may be underprivileged or deprived, where school may enrich or compensate for the other areas of their life which

> are lacking, and may provide a constancy of environment not found at home. (Rushton, 1995, p 94, cited in Howarth et al, 1998, p 50)

Existing literature (Gregg and Machin, 1998; Hobcraft, 1998) reveals severe disadvantages for children growing up in poverty with regard to their educational prospects. This chapter contributes, with German data, a special focus for measuring the income situation of children and thereby provides a more differentiated picture than gained with traditional research designs.

Although poverty rates among children in Germany appear less dramatic when compared to other countries (especially the US), the link between poverty and school attendance needs to be carefully investigated. This seems to be true in general for countries with relatively low child poverty rates where one could hypothesise that the educational prospects of children are negatively influenced by a low family income. However, a counter hypothesis would be that a relatively small variation in socioeconomic background is accompanied by relatively equal educational prospects for children.

In our analysis, we take a German Socioeconomic Panel Study (GSOEP) subsample of 14-year-old children to test whether at this stage of young adolescence in West Germany[1] a correlation can be verified between family income (including poverty information) and different educational prospects, indicating further differences in individual careers in the job market. At the age of 14 young adolescents are still at school; but the different tracks (*Hauptschule [HS]*, *Realschule [RS]* and *Gymnasium [GYM]*[2]) are mainly preset towards different individual careers, preparing for either direct transition to work, later apprenticeship or further educational levels. Special attention is given to the question of whether West German adolescents of 14 at the lower end of economic well-being have equal chances to be educated on the university preparation track at a *Gymnasium* or whether they are significantly disadvantaged in achieving higher educational levels.

Review of the literature and hypotheses

For West Germany, several studies (Büchel and Wagner, 1996; Büchel and Duncan, 1998; Wagner et al, 1998; and Merz and Schimmelpfennig, 1999) analyse the impact of parental income on school attendance. However, these studies neither introduce lag elements in income observation nor test for any special impact of poverty, even though there is a clear link between income of the parents (and their educational level) and educational attainment of children[3]. But as far as we know, a special non-linear impact of poverty has not yet been studied.

Retrospective longitudinal data about pupils in Dresden (see Becker and Nietfeld, 1999) shows a substantial impact of parental unemployment on the probability of East German pupils being able to switch to *Gymnasium*. Overall, the data state that sociocultural and family related factors seem to outweigh the relevance of variables measuring socioeconomic changes caused by the transformation of Germany to a united republic. Further aspects that affect the social development of children are whether single parents or complete families are running the household, the number of siblings, whether immigrant families have recently arrived, whether sufficient housing space for all members of a given household is available, parental education levels, labour market participation, occupational status of parents, and regional disparities (Bundesministerium für Familie, Senioren, Frauen und Jugend, 1998, pp 88ff, 93; Duncan et al, 1998; Weick, 1999, p 43ff; Carlson and Danziger, 1999)[4].

Looking at international evidence, Blau (1999) states with respect to the impact of family income on children's development that parents' permanent income has a substantially larger effect on cognitive, social and emotional development than current income. But he also confirms that family background characteristics are even more important. Duncan et al (1998) show that especially at younger ages the economic situation is relevant for later educational attainment. However, the impact of economic well-being on school attendance diminishes with increasing age of children.

Hypotheses drawn from recent literature suggest that (1) the economic situation has a higher impact on younger children than on adolescents[5]; and (2) that poverty (an income below a certain threshold) matters more than other income levels[6]. Low-income families tend to push their children into lower education tracks in order to speed up their transition to economic independence (*Bundesministerium für Familie, Senioren, Frauen und Jugend*, 1998, p 93; Weick, 1999, p 45). Low incomes also produce economic pressures that lead to conflict between family members and, as a consequence, can have negative impacts on the further cognitive development of children, especially to the self-confidence and achievement of boys (Duncan et al, 1998, p 409, Büchel and Duncan, 1998). However, there are also opposite tendencies as parents with low incomes also try to secure better living conditions for their children. We therefore expect only modest direct effects of family income on the school attendance of the 14-year-old adolescents.

Taking into account the findings from the literature, we will add empirical results concerning the impact of childhood poverty and income position on the school attendance of teenagers. For this purpose it is necessary to use *longitudinal* microdata, which allows the bringing together of *past* poverty experience with the *current* educational behaviour of children, which is of *future* relevance in terms of occupational and economic success.

For our research questions, one needs to pay special attention to different concepts of income, income dynamics and the timing of poverty, for example, the duration and re-occurrence of poverty over a longer period of time. Therefore, not only recent income information – such as the annual income of previous year (t_0) – needs to be taken into account but also income levels and poverty for two (t_{-1}), three (t_{-2}) or even more years previously. Of special interest is the relevance of long-term poverty, which can be expected to have a significant impact on lower *Gymnasium* participation rates for the 14-year-old adolescents.

For the sample of 14-years-olds which will be used throughout the following analyses, this t_{-2} measure represents the material standard of living at age 11. In most of the German federal states the decision to follow one of the three mentioned educational tracks usually occurs after fourth grade. Since most children start school at the age of 6 or 7, the t_{-2} measure may also be regarded as the initial measure of economic well-being at the time the decision for further school attendance was made. Thus, we pay special attention to this point in time in our analyses.

Data and methods

The microdata used for the analyses comes from the GSOEP. This survey was begun in Western Germany in 1984 with a sample of 5,921 households including 12,245 respondents and a total of 16,252 household members. The survey oversamples the main immigrant population at that time (Turks, Greeks, Italians, Yugoslavs and Spaniards). In June 1990 an East German subsample was integrated into the study, and in 1994/95 another subsample covering immigrants to West Germany since the middle of the 1980s was added.

For technical reasons our analyses are restricted to the original West German subsample (including the foreigners): first, we used pooled data for the period of the mid-1980s to the mid-1990s, as the East German subsample was not available before 1990; and there were some institutional changes in the East German school system during the early years after unification. Second, we used a permanent income measure over an eight-year period (definition see below) which has not been available for any other observations[7].

Starting at the age of 17, all people living in GSOEP households are asked for an individual interview. In addition, the head of household or the person who knows best about the general living conditions of a given household (main respondent) is requested to take part in a household interview. Information on the educational behaviour of children up to age 16 – thus, including our population of the 14-year-olds – is collected by means of this household questionnaire.

Because the number of 14-year-old adolescents is too small for an analysis for every sample year, we pooled the observations for 11 consecutive years (1986-96). Our final data set contains a summary of all West German children in the GSOEP who turned 14 years old between 1986 and 1996 (t_0). All descriptive variables such as family type, number of children living in the household and the characteristics of the head of household are related to the year when the children became 14 years old. Furthermore, only those children are included who follow the main tracks of schooling: *Hauptschule*, *Realschule* and *Gymnasium*. Other children at *Gesamtschule*, *Waldorfschule* or with missing values are omitted from the analyses.

Measures of economic well-being refer to post-government annual incomes after taxes and including transfers. Household rent is also included in our income measure (Burkhauser et al, 1999). All income measures are expressed in real prices of 1991. To take account of economies of scale of living together, post-government income is transformed to *equivalent* income, according to the revised OECD scale as recommended by Eurostat (1994)[8].

To get further information about income dynamics and permanent poverty, we included only those children for whom information on income for two previous years was available. As our income variables t_0 refer to annual incomes for the year before the interview took place, we therefore cover for all observed 14-year-old children for at least three years (t_{-2}, t_{-1}, t_0) of income development[9]. An alternative income measure to test for the long-term impact of income and poverty on schooling behaviour is permanent income. We calculate this measure as the average across all annual equivalent income measures for a given individual in a balanced design over the period t_{-7} to t_0, thus covering the age profile of a given

14-year-old since he or she was 6 years old. To test for differences within this period we also look at a permanent income defined for two sub-periods: a first one looks at the period t_{-7} to t_{-4} (age 6 to 9), a second one at the period t_{-3} to t_0 (age 10 to 13).

For calculating poverty head-count rates, we define the poverty thresholds at 50% of median equivalent income. This poverty line is not derived from the pooled data set of the 14-year-old children but rather from the entire West German population. Poverty among our population of teenagers is thus defined in relation to the complete cross-sectional population of any given year.

After pooling all observations over an 11-year-period from 1986 to 1996, we end up with a sample of 1,495 children aged 14 with valid information about household income for at least three consecutive years (t_{-2}, t_{-1}, t_0). The population used for the analyses on *permanent* income is made up by 679 observations only, the big difference in number of cases being caused by the necessity to restrict the sample to the period from 1991 to 1996[10]. All descriptive results are appropriately weighted[11] in order to account for selectivity processes over the observed time period in the survey[12].

Empirical results

The distribution of our sample of 14-year-old pupils (pooled over 11 years of panel data) across the main educational tracks – *Hauptschule*, *Realschule*, and *Gymnasium* – is about the same as reported above from official statistics for 1995 (see Table 6.1)[13]. One third of the pupils are educated at *Hauptschule*, 30% are attending *Realschule,* and the largest group (37%) is on the track for further higher education, thus attending *Gymnasium*[14]. Further differentiation according to social characteristics confirms some well-known bivariate relationships (Büchel and Wagner, 1996; Wagner et al, 1998). Girls have a higher probability than boys of being educated at *Gymnasium* and at *Realschule*. More than half of the immigrants are on the *Hauptschule* track (ie, the school form with the lowest requirements), and only 20% of them are educated at *Gymnasium*. Children from single-parent households are not very different from others; children with two and more siblings are more likely to be found at *Hauptschule* and less likely to attend *Gymnasium*. Children living in owner-occupied housing are more likely to go to *Gymnasium,* and children growing up with insufficient living space (less than one room per capita in the household) are more often found at *Hauptschule*.

One of the biggest impacts on pupils' school attendance is the educational level achieved by their parents: about 80% of children living in households where the head has finished higher education tracks (*Abitur*) are also educated at *Gymnasium*. Further impacts on school attendance are connected with the occupational background of parents. Children of blue-collar workers are much less, and children of civil servants (*Beamte*) are much more, represented at *Gymnasium* level than others.

Finally, the results for our short-term income measure in t_0 clearly confirm our expectation: of those children whose equivalent household income is below median, 47% attend *Hauptschule,* whereas 52% of those with above-median income in t_0 go to *Gymnasium*. Most interestingly, the correlation of long-term income and school attendance seems to be even stronger. Sixty per cent of those children with above-median permanent income are in fact attending *Gymnasium*, while only 17% are educated at *Hauptschule*.

The net equivalent income of a household is highly correlated with a pupil's educational track. Pupils of age 14 educated at the *Gymnasium* are living in families whose mean equivalent income is about 1.5 times higher than that of other families (Table 6.2), and pupils at the *Realschule* enjoy also about 10-15% higher family incomes than those at the *Hauptschule*. This relationship remains the same if we look at the different incomes of the 14-year-old adolescents in the previous year (t_0), or two years (t_{-1}) or three years (t_{-2})[15].

Table 6.3 breaks down school attendance by quintile shares. This table is the first one that concentrates on the distinction between *Gymnasium* on the one hand, and both other school types (*Hauptschule* and *Realschule*) on the other hand. This reduced categorisation is done to distinguish between those children with existing options to the highest occupational positions (requiring a university degree) and those without these expectations[16].

With higher incomes, there is a clear increase in the number of pupils who are educated at *Gymnasium*. In the lowest quintile, just about every sixth pupil is educated at the *Gymnasium,* whereas in the highest income quintile the proportion is nearly 70%. The differences between the results of column 1 (t_0) and column 2 (t_{-2}) are quite low. In the short-term sample focusing on t_0, the relation of the participation rates in the highest and lowest quintile is about 4.16, whereas in the long-term sample this relation is 4.25, which indicates an even stronger long-term effect. However, the difference is rather small. The overall result gives some empirical support to the argument that a remarkable portion of parents

Table 6.1: Social background and school attendance at age 14 in West Germany (1986-96) (%)

	Total	GYM	RS	HS
Total*	100.0	36.8	29.8	33.4
Boys	48.4	34.1	28.8	37.0
Girls	51.6	39.3	30.8	29.9
Foreigner	11.2	19.2	24.4	56.4
German	88.8	39.0	30.5	30.5
Born abroad	3.5	20.8	21.9	57.3
Single-parent	9.1	37.8	24.2	38.0
Complete family, 1 child	33.9	37.0	30.1	32.9
Complete family, 2 children	35.9	40.0	32.0	27.9
Complete family, 3+ children	21.1	30.6	28.0	41.4
Owner-occupier	57.8	44.0	30.6	25.4
Tenant	42.2	26.9	28.8	44.2
Less than 1 room per capita	27.8	22.1	29.8	48.2
1 room per capita	29.9	31.8	32.5	35.7
More than 1 room per capita	40.7	50.4	27.9	21.7
Abitur (HoH)	16.9	79.0	11.8	9.2
Other education level (HoH)	83.1	28.3	33.4	38.3
Blue collar (HoH)	34.2	16.9	29.9	53.2
Self-employed (HoH)	11.5	44.8	29.8	25.4
White collar (HoH)	32.1	47.2	34.8	18.0
Public servant (HoH)	12.2	74.4	16.0	9.6
Not employed (HoH)	9.9	17.2	29.6	53.1
Income at t_0 <= median	50.0	21.3	31.7	47.0
Income at t_0 > median	50.0	52.3	28.0	19.7
Permanent income** <= median	50.0	23.3	32.8	44.0
Permanent income** > median	50.0	59.9	23.4	16.8

HS=*Hauptschule*, RS=*Realschule*, GYM=*Gymnasium*; HoH=Head of Household.

* Total, n=1,495; ** Permanent income at age 6-13 (t_{-7}-t_0, n=679).

Source: GSOEP; authors' calculation

with low incomes take care of their children's future and that they invest in higher educational tracks which improve the chances to leave lower income ranges. Because in Germany there is no fee for better schooling, except for some private schools, this result seems very plausible.

Table 6.2: Post-government equivalent income and school attendance at age 14 in West Germany (1986-96)

	Total	GYM	HS, RS	(N)
		Mean (in DM)		
Post-government equivalent income at ...				
Age 13 (t_0)	27.458	34.714	23.234	(1,495)
Age 12 (t_{-1})	27.167	33.953	23.215	(1,495)
Age 11 (t_{-2})	26.361	33.368	22.281	(1,495)
Permanent income at ...				
Age 10-13 (t_{-3}-t_0)	29.052	35.383	24.534	(679)
Age 6- 9 (t_{-7}-t_{-4})	25.621	30.678	22.011	(679)
Age 6-13 (t_{-7}-t_0)	27.337	33.030	23.272	(679)

HS=*Hauptschule*, RS=*Realschule*, GYM=*Gymnasium*.

Note: Income is annual income after taxes and transfers in prices of 1991 (DM) using the revised OECD equivalence scale.

Source: GSOEP; authors' calculation

Table 6.3: Relative income positions (quintiles) and school attendance at age 14 in West Germany (1986-96)

	Pupils at *Gymnasium* according to welfare level at ...		
Quintiles	Age 13 (t_0)	Age 11 (t_{-2})	Age 6-13 (t_{-7}-t_0)
Lowest quintile	16.4	17.3	18.5
Second quintile	19.7	15.4	28.1
Third quintile	31.5	35.0	33.2
Fourth quintile	48.1	47.0	49.7
Highest quintile	68.3	69.7	78.6
Total (t_0)	36.8	36.8	41.7
(N)	(1,495)	(1,495)	(679)

Note: Quintiles are calculated from Annual Equivalent Income (Table 2). Quintile thresholds refer to the pooled data set of 14-year-old children, not to the entire cross-sectional population.

Source: GSOEP; authors' calculation

Moreover, the relative income position from age of 11 to the age of 13 (the age previous to t_0 in our sample of children at age 14) is far from being stable over time (Table 6.4a). Within two years more than half of the children in the second and third quintile[17] experienced changes in their household income positions from one quintile to another. In the lowest quintile about two thirds remained in this position. At the top of the distribution, relative income positions are more stable.

As a tendency, the income position of those children following the *Gymnasium* track is more stable over time than that of children following the *Hauptschule*. This is especially true for the highest quintile. Table 6.4b shows the same type of income mobility over a longer period. The effects are most similar to those presented in Table 6.4a.

Table 6.5 gives descriptive figures for the relation between poverty and school attendance. The poverty risk for the pupils who attend the *Gymnasium* is smaller than for all chosen poverty concepts – the poverty rate in the year of observation, in the previous year, the rate two years previously (when the decision was made whether or not to send children to *Gymnasium)* as well as the poverty rate based on permanent incomes (second panel of Table 6.5). The latter measure shows the largest difference in poverty risks between the two analysed groups of pupils: the poverty rates among pupils attending *Gymnasium* are three times lower than those of other children of the same age.

Table 6.6 presents results from logistic regressions that analyse the chances to attend *Gymnasium,* controlling only for income poverty indicators[18]. In panel 1, results for the *log* income as the only independent variable are displayed. The coefficient is positively significant for all three income measures (t_0, t_{-2} and 'permanent income'). Consistent with existing literature, it is not surprising that the size of the coefficient is the biggest for permanent income. The same is true for the three poverty indicators in panel 2. However, the significance level is much smaller for the long-term sample; this is probably caused by the smaller sample size and, in particular, by the small number of poor people within this sample. Panel 3 shows that there are different effects of short- and long-term poverty. Long-term poverty negatively affects children's chances of attending *Gymnasium* much more than short periods spent in poverty. Again, this result is in line with the international literature.

In panel 4, covariates are made up by dummy variables for income quintiles; additionally, the lowest quintile is split in the lower end (poverty population) and the population living just above the poverty threshold. At the upper end of the income distribution, we find very strong positive

Table 6.4a: Short-term income dynamics (quintiles) and school attendance at age 14 in West Germany (1986-96)

	Quintiles at age 11 (t_{-2})					
Total GYM HS, RS	**Lowest**	**Second quintile**	**Third quintile**	**Fourth quintile**	**Highest**	**Total**
Quintiles at age 13 (t_0)						
Lowest	**63.0**	24.7	7.6	4.5	1.1	20.0
GYM	**67.0**	10.7	4.5	10.9	6.9	8.9
HS, RS	**62.2**	27.4	8.2	2.1	0.0	26.5
Second quintile	25.0	**48.0**	20.2	3.5	3.2	20.0
GYM	20.8	**29.9**	32.0	6.5	10.9	10.7
HS, RS	26.0	**52.5**	17.3	2.8	1.3	25.4
Third quintile	8.5	22.5	**46.2**	19.5	3.3	20.0
GYM	5.1	14.5	**55.9**	18.7	5.8	17.2
HS, RS	10.1	26.2	**41.7**	19.9	2.1	21.7
Fourth quintile	2.2	3.7	20.9	**55.9**	18.1	20.0
GYM	1.3	4.9	16.6	**58.1**	19.1	26.1
HS, RS	2.9	2.6	24.9	**52.4**	17.2	16.4
Highest	1.3	1.6	5.1	18.2	**73.8**	20.0
GYM	0.0	1.2	3.4	14.8	**80.7**	37.1
HS, RS	4.1	2.6	8.7	25.6	**59.1**	10.0
Total	20.0	20.0	20.0	20.0	20.0	100.0
GYM	9.4	8.4	19.0	25.5	37.7	100.0
HS, RS	26.2	27.0	20.6	16.7	9.5	100.0

HS=*Hauptschule*, RS=*Realschule*, GYM=*Gymnasium*;

Note: Quintiles are calculated from Annual Equivalent Income. Quintile thresholds refer to the pooled data set of 14-year-old children (n=1,495), not to the entire population.

Source: GSOEP; authors' calculation

relations between household income and the quality of educational attainment of children. The chances of being able to attend *Gymnasium* then become lower step-by-step with lower parental incomes down to a level just above the poverty line, although some of these coefficients are not significant. A most interesting result is the atypical pattern for the poor: in the annual income approach, their children have better chances of being able to attend *Gymnasium* than the children living also in low income situations but just above the poverty line. This could be caused by the fact that the poor population is heterogeneous with respect to socioeconomic status (SES) background. For example, a single parent studying at a university most probably faces a higher poverty risk, but this does not necessarily interfere with the chance to send his or her

Table 6.4b: Long-term income dynamics (quintiles) and school attendance at age 14 in West Germany (1986-96)

	Quintiles at age 6-9 (t_{-7}-t_{-4})					
Total GYM, HS, RS	**Lowest**	**Second quintile**	**Third quintile**	**Fourth quintile**	**Highest**	**Total**
Quintiles at age 10-13 (t_{-3}-t_0)						
Lowest	**67.2**	25.4	5.1	1.5	0.8	20.0
GYM	**74.0**	18.7	7.3	0.0	0.0	6.6
HS, RS	**66.2**	26.4	4.7	1.8	0.9	29.6
Second quintile	25.3	**43.7**	19.9	8.8	2.2	20.0
GYM	28.2	**28.3**	32.2	7.3	4.0	16.4
HS, RS	23.8	**51.8**	13.5	9.6	1.3	22.5
Third quintile	5.2	23.8	**44.9**	16.9	9.2	20.0
GYM	8.8	23.8	**35.5**	15.8	16.1	17.4
HS, RS	3.1	23.8	**50.3**	17.6	5.3	21.5
Fourth quintile	2.2	4.5	26.9	**55.1**	11.3	20.0
GYM	0.8	0.0	28.6	**53.8**	17.6	22.5
HS, RS	4.1	8.5	25.4	**56.2**	5.9	18.3
Highest	0.0	2.5	4.0	15.7	**77.8**	20.0
GYM	0.0	3.3	1.6	12.7	**82.4**	37.0
HS, RS	0.0	0.0	11.8	25.6	**62.7**	8.1
Total	20.0	20.0	20.0	20.0	20.0	100.0
GYM	11.1	11.2	19.0	20.8	37.9	100.0
HS, RS	26.4	26.1	20.8	18.8	7.8	100.0

HS=*Hauptschule*, RS=*Realschule*, GYM=*Gymnasium*;

Note: Quintiles are calculated from Permanent Equivalent Income. Quintile thresholds refer to the pooled data set of 14-year-old children (n=679), not to the entire population.

Source: GSOEP; authors' calculation

child to *Gymnasium*. The most important message from the permanent income analysis (third column) is that German children living in poverty do not show a significantly higher risk of failing the *Gymnasium* entrance requirements than those living in intermediate financial circumstances. This is evidence of the success of one the main aims of German education policy, namely to offer access to higher education to underprivileged groups by fully financing the school system by public means.

Table 6.7 brings together all the non-monetary determinants of school attendance and our income measures (based on dummies). The table shows that the main effects that we know from the bivariate analyses remain stable when controlling for important non-monetary SES measures. There are strong positive impacts on the probability of children to be

Table 6.5: Poverty and school attendance at age 14 in West Germany (1986-96)

	Total	GYM	HS, RS	(N)
Poverty rates based on *annual* income at ...				(1,495)
Age 13 (t_0)	7.8	5.6	9.1	
Age 12 (t_{-1})	8.2	6.6	9.1	
Age 11 (t_{-2})	6.9	5.5	7.8	
N-times-poor (t_{-2}-t_0)	100.0	100.0	100.0	
Never	86.9	90.8	84.5	
1 time	6.6	4.3	8.0	
2-3 times	6.5	4.9	7.5	
Poverty rates based on *permanent* income				(679)
Age 6-13 (t_{-7}-t_0)	2.6	1.2	3.6	
N-times-poor (t_{-7}-t_0)	100.0	100.0	100.0	
Never	82.7	88.2	78.7	
1-3 times	14.7	10.2	18.1	
4-8 times	2.6	1.6	3.2	

HS=*Hauptschule*, RS=*Realschule*, GYM=*Gymnasium*.

Source: GSOEP; authors' calculation

educated at the *Gymnasium* caused by higher education of the parents, living in metropolitan areas, living in mid-western German federal states, and parents who are working as civil servants. Significant negative effects are observed for parents born abroad and parents who are blue-collar workers or are unemployed. Controlling for income measures, we find similar effects as presented in the previous table. Therefore, we can state that children living in poverty do not show significantly lower *Gymnasium* participation rates than children living in families with intermediate incomes even when controlling for various non-monetary background information about the family situation. Focusing on permanent incomes, similar chances are observable for all three lower income quintiles.

It is true in Germany, as probably everywhere in the world, that higher-educated parents and those with high incomes show a much greater tendency to send their children to better schools. A probably unexpected result, however, is that German children living in poverty do not have a statistically significant lesser chance of getting on to the Gymnasium track, which offers the best occupational prospects. We conclude with this important impact of the public school system in Germany on our results.

Table 6.6: Coefficients from logistic regression on attending *Gymnasium* at age 14 using different income and poverty measures, West Germany (1986-96)

Variables[a]	*Annual* income at age 13 (t_0)	*Annual* income at age 11 (t_{-2})	*Permanent* income age 6-13 (t_{-7}-t_0)
Log income	1.74*** (0.15)	1.75*** (0.15)	2.57*** (0.27)
Constant	-18.34*** (1.52)	-18.32*** (1.55)	-26.52*** (2.75)
-2 log likelihood	1,659	1,668	740
Poor	-0.62** (0.22)	-0.54* (0.23)	-1.22+ (0.63)
Constant	-0.69*** (0.19)	-0.72*** (0.19)	-0.42* (0.19)
-2 log likelihood	1,820	1,844	850
Short-term poor[b]	-0.55* (0.23)		-0.47* (0.23)
Long-term poor[c]	-0.65* (0.25)		-10.14* (0.55)
Ref.: never poor			
Constant	-0.68*** (0.19)		-0.34+ (0.20)
-2 log likelihood	1,816		846
Lowest quintile poor	-0.51* (0.25)	-0.62* (0.26)	-0.88 (0.65)
Lowest quintile not poor	-1.00*** (0.24)	-1.28*** (0.23)	-0.63* (0.30)
2nd quintile	-0.65*** (0.19)	-0.84*** (0.19)	-0.27 (0.28)
Ref: 3rd quintile			
4th	0.67*** (0.18)	0.41* (0.18)	0.73** (0.28)
Highest quintile	1.49*** (0.19)	1.38*** (0.19)	2.15*** (0.31)
Constant	-0.82*** (0.23)	-0.60** (0.23)	-0.74** (0.28)
-2 log likelihood	1,632	1,621	733
(N)	(1,495)	(1,495)	(679)

[a] All models depicted in this table include dummy variables for calendar years (see full models as shown in Table 6.7).

[b] Models based on *Annual* Income: 1 time poor; Models based on *Permanent* Income: 1-3 times poor.

[c] Models based on *Annual* Income: 2-3 times poor; Models based on *Permanent* Income: 4-7 times poor.

Standard errors in parenthesis. Significance Level: + <0.10, * <0.05, ** <0.01, *** <0.001.

Source: GSOEP; authors' calculation

Conclusions

The design of our research approach is characterised by extending the dimensions of income measurement when analysing the relation between parental income and educational prospects. A special focus was set on the lower tail of income distribution.

Introducing lagged income information shows similar results as using current cross-sectional income information. However, the positive correlation between income situation and quality of children's school attendance is somewhat stronger when applying the first approach. This means that – as theoretically expected – the parental income situation at the time of school decision making is more influential than the financial background after enrolment into a specific school form.

Introducing longitudinal income information as a permanent income measure – given by the average of consecutive yearly incomes – has two advantages compared to the traditional single cross-sectional observation approach. From a methodological point of view, the outlier problem is strongly diminished. From a content point of view, this measure is expected to catch the financial background of a family in a much more valid way than measuring income in a single year. Indeed, our results show that the plausibility of the obtained results is enhanced when following this approach.

Introducing a split of the lowest net equivalent household income quintile into poor and non-poor families shows most important results: the standard approach that does not differentiate low income families (in the lowest quintile) of course leads to the expected results. This shows the lowest educational prospects for children living in a household of the lowest income quintile. However, the missing split into poor and non-poor would hide a most interesting heterogeneous social structure of the German poor families with adolescent children. This is contrary to the behaviour of families living just above the poverty threshold who typically do not send their children to the *Gymnasium*. Among the 'real' poor there is a substantial portion of families who are able to keep educational options open for their children and, in doing so, can offer promising long-term perspectives to their children. We used a poverty measure based on permanent incomes – which is considered to be the most valid one in our research context – over a period of eight years (age 6 to 14). Controlling for various non-monetary family characteristics, the chances of poor children being able to attend *Gymnasium* are not significantly lower than those for children living in households with intermediate incomes. To repeat, this is an indication of the success of Germany's socially aware education policy, which offers publicly financed access to all schools to achieve equal opportunities for all children.

Table 6.7: Coefficients from logistic regressions on attending *Gymnasium* at age 14 using annual and permanent income measures, West Germany (1986-96)

	Annual income		Permanent income	
Variables	**Excluding income measures**	**Including income measures (t_{-2})**	**Excluding income measures**	**Including income measures**
Community size 20.-100.000	0.31 (0.17)+	0.29 (0.17)+	0.33 (0.24)	0.21 (0.25)
Community size 100.-500.000	0.52 (0.21)*	0.43 (0.22)*	0.17 (0.33)	-0.02 (0.35)
Community size >500.000	0.93 (0.22)***	0.82 (0.22)***	0.87 (0.32)**	0.63 (0.33)+
Ref: Community size <20.000				
Region-North	0.10 (0.20)	0.11 (0.20)	0.34 (0.29)	0.32 (0.30)
Region-Mid West	0.42 (0.15)**	0.48 (0.16)**	0.75 (0.23)**	0.83 (0.24)***
Ref: Region-South				
Abitur (HoH)	1.20 (0.18)***	1.01 (0.19)***	1.05 (0.28)***	0.75 (0.30)*
Age (HoH)	0.02 (0.01)+	0.02 (0.01)+	0.03 (0.02)+	0.03 (0.02)+
Foreigner	-0.25 (0.19)	-0.21 (0.19)	-0.50 (0.29)+	-0.46 (0.29)
Male	-0.20 (0.13)	-0.19 (0.13)	-0.04 (0.19)	-0.04 (0.20)
Lone-parent	0.12 (0.29)	0.23 (0.29)	0.09 (0.44)	0.19 (0.44)
Family, 2 children	-0.00 (0.16)	0.07 (0.16)	-0.01 (0.24)	0.10 (0.25)
Family, 3+ children	-0.21 (0.20)	-0.06 (0.20)	-0.32 (0.29)	-0.09 (0.30)
Ref: Family, 1 child				
Not employed (HoH)	-1.10 (0.25)***	-0.83 (0.27)**	-1.01 (0.37)**	-0.73 (0.39)+
Blue collar (HoH)	-1.13 (0.18)***	-0.91 (0.19)***	-0.97 (0.27)***	-0.74 (0.28)**
Self-employed (HoH)	0.15 (0.23)	0.09 (0.23)	0.32 (0.33)	0.16 (0.35)
Public servant (HoH)	0.63 (0.24)**	0.64 (0.25)*	0.81 (0.36)*	0.82 (0.37)*
Ref: White collar (HoH)				

Table 6.7: Contd.../

Variables	Annual income: Excluding income measures	Annual income: Including income measures (t_{-2})	Permanent income: Excluding income measures	Permanent income: Including income measures
Owner-occupier	0.43 (0.17)*	0.12 (0.18)	-0.39 (0.24)	-0.07 (0.28)
More than 1 room per capita	0.50 (0.16)**	0.42 (0.16)**	0.55 (0.22)*	0.38 (0.23)
1986	-0.03 (0.29)	0.10 (0.29)	–	–
1987	-0.35 (0.30)	-0.23 (0.31)	–	–
1988	0.02 (0.30)	0.15 (0.31)	–	–
1989	-0.11 (0.31)	-0.08 (0.32)	–	–
1991	-0.61 (0.34)+	-0.73 (0.35)*	-0.87 (0.36)*	-0.92 (0.38)*
1992	-0.22 (0.31)	-0.28 (0.32)	-0.40 (0.32)	-0.30 (0.33)
1993	0.16 (0.31)	0.02 (0.31)	-	-
1994	-0.21 (0.32)	-0.26 (0.32)	-0.42 (0.33)	-0.35 (0.34)
1995	-0.01 (0.31)	0.10 (0.31)	-0.10 (0.32)	0.01 (0.33)
1996	-0.07 (0.32)	-0.14 (0.32)	-0.31 (0.32)	-0.26 (0.33)
Ref: 1990/1993				
Lowest quintile, in poverty	–	-0.46 (0.30)	–	-0.54 (0.73)
Lowest quintile, not in poverty	–	-0.86 (0.26)***	–	-0.20 (0.37)
Second quintile	–	-0.54 (0.21)**	–	0.09 (0.31)
Fourth quintile	–	0.11 (0.21)	–	0.70 (0.32)*
Highest quintile	–	0.65 (0.22)**	–	1.47 (0.35)***
Ref: Third Quintile				
Constant	-1.96 (0.59)***	-1.91 (0.61)**	-2.48 (0.86)**	-2.65 (0.93)**
-2 log likelihood	1,461	1,426	668	644
(N)	(1,478)	(1,478)	(670)	(670)

Standard errors in parenthesis. Significance level: + <0.10, * <0.05, ** <0.01, *** <0.001.
HoH=Head of household.
Source: GSOEP; authors' calculation

Notes

[1] Due to the outstanding circumstances in East Germany, which were caused by the transition from a planned to a market economy (including institutional changes in the school system), we do not analyse East German pupils. Nevertheless, the panel data set used for this paper (GSOEP) includes appropriate microdata on East Germany since 1990 (beginning on the eve of unification) as well. For an analysis on East Germany, see Becker and Nietfeld (1999).

[2] In principle, the German school system offers three tracks with different qualification levels: the *Hauptschule* (HS) and *Realschule* (RS) are mainly preparing for a low skill job or an apprenticeship qualifying for intermediate career tracks, whereas the *Gymnasium* (GYM) prepares for university. In 1960, 70% of all children at the age of 13 in West Germany were educated at HS, 11% at *Realschule*, and only 15% at the *Gymnasium* (and 4% at other kinds of schools). These relationships changed dramatically over the following three dozen years. In 1998, only 21% of the 13-year-old children in Germany (including East Germany) were enrolled at HS, another 17% were educated in integrated classes for HS and RS (including *Integrierte Gesamtschule* and *Waldorfschule*); 24% were attending RS and 30% a *Gymnasium* (another 7% were educated in other types of schools (cf Statistisches Bundesamt, 2000, p 59). All in all, in Germany the percentage of young adults who receive a university degree or another kind of higher qualification is about average compared to the European standard.

[3] See also Dunn and Couch (1999) for intergenerational analyses concerning earnings and Couch and Dunn (1997) concerning the relationship between labour market status of parents and educational outcomes of their children.

[4] Bauer and Gang (1999) do not find major sibling effects concerning rivalry, thus we do not control for child parity and the sex of siblings. Nevertheless, there is the need to control for number of siblings or family size and household composition.

[5] "Family economic conditions in early and middle childhood appeared to be far more important for shaping ability and achievement than were economic conditions during adolescence" (Duncan et al, 1998, p 408).

[6] "... increasing the incomes of children whose family incomes are below or near the poverty line will have a larger impact on early-childhood ability and

achievement than would increasing the incomes of children in middle-class and affluent families." (Duncan et al, 1998, p 409)

[7] Unfortunately, from a substantive point of view this also excludes the new subsample of immigrants to Germany, which was started in 1994 (see Burkhauser et al, 1997 for a description of these data and Frick and Wagner (Chapter Eleven) for some substantive analyses comparing living conditions of immigrant children to those of native born German children).

[8] This approach gives a weight of 1 to the head, 0.5 to other adult household members aged over 14, and 0.3 to children up to 14 years of age. For more detailed discussion of differences in the empirical results due to the chosen equivalence scale as well as other aspects, see Atkinson et al (1995).

[9] If one of the reported annual incomes at $t_{0,}$ $t_{-1,}$ or t_{-2} was less than DM 500 (which is less than the support which is given by the German social assistance scheme), the observation was dropped ('bottom trimming').

[10] Again, we applied a 'bottom trimming' at DM 500 in each single year of the eight years observation period.

[11] We apply the cross-sectional weights for year t_0.

[12] Nevertheless, the two samples are not 'identical'. The smaller sample that covers more years is a positive selection when compared to the bigger sample which is used for the analysis of annual incomes at ages 11 to 13 (cf. for instance Table 6. 3, Total line). In the smaller sample the share of pupils who are attending Gymnasium is higher. This can partly be attributed to a larger standard error, but there is a real selection as well. Due to re-migration of 'guestworker families' in the long-term sample, the share of foreigners is smaller than in the short-term sample.

[13] The distribution reported above refers to all 13-year-old pupils in Germany in 1995, whereas our sample of 14-year-old pupils includes only West Germans pooled over 11 years (1986-96).

[14] Pupils 'visiting' other kinds of schools such as Integrierte Gesamtschule, Waldorfschule or Behindertenschule etc. were excluded from our analyses. This group covered about 7% of the 13-year-old pupils in Germany (Statistisches Bundesant, 2000, p 59).

[15] The small increase in real incomes from t_{-2} to t_0 may be the result of real welfare improvements achieved mainly during the second half of the 1980s.

[16] The results of Table 6.3 show that the long-term sample (N=679) is a positive selection compared to the short-term sample (N=1,495) because the overall share of pupils who are attending *Gymnasium* is about 37% in the short-term and about 42% in the long-term sample. This is due to a higher share of foreigners in the short-term sample, because in the long-term sample migration makes the share of foreigners smaller. A higher panel mortality of low-income families could matter, too.

[17] Each quintile covers 20% of all pupils at age 14 ranked according to equivalent income.

[18] In addition, we control for the different calendar years of observations by plugging in dummy variables. We do not find strong calendar effects (not documented; see also results in Table 6.7).

References

Atkinson, A.B., Rainwater, L. and Smeeding, T.M. (1995) *Income distribution in OECD-countries: the evidence from the Luxembourg Income Study*, Paris: OECD.

Bauer, T. and Gang, I. (1999) 'Siblings, their sex composition and educational attainment in Germany', in T.A. Dunn, J.R. Frick and J.C. Witte (eds) Proceedings of the 1998 Third International Conference of Socio-Economic Panel Study Users, *Vierteljahrshefte zur Wirtschaftsforschung*, vol 68, no 2, pp 215-21.

Becker, R. and Nietfeld, M. (1999) 'Arbeitslosigkeit und Bildungschancen von Kindern im Transformationsprozeß. Eine empirische Studie über die Auswirkungen sozioökonomischer Deprivation auf intergenerationale Bildungsvererbung', *Kölner Zeitschrift für Soziologie und Sozialpsychologie*, vol 51, no 1, pp 55-79.

Blau, D.M. (1999) 'The effect of income on child development', *The Review of Economics and Statistics*, vol 81, no 2, pp 261-76.

Bradbury, B. and Jäntti, M. (1999) 'Child poverty across industrialized nations', Economic and Social Policy Series No 71, Florence: UNICEF International Child Development Centre, Innocenti Occasional Papers.

Bradshaw, J. (1999) 'Child poverty in comparative perspective', Paper given at Developing Poverty Measures: Research in Europe Defining and Measuring Poverty, University of Bristol, 1-2 July.

Büchel, F. and Duncan, G.J. (1998) 'Do parents' social activities promote children's school attainments? Evidence from the German Socio-Economic Panel', *The Journal of Marriage and the Family*, vol 60, pp 95-108.

Büchel, F. and Wagner, G. (1996) 'Soziale Differenzen der Bildungschancen in Westdeutschland – Unter besonderer Berücksichtigung von Zuwandererkindern', in W. Zapf, J. Schupp and R. Habich (eds) *Lebenslagen im Wandel: Sozialberichterstattung im Längsschnitt*, Frankfurt am Main/New York, NY: Campus, pp 80-96.

Bundesministerium für Familie, Senioren, Frauen und Jugend (1998) 'Bericht über die Lebenssituation von Kindern und Leistungen der Kinderhilfen in Deutschland – Zehnter Kinder- und Jugendbericht', *Bundestagsdrucksache* 13/11368, Bonn.

Burkhauser, R.V., Butrica, B.A. and Daly, M.C. (1999) 'The PSID-GSOEP equivalent file: a product of cross-national research', in W. Voges (ed) *Dynamic approaches to comparative social research: Recent developments and applications*, Aldershot: Ashgate Publishing Ltd, pp 53-66.

Burkhauser, R.V., Kreyenfeld, M. and Wagner, G.G. (1997) 'The German socio-economic panel: a representative sample of reunited Germany and its parts', in T. Dunn and J. Schwarze (eds) Proceedings of the 1996 Second International Conference of Socio-Economic Panel Study Users, *Vierteljahrshefte zur Wirtschaftsforschung*, vol 66, no 1, pp 7-16.

Burniaux, J.-M., Dang, T.-T., Fore, D., Förster, M., d'Ercole, M.M. and Oxley, H. (1998) 'Income distribution and poverty in selected OECD countries', Economics Department Working Papers No 189, Paris: OECD.

Carlson, M. and Danziger, S. (1999) 'Cohabitation and the measurement of child poverty', *Review of Income and Wealth*, vol 45, no 2, pp 179-91.

Cornia, G.A. (1997) 'Child poverty and deprivation in the industrialized countries from the end of World War II to the end of the Cold War era', in G.A. Cornia and S. Danzinger (eds) *Child poverty and deprivation in the industrialized countries, 1945-95*, Oxford: Clarendon Press, pp 25-63.

Couch, K.A. and Dunn, T.A. (1997) 'Intergenerational correlations in labor market status: a comparison of the United States and Germany', *Journal of Human Resources*, vol 32, no 1, pp 210-32.

Duncan, G.J., Yeung, J.W., Brooks-Gunn, J. and Smith, J.R. (1998) 'How much does childhood poverty affect the life chances of children?', *American Sociological Review*, vol 63, pp 406-23.

Dunn, T. and Couch, K. (1999) 'Intergenerational correlations in earnings in three countries: the United Kingdom, Germany and the United States', in T.A. Dunn, J.R. Frick and J.C. Witte (eds) Proceedings of the 1998 Third International Conference of Socio-Economic Panel Study Users, *Vierteljahrshefte zur Wirtschaftsforschung*, vol 68, no 2, pp 290-6.

Eurostat (1994) 'Poverty statistics in the late 1980s: research based on micro-data', Theme: Population and social conditions; Series: Accounts, surveys, and statistics, Luxembourg: Eurostat.

Gregg, P.A. and Machin, S.J. (1998) 'Child development and success or failure in the youth labour market', Discussion paper No 397, London: Centre for Economic Performance.

Habich, R. and Krause, P. (1997) 'Armut', in Statistisches Bundesamt (ed) *Datenreport 1997: Zahlen und Fakten über die Bundesrepublik Deutchsland*, Bonn: Bundeszentrale für politische Bildung, pp 515-25.

Hobcraft, J. (1998) 'Intergenerational and life-course transmission of social exclusion: influences of childhood poverty, family disruption, and contact with the police', London: CASE paper No 15, London School of Economics.

Howarth, C., Kenway, P., Palmer, G. and Street, C. (1998) 'Monitoring poverty and social exclusion. Labour's inheritance', New Policy Institute, York: Joseph Rowntree Foundation.

Merz, M. and Schimmelpfennig, A. (1999) 'The demand for higher education in Germany', *Vierteljahrshefte zur Wirtschaftsforschung*, vol 68, no 2, pp 204-8.

OECD (1998) *Education at a glance*, OECD Indicators 1998, Paris: OECD, Centre for Educational Research and Innovation.

Rushton, A. (1995) 'Get them young: the impact on early intervention on social and emotional development', in P. Farell (ed) *Children with emotional and behavioural difficulties: Strategies for assessment and intervention*, London: The Falmer Press.

Statistisches Bundesamt (2000) *Datenreport 1999: Zahlen und Falken über die Bundesrepublik Deutschland*, Bonn: Bundeszeutrale für politische Bildung.

Wagner, G.G., Büchel, F., Haisken-DeNew, J.P. and Spiess, C.K. (1998) 'Education as a keystone of integration of immigrants: determinants of school attainment of immigrant children in West Germany', in H. Kurthen, J. Fijalkowski and G.G. Wagner (eds) *Immigration, citizenship, and the welfare state in Germany and the United States – Immigrant incorporation*, vol 14 (A) of Industrial Development and Social Fabric Series of JAI Press Inc, Stamford, CT and London, pp 15-35.

Weick, S. (1999) 'Relative Einkommensarmut bei Kindern. Untersuchungen zu Lebensbedingungen und Lebensqualität in Deutschland von 1984 bis 1996', Justus-Liebig-Universität Gießen, Fachbereich Gesellschaftswissenschaften, Educational Research and Innovation, Dissertation.

SEVEN

Inequalities in the use of time by teenagers and young adults

Anne H. Gauthier and Frank F. Furstenberg Jr

Introduction

Teenage and early adulthood is a period marked by increasing independence from parents and increasing freedom among young people regarding lifestyle and use of time. It is also a fundamental period for acquiring human, social, and cultural capital (Buchmann, 1989). And yet, not all young people experience their transition to adulthood successfully. While the majority of young people prepare successfully for their future adult roles, others miss out on good opportunities, fail to reach their educational potential, may become entrapped in problem behaviour, and face the risk of permanent exclusion from mainstream society (Macdonald, 1997). Inequalities in the everyday life of young people are substantial and consequential (Green, 1998).

This chapter examines some of these inequalities by analysing the patterns of time use of teenagers and young adults, aged 15 to 24 years old, in four industrialised countries: Austria, Canada, Finland, and Italy. Our aim is to document the inequalities among young people, both between and within countries, as revealed by their patterns of time use. The data used in this chapter provides an extremely rich window into the world of young people, but is unfortunately not completely adequate to capture important differences in the nature and quality of young people's experiences and daily activities. The chapter summarises a first exploration of time budget data to approach the complex topic of inequalities and social exclusion.

Literature

The literature on successful ageing demonstrates the positive impact of physical activities, social contacts and volunteer work on elderly people's health and well-being (Palmore, 1979; Rowe and Kahn, 1998). Similarly, the literature on youth points to the importance of formal education, structured extra-curricular activities and voluntary work in keeping young people out of trouble and providing them with the essential skills to enter the labour market and adulthood (Carnegie Corporation, 1992). Participation in structured leisure activities, such as extra-curricular, volunteer and community activities has been found to be associated with higher educational achievement and lower risk of delinquency (Furstenberg and Hughes, 1995). Parents' involvement with their children, family activities, social contacts with friends, participation in arts, cultural activities and sport have also been shown to have a positive effect on youth development (Larson and Verma, 1999). Obviously, the benefits of such activities are dependent on their context and duration. Studying hard may improve one's chance of getting a good job, but may also be associated with anxiety and stress (Larson and Verma, 1999). Similarly, while meeting with friends contributes to young people's networking and independence, hanging out with friends all day long may have negative consequences. And while a 'healthy' balance between structured and unstructured activities may be hard to define, the way young people use their time has undoubtedly long-lasting impacts.

Our knowledge of the way teenagers and young adults use their time is very limited, especially when it comes to cross-national studies. In our review below we refer to four main studies: Alsaker and Flammer (1999), Larson and Verma (1999), WHO (1996) and European Commission (1997). The Alsaker and Flammer study was based on a sample of around 200 teenagers aged 11 to 15 years old in each of 12 European and North American countries. The study used diaries to collect data on teenagers' daily activities. The Larson and Verma study also relied on time budget data, but was based on secondary rather than primary data. The study covered the time use of children and teenagers in non-industrial, transitional and industrialised countries. The WHO study was focused on school children aged 11 to 15 years old in 24 countries. It collected data on young people's participation in activities such as sports, television and computer games. Finally, the Eurobarometer survey was focused on young people aged 15 to 24 years old in member states of the European Union (EU), and questioned them about activities that they regularly did. While the WHO and Eurobarometer surveys provide valuable cross-nationally comparable data, their reliance on so-called stylised questions (about time spent on activity 'x' or regularity of participation in activity 'x') results in less accurate estimates of the patterns of time use of young people than time budget diaries (Robinson and Godbey, 1997).

Variations between countries

We know that the amount of time children and teenagers devote to education increases with industrialisation, while time spent on labour (paid or unpaid) decreases (Larson and Verma, 1999). We also know that time spent on education varies substantially across countries at a similar level of industrialisation. Teenagers in Japan, for instance, spend on average 2½ hours per day on school homework, as compared to ½ hour for American teenagers (Larson and Verma). Cross-national differences in public investment into education and the value placed on education by societies and parents may explain such large variations in the patterns of time use of young people.

Large differences between countries were also found in youth participation in arts, sports and volunteer activities. Among teenagers aged 11 to 15 years old, German, Swiss and Norwegian young people report spending more than 20 minutes per day on average playing music, as compared to less than 10 minutes for American and Romanian young people (Alsaker and Flammer, 1999). Among young people age 15 to 24 years old, more than 15% of those in Denmark, Luxembourg and Finland reported regularly playing a musical instrument during their leisure time, as compared to less than 10% in Belgium, Greece, Portugal and Spain (European Commission, 1997). Playing a musical instrument is obviously a specific activity, but it is also a good example of an activity that is very rich in cultural capital.

With regard to sport, American and Norwegian adolescents in the Alsaker and Flammer's study reported spending more time on this activity than adolescents in other countries. Time spent doing sport was especially low in Bulgaria, France, Romania and Russia. Inter-country variations in sport participation were somewhat smaller among the 15 to 24 years old according to the Eurobarometer survey. The percentage of young people reporting regularly doing sport ranged from 39% in Greece to about 52% in Denmark. Finally, participation in voluntary and special-interest organisations reached about 50% of young people across all EU countries (including sport clubs and associations). Participation tends to be relatively high in the Scandinavian countries, while being lower in Southern Europe. The exception is participation in religious or parish organisations, which was found to be very high in Italy. As mentioned earlier, after-school activities and participation in organisations are known to have long-term beneficial impact on children and young people.

Variations within countries

In addition to variation between countries, the patterns of time use of young people are also known to vary substantially within countries. Data from the Eurobarometer survey suggest that reading, doing sport, going to the cinema, theatre, or to concerts, playing a musical instrument, using the computer and participating in community or volunteer organisation is done more regularly by people with higher levels of education. On the other hand, watching television and doing some work for money (during leisure time) is done less regularly by people with higher levels of education. Canadian data also suggests a higher volunteer participation rate among people with higher levels of education (Hall et al, 1998). Parents' education also matters. In the United States, children and teenagers of highly educated parents were found to be spending more time doing housework, reading, studying, doing Church-related activities and socialising (including community activities), but less time watching television (Hofferth, 1998). American teenagers aged 12 to 14 years old were also found to be less likely to be in self-care (home alone) when their parents had higher levels of education (Smith and Casper, 1999).

Thus, while the above literature provides some information about the magnitude of between and within country differences in the everyday experience of teenagers and young adults, it is limited in two major ways. First, the empirical evidence is either based on very small samples of individuals (the Alsaker and Flammer study) or on questions that only approximate the daily patterns of time use of young people (WHO and Eurobarometer surveys). Second, the empirical evidence has not been linked to other sources of inequality in the everyday experience of young people at the international level (differences between countries in the support for young people) and national level (income inequalities). We are therefore undertaking to analyse large-sample time-use surveys from four countries and to frame the analysis in terms of international and national welfare and income inequalities.

Theoretical framework

As mentioned above, considerable evidence suggests that youth involvement and participation in activities related to the acquisition of social and human capital is a fundamental dimension of young people's successful transition into adulthood. Accordingly, we propose using a social and human capital theoretical perspective to analyse the patterns of time use of young people (Coleman, 1988; Furstenberg and Hughes, 1995; Teachman et al, 1997). This perspective identifies two main determinants of patterns of time use: individual determinants and societal determinants. The former refers to factors such as the individual's own family background, gender, age, household type, income and residence. These factors have been shown to influence the allocation of time of young people and particularly their level of participation in activities related to the acquisition of social and human capital. On the other hand, societal determinants refer to factors such as institutions, policies, norms and values: factors that have also been shown to influence the allocation of time of young people. Laws regarding the minimum age for leaving school, the minimum number of hours of school per year, policies regarding access to higher education, policies regarding youth employment and the degree of public financing of leisure and volunteer organisations are all societal factors that may affect young people's use of time (Gauthier and Furstenberg, 1999).

We obviously know that countries differ substantially with regard to both public policy and socioeconomic characteristics. They vary in their levels of services, infrastructure and financial support for young people (Green, 1998). And they tolerate different levels of income inequality (Atkinson et al, 1995). On the basis of the above theoretical framework, we can therefore expect these country characteristics to significantly influence the patterns of time use of young people. We furthermore know that country characteristics such as public expenditure for young people and degree of income inequality are not random but are instead associated with specific welfare regimes and political orientation. For instance, social democratic welfare states (such as Sweden) tend to devote a larger share of their national resources to public expenditures than liberal welfare states do (such as the US). They also tend to have lower youth unemployment rates and lower levels of income inequality. Young people residing in social democratic welfare states are therefore provided with different opportunities, and are subjected to different constraints to their counterparts residing in liberal welfare states[1]. We hypothesise that three major factors influence the patterns of young people's time use. (1) There is the level of public support for young people (in the form of financial support and the provision of services) that will determine the availability and affordability of higher education, as well as cultural and recreational activities. (2) There is the degree of income inequality that will determine whether certain activities are open to all young people (regardless of income) or only to the well-to-do. (3) There is the level of income or wealth of a country that will determine the extent to which young people have access to independent sources of income and can therefore afford to devote a larger share of their time to leisure activities, especially expensive leisure activities. These three factors are expected to influence both between- and within-country variations in patterns of time use as follows.

(1) Level of public spending: we can expect young people who reside in high public spending countries to benefit from high state support in the form of financial support and education subsidies, and therefore not only to have greater opportunities to access higher education, but also to have less of a need to combine education and paid employment. In terms of patterns of time use, we can therefore expect students in high public spending countries to be less likely to devote time to paid work than their counterparts in low public spending countries. Furthermore, because high public spending countries tend also to have lower levels of youth unemployment, we can hypothesise that students in high public spending countries will be facing lower competition on the labour market, and will therefore have less incentives to study very hard in order to secure a job. In contrast, students in low public spending countries may be expected to face a tighter labour market (because of high levels of youth unemployment), and therefore to have greater incentives to study very hard in order to be better equipped to compete on the labour market. In short, we can expect students in low public spending countries to be devoting more hours to education than students in high public spending countries, and to be devoting more hours to paid work[2].

Financial support and education subsidies are, however, only one form of public support. In addition, young people who reside in high public spending countries may also be expected to benefit from subsidised cultural and recreational services. Consequently, we can expect young people residing in such countries to devote more of their leisure time to activities related to the acquisition of cultural and social capital, as compared to their counterparts in low spending countries.

(2) Income inequality: the degree of income inequality tolerated in a society is obviously not independent of the level of public expenditure. High public spending countries tend also to pursue income redistribution policies and tend therefore to display lower degrees of income inequality than low spending countries. Consequently, we can expect to observe fewer intra-country differences in the everyday life of young people in high public spending countries than in low spending countries. In particular, because the cultural and recreational facilities are heavily subsidised, we expect all young people in high public spending countries to have the means and opportunities to participate in cultural and recreational activities, instead of only young people with higher income. Participation rates in specific forms of leisure activities such as going to museums, playing a musical instrument, travelling and having hobbies are expected to be higher in countries with lower income inequalities than in countries with higher income inequalities.

(3) Level of wealth: young people who reside in high income and high wealth countries may be assumed to have access to independent sources of income to purchase goods and services. Because of these independent sources of income, they are expected to have less of a need to combine school and paid work, and are, moreover, expected to devote a larger proportion of their leisure activities to 'high-end' forms of activities (ie, high consumption and expensive leisure) than young people residing in less well off countries.

Unfortunately, the world is a much more complex one, and it would be difficult to find countries that typify perfectly the characteristics outlined above. Nonetheless, the four countries that are analysed in this chapter differ significantly with regard to these characteristics (especially public spending and income inequalities) and therefore provide us with a sort of 'natural experiment'. In commenting on our results, we will therefore refer to some of these characteristics and their related expected effects on the patterns of time use of young people. This chapter examines the countries as case studies; we, however, do not statistically test the impact of welfare and economic characteristics on the patterns of time use by young people.

The four countries represented – Austria, Canada, Finland, and Italy – were selected for two main reasons. First, and as will be discussed below, the time budget surveys carried out in these four countries all have a large sample of respondents, including teenagers, and have, moreover, been carried out over the 12 months of the year (Austria is the exception). Second, and perhaps of more importance, these four countries belong to different models of welfare states and they consequently have very different levels of public spending and different levels of income inequality (see Table 7.1).

Of the four countries, Finland devotes most resources to public expenditures. It also has a small degree of income inequality (as measured by the Gini coefficient and the child poverty rate) and a low youth unemployment rate. Austria resembles Finland with a low degree of income inequality, low child poverty (although not as low as in Finland), low youth unemployment, and high public spending (not as high as in Finland). Canada presents a very different case. It has a low level of public expenditure (although it devotes more of its GNP to education), has a high level of income inequality and a high youth unemployment rate. On the other hand, Canada has the highest level of national income. Finally, Italy has the lowest level of public expenditure, high income inequality and low spending into education. As discussed above, we are not suggesting that these four countries 'typify' welfare state models or high/low public spending countries. We are simply relying on the fact that they differ with regard to our three key time-use determinants (public spending, income inequality, general level of income) in order to shed light on the between- and within-country variations in the patterns of time use of young people.

Method and data

In this study we rely on diaries to analyse the patterns of time use of young people. We furthermore restrict our analysis to non-married students aged 15 to 24 years old[3]. Our data comes from time-budget surveys that have been carried out between 1987 and 1992 (see Table 7.2). Time-budget surveys are unusual types of surveys that rely on dairies to collect detailed information on people's daily activities. This means that, unlike most other types of surveys, time budget surveys do not only record people's employment status. They also collect precise information about time spent in school, in paid employment, as well as time spent doing other activities such as volunteering, doing unpaid work, attending meetings and socialising with friends and relatives. A typical time-use survey collects information on all activities that took place during a 24-hour period: the time that the activity started, the time it ended, the nature of the activity, where it took place and with whom the activity

Table 7.1: National characteristics

	Austria	Canada	Finland	Italy
Gini coefficient[a]	23.1 (1987)	31.5 (1994)	25.6 (1991)	31.2 (1991)
Child poverty[b]	5.6 (1987)	7.4 (1991)	1.9 (1991)	9.5 (1991)
Youth unemployment rate rate (20-24)[c]	5.4 (1992)	12.9 (1992)	5.6 (1987)	18.8 (1989)
GDP per capita[d]	23,077 (1997)	23,761(1997)	20,488(1997)	21,265 (1997)
Public expenditure on non-aged[e]	37.4 (1985)	36.5 (1985)	40.7 (1984)	33.8 (1985)
Expenditure on education[f]	5.7 (1992)	7.6 (1992)	5.5 (1987)	4.1 (1989)

Notes and sources: [a] World Bank. Online *World Development Report 1998/99*.
[b] Poverty among children age 0-17 years old, computed on the basis of 50% of the median income adjusted for family size (from Rainwater and Smeeding, 1995 and Micklewright and Stewart, 1999).
[c] Unemployment rate of young people aged 20 to 24 years old (from ILO *Yearbook of Labor Statistics)*.
[d] OECD online data for 1997 (based on Parity Purchasing Power) in US dollars.
[e] Total public expenditure minus public expenditure on age, disability and survivors pension as a percentage of GDP (computed from data included in the *Comparative Welfare States Data Set* by Huber, Ragin, and Stephens, 1997).
[f] Expenditure on education as a percentage of GNP (from Unesco online data).

was carried out. Diaries therefore provide information about time spent on each activity and its context (What? With whom? Where?). Diaries have been shown to provide more reliable estimates of time use than stylised questions about time spent on specific activities (Juster and Stafford, 1991; Robinson and Godbey, 1997). Since the 1960s, time-budget surveys have been carried out in most industrialised countries. They have, moreover, followed a methodology established in the 1960s by a group of researchers under the direction of Szalai in Hungary (Szalai, 1972).

Because of this common methodology, data from the four time-budget surveys used in this chapter are highly comparable. There are differences between surveys in the actual way by which the diaries were collected (phone, mail back, visit) but the literature suggests that these different modes of data collection do not affect the comparability of the data (Robinson and Godbey, 1997). Some possible sources of non-comparability, however, exist, among which are the sampling design, the response rate and the coverage of 12 months of the year. These sources of variation will be important to bear in mind when analysing the data.

With regard to the coding of the daily activities, most surveys have used variants of the typology developed by the Szalai team in the 1960s.

Table 7.2: Time-use surveys

Country	Title of the Survey	Year of the Survey	Age range[a]	No of cases[b]	Res-ponse rate[c]	Mode of data collection	Survey period
Austria	Zeitverwendung (Time Use) (Micro census survey)	1992	15-24	3,525	47%	1-day diary (self-completed and house visit)	2 months (March and September)
Canada	Time Use, (General Social Survey, Cycle 7)	1992	15-24	1,476	77%	1-day diary (phone)	12 months (January to December)
Finland	Time-use survey	1987	15-24	2,614	74%	2-day diary (self-completed)	12 months (January to December)
Italy	L'Uso del Tempo in Italia (The use of time in Italy)	1988/9	15-24	5,841	70%	3-day diary (self-completed)	12 months (June 1988 to May 1989)

[a] This is the age range used in this paper. The original surveys covered a wider range.

[b] Number of cases for the age range used in this paper.

[c] This is the response rate for the total sample.

Source: Fisher (2000)

In this chapter, we distinguish three broad categories of activities and 11 sub-categories of activities (further details are provided in the Appendix)[4]:

- *Committed time:* 1 paid employment, 2 education, 3 housework, 4 caring for another person.
- *Personal time:* 5 personal needs.
- *Discretionary time:* 6 social activities, 7 civic and religious activities (including volunteer work), 8 active leisure (sport), 9 passive leisure (including watching television), 10 hobbies and cultural activities, 11 leisure travel.

While this typology will allow us to measure between- and within-country differences in the patterns of time use of young people, as will be seen later, it is, however, not perfectly suited to the analysis of differences in investment in human and social capital.

Because most surveys collected a one-day diary, the method of analysis consists in constructing 'synthetic' weeks. This is done by computing the weekly averages of respondents' having filled out their diaries on different days of the week and then by giving an equal weight to each day of the

Table 7.3: Sample characteristics[a]

Characteristics	Austria	Canada	Finland	Italy
Total number of cases (non-married students aged 15-24 years old)	1,153	587	1,000	2,647
Non-married students age 15-24 as a percentage of the total population aged 15-24	33	38	38	45
% men among non-married students aged 15-24	48	49	45	52
Mean age of non-married students aged 15-24	17.7	18.1[b]	17.9	17.9

[a] For Austria, the sample is restricted to the months of March and September; for Canada the sample is restricted to September and June; for Finland the sample is restricted to September and May

[b] The age of respondents in Canada is coded by category (15-17, 18-19, 20-24). A weighted average using the mid-age of each category was used.

week (Pentland et al, 1999). The assumption here is that while data at the individual level may not accurately capture the individual's allocation of time, it does so at the aggregate level, when we compare sub-groups of people who share similar demographic, social and economic characteristics (Robinson, 1977). In addition to mean patterns of daily activities for various sub-groups of respondents, our analysis also includes a discussion of participation rates in specific activities[5].

The description of our sample appears in Table 7.3. The samples are relatively large, ranging from nearly 600 young people in Canada to more than 2,500 in Italy. Non-married students aged 15 to 24 years old represent between 33% to 45% of the total population of that age. In all countries the average age is around 18 years old. The samples are about equally distributed between men and women. It should be noted that we are restricting the analysis to young people who were students at the time of the survey[6].

Results

Overall patterns of time use

The average pattern of time use of non-married students aged 15 to 24, by gender and country appears in Table 7.4. On average, young people devote 7.1 hours per day (30%) to committed activities, 10.8 hours (45%)

Table 7.4: Summary results: patterns of time use by gender and country

		Hours per day				%			
Country	Gender	Committed	Personal	Discretionary	Total	Committed	Personal	Discretionary	Total
Austria	Men	7.2	10.9	6.0	24.0	30	45	25	100
Canada	Men	7.8	9.9	6.3	24.0	32	41	26	100
Finland	Men	6.0	10.9	7.1	24.0	25	46	30	100
Italy	Men	6.5	11.4	6.1	24.0	27	47	26	100
Austria	Women	7.8	11.1	5.1	24.0	32	46	21	100
Canada	Women	8.1	9.9	5.9	24.0	34	41	25	100
Finland	Women	6.4	10.9	6.7	24.0	27	45	28	100
Italy	Women	7.1	11.5	5.4	24.0	30	48	22	100
	Average[a]	7.1	10.8	6.1	24.0	30	45	25	100

[a] Simple average, with equal weighting for every country and gender.

to personal activities and 6.1 hours (25%) to discretionary activities. The country and gender variations are, however, large. Time spent on committed activities varies between a minimum of 6.0 hours for Finnish men and a maximum of 8.1 hours for Canadian women. Time spent on personal activities varies between a minimum of 9.9 hours for Canadian men and women to a maximum of 11.5 hours for Italian women, that is, a difference of about 1½ hours per day. And time spent on discretionary activities varies between a minimum of 5.1 hours for Austrian women to a maximum of 7.1 hours for Finnish men. Overall, across these three broad categories of activities, the degree of dissimilarity is greatest between Canada and Finland, for men, and between Austria and Finland for women. On the other hand, the pattern of time use of men and women is most similar in Canada and most dissimilar in Austria[7].

Committed time

Countries vary significantly not only in the total amount of time devoted to committed activities but also in the structure of the committed time. Time spent on education, paid work, housework and caring, as well as the related participation rates, appear in Table 7.5.

Not surprisingly, education (time spent in school, studying and doing homework) occupies most of students' committed time. Students spend on average 4.8 hours per day on education[8]. The variation across countries is, however, large. Canadian men and women spend by far the largest amount of time on education (5.4 hours), and Finnish men and women the smallest (4.1 hours). Participation rate in education is also highest in Canada, and lowest in Austria and Finland[g].

In addition to education, students spend on average 1.1 hours per day on paid work. Again, Canadian men and women spend the largest amount of time on that category of activity (1.6 hours). Italians and Finns spend the least amount of time on paid work (between 0.7 and 1.0 hours). Participation rates follow a similar pattern, ranging between 72% for Canadian men and 55% for Italian women. Canadian men and women spend therefore their time in a very unique way, by devoting the largest amount of time to education and the largest to paid work. We will come back to this finding later in the chapter.

Students spend on average 1.1 hours on housework. The gender dimension is unmistakable. Women in all countries spend more time on housework than men and have a higher participation rate. The largest gender gap is observed in Italy, with nearly one hour per day, and the smallest one in Canada, less than 20 minutes per day.

Finally, students spend almost no time on child caring activities. This is not surprising considering that we have restricted our sample to non-married students. Caring for children other than their own (for younger siblings, or for neighbours) is likely to have been reported by students as paid work, provided that it was paid.

Personal time

Time spent on personal activities varies between 9.9 hours for Canadian men and women and 11.5 hours for Italian women. Of all the eleven categories of activities examined in this chapter, personal activities display the lowest coefficient of variation (across countries). Sleep dominates this category of activity in all countries and its duration is remarkably equal across countries (the breakdown by sub-category is not shown here). Only in Canada is time devoted to sleep shorter. Eating is the second most important category. In decreasing order, one finds Italy, Austria, Finland and Canada. Time spent dressing and bathing shows a clear gender difference, with women spending more time on this activity than men. Finally, time spent on personal services (eg, going to the doctor or dentist) is very small in all countries.

Table 7.5: Patterns of time use, non-married students age 15-to 24-years-old (average hours per day and participation rates)

Mean hours per day Country	Gender	Work	Educ.	House	Care	Personal	Social	Civic	Active	Passive	Hobbies	Travel	Total
Austria	Men	1.4	4.8	1.0	0.0	10.9	1.6	0.2	0.9	1.9	1.1	0.2	24.0
Canada	Men	1.6	5.4	0.8	0.0	9.9	1.5	0.1	0.9	2.4	0.8	0.6	24.0
Finland	Men	0.8	4.1	1.0	0.0	10.9	1.0	0.1	0.7	2.9	1.4	1.0	24.0
Italy	Men	1.0	5.0	0.5	0.0	11.4	1.2	0.2	1.3	2.2	0.7	0.6	24.0
Austria	Women	1.3	4.7	1.6	0.1	11.1	1.4	0.1	0.5	1.8	1.0	0.1	24.0
Canada	Women	1.6	5.4	1.1	0.1	9.9	1.9	0.3	0.4	1.9	0.9	0.6	24.0
Finland	Women	0.7	4.1	1.5	0.1	10.9	1.3	0.1	0.5	2.2	1.8	0.8	24.0
Italy	Women	0.8	5.0	1.4	0.0	11.5	1.0	0.2	1.0	2.1	0.6	0.5	24.0

Mean hours per day (%) Country	Gender	Work	Educ.	House	Care	Personal	Social	Civic	Active	Passive	Hobbies	Travel	Total
Austria	Men	6	20	4	0	45	7	1	4	8	5	1	100
Canada	Men	7	22	3	0	41	6	1	4	10	3	2	100
Finland	Men	3	17	4	0	46	4	0	3	12	6	4	100
Italy	Men	4	21	2	0	47	5	1	5	9	3	2	100
Austria	Women	5	20	7	1	46	6	0	2	8	4	1	100
Canada	Women	7	22	5	0	41	8	1	2	8	4	2	100
Finland	Women	3	17	6	0	45	6	1	2	9	7	3	100
Italy	Women	3	21	6	0	48	4	1	4	9	3	2	100

Participation rate (%) Country	Gender	Work	Educ.	House	Care	Personal	Social	Civic	Active	Passive	Hobbies	Travel
Austria	Men	61	68	59	1	100	51	8	35	80	58	24
Canada	Men	72	77	66	1	100	57	12	36	86	44	61
Finland	Men	60	71	67	0	100	62	4	40	92	83	68
Italy	Men	57	75	41	2	100	61	11	56	90	48	59
Austria	Women	62	72	74	6	100	59	5	26	77	56	18
Canada	Women	70	79	71	5	100	75	14	24	74	43	57
Finland	Women	58	73	87	5	100	80	6	40	92	90	65
Italy	Women	55	78	75	3	100	60	13	52	88	44	57

Discretionary time

Time spent on leisure activities also appears in Table 7.5. In all cases, passive activities dominate this category. This category of activities is followed in decreasing order by social activities, hobbies/cultural activities, active leisure, travel, and civic and religious activities. Time spent on social leisure activities varies between 1.9 hours for Canadian women and 1.0 hour for Finnish men and Italian women. Participation rates, on the other hand, displays a different country ranking. On average, participation in social leisure activities is highest in Finland and lowest in Austria. Participation rates are also higher for women than men. Time spent on hobbies and cultural activities varies between 1.8 hours per day for Finnish women and 0.6 hours for Italian women. Overall, Finnish men and women devote the largest amount of time to this activity. They also have the highest participation rate. Time spent on active leisure varies between 1.3 hours for Italian men and 0.4 hours for Canadian women. Overall, Italian men and women spend the largest amount of time on this type of activity. They also display the highest participation rate. In all countries, women devote less time to active leisure than men. Time spent on passive leisure activities varies between 2.9 hours for Finnish men and 1.8 hours for Austrian women. Participation rates are very high, exceeding 70% in all cases. In all countries, men devote more time to passive activities than women. Time spent on leisure travel varies between 1 hour for Finnish men and 0.1 hours for Austrian women. Participation rates are relatively high in all countries, around 50% and 60%, with the exception of Austria. Finally, time spent on civic and religious activities varies between 0.3 hours per day for Canadian women, to 0.1 hours for Canadian and Finnish men, and Austrian and Finnish women. Italy and Canada devote the largest amount of time to this activity. Participation rates are very low, even in Canada and Italy. The highest participation rate is observed for Canadian women, with 14%.

Discussion

To what extent can we relate our empirical findings to the theoretical framework set at the beginning of this chapter? To recall, we hypothesised that three macro-characteristics had a potential impact on the time use of young people: the level of public spending, the degree of income inequality, and the level of national income. Results provide relatively strong support for the hypothesised relationships between patterns of time use and the first two macro-characteristics, but provide no support for the hypothesised relationship between patterns of time use and the level of national income.

According to our theoretical framework, we were expecting young people residing in high public spending countries to be less likely to combine school and paid employment, and to be less likely to devote long hours to education. These hypothesised relationships are mainly supported. Canadian men and women reside in a country that devotes a relatively small share of national resources to public spending. They also devote the longest hours to education and the longest hours to paid work. Finnish men and women, on the other hand, reside in a country that devotes the highest share of national resources to public spending. They also devote the shortest hours to education and devote relatively little time to paid work. Italian men and women also devote a small amount of time to paid work (despite facing low public spending). The very high levels of youth unemployment observed in Italy may be severely restricting the job opportunities of Italian students[10].

We also hypothesised that young people residing in high public spending countries would be more likely to devote a larger share of their leisure time to activities related to the acquisition of cultural and social capital. Our various sub-categories of leisure activities do not allow us to easily identify activities that are rich in terms of cultural and social capital. The closest category is that of 'hobbies and cultural activities' which is unfortunately a very heterogeneous category including activities such as camping, caravanning, day trips to towns and cities, visiting areas of natural beauty, visiting zoos, museums, stately homes, and exhibitions, and going to a library. Results for this category of activities match our expectations. Finnish men and women devote the largest amount of time to this category of activity, while Canadian men and women (along with Italian men and women) devote the least amount of time to this category of activity.

With regard to income inequality, we hypothesised that the patterns of time use of young people residing in countries with lower degrees of income inequality would display more homogeneity, that is, fewer intra-country differences in their everyday life. Furthermore, we hypothesised that the participation rates in cultural and recreational activities would be higher in countries with lower degrees of income inequalities because of the more equal access to such activities (as opposed to a more elite access in countries with high income inequalities). Again, our data unfortunately makes it difficult to identify these cultural and recreational activities. The 'hobbies and cultural activities' referred to above appear to match our expectations with much higher participation rates in Finland than in Canada and Italy. The hypothesised relationship is, on the other hand, not supported in the case of 'active leisure', possibly because of the once again heterogeneous nature of this sub-category of activities (including both structured and unstructured active leisure).

Finally, we hypothesised that young people residing in high income and high wealth countries would have less need to combine school and paid work, and would, moreover, be expected to devote a larger proportion of their leisure activities to 'high-end' forms of activities (ie, high consumption and expensive leisure). These hypotheses would therefore suggest significant differences between Austria and Canada, on the one hand (high income levels), and Finland and Italy (lower income levels), on the other. Contrary to our hypotheses, Canadian men and women are more, not less, likely to combine education and paid work. Moreover, Canadian men and women do not devote a larger proportion of their leisure time to 'high-end' activities (if we approximate these by 'hobbies and cultural activities'). The opposite was, in fact, observed. Two points ought to be made. First, although Canada has a high level of income, it has also a high degree of income inequality and a low level of public spending. These characteristics may have confounded the impact of high-income level. Second, all four countries do not differ widely with respect to their national income. The inclusion in the analysis of countries with much lower levels of income may have allowed us to test this hypothesis more carefully.

Conclusions

The literature on youth development stresses the importance of education and participation in organised after-school activities. The human, social and cultural capital skills acquired through such activities appear to be associated with higher educational achievement and a more successful transition into adulthood. Yet, we know very little about the ways young people spend their time and even less about the magnitude of the related between- and within-country differences. Results presented in this chapter suggest that, overall, young people in different countries spend their time in a remarkably similar way. Non-married students aged 15 to 24 years old devote about 45% of their time to personal activities, 30% to committed activities and 25% to discretionary activities. However, a closer look at the data reveals non-negligible differences. Young people in Canada spend more time studying and working than young people in Austria, Italy and

Finland. On the other hand, young people in Finland spend the least amount of time on committed activities, but the largest amount of time on discretionary activities. Young Italians spend also more time on active leisure, and on civic and religious activities (together with Canadians) than young people in the other countries. Finally, young people in Finland stand out as spending limited time on education but more time on hobbies and cultural activities, as compared to the other countries.

These results are suggestive of a relationship between young people's time use and country characteristics, such as level of public spending and income inequality. As mentioned at the beginning of this chapter, the analysis presented here constitutes a first exploration of between- and within-country differences in patterns of time use of young people. The addition of more countries to the analysis, and the development of a more detailed typology of activities, is expected to shed further light on the determinants of the everyday experiences of young people, and particularly on their underlying inequalities.

Notes

[1] It may be tempting here to link the time-use theory with the welfare state one. While this is partly implied in the theoretical framework discussed below, it is not essential to our argument.

[2] Of course, institutional factors such as the compulsory number of days of school during the year and the compulsory number of hours of lectures per year can have a direct impact on the patterns of time use of students.

[3] Most of these young people will be living in their parental house (less so among the 20- to 24-year-olds) and will be childless at the time of the survey. The way the background and demographic variables were coded allowed us to distinguish young people's labour-force status (student) and marital status (not married). It was, however, not possible to distinguish their living arrangement (living with their parents or independently) nor their family status (with or without children).

[4] Data for some specific codes are missing in some surveys (the most frequent ones being time spent in pubs and bars). The typology used in this chapter is a variant of those suggested by Juster and Stafford (1985) and Carnegie (1992).

[5] Participation rates refer to the percentage of young people who happened to take part in one specific activity the day that they filled out the diary. For activities

done everyday by everybody, the participation rate is 100% (eg, sleeping). For other activities, the participation rate is lower, and includes a high percentage of people who did not participate the day that they filled out the diary. These non-participants include people who never carry out this activity, and people who just happened not to carry out this activity on that particular day.

[6] In most surveys, the employment/educational status of respondents was measured by reference to the main activity during the week prior to the survey. This means that we excluded students who were holding a summer job (and declared themselves employed instead of students) and included students who were on vacation but not holding any job (and not attending school either). For example, the Canadian sample had almost no students in the months of July and August, while the Finnish sample had a significant number of students during the months of June, July and August – although none of them reported studying. For reasons of cross-survey consistency, we restricted the Canadian sample to the months of September to June and the Finnish sample to the months of September to May. This procedure is equivalent to restricting the sample to the school year as opposed to the full year. In Austria the sample was already restricted to the two months during which the data collection took place – March and September. A closer look at the data revealed that the percentage of students who were attending classes in March was very high, but very low in September. In the absence of better data, we can only assume that the patterns of time use based on these two months approximate the patterns of time use throughout the entire school year (which appears to be the case in Canada and Finland). Finally, in Italy we know that the data collection was spread over 12 months; however, which month each diary was collected in was not coded in the Italian dataset. Consequently, we were not able to filter out the summer months, nor were we able to analyse the distribution of cases by month. This is most likely to lead to an underestimation of the time spent on education in Italy, although we have no way of checking this.

[7] The similarity and dissimilarity were computed on the basis of the three categories of activities using the Euclidean distances.

[8] Time spent travelling to and from school has been coded as time spent to and from work. In our analysis, time spent travelling to and from school has therefore been included in the paid work category. While this coding results in an over-estimation of time spent on paid work, the magnitude of the bias is relatively equal across countries.

[9] The smaller amount of time devoted to education by Finnish students in line with data reported elsewhere. For example, data from the OECD (2000) indicates that, while students at upper secondary level in Finland received 428 hours of instruction in 1998, the comparable figures for Austria, Italy and the US were 616, 612 and 943 respectively (data for Canada is not available). Our time use data also reveals that, even on school days, Finnish students devote less time to classes and homework than students in the other three countries (data not shown in this chapter).

[10] Two other phenomena may account for the limited amount of time that young Italians devote to paid work. First, there is the possible involvement of Italians in the informal economy, or even in illegal work. Although people involved in the informal economy or in illegal work may be paid for their work, it is unclear if they report it as paid work in the diaries, or as another type of activity. If they do not report that type of activity as paid work, then we are under-estimating time spent in paid work. Second, there is also the issue that young Italians tend to stay in their parental home for an extended period and that they are thus highly dependent on their family in financial terms (Sgritta, 1999). Such a dependency may in turn provide a disincentive to young people to get a paid job and earn their own money. Empirical evidence is unfortunately lacking to support either explanation.

References

Alsaker, F.D. and Flammer, A. (1999) *The adolescent experience in twelve nations: European and American adolescents in the nineties*, Hillsdale, NJ: Lawrence Erlbaum.

Atkinson, A.B., Rainwater, L. and Smeeding, T.M. (1995) *Income distribution in OECD countries. Evidence from the Luxembourg Income Study*, Paris: OECD.

Buchmann, M. (1989) *The script of life in modern society; entry into adulthood in a changing world*, Chicago, IL: University of Chicago Press.

Carnegie Council on Adolescent Development (1992) *A matter of time; risk and opportunity in the nonschool hours*, New York, NY: Carnegie Corporation of NY.

Coleman, J.S. (1988) 'Social capital in the creation of human capital', *American Journal of Sociology*, vol 94, pp S95-S120.

Council of Europe (1998) *European youth trends 1998*, Strasbourg: Council of Europe Experts in Youth Research.

European Commission (1997) *Young Europeans; Eurobarometer 47.2*, Brussels: European Commission, DG XXII.

Eurostat (1999) *On-line stastistics on social protection.*

Fisher, K. (2000) *Technical details of time use studies*, Release 2, 30 June, Institute for Social and Economic Research, University of Essex, online.

Furstenberg, F.F. Jr and Hughes, M.E. (1995) 'Social capital and successful development among at-risk youth', *Journal of Marriage and the Family*, vol 57, no 3, pp 580-92.

Gauthier, A.H. and Furstenberg, F.F. Jr (1999) 'Time use by young adults', Paper presented at the meeting 'Transition to Adulthood', Philadelphia, April.

Green, D.R. (1998) *Taking steps: Young people and social protection in the European Union; A report for the European Youth Forum*, Strasbourg: Council of Europe.

Hall, M., Knighton, T., Reed, P., Bussière, P., McRae, D. and Bowen, P. (1998) *Caring Canadians, involved Canadians: Highlights from the 1997 National Survey of Giving, Volunteering and Participating*, Ottawa, Canada: Statistics Canada.

Hofferth, S. (1998). 'Changes in American children's time, 1981-1997', Manuscript.

Huber, E., Ragin, C. and Stephens, J.D. (1997) *Comparative welfare states data set*, US: Northwestern University and University of North Carolina.

International Labor Office (annual) *Yearbook of Labour Statistics*, Geneva: ILO.

Juster, F.T. and Stafford, F.P. (eds) (1985) *Time, goods, and well-being*, Ann Arbor, MI: Institute for Social Research, University of Michigan.

Juster, F.T. and Stafford, F.P. (1991) 'The allocation of time: empirical findings, behavioral models, and problems of measurement', *Journal of Economic Literature*, vol XXIX, pp 471-522.

Larson, R.W. and Verma, S. (1999) 'How children and adolescents spend time across the world: work, play, and developmental opportunities', *Psychology Bulletin*, vol 125, no 6, pp 701-36.

Macdonald, R. (ed) (1997) *Youth, the underclass, and social exclusion*, London: Routledge.

Micklewright, J. and Stewart, K. (1999) *Is child welfare converging in the European Union?*, Occasional Paper No 69, Florence: International Child Development Center, UNICEF.

OECD (1999) On-line statistics on GDP per capita.

OECD (2000) *Education at a glance; OECD indicators: Education and skills*, Paris: OECD.

Palmore, E. (1979) 'Predictors of successful aging', *The Gerontologist*, vol 19, no 5, pp 427-31.

Pentland, W.E., Lawton, M.P., Harvey, A.S. and McColl, M.A. (eds) (1999) *Time-use research in the social sciences*, New York, NY: Plenum Press/Kluwer Academic.

Rainwater, L. and Smeeding, T.M. (1995) *Doing poorly: The real income of American children in a comparative perspective*, Luxembourg Income Study Working Paper No 127, Luxembourg: LIS.

Robinson, J.P. (1977) *How Americans use time: A social-psychological analysis of everyday behavior*, New York, NY: Praeger.

Robinson, J.P. and Godbey, G. (1997) *Time for life: The surprising ways Americans use their time*, College Park, PA: Pennsylvania State University Press.

Rowe, J.W. and Kahn, R.L. (1998) *Successful aging*, New York, NY: Pantheon Books.

Sgritta, G.B. (1999) 'Too late, too slow: the difficulty of becoming adult in Italy', Paper presented at the conference 'The transition to adulthood', Marbach Castle, Germany.

Smith, K.E. and Casper, L.M. (1999) 'Home alone: reasons parents leave their children unsupervised', Paper presented at the Annual meeting of the Population Association of America, New York, March.

Szalai, A. (ed) (1972) *The use of time: Daily activities of urban and suburban populations in twelve countries*, Paris: Mouton.

Teachman, J.D., Paasch, K. and Carver, K. (1997) 'Social capital and the generation of human capital', *Social Forces*, vol 75, no 4, pp 1342-59.

Unesco (1999) On-line statistics on public expenditure on education.

World Health Organisation (1996) *The health of youth; A cross-national survey*, Geneva: WHO.

Appendix: Categories of activities

Major category	Sub-category	Variable name[a]	Description
Committed time	1. Paid work	AV1	Paid work
		AV2	Paid work at home
		AV3	Second job
		AV5	Travel to/from work
	2. Education	AV4	School/classes
		AV33	Study
	3. Housework	AV7	Routine housework
		AV6	Cooking, washing up
		AV10	Shopping
		AV12	Domestic travel
		AV8	Odd jobs
		AV9	Gardening, pets
	4. Caring	AV11	Childcare
Personal time	5. Personal needs	AV13	Dressing/bathing
		AV16	Sleep
		AV15	Meals, snacks
		AV14	Personal services
Discretionary time	6. Social activities	AV25	Dances, parties
		AV26	Social club
		AV27	Pub
		AV28	Restaurant
		AV29	Visiting friends
		AV38	Entertaining friends
		AV37	Conversation
	7. Civic and Religious activities	AV22	Religious activities
		AV23	Civic activities
	8. Active leisure (sport)	AV19	Active sport
		AV21	Walking
	9. Passive leisure	AV30	Listening to radio
		AV31	Television, video
		AV32	Listening to tapes, etc
		AV20	Passive sport (spectator)
		AV36	Relaxing
	10. Hobbies (incl. Cultural activities)	AV18	Excursions
		AV24	Cinema, theatre
		AV34	Reading books
		AV35	Readings papers, magazines
		AV39	Knitting, sewing, etc
		AV40	Other hobbies and pastimes
	11. Leisure travel	AV17	Leisure travel

[a] The variable names correspond to the harmonised variables in the World5 version of the time use archive.

Notes: AV14 (Personal services): includes personal care services, medical/dental care and other personal care activities. AV10 (Shopping), includes everyday shopping, shopping for durable goods, governmental/financial services, other professional services, repair services, waiting/queuing for services and other services.

EIGHT

Gender inequality in poverty in affluent nations: the role of single motherhood and the state

Karen Christopher, Paula England, Sara McLanahan, Katherin Ross and Timothy M. Smeeding

Introduction

Women have higher poverty rates than men in almost all societies (Casper et al, 1994). In this chapter, we compare modern nations on this dimension. We use the Luxembourg Income Study (LIS) to compare women's and men's poverty rates in eight Western industrialised countries circa the early 1990s: the United States, Australia, Canada, France, West Germany, the Netherlands, Sweden, and the United Kingdom. We define individuals to be in poverty if they live in households with incomes below half the median for their nation. We examine, for each country, the ratio of women's to men's poverty rate. We then use simple demographic simulation methods to estimate how this gender disparity is affected by how prevalent single motherhood is, and by state tax and transfer programmes that may particularly help households headed by women.

Our guiding framework emphasises a web of interdependencies. Individuals rely on others (family members, employers, or the state) to obtain money and what it can buy. In addition, we have relationships with other people – as friends, spouses, employees, fellow citizens or neighbours – and in this we are reliant on the labour of those who reared these people. In this second emphasis, our analysis is inspired by feminist interrogation of who pays the costs of children (England and Folbre, 1999; Folbre, 1994a; 1994b). In this view, an important reason why more women than men are in poor households is because women are paying more of the costs of children than men. Folbre (1994a) argues that many members of society share in the benefits of children being brought up well. Most of us are dependent upon those who rear children for our ability to find caring friends, a spouse, trustworthy neighbours or employees. But we seldom recognise this dependency, and market mechanisms don't get all the beneficiaries to pay the parents or others who reared children. Often when services have this 'public good' aspect, as for example with national defence or highways, the state steps in to socialise the costs. Many social welfare programmes, in effect, socialise some of the costs of rearing children.

But states differ in how much they do this, and this may affect how much individual mothers bear the costs of children relative to individual fathers, and relative to male and female taxpayers. Single motherhood also affects the distribution of the costs of children between individual mothers and fathers, since in the case of nonmarital births and divorce, individual fathers often contribute little or nothing to the labour of rearing children and little to the financial costs. If women are poorer than men because many of them are raising children alone, this is evidence that mothers are bearing a disproportionate share of the costs of children relative to fathers or other citizens. The prevalence of single mothers and the way they (and others) are treated by social policies both affect the sex gap in poverty rates.

Past literature on gender inequality in poverty rates

Individuals get income from three main sources: the family, the market and the state. Households get their money primarily from members selling their labour or receiving transfers from government programmes[1]. Family members generally pool income, so the family serves to redistribute income within households. Those who either work for earnings or receive government transfers share these types of income with those who receive less or no income from outside the household.

Women have a higher poverty rate than men in almost all nations. (Sweden is the exception among the countries in our sample.) In thinking about possible causes of the gender gap in poverty rates, it is crucial to understand that poverty is measured at the *household or family level* in most government and academic statistics. An individual is in poverty if s/he lives in a household whose total income falls below the poverty line. In households with an adult couple, either both partners are in poverty or neither is in poverty. So, if all adults were married to or cohabiting with a person of the other gender, there would be no gender gap in poverty[2]. Thus, the gender gap in poverty exists because single women are poorer than single men. And for any size of the gender gap among singles, the overall gender gap will be larger if a higher proportion of the population is single.

Why are single women's households poorer than single men's? There are two main reasons – women's lower income and the fact that more single women live with children. Having children in the household affects the likelihood of poverty in one definitional way. Since the poverty line is adjusted for household size, the presence of children in a household raises the income necessary for the household to escape poverty and thus, income equal, single adults who live with children are more likely to be poor than those who live alone. Single women are much more likely to live with children than single men, since women usually have custody of the children in cases of divorce or nonmarital births. Thus, even if single men and women had equal earnings, more of the women than the men would be in poverty by virtue of supporting children.

Single women's greater poverty also comes from their lower earnings. Since single individuals typically do not have adult household members to transfer income to them, most are reliant on either government transfers or earnings. Although research on the gender gap in pay has seldom examined patterns separately by marital status, it is safe to assume that single women earn less than single men for many of the same reasons that women earn less than men more generally. (For a comparative overview of gender inequality in employment and earnings in modern nations, see Gornick, 1999.)

Jobs are still quite segregated by gender, both because a myriad of social forces encourage individuals to seek out gender-typical jobs and because of sex discrimination in hiring and job placement by employers (Jacobs, 1989; Reskin and Roos, 1990). Segregated jobs create a gender gap in pay because, even though 'female' jobs require as much education, on average, as 'male' jobs, they pay less (England, 1992). The low pay in 'women's jobs' may arise because of crowding, the greater excess of supply relative to demand in female jobs than in male jobs, resulting from the exclusion of women from 'male' jobs (Bergmann, 1986). In addition, there is evidence that sex bias affects employers' decisions about how much to pay 'women's jobs' relative to jobs dominated by men; this is the type of discrimination at issue in 'comparable worth' (England, 1992; Sorensen, 1994).

Parenthood reduces women's but not men's pay, also contributing to the gender gap in pay. Motherhood lowers the pay of women because some women leave the labour force or work part-time when they have children. In the case of single mothers this may require living on government transfer payments. When mothers return to work full-time, their earnings suffer from the accumulated deficit in experience and seniority. However, even after adjustments for prior experience, motherhood lowers women's earnings (Budig and England, 1999; Waldfogel, 1997, 1998). This may be because childcare leaves mothers with less energy when they go to work, cutting into their productivity because they trade off higher wages for 'mother-friendly' jobs[3], or because employers discriminate against mothers.

Nations differ in how their welfare states deal with these issues. Orloff (1993, p 319) suggests the utility of classifying welfare states along "a general dimension of self-determination" that would consider how much the state allows individuals to be independent from either markets or marriages. This contrasts with conceptualisations, like Esping-Andersen's (1990) Marxist-inspired notion of 'decommodification', which focuses on how much independence from markets the state provides. A feminist critique of this formulation is that it implicitly assumes that men's (or women's) dependence on capitalist employers is more problematic than wives' dependence upon husbands for money. In her discussion of the gendered nature of welfare states, Orloff (1993) focuses on how much the state facilitates women's independence from *either* employers or husbands. Her work implies that a large gender gap in poverty is not a *necessary* consequence of a high incidence of single mothers. This is because welfare states can ameliorate poverty among single mothers, either through policies that help women combine employment with motherhood, through enforcement of obligations that noncustodial fathers pay child support, and/or through transfer payments that pull single mothers out of poverty.

The thrust of the literature on welfare states is that the US and other Anglo-Saxon nations provide fewer supports for mothers' employment as well as less generous and universal income support. Nordic nations provide the most, with other nations intermediate. One might infer from this that nations in which the welfare state is doing more for women (and mothers) have lower gender gaps in poverty. However, state policies are not necessarily the cause of national differences in the gender gap in poverty. In part this is because there are other determinants of women having higher poverty than men, such as the proportion of women who are single mothers and the relative treatment of men and women in private-sector labour markets. Also, having relatively generous programmes for single women (including single mothers) will not necessarily equalise poverty rates for women *relative to* men. It could be that welfare states that have generous policies for single women also have generous policies for single men, and therefore that generous welfare states do nothing to close the gender gap in poverty.

Our goal is to assess the extent to which national differences in the gender gap in poverty come from differences in family structure (the proportion of people who are single, and whether single women are mothers) and governmental transfers more favourable to women versus men. The past research that comes closest to addressing our question is that of Casper et al (1994). Using data from the mid-1980s, they showed nations arrayed as follows, in descending order of the size of their ratio of women's to men's poverty rate. The US, Australia, West Germany, Canada, and the UK all had a sizeable gender gap. In Italy and the Netherlands women's poverty rate was about the same as men's. In Sweden, women's poverty rate was actually less than men's. Like Casper et al (1994), we use LIS data, but we use a more recent wave of data for each country. We analyse the same countries except that we have added France because it is well known for welfare state policies directed at children, and we excluded Italy[4].

Casper et al (1994) used logistic regression to predict individuals' poverty from several variables; most describe household composition and one dummy variable indicates whether are not individuals are employed. They then performed a decomposition showing that nations with more women relative to men living in households with children – which occurs when there are more single mothers – have larger sex gaps in poverty. They found that the high levels of employment among single females in Sweden are important in reducing women's poverty relative to men's. They speculate that the near equal poverty rates of the Dutch must come from generous transfer programmes, since they show that the Netherlands has low female employment and relatively high rates of single motherhood, both factors that would tend to increase women's poverty relative to men's.

Our analysis, like that of Casper et al (1994), examines the effect of a nation's family patterns (eg, prevalence of single mothers) on the gender gap in poverty. On this question, our contribution is in more detailed measures of family status categories and use of more recent data. Their analysis did not examine the contribution of the state to men's and women's poverty. Their conclusion, that the relatively low gender gap in poverty in the Netherlands is explained by welfare policies, was largely speculative. We assess this more directly through our simulations that examine each nation's ratio of women's to men's poverty including and excluding transfer payments, after standardising poverty rates for demographic differences between nations in the proportion of people in various family status categories.

Data, measures and method

We use the LIS. This data set contains information on household income for over 25 nations in 90 databases covering the period 1967 to 1995, and new waves of data continue to be added (LIS, 1996). The LIS consists of a set of household income surveys representing the civilian non-institutionalised population of each nation. We use the most recent wave for each of eight nations; most are from early- to mid-1990s. The US database is the March 1995 Current Population Survey with annual income information for 1994. The other nations we examine are Australia (1994), Canada (1994), West Germany (1994), France (1989), the Netherlands (1991), Sweden (1992) and the UK (including England, Scotland, Wales and Northern Ireland, 1995)[5].

In order to avoid including students and retirees, whose poverty is driven by very different factors than that of 'prime-age' adults, we limited our sample to adults from age 25 to 54. Although our measures of poverty and household type are defined at the household level, individual men and women are the units of analysis[6].

The measure of economic poverty we use here considers an individual in poverty if she or he lives in a household with a (size-adjusted) disposable money income that is less than half the median for households in the nation. This is a relative notion of poverty that compares the economic well-being of individuals to other residents of the same nation (not to those in other countries or to some absolute standard). We measure poverty at the household level. One limitation of measuring poverty at the household level is the implicit assumption of perfect pooling between household members. This ignores that an individual who brings money into the household may not share perfectly, but may retain disproportionate power over how money is spent and may consume more than other family members. There is a strong theoretical and an inconclusive but suggestive empirical literature proposing that women may have less decision-making power over how money is to be spent and in bargaining over other issues when they are dependent on their husbands for money.

(For reviews, see England and Kilbourne 1990; Lundberg and Pollak 1996.) On the other hand, to assume no pooling would even more seriously distort individuals' ability to consume and to participate in societies in ways that require money. The nonemployed wife of a corporate executive with extremely high earnings would be classified in poverty if we took an individual rather than household definition of poverty. Thus, we think the household definition is preferable, as long as we do not forget that those who earn or otherwise receive money from outside the household may gain more from it than other household members.

The forms of income that go into the determination of whether a household is in poverty are cash and near-cash income. LIS data sets contain variables for earnings, pensions, many types of government transfers, and other sources of income such as property income and child support payments. These were added to form total household income. We also include near-cash transfers such as food stamps[7] and cash denominated housing allowances in our definition of household income. This gross income was then converted to 'disposable income' by subtracting out income and payroll taxes. For our simulation designed to assess the effect of welfare state's tax and transfer programmes on gender inequality in poverty, discussed below, we compare ratios of women's to men's poverty computed using this disposable (post-tax, post-transfer) income to those computed using pre-tax, pre-transfer income. (For both we take the poverty line to be half of median disposable income.) Even post-transfer income excludes non-cash benefits such as healthcare, childcare and education; they are not measured by the LIS.

Before comparing a household's income to the poverty line for the relevant nation to determine whether the household is in poverty, income was adjusted by a commonly used equivalence scale. (The US governmental poverty line, which we do not use, is also constructed with an equivalence scale.) Equivalence scales adjust income for family size. However, instead of a simple linear transformation like per capita income, they are calibrated to reflect the notion that while a larger family needs more income than a smaller family, given economies of scale, a family of four doesn't need twice of what a family of two needs. Details on our choice of an equivalence scale are in the Appendix. The Appendix also includes calculations showing that our basic substantive conclusions are fairly robust regardless of whether our measure of family size weights each adult and child as 1, or weights children 25% more or less than adults. The former assumes that households need more money per child than per adult because children need childcare, while the latter assumes children consume less of some goods, such as food.

To assess how much between-nation differences in household composition affect the degree of gender inequality in poverty, we perform a simple demographic simulation making use of post-tax, post-transfer (disposable) income. To do this, we first classify the individual women and men who are our units of analysis by the household type they live in, that is, whether they are part of a male-female couple or not and by the presence or absence of children under age 18 in the household. As shorthand, we will refer to both married and cohabiting male-female couples as 'married'[8]. Whether individuals are classified as 'parents' is determined not by whether they have biological children, but by whether a child under 18 lives in their household. So, for example, single fathers who do not live with their children are classified as male single non-parents. This yields four household types for each sex: married parents, married non-parents, single parents and single non-parents. The overall poverty rate for women is a weighted average of the poverty rate for women in each of the four household-type categories, and analogously for men.

Our analysis begins with a simple calculation of poverty rates for men and women. The measure of the gender gap in poverty that we use is the ratio of women's poverty rate to men's poverty rates, called the 'gender-poverty ratio'. (We take this term from McLanahan et al, 1989.) We also examine these ratios for subgroups such as singles and single parents.

We then move to simulations designed to assess the effects of welfare state tax and transfer policies, and the effects of household composition on cross-national differences in gender inequality in poverty. First, to assess the effects of tax and transfer policies, we compare the gender-poverty ratio if income is pre-tax and pre-transfer to the gender-poverty ratio if it is post-tax and post-transfer. If we are willing to assume no behavioural response (in labour supply, marriage, cohabitation or fertility) to policies, this tells us whether overall the tax and transfer policies help women or men more, as regards being or not being in poverty.

Second, we assess the effects of family composition on nations' sex-poverty ratios by performing a simulation that gives every other nation the US proportion of men and women in each household type, but retains the nation's own poverty rates within household types. In essence, we weight a country's gender- and household-type-specific poverty rates by US weights for family demography. This gives us the gender-poverty ratios other nations would have if they had the US household composition.

Results

Table 8.1 shows the raw gender gap in poverty in various sub-groups. The first two columns examine poverty rates among all men and women ages 25-54 and the third shows the 'gender-poverty ratio', that is, women's poverty rates divided by men's poverty rates.

Looking at the poverty rates, we see that men in Sweden and the Netherlands have substantially lower poverty rates than men in the other countries (under 5%), while US and Canadian men have the highest poverty rates (11%). The rank order of countries by women's poverty rates is similar, with the lowest women's poverty in Sweden (3%) and the Netherlands (6%) and highest rates in Canada (13%) and the US (15%).

Only Sweden has a gender-poverty ratio of less than one, indicating that Swedish men are more likely to live in poverty than Swedish women. But both sexes have very low poverty, so the difference is not large in percentage point terms (4% for men and 3% for women). In all other countries, women have higher poverty rates then men; the country with the next lowest gender-poverty ratio is France, where women are 11% more likely than men to live in poverty. Gender-poverty ratios are higher than this in Canada, the Netherlands, Germany and the UK, where women are between 13% and 20% more likely to live in poverty than men. The two outliers are Australia and the US, where women are respectively 30% and 38% more likely to live in poverty than men.

Table 8.1 also shows poverty rates and ratios for single men and women. We examine singles separately because the overall gender gap in poverty is driven entirely by the gap among singles, weighted by what proportion of people are single, as discussed previously. Nations' rankings in single men's poverty rates are quite similar to the ranking for all (single and married) men. The same holds for single women. The low poverty of single women in Sweden (5%) is striking. Even single men in all countries have higher poverty rates, and the poverty rates of single women in other countries are in an entirely different ballpark than that of their Swedish counterparts, from 13% in the Netherlands to a high of 32% in the US. In all countries but Sweden, single women have higher poverty than single men. In all countries but Sweden and France, single women's poverty is more than 50% higher than men's.

Table 8.1 also shows the poverty rates for single mothers. Swedish single mothers are outliers with a poverty rate of only 3%. Rates of poverty for single mothers are very high in all other countries, from a

Table 8.1: Poverty rates[a] and sex-poverty ratios[b] for all adults, single adults, and single mothers and fathers

		Male poverty rates	Female poverty rates	Sex-poverty ratio poverty	Single male poverty rates	Single female poverty rates	Singles' sex poverty ratio	Single mothers poverty rates	Single fathers poverty rates[c]	Single mothers/ single men	Single mothers/ single fathers
AS	1994	0.082	0.107	1.30	0.148	0.247	1.67	0.386	0.275	2.60	1.40
CN	1994	0.116	0.131	1.13	0.174	0.291	1.68	0.405	0.171	2.33	2.37
FR	1989	0.096	0.107	1.11	0.132	0.164	1.24	0.247	0.111	1.87	2.23
GE	1994	0.083	0.098	1.18	0.118	0.226	1.92	0.391	0.111	3.31	3.52
NL	1991	0.049	0.056	1.14	0.081	0.132	1.63	0.257	0.000	3.17	NA[d]
SW	1992	0.040	0.029	0.73	0.093	0.048	0.52	0.034	0.069	0.37	0.49
UK	1995	0.091	0.109	1.20	0.136	0.214	1.57	0.319	0.200	2.35	1.60
US	1994	0.110	0.151	1.38	0.166	0.320	1.93	0.471	0.223	2.84	2.11

[a]Poverty rates are the proportion of non-elderly adults aged 25-54 whose disposable family incomes fall below the poverty line. 'Single' means not married or part of a cohabiting male/female couple.

[b]The sex-poverty ratio is the female poverty rate divided by the male poverty rate.

[c]Single fathers are men living with a child under the age of 18 and without an adult female. Single mothers are defined analogously. Single fathers' rates should be interpreted with caution because some Ns are < 30.

[d]This ratio cannot be computed since the denominator is 0.

Note: AS=Australia, CN=Canada; FR=France; GE=Germany; NL=the Netherlands; SW=Sweden; UK=United Kingdom; US=United States.

Table 8.2: Ratio of women's to men's poverty rate in eight nations and under simulations

Ratio based on:	US 94	AS 94	CN 94	FR 89	GE 94	NL 91	SW 92	UK 95
Pre-transfer, pre-tax income	1.42	1.37	1.15	1.12	1.19	1.34	.92	1.30
Post-transfer, post-tax (disposable) income	1.38	1.30	1.13	1.11	1.18	1.14	.73	1.20
% tax and transfer system changes ratio	–3%	–5%	–2%	–1%	–1%	–15%	–21%	–8%
Post-transfer, post-tax income with US household composition	1.38	1.39	1.21	1.19	1.40	1.48	0.79	1.16
% US household composition changes ratio	0%	7%	7%	7%	19%	30%	8%	3%

Note: The first row gives the ratio of women's to men's poverty rates for each country when we do not add government transfers to or subtract payroll taxes from income. The second row gives the ratio of women's to men's poverty rate for disposable income (post-transfer, post-tax). The third row gives the percentage change in the ratio of women's to men's poverty rate due to the nation's tax and transfer system (ie the percentage change between row 1 and 2). Using disposable (post-transfer, post-tax) income, the fourth row gives the ratio of women's to men's poverty rate each nation would have if it kept its own poverty rates for men and women within each household type, but had the proportion of men and women in each household type observed in the US. The last row gives the percentage change between rows 2 and 4. This is the percentage by which the sex-poverty ratio for disposable income would be increased if the nation had the US distribution of people across household types, but kept its own sex-specific poverty rates within each household type.

AS=Australia, CN=Canada; FR=France; GE=Germany; NL=the Netherlands; SW=Sweden; UK=United Kingdom; US=United States.

low of 25% in France and the Netherlands to a high of 47% in the US. Single fathers have poverty rates lower than single mothers. But the poverty rates of single fathers are quite high, in the 10-30% range except for the low rates of Sweden and the Netherlands[9].

These descriptive statistics allow several generalisations: women's poverty rate is higher than men's everywhere except Sweden. However, there are large national differences in the extent of inequality between women's and men's rates of poverty. Single women, particularly single mothers, have higher poverty rates than most other groups of men or women in all nations but Sweden. But the extent to which single women and single mothers have 'surplus' poverty varies by nation.

Next we want to assess how much differences between nations in their gender-poverty ratio are driven by differences in their tax and transfer policies, and how much by the prevalence of single motherhood. To do this, we perform data based simulations, presented in Table 8.2.

First, we want to assess whether, all in all, tax and transfer payment policies help reduce women's poverty relative to men's. That is, we want to know if they change the ratio of women's poverty rate to men's. For that to be true, the policies would have to raise proportionately more women than men above the poverty line. To examine this, we first compute hypothetical poverty rates for women and men in each nation based on their income before subtracting taxes and before adding government transfers. The ratio of women's to men's poverty in the first row of Table 8.2 comes from these calculations. It can be compared to the second row in the table which gives the gender-poverty ratio when each household's actual disposable (post-tax, post-transfer) income is used.

Table 8.2 shows that in all cases the actual ratio of women's to men's poverty is lower than it is before taxes and transfers, implying that every nation's welfare state pulls proportionately more single women than single men out of poverty. However, in most nations the reductions are very small. If we count any reduction of less than 5% as trivial, then the welfare states of the US, Canada, France and Germany are not redistributive between men and women, at least across the poverty line. They reduce the sex-poverty ratios by 3%, 2%, 1%, and 1% respectively. The tax and transfer systems of Australia and the UK are slightly more friendly to women relative to men as regards poverty; they reduce the sex-poverty ratio by 5% and 8% respectively. The nations with tax and transfer systems that help women out of poverty the most, relative to men, are the Netherlands and Sweden, whose systems reduce the ratio of women's to men's poverty by 15% and 21% respectively (Table 8.2). Thus, the fact that the US has the highest ratio of women's poverty to men's poverty can be attributed in part to its less gender-redistributive system of tax and transfer policies as regards poverty. This is particularly true in comparison with the Netherlands and Sweden.

The two nations whose welfare states reduce the gender gap in poverty the most, Sweden and the Netherlands, also have the lowest poverty rates of both men and women. However, the Netherlands has much higher poverty of single mothers (25%, similar to that of France) than Sweden (3%). The policies of most of the nations are scarcely redistributive across gender lines. Some nations, such as France and Germany, may have relatively generous welfare systems compared to the US, but because they help men nearly as much as women, they scarcely reduce the gender inequality in poverty produced by the family and market.

We next address the question of the effect of family demography on the ratio of women's to men's poverty. To do this, we can standardise any nation's poverty rates to the demography of any other. To avoid too many comparisons, and because the US has the worst gender gap in poverty, we use the US as a comparator. The fourth row of Table 8.2 gives the hypothetical ratio of women's to men's poverty for each nation if it were given the family demography of the US.

To calculate this, we first divide the individuals in each nation into eight gender-specific household types. That is, we divide each gender into married parents, married non-parents, single parents and single non-parents. The US poverty rate for each of these groups is computed from the LIS US data. Then we create hypothetical male and female poverty rates for the other nations under the assumption that they had the US family demography. To do this, for each gender, in each nation, we take a weighted average of that nation's observed poverty rates. If we used that nation's proportion of persons of that gender who are in that household category, we would get the nation's observed (disposable, ie, post-tax, post-transfer) poverty rate. However, by using US household category proportions as weights, we get the poverty rate the nation would have if it had US family demography. The gender-poverty ratios corresponding to these hypothetical rates are row 4 of Table 8.2. By comparing them to row 2, the nation's actual post-transfer, post-tax ratios, we see how much their gender inequality in poverty would be increased if they had the US family demography. Close examination of the detailed numbers leading to these rates and ratios makes clear that it is largely the US higher proportion of single mothers that drives the differences between the gender-poverty ratios with the nation's own versus the US family demography (row 2 versus row 4 in Table 8.2). The last row of the table gives the percentage by which the gender-poverty ratio is increased when each nation is given the US family demography (as weights) but keeps its own poverty rates within household types.

The last rows of Table 8.2 show that every nation would have a higher ratio of women's to men's poverty if they had the US household family composition. This is largely due to the high percentage of US women who are single mothers, about 12%. In Sweden, France, Germany and the Netherlands only 5% of women are single mothers. The Anglo-Saxon nations have higher rates with Australia at 8%, Canada at 9%, the UK at 11%, and the US the highest at 12%. We see that, given that the UK has a similar proportion of single mothers to the US, if they had the US family demography their gender-poverty ratio would go up only 3%.

But the ratios of Australia, Canada, France and Sweden would all go up 7-8%. The ratios for Germany would go up 19% and the Netherlands would go up 30%. Despite the fact that Germany and the Netherlands have about the same proportion of single mothers as France and Sweden, the ratio of women's to men's poverty would go up much more in the former than the latter two nations if they had the US family composition. This is largely because single mothers have higher poverty relative to single men in Germany and the Netherlands than in France and Sweden.

Conclusions

Women have higher poverty than men in every nation besides Sweden. However, the ratio of women's poverty to men's among the nonelderly differs by nation, being highest in the US (1.38), followed by Australia (1.30). In this chapter, we explored the operation of the welfare state and family demography as they affect these gender-poverty ratios.

To assess how nations' welfare states affect gender inequality in poverty, we compared the hypothetical gender-poverty ratios if the state had no taxation and transfers (that is the ratios calculated from pre-transfer, pre-tax income) to the actual ratios (calculated on disposable, ie post-transfer, post-tax income). Systems of taxation and transfer payments are the major way that welfare states affect the distribution of income. While our analysis does not consider the effects of specific programmes, it provides a good 'bottom line' assessment of whether tax and transfer systems bring proportionately more women or men out of (or into) poverty. The US, Australia, Canada, France and Germany all reduce the ratio of women's to men's poverty rates by 5% or less through their tax and transfer systems. Thus, in these countries the welfare state does little to reduce the gender inequality in poverty produced by single motherhood and labour market inequalities. The UK reduces its gender-poverty ratio from 1.30 to 1.20, by 8%, with its tax and transfer system. The nations whose welfare states do the most for women relative to men are the Netherlands and Sweden. In Sweden, women have no higher poverty than men even when we look at pre-tax, pre-transfer income, but after taxes and transfers are included in income, women's poverty goes down even more relative to men's.

One might object to our analysis because it embodies the unrealistic assumption that there are no behavioural effects of welfare, such as women deciding not to be employed or not to get married because of the availability of transfers for single mothers. However, if such behavioural effects exist, and particularly affect women, then our analysis will exaggerate the beneficial effects of transfers on women's poverty rates relative to men's. If this is true, we may be exaggerating the helpful effect of the state on gender equality in freedom from poverty in Sweden and Netherlands. But the conclusion seems quite safe that the welfare states of the other five nations (the US, Australia, Canada, France and Germany) make no more than trivial redistribution that reduces the gender disparity in poverty rates.

Our analysis also examined the effect of household demography on gender inequality in poverty. Poverty, as we measure it, applies to all members of a household, so married couples cannot contribute to a gender gap in poverty, and any gap must come from disparities between single men and women. In particular, single mothers have higher poverty than other groups everywhere but Sweden (although the extent of their surplus rates varies). Single women are more likely to be supporting children than single men, yet have lower earnings on average. Thus, nations with a higher percent of women who are single mothers will generally have a higher gender gap in poverty. We examined how much household composition drives differences between nations in the degree of gender inequality in poverty. To do this, we compared the actual gender-poverty ratios to those each nation would have if it had the proportion of men and women in each household category (single with kids, single without kids, married with kids, and married without kids) that the US has. This simulation showed that every nation would have more gender inequality in poverty if it had US family demography. The major factor in the increase is the higher proportion of American women who are single mothers. Indeed, the poverty rates of Australia, Germany and the Netherlands are such that if they had US demography but their own poverty rates within household types, they would have higher gender inequality in poverty than the US.

Sweden is doubly blessed, with family demography and the state contributing to women's low poverty relative to men's. Even if single mothers did have higher poverty than other groups in Sweden, its lower proportion of single mothers relative to the US would give it a lower ratio of women's to men's poverty than in the US. Its welfare state is also important to gender equality, as seen by the fact that taxes and transfers reduce the ratio of women's poverty to men's below its already low level.

France is also known for its ample government transfers and services for families with children. We thought at first that this must be what produced its relatively low poverty rates among single mothers and low sex-poverty ratio among singles (Table 8.1). However, our simulations make clear that state transfers of income are not what generates France's greater gender equality compared to the US. Taxes and transfers do little to reduce the gender disparity in poverty in either France or the US. Apparently, the French system is more generous to both men and women, while the US system is stingy to both, but neither does much redistribution by gender. The superiority of France to the US in gender equality in poverty comes in part from its lower prevalence of single mothers.

The Netherlands is a particularly interesting case with forces pulling for and against gender equality in poverty. Dutch single mothers have high poverty rates. Before taxes and transfers the Dutch gender-poverty ratio is as high as any nation but the US and Australia, in part because all mothers, single and married, have low employment rates. But the Netherlands has fewer single mothers than the US or other Anglo-Saxon nations, which lowers their gender inequality in poverty. Their tax and transfer system also works against gender inequality in poverty more than that of any nation besides Sweden.

If Sweden is doubly blessed, the US is 'doubly damned', with high levels of single motherhood and a welfare state that is relatively stingy and redistributes little if at all by gender. Both the high rates of single motherhood and the lack of gender redistribution by the welfare state contribute to the highest gender disparity in poverty. It is important to remember that the income data used here exclude noncash transfers, such as healthcare and childcare. Analyses that included these would make the US look even worse relative to other nations in poverty rates and gender inequality in poverty. All other affluent nations have universally available healthcare and more state childcare funding than the US. Universally available healthcare and childcare are particularly beneficial to single mothers for their direct benefits, as well as because they make employment pay where it otherwise would not because of childcare costs and loss of welfare-provided healthcare for children.

Single motherhood is growing in most industrial nations. As this occurs, gender inequality in poverty will increase if women's employment and earnings and/or state subsidisation of the costs of rearing children do not increase to compensate for women's loss of access to men's earnings. This is an important concern for public policy, both out of a concern for gender equity in bearing the costs of children, and also because the higher poverty of single mothers means poverty for their children.

Notes

[1] Some individuals also receive market income from property – dividends from stock, rents from real estate, etc, although this affects a fairly small proportion of households in modern nations. Pensions received later in life are a delayed payment for work in labour markets, so we consider them as part of an individual's own market earnings. Self-employment earnings mix a return to labour and capital, but we consider them together with labour earnings.

[2] US government poverty statistics consider cohabiting unmarried couples as if they were two households. Following the convention of most other governments, in this chapter we will consider cohabiting different-sex couples and married couples together, referring to them as married. This reflects the assumption that cohabiting couples generally pool income.

[3] A recent analysis by Budig and England (1999) casts doubt on the hypothesis that the motherhood penalty arises because mothers trade off wages for mother-friendly jobs. Entering a large number of occupational characteristics and dummy variables for industry into a regression predicting women's earnings showed that the presence or absence of these controls had no effect on the size of the coefficient measuring the effect of number of children on wages.

[4] We omitted Italy because a few anomalies in the most recent wave of data require correction.

[5] The LIS databases for the other nations are: Australia 1994 (Housing and Income Survey), Canada 1994 (Survey of Consumer Finances), France 1989 (Enquête Budget, or Budget Survey), West Germany 1994 (German Social and Economic Panel), the Netherlands 1991 (Income Distribution Survey), Sweden 1992 (Household Income Distribution Survey), and the UK (1995 Family Expenditure Survey). Each national database is sent to LIS in its cleaned and edited form. At LIS, the data are harmonised by reclassifying the income and demographic variables into homogeneous types of income and family/household characteristics. These consistently defined income and household types allow the researcher to carry out analysis of a particular research question in several countries on a comparable basis.

[6] We only include individuals whom LIS classified as heads of households or the spouses or cohabitants of heads. Single adults living alone or with children were classified as heads, and one person in each different-sex couple was called the

head (with decision rules varying by country). Thus, the individuals who are omitted from our analysis are adults who are neither a single head nor part of a married or cohabiting different-sex couple. For example, if a single or married mother lives with her mother, the grandmother is not a unit in our analysis. However, any income provided by these extra adults is included in our measure of household income, and the presence of the adult is taken account of when the equivalence index is used to size-standardise the household's income before determining if it is in poverty.

[7] In including food stamps, our procedure differs from the US government poverty series, which excludes food stamps income before determining if it is in poverty.

[8] Only the data from the Netherlands identified same-sex couples; we did not include them in our analysis since no other nations' data sets allow us to identify same-sex couples.

[9] Caution is needed interpreting rates for single fathers, as the data sets in many countries have quite small sample sizes of single fathers, sometimes fewer than 30.

References

Bergmann, B.B. (1986) *The economic emergence of women*, New York, NY: Basic Books.

Budig, M. and England, P. (1999) 'The Wage Penalty for motherhood', Paper presented at the 1999 annual meetings of the American Sociological Association, Chicago.

Buhmann, B., Rainwater, L., Schmaus, G. and Smeeding, T. (1988) 'Equivalence scales, well-being, inequality and poverty', *Review of Income and Wealth*, June, vol 34, no 2, pp 115-42.

Casper, L.M., McLanahan, S.S. and Garfinkel, I. (1994) 'The gender-poverty gap: what we can learn from other countries', *American Sociological Review*, vol 59, pp 594-605.

Citro, C.F. and Michael, R.T. (1995) *Measuring poverty: A new approach*, Washington, DC: National Academy Press.

England, P. (1992) *Comparable worth: Theories and evidence*, New York, NY: Aldine.

England, P. and Folbre, N. (1999) 'Who should pay for the kids?', *Annals of the American Association of Political and Social Sciences*, vol 563, pp 194-207.

England, P. and Kilbourne, B. (1990) 'Markets, marriages, and other mates: the problem of power', in R.Friedland and A.F. Robertson (eds) *Beyond the marketplace: Rethinking economy and society*, Hawthorne, NY: Aldine de Gruyter, pp 163-89.

Esping-Andersen, G. (1990) *Three worlds of welfare capitalism*, Cambridge: Polity Press.

Folbre, N. (1994a) 'Children as public goods', *American Economic Review*, vol 84, no 2, pp 86-90.

Folbre, N. (1994b) *Who pays for the kids? Gender and the structures of constraint*, New York, NY: Routledge.

Gornick, J. (1999) 'Gender equality in the labor market: women's employment and earnings', in D. Sainsbury, *Gender and welfare state regimes*, Oxford: Oxford University Press.

Jacobs, J. (1989) *Revolving doors: Sex segregation and women's careers*, Stanford, CA: Stanford University Press.

Lundberg, S. and Pollak, R.A. (1996) 'Bargaining and distribution in marriage', *Journal of Economic Perspectives*, vol 10, pp 139-58.

Luxembourg Income Study (1996) *LIS user guide*, Syracuse, NY: Luxembourg Income Study, Syracuse University.

McLanahan, S., Sorensen, A. and Watson, D. (1989) 'Sex differences in poverty 1950-1980', *Signs: Journal of Women in Culture and Society*, vol 15, no 11, pp 102-22.

Orloff, A.S. (1993) 'Gender and the social rights of citizenship', *American Sociological Review*, vol 58, pp 303-28.

Reskin, B.F. and Roos, P.A. (1990) *job queues, gender queues: explaining women's Inroads into Male Occupations*, Philadelphia, PA: Temple University Press.

Sorensen, E. (1994) *Comparable worth*, Princeton, NJ: Princeton University Press.

Waldfogel, J. (1997) 'The effect of children on women's wages', *American Sociological Review*, vol 62, pp 209-17.

Waldfogel, J. (1998) 'Understanding the "family gap" in pay for women with children', *Journal of Economic Perspectives*, vol 12, no 1, pp 137-56.

Appendix

Equivalence scales to adjust for family size

Equivalence scales adjust the poverty line for family size. Buhmann et al (1988) propose that income be adjusted for family size in the following way:

Adjusted Income = Disposable Income/Size^{E}

The equivalence elasticity, E, varies between 0 and 1. The smaller the E, the larger the economies of scale assumed by the equivalence scale. An E of 0 makes no size adjustment; the poverty line is the same regardless of family size. With an E of 1, adjusted income becomes per capita income (with no economies of scale). We use an equivalence scale of 0.5, as this is the middle ground between no adjustment for size and per capita income, and this figure is commonly used in cross-national poverty research. The official poverty rate used by the US government is based on an equivalence scale of 0.56, but produces similar poverty rates to the equivalence scale of 0.5.

A separate issue is how adults are to be weighted relative to children. The simplest procedure, which we use in Tables 8.1 and 8.2, weights both adults and children as 1 to get Size. However, some (eg, Citro and Michael 1995) argue that children should be weighted less because they consume less of some goods, for example food, and thus a family needs less income for an additional child than an additional adult. On the other hand, children need intensive care that adults do not. This care is paid for by families (or the state) either in cash for childcare or in the opportunity cost of a family member's time spent caring for children rather than earning a wage. To test how sensitive our conclusions are to the relative weight given to children and adults, Table A-1 presents the results in Table 8.2 (in bold) and compares them to results when children are weighted 0.75 (top number in each cell) and 1.25 (lower number in each cell). In all cases adults are weighted 1 and E=0.5. An examination of Table A-1 suggests that how children are weighted changes numbers somewhat, but our basic conclusions are unchanged, and it is surprising how little the weights change the gender-poverty ratios.

Appendix Table A-1: Ratio of women's to men's poverty rate in eight nations and under simulations, using an equivalence scale in which children are weighted .75, 1, and 1.25 that of adults

Ratio based on:	US 1994	AS 1994	CN 1994	FR 1989	GE 1994	NL 1991	SW 1992	UK 1995
Pre-transfer,	1.43	1.37	1.14	1.13	1.16	1.34	.90	1.29
pre-tax income	**1.42**	**1.37**	**1.15**	**1.12**	**1.19**	**1.34**	**.92**	**1.30**
	1.41	1.35	1.14	1.10	1.17	1.32	.93	1.30
Post-transfer,	1.39	1.26	1.10	1.09	1.17	1.11	.70	1.10
post-tax	**1.38**	**1.30**	**1.13**	**1.11**	**1.18**	**1.14**	**.73**	**1.20**
(disposable) income	1.36	1.35	1.15	1.12	1.18	1.23	.76	1.26
% that tax and	-2%	-8%	-3%	-4%	1%	-17%	-22%	-15%
transfer system	**-3%**	**-5%**	**-2%**	**-1%**	**1%**	**-15%**	**-21%**	**-8%**
changes ratio	-3%	-0%	1%	1%	1%	-7%	-18%	-3%
Post-transfer,	1.39	1.36	1.20	1.11	1.37	1.37	.88	1.08
post-tax income	**1.38**	**1.39**	**1.21**	**1.19**	**1.40**	**1.48**	**.79**	**1.16**
with US household	1.36	1.48	1.25	1.20	1.44	1.66	.80	1.24
composition								
% US household	0%	8%	9%	4%	17%	23%	26%	-2%
composition changes	**0%**	**7%**	**7%**	**7%**	**19%**	**30%**	**8%**	**3%**
ratio	0%	10%	9%	7%	22%	35%	5%	-2%

Note: The first number in each cell is the ratio when children are weighted 0.75 in the equivalence scale, the second when weighted 1 (bolded numbers are those in Table 8.2), and the third when weighted 1.25. See Appendix for description of equivalence scale.

Note: The first row gives the ratio of women's to men's poverty rates for each country when we do not add government transfers to or subtract payroll taxes from income. The second row gives the ratio of women's to men's poverty rate for disposable income (post-transfer, post-tax). The third row gives the percentage change in the ratio of women's to men's poverty rate due to the nation's tax and transfer system (i.e. the percentage change between row 1 and 2). Using disposable (post-transfer, post-tax) income, the fourth row gives the ratio of women's to men's poverty rate each nation would have if it kept its own poverty rates for men and women within each household type, but had the proportion of men and women in each household type observed in the US. The last row gives the percentage change between rows 2 and 4. This is the percentage by which the gender-poverty ratio for disposable income would be increased if the nation had the US distribution of people across household types, but kept its own sex-specific poverty rates within each household type.

AS=Australia, CN=Canada; FR=France; GE=Germany; NL=the Netherlands; SW=Sweden; UK=United Kingdom; US=United States.

PART 3

Country studies and emerging issues

Introduction

The third part of this volume presents several innovative national studies that highlight country-specific developments, data developments or methodological breakthroughs that are interesting for an international audience. The first two chapters analyse the evolution of child poverty in nations that have undergone important socioeconomic transitions in the last decade. Jane Falkingham focuses on the impact of economic change on child welfare in Central Asia by taking a multidimensional view of child well-being in these transition nations. The selected indicators include both economic measures of poverty, based on incomes and expenditures, and selected capability-based indicators, reflecting children's health, survival, educational attainment, personal development and their social exclusion. This data was collected by the World Bank in a uniform survey and provides an opportunity to study economic well-being and child outcomes more efficiently and effectively for this set of nations than can currently be achieved by the rich country studies, which do not have this unique type of data.

The results of the study reveal that the cost of economic transition has been particularly high in Central Asia, and children are clearly among those who have suffered the most. Child poverty rates exceed those of the general population, children's nutritional status is poor and its consequences are akin to those observed in parts of sub-Saharan Africa. Still, infant mortality has fallen in Central Asia and remains low compared to other countries in a similar economic situation. Further, immunisation programmes have continued near-universal coverage, and primary school enrolments have been maintained at a reasonably high level. Nevertheless, Falkingham notes that the combined impact of low social spending and low household income might be beginning to take its toll. Children whose families are not able to contribute towards their education and childcare increasingly face the risk of being excluded from access to these services. Even when they continue to have access, low social spending starts to reduce the quality of these services. Falkingham observes that:

> Given that in the Central Asian region children take pride of place within the family and culturally prioritised within the family's hierarchy of needs, the observed levels of malnutrition among young children and growing absences from school are indicators of a society in severe distress. (p 251)

Falkingham concludes that governments in Central Asia need to intervene to minimise the multiple risk of the material and capability poverty children face during transition. International aid could fund properly delivered food, medicine and other services, which would help these nations overcome the sobering situation. The chapter also puts into perspective the differences between child poverty in poor nations such as those she studies and the richer nations' children covered in the other chapters in the book. It also suggests that rich nations could undertake similar studies to the one that the World Bank funded here, permitting direct family-by-family linkages of economic and social status with levels of child outcomes.

Far less distressing is Brian Nolan's analysis of the evolution of child poverty and deprivation in Ireland. During the late 1980s and early 90s, economic growth reached record levels in Ireland. In this context, Nolan examines the level and trend in child poverty in this period of increased prosperity. Although the gap between relative income poverty rates for children and adults remained relatively stable between 1987 and 1994, Nolan finds that the poverty rates for children based on the 50% and 60% of median poverty lines declined in the period between 1994 and 1997, while those for adults increased, thus producing a significant narrowing of that gap. Nolan attributes the declining relative poverty rates for children at the two higher lines to the impact of falling unemployment. Nonetheless, the child poverty rate based on the 40% line increased, reflecting that this line was now higher than the support for families provided by some social-welfare programmes. Nolan also used a range of non-monetary indicators together with income to present a more comprehensive picture of the evolution of child poverty in Ireland. Those measures that combine poverty lines with experience of basic deprivation confirm that children were at a substantial disadvantage vis-à-vis adults in 1994. Unlike the poverty lines, these combined measures showed no narrowing in that gap between 1994 and 1997, mainly because deprivation levels for adults declined on average more rapidly than for children. Thus, the Nolan study addresses child-poverty progress in an era of rising incomes.

Joachim R. Frick and Gert G. Wagner's chapter discusses the living conditions and the long-term prospects of immigrant children, an emerging issue throughout the industrialised world. Frick and Wagner compare the situation and prospects of immigrant children in Germany to those born to native-born German parents. Both monetary and non-monetary indicators show a "remarkable difference" in terms of living conditions between native-born German children and those born to immigrants and foreigners. The authors also find that, according to some of the indicators used in this study, the position of children in the eastern part of Germany – the former German Democratic Republic – is quite similar to the situation of non-native children in the western part of Germany – the states of the former Federal Republic of Germany. Although children of foreigners and immigrants are in both regions heavily subsidised by public transfers, constituting about 20% of their post-tax and post-transfer income, their relative income position is between 25% and 30% lower than the overall population.

Where there seems to have been some improvement in the position of children of immigrants and foreigners over the period 1985/86 to 1995/96, Frick and Wagner remark that the position of children of ethnic Germans has deteriorated over the same period of time. The group most exposed to poverty are children in lone-parent families, which can be explained by the low labour-force participation rates of lone mothers, caused in the past by insufficient childcare arrangements. Frick and Wagner remark that, given the overall richness of the German economy and society, poverty rates are surprisingly high among all children, regardless of the fact that they are native or foreign-born. They conclude that "the German welfare state fails – or at least has major difficulties – in giving equal chances to all children". While this comment bears some truth, it must be taken in light of the counterfactual situation of these children without immigration, or unity for Eastern German children with West Germany's economic support.

Hugh Davies and Heather Joshi study the cost of children in terms of adults' forgone income in Britain. In practice, this means mothers' incomes. Their previous research for the mid-1980s had found that motherhood reduced women's participation in the labour market and often confined their hours of work to part-time jobs. As a result, hourly earnings were lowered and, over a lifetime, mothers would earn less than childless women through having fewer years of earnings, lower hours of work and lower rates of pay. However, the developments of the 1990s tended to reduce the extent to which British mothers stayed away from the labour market while they raised children. Some of the developments on the wages front would have increased the cash penalties of not earning, particularly not earning full-time. In this study Davies and Joshi use a simulation model to generate lifetime earnings of illustrative women and their husbands, using parameters based on data observed in the mid-1990s. They report that British women with less earning power, and those of middle earning power and more than one child, are less likely to combine child rearing and work. Maternity leave and more 'family friendly' enterprise policies have increased the employment continuity around the time of childbirth, but another important factor was the increased availability of childcare in Britain. British women who can afford it increasingly take advantage of this possibility. Expenditures on childcare are increasingly substituting for self-provisioning and Davies and Joshi conclude that "the indirect costs of motherhood are thus being transformed for more women into the direct cost of day care".

Richard Percival and Ann Harding examine the public and private costs of children in Australia, estimating the private cost of children in two-parent families and comparing them to selected public costs. Private costs of children refer to amounts that parents actually spend on their children. Indirect costs, such as the reduction of working hours and paid labour-force participation mentioned in the study by Davies and Joshi, are not taken into account by Percival and Harding. Rather, they estimate the cost of a child as the difference in average expenditures between households where only a couple is present, and households where a couple and one or more children are present, given that households enjoy an equivalent standard of living. The measure of the material standard of living was the proportion of the total expenditure spent on a basket of goods that included food consumed at home, fuel and power. The costs of the children reported in the study are averaged estimates derived from reporting what parents spend to meet all household costs. The analysis was restricted to couple households, and therefore the results do not indicate what the cost of children would be in other types of household. Considering these restrictions, the Percival and Harding study produces some important findings. As expected, they find that the average costs of children in Australian families varied according to the age of the child, the income of the parents and the number of children in the family, and that government assistance to families in the form of cash transfers, outlays on education, health and childcare increased in magnitude as children grew older. They also find that government outlays were particularly important for lower-income families, amounting to 75% of total outlays for children living in the bottom-quintile families.

The chapter by Candace Currie studies the impact of social inequality during childhood and adolescence, in terms of impairment to health and well-being, using data from the 1997/98 WHO-HBSC[1] cross-national survey. As far as we know, this data source has never before been employed to study the impact of child poverty on health outcomes. The conceptual framework taken in the chapter uses economic well-being as a predictor of child health and social well-being, with the latter measured against a number of psychosocial health indicators self-reported by children. These include, for example, reported health, reported happiness, reported symptoms, reported self-confidence and helplessness. Health behaviours, such as smoking, alcohol use, physical activity and nutrition are considered to be health 'outcomes'. Currie finds that countries in which a relatively high proportion of children experience low material household affluence correspond powerfully to countries where high levels of poor self-reported health and happiness exist. Patterns of association within countries are also visible, although less dramatic. The most evident associations are between perceived household wealth and perceived physical and psychosocial health, including confidence and helplessness. This study illustrates the potential as well as the limitations offered by the WHO-HBSC cross-national survey. Currie suggests that even more possibilities will be offered to her line of research by the next HBSC cross-national survey in 2001/02 which will include a wider range of indicators of positive health and indicators of social capital, in addition to the current measures of socioeconomic circumstances, health and well-being. We conclude that this paper only scratches the surface of the types of analyses that could be carried out with the HBSC data.

Notes

[1] World Health Organisation – *Health Behaviour in School-Aged Children.*

NINE

The impact of economic change on child welfare in Central Asia

Jane Falkingham[1]

Introduction

There is a growing literature on the welfare impact of economic transition in Central and Eastern Europe (CEE) and the former Soviet Union (FSU) (Falkingham et al, 1997; Milanovic, 1998; UNDP, 1999). Most has concentrated on household welfare[2]. This paper, however, takes as its focus the impact of recent economic changes on the welfare of children. Why children? First, children are worthy of attention in terms of their numerical significance. The five Central Asian Republics (CARs) together contain over 23 million people aged under 18 and children constitute two fifths of the region's population. Second, and more important, today's children are tomorrow's adults. The experiences of today's young people will, to a large degree, determine the shape of the region's future. As such, it is essential to understand how the recent economic transition has affected the risks they face during their own transition through childhood to adulthood. Any lost development during the period of childhood cannot easily be recouped later in life, resulting in a generation at risk of social exclusion.

This chapter takes a multidimensional view of child well-being. The indicators discussed include both economic measures of poverty based on incomes and expenditures and selected capability-based indicators, reflecting the health and survival, and the education and personal development of children and their social inclusion/exclusion. We begin with a brief discussion of the demographic significance of children in the Central Asian context. This is followed by a discussion of the recent macroeconomic changes in the region and the possible ways in which these changes may impact upon the welfare of children. The available evidence concerning recent trends in both the material poverty and capability welfare of children in Central Asia is then presented and conclusions drawn.

Children in Central Asia

Children are at the heart of Central Asian society and culture. The five CARs together contain over 23 million people aged under 18, and children make up between 35% (in Kazakhstan) and 48% (in Tajikistan) of the national populations. These youthful Central Asian populations contrast sharply with those of the European republics of the FSU and CEE, where children account for between one fifth and one quarter of the population.

The CARs have relatively high fertility, with women in the region (at least until 1990) typically giving birth to 4-5 children. The birth rate, however, declined significantly in all the CARs during the early 1990s, following independence – by between one quarter in Uzbekistan and one half in Tajikistan. The fall in births has resulted in a sharp drop in both the number of children under five and the share of under-five-year-olds in the total population (Figure 9.1). This trend has been most marked in Tajikistan where children under five made up 18% of the population in 1990, but 'just' 13.5% by 1998.

Despite recent declines in the birth rate, children under age five still constitute one out of every ten people in Central Asia, and children under 16 account for two out of every five. Given this, any economic change which impacts upon the population will by definition affect children. Equally, any change that affects children will also affect the majority of households. In Kyrgyzstan, in 1996, 70% of households contained at least one child under 16 and 86% of individuals lived in a household containing at least one child under 16. Below we review recent macroeconomic trends in Central Asia and the transmission mechanisms whereby such changes may affect children and families.

Macroeconomic change and child welfare

Recent macroeconomic trends

During the Soviet period, Central Asia received large transfers from central government. It is estimated that such transfers represented around 10% of regional gross domestic product (Bauer et al, 1998). The withdrawal

Figure 9.1: Share of children aged under five in total population, Central Asia 1990-98

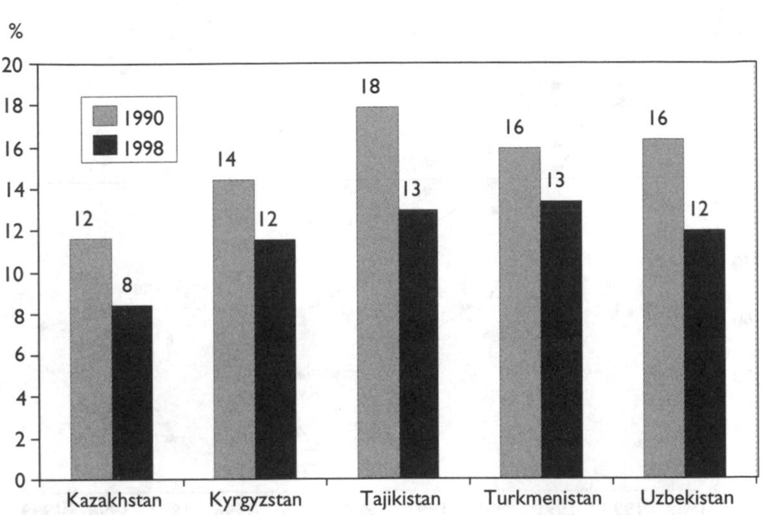

Source: Transmonee database, UNICEF

of subsidies from Moscow following independence, combined with the interruption of inter-republican trade within the former USSR and the impact of tight government-stabilisation policies, resulted in severe economic depression across the region. There were signs of recovery in the mid-1990s, but the recent turmoil within the Russian economy, with the subsequent loss of the region's export markets to Russia and exchange-rate instability following the collapse of the rouble, has halted any progress.

The general picture since independence has thus been one of falling output – a smaller 'cake'; declining real wages and growing unemployment leading to rising inequality – a more unevenly shared cake; and a drop in real government expenditure on social services – resulting in a smaller slice of the cake to fund expenditures on children.

Falling output

Figure 9.2 shows the change in real GDP since 1989[3]. Growth was negative in all countries in the region up to 1995, since when there has been a gradual reversal of fortunes, with the exception of Turkmenistan, which experienced a 25% drop in GDP in 1997. Recovery has been slow and, despite recent improvements, real output remains significantly

Figure 9.2: Cumulative change in real GDP in Central Asia, 1989-99 (1989=100)

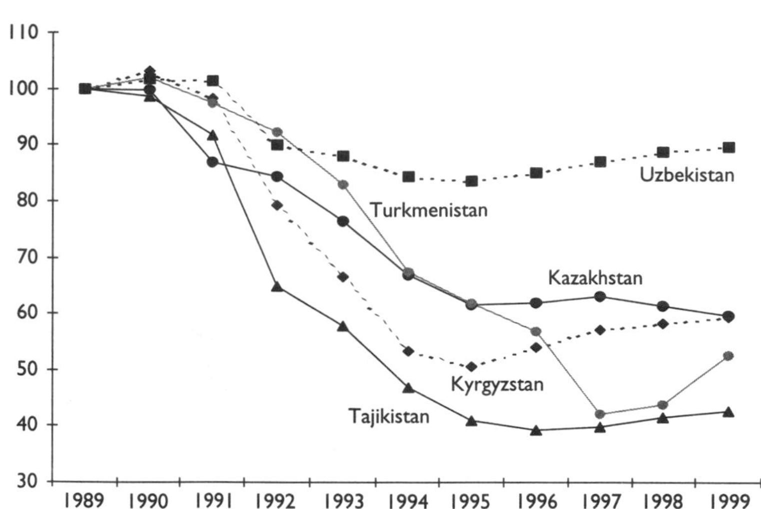

Source: 1989-98 from Transmonee database, UNICEF; projections for 1999 from EBRD Transition Report Update, April 1999

below pre-transition levels. In 1999, real GDP was still below half its pre-transition level in Tajikistan and Turkmenistan and a third below in Kyrgyzstan and Kazakhstan.

The diversity of experience in Figure 9.2 reflects the fact that the CARs vary greatly in their initial resource endowments and also have followed different policy directions since independence. Kazakhstan and Turkmenistan possess the most favourable endowments for long-term growth, with considerable oil and gas reserves. However, exploitation has been hampered by the lack of infrastructure, in particular pipelines to markets outside the FSU. Tajikistan has abundant hydroelectric reserves, as well as substantial deposits of coal, gold and silver. Until recently, however, the country has been engaged in a protracted civil war and, since the establishment of peace, problems of accessibility to both reserves and markets have hindered exploitation. The other main export commodity in the region is cotton. Uzbekistan is the world's fifth largest cotton producer and second largest cotton exporter, and also has significant gold reserves. Unlike energy reserves, both of these commodities are easy to export and Uzbekistan has benefited from the buoyant international markets for cotton and gold. This goes some way towards explaining the

Table 9.1: Selected macroeconomic indicators in Central Asia since independence

	Real GDP (Index 1991 =100)		Price inflation (% change in end year consumer prices)		Real wages (Index 1991 =100)		Registered unemployment (%)	
	1993	**1998**	**1993**	**1998**	**1994**	**1997**	**1993**	**1998**
Kazakhstan	87	65	2,169	2	32.9	36.6	0.6	4.1[a]
Kyrgyzstan	68	65	1,363	18	59.4	49.1	0.2	3.2[a]
Tajikistan	63	44	7,344	3		5.0[b]	1.2	3.1
Turkmenistan	85	46	9,750	20	52.9	30.9		3.0[c]
Uzbekistan	87	88	885	40			0.3	0.6

Notes: [a]1997, [b]estimate in Mills (1998), [c]1995
Source: EBRD *Transition Report Update* (1999)

comparatively small loss of output experienced by Uzbekistan in contrast to the other CARs.

Furthermore, the pace of transition has not been consistent across the region (Table 9.1). Kyrgyzstan and Kazakhstan were quick to embrace market reform and liberalised prices in 1992-93. Privatisation of small and medium enterprises is now well advanced in both countries (EBRD, 1999). In December 1998, Kyrgyzstan became the first country in the FSU to join the World Trade Organisation. In contrast, Uzbekistan and Turkmenistan have been slow, even reluctant, to reform, while in Tajikistan reform was delayed by civil war. However, since the signing of the peace agreement in mid-1997, the privatisation process in Tajikistan has accelerated. It is notable that Uzbekistan, the slowest reformer, has also suffered the lowest loss of output. It remains to be seen whether the gradual strategy pursued by Uzbekistan has long-term costs in terms of the potential for economic growth that will outweigh the short-term benefits (Pomfret, 1999).

Growing unemployment

The falls in output have been accompanied by a reduction in employment opportunities and the emergence of unemployment across the region. It should be noted that the figures on registered unemployment in Table 9.1 represent only a fraction of real unemployment in the CARs. For many people there is little incentive to register, as few are entitled to any benefits and few vacancies are available. Furthermore, official registered unemployment does not take account of the very extensive under-employment in many state-owned enterprises and agricultural collectives. Many employees are still on the 'payroll' even although they have not been paid for several months, or, in extreme cases, years. The true level of unemployment is thought to be much higher. Using the International Labour Organisation (ILO) definition[4], unemployment is estimated to be around 30% in Tajikistan (Mills, 1998), 20% in Kyrgyzstan (EBRD, 1998), 11% for men and 6% for women in Uzbekistan (Coudouel, 1998), and 6% in Kazakhstan (World Bank, 1998).

There is some evidence that women are disproportionately bearing the cost of a shrinking labour market. Women's labour-force participation rates in the Soviet period were much higher than in other industrialised countries. Since independence, however, a greater proportion of female employees have been laid off and more are on unpaid leave than their male counter-parts. In Kazakhstan in 1995, 60% of the people 'discharged' from state enterprises were women (Tadjbakhsh, 1999) while in Kyrgyzstan an ILO survey found that women accounted for nearly two thirds of job losses (Evans-Klock and Samorodov, 1998). The same ILO survey also found that for every three employed women in Kyrgyzstan, one was listed as being on maternity leave. It is argued that most of the women listed as on maternity leave should actually be classified as either having left the labour force or in disguised unemployment (Evans-Klock and Samarodov, 1998, p 62).

Once out of work, women experience greater difficulty in re-entering the labour market. Evans-Klock and Samorodov (1998) report clear evidence of gender bias in hiring decisions. On average, women were hired for just one out of every four new jobs in Kyrgyzstan, with no significant difference in hiring preferences between privatised and state enterprises. The ILO survey also found that when in work, women were much less likely than men to receive training from their employers. In Kyrgyzstan one out of two employees were women, but on average only one in four trainees were women.

Rising unemployment has resulted in a growth in the number of children living in households where one or more members are unemployed and the emergence of workless households, where no member of the household is gainfully employed (either because of unemployment or being out of the labour market). Using the ILO definition of work, in Kyrgyzstan in 1996 a staggering 34% of children aged under than 10 lived in a household where no one was employed (author's own analysis of the Kyrgyz Living Standards Survey; KLSS). This trend is of concern for several reasons, the most obvious being the association with the risk of children being poor. Further, the lack of connection with the labour market may negatively affect children's aspirations in terms of future employment, and the contacts and networks available to them for securing employment. Lack of work may also result in increased tension within the family with subsequent negative impact on psychosocial well-being of the children.

Falling real wages

Real wages have declined even further than real output. It is estimated that in Tajikistan average real wages in 1998 were only 2% of their pre-1989 level. Elsewhere, the level of real wages has fallen to between a third to a half of their pre-independence value, except in Uzbekistan, where the latest International Monetary Fund (IMF) estimates show the average wage in 1997 was worth 123% that in 1991 (IMF, 1998). Again, there is some evidence that women's wages have fallen more than men's. In the Soviet period a high proportion of public-sector workers were women (especially in education and health). These are now the sectors where wages have not been paid and where real pay rates have suffered the greatest fall in value.

Lower real wage levels have obvious implications for child welfare in terms of the material resources available to families. Furthermore, there is evidence that a greater proportion of income earned and controlled by women is spent on children than income earned by men. Thus the greater decline in the relative value of women's wages may mean that the proportion of household resources 'enjoyed' by children may also be shrinking.

Rising inequality

In common with other countries in transition, the CARs have witnessed a rise in the inequality of incomes. In the Soviet Union the overall distribution of income was much more egalitarian than in most market economies (Atkinson and Micklewright, 1992; Milanovic, 1998). In 1989 it is estimated that the Gini coefficient for per capita income in the CARs, calculated from the Family Budget Surveys, ranged from 0.29 in Kyrgyzstan and Kazakhstan to 0.31 in Tajikistan and Turkmenistan, with Uzbekistan occupying a middle position of 0.30. By 1993 the Gini coefficient had increased to 0.33 in Kazakhstan and Uzbekistan, 0.35 in Kyrgyzstan and 0.36 in Turkmenistan. To put these figures into perspective, the increase in inequality in Kyrgyzstan, where the coefficient increased by 0.017 per annum, occurred at a rate two and a half times as fast as that recorded in the fastest inequality-increasing Western countries in the 1980s. The level of inequality in 1993, with a Gini coefficient of 0.35, overtook that of India (0.34 in 1992).

The growth in income inequality is the result of a number of factors, including restructuring of economic activity and a greater proportion of income coming from the private sector, a shift in the distribution of wages, the growth of open unemployment, and the redistribution of wealth and privatisation of state assets (Falkingham, 1999).

Other dimensions of inequality have also grown. As already noted, gender disparities have widened as women's employment opportunities and wages have deteriorated relative to men's. In addition to decline in the economic sphere, women's participation in public life has also contracted – in 1989 30% of parliamentarians were women, by 1998 women deputies had fallen to just 5% across the region (Tadjbakhsh, 1999). This may have a negative impact on child welfare, as power structures dominated by men may be less sensitive to issues viewed to be women's responsibility such as child rearing and other reproductive functions. Furthermore, reduced female participation may adversely affect girl children in terms of role models and their aspirations.

Falling government expenditure

The fall in GDP has been accompanied by a growing incapacity of governments throughout the region to mobilise resources. Government revenues have fallen due to the loss of union budget transfers and the erosion of the tax base due to declining output. The ability to raise taxes has been further hampered by the dramatic growth of the informal sector. For example, tax collection rates reached a low of about 13% of GDP in Kazakhstan in 1997 (EBRD, 1998).

As a result of lower revenues, and despite all countries in the region running fiscal deficits, government expenditures as a share of GDP have fallen sharply. Between 1991 and 1997 government expenditures as a share of GDP in Tajikistan fell by nearly two thirds from 50% to 17%. Elsewhere proportionate declines have ranged from around a third in Uzbekistan to a fifth in Kyrgyzstan.

The collapse in GDP combined with lower government spending has

Table 9.2 Changes in social spending in Central Asia since Independence

	Government expenditure as % GDP		Social Security expenditure as % GDP		Education expenditure as % GDP		Healthcare expenditure as % GDP	
	1991	1997	1991	1996	1991	1996	1991	1996
Kazakhstan	32.9	20.3	4.9	0.6	7.6	3.2	4.4	2.7
Kyrgyzstan	30.3	26.3	5.5	3.8	8.0[a]	5.4	5.0	2.9
Tajikistan	49.6	17.0	3.0[b]	0.2[d]	11.1[b]	3.3	6.0	1.1[c]
Turkmenistan	38.2	29.2	3.2	0.8	9.6	2.8	5.0	1.5[c]
Uzbekistan	52.7	32.8	7.7	2.5	10.2[b]	7.4[c]	5.9	3.1

[a]1990; [b]1992; [c]1995; [d]1997

Sources: Column 1 EBRD (1999); Columns 2 & 3 Mehrotra (1999); Column 4 Transmonee Database, UNICEF

meant that real allocations to the social sectors have declined precipitously (Table 9.2). Spending on social protection has fallen dramatically, while the level of real spending in the health and education sectors has declined sharply to between only a quarter to a third of pre-independence levels. This has important implications for child welfare, as children are the main beneficiaries of social spending.

Prior to independence, a wide variety of cash transfer payments were provided and it is estimated that social transfers made up 14% of total gross income (Atkinson and Micklewright, 1992). The majority of these payments were for families with children, including one-off birth payments, payments for mothers on maternity or childcare leave, monthly allowances for children aged 0-18 months and 15-16 years, additional benefits for single mothers and mothers of more than 4 children, payment for expenses related to the education of disabled children and several others. The other main group of beneficiaries was older people, with a range of old age and work-related pensions.

The economic dislocation during transmission has weakened the ability to continue to provide a universal system of benefits to all families with children. Table 9.2 shows that government spending on social protection has declined sharply. With fewer resources and a growing number of people in 'need', targeting of family allowances has now been introduced in all the countries – with payments in most cases being limited to families where the per capita income is less than some notional subsistence level

Figure 9.3: Pathways between macroeconomic change and its impact on child welfare

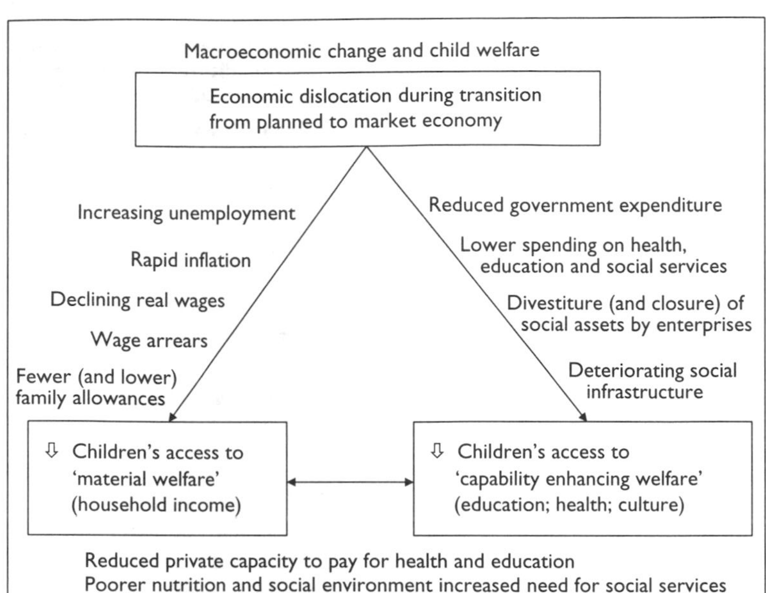

(often the minimum wage). In addition, the real value of the benefits paid has fallen. Lower social spending has also negatively affected other sectors such as health and education, which are vital for children's long-term development.

The welfare impact of macroeconomic change – possible transmission mechanisms

Figure 9.3 illustrates the mechanisms by which recent macroeconomic changes may impact upon the well-being of children and their families. First, there is the direct impact on the level of material well-being enjoyed by children as measured by household income. Increasing unemployment, rapid inflation, growing wage arrears and declining real wages when they are paid, as well as tighter eligibility for family allowances and lower levels of benefit when in payment, all combine to reduce the resources available to households and increase the risk of child poverty.

Second, reduced government expenditures on social services along with the closure of some services that were previously provided by the enterprise (eg, kindergartens) and deteriorating social infrastructure (roads, transport, etc) reduce the 'benefits-in-kind' that children and households receive. The outcome of lower government spending on social services such as education and basic healthcare may either result in a drop in quality or a drop in quantity or both. One possible response is that providers (schools, hospitals, doctors and teachers) may turn to their clients to make good the shortfall in public spending by introducing charges for services such as textbooks, school meals, immunisations, drugs and regular health checks. If families are not in a position to pay these charges, this may result in children's loss of access to health and education and a consequent drop in child 'capability' well-being, the definition of which is discussed later.

Furthermore, lower household income may itself result in poor child nutrition. Deteriorating child health may in turn then increase the need for healthcare services, which are already under resource pressure and which families cannot afford to purchase, so setting up a vicious circle of 'increased need and reduced ability to pay'. The combination of lower household resources and lower government expenditure will impact upon children differently at different stages of the lifecycle – although low household income and 'living in poverty' will affect all members negatively regardless of age.

Figure 9.4 presents a typology of the risks across the lifecycle that may result from lower public and private spending on social services and their possible outcomes and indicators. The list is far from complete but serves to emphasise the important relationship between macroeconomic change and child welfare.

The key risks for younger children flow from reduced access to healthcare services combined with low income, and the main outcomes are poorer health and nutrition status. As children get older, risks are increasingly connected to reduced access to both education and health spending. Outcomes on schooling are three-fold. First, decreased access may reduce enrolment. Parents who are unable to afford the cost of textbooks, uniforms, or even shoes, may simply withdraw their children altogether. Second, even if enrolled, children may not actually attend school regularly, either for the reasons given above or because the children are needed as family labour (working in the home looking after younger children, or on family land or in the hired labour market to supplement household income). Finally children may be enrolled and attending school, but may not actually be learning anything; the teacher may be absent on a second job (that actually pays wages), there may be no textbooks, it

Figure 9.4: Typology of risk, outcomes and indicators faced by children in transition across the lifecycle

Age	Risks	Outcomes	Indicators
0-1	↓ pre and ante natal care	↑ morbidity and mortality	Low birth weight Infant mortality rate
1-4	↓ immunisation ↓ pre-school provision ↓ milk kitchens	↑ morbidity ↓ nutritional status	Immunisation rates Child mortality rate Anthropometric measures
5-9	↓ access to free education (charges; ↑ bus fares; ↑ cost of uniform; family ↓ income) ↓ school meals ↓ child sanatoria	↓ school enrolement ↓ school attendance ↓ learning achievement ↓ nutritional status ↑ morbidity	Enrolement rates Test scores Age-specific mortality rates
10-14	↓ access to 'free' education school absenteeism as ↑ family labour (synergy with ↓ family income) ↓ summer pioneer camps	↓ school enrolement ↓ school attendance ↓ learning achievement ↑ morbidity	Enrolement rates Test scores Age-specific mortality rates
15-19	↓ participation in schooling beyond compulsory period (synergy with ↓ family income) ↓ vocational training ↓ youth clubs	↓ qualifications ↑ job opportunities ↑ youth unemployment ↑ informal activity ↑ dillusion and social exclusion ↑ drug and alcohol abuse ↑ sexual activity	Qualifications Youth unemployment rates Suicide rate Juvenile crime rates Teen pregnancy rate STD incidence and prevalence

may be too cold to concentrate due to lack of heat, or the child may be anaemic and/or malnourished and too lethargic to learn.

In addition, adolescent children may also face the risk of lower participation – in education, the labour market and civil society – and the subsequent outcome of increased feelings of social exclusion and a rise in anti-social behaviour. In the next section the evidence for recent changes in both material and capability welfare of children is examined, using some of the indicators highlighted in this typology.

Material poverty

Poverty in Central Asia

Prior to independence, the CARs were among the poorest in the FSU. Atkinson and Micklewright (1992), using data from the Family Budget Surveys (FBS) and taking a per capita income of less than 75 rubles as the national 'poverty threshold', estimated that for the FSU as a whole 31 million people, or 11% of the population, were poor by this standard. However, within Central Asia over half (51%) of those living in Tajikistan were poor by this standard – 44% in Uzbekistan, 35% in Turkmenistan, 33% in Kyrgyzstan and 16% in Kazakhstan. Thus even before the turmoil of the early 1990s a significant proportion of the population were surviving on a low income. Since the break-up of the Soviet Union, the absolute number of people, as well as the proportion of the population, who are poor has increased. In addition to exacerbating the disadvantage of the 'old poor' – pensioners, families with large numbers of children and single-parent-family children (Braithwaite, 1995) – the economic dislocation of transition has also given rise to new groups of poor, including the families of workers 'on leave without pay', the long-term unemployed, agricultural workers, young people in search of their first job, and a growing number of refugees, both economic refugees and persons displaced as a result of civil conflict.

Since 1993, World Bank sponsored *Living Standard Measurement Surveys* (LSMS) have been held in four of the Republics – Kazakhstan, Kyrgyzstan, Turkmenistan and Tajikistan[5]. The LSMS are nationally representative multipurpose surveys, which collect detailed information on a range of topics, including income, expenditure and consumption as well as use of education, health and employment. The strength of such surveys is that they allow detailed analysis of the determinants of various outcomes as well as the measurement of living standards. As Grosh (1991) notes, an

Table 9.3: Poverty indicators in the Central Asia republics

	Poverty rate (% poor)	Gini coefficient
Kazakhstan (1996)[a]		
Households		0.35
Individuals	34.6	
Kyrgyzstan (1996)[b]		
Households	60.5	0.46
Individuals	68.7	
Kyrgyzstan (1993)[b]		
Households	39.7	0.58
Individuals	45.4	

Notes: [a]Welfare indicator: per capita household expenditure. Poverty line: Government's subsistence minimum (prozhitochnyi minimum) for single adult. [b]Welfare indicator: total household expenditure. Poverty line: household specific 'high cost' poverty basket (reflecting composition of household by sex and age).

Sources: World Bank, 1995, 1998; Mimeo: Kyrgyzstan Analysis Report, Spring 1996 LSMS

LSMS survey permits analysis of links between different aspects of household well-being, for example, "the impact of education on nutrition, the effect of health on employment, and the relationship between income and fertility". Thus they allow us to look at both incomes and outcomes. Table 9.3 presents some information on the incidence of poverty for Kazakhstan (1996) and Kyrgyzstan (in 1993 and 1996). In all three surveys, and in contrast to the results from the FBS mentioned earlier, household expenditure rather than income has been taken as the welfare indicator. Note that the definition of the poverty line varied between the two countries, hence the numbers are not directly comparable cross-nationally. Nevertheless, the survey evidence clearly shows an increase in the incidence of poverty in Kyrgyzstan (the only country for which there is currently survey data over time), from 40% in 1993 to 61% in 1996. Over a third of individuals are estimated to be living below the subsistence level in Kazakhstan in 1996.

Elsewhere in the region poverty is also widespread. Uzbekistan appears to be in the most favourable position with overall incidence of poverty with 'only' 30% of the population being poor in 1995, estimated from a household survey conducted by the European University Institute (Coudouel, 1998). The 1996 United Nations Development Programme (UNDP) Human Development Report for Turkmenistan estimates that over half the population are poor. There is as yet no reliable evidence of the extent of poverty in Tajikistan, although a recent survey carried out by ECHO in August 1997 found one in every six households to be 'food insecure' (Freckleton, 1997). It is estimated that as many as 85% of the population of 6 million could be considered poor, and of these 700,000 (12%) are extremely poor and a further 300,000 (or 5% of the population) are 'helplessly destitute' (Mills, 1998). Of course, poverty rates depend both upon the poverty line chosen and the definition of income (or expenditure) that is compared against this line. Nevertheless the above data indicate that a significant proportion of people in Central Asia are surviving on a low level of material resources.

Child poverty

Given that children make up 40% of the population of the region, even without further information it would be safe to say child poverty is likely to be a common problem. However, evidence from available survey data shows that poor households are generally larger than non-poor households, and that households with a large number of children are most at risk of poverty.

In Kazakhstan, those households in the bottom fifth of the income distribution had, on average, two thirds more children than those at the top of the distribution. Families with young children were disproportionately represented in the lower quintiles, with over 40% of bottom quintile households having small children compared to less than a quarter of all households (World Bank, 1998). In Kyrgyzstan, although children under 16 constituted 37% of the total survey population, they made up 43% of the poor. Thus it appears that children are more at risk of living in poverty than other groups.

Little of the available published data is analysed by age groups. Figure 9.5 shows the incidence of poverty among children of different age groups, using data from the LSMS for Kyrgyzstan in 1993 and 1996. There are several points to note: first, the poverty rate is higher among children than in the population in general; second, younger children are more likely to be poor than older children; and third, child poverty rates increased markedly between 1993-96.

Capability poverty

It is increasingly recognised that material resources, or rather the lack thereof, reflect just one, albeit very important, dimension of poverty. Monetary measures fail to capture other important aspects of individual

Figure 9.5: Percentage of children living in poverty, Kyrgyzstan (1993-96)

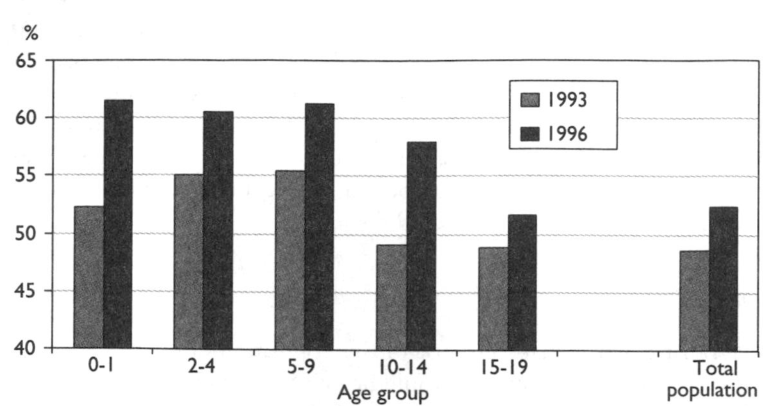

Source: Author's analysis of KMPS (1993) and KLSS (1996)

well-being such as community resources, social relations, culture, personal security and the natural environment. Dreze and Sen (1995) have defined capabilities as the alternative combinations of 'functionings' – or 'doings and beings' a person achieves – from which a person can choose. Micklewright and Stewart (1999) identify four key functionings that a child needs in order to lead what Amartya Sen has referred to as a 'good life': material well-being, health and survival, education and personal development, and social inclusion/participation.

McKinley (1997) has proposed a system of complementary poverty measures which focus on capability poverty, incorporating access to public services, assets and employment, as well as income poverty, covering the ability to 'purchase' food, clothing and shelter. Capability poverty focuses on an individual's capacity to live a healthy life, free of avoidable morbidity, having adequate nourishment, being informed and knowledgeable, being capable of reproduction, enjoying personal security, and being able to freely and actively participate in society. Material resources at some level are generally necessary for some of these activities, but they alone are not sufficient. Therefore, capability poverty goes beyond income poverty in terms of measuring actual well-being.

Capability poverty can be measured directly in terms of capabilities themselves; for example, the percentage of children who are underweight; or indirectly in terms of access to opportunities, or the means of capabilities, such as access to trained health personnel at birth, and access to education

Figure 9.6: Infant mortality rates in Central Asia (1989-97) (deaths under age one per 1,000 live births)

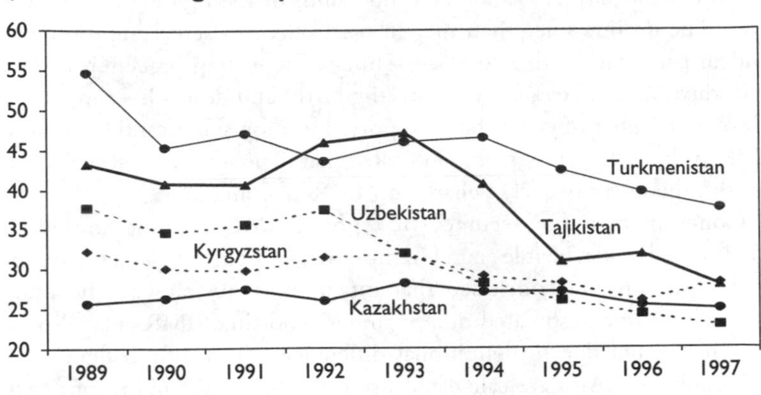

Source: Transmonee database, UNICEF

and other public services. As discussed earlier, with the introduction of charges for healthcare, textbooks, school lunches and bus fares, many children's access to basic social services has been severely eroded; and it is likely that this will be reflected in a deterioration of the indicators of child capability poverty. Following the approach adopted in Figure 9.4, the evidence is now examined concerning recent trends in capability poverty for children at different stages of the life course.

Children under 1

Infant mortality

The ultimate indicator of capability poverty is mortality. As Sen (1998) points out, all other 'capabilities' are contingent on being alive. Figure 9.6 presents information on the level and trend in infant mortality in the CARs. There are two points to note. First, infant mortality rates (IMR) in the region are relatively high compared to elsewhere in the FSU and CEE. For example, in 1997 IMR in the CARs varied from 22.8 per 1,000 live births in Uzbekistan to 37.5/1,000 in Turkmenistan. These compare with rates of 17.2/1,000 in Russia, 15.4/1,000 in Armenia, 14.0/ 1,000 in Ukraine and 10.2/1,000 in Poland (UNICEF, 1999). Second, although still relatively high, recorded infant mortality has fallen in all the republics since independence.

The trend in IMR has not been uniform across the region. Infant mortality rose in Tajikistan between 1991 and 1993 and since then has fallen dramatically. 1993 marked the zenith of the fighting in the civil war. The decline since then may in part reflect an actual improvement and in part may be due to a worsening of reporting procedures. The introduction of a charge for registering births and deaths has caused the absolute number of events being reported to drop significantly. Because IMR is the only demographic indicator that depends on both births and deaths, the effect of such a charge on IMR is ambiguous.

Concerns over the accuracy of reported IMR are not limited to Tajikistan. Becker, Hemley and Urzhumova (1996) investigated the trends in Kazakhstan and concluded that infant mortality rates in the mid-1990s were underestimated due to under-reporting. IMR may also be underestimated due to definitional differences. The official figures on IMR for the CARs are calculated using the Soviet definition of a 'live birth' which tends to underestimate IMR as compared to the WHO definition. Estimates from the recent Demographic and Health Surveys (DHS) indicate rates that are significantly higher than the official figures, with IMR of 40/1,000 for Kazakhstan in 1995, 49/1,000 for Uzbekistan in 1996, and 61/1,000 for Kyrgyzstan in 1997. Such figures compared with IMR of 44/1,000 in Nicaragua, 47/1,000 in Indonesia and 57/1,000 in Egypt (UNDP, 1998).

Children under 5

Nutritional status

The trends in material poverty noted above may impact upon children's nutritional status, with subsequent long-term developmental consequences. The DHS contain valuable information on the nutritional status of young children (aged under 36 months) for the three republics in which the surveys have been conducted. Figure 9.7 below shows information for the three standard indices of physical growth: height-for-age (percent stunted reflects chronic undernutrition), weight-for-height (percent wasted reflects acute or recent malnutrition), and weight-for-age (percent underweight is a good overall indicator of the child population's nutritional health). In a healthy, well-nourished population of children, it is expected that 2.3% of children will fall below two standard deviations of the reference population and will be classified as stunted, wasted or underweight. The figures also present data on the proportion of children under 3 with moderate or severe anaemia.

Figure 9.7: Nutritional status of children in Central Asia

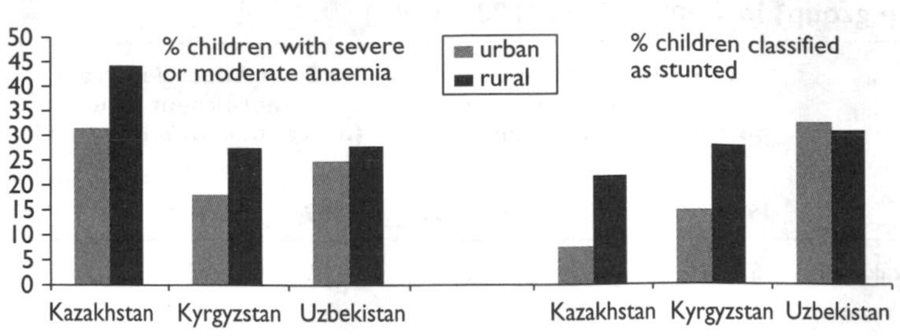

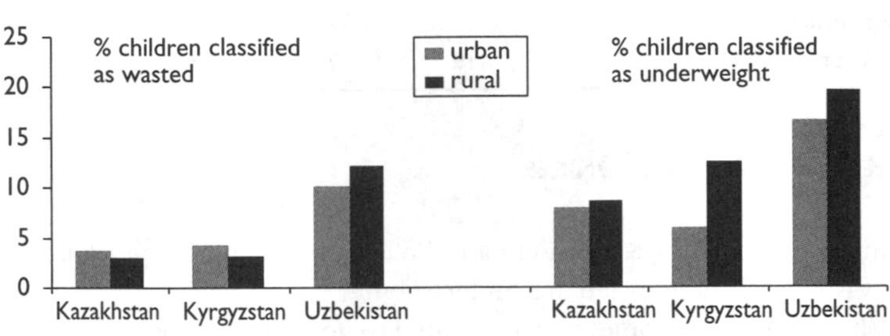

Source: Kazakhstan DHS 1995, Uzbekistan DHS 1996, The Kyrgyz Republic DHS 1997

It is clear from Figure 9.7 that the nutritional status of children in the CARs is a major cause for concern. The percentage of children classified as stunted is significantly greater than the WHO standard of 2.3% in all instances. Forty-four percent of children under 3 years old suffered from moderate or severe anaemia in rural areas in Kazakhstan in 1995 and nearly a third in urban areas. Elsewhere in the region the proportion ranges from a fifth to a quarter. It is particularly worrying to note that the proportion of children classified as stunted or wasted is highest in Uzbekistan. Yet on other (economic) indicators Uzbekistan appears better off than its neighbours. Ismail and Micklewright (1997), using an alternative data set, report significantly lower levels of malnutrition which are perhaps more in line with other evidence for Uzbekistan than those from the DHS.

Data on the nutritional status of children in Tajikistan from a survey conducted by German Agro Action in 1998 (Schumacher, 1998) present a disquieting picture. On all measures children's nutritional status has worsened over the two years 1996-98, and according to each measure the position in Tajikistan is significantly worse than elsewhere in the region. Over four out of every ten children under age five in Tajikistan are stunted

Table 9.4: Changes in school enrolment rates (% of the relevant age group) in Central Asia (1989-1997)

	Kindergarten net enrolment rate (percentage of 3-6 year olds)			Basic education gross enrolment rate (percentage of 7-15 year olds)		
	1989	1997	% change 1989-97	1989	1997	% change 1989-97
Kazakhstan	52.2	11.7	-78%	93.9	89.2	-5%
Kyrgyzstan	31.3	7.0	-78%	92.5	89.2	-4%
Tajikistan	16.7	7.7	-54%	94.1	85.5	-9%
Turkmenistan	36.0	21.0	-42%	94.3	83.1	-12%
Uzbekistan	38.5	22.7 [a]	-41%	92.2	89.7	-3%

Note: [a] 1996

Source: Transmonee, database UNICEF

(compared to 16% in Kazakhstan and 25% Kyrgyzstan), over one in ten are wasted and three in ten are underweight.

What of other outcomes that are related to government social spending as well as family resources? The decrease in real spending on education, combined with the divestiture of social assets from the newly privatised enterprises has resulted in a fall in the proportion of children under five enrolled in pre-school (see Table 9.4 above).

Prior to independence, attendance at kindergarten was widespread. About one half of children in the target age group were enrolled at kindergartens in Kazakhstan, and around a third in Uzbekistan, Turkmenistan and Kyrgyzstan. Enrolment was lowest in Tajikistan at less than one sixth. Since independence, rates have fallen dramatically in both Kyrgyzstan and Kazakhstan to a quarter of the level in 1989. This is in part due to the closure of enterprise based (employer-provided) kindergartens. However, enrolments have fallen by more than the drop in capacity, suggesting a fall in demand for kindergarten places as well as their supply (Klugman et al, 1997).

The decline in enrolment in kindergartens is particularly worrying given the part that they can play in raising child welfare, both in terms of freeing the parent to participate in other activities, specifically paid employment, and the developmental value of pre-school education, as well as their role in health interventions.

Children 5 to 14

Enrolment rates

The countries of the FSU, including Central Asia, began the transition with near-universal literacy. Table 9.2 shows the drop in government expenditure on both education and health services. These falls in real spending are in turn reflected in the changes in enrolment rates presented below. The trends shown in Table 9.4 indicate that several of the countries of Central Asia have suffered serious reversals in education between 1989 and 1997.

Basic education continues to be compulsory throughout the CARs, and enrolment rates for 7-15-year-olds have remained high, although they have declined from the near universal levels of the Soviet era. In Turkmenistan enrolment in primary schools fell by 12% between 1991 and 1997.

School attendance

Enrolment rates tell only part of the story. There is a growing problem of declining school attendance. In part this is due to increased child labour, particularly in rural areas. However, the poverty of families has also become a barrier to school attendance. The meaning of 'free' education has shifted. The real costs of education faced by families have risen as the cost of textbooks, supplies, meals and transportation are increasingly being passed onto the student, with the result that many poor parents can no longer afford to send their children to school. When children in Kyrgyzstan were asked why they had discontinued with their studies, the majority (68%) reported that they had finished/graduated. However among those who gave other reasons, over half said they had to leave school to earn money to live and 5% said it 'cost too much'.

Children 15 to 19

Education

Enrolment rates have also fallen in post-compulsory education establishments. The proportion of 15-18-year-olds attending general secondary schools has fallen by just over 10% in Kyrgyzstan, Kazakhstan and Turkmenistan and by a quarter in Uzbekistan. Perhaps of greater

Table 9.5: Changes in secondary, technical and vocational school enrolment rates (% of 15-18 year olds) in Central Asia (1989-1997)

	General secondary enrolment rate (percentage of 15-18-year-olds)			Technical and vocational enrolment rate (percentage of 15-18-year-olds)		
	1989	1997	% change 1989-97	1989	1997	% change 1989-97
Kazakhstan	30.4	26.5	-13%	42.4	25.7[c]	-39%
Kyrgyzstan	36.6[a]	32.4	-11%	27.3	13.2	-52%
Tajikistan	41.5	22.5	-46%	20.2	12.4[b]	-39%
Turkmenistan	39.0	34.4[b]	-12%	25.8	7.9	-69%
Uzbekistan	37.5	28.6	-24%	32.4	n/a	

Notes: [a]1990; [b]1995; [c]1996.

Source: Transmonee database, UNICEF

concern, however, is the drop in technical and vocational enrolment. There have been substantial declines across the region with enrolment rates down by over two-thirds in Turkmenistan, by a half in Kyrgyzstan and by 39% in Kazakhstan and Tajikistan.

One of the reasons for the fall in enrolment in technical and vocation establishments is that the skills they provide are increasingly seen as irrelevant. The system is still largely geared up to train young people for positions needed under the central planning system. Training is generally oriented towards obsolete Soviet technology and not the new skills needed in a market economy such as accountancy, marketing and management. The combined effect is significantly fewer 15 to 18-year-olds in education. Has the labour market been able to absorb this extra supply?

Youth unemployment rates

In the past, youth unemployment was virtually unknown. Young people were allocated to jobs after finishing education as part of the central planning process (Evans-Klock and Samorodov, 1998). Since independence this mechanism has broken down. Public enterprises are increasingly unable to take on new staff and competition for jobs with new private businesses is fierce.

As Table 9.1 illustrated, unemployment in general has risen across the region. There is little evidence on official unemployment rates by age, which makes it difficult to judge whether younger workers have suffered disproportionate job losses during the economic recession. However, data from the two rounds of the ILO surveys in Kyrgyzstan in 1992 and 1995 show that the share of employment among workers under age 25 had dropped substantially. In 1992 they made up a quarter of the work force, but by 1995 they constituted only one fifth (Evans-Klock and Samorodov, 1998). In Kazakhstan, in 1996, young people aged below 20 accounted for 15% of all registered unemployed.

Growing social exclusion?

The combined impact of lower household income, greater school absenteeism, fewer job prospects and an uncertain future has resulted in an increase in anomie. The rise in the number of young people who feel alienated from society and unable to cope with the multiple problems of unemployment, poverty and family tension and breakdown is reflected in a number of recent trends: an increase in alcoholism and drug abuse among children and young people; a rise in suicide rates; an increase in juvenile crime rates; and an increase in teenage pregnancy.

A disturbing increase in suicides committed by children and teenagers has been documented in Kazakhstan. From a level of 6.1 suicides per 100,000 children under age 20 in 1990 for boys and 2.6 for girls, by 1994 the incidence had increased to 7.8 for boys and 3.0 for girls (Bauer et al, 1998). The increase was even greater for young men in their 20s. A similar rise in adolescent male suicide rates has been found in Russia, with rates rising from 8.9/100,000 in 1990 to 13.4/100,000 in 1997 (UNICEF, 1999). Elsewhere in Central Asia, suicide rates are much lower than in Kazakhstan. Nevertheless, there is some evidence of an increase in psychological stress among teenagers. In the city of Khudjand in Tajikistan, a telephone hot-line has been set up by the 'Association of Business Women' (a local non-governmental organisation) for young women who have or are contemplating attempted suicide. The main reason cited by callers in 1996/97 was 'depression' (43%) followed by 'the difficult material situation of the family' (30%).

Another indicator of growing detachment from 'traditional' society is the increase in the number of out-of-wedlock births and the share of births to young mothers. The proportion of all births that occur to women under 20 is rising in all countries in the region. Women under 20 now account for one in eight births in Kazakhstan, one in nine in Kyrgyzstan, and one in ten in Uzbekistan. Teenage pregnancy carries physical, economic and social risks both for the young mother and the child. Both may face ostracism from society – especially in Central Asia. Children of teenage mothers have been found to be more likely to be of low birth weight or to die in the first year of life, are at greater risk of physical abuse and accidental injury, and do less well in education. The mother herself is more likely to drop out of school, with a subsequent negative impact on lifetime earnings potential. Thus the rise in teenage pregnancy could have long run developmental consequences for both the individuals involved.

Conclusions

Much has been written on the meaning of transition. Economists when referring to transition usually mean the shift from a centrally planned economy to a market orientation. In political terms the 'transition' may be one from dictatorship to democracy. From a welfare perspective the current transition in Central Asia is from a universal welfare state to a residual one and from an equitable distribution of income to rising inequality. However, from a child's perspective the recent transition may simply be from a position of security to one of uncertainty.

The human cost of economic transition has been high. Children, far from being protected from its impact, have been among those who have suffered the most. Child poverty rates exceed those of the general population. Child nutritional status is poor and levels of stunting and wasting are now more akin to those observed in parts of sub-Saharan Africa.

Yet infant mortality has fallen and remains low in comparison to other low and middle-income countries. Immunisation programmes have continued near universal coverage, and primary school enrolments have been maintained at a reasonably high level. However, there are signs that the combined impact of low social spending and low household income is beginning to take its toll. Children whose families are not able to contribute towards their education or healthcare costs face the risk of being excluded from access to these vital services. Even where they do gain access to them, the quality of the learning experience is endangered by other factors. It is not sufficient to sit in a cold school building to learn. Older children face the prospect of leaving school to enter an uncertain labour market. Job opportunities are scarce and training often inappropriate. Home life for some children is also not as secure as in the past, as financial pressures fuel domestic tensions.

Given that in the Central Asian region children take pride of place within the family and culturally children are prioritised within the family's hierarchy of needs, the observed levels of malnutrition among young children and growing absences from school are indicators of a society in severe distress. Families alone have been unable to protect children from the negative outcomes associated with transition. Governments in Central Asia need to intervene, both to protect the future human capital of their countries, and to minimise the multiple risks of material and capability poverty children face during transition. We need to ensure that the transition children experience is one that offers both opportunity and freedom and not simply uncertainty and insecurity.

Notes

[1] This chapter is based on work originally commissioned by the Central Asia regional office, UNICEF as part of a situational analysis of the welfare of children and women in the region. The support and advice of colleagues in UNICEF-CARK, and in particular Simon Stratchan, is gratefully acknowledged. The paper has also benefited from comments by John Micklewright and Ceema Namazie.

[2] The UNICEF MONEE Project Regional Monitoring Reports are a notable exception to this.

[3] There are considerable problems in compiling a consistent series of data on economic performance across time, both due to changes in definition and variation in data quality. Absolute numbers should perhaps be treated with caution. However, the overall trends are clear.

[4] The ILO definition of unemployed refers to all those aged 16 and over who are without a job, and who are available to start work in the next two weeks and who have been seeking a job in the last four weeks or are waiting to start a job already obtained.

[5] Unfortunately data are not available for Tajikistan as fieldwork has only recently been completed (June 1999), and the data file for Turkmenistan is not publicly available.

References

Atkinson, A.B. and Micklewright, J. (1992) *Economic transformation in Eastern Europe and the distribution of income*, Cambridge: Cambridge University Press.

Bauer, A., Boschmann, N., Green, D. and Kuehnast, K. (1998) *A generation at risk: Children in the Central Asian republics of Kazakstan and Kyrgyzstan*, Manila: Asian Development Bank.

Becker, C.D., Hemley D. and Urzhumova, D. (1996) *Demographic change in a period of social and economic crisis: standardized mortality trends in Kazakstan, 1975-1995*, The Economics Institute, Boulder CO, Working Paper, November.

Braithwaite, J. (1995) 'The old and new poor in Russia: trends in poverty', in *Poverty in Russia: An assessment, Vol II*, (Report no. 14110-RU), Washington, DC: World Bank.

Coudouel, A. (1998) Living standards in Uzbekistan, PhD Dissertation, Florence: European University Institute.

Dreze, J. and Sen, A. (1995) *The political economy of hunger. Selected essays*, Oxford: Oxford University Press

EBRD (1998) *Transition report*, London: EBRD.

EBRD (1999) *Transition report update April 1999*, London: EBRD.

Evans-Klock, C. and Samorodov, A. (1998) *The employment impact of privatisation and enterprise restructuring in selected transition economies*, Geneva: International Labour Office.

Falkingham, J., Klugman, J., Marnie, S. and Micklewright, J. (eds) (1997) *Household welfare in Central Asia*, Basingstoke: Macmillan Press.

Falkingham, J. (1999) *Welfare in transition: Trends in poverty and well-being in Central Asia*, CASE Discussion paper 20, London: Centre for Analysis of Social Exclusion, London School of Economics.

Freckleton, A. (1997) *Who's needy: An assessment of household food insecurity in Tajikistan*, Dushanbe: ECHO.

Grosh, M. (1991) *The household survey as a tool for policy change: Lessons from the Jamaican Survey of Living Conditions*, LSMS Working Paper No 80, Washington DC: World Bank.

International Monetary Fund (IMF) (1998) *Republic of Uzbekistan: Recent economic developments,* IMF Staff Country Report No 98/116, Washington, DC: IMF.

Ismail, S. and Micklewright, J. (1997) *Living standards and public policy in Central Asia: What can be learned from child anthropometry?*, Discussion Paper 62, Florence: UNICEF International Child Development Centre.

Klugman, J., Marnie, S., Micklewright, J. and O'Keefe, P. (1997) 'The impact of kindergarten divestiture on household welfare', in J. Falkingham, J. Klugman, S. Marnie and J. Micklewright (eds) *Household welfare in Central Asia*, Basingstoke: Macmillan Press, pp 183-201.

McKinley, T. (1997) *Beyond the line: Implementing complementary methods of poverty measurement*, UNDP Technical Support Document Number 3.

Mehrotra, S. (1999) 'Public spending priorities and the poor in Central Asia', in UNDP *Central Asia 2010*, New York, NY: UNDP, pp 48-57.

Micklewight, J. and Stewart, K. (1999) *Is the well-being of children converging in the European Union?*, Discussion Paper 69, Florence: UNICEF International Child Development Centre.

Milanovic, B. (1998) *Income, inequality and poverty in transition*, Washington, DC: World Bank Regional and Sectoral Study.

Mills, M. (1998) Tajikistan: A poverty note, Mimeo Paper, Washington, DC: World Bank.

Pomfret, R. (1999) 'Development strategies and prospects for the future', pp 58-65 in *Central Asia 2010*, New York, NY: UNDP.

Schumacher, B. (1998) *German Agro Action, nutrition health and food security survey*, Dushanbe, Tajikistan: German Agro Action.

Sen, A. (1998). 'Mortality as an indicator of economic success and failure', *Economic Journal*, vol 108, no 446, pp 1-26.

Tadjbakhsh, S. (1999) 'Impact of restructuring on women in Central Asia', in UNDP *Central Asia 2010: Prospects for human development*, New York, NY: UNDP.

UNDP (1998) *Human development report 1998*, New York, NY: Oxford University Press.

UNDP (1999) *Transition 1999. Human development report for Europe and the CIS*, New York, NY: UNDP.

UNICEF (1999) The MONEE project regional monitoring report No 6, Florence.

World Bank (1995) *The Kyrgyz Republic poverty assessment and strategy*, Report No 14380-KG, Washington, DC.

World Bank (1998) *Kazakhstan living standards during the transition*, Report No 17520-KZ, Washington, DC.

TEN

The evolution of child poverty in Ireland

Brian Nolan

Introduction

This chapter uses new data to explore the evolution of child poverty in Ireland over the past decade. The relative position of households with children deteriorated sharply in Ireland during the 1980s, as analysed in detail in Nolan and Farrell (1990). The macroeconomic environment has been very different since then, with stagnation replaced by economic growth reaching record levels since 1994. How have children fared? We seek to answer this question using household survey data up to 1997.

We begin with a very brief discussion of the macroeconomic and policy context and the data to be employed. We then present relative income poverty rates for Irish children from the early 1970s up to 1997. Non-monetary indicators of deprivation are then used to show that relative income poverty rates provide a rather partial picture in a situation of rapid growth. Finally, the implications for poverty measurement and policy are highlighted.

The macroeconomic and policy context

The central feature of the Irish economy from the 1970s has been exceptionally pronounced fluctuations in economic growth. Following a misplaced fiscal pump priming in the late 1970s, there was little or no economic growth from 1980 to 1987 as the government struggled to bring the public finances under control. In each of the years from 1987 to 1994, on the other hand, growth in real Gross Domestic Product (GDP) exceeded both the European Union and OECD average. Economic growth has been even more rapid since then, with GDP increasing by 7% to 8% per annum – the 'Celtic Tiger' phenomenon. The factors producing this growth are many and the balance between them debated (see for example Bradley et al, 1997; Barry 1999).

Unemployment rose very rapidly during the 1980s, reaching 18% of the labour force, with long-term unemployment accounting for a particularly high proportion. Unemployment proved initially resistant to the renewal of economic growth, still remaining as high as 16% by 1994, but subsequently fell rapidly, down to 11% by 1997 (and has fallen a good deal further since then). Again with something of a lag, long-term unemployment has also now fallen very considerably.

As well as unemployment, tax and social security policies during the 1980s tended to disadvantage families with children. Up to the late 1980s, social security pensions were seen as targeting resources to a needy group without distorting financial incentives to work and received priority over unemployment compensation. Since then, however, the rates of social welfare support for different contingencies have been brought much closer together. On the tax side, erosion of the real value of allowances and bands pulled an ever-increasing proportion of the population into the tax net. From the mid-1980s no account was taken of the presence of children in determining the amount of tax paid by those in the tax net, as support was concentrated in the universal (and untaxed) Child Benefit.

Child poverty has come to be recognised as a major challenge facing Irish policy makers and options for improving the situation for families with children are being intensively canvassed. In particular, there has been on-going debate about the potential of substantial increases in Child Benefit (see for example Callan et al, 1995). The best way of assisting families with the costs of childcare have also been the focus of debate, not least in the recent report by the expert Commission on the Family (1998). This makes it all the more timely to be able to explore here how Irish children have fared in recent years.

The data

The data on which we primarily rely come from two waves of the Living in Ireland Survey, the Irish element of the European Community Household Panel (ECHP). The 1994 Living in Ireland Survey was the first wave and used the Electoral Register as the sampling frame. This survey obtained information for 4,048 households, 62% of valid addresses contacted. To ensure representativeness the sample has been reweighted using weights derived from the much larger Labour Force Survey. Results from this survey on household poverty have been published in Callan et al (1996), which also contains a comprehensive description of the survey itself.

The second data set is from 1997, the fourth wave of the Living in Ireland Survey. The wave-on-wave attrition rate in the Irish panel was quite high; of the original 14,585 individuals in the 1994 sample, only 63% (9,208) were still in completed Wave 4 households. However, intensive validation and the construction of longitudinal weights suggest that the overall impact of attrition on the sample structure is slight. In particular, there is no evidence that households with specific characteristics related to the measurement of poverty (in terms of income or deprivation levels or social security recipiency) have been selectively lost from the sample. A comprehensive description of the 1997 survey, the reweighting procedure and these validation exercises is in Callan et al (1999).

In terms of income, Eurostat's main focus in the ECHP is on disposable income in the calendar year before the interview. However, the Irish questionnaire also collected details on income currently being received, and it is this current income measure that we use here. A range of questions about a range of non-monetary indicators of lifestyle and deprivation were also included, which as we shall see prove particularly useful in assessing the living standards of households. In providing a longer-term perspective we also draw on results from another household survey carried out by the Economic and Social Research Institute in 1987, employed in earlier research on poverty summarised in Nolan and Callan (1994), and the 1973 and 1980 Household Budget Surveys (CSO, 1980, 1984) carried out by the Central Statistics Office (CSO). These are the only years before 1994 for which household surveys gathering detailed income data on a large representative national sample were carried out in Ireland.

Relative income poverty for Irish children

A relative standard for measuring poverty in developed countries is by now widely though not universally accepted. The definition of poverty employed in the National Anti-Poverty Strategy recently adopted by the Irish government is typical:

> People are living in poverty if their income and resources (material, cultural and social) are so inadequate as to preclude them from having a standard of living which is regarded as acceptable by Irish society

> generally. As a result of inadequate income and resources people may be excluded and marginalised from participating in activities which are considered the norm for other people in society. (NAPS, 1997, p 3).

In actually implementing such a definition, the most common approach has been to define a poverty line in terms of income and regard those with incomes below the line as poor. To derive income poverty lines, the approach widely adopted in comparative studies of poverty across industrialised countries has been to take a proportion of mean or median income. (Some studies do of course apply a common real income standard over time or across countries; we mention the implications of such an approach in the Irish case below.)

We therefore begin by concentrating on poverty measured vis-à-vis relative income poverty lines. We follow conventional practice in adopting the household as the income and resources sharing unit throughout this study, treating all members of a particular household as having the same standard of living. Some analysis of the situation of individuals within households has been undertaken using ESRI survey data (see Rottman, 1994; Cantillon and Nolan, 1998), but we do not explore these issues here. A child is therefore poor if he or she lives in a poor household.

Again following conventional practice, equivalence scales are used to adjust household income for the differences in 'needs' associated with differing size and composition, calculating the total number of 'equivalent adults' in the household. To assess the sensitivity of the findings, three scales are used here. Where the first adult in a household is given the value 1, the first scale – derived from Irish social security rates – gives each additional adult a value of 0.66 and each child a value of 0.33. The second scale, often employed in UK research, gives each additional adult a value 0.6 and each child 0.4. The third scale, often called the 'OECD scale', attributes to each additional adult a value of 0.7 and each child 0.5. In calculating these scales, we follow the Hagenaars et al study for Eurostat (1994) in defining children as those aged under 14 years of age.

In constructing relative income poverty lines, a number of other choices have to be made. One is whether the mean or the median income is to be used; we use mean income here, but have also examined elsewhere trends with median income-based poverty lines. Mean income per equivalent adult can then be calculated either by taking the average over households or the average over individuals (attributing the equivalised income of the household to each individual in it). A case can be made for either approach and here we look at results for both. We use three

Table 10.1: Percentage of Households and Persons Below Relative Income Poverty Lines, Ireland (1973-1997)

	1973	1980	1987	1994	1997
Percentage of households below line[a]					
40% line	9.1	8.0	6.2	5.0	7.6
50% line	18.8	17.6	16.3	18.5	21.9
60% line	27.3	27.6	28.5	34.6	36.5
Percentage of persons in those households					
40% line	7.6	8.5	6.8	6.8	10.0
50% line	15.5	16.2	18.9	20.7	21.7
60% line	25.5	26.7	29.8	34.0	35.3

[a] Equivalence scale 1/0.66/0.33

cut-offs – 40%, 50% and 60% of mean income – in order to test the sensitivity of conclusions to the precise location of the poverty line.

We now look briefly at overall trends in relative income poverty over the whole period from 1973 to 1997, to put recent developments and the pattern for children in longer-term context. Table 10.1 shows the percentage of households falling below the relative income poverty lines (with the 1/0.66/0.33 scale) for the years 1973, 1980, 1987, 1994 and 1997, and then the percentage of individuals living in those households. We see that the percentage of households below the 50% line fell between 1973 and 1987, then rose to 1994 and again between 1994 and 1997. The percentage of persons in households below that line rose slightly between 1973 and 1980, more rapidly between 1980 and 1987, and continued to rise to 1994 and again to 1997. There is no consistent pattern in the trends over time with the 40% line, but with the 60% line there is a consistent increase from one observation to the next in the percentage of persons in households falling below these lines. (As detailed in Callan et al, 1996, 1999, this is not invariably found with the other equivalence scales we have employed.) The key factors underlying these trends will appear in the course of our analysis of what has been happening to children, to which we now turn.

Table 10.2 shows the percentage of Irish children and adults living in households below each of these relative income lines, with the 1/0.66/0.33 equivalence scale and averaging across households, in each of the years for which we have such results. We see that from 1973 to 1987, the risk of relative income poverty for children increased at all three cut-offs. From 1987 to 1994, that risk was unchanged at the 40% relative income cut-off, but increased again at both the 50% and 60% lines. Between

Table 10.2: Relative income poverty rates for adults and children, Ireland (1973-97)

	1973 HBS	1980 HBS	1987 ESRI	1994 LII	1997 LII
		% Children below relative income line[a]			
40% line	8.1	10.1	7.6	7.6	13.2
50% line	16.2	18.5	25.5	29.6	26.0
60% line	27.5	29.5	37.8	40.6	37.2
		% Adults below relative income line[a]			
40% line	7.4	7.7	6.5	6.5	9.1
50% line	15.1	15.2	16.1	18.0	20.5
60% line	24.4	25.4	26.5	32.0	34.4

[a] Equivalence scale 1/0.66/0.33.

1994 and 1997, however, the risk for children rose with the lowest relative line but fell markedly with the 50% and 60% lines.

By comparison, the risks for adults are much less volatile over the whole period. The risk for adults was broadly unchanged between 1973 and 1987, and then increased at the 50% and 60% lines to 1994, and at all three lines from there to 1997. In terms of the position of children versus adults, then, children had a slightly higher risk in 1973, but by 1987 a much more substantial gap had opened up with children at much higher risk using the 50% or 60% line. This gap persisted in 1994. However, since the risk for adults rose but that for children fell between 1994 and 1997 with the 50% and 60% lines, the gap between risks for children versus adults narrowed significantly over these three years. With the 40% line, on the other hand, the risk for children not only rose, it did so more rapidly than for adults and produced a widening gap.

The child poverty rate is rather sensitive to the scale used, as we see when we derive the corresponding results with the alternative equivalence scales described earlier. The other two scales both incorporate higher 'costs for children' and show higher child poverty rates. With the so-called OECD scale, for example, about 32% of children were in households below half average equivalent income in 1997, compared with 26% with the 1/0.66/0.33 scale. However, the overall trend of rising child poverty rates up to 1994 followed by a decline to 1997 is also found with each of the other two scales. If we average across persons rather than households in deriving the poverty lines, the poverty rates for children in 1997 are about 2 percentage points lower than those shown in Table 10.1, but the same trends in the gap between adults and children are seen.

Table 10.3: Households below 50% relative income poverty line by labour force status of head, Ireland (1994 and 1997)[a]

	1994 %	1997 %
Employee	6.2	12.7
Self-employed	6.7	7.7
Farmer	8.9	3.8
Unemployed	32.6	21.1
Ill/disabled	9.5	9.8
Retired	10.5	15.7
Home duties	25.5	28.9
All	100	100

[a] Equivalence scale 1/0.66/0.33.

The households in which poor children live

To understand why children find themselves in households below the relative income lines and why this has been changing over time, we can look at the characteristics of these households across a number of dimensions. Callan et al (1989) showed that the dominant factor increasing income poverty rates for families with children in the 1980s was unemployment. From 1987 to 1994, the percentage of households headed by an unemployed person in our samples fell only marginally, while their risk of being below half average income increased slightly. As a result, unemployment continued to be the dominant factor underlying income poverty for families with children. Over the 1994 to 1997 period, however, unemployment fell markedly and a rather different pattern emerged.

Table 10.3 shows that considerable changes took place in the composition of the households below the 50% line over this short period. We see that households headed by an unemployed person accounted for a substantially lower proportion of all those below that line by 1997, down from one third to just over one fifth. This reflected the substantial decline in the level of unemployment. Households headed by an employee or by a retired person, on the other hand, saw an increase in their poverty risk and as a result became more important among those below the line.

Focusing on children, Table 10.4 shows that in 1994, 20% of all children lived in households where the head was unemployed. By 1997 this had fallen to 14%, balanced by an increase in the percentage living in households where the head is an employee. The table also shows that the

Table 10.4: Children by labour-force status of household head and poverty risk (with 50% income poverty line), Ireland (1994 and 1997)

	% of all children		% of these falling below 50% line	
	1994	1997	1994	1997
Employee	48.8	53.3	6.3	8.7
Self-employed	11.3	11.4	18.4	19.4
Farmer	7.8	8.4	31.5	12.0
Unemployed	19.5	13.6	72.2	75.9
Ill/disabled	2.6	4.8	64.5	66.8
Retired	1.1	0.5	24.4	42.4
Home duties	8.8	8.0	66.1	55.4
All	100.0	100.0	29.5	26.0

poverty risk associated with unemployment for the household head actually rose; 76% of children in households headed by an unemployed person were below half average income in 1997, compared with 72% in 1994. However, this was more than offset by the decline in the numbers involved. As a result, only 10% of all children in 1997 were in households both headed by an unemployed person and below half average income, compared with 14% in 1994. This in itself would account for the scale of the overall decline in child poverty with this relative line.

With the 60% relative income line, a very similar pattern is seen. As in the 1980s, the risk for children of being below the 50% and 60% lines if the household head was unemployed was very high. However, just as the dramatic rise in unemployment between 1980 and 1987 pushed many households with children into relative income poverty, the fall in unemployment between 1994 and 1997 has pulled them over the relative income lines.

The other key factor in narrowing the gap in relative income poverty rates between adults and children with these lines has been the fact that those continuing to be dependent on social welfare have lagged behind. While income support rates have increased significantly in real terms, they have not kept up with the very rapid rise in average incomes. This is reflected in a significant increase in relative income poverty rates for households headed by someone aged 65 or over, documented in Callan et al (1999), and is the main reason that relative income poverty rates for adults have risen during the boom.

Table 10.5: Breakdown of children in households below 50% income poverty line by household composition, Ireland (1994 and 1997)[a]

	1994 %	1997 %
2 adults 1 child	3.2	6.2
2 adults 2 child	8.2	11.8
2 adults 3 child	13.8	24.3
2 adults 4+child	17.5	13.4
1 adult+children	11.8	9.0
3+ adults+child(ren)	45.5	35.3
All	100	100

[a] Equivalence scale 1/0.66/0.33

As a result of both these factors, the position of families with children on average has generally improved relative to, for example, pensioners or widows. With the 40% relative income line, however, the poverty rate for children actually increased between 1994 and 1997. This is mainly because of the precise location of that line vis-à-vis social welfare support rates, in a situation where the latter are lagging behind. The support for families provided by social welfare programmes had previously been comfortably above the 40% line, so many of those below that line were relying on, for example, very low incomes from farming or other self-employment. With mean income increasing so rapidly between 1994 and 1997, the 40% line more or less 'caught up' with some social welfare support rates for families over the period. Poverty risk at this line then increased sharply for children in households headed by an unemployed person, or by a parent not in the workforce.

Turning to household size and composition, Table 10.5 shows the type of household in which children below the 50% relative income line lived in 1994 and 1997. We see that in 1994, about 46% of these children lived in households comprising three or more adults with children, while a further 18% were in households of two adults plus four or more children. (Recalling that the definition of child being used is anyone under 14 years of age, many of the former group are households of two parents with older offspring as well as under-14s.)

By 1997, a considerably higher proportion of the children below this line were in households comprising two adults with one to three children. It is worth noting that, despite Ireland's rapidly-increasing lone parenthood

Table 10.6: Mean family size for children in households below relative income poverty lines, Living in Ireland Surveys (1994 and 1997)[a]

	1994	1997
Children in households:	Mean number of children in family	
Below 40% line	3.08	2.97
Below 50% line	3.07	2.77
Below 60% line	2.99	2.65
Above 60% line	2.42	2.15
All	2.65	2.34

[a] Equivalence scale 1/0.66/0.33

rate, only about one in ten of the children in households below the 50% line were in single-adult households, and this did not increase between 1994 and 1997.

Children below the income poverty lines are in larger families on average than other children. Table 10.6 shows that children in households below the 60% line in 1994 had an average family size (in terms of number of children aged under 14) of about three, compared with 2.4 for those in households above that line. By 1997 the average number of children had fallen, both for those above and below the relative income lines, but the gap between them remained.

With average incomes increasing rapidly in real terms from 1994, these trends in relative income poverty have to be seen in their quite unusual context. As explored in detail in Callan et al (1999), the numbers falling below poverty lines held fixed in real terms have declined dramatically, particularly between 1994 and 1997. An increase in relative income poverty in such a situation has to be regarded rather differently to one where average incomes are stagnant or even falling. We now go on to explore the implications of this combination of real and relative income trends, by looking beyond income to non-monetary measures of living standards.

Using non-monetary indicators in measuring child poverty

So far we have focused on household incomes, but we now wish to broaden that focus. Poverty is conventionally defined in terms of exclusion due to lack of resources, but low income on its own may not be an entirely satisfactory measure of such exclusion. The hypothesis that those falling below a specified income poverty line are not able to participate fully in the life of the community requires validation. Indeed, Ringen's (1987, 1988) stringent critique of the use of income poverty lines is based precisely on the argument that low income is unreliable as an indicator of poverty, because it often fails to distinguish households experiencing deprivation and exclusion. This is not primarily because of the (real) difficulties in measuring income accurately, but more because a household's command over resources is affected by much more than its current income. Long-term factors, relating most importantly to the way resources have been accumulated or eroded over time, as well as current income play a crucial role in influencing the likelihood of current deprivation and exclusion.

Two complementary routes can be pursued in moving away from reliance on income at a particular point in time. The first is to measure income as it evolves over time by means of longitudinal surveys. The second is to measure various aspects of living standards and deprivation directly through non-monetary indicators. The use of such indicators was pioneered by Townsend (1979) and they have been used in studying poverty from a cross-section perspective in for example Mack and Lansley (1985), Mayer and Jencks (1988), Mayer (1993), Muffels (1993), Callan, Nolan and Whelan (1993), Halleröd (1995) and Nolan and Whelan (1996). These studies have sought to use non-monetary indicators in rather different ways. They all face hard questions such as how the most satisfactory indicators for the purpose are to be selected, whether they are to be combined into a summary deprivation measure and if so how, and how they are then to be employed in exploring poverty.

It may be particularly important to know the extent to which distinct dimensions of deprivation can be identified, since some may be better than others as measures of generalised deprivation and exclusion. In earlier research with data for Ireland, three such dimensions were identified (Nolan and Whelan, 1996):

- *Basic life-style deprivation* – enforced absence of basic items such as food or clothing, considered by most people to be necessities.
- *Secondary life-style deprivation* – enforced absence of items such as cars, telephone and holidays commonly possessed but not considered by a majority of people to be necessities.
- *Housing deprivation* – enforced absence of items relating to housing such as having an indoor toilet, hot and cold running water, or a bath/

shower, generally considered to be necessities; but absence bore a weak relationship to other types of deprivation.

The key finding emerging from in-depth analysis of these deprivation indicators is that current income is only one of the factors influencing deprivation levels. Other variables which proved significant in predicting deprivation levels included the household's level of financial savings, whether it rented or owned its accommodation, the value of the house, the extent of unemployment experienced over the household head's career, and his or her social class origin and educational qualifications. This brings out the fact that current living standards are influenced by the accumulation or erosion of resources over a long period and highlights the importance of a dynamic perspective. The housing indicators were also seen to be quite distinctive, with single people and farm households particularly likely to experience this but not the other forms of deprivation. Such indicators are thus less likely to be suitable as indicators of generalised deprivation – although in many surveys they are the only ones included.

In seeking to identify those excluded due to a lack of resources, we have concentrated on the basic deprivation index. These items clearly represented socially perceived necessities, they were possessed by most people, they reflect rather basic aspects of current material deprivation, and they cluster together, which lends support to the notion that they are useful as indicators of the underlying generalised deprivation we are trying to measure. Focusing on households that are both at relatively low income levels and experiencing basic deprivation should then give a better indication of the scale of generalised deprivation or exclusion due to lack of resources than those below income lines alone. This way of identifying those most in need has already proved important from a policy perspective, being incorporated in the global poverty reduction target adopted in the Irish National Anti-Poverty Strategy, which forms the benchmark against which progress in combating poverty is assessed (NAPS, 1997).

Between 1987 and 1994 there was little change in the extent of poverty overall shown by these combined income and deprivation measures. Table 10.7 shows for 1994 and 1997 the percentage of households falling below 40%, 50% and 60% of mean equivalent income (using equivalence scale 1/0.66/0.33) and experiencing enforced basic deprivation. We see that there has been a marked fall in the percentage below the relative income lines and experiencing basic deprivation with the highest, 60% income line. The percentage below that line and experiencing basic deprivation has fallen from 15% to 10%. The percentage below the 50% relative

Table 10.7: Percentage of households and persons below relative income thresholds and experiencing basic deprivation in 1994 and 1997[a]

Relative income line	% of households below line and experiencing enforced basic deprivation	
	1994	1997
% of households		
40% line	2.4	3.0
50% line	8.9	7.3
60% line	14.9	9.9
% of persons		
40% line	3.4	4.6
50% line	11.2	8.5
60% line	17.0	11.0

[a] Equivalence scale 1/0.66/0.33

income line and experiencing basic deprivation has also fallen, though less sharply, while the percentage below the 40% line and experiencing such deprivation has risen slightly. Thus, combining relative income poverty lines with a deprivation criterion held fixed from 1987 to 1997 gives a very different picture for all households to that described above with the income lines alone.

What about children? The available indicators were designed to measure the extent and nature of deprivation at the level of the household rather than the individual. As in using household income to measure poverty, the assumption is made that pooling of resources within the household equalises living standards and poverty risk for all household members. The situation where children are in poverty because of insufficient sharing of resources within the household will not be captured, either with conventional income measures or with the deprivation indicators we have available here. (Some indicators specifically designed to capture deprivation among children are however being included in the 1999 wave of the Living in Ireland survey; see Cantillon and Nolan (2001) for a discussion.) On that basis, we can see what these indicators, together with income, tell us about the households in which children live.

Table 10.8 shows the percentage of children and adults in households below the relative income lines and experiencing basic deprivation in both 1994 and 1997. We see first that the poverty rates on this basis are a good deal higher for children than for adults. For example, 17% of all

Table 10.8: Percentage of children and adults in households below relative income thresholds and experiencing basic deprivation in 1987 and 1994[a]

Relative income line	% in households below line and experiencing enforced basic deprivation	
	1994	1997
% of children		
40% line	4.1	8.6
50% line	17.9	14.9
60% line	23.5	16.9
% of adults		
40% line	3.2	3.6
50% line	9.0	6.8
60% line	14.8	9.4

[a] Equivalence scale 1/0.66/0.33

adults but 24% of all children were in households below the 60% relative income line and experiencing basic deprivation in 1994. These are rather wider gaps between children and adults than shown by the relative income lines in that year, discussed earlier.

In terms of trends over the 1994-97 period, we see that the percentage of children in households below the 40% income line and experiencing basic deprivation rose sharply between 1994 and 1997, but that with the 50% and especially the 60% income line the percentage fell. This is similar to the direction of change shown for children by the corresponding income lines alone, though the scale of the fall is much greater when we look at the numbers below the 60% line and experiencing basic deprivation than just those below that income line.

It is worth noting that for adults, on the other hand, there is a marked contrast between trends with the income lines alone and those with the income plus deprivation measures. For adults, we see that the percentage falling below the 50% and 60% income lines and experiencing basic deprivation fell by at least as much as for children between 1994 and 1997, despite the fact that as we saw earlier their income poverty rates rose. This pronounced fall in deprivation, at a time when relative income poverty was rising, is attributable to the very rapid rates of income growth experienced over the period. As explored in detail in Callan et al (1999), the contrast brings out that in such a period of rapid growth, relative income lines on their own may miss out on an important part of the story. The official global poverty reduction target adopted in 1997 by the

Irish Government's National Anti-Poverty Strategy focuses on the numbers falling below 50% or 60% of mean income and experiencing basic deprivation. As a result of the decline in these measures now shown by the 1997 data, this target has recently been rebased to aim at a greater fall than initially envisaged (see NAPS 1999). Had the target been framed simply in terms of relative income poverty, on the other hand, the 1997 data would have suggested that poverty got worse over the period.

Here is not the place to explore the best way to frame such targets – we argue in Callan et al (1999) for a tiered set of targets encompassing real income levels, deprivation indicators that adjust over time to enhanced expectations and relative income levels. The point of most relevance here is that in terms of the (50% or 60%) relative income lines combined with basic deprivation measures, the position of children improved between 1994 and 1997, but the pronounced gap between them and adults did not narrow in the same way as the corresponding relative income poverty rates. Explaining why this happened will be a priority for future research with these data sets.

The final issue to be addressed is whether the children identified by the combined income and deprivation measures as poor are in the same types of households as those below the relative income poverty lines. Table 10.9 compares the children in households below half average income with those falling below the higher 60% line but also experiencing basic deprivation, in both 1994 and 1997, in terms of the labour-force status of the head of the household in which they live. We see that unemployment is more prominent and self-employment (including farming) less important for those below the higher income line and experiencing basic deprivation.

Conclusions

Assessed vis-à-vis relative income poverty lines, child poverty had risen substantially in Ireland by the late 1980s and a substantial gap had opened up between poverty rates for children and for adults. This reflected a combination of the effects of macroeconomic trends – notably rapidly rising unemployment – and improved pensions for the elderly. This chapter has employed new data from the 1994 and 1997 waves of the Irish element of the ECHP Survey to explore the evolution of child poverty since then. With Ireland's recent exceptional rates of economic growth from 1994, we have been particularly interested in bringing out what has happened to child poverty in a booming economy.

Overall relative income poverty rates rose both between 1987 and 1994

Table 10.9: Breakdown of children in 'poor' households by labour force status of household head, Ireland (1994 and 1997)[a]

	1994		1997	
	Below 50% line	Below 60% plus deprivation	Below 50% line	Below 60% plus deprivation
	%	%	%	%
Employee	10.4	12.0	17.7	16.1
Self-employed	7.1	1.7	8.5	4.0
Farmer	8.3	3.2	3.9	0
Unemployed	47.8	52.0	39.7	53.2
Ill/disabled	5.6	5.8	12.3	10.4
Retired	0.9	0.7	0.9	0.6
Home duties	19.8	24.7	17.0	15.8
All	100	100	100	100
% of all children	29.6	23.5	26.0	16.9

[a] Equivalence scale 1/0.66/0.33

and between 1994 and 1997. Unemployment was almost as important a factor underlying relative income poverty in 1994 as in 1987, but by 1997 had declined significantly. Social welfare support rates – though increasing substantially in real terms – lagged behind average incomes between 1994 and 1997, and this played a central role in increasing relative income poverty rates. With average incomes increasing rapidly in real terms, the numbers falling below poverty lines held fixed in real terms declined dramatically, particularly between 1994 and 1997.

The gap between relative income poverty rates for children and adults was fairly stable between 1987 and 1994. From 1994 to 1997, however, the poverty rates for children declined with the 50% and 60% relative income poverty lines while those for adults increased, producing a significant narrowing in that gap. With the 40% line the poverty rate for children increased, reflecting the fact that this line was now as high as the support for families provided by some social welfare programmes. Declining relative income poverty rates for children with the two higher lines were attributable to the impact of falling unemployment.

A range of non-monetary indicators was also employed, together with income, to characterise more comprehensively the evolution of child poverty. Like relative income poverty lines, measures combining those lines with experience of basic deprivation showed children at substantial disadvantage vis-à-vis adults in 1994. Unlike those relative lines, however, these combined income and deprivation measures showed no narrowing in that gap between 1994 and 1997, with deprivation levels for adults declining more rapidly than children on average.

Ireland's experience is best seen in a comparative perspective, which the present chapter has not explored because other chapters in this volume have such a comparative picture as their central focus. A priority for further research will be to use the ECHP data to study both income and deprivation dynamics, extending results for Ireland already produced in the course of UNICEF's Child Income Dynamics project.

References

Barry, F. (ed) (1999) *Understanding Ireland's economic growth*, London: Macmillan.

Bradley, J., FitzGerald, J., Honohan, P. and Kearney, I. (1997) 'Interpreting the recent Irish growth experience', in D. Duffy, J. FitzGerald, I. Kearney and F. Shortall (eds) *Medium-term review: 1997-2003*, Dublin: The Economic and Social Research Institute.

Callan, T., Nolan, B., Whelan, B.J, Hannan, D.F. and Creighton, S. (1989) *Poverty, income and welfare in Ireland*, General Research Series No 146, Dublin: The Economic and Social Research Institute.

Callan, T., Nolan, B. and Whelan, C.T. (1993) 'Resources, deprivation and the measurement of poverty', *Journal of Social Policy*, vol 22, no 2, pp 141-72.

Callan, T., O'Neill, C. and O'Donoghue, C. (1995) *Supplementing family incomes,* Policy Research Series Paper No 23, Dublin: The Economic and Social Research Institute.

Callan, T., Nolan, B., Whelan, B.J., Whelan, C.T. and Williams, J. (1996) *Poverty in the 1990s: Evidence from the Living in Ireland Survey*, General Research Series Paper 170, Dublin: Oak Tree Press.

Callan, T., Layte, R., Nolan, B., Watson, D., Whelan, C.T., Williams, J. and Maitre, B. (1999) *Monitoring poverty trends: Data from the 1997 Living in Ireland Survey*, Dublin: Stationery Office/Combat Poverty Agency.

Cantillon, S. and Nolan, B. (1998) 'Are married women more deprived than their husbands?', *Journal of Social Policy*, vol 27, no 2, pp 151-71.

Cantillon, S. and Nolan, B. (2001) 'Poverty within households: measuring gender differences using non-monetary indicators', *Feminist Economics*, vol 17, no 1.

CSO (1980) *Household budget survey 1973: Detailed results*, Dublin: Stationery Office.

CSO (1984) *Household budget survey 1980: Detailed results*, Dublin : Stationery Office.

Commission on the Family (1998) *Strengthening families for life, final report*, Dublin: Stationery Office.

Hagenaars, A., de Vos, K. and Zaidi, M.A. (1994) *Poverty statistics in the late 1980s: Research based on micro-data,* Luxembourg: Office for Official Publications of the European Communities.

Halleröd, B. (1995) 'The truly poor: Direct and indirect measurement of consensual poverty in Sweden', *European Journal of Social Policy*, vol 5, no 2, pp 111-29.

Mack, J. and Lansley, S. (1985) *Poor Britain*, London: Allen and Unwin.

Mayer, S. (1993) 'Living conditions among the poor in four rich countries', *Journal of Population Economics*, vol 6, pp 261-86.

Mayer, S. and Jencks, C. (1988) 'Poverty and the distribution of material hardship', *Journal of Human Resources*, vol 24, no 1, pp 88-114.

Muffels, R. (1993) 'Deprivation standards and style of living indices', in J. Berghman and B. Cantillon (1993) *The European face of social security*, Aldershot: Avebury.

National Anti-Poverty Strategy (1997) *Sharing in progress: National anti-poverty strategy*, Dublin, Stationery Office.

National Anti-Poverty Strategy (1999) *Social inclusion strategy: 1998/99 annual report of the Inter-Departmental Policy Committee of the National Anti-Poverty Strategy*, Dublin, Stationery Office.

Nolan, B. and Farrell, B. (1990) *Child poverty in Ireland*, Dublin: Combat Poverty Agency.

Nolan, B. and Callan, T., (eds.), (1994) *Poverty and policy in Ireland*, Dublin: Gill and Macmillan.

Nolan, B. and Whelan, C. (1996) *Resources, deprivation and poverty*, Oxford: Clarendon Press.

Ringen, S. (1987) *The possibility of politics*, Oxford: Clarendon Press.

Ringen, S. (1988) 'Direct and indirect measures of poverty', *Journal of Social Policy*, vol 17, pp 351-66.

Rottman, D.B. (1994) *Allocating resources within Irish families*, Dublin: Combat Poverty Agency.

Townsend, P. (1979) *Poverty in the United Kingdom*, Harmondsworth: Penguin.

ELEVEN

Living conditions of immigrant children in Germany

Joachim R. Frick and Gert G. Wagner

Introduction

In 1995, the proportion of foreign-born persons in Gemany was about 9% of the entire population[1]; in West Germany, where more or less all the immigrants are living, the proportion of foreign born is about 12%. As a result of this, the number of children born to immigrants is of a significant magnitude, especially since the fertility rate among immigrant women is higher than that among native German women (cf Deutscher Bundestag, 1998a, p 55ff). But, despite an ongoing influx of immigrants, Germany does not consider itself an 'immigrant society'.

Due to the specific German regulations on granting citizenship, children born to foreign immigrants in Germany are considered as 'immigrant children' regardless of their respective place of birth (abroad or within Germany after their parents immigrated). In contrast to countries like the United States, where citizenship is granted to people born within the US (*ius solis*), children born in Germany do not automatically receive German citizenship. Instead they receive the nationality of their parents (*ius sanguinis*).

The most relevant immigrant groups in Germany are made up of migrant workers from Mediterranean countries who came during the period from the 1960s to the early 1970s (so-called *guestworkers*) and of immigrants from Eastern Europe since the fall of the Berlin wall in October 1989, especially 'Ethnic Germans' (*Aussiedler*). As a result of the specific German concept of ethnicity and citizenship, it is worthwhile differentiating immigrant children. Figure 11.1 shows our concept of

Figure 11.1: Immigration status in Germany

Citizenship (child or parents)	Place of birth (child or parents) In Germany	Abroad
German	(A) Native-born German	(B) German immigrant (mainly *Aussiedler*)
Non-German	(C1) Native-born foreigner 'Second and third generation'	(C2) Foreign-born foreigner ('classic' case of immigrant)

'immigration status' based on the combination of citizenship and country of birth of children and their parents.

The aim of this chapter is to describe and analyse short and long-term prospects for children in Germany. The *Kinder-und Jugendbericht* (child and youth report) for 1998 shows clear signs of a worsening economic situation for children in Germany. Unfortunately, this official report fails to provide sufficient information on immigrant children. The proportion of children living in households receiving welfare increased to about 7% in 1997, about twice that for the entire population. The report also states that the positive correlation of child poverty with (future) malnutrition, drug abuse, crime intensity and so on, requires an improvement and a targeting of social policy. It is expected, that the additional costs involved would pay off in the long run, due to a reduction of the otherwise higher costs of fighting the above mentioned negative developments (Deutscher Bundestag, 1998b, p 95).

Our analysis pays special attention to the differences in the situation of children born to immigrants and foreigners as compared to those born to native-born German parents. For the short run, we analyse income position, poverty risk, and some selected living conditions, such as individual housing situations. Our indicator for the long-run prospects is based on current educational enrolment of teenagers, which is closely linked to their future development. This indicator is also most likely correlated with current and past income and poverty (cf Büchel et al, Chapter Six).

This chapter is organised as follows. First, we give a brief review of regulations and the structure of immigration into (West) Germany throughout the past decades. We then discuss some methodological aspects and show the results of our empirical research, which is based on data from the German Socio-economic Panel (GSOEP). The population under consideration is made up of all children up to 16 years of age living in private households in Germany. Finally, we draw some conclusions from our empirical findings.

General features of immigration to (West) Germany

In 1950, residents with a non-German nationality represented only about 1% of the West German population. As such, the proportion of foreigners and immigrants was quite small compared to that of most other European countries[2]. The role of foreigners changed dramatically over subsequent decades. With only a few exceptions, the foreign population grew substantially in all European countries. This was especially true for West Germany, where the proportion of foreigners in 1995 was more than 12 times as high as in 1950. The following paragraphs illustrate the most essential features of this process[3].

In the late 1950s, the West German *guestworker* system was introduced to ease labour-market shortages. Treaties with Italy, Turkey, Yugoslavia, and other Mediterranean countries led to huge inflows of foreign labourers. In 1970, almost 2.9 million foreigners, equalling almost 5% of the total population, lived in the then Federal Republic of Germany (Fassmann and Muenz, 1994).

Between 1988 and 1994 more than 1.5 million *Aussiedler* immigrated to Germany, representing about 2% of the current population of the western states. Their integration into German society was supported by German language courses, financial aid and full integration with the retirement system (without any prior contribution).

The majority of asylum seekers in European countries between 1988 and 1993 were absorbed by Germany. The demands that this large number of asylum seekers put on resources led to a change in German asylum law. Since 1993, individuals entering Germany via safe countries have no longer been allowed to apply for asylum.

By 1993, foreign residents made up 8.6% of the population of reunited Germany, despite the fact that Germany's official policy to encourage foreign workers to immigrate from non-EU member states was terminated in November 1973. Since the Second World War, West Germany has accepted a larger number of foreign nationals than any other country in Western Europe. Even this enormous growth in foreign residents understates the number of new residents who have immigrated to the western states of Germany over the last decade. All ethnic Germans who moved from Eastern Europe to Germany (*Aussiedler*) were immediately granted full citizenship. This group is not included in the above mentioned 8.6% proportion of foreigners. When these ethnic Germans are included, the overall proportion of residents who were not born in Germany is about 10% (12% in West Germany), half of whom have arrived since 1984. Due to the age composition of immigrants and foreigners, and their (up to now) higher fertility rates, the structure among children is heavily influenced by immigration. In united Germany, one out of five children up to 16 years of age was born outside of Germany or is a foreigner; in West Germany this is the case for one in four children.

The German concept of citizenship is closely related to history: "Political fragmentation led Germans to think of their nation not as a political or geographical unit, but as a cultural, linguistic and ethnic one" (Hailbronner, 1992). The policy implication of this concept of citizenship is that German citizenship is possible for those who can trace their ancestry to German roots, while non-ethnic Germans, even if they are born in Germany, do not automatically receive German citizenship. The *ius sanguinis* (right of blood) allows people of German origin who live outside the borders to claim German citizenship. In practice, however, this right of blood applies almost exclusively to ethnic Germans in Eastern Europe and German people who lived under communist rule in the former East Germany.

A very interesting result of this German concept of ethnicity and the regulations for citizenship is that more than one in four foreigners living in Germany in 1995 is native-born, and at the same time about 45% of all immigrants are German citizens, mainly *Aussiedler*.

Data and methods

The microdata used for the empirical analyses in this chapter come from the GSOEP. The survey was started in 1984 in West Germany and was extended to the then German Democratic Republic (East Germany) in June 1990 just before unification (cf Wagner et al, 1993).

The 1984 West German GSOEP explicitly oversampled foreigners to a great extent, since a higher dropout rate was to be expected (mostly due to remigration) and to ensure a sufficient number of observations for detailed analyses. Nevertheless, due to massive immigration since 1983, when the original sample was drawn, the representation of immigrants within the GSOEP data constantly worsened. This was so because the ongoing panel study did not cover new immigrants unless they joined existing survey households. This situation might happen fairly often in the case of family reunification, which can be observed very frequently in GSOEP *guestworker* families. However, given the structure of immigration, especially since the late 1980s, there were a lot of new immigrants such as the ethnic Germans (contributing about 50% of net immigration in the period 1984 to 1994) and asylum seekers, refugees, etc who mostly settled down in newly created households[4]. To overcome this unsatisfactory situation, a new subsample was introduced in GSOEP for the years 1994/95, the so-called 'immigrant sample' (cf Burkhauser et al, 1997). Due to federal data privacy laws in Germany, ethnic Germans cannot be identified as immigrants in the big cross-sectional surveys of the Federal Statistical Office, whereas this is possible with the new GSOEP subsample.

For this chapter we exploit data for the years 1985/86 for West Germany and the years 1995/96 for the new unified Germany (East and West Germany, including the most recent immigrant population in 1994)[5]. Due to a very small influx between 1984 and 1985, we considered the GSOEP to be representative for the years 1985/86. This has the advantage that by that time we already had more information on our respondents than was the case in the very first wave in 1984. The data for the period 1995/96 again is representative for the population in Germany, whereas the years in between are likely to be biased due to non-covered immigration. Some of our following analyses for 1995/96 focus on the child population in unified Germany, while some concentrate on West Germany to allow for a better comparison with the situation in the previous decade, 1985/86.

While in the GSOEP all adult members of a given household are interviewed personally, information on children aged up to 16 years is gathered from questions asked of the main respondent (mostly the head of household). Thus, we have rather restricted data on the youth population covering age, gender, and some more detailed information concerning enrolment in pre-school, school or other educational settings. Nevertheless, due to the fact that the GSOEP is a household related survey interviewing all adult household members, we do have a great deal of data on the household as a whole.

Without any doubt, individual well-being depends on monetary as well as non-monetary factors. Nevertheless, for the short-term perspective we are dealing mainly with disposable household income and poverty status as the major indicators for economic well-being of individuals, since many non-monetary conditions are highly correlated with income.

In addition, we will focus on some non-monetary indicators, such as those concerning the children's housing situation.

The income situation of a household is depicted by annual income measures, referring to the year prior to the interview[6].

- Pre-government income is a measure of market income, which includes income from employment of any kind, private transfers, assets (income from interest, dividends or rent), and imputed rental value of owner-occupied housing.
- Post-government income is our measure of disposable income. It is given by pre-government income minus taxes and social security contributions, plus public transfers and pensions of all sources.
- Public transfers are the sum of all – mostly means-tested – transfers received by all household members throughout the previous year. This measure is an insufficient indication for addressing the question: "How costly are immigrants to society?"

In order to adjust income for differences in family or household size, we apply a straightforward equivalence scale, following Atkinson, Rainwater, and Smeeding (1995). We calculate an adjusted 'equivalent income' as follows:

$$(1) \qquad Y_{eq} = Y_{disp} \,/\, S^{\varepsilon}$$

where Y_{eq} is equivalent income, Y_{disp} is disposable household income, S is family size, and ε is the equivalence elasticity. For the following calculations we use $\varepsilon = 0.5$, which gives the square root of household size.

One indicator of economic well-being is the poverty status of households and individuals living therein. We apply two poverty measures: the head-count ratio (percentage of population with income below a certain poverty line) as well as the poverty index P_{α} with $\alpha = 2$, as suggested by Foster, Greer, and Thorbecke (1984), which also takes into account the intensity and inequality of poverty. Based on the poverty aversion parameter α, this index gives additional weight to the poorest poor[7]:

$$(2) \quad \textit{Head-count Ratio:} \quad H = \frac{1}{n} \sum_{i=1}^{q} [((z-y_i)/z]^{0} = \frac{q}{n}$$

$$(3) \quad \textit{Poverty Index:} \quad P_{\alpha=2} = \frac{1}{n} \sum_{i=1} [((z-y_i)/z]^2$$

where q is the number of poor, n is total population, z depicts the poverty line, and y_i is individual income. In order to show the sensitivity of our results to the chosen poverty line, we allow the underlying poverty

Table 11.1: Composition of the resident child population in West Germany (up to 16 years of age)

	1985/86 West Germany	1995/96 West Germany	1995/96 Germany
Immigrant status			
Native-born German	84.3	76.8	80.5
German immigrant	2.1	6.1	5.6
Foreigner	13.6	17.1	13.9
Total	100.0	100.0	100.0

Source: GSOEP; authors' calculations

threshold to be 50% and 60% of median income of the entire population (including adults).

Empirical results

Non-monetary living conditions of children by immigrant status

Table 11.1 depicts the composition of the resident population (up to 16 years of age) in Germany in 1985/86 and 1995/96 with respect to immigration. In 1985/86, the group of non-natives was clearly dominated by foreigners (mostly children of *guestworkers*); the proportion was almost 87%. On the other hand, German immigrants contributed only 13% to this population of foreign or foreign-born children. This changed drastically over the next ten years, due to the massive influx of 'Ethnic Germans' *(Aussiedler)* from the former Soviet Union, Poland and Romania. Although the population of both groups of non-natives grew substantially until 1995/96, the German immigrants doubled their share to 26%. The number of native-born Germans among all children in the mid-1990s was down to 77% in West Germany. Due to the very few foreigners and immigrants in East Germany, this figure is different for united Germany, where the proportion of native-born children is still around 80%.

Table 11.2 displays some key descriptive statistics for the years 1985/86 and 1995/96. Immigrant children, especially foreigners, are much more concentrated in the larger cities than their native-born German counterparts. This is most likely influenced by network-oriented migration behaviour, where a lot of new migrants tend to move into areas and neighbourhoods where fellow aliens live. Additionally, immigrants who stick to their traditional way of life (this is the case, for example, for a

Table 11.2: Living conditions of children in Germany by immigrant status

	1985/86				1995/96				
	West Germany				West Germany				East Germany
	Native-born German	German immigrant	Foreigner	Total	Native-born German	German immigrant	Foreigner	Total	Total
Community size									
< 20,000 inhabitants	46.4	34.5	30.3	43.9	46.5	43.0	30.7	43.6	53.2
20-100,000 inhabitants	28.3	24.5	26.2	27.9	28.3	24.8	34.9	29.2	18.5
100-500,000 inhabitants	14.5	12.0	19.1	15.1	13.9	22.4	14.5	14.5	17.0
> 500,000 inhabitants	10.8	29.1	24.3	13.0	11.3	9.8	20.0	12.7	11.3
Regional distribution									
North	21.0	16.4	19.7	20.7	23.5	26.5	16.6	22.5	0
Mid-West	42.5	52.1	38.5	42.1	42.1	56.0	41.6	42.8	0
South	36.5	31.5	41.9	37.1	34.5	17.4	41.8	34.7	0
East	0	0	0	0	0	0	0	0	100.0
Housing situation									
Owner-occupier (in %)	53.1	29.6	14.2	47.2	55.7	27.4	29.6	49.5	33.5
# of rooms per capita	1.12	0.97	0.83	1.07	1.15	0.95	0.91	1.09	1.00
<1 room per capita (in %)	27.8	45.1	66.5	33.5	26.0	52.1	51.1	32.0	36.6
m^2 per capita	27.6	23.0	18.6	26.2	29.2	23.0	22.4	27.6	23.0
'too small' (in %)[a]	21.5	20.5	33.8	23.2	28.4	28.3	48.4	31.8	37.6
Household structure									
Lone parent	6.5	(12.3)	(2.7)	6.1	9.3	9.5	4.4	8.5	8.5
Multi-adult 1 child	33.9	34.3	22.9	32.4	27.6	21.6	22.7	26.4	34.3
Multi-adult 2 children	41.4	35.4	41.9	41.3	40.4	37.3	41.9	40.5	43.9
Multi-adult 3+ children	18.2	17.9	32.3	20.1	22.7	31.6	30.9	24.6	13.3

Table 11.2: contd.../

	1985/86				1995/96				
	West Germany				West Germany				East Germany
	Native-born German	German immigrant	Foreigner	Total	Native-born German	German immigrant	Foreigner	Total	Total
Unemployment experience in previous year[b]									
No employable person	2.9	(8.4)	1.9	2.9	1.6	(0.4)	2.8	1.8	0
Index = 0% (no unemployment)	83.5	76.5	79.1	82.7	79.0	77.4	65.5	76.6	58.5
Index = 1-50%	9.3	(8.7)	12.4	9.7	16.8	13.9	22.3	17.6	32.0
Index = 50-100%	4.3	(6.4)	6.6	4.7	2.5	8.2	9.4	4.0	9.5
Current unemployment[c]									
Households with unemployed (in %)	7.6	18.4	15.4	8.9	5.7	14.4	16.8	8.1	29.3
Parental education[d]									
Without Secondary Education	9.8	(4.8)	55.6	15.9	9.9	27.1	37.4	15.6	(1.7)
Completed Secondary Education	49.9	65.7	29.7	47.5	48.7	50.8	33.6	46.2	53.3
Some Post-Secondary Education	40.3	29.5	14.7	36.6	41.5	22.1	29.0	38.1	45.0

Notes: Values in parentheses: n < 30. [a] Evaluation by head of household. [b] Months in unemployment as a share of months with potential employment of all employable household members during the previous year. [c] At least one household member is officially registered as unemployed in the month of the interview 1986 and 1996, respectively. [d] Highest educational level achieved by parents.

Source: GSOEP, authors' calculations

large part of the big Turkish community in Berlin) have a sure supply of their daily-life requirements. This also lowers the pressure to integrate with German society, which tends to result in the establishment of 'immigrant communities'.

The regional distribution of children in West Germany did not change very much in the ten-year period under consideration. Additionally, there are no big differences between the native German-born population and the other groups. Only about one fifth of all immigrants and foreigners live in the north, about 40% live in the midwestern part of West Germany, and about 35% live in southern regions. Within the immigrant groups, however, we can find some changes in the patterns. Most of the recent German immigrants have settled in the northern part of Germany, which is not as attractive for foreign immigrants who still prefer the southern part of Germany, perhaps because it is closer to the Mediterranean countries that are still the major countries of origin. Another argument is that the typical jobs for *guestworkers* are predominantly in these areas (eg, automobile industry).

Corresponding to the higher proportion of native German children living in small towns (of less than 20,000 inhabitants), this group also shows the highest proportion of owner-occupied housing. In 1985/86, more than 50% of these children lived in homes owned by their families. Owner-occupation among foreigners doubled over the 1985/86-1995/96 period, from 14% to about 30%. East German children (in the mid-1990s) showed only a slightly higher proportion of owner-occupiers, while German immigrants could barely match this standard. Since, on average, self-occupied housing is more spacious than rented homes, it is not surprising to see that foreigners also improved their situation concerning flat size and number of rooms per capita. But there also seems to be an adoption of German standards regarding the size of housing units[8]. Although foreigners clearly improved their housing conditions by means of objective indicators, the percentage of those who complained about their apartment or house being 'too small' increased from a third to about 50%.

In line with the traditionally high relevance of family networks, as well as high fertility rates among foreigners, we find lone parents to be less common among children of foreigners compared to both other groups. On the other hand, children of foreign immigrants had a much greater chance of living in a household with three or more offspring in 1985/86. Due to the massive influx of *Aussiedler* over the period observed, the proportion of multiple-children families for German immigrants clearly increased until 1995/96. The situation in East Germany is different; the majority of children live in families with one or two children, and larger families are rare.

Parental education is very important for the long-run prospects of children. Not surprisingly, the educational background of children of foreign immigrants is far worse than the background of German children[9]. Even the impressive improvement between 1985/86 and 1995/96 does not eliminate this difference. More than a third of foreigners' children have poorly educated parents (less than secondary education). Nevertheless, this situation seems to be partly the result of an increasing number of 'second generation immigrants' among these foreign parents, 29% of whom had some post-secondary education. Another interesting aspect is the worsening of the educational background of German immigrants due to presence of the recently immigrated *Aussiedler*. Meanwhile, the parents of German immigrant children had an educational level comparable to that of foreign immigrants. The proportion of parents with some post-secondary education is the smallest in this group. Again, East German children do not differ that much from West German natives.

Unemployment is much more common in households of both immigrant groups than it is in households of native-born German children in West Germany; this is true for the snapshot of current unemployment in the month of the interview as well as for the unemployment index based on the previous year. A dramatic unemployment problem exists in East Germany, where almost 30% of children were affected by unemployment in the month of the interview. In West Germany, households of foreigners are affected most by unemployment, especially in the most recent period; the number of foreign children living in households without unemployment is only two thirds. Almost every tenth child in this group lives in a household severely struck by unemployment, as is the case in East Germany.

After going through a list of non-monetary indicators, we now concentrate on income and poverty indicators (Table 11.3). The overall picture in terms of all measures employed is that immigrant and foreigner children tend to be in a significantly worse position than native-born children in West Germany. Nevertheless, for the period 1995/96 we point out that children in East Germany are very much like non-native children in West Germany. The following discussion of some selected measures sheds more light on this issue by also looking at distribution aspects.

Table 11.3: Income and poverty measures for children in Germany by immigrant status

	1985/86				1995/96				
	West Germany				West Germany				East Germany
	Native-born German	German Immigrant	Foreigner	Total	Native-born German	German Immigrant	Foreigner	Total	Total
Assets[a]									
Saving account	79.6	80.1	60.7	77.0	78.6	50.8	55.0	72.9	81.7
Savings w/building societies	54.1	53.3	30.7	50.8	57.6	44.8	38.5	53.5	51.4
Life insurance	70.3	61.0	31.6	64.7	77.1	52.7	48.6	70.7	71.9
Financial assets	19.0	11.4	6.6	17.1	28.2	6.1	12.2	24.1	17.2
Operating assets	10.6	6.8	2.5	9.4	9.2	0.7	2.2	7.5	7.9
None	10.0	19.9	27.6	12.7	8.9	26.1	23.9	12.5	8.0
Pre-government income[b]	32,650	25,800	24,699	31,425	35,715	25,081	27,986	33,741	26,979
Post-government income[b]	26,538	21,973	20,239	25,586	28,825	21,747	23,500	27,480	23,862
Public transfers[b]	1,808	1,898	2,051	1,843	1,973	3,213	2,443	2,129	3,648
Public transfers as a % of post-government income	11.1	13.2	14.1	11.5	12.4	20.4	20.4	14.3	21.1
Relative equivalent pre-government income position[c]	108.7	90.1	82.3	104.7	104.3	75.2	87.6	99.8	78.6
Relative equivalent post-government income position[c]	94.7	78.4	72.2	91.3	92.4	69.7	75.3	88.1	76.5

Table 11.3: contd.../

	1985/86				1995/96				
	West Germany				West Germany				East Germany
	Native-born German	German Immigrant	Foreigner	Total	Native-born German	German Immigrant	Foreigner	Total	Total
Measures based on equivalent post-government income									
Lowest quintile	17.8	28.9	32.5	20.0	18.0	20.7	30.2	20.2	19.0
Second lowest quintile	19.0	21.5	25.3	20.0	15.6	37.7	25.6	18.7	25.9
Middle quintile	20.3	16.9	19.3	20.0	19.6	22.2	12.5	18.5	26.2
Second highest quintile	21.0	19.1	14.2	20.0	23.0	12.0	10.3	20.2	19.3
Highest quintile	22.0	13.6	8.8	20.0	23.8	7.4	21.4	22.4	9.7
Decile ratios									
90:10	3.04	2.89	2.88	3.07	4.71	2.58	6.12	4.58	3.02
90:50	1.74	1.78	1.70	1.76	1.89	1.66	2.17	1.91	1.59
50:10	1.75	1.63	1.70	1.75	2.49	1.55	2.82	2.40	1.90
Poverty head count ratio using a poverty line at ...									
50% of median	8.5	10.2	15.7	9.5	15.2	13.7	23.9	16.6	15.4
60% of median	16.2	24.5	30.0	18.3	21.4	28.6	36.2	24.4	23.9
Poverty index ($P_{\alpha=2}$) using a poverty line at ...									
50% of median	.0151	.0270	.0122	.0149	.0328	.0248	.0674	.0382	.0216
60% of median	.0207	.0334	.0234	.0214	.0438	.0347	.0832	.0500	.0320

[a] Fraction of households holding specific assets in the previous year (in %). [b] Mean of Equivalent Income in 1991 DM. [c] Total population=100.

Source: GSOEP, authors' calculations

Stock of assets

The upper panel of Table 11.3 shows the portfolio of assets owned by households with children in Germany. In particular, this information on assets documents the integration process of children born to foreigners. In the mid-1980s, less than a third lived in households which had life insurance, and only 6% owned financial assets. Ten years later these proportions increased to almost 50% and 12%, respectively. Although native-born children live in much better endowed households, this panel shows that a relevant section of foreigner households meanwhile made their living fairly well. On the other hand, the influx of ethnic Germans during the last few years on average resulted in a worse situation for children in immigrant households. While less than a fifth of this group held no assets at all in 1985/86, that proportion increased to more than 26% in 1995/96.

Income levels and income distribution

The lower panels of Table 11.3 show average pre- and post-government incomes (in 1991 DM) for each of the sub-groups in West Germany in both periods as well as for East German children in 1995/96. Although East German incomes are adjusted for purchasing power differences, they are lower than those for the West German native-born population, and barely match the income of children born to German immigrants and foreigners in West Germany. Looking at the equivalent weighted amount of public transfers received, we find not only the highest absolute value for East German children, but also the highest dependency rate, measured by public transfers as a percentage of post-government income. On the other hand, children of foreigners tend to live in households that receive less public transfers in absolute terms.

Relative income positions based on post-government income are below the population average for all children (because households without children, on average, are better off than those with children). While the position of native-born German and foreigner children remains fairly stable over the ten-year period, there is a remarkable drop for German immigrant children from almost 80% down to less than 70%, which perfectly fits the results for their higher dependency on public transfers.

Quintile proportions as well as decile ratios show that the income distribution for households with children widened considerably in the period under consideration. The income distribution based on the entire population in (West) Germany became less equal as well, but this increase in inequality was much more pronounced for households with children than for other households. While the 90:10 decile ratio for those up to 16 years of age increased by almost 50% (from 3.07 to 4.58), this change was 26% for the entire population (from 3.32 in 1985 to 4.18 in 1995, not shown in Table 11.3). The most impressive change is the drastic increase in inequality among children born to foreigners. This inequality is not only evident by looking at the development of the 90:10 decile ratio (from 2.88 in 1985/86 to 6.12 in 1995/96); the top quintile proportion also increased significantly, from 8.8% to 21.4% over this period. Clearly, there seems to be a sub-group within this foreign-born group that literally has made it to the top, while almost a third of this group were in the lowest quintile. Also interesting is the increasing inequality among native-born children in the lower tail of the income distribution, which is expressed by the 50:10 decile ratio. While this ratio was only 1.75 in the mid-1980s, it grew to 2.49 in the mid-1990s.

The proportion of East German children in the highest quintile was less than 10% in 1995/96. Given that they also had a low average equivalent post-government income, it seems surprising that their poverty rates do not differ from those of native-born children in West Germany. This is a result of the much flatter income distribution. East German children in 1995/96 show decile ratios comparable to those in West Germany about a decade ago.

One important conclusion to be drawn from these selected descriptive analyses is that in 1995/96, children born to immigrants and foreigners in West Germany, on average, lived under conditions which were less favourable than those for native-born children, but the difference from East German children was much smaller. From a theoretical as well as from a political point of view, it is important to know if the weak position of immigrant children is due to the immigration status *per se* (for example, resulting from discrimination) or due to social structure, such as the poorer qualification level of immigrant parents[10]. For this purpose, we estimated ordinary least square regression models on equivalent post-government income, simultaneously controlling for the partial effects of a set of independent variables such as parental age, highest educational level of parents, regional information, community size and household or family type. The results of these regression models for West Germany in both periods 1985/86 and 1995/96 have not been tabulated in this chapter due to space constraints (for full results cf Frick and Wagner, 2000).

Controlling for immigration of any kind, we found a negative and significant coefficient, which support the hypothesis of some discrimination against immigrants, but this could also be a result of the non-observed effects of 'ability'. In 1985/86 immigrants received about 7% less income than other households (after controlling for the household structure by an equivalence scale and by dummy variables for household types). This negative effect almost doubled to 13% in 1995/96.

Analysing immigrants by area of origin shows those from Western countries to be very different from the other immigrants. Although this group is fairly small, they have about the same income position as native-born Germans in 1985/86 and an even better one in 1995/96. These immigrants are a positive selection. For the first period, the coefficients for all other groups of immigrants are, as expected, negative; statistically significant are the income deviations for those from European countries that are not part of the EU (about 10%) and those from Eastern Europe (about 14%). This structure was confirmed within ten years, with all depicted results being even more pronounced. Additionally, the coefficient for children coming from 'other' countries is also significantly negative, due to the included asylum seekers and refugees.

If a society is successfully integrating immigrants, their level of economic well-being should improve with the duration of stay in the host country. In the regression analysis we control this factor by brackets of years since the parents' migration. As expected, children born to newly arrived immigrants (those who had been in Germany no longer than five years) lived on a significantly lower income. In 1985/86, this income differential was about a fifth of that of native-born German children; within ten years this gap widened to more than a third. We may, however, be witnessing the beginning of a long-term integration success story. Whereas in 1985/86 all children born to immigrants and foreigners – no matter when their parents had come to Germany – lived on lower incomes than native-born German children, in 1995/96 there were no more significant income differentials for those whose parents had lived in Germany for more than 20 years or had been born in the country.

Poverty

The poverty head-count ratio, based at a poverty threshold of 50% of median income (see Table 11.3), of native-born children nearly doubled from 1985/86 to 1995/96, from 8.5% to 15.2%, whereas the corresponding rate for German immigrant children only increased from 10% to 14%. Again, children born to foreigners experienced a higher increase, from

16% to 24%. Additional information on poverty comes from the poverty index ($P_{\alpha=2}$), which also gives information on the degree of poverty. For native-born children, this index, when based at a poverty line at 50% of median income, confirms the head-count ratio results when it doubles from 0.0151 to 0.0328. On the other hand, for children of foreigners, the index skyrocketed from 0.0122 to 0.0674, while it remained stable for German immigrants.

Again, we employed regression models to validate these descriptive findings. The results of logistic regression models, which analyse the multiple determinants of poverty, are in line with those of the regressions on income. Nevertheless, since by definition the analysis of relative poverty concentrated on the lower end of the income distribution, there are a few notable exceptions.

Children with 'pure' foreign parents (ie both parents are foreigners) were most exposed to poverty, while 'pure' German immigrants as well as 'mixed' foreigners seemed at less risk of falling into poverty even than native-born German children. The children of immigrants from European non-EU countries (mostly Turkey and the former Yugoslavia) as well as from the 'other' category (including asylum seekers and refugees) had the greatest chance of being poor. On the other hand, children in households coming from EU-countries and other Western industrialised countries again proved to be in a positive selection, having a poverty risk lower than that of native-born German children.

Not surprisingly, those who immigrated most recently (during the last five years) were in the worst position. Compared to the reference group and with all other things being equal, children in this group exhibited a poverty risk about four times as high in 1985/86 and almost three times as high in the mid-1990s. For the 1985/86 estimation, this effect erodes somewhat with extended duration of stay in Germany, and was no longer significant for those whose parents had entered Germany more than 20 years ago (the *guestworker* of the 1960s). The picture for the second period 1995/96 is somewhat different. A significant poverty boosting effect can only be seen for those children with recently immigrated parents.

Educational enrolment

There is no formal discrimination against foreign-born or foreign-national children in the German educational system. However, there are no specific anti-discrimination measures, or special training for children who are not native German-speakers.

Table 11.4: Educational enrolment of 13- to 16-year-old children in Germany, by immigrant status

	1986				
	West Germany				East Germany
	Native-born German	German immigrant	Foreigner	Total	Total
Type of school					
Hauptschule	33.8	35.8	56.6	36.5	na
Realschule	24.4	8.4	13.1	22.7	na
Gymnasium	24.2	25.8	13.6	23.0	na
Other[a]	17.6	30.0	16.7	17.8	na
Total	100.0	100.0	100.0	100.0	na
	1996				
	West Germany				**East Germany**
	Native-born German	**German immigrant**	**Foreigner**	**Total**	**Total**
Type of school					
Hauptschule	26.5	28.8	39.2	28.7	7.5
Realschule	24.8	22.3	25.1	24.6	36.7
Gymnasium	32.3	25.9	18.9	29.5	36.9
Other[a]	16.4	23.0	16.8	17.2	19.2
Total	100.0	100.0	100.0	100.0	100.0

[a]This category includes *Waldorfschule*, *Gesamtschule*, special schools for the disabled, as well as vocational training.

Source: GSOEP, authors' calculations

Table 11.4 gives some insight into the educational enrolment of the sub-group of 13 to 16-year-old children who were most likely on their final school track. In other words, the school where they were educated at this age was most likely the one from which they would receive their final degree. The German school system differentiates three major levels: *Hauptschule* is the lowest level with graduation after nine years of school, *Realschule* ends after tenth grade, and successfully finishing *Gymnasium* qualifies students for university access (cf Wagner et al, 1998). Pupils who successfully finish *Hauptschule* or *Realschule* are mostly looking for an apprenticeship to go on with vocational training. Without any doubt, in a tight apprenticeship market the odds are against those with a *Hauptschule*-degree. Thus, it is interesting to see which type of school a child is attending, since this is a good indicator for further development and future economic success.

Over the period 1985/86 to 1995/96, the proportion of foreign children attending *Gymnasium* increased from 14% to 19% (see also Jeschek, 1999). Nevertheless, this is still a lower proportion in comparison to both other groups, with a third of natives and a quarter of German immigrants attending this type of school. Most impressive is the clear reduction in the proportion of foreigners attending the lowest school level (*Hauptschule*). This proportion dropped from 57% to 39%.

For a multiple analysis of the determinants of school enrolment, we employed a logistic regression model to estimate the probability of attending the highest school level, *Gymnasium* (for tabulated results cf Frick and Wagner, 2000). Not surprisingly, this model confirms the well-known positive intergenerational correlation of education (cf Wagner et al, 1998).

More important for our research was the impact of immigration-specific variables on school enrolment. In both periods there was a significantly higher probability of being able to attend Gymnasium for children of 'mixed' parent couples of foreigners and Germans. On the other hand, in the mid-1980s there was a significantly lower *Gymnasium* attendance of children with 'purely' foreign parents. Ten years later, this effect still existed, though clearly reduced and no longer significant. Accounting for country of origin, children from non-EU countries (Turkey and former Yugoslavia) had a reduced probability for attending *Gymnasium* in the 1980s, while during 1995/96 the figures again confirm that children from western industrialised countries were in an advantageous position.

If integration were an ongoing process, one would expect that this situation would improve with extended duration of stay within the host country. In 1995/96, children whose parents had lived in Germany for ten to twenty years had an even higher probability of attending *Gymnasium* than the native-born German children.

Conclusions and outlook

Based on our empirical findings, we can draw the following conclusions. With respect to non-monetary as well as monetary indicators, there is still a remarkable difference in living conditions between native-born German children and those born to immigrants and foreigners. While the integration process of foreigners' children over the period 1985/86 to 1995/96 showed some signs of improvement, the children of ethnic Germans were a new problem group that was not sufficiently addressed by German politicians. When evaluating these differences within West

Germany, one also needs to take into account the position of children in East Germany, where monetary indicators show some similarities with the situation of non-native children in West Germany.

Given the overall richness of the German economy and society, poverty rates among children are surprisingly high. This is true for all children, whether they are native or foreign-born. From 1985/86 to 1996/96, the poverty head-count rates for West Germany (poverty line at 50% of median equivalent income) on average increased from about 10% to almost 17%; the 1995/96 average for children in East Germany was about 15%. Foreign-born immigrant children have a significantly higher poverty risk of about 24%, though among this group there seems to be an increasing concentration at the upper end of the income distribution as well. Although children of foreigners and immigrants in West Germany, as well as East German children, are heavily subsidised by public transfers, which make up about a fifth of their post-government income, their relative income position was only between 70% and 75% of the entire population. The group most exposed to poverty was made up of children of lone parents. Obviously, the German welfare state failed – or had major difficulties – in giving equal chances to all children. This high poverty risk of lone parents and their children was mostly due to the low labour-force participation rates of lone mothers. This very often is caused by insufficient child day care facilities, preventing lone parents from finding adequate jobs or even forcing them to stay out of the labour market (cf Spiess, 1997).

There is no formal 'discrimination' against immigrant children by the German school system. However, due to the strong intergenerational correlation concerning educational attainment, it is a problem that the educational level of immigrant parents as well as of foreign parents living in Germany is still clearly below the population average, although there are some signs of improvement. As a result of the low educational level of their parents, children born to immigrants and foreigners in Germany are on less favourable educational tracks more often than native-born German children. The long-term problem arising from this will be a persistently high number of rather poorly-qualified persons in the future work force who will face severe labour market problems and as such will be a problem for the German economy as a whole. In other words, the German educational system – including pre-school, school and vocational training – needs to provide equal opportunities for all children regardless of their social background. If necessary, there should be additional incentives for children born to immigrants and foreigners to overcome language disadvantages. In this context, some recently introduced institutional changes might be helpful as well: the facilitation of the naturalisation process for long-term resident aliens and the option for (temporary) dual citizenship for native-born children of foreigners.

Notes

[1] This accounts only for immigrants who arrived after 1949, the year the Federal Republic of Germany was founded.

[2] However, after the Second World War a lot of refugees came from former German 'settlements' in order to live in (West and East) Germany. But they were not treated as a 'foreign born' population; more importantly, they mostly spoke German, which is not the case for all 'ethnic Germans' who entered the country since the late 1980s.

[3] We concentrate on West Germany, since the proportion of foreign-born residents in East Germany (former GDR) is of negligible size.

[4] As long as these persons live in institutions (eg, refugee camps), they are not part of the GSOEP target population of private (non-institutionalised) households.

[5] In order to get more stable results, we pooled information over two years. The numbers of observations for these analyses are: 6,566 for the period 1985/86, and 5,648 in West Germany and 2,122 in East Germany for the period 1995/96.

[6] These annual income measures are part of the PSID-GSOEP Equivalent Data File produced by Cornell University in Ithaca, NY and the DIW in Berlin. For more information on this project see Burkhauser, Butrica and Daly, 1999. All income measures are cpi-adjusted in 1991 DM. Additionally, income measures for East Germany are adjusted for purchasing power differences.

[7] For the head count ratio, it does not matter if a poor person's income is only one monetary unit below the poverty line or 100 units, whereas the poverty index would be rather small in the first case, but would clearly increase if the latter were true.

[8] This information comes from the head of household and as such does not necessarily match the impression of the children.

[9] With respect to education, the parental population of our sample was very heterogeneous. Educational levels achieved in foreign countries are hard to compare with those in the German system. Thus, parental educational status in our analysis is based on the International Standard Classification of Education (ISCED) and gives the highest educational status achieved by a child's parents. Due to problems of comparing educational degrees received within Germany with those from abroad (see eg Reitz et al, 1999), we differentiated only three levels of education: 'without secondary education', 'secondary education', and 'some post-secondary education'.

[10] Based on GSOEP data, Büchel, Frick and Voges (1997) showed that in a bivariate comparison, immigrants to Germany have a higher probability of social assistance take-up when comparing them to natives. Nevertheless, when controlling for a variety of socioeconomic characteristics, this difference is clearly reduced.

References

Atkinson, A.B., Rainwater, L. and Smeeding, T.M. (1995) *Income distribution in OECD countries: The evidence from the Luxembourg Income Study*, Paris: OECD.

Büchel, F., Frick, J. and Voges, W. (1997) 'Der Sozialhilfebezug von Zuwanderern in Westdeutschland', *Koelner Zeitschrift fuer Soziologie und Sozialpsychologie*, vol 49, no 2, pp 272-90.

Burkhauser, R.V., Kreyenfeld, M. and Wagner, G.G. (1997) 'The German Socioeconomic Panel: a representative sample of reunited Germany and its parts', in T. Dunn and J. Schwarze (eds) Proceedings of the 1996 Second International Conference of Socioeconomic Panel Study Users, *Vierteljahrshefte zur Wirtschaftsforschung*, vol 66, no 1, pp 7-16.

Burkhauser, R.V., Butrica, B.A. and Daly, M.C. (1999) 'The PSID-GSOEP equivalent file: a product of cross-national research', in W. Voges (ed) *Dynamic approaches to comparative social research: Recent developments and applications*, Aldershot: Ashgate, pp 53-66.

Deutscher Bundestag (1998a) *Demographischer Wandel: Zweiter Zwischenbericht der Enquete-Kommission 'Demographischer Wandel' – Herausforderungen unserer älter werdenden Gesellschaft an den einzelnen und an die Politik*, Bonn.

Deutscher Bundestag (1998b) 'Zehnter Kinder- und Jugendbericht', *Bundestags-Drucksache* 13/11368 vom 25.8.1998.

Fassmann, H. and Muenz, R. (1994) 'Patterns and trends of international migration in Western Europe', in H. Fassmann and R. Muenz (eds) *European migration in the late twentieth century*, Aldershot, Brookfield: Elgar, pp 3-33.

Foster, J., Greer, J. and Thorbecke, E. (1984) 'A class of decomposable poverty measures', *Econometrica*, vol 52, no 3, pp 761-6.

Frick, J.R., Smeeding, T.M. and Wagner, G.G. (1999) 'Immigrants in two modern nations: characteristics of the foreign and native-born populations in Germany and the United States', in T.A. Dunn, J.R. Frick and J.C. Witte (eds) Proceedings of the 1998 Third International Conference of Socioeconomic Panel Study Users, *Vierteljahrshefte zur Wirtschaftsforschung*, vol 68, no 2, pp 297-307.

Frick, J.R. and Wagner, G.G. (2000) 'Short term living conditions and long term prospects of immigrant children in Germany', DIW-Discussion Paper No 229, Berlin.

Hailbronner, K. (1992) 'Citizenship and nationhood in Germany', in W. Brubaker (ed) *The politics of citizenship in France and in Germany*, Cambridge: Cambridge University Press, pp 67-79.

Jeschek, W. (1999) 'Integration junger Ausländer in das Bildungssystem verläuft langsamer', *DIW-Wochenbericht*, vol 66, no 22, pp 408-18 .

Reitz, J., Frick, J.R., Calabrese, T. and Wagner, G.G. (1999) 'The institutional framework of ethnic employment disadvantage: a comparison of Germany and Canada', *Journal of Ethnic and Migration Studies*, vol 25, no 3, pp 397-444.

Spiess, C.K. (1997) 'American and German mothers' child care choice: does policy matter?', in T.A. Dunn and J. Schwarze (eds) Proceedings of the 1996 Second International Conference of Socioeconomic Panel Study Users, *Vierteljahrshefte zur Wirtschaftsforschung*, vol 66, no 1, pp 125-35.

Wagner, G.G., Burkhauser, R,V. and Behringer, F. (1993) 'The English language public use file of the German Socioeconomic Panel Study', *Journal of Human Resources*, vol 28, no 2, pp 429-33.

Wagner, G.G., Büchel, F., Haisken-DeNew, J.P. and Spiess, C.K. (1998) 'Education as a keystone of integration of immigrants: determinants of school attainment of immigrant children in West Germany', in H. Kurthen, J. Fijalkowski and G.G. Wagner (eds) *Immigration, citizenship, and the welfare state in Germany and the United States: immigrant incorporation*, Industrial Development and Social Fabric Series Vol 14 A, Stamford, CT/London: JAI Press Inc, pp 15-35.

TWELVE

Who has borne the cost of Britain's children in the 1990s?

Hugh Davies and Heather Joshi[1]

Introduction

This chapter is about the cost of children in terms of adults' forgone income in Britain. In practice, this means mothers' incomes. In the 1980s (and the three preceding decades) the lifetime employment of British women appeared to conform to a stylised trajectory. Motherhood reduced women's participation in the labour market and often confined their hours of work to part-time jobs. Hourly earnings were lowered by taking part-time jobs and by interrupted employment experience. Over a lifetime, therefore, mothers would earn less than childless women through having fewer years of earnings, fewer hours of work when employed and lower rates of pay. Estimates were made of the forgone earnings of a hypothetical mother with various numbers of children (Joshi, 1990). These suggested that the typical mother of two children earned only about half as much as her childless counterpart after the age of childbearing. The missing half represents the earnings opportunity cost of motherhood. This has ramifications for taxation, benefits, pensions and the distribution of income within the family and upon divorce. These were explored with a simulation model, and the findings summarised by Joshi, Davies and Land (1996).

We also discovered that our central trajectory of a British mother with middle-level qualifications, whom we called 'Mrs Typical' did not appear to be so typical internationally and that it did not apply right across the British social spectrum. The earnings profile was similar to those for Germany (West) and the Netherlands and to that of lower skilled women in both France and Britain; but it was much more disrupted than the profile for Sweden and for women in France with a high initial labour force attachment and for graduates in Britain. The latter all achieved greater, if not complete, employment continuity, presumably facilitated by maternity leave, public or private day care and other supportive measures.

The lifetimes simulated in all this previous work take place in a time warp where the parameters of participation, hours and pay relationships observed in 1980 are frozen in perpetuity. We now take parameters based on data observed in the mid-1990s, and investigate their implications for lifetime earnings and forgone earnings due to motherhood. How is the earnings opportunity cost of children distributed between the two parents and the state? Given that children do not always have two parents, we also investigate how lone motherhood affects a woman's lifetime earnings.

Rising participation of women in the 1980s and 1990s was particularly marked among mothers of pre-school children. The archetypal biography of Mrs Typical, staying out of employment until her youngest child goes to school, has become less typical. Although public provision of day care remained low by most international standards, the use of privately purchased childcare grew rapidly in the 1990s (Finlayson et al, 1996). The qualification level of British women has continued to improve relative to men, and relative rates of pay for identically qualified and experienced men and women have also improved, although the pay penalty to part-time employment has worsened. Many of these developments would tend to reduce the extent to which British mothers have been staying away from the labour market while they raise children. Some of the developments on the wages front would have increased the cash penalties of not earning, particularly not earning full-time.

The plan of the chapter is as follows. The next section outlines our method and assumptions. There follow two sections concerning the magnitude and distribution of the forgone labour market income costs of children in intact marriages. Sections on divorce and teenage mothers come next.

Method and assumptions

Our simulation model generates the lifetime earnings of illustrative women and their husbands from econometric functions and then applies tax, benefit and pension rules to these simulated gross earnings, with and without redistribution within a couple. Participation and earnings functions were estimated on data from the British Household Panel Survey (BHPS). The data mainly came from the 4th Wave (1994).

Participation is modelled by a multinomial logit, which distinguishes between part-time and full-time work. A woman is assumed to be employed when the predicted probability of any employment exceeds 0.5. If employed, she is assigned to full- or part-time states by whichever has the higher probability. Hours of paid work depend on sex, occupational grade and whether part-time or full-time. The wages for female participants are obtained from separate wage equations for full-time and part-time jobs.

The couples

Our simulations allow for three occupational levels. Our central figure has some schooling beyond the minimum: think of her as a secretary. We compare her with a graduate (perhaps a teacher), and another woman, who left school with no qualifications and takes only low-skill jobs, such as a shop assistant. We also created a husband for each woman. In this exercise we concentrate on couples in the same skill band, although we also include a man in a high-level occupation married to a woman in a low-level occupation, a combination that is becoming less common as women's skill levels increase in successive cohorts. We assume that there are no interruptions to earnings histories, apart from those due to childcare responsibilities. Our illustrative people are not averages, rather they are 'typical' individuals in a hypothetical world where uninterrupted male careers are the norm.

We simulate four types of fertility history: married women with no, one, two and four children. A woman marries at age 20, 22 or 24, depending (positively) on her occupational level. If she has two children, these are born three years after marriage and three years after that. If she has four children, they arrive at two-year intervals. In most of the following we give results here only for women with two children. Although these marriage and fertility assumptions do not reflect the trend towards later childbearing in the 1990s, we keep them to facilitate comparisons with previous work. In each case the man is assumed to be two years older than his wife. Men are assumed to live up to age 78 and women up to age 81.

Lone mothers

We look at the two main entry routes into lone motherhood – via divorce and from births out of wedlock, among the latter, we focus on women who are teenagers at the birth of their first child. We take two examples of divorces, occurring after the birth of two children (or at a corresponding age if the women has no children). The first is a relatively short duration marriage assumed to end after 8 years, and the other later divorce after 18 years of marriage when the youngest child, if any, is aged 2 and 12 respectively. We also allow for one example of remarriage, occurring 10 years after an early divorce. Divorcing fathers are assumed to remarry almost immediately, and to father two children in their second marriage – one born the year after the divorce and the second two years after that. These assumptions affect the amount of child support payable (see below).

Although there are many very short duration marriages, we have not found it interesting to simulate them, particularly as they typically do not involve children. Furthermore, available data suggest that if divorced women remarry, they tend to do so quickly and at a younger age, and tend to have their second or third child in their early 30s (Office for National Statistics, 1999). Thus there is little advantage to simulating a history involving a very short marriage, since it would be very similar to that of the average continuously married woman.

The simulations allow for two types of lone mothers who were not previously married. We concentrate on teenage motherhood – in 1997, there were 56,000 live births to teenage mothers in Britain, the highest rate in Europe (Social Exclusion Unit, 1999). The importance of childbirth at young ages is indicated by the fact that more than a third of lone mothers are under 25 (Haskey, 1998, p 10). In both the teenage motherhood scenarios simulated, the woman has her first child when she is 18 and unpartnered. In the first case the woman never marries (or cohabits) and she has a second child when she is 21, while in the second case the woman enters an enduring marriage when she is 20 (22 if mid-skill) and has her second child two years after the marriage. In either case, the women are assumed to seek (and obtain) employment in accordance with the predictions of our labour supply model. To highlight the cases of women who bring up children without the support of a partner, we have assumed that the fathers of the children born outside wedlock in these cases, are unemployed or on very low wages, so that they contribute only minimal child support. In the case of the young mother who marries when her child is two, we assume that the husband is not the father of the first child, and is continuously employed. In this case, therefore, the teenage start to childbearing might be expected to have a relatively small effect on the woman's lifetime income.

In the simulations of teenage mothers, there are no highly educated cases, since a woman who has a child at age 18 is unlikely to graduate from university (or attain other advanced qualifications) at the normal age.

Timing

The simulations reported here take place in a time warp, as in a life table. There is no inflation or economic growth: earnings levels are calibrated to January 1998 levels.

Institutional features

Our model calculates the major components of the (direct) tax, benefit and pension systems as they apply to those who do not suffer from long-term illness or disability. We assume that all relevant tax and benefit rates are fixed at their April 1998 levels, except for child support. Rules for tax, benefit and pension schemes are generally fixed to be those faced by someone entering the labour force in 1998. We have included policies that are not yet in effect in two areas: child support and pension splitting.

Child support. The 1991 Child Support Act set up the Child Support Agency (CSA). This legislation established a formula for calculating how much an absent parent (usually a father) should contribute towards the upkeep of his children. The legislation was deeply unpopular with all concerned. Despite various attempts to simplify the procedures and the formula for calculating entitlement to child support, the CSA never managed to get on top of its caseload and became a byword for bureaucratic incompetence. The government has proposed a new system for child support (DSS, 1999). This is based on a very simple formula – in particular, neither the income of the man's ex-spouse nor that of his current spouse enters into the calculation. The payment is based entirely on the man's net income and on the numbers and ages of his children in the receiving family, and the numbers and ages of the children in the family in which he is currently resident. There is a lower limit for the amount of payment: even a father on low earnings or dependent entirely on benefits must pay £5 a week child support. Our calculations assess liability for child support in this new system, and have assumed compliance with the new legislation. This is in line with the implicit assumption of our model that the rules of the tax/benefit system are applied perfectly throughout – there is no tax evasion or failure to claim (or pay) benefit.

Pension splitting. Traditionally, in English law a divorcing couple have no claim on each other's pensions. Legislation has recently been introduced to enable occupational pensions (including the state earnings-related pension, SERPS) to be split as part of the divorce settlement. The new law enables, but does not require, pension assets to be treated like other assets and divided on divorce. In our simulations, we have, however, assumed that couples split the value of their earnings-related pension rights equally and that the value transferred is used to purchase a pension (rather than being traded-off against other assets). For a more detailed discussion of pension splitting, see Davies and Joshi (1999).

Family transfer

In view of the assumed function of marriage as a mechanism pooling resources and supporting 'dependants', one potential source of a woman's income is a share in the earnings of her husband. Our analysis will explicitly quantify the importance of the conventional assumption that income is shared equally between the partners in a marriage. We refer to the implied transfer of purchasing power as the 'family transfer', without suggesting that the transfer is entirely altruistic or un-reciprocated. We think of a person's income over the lifecycle as deriving from three sources: the market (here the labour market only), the state and any transfer that they might receive from a partner. We do not make allowance for any economies of scale in consumption that may be realised by sharing living arrangements or for the expenditure costs of children – there is no equivalisation of incomes in this chapter.

Earnings cost of children: intact marriages

Our simulations generate a set of earnings profiles. Figure 12.1 shows the earnings trajectories of the four types of woman with zero, one, two and four children. Long breaks in earnings are apparent for most of the low skilled mothers. Mothers of four in all types have more part-time employment than do those with fewer children. The mid-skill mother of two (and one) loses earnings relative to her childless counterpart mainly through spells of part-time work. Once she returns to full-time work her earnings do not take long to catch up. The same goes for the graduate mothers, although the period of reduced earnings is shorter. Note that the vertical axes are on different scales. The mid-level earnings profile is only modestly above and steeper than that of the low skilled (plateauing at £14,000 pa 1998 prices for a continuously full-time employed worker, compared with £11,000 for the least skilled). The graduate earnings profile, by contrast, soars to more than double (£29,000). This is a widening gulf between the highly educated and the rest compared to our simulations for the 1980s.

Figure 12.1: Earnings profiles for childless women and mothers at various skill levels

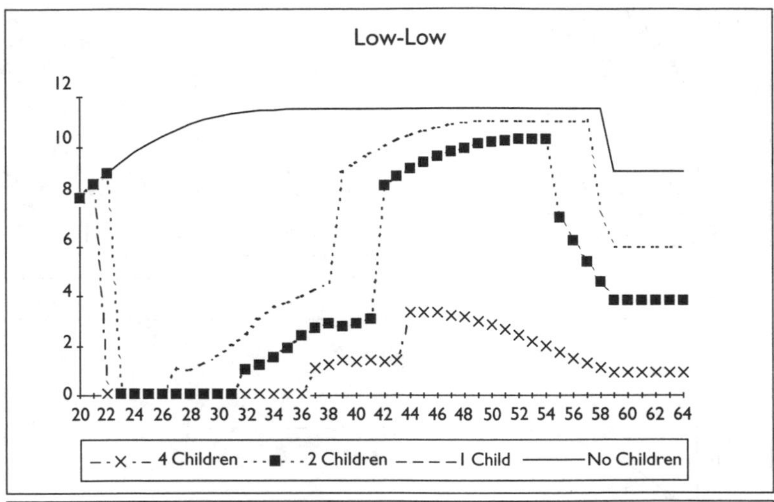

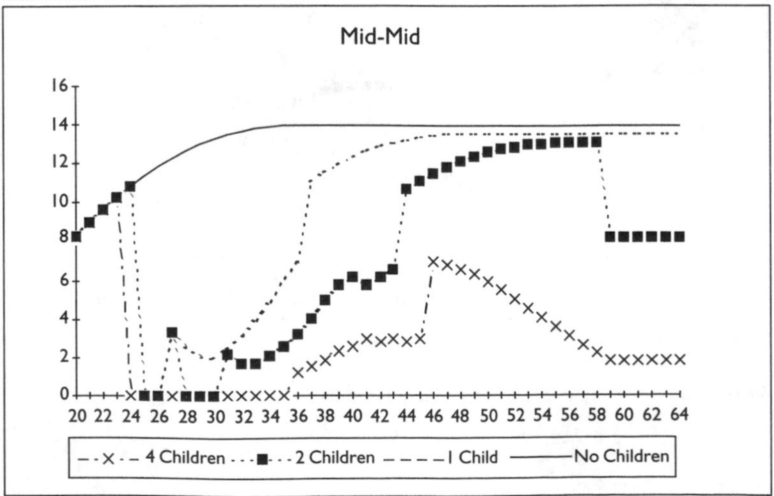

Figure 12.1: cont.../

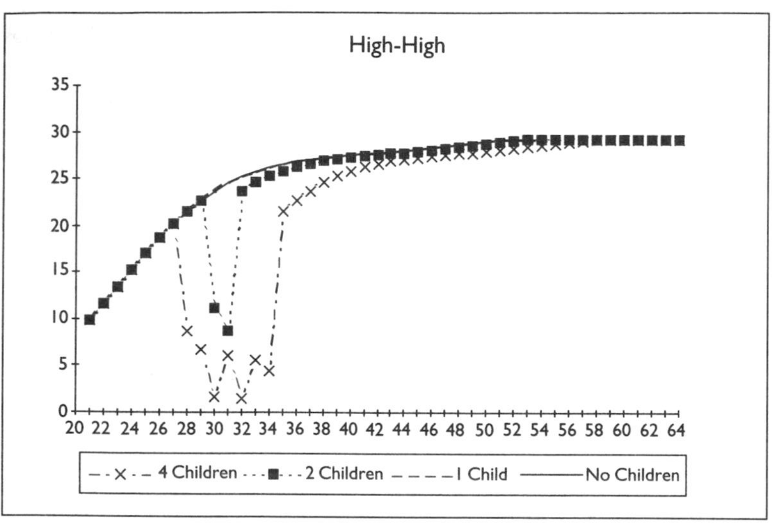

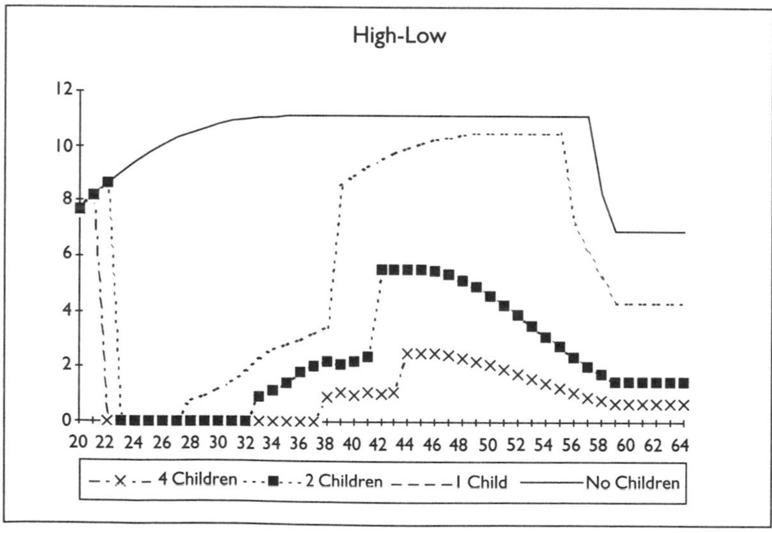

Source: Authors' calculations from simulation model

Table 12.1: Forgone earnings cost of motherhood

Type of marriage	Unbroken	Short	Long	Remarries
£000s, 1998				
Both low-skill	255	223	214	268
Both mid-skill	257	180	200	230
Both high-skill	39	39	39	39
He high, she low	334	223	222	336
As percent of potential earnings after first birth				
Both low-skill	58	49	47	61
Both mid-skill	47	33	37	42
Both high-skill	4	4	4	4
He high, she low	78	49	48	78

Note: Forgone earnings cost is gross earnings for childless woman minus gross earnings for mother with same marital history.
Source: Authors' calculations from simulation model

The areas in the graphs in Figure 12.1 between the line for the childless woman's earnings and those of the various mothers represent the earnings forgone as a result of responsibility for children, because the women being compared are otherwise identical. The closer the lines, as in the High-High couple, the less the earnings forgone; the bigger the gap, as for the low skilled woman, the bigger the sum forgone. The (undiscounted) totals represented by the areas for the two-child cases are shown in the 'Unbroken' column ofTable 12.1. In the central case, the mid-skill mother of two forgoes £257,000, or 47% of her earnings after the age of childbearing. This is almost identical to the sum (£258,000 at 1998 prices) we obtained in our 1980-based estimates, although it is a lower fraction of potential earnings than the 55% we obtained earlier. In the present estimates a similar absolute sum is forgone by the woman with two children in a low-skilled couple, representing a higher proportion (58%) of her lifetime earnings. This is a higher cash sum than the earlier estimate but, as for the mid-skilled woman, it represents a lower fraction of potential earnings after the first birth than the 62% we previously obtained. The graduate mother of two forgoes £39,000, amounting to just 4% of her potential earnings after motherhood, as compared to 18% in the 1980 simulations.

Table 12.1 also shows the earnings costs of two children for the simulated divorced women. Before picking up their story, we turn to the distribution of the forgone earnings costs in cases with intact marriages.

Table 12.2: Who bears the cost of two children: unbroken marriages (percentage of woman's labour market cost)

	Woman	Man	State
Both low-skill	36	35	30
Both mid-skill	34	33	33
Both high-skill	10	10	79
He high, she low	37	36	28

Note: Labour market cost is forgone earnings cost adjusted for earnings-related pension contributions and receipts.
Source: Authors' calculations from simulation model

Distribution of the earnings costs

The costs of the mother's forgone earnings do not fall entirely during the years she is of labour force age, and they do not entirely fall on her. Some losses may be deferred insofar as earnings-related pensions are reduced by motherhood. We treat earnings-related pension as deferred labour income and define labour market income as gross earnings less pension contributions plus pension payments. Losses may also be spread to other people insofar as there are transfer payments each year, to or from the state through taxes and benefits and, if her partner pools his income, within the family. If the net marginal rate of tax less benefit is around 33% and all family income is split, then every pound not earned by a mother will have an incidence that is roughly split in three equal portions between herself, her partner and the state.

Table 12.2 shows who bears the labour income cost of two children in an unbroken marriage, on the assumption of perfect pooling within marriage. The estimates for the low-and mid- skilled couples show the neat three-way split between mother, father and state. For the graduates, the contribution of the state has gone up to 79%.

This reflects the fact that the total lost earnings has become quite small for the higher paid, and so child benefit is a large fraction of forgone labour income. Furthermore, the better paid women pay higher average tax rates on a year's earnings, so that any time they do take out of the labour force is more expensive for the state than is the time of low-skilled women. The contributions of the man and the woman are nearly identical, but not quite. We assume there is complete pooling of revenue while both are alive, but we also assume that the woman outlives the man and therefore spends some years experiencing a reduced pension without being able to split the deficit with her now deceased spouse. To the extent that the marginal pound earned by a woman is not put into a family pool (and our participation estimates suggest it is not), the split between man and woman can be assumed to take different values, which we have not so far explored. If there has been a shift away from family transfers spreading the net earnings costs of motherhood between men and women, as Folbre (1994) suggests, then women's apparent gains might have to be reconsidered. It is also worth noting that greater continuity of employment involves other costs, notably those of providing maternity leave and childcare. We have not attempted to quantify either of these, but some of them may fall on the employer. Many people believe that the private costs of purchased childcare fall disproportionately on mothers.

Divorce

Income in cases with divorce

In considering divorce, we look only at cases involving two or zero children, on the assumptions set out above.

Divorce may have two effects on labour supply: on the one hand, lone-parenthood increases the burden of domestic work and may make the organisation of childcare difficult, thus decreasing labour supply; on the other hand, the loss of income from a partner will tend to increase labour supply. (Unless there is also an entitlement to strongly means-tested benefit that tends to inhibit employment.) Our calculations take no account of childcare, domestic work or any selection effects in divorce towards less contributive husbands.

We first look at the lifetime income costs of divorce, on the assumption that equal sharing prevailed in the marriage. We define the cost of divorce for the woman in terms of the difference between the outcomes had she divorced and had she remained married. After divorce, the woman is presumed to lose the family transfer and the survivor's pension she would have received had the marriage been ended by the death of the husband. This initial loss may be offset from a number of sources: increased labour supply by the woman, greater net benefits from the state, and child support payments and pension share from the ex-husband. Table 12.3 quantifies these effects.

Our simulated low- and mid-skill divorcees who remain unmarried after divorce have greater labour supply than their continuously married

Table 12.3: Costs of divorce: Woman with two children

Type of marriage	Short	Long (£000s, 1998)	Remarrried
Low-skill woman, divorced from low-skill man			
Initial loss from divorce	138	91	138
Offsetting income increases			
Fom labour market	48	58	-14
From child support	22	7	22
From pension share	2	5	2
From tax/benefit system	23	-11	29
From second husband			96
Net cost of divorce	43	32	3
Mid-skill woman, divorced from mid-skill man			
Initial loss from divorce	207	157	207
Offsetting income increases			
Fom labour market	80	61	27
From child support	29	8	29
From pension share	27	50	27
From tax/benefit system	-8	-21	4
From second husband			144
Net cost of divorce	78	60	-25
High-skill woman, divorced from high-skill man			
Initial loss from divorce	90	80	90
Offsetting income increases			
Fom labour market	0	0	0
From child support	46	12	46
From pension share	12	7	12
From tax/benefit system	18	15	-1
From second husband			70
Net cost of divorce	13	45	-39

Note: Costs of divorce calculated as difference from outcome for woman with unbroken marriage and identical fertility.

Source: Authors' calculations from simulation model

counterparts. The most dramatic labour supply response to divorce is displayed by the low-skill woman who is divorced from a high-skill man after a 'short' (eight-year) marriage. After divorce, she does little part-time work in the labour market. She tends to take either no employment or full-time employment, whereas her continuously married counterpart never resumes full-time work after she has her children. The high-skill woman is simulated to remain in full-time employment after the divorce – the same behaviour as if she had remained married.

The state tax/benefit system has varied effects on divorced women *vis-à-vis* their continuously married counterparts. The high-skill women gain from the tax/benefit system: as their earnings have not increased, neither have their taxes, and they get a tax allowance of equal value to the Married Couple's Allowance which would have formerly been shared with a husband. In the tax/benefit rules simulated here, (untaxed) child benefit is paid at a higher rate to lone mothers than to married mothers. The low-skill women from the low-skill couple who have short marriages, increase their labour supply relatively little, and are net gainers from the state. In other cases, large increases in labour supply lead to tax increases, which more than offset the higher benefit levels. Recent and forthcoming changes in the tax and benefit system are likely to affect these findings. In particular, the relatively low paid will benefit from the new Working Families Tax Credit – a more generous benefit than the Family Credit it is replacing. Turning to the offsetting income increases provided by the father, we see that, as expected, child support provides a much larger contribution in the case of short marriages (where the children are dependent for longer after their parents divorce). Child support payments offset only a relatively small fraction of the lost family transfer in the couples with low- or mid-skill men, whereas over half the lost family transfer is made up from child support payments in the case of the high-skill couple who divorce after a short marriage. The total of the offsetting income provided by fathers includes the ex-wife's assumed share of his pension.

Remarriage has substantial effects, according to our simulations. The women who remarry increase their lifetime labour supply much less than divorcees who do not, and in some cases supply less market labour than their continuously married counterparts. We assume that they benefit from the family transfer provided by their second husbands. This is shown explicitly in Table 12.3 in the 'from second husband' rows, and it offsets a large fraction of the initial loss. Remarriage does not affect entitlement to child support or to a share in the ex-husband's pension, and this is what accounts for the income increase shown in some of the 'net cost of divorce' rows of Table 12.3.

It may be worth repeating that these estimates of cost of divorce are based on a large number of assumptions. In particular, we are not looking at the most pessimistic scenario with respect to employment after divorce, and we are also being optimistic about the payment of child support (see Jarvis and Jenkins, 1999). We may also have overstated the 'payoff' to staying married if those who are supposed to enjoy a 'family transfer' in fact receive less than we have assumed.

Costs of children in cases with divorce

What is the effect of divorce on the revenue cost of children? We calculate the cost of children for a divorced woman by comparing her income with that of a childless counterpart experiencing the same marital history, and the costs are shown alongside those for the women with unbroken marriages in Table 12.1. The revenue costs of children are generally lower for the cases involving divorce, and higher with remarriage. This is because divorce does not increase the labour supply of childless women much (in our simulations all childless women have high employment propensities), but it increases the labour supply of mothers. For divorced women, therefore, the gap between the labour supply of the mothers and their childless counterparts is smaller than for the continuously married. For re-marriage, just the opposite holds.

The workings of the tax/benefit system and of the child support and pension splitting mechanisms discussed above mean that the net income cost of children is very substantially smaller than the gross income cost for the illustrative cases of divorce, especially after a short marriage. Indeed, according to these simulations, the high-skill women stand to gain income from having children, if they also divorce.

The distribution of the revenue cost of two children in divorced cases is shown in Table 12.4. It should be emphasised that we are here concerned only with the revenue cost. We take no account of the fact that the divorced woman will have to provide for the children entirely from her own resources, while her married counterpart may share the expenditure costs of children (as well as income) with her spouse (see Jarvis and Jenkins, 1999). In this table we distinguish between the father of the children and the mother's second husband, and we also include explicitly the amount contributed by the father after the divorce from child support. Apart from the cases of high-skilled men, the fathers contribute a much higher proportion of the revenue costs where the marriage is longer-lived: indeed the mid-skill couple who divorce after a long marriage almost preserve the equal three-way split we remarked upon above in the case of the unbroken marriage. Generally, it seems that (if the putative family transfer actually takes place) marriage provides a better vehicle for sharing the costs of children between man and woman than the post-marital sharing mechanisms modelled here (child support and pension splitting). Nevertheless, for the low- and mid-skill fathers who divorce after a short marriage, over half the amount they are simulated to contribute to the revenue costs of their children comes in the form of child support

Table 12.4: Who bears the revenue cost of children in cases of divorce? (percentages of woman's labour market cost)

Type of marriage	Short	Long	Remarries
Low-skill couple			
Woman	35	38	30
Father	18	28	15
Second husband	0	0	16
State	47	34	39
Of father's share, due to:			
Child support	10	3	8
Mid-skill couple			
Woman	28	32	27
Father	28	33	22
Second husband	0	0	11
State	45	36	40
Of father's share, due to:			
Child support	16	4	12
High-skill couple			
Woman	–161	–48	–127
Father	166	71	166
Second husband	0	0	–26
State	96	77	87
Of father's share, due to:			
Child support	129	34	129
Mixed-skill couple (man high, woman low)			
Woman	33	38	31
Father	28	30	19
Second husband	0	0	20
State	39	32	31
Of father's share, due to:			
Child support	20	5	13

Source: Authors' calculations

payments. If the new system does indeed secure a high level of compliance, this will constitute a non-negligible source of income as contrasted with the status quo in which only about a quarter of fathers pay child support. The state generally bears a larger share of the (lower) income costs of children in these divorce simulations than in the cases where the marriage is unbroken. In interpreting the rather peculiar-looking results for the high-skill couple, it is necessary to bear in mind that these are percentages of (small) income *increases*. Where the woman remarries, her second husband makes a substantial contribution if she is low- or mid-skilled (greater than that of the father if she is low-skilled). The second husband

Table 12.5: Teenage mothers: Who bears the revenue cost of two children?

	Never married	Married later
Low-skill woman		
Labour market costs (£000s, 1998)	*391*	*435*
As percent of base earnings	76	88
Paid by (percentages)		
mother	48	41
father	1	1
husband		38
state	51	20
Mid-skill woman		
Labour market costs (£000s, 1998)	*350*	*580*
As percent of base earnings	55	92
Paid by (percentages)		
mother	49	41
father	1	1
husband		36
state	50	22

Note: The costs are defined relative to a childless woman with same marital history.

Source: Authors' calculations

of the simulated high-skill woman gets a share of her income gain from the children.

Teenage mothers

Another way in which childrearing may depart from the model nuclear family is if it starts outside wedlock. As discussed above, we consider two scenarios for teenage mothers (for low- and mid-skilled women only). In the first scenario, the woman never marries and her counterpart is the childless unmarried woman. In the other case, the woman marries some time after the birth of the first child, and her counterpart is a woman who marries at the same age as she does, but never has children.

Table 12.5 shows the cost of forgone labour market income to these teenage mothers. Our participation model projects that these teenage mothers who never marry do not take employment while they have dependent children, but they return to part-time work (if they are low-skilled) or full-time work (if mid-skilled) thereafter and continue in employment until pension age. This means that the low-skill teenage mothers lose £391,000 gross earnings and the mid-skilled £350, 000 – substantially more than the sum of around a quarter of a million simulated for those who start childbearing later within marriage (23 for the low-skilled couple and 25 for the mid-skilled). The extra losses arise therefore from starting childbearing five or eight years earlier and illustrate the earnings gains to be made from deferring motherhood. Whatever their skill level, the simulated lone mothers must themselves bear just under half of the labour market cost. They receive very little monetary help from the fathers of their children – although it must be born in mind that these cases have been deliberately selected to illustrate this possibility. If the fathers contribute substantially more, however, the main effect will be a reduction in the state's contribution. By far the largest element in the state's contribution comes from Income Support, the means-tested social safety net, and this will be reduced pound for pound by any increase in the father's contribution above the £10 per week disregard.

For the teenage mothers who find a husband, things are rather different in our simulations. Although these women take up part-time employment for six years while they have dependent children and stay in employment until state pension age, they never return to the labour market full-time and their forgone labour market income is greater than that of those who never married. It is the presence of the husband (presumably sharing his income) which enables this lower level of labour market activity. The husband (and father of the second child) contributes over a third of the forgone labour income, and the state provides a much smaller fraction of the total – when she marries an employed man, the woman will no longer be eligible for Income Support.

It is interesting to compare teenage mothers with other young women who reverse the order of marriage and childbearing (Rake, 2000). If we assume perfect pooling while married, the women who get married at 19 and have their first child when they are 21 have substantially higher lifetime incomes than the teenage mothers who get married at 21. They get about 27% more than the teenage mothers in the low-skilled case and 35% if mid-skilled.

The calculations discussed above make no allowance for any selection effects. It is possible that teenage mothers are not a random sample of their skill group, and that the labour market earning potential of the childless counterpart assumed here may be too optimistic.

Conclusions

Highly qualified women in Britain in the 1990s appear to be even more attached to full-time employment than they were in the 1980s. Most women of middle level earning power are now also more likely than not to be in the labour force (although on a part-time basis) during most of the years when they have young children. Those of lesser earning power do not appear to have increased their attachment to the labour force during the child-rearing years by much. Our method of simulating the lifetime earnings of illustrative individuals suggests that the earnings costs of motherhood have gone down for women of high earning power and have gone down or stayed about the same for women of middle earning power depending on whether they have one or two children. For the least qualified, they have tended to go up. This adds new evidence to a number of other sources that the experience of employment after childbearing is becoming polarised (see Dex et al, 1996). Motherhood is no longer the social leveller it was, since the earnings of two-earner families will tend to grow relative to families with only one breadwinner, who is increasingly likely to be less well paid himself.

The high level of employment continuity around the time of childbirth, which we have simulated for the more highly skilled mothers, is partly due to the growth of maternity leave. Employers have also been introducing various other 'family friendly' practices, particularly for the benefit of more skilled workers (Forth et al, 1997). Another development running parallel to the increase in career continuity is the increased use of childcare. Those who can afford these largely private childcare arrangements seem to be making them (although informal childcare arrangements are still very common, particularly for mothers with part-time jobs). The indirect costs of motherhood are thus being transformed, for more women, into the direct costs of day care. Our calculations have not included childcare costs. They may well be replacing the forgone earnings costs calculated here. It is also believed that such expenditure falls disproportionately on women.

The simulations suggest that Britain is becoming one of those countries where the number of children, rather than the age of the youngest, is the most important predictor of labour-force participation. Although this does not apply across the board, it may have implications for projections of the labour force as well as of fertility.

A few words of caution about the results are in order. Our 'first past the post' method of assigning employment status to our illustrative cases ignores cases at the other side of the distribution and may produce some distortion – it would be desirable to extend the model to simulate a distribution of individuals not just 'representatives'. We have not, so far, made any allowance for interruptions to husbands' earnings, or for interruptions to women's earnings from other sources than childbearing. The simulations reported here do not allow for the re-timing of fertility in the 1990s to later ages, which our model shows to induce greater employment continuity and hence lower forgone earnings. Here we have not calculated the costs of direct expenditures or of the non-market time involved in bringing up children, but see Joshi and Davies (2000) for an attempt to do so.

We have shown how lifelong married couples may share the earnings costs of motherhood by pooling family income. If the marriage is ended prematurely the lone mother is left to manage without the pooling. Our simulations show that the structure of her income sources also changes. She is likely to earn more, in the long term, than if she had remained married, but also to draw more benefit from the state. On the basis of new legislation, she is likely to be entitled to a share of the husband's pension and, on an optimistic assumption, to draw child support payments from him. The contributions of the fathers through child support and pension splitting do not, however, come close to compensating for the lost family transfer. While the share of these revenue costs borne by divorced women (on these assumptions) may not be much greater than that borne by married mothers, it is greater for the young unmarried mothers we have simulated. Our results suggest that remarriage is an attractive financial option for divorced women (especially if they are not highly skilled) and that marriage is similarly attractive for the teenage mothers. This is mainly because of the assumption of income pooling, and so these results again serve to emphasize the importance of this assumption, and the deprivation likely to be suffered by women in marriages where pooling is incomplete or not practised.

The expenditure and time costs are likely to change considerably with changes in marital status. Our results may therefore understate the losses from divorce, even leaving aside issues of emotional costs and benefits of building or breaking up a family.

We have not attempted to quantify the undoubted benefits of raising children in Britain, but we have tried to apportion the costs of lost earnings between three of the parties who have an interest: mothers, fathers and the state, assuming a public interest in producing the next generation of citizens. On the initial assumption of lifelong and income-pooling marriage, the costs are spread fairly evenly between mothers, fathers and the Exchequer (apart from the graduate mothers who hardly forgo any earnings anyway). For cases of divorce and out of wedlock childbearing, the father's contribution would tend to diminish, but may not disappear if child support is actually paid. The prospect of pension splitting is another route through which fathers absent from their children may help to pay for their costs, but this makes a relatively minor overall contribution in our simulations. The state's share in the earnings cost of two children (through forgone tax and benefit paid out) rises from around one third in the case of intact marriages, through a bit more than 40% for the early divorce to around 50% in the case of unmarried teenage motherhood. This is abated if the mother remarries. Because we do not observe intra-family transactions, or know if the child support arrangements now being recommended will be observed, our estimated allocation between mother and father is hypothetical. The full answer to the question in our title needs these estimates to be supplemented with data on expenditures, particularly the expenditures on childcare which are increasingly substituting for the self-provisioning which results in the earnings shortfall we have analysed here.

Children reduce income, but they raise the need for also it. The lower income is when they are dependent upon it, the less expenditure there will be on the children. In this way, particularly if the reduction in income leads to child poverty, the children themselves also bear part of the cost. If reduced income stretches into old age, the mother may then become dependent on her offspring. Both these considerations suggest that the incidence of the income cost of children may spread from the parents to the children, but these intergenerational transfers have been beyond the scope of this chapter.

Note

[1] This is a shortened version of the paper presented at the 1999 Conference. The full paper is available as Davies and Joshi (1999). We are grateful to the Leverhulme Trust for supporting this research, under the project 'Living Arrangements and Livelihoods over the Life Cycle' (grant F/353/G), and to the ESRC Data Archive for access to data from the British Household Panel Survey. Romana Peronaci contributed valuable assistance.

References

DSS (Department of Social Security) (1999) *Children's rights and parents' responsibilities*, Cm 4349, London: DSS.

Davies, H.B. and Joshi, H.E. (1999) *Who bears the cost of Britain's children in the 1990s?*, Birkbeck College Discussion Paper in Economics 27/99.

Dex, S., Joshi, H. and Macran, S. (1996) 'A widening gulf among Britain's mothers', *Oxford Review of Economic Policy*, vol 12, no 1, pp 65-75.

Finlayson, L.R., Ford, R. and Marsh, A. (1996) 'Paying more for childcare', *Labour Market Trends*, July, pp 296-303.

Folbre, N. (1994) *Who pays for the kids? Gender and the structures of constraint*, London: Routledge.

Forth, J., Lissenburgh, S., Callender, C. and Millward, N. (1997) *Family friendly working arrangements in Britain, 1996*, DfEE Research Report RR16, Sudbury.

Haskey, J. (1998) 'One parent families and their dependent children in Great Britain', *Population Trends*, No 91, Spring.

Jarvis, S. and Jenkins, S. (1999) 'Marital splits and income change: evidence from the British Household Panel Survey', *Population Studies*, vol 53, no 2, pp 237-54.

Joshi, H.E. (1990) 'The opportunity cost of childbearing: an approach to estimation using British data', *Population Studies*, vol 44, pp 41-60.

Joshi, H. and Davies, H. (2000) 'The price of parenthood and the value of children', in N. Fraser and J. Hills (eds) *Public policy for the 21st century: Social and economic essays in memory of Henry Neuburger*, Bristol: The Policy Press, pp 63-76.

Joshi, H.E., Davies, H.B. and Land, H. (1996) *The tale of Mrs Typical*, London: Family Policy Studies Centre.

Office for National Statistics (1999) *Population Trends*, Spring.

Rake, K. (ed) (2000) *Women's incomes over the lifetime*, London: The Stationery Office.

Social Exclusion Unit (1999) *Teenage pregnancy*, Cm 4342, London: The Stationery Office.

THIRTEEN

The public and private costs of children in Australia, 1993-94

Richard Percival and Ann Harding

Introduction

The costs of children are of immense importance in a wide range of social and economic policy areas. Studies of income distribution and poverty, for example, usually incorporate assumptions about the estimated costs of children by applying equivalence scales to the incomes of families. The likely costs of children are one critical factor affecting the level of payments or rebates for children in the social security and the income tax systems. The estimated costs of children also have implications for the legal system, affecting awards for child support or child maintenance after accidents or medical problems. As Saunders notes: "there is thus an ongoing need to ensure that the best possible estimates of the costs of children are available so as to inform public debate and policy formulation on these important issues" (1999, p 63).

There is not, however, any consensus about the best way to measure the costs of children. Recent Australian studies have used the budget standards approach (Saunders, 1999) and the extended linear expenditure system approach (Valenzuela, 1999). This study uses a variant of the approach originally developed by Engels and since used by Espenshade (1984) and others to estimate how much children actually cost their parents[1].

The purpose of this study is to estimate the private costs of children in Australian two-parent families and to compare them to selected public costs. In the study, the private costs of children were taken to be money expenditures – that is, the amounts that parents actually spent on their children. Thus, the indirect costs of children – caused, for example, by mothers reducing their hours of paid labour-force participation – were not taken into account in any way.

Estimating the costs of children is inherently difficult, as many items of family expenditure are often shared among all family members or incurred indirectly by parents. In practice, it is also likely that there are wide variations in the amounts that parents spend on their children, both as family incomes vary and as the sense of what it is proper to spend varies. Not surprisingly, discussion of the costs of children is often directed towards what should be spent, as much as to what is spent.

As a key focus of the study was on what families in Australia do spend on their children, an approach was required which would make use of available information on family expenditure patterns and which would allow the costs of children to be calculated separately from other expenditures by their parents.

In this chapter we first outline the methodology and data source used in estimating the public and private costs of children, and then examine the private costs to parents of children by age of the child and number of children living in the household. In the next section we contrast the private and public costs of children, looking at government outlays on cash transfers, health, education and childcare.

Methodology

Estimating the private cost of children

The methodology used in this study to estimate the costs of children generally follows that developed by Espenshade, following Engel, to estimate the costs of parental expenditures on children in the United States (1984). This methodology was subsequently used by Lee (1988) to provide estimates of the costs of children in Australia in 1984.

Broadly, the methodology estimates the cost of a child as the difference in average expenditures between households where only a couple is present, and households where a couple and one or more children are present, given that the households enjoy an equivalent standard of living.

As Espenshade points out (1984, p 19) the central problem in estimating the cost borne by parents in raising children is that it is difficult to separate the costs of each family member from the total costs of the household. In many instances these costs cannot be easily assigned to particular individuals (eg, housing costs or electricity costs). As well, many expenditure items that are directly for children are simply recorded as expenditure items by their parents (eg, food costs).

One solution to this problem is to use an index of the material standard of living of different families. Such an index allows families with the same standard of living to be compared, even though their family composition and incomes may differ. The problem, of course, is how to determine when families have a similar standard of living – ie how to construct such an index. Simply comparing gross incomes is not sufficient, as families with the same income may have widely differing demands placed on that income and, hence, differences in their standards of living.

Once it is possible to tell if differently constituted families have the same standard of living, it is reasonably straightforward to estimate the costs of their children. Suppose we follow Engel and assume, for example, that the proportion of total expenditure devoted to food is an adequate indicator of the material standard of living of a family. Then consider two families, the first a couple with no children and a weekly expenditure of $500 and the second a couple with one child and a weekly expenditure of $600. If both spend 15% of their total expenditure on food then the difference in their expenditures can be said to equal the cost of the child in the second family – ie $100 per week.

For the purposes of the study this comparison was generalised in the form of two regression equations. The first was used to estimate total household consumption expenditure, given information on parental incomes and the number (and ages) of the children. The second estimated household living standards, given information on household consumption expenditure and the number (and ages) of the children – see Percival and Harding (2000) for more details of the regression coefficients.

The methodology used in this study to calculate the cost of children relies on being able to determine when families of different sizes and with different incomes have similar living standards. In his earlier work on costs of children Espenshade examined several different methods that had been used to determine family living standards (1972, pp 63-74). These included per capita income, level of adult expenditure, proportion of income saved and the proportion of income spent on food. After considering each, Espenshade concluded that the most appropriate measure to use was the proportion of family income spent on food (the so-called 'Engel estimator').

However, using the proportion of total expenditure devoted to food as the indicator of living standards has been the subject of extensive criticism. In particular, Deaton and Muellbauer (1986) argued that the Engel method is fundamentally incorrect in assuming that food share indicates the welfare level of households of different sizes (p 741). They also argued that it can be theoretically shown that the Engel method will produce estimates higher than the 'true' cost of children.

Since the publication of the paper by Deaton and Muellbauer, the Engel approach has often been described as establishing an upper bound to child cost estimates. However, there are grounds for viewing this widely held assertion with some caution. In particular, as Bradbury points out, the argument that the Engel approach establishes an upper bound to child costs relies on the assumption that food constitutes a relatively high proportion of total child expenditures. However, as this would more typically be the case in developing countries (which are the focus of Deaton and Muellbauer's analysis), in more developed countries such as Australia such a conclusion is less certain (Bradbury, 1994, p 2).

What is perhaps more likely to be correct is that an Engel estimator will over-estimate the costs of larger families. This is because there are likely to be greater economies of scale present in a household's non-food consumption than there is in their food consumption.

A number of other indexes of standard of living have been proposed, including the level of total expenditure devoted to 'adult goods' (Rothbarth, 1943). However, Bradbury has shown that, theoretically, this approach will most likely overestimate the cost of children (Bradbury, 1997, p 76).

Given this uncertainty in the literature, this study has used the general Espenshade approach. However, the estimator of comparable living standards used was a variation on the Engel method, with the food-at-home share estimator being expanded to include other basic expenditure items (such an estimator is sometimes referred to as an ISO-PROP estimator, following Watts, 1977). (Estimated costs of children were also produced using alternative estimators – see Percival et al, 1999.)

The Basic Goods Estimator was used as investigation found that it was able to provide a better fit for the data and its use answered, at least in part, one of the more telling criticisms of the Engel estimator – that it imposes the relative lack of economies of scale that exist in food consumption on all other items of non-food consumption. By using the Basic Goods Estimator, at least some account is taken of household economies of scale.

The items included in the Basic Goods Estimator are listed in Table 13.1. The expenditure items included in the 'basket' were selected to meet two criteria:

Table 13.1: Basic goods 'basket' used in ISO-PROP estimator

- Food at home
- Fuel and power
- Household non-durables for use inside the home
- Postal, telephone and telegram charges
- Personal care products and services

- that each item be capable of being readily observed as a household necessity;
- that there should be a mix of items likely to introduce either an 'upward' or a 'downward' bias to the estimates – as Whiteford sets out, upward biases are likely to result if an item is consumed more by a child than an adult and downward biases where the item is subject to economies of scale (such as housing) (Whiteford, 1985, p 52).

Not included in the basket were the costs of housing, clothing and health. While these have often been included by other researchers when compiling a basket of basic goods (see, for example, Betson, 1990; Merz and Faik, 1992), their use is problematic.

Housing was not included as it has characteristics that set it apart from other essential expenditures. As a recent study (which did not include the costs of housing in any of several baskets of basic goods) noted, expenditure on housing is 'peculiar' (Carlucci and Zelli, 1998). What makes it peculiar is that it can differ markedly between households that are similar in every other aspect other than their tenure type. As well, in contrast to other 'basket' items, the housing costs of many families, particularly those with children, tend to diminish across the life-cycle. That is, families with older children are much more likely to have lower relative housing costs, given that expenditure by home purchasers will, over time, be reduced by the effects of inflation and, as well, will increasingly go to paying off the capital component of their mortgage. For these reasons, it would seem that the inclusion of housing in the measure of living standards is likely to introduce significant distortions.

Clothing was excluded from the basic basket of goods because, in contrast to other basic expenditures, its share of total expenditure raised as household expenditure increased. This mirrors the finding of Carlucci and Zelli (1998), who categorised clothing as a 'comfort' good, rather than a 'necessity' good. (Some clothing is, of course, a necessity. However, it is also in many instances very much a luxury item. Unfortunately, when compared to food, it is more difficult to separate out what is basic expenditure on clothing from what is luxury expenditure. There would also appear to be more scope for wealthier households to increase their expenditure on clothing than there is to increase their expenditure on food at home.)

Finally, household expenditure on health was not included in the basic basket of goods, given the role played by the Medicare system in Australia in meeting all or most of the basic components of these expenses.

Estimating the public costs of children

In estimating the public costs of children many similar difficulties were encountered as when estimating the private costs – including how to precisely identify which government outlays were upon children and which were upon adults. After consideration of the options, we decided to examine three types of government outlays on services for children – education[2], health and childcare.

The estimated value of the publicly subsidised health, education and childcare services used by households in 1993-94 has already been calculated by the Australian Bureau of Statistics (ABS, 1996), using a standard fiscal incidence study methodology. Their estimates are included in the publicly available Household Expenditure Survey (HES) unit record file, and we have thus used the ABS estimates of education, health and childcare as our starting point (ABS, 1994). A problem for this study, however, is that the HES data simply show, for example, the total value of public health outlays consumed by a household (rather than the total value of health services consumed by the children living within a household).

As a result, the public costs of children for health, education and childcare subsidies were estimated by extending the methodology used to estimate private child costs. This involved treating the ABS estimates of public health, education and childcare subsidies as additional household expenditure items. Thus, the public health costs of, for example, a family with one child were defined as the difference between that family's public health costs and those of a couple-only family at a similar level of material standard of living (defined as set out in the preceding section)[3].

In addition to the above non-cash benefits, we also looked at cash transfers specifically for children. As receipt of Family Payment was one of the recorded sources of income on the HES, their value was estimated directly from the HES, averaged by family type and family income quintiles.

Data source

The data source used in this study was the publicly released 1993-94 HES unit record file. This survey collected information on household expenditures, incomes and a wide range of other socioeconomic characteristics. In total, some 8,389 confidential records were included in the publicly released file, representing some 6.6 million households.

However, for this study only couple households where the spouse was aged between 25 and 54 years and where there were either no other persons present or where there were one or more dependent children under 18 years of age were included. This restriction was imposed to reduce any age-related effects that might be associated with the two different types of families – those with and those without children – having different characteristics.

Also excluded from the analysis were households:

- whose principal source of income was from self-employment or reported as being from 'private sources' (eg, from interest or superannuation);
- with negative or zero consumption expenditure;
- with negative or zero income;
- where the ratio of household total expenditure to household total income was greater than two.

The final data set thus defined contained 2,658 records, representing some 1.976 million families.

Distribution of incomes

The analysis began with an examination of the data to determine the number and distribution of records by income ranges. Income was defined as total current household income – that is, income from all sources before deductions for income tax or other compulsory payments are made. (Excluded by the ABS from the definition of current income are amounts such as lump-sum receipts, windfall gains, and withdrawals from savings [ABS, 1995, p 35].)

Most apparent from the analysis was a decline in the number of records as income increased, particularly above $75,000, and as the number of children per household increased. Also apparent was the smaller number of households with older children present – most probably a result of their being more likely to live in households with non-dependent children or other relatives present (and thus be excluded from the analysis).

Because of this decline in the number of records, reporting of child costs by the number of children in a family was restricted to 1, 2 or 3 children. (However, families with larger numbers of children were included in the analysis that estimated the equations.)

Definition of expenditure

In this study, expenditure was defined as current household expenditure. This is total household expenditure as recorded on the HES less the following:

- repayment of mortgage principal for the family home;
- other capital housing payments (includes additions, extensions and renovations to family home, and purchase of other dwellings); and
- expenditure on superannuation and life insurance.

The reason for excluding these items is that they represent saving, rather than consumption.

However, it needs to be acknowledged that expenditure on at least some of the above items could be expected to be influenced by the presence of children in the family – that is, they could be said to have a non-discretionary element. For example, in the case of life insurance, it is quite possible that families with children are more likely to purchase these products.

Similarly, in the case of housing, once the decision has been made to become a homeowner, the subsequent housing costs are not discretionary, including those that represent a form of saving.

What would be the effect of including items of non-current expenditure in the cost estimates? Most likely this would see some increase in the costs of older children. For example, typical housing repayment patterns show that, over time, an increasing proportion goes towards paying-off the mortgage principal. As a result, the housing costs of older families (who would be more likely to have older children) could be biased towards greater repayment of this mortgage component. This may, however, be offset by the methodology not directly comparing families at the same point in their lifecycles. That is, couples with older children, who would be older themselves, are not compared with older couples without children. Instead, they are compared to couples without children of all ages. It is also possible that families with older children could be more likely to be paying for home extensions and renovations.

Costs of children

The first step in estimating the cost of children was to use Ordinary Least Squares (OLS) regression to model equations to predict family expenditure as a function of family composition and income, and family living standards as a function of family composition and expenditure. Solving these equations allowed child costs to be estimated at different income levels and for different family compositions. For the subsequent analysis, our restricted population of couples with children was divided into quintiles, with the 20% of such couple households with the lowest gross incomes being placed in the bottom quintile.

In this section, government outlays on Family Payments, which underlie the level of private spending on children, are included as part of the direct costs of children. In the following section, which looks at the public and private costs of children, their value is calculated separately and added to the indirect public costs of children.

Costs of children by age

The costs of children were first estimated for a single child in each of the defined age and income ranges.

The results are shown in Table 13.2 and in Figure 13.1. As expected, the direct costs of children increased with the age of the child and with the level of family income. The lowest direct costs of $52 a week were estimated for children aged between zero and four years living in families in the bottom quintile (with average gross incomes of $410 a week). The highest costs of $280 a week were estimated for 15- to 17-year-old children living in top quintile families. Wealthier families were found to spend a greater amount on their children, whatever their ages. Generally speaking, families in the top quintile spent more than twice as much on their children as families in the bottom quintile.

Table 13.2: Estimated average costs of a single child, by age of child and quintile of gross family income, Australia (1993-94)

Gross income Quintile	Average income	Age of child 0-4	5-9	10-14	15-17
		($ pw)	($ pw)	($ pw)	($ pw)
1 (lowest)	$410	52	62	89	127
2	$620	70	82	111	154
3	$810	86	99	132	178
4	$1,030	104	119	154	204
5 (highest)	$1,700	157	177	219	280

Source: ABS (1994) and authors' calculations

Figure 13.1: Estimated average costs of children, by age of child and quintile of gross family income, Australia (1993-94)

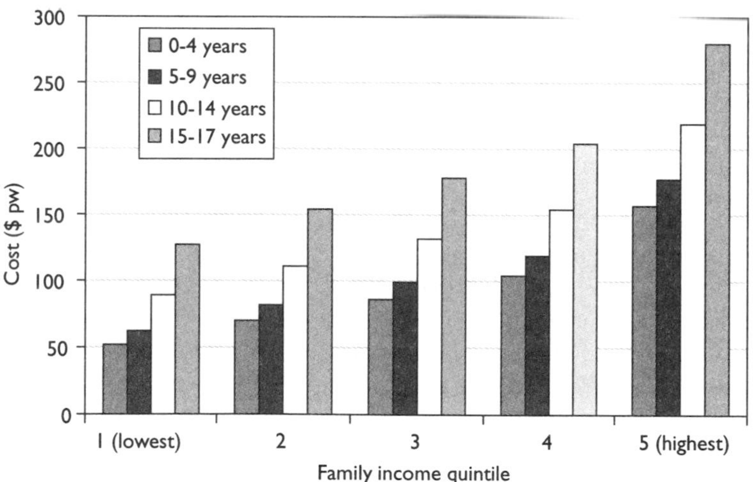

Source: ABS (1994) and authors' calculations

Table 13.3: Estimated average costs of a single child as a proportion of total family income, by age of child, Australia (1993-94)

		Age of child			
Gross income quintile	**Average income**	**0-4**	**5-9**	**10-14**	**15-17**
		(%)	(%)	(%)	(%)
1 (lowest)	$410	12.7	15.1	21.7	31.0
2	$620	11.3	13.2	17.9	24.8
3	$810	10.6	12.2	16.3	22.0
4	$1,030	10.1	11.6	15.0	19.8
5 (highest)	$1,700	9.2	10.4	12.9	16.5

Source: ABS (1994) and authors' calculations

While there was a steady rise in the cost of a child as family income increased, when total costs were considered as a proportion of family income, there was a fall as incomes rose. However, the rate of decline was reduced as family income rose (Table 13.3 and Figure 13.2).

For families, the costs of a child as a proportion of their combined income ranged between a little over 9% (for a child aged up to four years in a top quintile family with a gross income of $1,700) to 31% (for a child aged 15 to 17 years in a bottom quintile family with an income of $410 per week). Interestingly, as Figure 13.2 illustrates, there is much less variation in the direct costs of children by quintile for older children which, in turn, means that the proportion of family income devoted to spending on older children falls sharply as family income increases. Top quintile families with a child aged 15 to 17 spent only a little more than twice as much as bottom quintile families on comparable children. As a result, expenditure on older children aged 15 to 17 years falls sharply from 31% of gross family income for bottom quintile families to 17% of income for top quintile families (Table 13.5).

In contrast, top quintile families with a young child aged 0 to 4 were estimated to spend about three times as much on their child as bottom quintile families (Table 13.2). As a result, expenditure on younger children as a percentage of income showed relatively little variation between the quintiles, ranging from 9% to 13% of gross income (Table 13.3).

Figure 13.2: Estimated average costs of children as a proportion of family income, by age of child and gross family income quintile, Australia (1993-94)

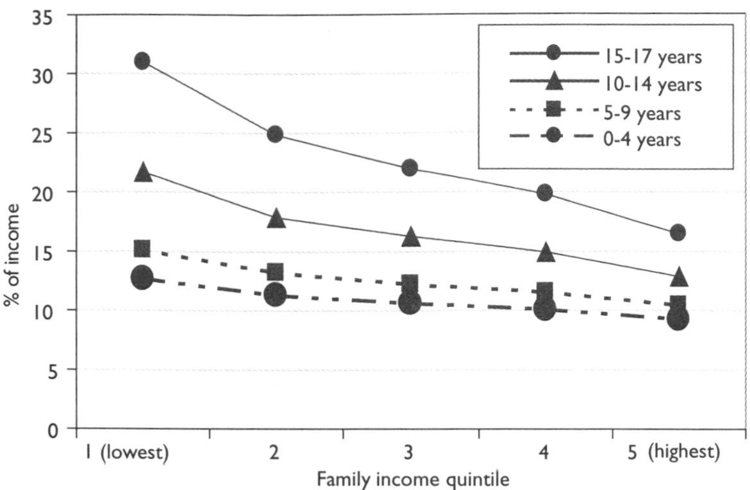

Source: ABS (1994) and authors' calculations

Costs of children by number of children in household

The next stage of the analysis was to consider the costs of children according to the number of children in the family. For this purpose, the estimates presented represent the costs of children averaged across all the age ranges. (An alternative would be to estimate average total costs for hypothetical families – for example, for a family with one child aged 4 years and another child aged 15, and so on.) It should be noted that this is not effectively an estimate of the average costs of children up to the ages of 17 years, as this would assume that family incomes remained constant across a child's different ages. This is, of course, not the case, as incomes typically tend to increase over the family lifecycle. To calculate such lifecycle costs would require the use of estimates of the average variations in family incomes over the child-rearing years. Espenshade has adopted such an approach in presenting estimates of the total parental expenditure on children (Espenshade, 1984).

It also should be noted that the under-representation of older children in the data included in the analysis may, given the higher costs of older

Table 13.4: Estimated average costs of children, by number of children and gross family income quintile, Australia (1993-94)

Gross income quintile	Average income	1 child	2 children	3 children
		($ pw)	($ pw)	($ pw)
1 (lowest)	$410	70	136	196
2	$620	91	173	242
3	$810	110	204	282
4	$1,030	132	240	328
5 (highest)	$1,700	191	338	453

Source: ABS (1994) and authors' calculations

Figure 13.3: Estimated average costs of children, by number of children and gross family income quintile, Australia (1993-94)

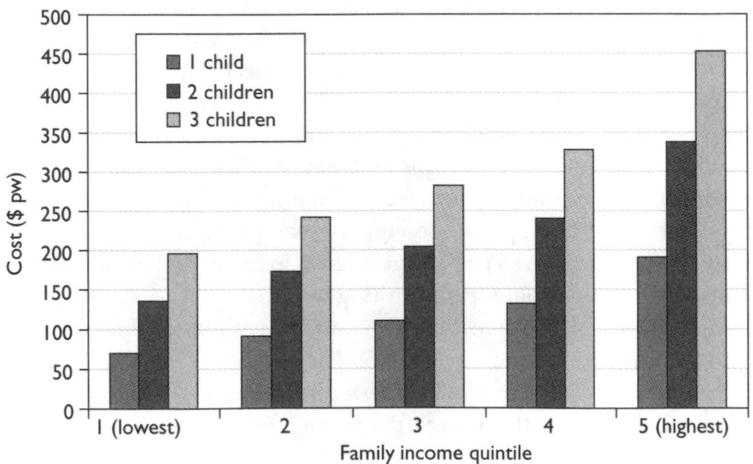

children, mean that the averaged costs presented in this section may be underestimated.

Figure 13.3 and Table 13.4 show the cost of children by the number of children. Again the cost of each child was found to rise with family incomes. Bottom quintile families with one child were estimated to spend $70 a week on that child, while top quintile families with one child spent $191 a week.

Table 13.5: Estimated average costs of children, as a proportion of income, by number of children and gross family income quintile, Australia (1993-94)

Gross income quintile	Average income	1 child	2 children	3 children
		(%)	(%)	(%)
1 (lowest)	$410	17.1	33.2	47.8
2	$620	14.7	27.9	39.0
3	$810	13.6	25.2	34.8
4	$1,030	12.8	23.3	31.8
5 (highest)	$1,700	11.2	19.9	26.6

Source: ABS (1994) and authors' calculations

As Table 13.5 shows, the cost of a single child amounted on average to between 11% and 17% of family income, for two children 20% to 33% of family income and, for three children, about 27% to 48%.

These results contrast with those recorded by Valenzuela using the same 1993-94 HES data, but using the extended linear expenditure system. Valenzuela found that the estimated cost ratios appeared stable across the income distribution – for example, she estimated that spending on the first child amounted to a uniform 18% of gross family income and that spending on three children remained at about 34% of income irrespective of income level (1999, p 75). In contrast, we have found much greater variation in child costs as a percentage of gross income for those at different points within the income spectrum (Figure 13.4).

The cost of each additional child in families with up to three children is shown in Table 13.6 and Figure 13.5. The cost of the first child was the greatest across all income levels (between $70 and $191). For a middle quintile family on $810 per week the average cost of a second child was approximately 85% of the cost of the first child, while the cost of the third child was approximately 71% of the first. The reduction in the average cost of each additional child was a result of both the expenditure constraints and the economies of scale that families experience as their size increases.

It was also found that, in proportional terms, the additional costs of each child diverged as incomes rose. That is, the gap between what families spent on a single child and the additional amounts they spent on subsequent children contracted as incomes rose. At bottom quintile incomes of $410 the cost of the second child was approximately 94% of that of the first, while the cost of the third child was approximately 86%

Figure 13.4: Estimated average costs of children, as a proportion of income, by number of children and gross family income quintile, Australia (1993-94)

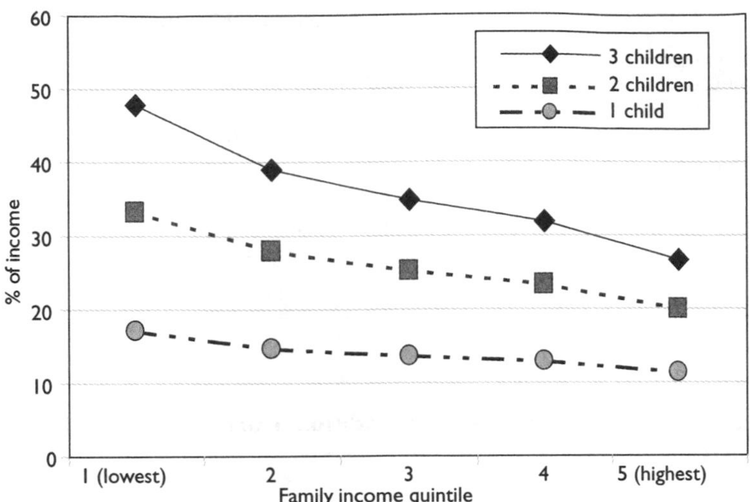

Source: ABS (1994) and authors' calculations

of the first. At top quintile incomes of $1,700, the cost of the second child was approximately 77% of that of the first, while the cost of the third child was approximately 60% of the first.

The results suggest economies of scale for additional children, particularly for middle to higher income families. As shown in Table 13.6 and Figure 13.5, the marginal cost of the second child was always lower than that of the first, while the marginal cost of the third child was lower again. This suggests that the costs of second and subsequent children are lower, as children can share rooms, pass on clothes and toys, and so on. It should also be emphasised, however, that the results also reflect the budget constraints faced by parents. In other words, the marginal costs of the third child are lower in part because at a given income level parents simply cannot afford to spend the same amount on the third child as on the second.

These results again contrast with those recorded by Valenzuela using the same 1993-94 HES data, but using the extended linear expenditure system. Valenzuela found equal cost requirements for the second and third child (1999, p 75), rather than the reduced cost requirements for the third child estimated in this study.

Table 13.6: Estimated average marginal costs of children, by number of children and gross family income quintile, Australia (1993-94)

Gross income quintile	Average income	Number of children 1st child	2nd child	3rd child
		($ pw)	($ pw)	($ pw)
1 (lowest)	$410	70	66	60
2	$620	91	82	69
3	$810	110	94	78
4	$1,030	132	108	88
5 (highest)	$1,700	191	147	115

Source: ABS (1994) and authors' calculations

Figure 13.5: Estimated average additional costs of each child, Australia (1993-94)

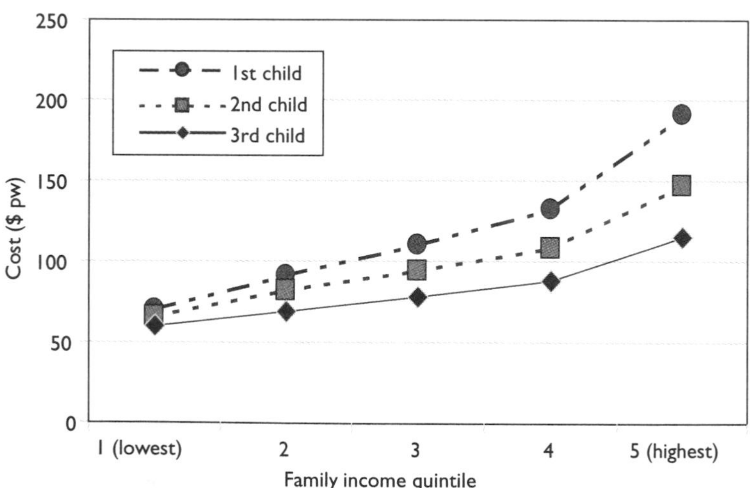

Source: ABS (1994) and authors' calculations

Equivalence scale estimates

The costs of children estimated in this study can be used to construct equivalence scales. How do they compare to those produced by other studies? It should be appreciated that this is a fairly rough comparison, as some of the results are for families at different income levels or are averaged across all families. Our estimates of the costs of children are substantially higher than those derived for Australia using the Extended Linear Expenditure System, and somewhat higher than those derived by Peter Whiteford based on an average from dozens of studies across the world (Bradbury, 1994 in Table 7). Our estimates accord fairly closely with the relativities implicit in the Australian income support system for lower families with children (Harding and Percival, 1999).

Valenzuela observes that studies based on the budget standards approach (which is based on what children need) tend to reveal highest costs than those coming from the ELES method (based on what families actually spend on their children) (1999, p 73). This is also indicated in Table 13.7, where the estimates of child costs based on the Budget Standards project conducted at the Social Policy Research Centre are higher than those produced by most of the other studies (McHugh, 1999).

Generally speaking, there is much greater consistency between the various equivalence scales in the estimated difference in costs faced by a couple with one child relative to a couple with no children. It is in the estimated increase in costs faced by couples with two and three children that the various methods produce very divergent results.

Public and private costs of children

How do the expenditures made by parents on their children compare with those made by government either directly or on their behalf? To answer this question, the principal income assistance program for parents of dependent children (Family Payment) and three types of government outlays on non-cash benefits for children (education, health and childcare) were considered. As shown in Table 13.8 below, like private outlays, government outlays on children increase with the age of the child. For example, while average government outlays on Family Payment, health, education and childcare for zero to four year olds in the lowest quintile are about \$61 a week, for 15- to 17-year-olds they are about \$124 a week.

Table 13.7: Comparison between various equivalence scale results

Study	Methodology	Income level	Type of couple family (2,0)	(2,1)	(2,2)	(2,3)
Valenzuela, 1999	ELES	$592 (1993-94$)	1.00	1.18	1.25	1.34
Bradbury, 1994	Rothbarth method (adult clothing)	Average for 1988-89 sample	1.00	1.16	1.28	1.35
Tran and Whiteford (1990)	ELES	$325 disp inc (1984$)	1.00	1.20	1.28	1.44
Whiteford average (Bradbury, 1994)	Average of wide range of methods	Various	1.00	1.20	1.38	1.51
Australian income support system	Actual payment rates	July 1999 rates	1.00	1.17	1.34	1.51
Percival and Harding, 1999	ISO-Prop (food at home, fuel, non-durables, postal, personal care)	$620 (1993-94$)	1.00	1.18	1.47	1.65
Henderson (head working) (Commission of Inquiry into Poverty 1975)	New York budget data	1950s	1.00	1.15	1.37	1.68
McHugh (1999)[a]	Budget standards	Low but adequate	1.00	1.25	1.58	1.73
OECD equivalence scale			1.00	1.29	1.59	1.88
Tran and Whiteford (1990)	ISO-Prop (food, clothing, housing and fuel)	1984	1.00	1.25	1.57	1.97

[a] These scales should only be regarded as very broadly indicative of the budget standards results, as the budget standard estimates change for children of different ages, gender etc.

Source: ABS (1994) and authors' calculations

Table 13.8: Private and public expenditure on children, by age of child and gross family income quintile[a]

Age of child	Gross family income quintile				
	1	2	3	4	5
0- to 4-year-olds					
Private	13	58	77	95	152
– Public (cash transfer)	39	12	9	9	5
– Public (non-cash)	22	22	23	23	23
Total public	61	34	32	32	28
Total public and private	74	92	109	127	180
5- to 9-year-olds					
Private	34	62	88	110	174
– Public (cash transfer)	28	20	11	9	3
– Public (non-cash)	58	58	58	57	57
Total public	86	78	69	66	60
Total public and private	120	140	157	176	234
10- to 14-year-olds					
Private	57	102	124	141	217
– Public (cash transfer)	30	9	8	13	2
– Public (non-cash)	88	87	86	85	82
Total public	118	96	94	98	84
Total public and private	177	198	218	239	301
15- to 17-year-olds					
Private	110	148	172	196	280
– Public (cash transfer)	17	6	6	8	0
– Public (non-cash)	107	106	105	104	102
Total public	124	112	111	112	102
Total public and private	234	260	283	308	382

[a] Public cash transfers comprise Family Payments and non-cash expenditure means government outlays on health, education and childcare.

Source: ABS (1994) and authors' calculations

There is also some variation in government outlays by the income level of the family. For example, government outlays for children aged 10 to 14 years in the bottom quintile are $118, about 40% higher than the $84 spent on 10 to 14 year olds living in top quintile families. Given the methodology used by the ABS to impute the usage and value of services received, the differences in expenditure are largely driven by Family Payment and by education[4]. Family Payment is means-tested, and higher income families are more likely to send their children to private schools. The average subsidy for a child attending a government secondary school in 1993-94 was about $5,260 a year, compared with $3,280 for a child attending a non-government secondary school.

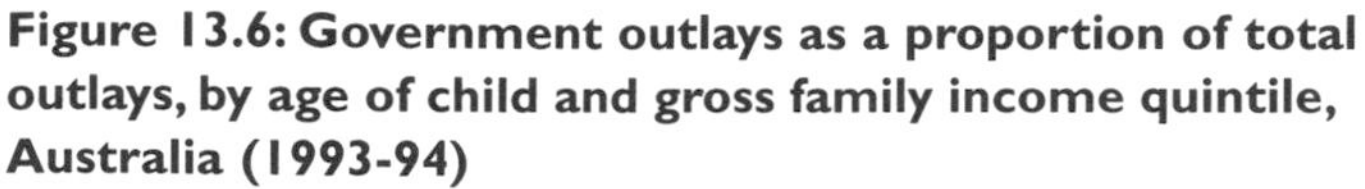

Figure 13.6: Government outlays as a proportion of total outlays, by age of child and gross family income quintile, Australia (1993-94)

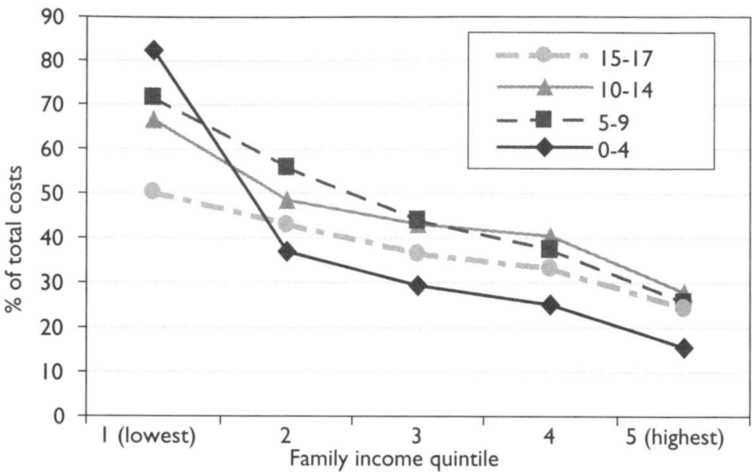

Source: ABS (1994) and authors' calculations

Government outlays on children are particularly important for lower income families. As shown in Figure 13.6, government spending exceeds private spending for families in the bottom quintile for children of all ages. For example, bottom quintile parents are estimated to spend only \$34 a week on children aged five to nine years, compared with the \$86 spent by government. (Note that the 'parental' expenditures actually financed by cash transfers from government have been deducted from total parental expenditures here, to give a more accurate picture of the relative contributions of government and parents. A similar methodology is used in Bainbridge and Garfinkel, 1999.)

The relative importance of government spending falls as family income increases so that, for top quintile families, government expenditure on 5- to 17-year-olds is about one third of all expenditure. On the whole, the results suggest that the efforts of government move in tandem with the efforts of parents, with the contribution of both increasing as children grow up and become more expensive.

How important are the contributions made by government for larger families? As Table 13.9 again suggests, the government shoulders a significant part of the costs of children, especially for low-income families.

Table 13.9: Private and public expenditure on children, by number of children and gross family income quintile[a]

	Gross family income quintile				
Number of children	**1**	**2**	**3**	**4**	**5**
One child					
Private	38	78	101	123	188
– Public (cash transfer)	32	13	9	9	3
– Public (non-cash)	65	64	64	63	63
Total public	97	77	73	72	66
Total public and private	135	155	174	195	254
Two children					
Private	73	138	183	221	328
– Public (cash transfer)	63	35	21	19	10
– Public (non-cash)	129	128	128	127	125
Total public	192	163	149	146	135
Total public and private	265	301	332	367	463
Three children					
Private	93	174	245	297	439
– Public (cash transfer)	103	68	37	31	14
– Public (non-cash)	193	192	191	190	188
Total public	296	260	228	221	202
Total public and private	389	434	473	518	641

[a] Public cash transfers comprise Family Payments and non-cash expenditure means government outlays on health, education and childcare.

Source: ABS (1994) and authors' calculations

For three-child families in the bottom quintile, for example, governmental outlays are $296 a week and parental outlays $93 a week. Thus, the contribution by government is roughly three times the contribution made by parents. Figure 13.7 indicates that the importance of the contribution of government expressed as a percentage of total outlays does not vary greatly by family size. In other words, the government does not provide all that much more assistance to three-child families than to one-child families, relative to the outlays of parents. However, once again, government outlays on children amount to a much lower percentage of parental outlays as family income increases.

Figure 13.7: Government outlays as a proportion of total outlays, by number of children and gross family income quintile, Australia (1993-94)

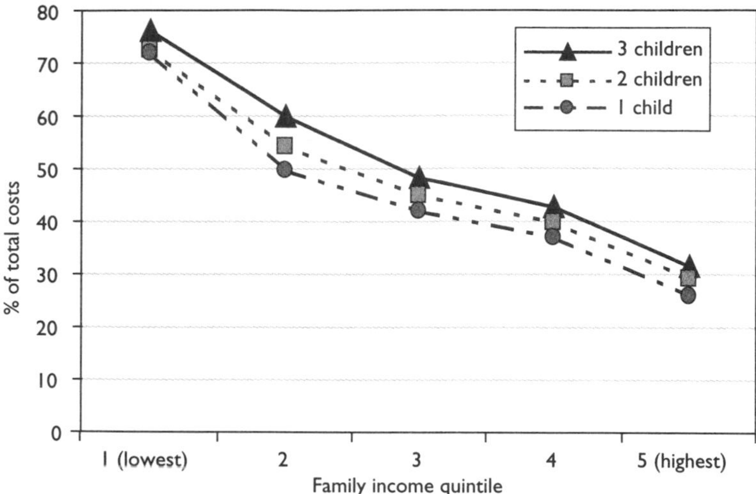

Source: ABS (1994) and author's calculations

Summary and conclusions

In this study we have estimated the direct costs of children in Australian two-parent families, where the costs of children were defined as parental expenditures on children up to 17 years of age. The level of expenditure was determined by comparing the expenditures of couple families with and without children at the same material standard of living. The measure of the material standard of living was the proportion of total expenditure spent upon a basket of goods that included food consumed at home and fuel and power. No account was taken of the indirect costs of children (eg, the forgone earnings due to mothers working part-time rather than full-time).

There were several important findings made in the study. Not unexpectedly, these included that the average costs of children in Australian families varied according to the age of the child, the income level of the parents and the number of children in the family. More specifically:

- The cost of a child was found to be lowest for children in the youngest age group (at $86 a week for zero to four year olds living in middle income families with an average gross income of $810 a week) and highest for children in the oldest age group (at $178 a week for 15- to 17-year-olds in the same middle income families);

- Higher income families spent more on their children than lower income families (eg, the costs of a five to nine year old child were estimated at $62 a week for families in the bottom income quintile, rising to $177 a week for families in the top income quintile);
- While the costs of children rose in line with rising family incomes, they nonetheless fell when expressed as a proportion of family income (particularly for older children aged ten and above);
- The average expenditure per child was found to be greatest for families with one child, and fell for families with either two or three children. The average cost of the first child was found to range between $70 and $191, according to family income, while the cost of a second child ranged between $66 and $147 per week and that of a third child between $60 and $115 per week.
- Government assistance to families in the form of cash transfers and outlays on education, health and childcare supported families by also increasing in magnitude, as children grew older. Government outlays were particularly important for lower income families, amounting to about 75% of total outlays for children living in bottom quintile families.

In assessing the results of the study, it must again be stressed that the costs of children that have been presented are averaged estimates derived from reporting of what parents spend to meet all household costs. Being averages, actual expenditures on children will often be considerably higher or lower for particular families than the estimates we present – that is, nothing in the study suggests a prescriptive level of parental expenditure. As well, as the analysis was restricted to couple households, it is not possible to say what the cost of children would be in other types of households (for example, those where there is only one adult or those where there are more than two adults).

Notes

[1] Much of the methodology used in this study for estimating the private costs of children was developed as part of an earlier report undertaken by the authors and Professor Peter McDonald of the Australian National University for the Department of Family and Community Services.

[2] Defined as public subsidies for pre-schools, primary schools, secondary schools, technical and further education institutes and tertiary institutes.

[3] See Percival and Harding (2000) and Percival et al (1999) for a detailed description of the methodology.

[4] Some recent research by NATSEM has indicated that the methodology used by the ABS to impute the value of hospital and medical services received overstates the benefits to high income families and understates the benefit of such services to low income families (Schofield, 1998; Harding et al, 2000). This is because usage of health services is imputed by the ABS solely on the basis of age, gender and State of residence, although recent research has suggested that family income is also a factor affecting usage.

References

ABS (Australian Bureau of Statistics) (1994) *Household Expenditure Survey 1993-94*, Unit Record Tape, Canberra, Australia.

ABS (1995) *Household Expenditure Survey 1993-94, Australia, User Guide*, ABS Catalogue no 6527.0, Australian Bureau of Statistics, Canberra, Australia.

ABS (1996) *1993-94, Household Expenditure Survey*, Australia: The Effects of Government Benefits and Taxes on Household Income, ABS Cat No 6537.0

Bainbridge, J. and Garfinkel, I. (1999) 'Cost of children study', mimeo, Washingon, DC: School of Social Work, Columbia University, December.

Betson, M. (1990) *Alternative estimates of the cost of children from the 1980-86 consumer expenditure survey*, Special Report Series No 51, Institute for Research on Poverty, University of Wisconsin-Madison.

Bradbury, B. (1994) 'Measuring the cost of children', *Australian Economic Papers*, June, pp 120-38.

Bradbury, B. (1997) *Family size and relative need*, Unpublished PhD Thesis, School of Economics, University of New South Wales.

Carlucci, M. and Zelli, R. (1998) 'Expenditure patterns and equivalence scales', Paper presented to the 25th General Conference of the International Association for Research in Income and Wealth, Cambridge, 23-29 August.

Commission of Inquiry into Poverty (1975) *Poverty in Australia: First main report*, AGPS, Canberra.

Deaton, S. and Muellbauer, J. (1986) 'On measuring child costs: with applications to poor countries', *Journal of Political Economy*, vol 94, no 4, pp 720-44.

Espenshade, T. (1972) *The cost of children in urban United States*, Princeton University, PhD, University Microfilms, Ann Arbor, Michigan.

Espenshade, T. (1984) *Investing in children: New estimates of parental expenditures*, Washington, DC: Urban Institutes Press.

Harding, A., Percival, R., Schofield, S. and Walker, A. (2000) 'The lifetime distributional impact of government health outlays', forthcoming Discussion Paper, National Centre for Social and Economic Modelling, University of Canberra.

Harding, A. and Percival, R. (1999) 'The private costs of children in 1993-94', *Family Matters*, No 55, Spring.

Lee, D. (1988) 'Estimates of direct expenditures on children in Australia: results from the Household Expenditure Survey 1984', Paper presented at the Conference of the Australian Population Association, Brisbane, 31 August-2 September.

McHugh, M. (1999) 'The costs of children: budget standards estimates and the child support scheme', Discussion Paper No 103, Social Policy Research Centre, University of New South Wales, Sydney.

Merz, J. and Faik, J. (1992) 'Equivalence scales based on revealed preference consumption expenditure microdata – the case of West Germany', Discussion Paper No 3, *Forschungsinstitut Freie Berufe*, University of Lunenburg, Lunenburg.

Percival, R. and Harding, A. (2000) 'The public and private costs of children in Australia, 1993-94', NATSEM Discussion Paper, National Centre for Social and Economic Modelling, University of Canberra, Canberra, forthcoming.

Percival, R., Harding, A. and McDonald, P. (1999) 'Estimates of the costs of children in Australian families, 1993-94', Report prepared for the Department of Family and Community Services, National Centre for Social and Economic Modelling, May.

Rothbarth, E. (1943) 'A note on a method of determining equivalent income for families of different composition', Appendix 4 in C. Madge (ed) *War-time patterns of saving and spending*, Cambridge: Cambridge University Press.

Saunders, P. (1999) 'Budget standards and the costs of children', *Family Matters*, no 53, Winter, pp 62-70.

Schofield, D. (1998) *Public expenditure on hospitals: Measuring the distributional impact*, Discussion Paper No 36, Canberra: National Centre for Social and Economic Modelling, University of Canberra.

Tran Nam, B. and Whiteford, P. (1990) 'Household equivalence scales: new Australian estimates from the 1984 Household expenditure survey', *The Economic Record*, September, pp 221-34.

Valenzuela, M.R. (1999) 'Costs of children in Australian households', *Family Matters*, no 53, Winter, pp 71-6.

Watts, H. (1977) 'The iso-prop index: an approach to the determination of deferential poverty income thresholds', in M. Moon and E. Smolensky (eds) *Improving measures of economic well-being*, New York, NY: Academic Press.

Whiteford, P. (1985) *A family's needs: Equivalence scales , poverty and social security*, Research Paper No 27, Development Division, Department of Social Security, Canberra.

FOURTEEN

Socioeconomic circumstances in Europe and North America among school-aged children

Candace Currie

Socioeconomic inequality and child well-being

In today's Europe, as well as in most other advanced countries, there is a rising proportion of people living in poverty and increasing socioeconomic inequality (Atkinson et al, 1995). This is the case, not only in the countries of Central and Eastern Europe (CEE), but also in west European welfare states and other highly developed countries such as Canada, the United States and Australia. High economic growth, in conjunction with rising unemployment and low paid jobs, has led to widening income gaps. These in turn have resulted in changing living conditions for children – for example, at least one parent out of work and resultant material hardship. In addition, in Europe and North America there have been changes in family structure and circumstances with an increase in lone-parent families, divorces and commuter families. A narrowing labour market and fragile social and family support networks place a higher proportion of children at potential risk of reduced health and well-being.

The transition countries of East Europe have experienced a dramatic change of social structure within the last decade. Starting from a comparatively equal distribution of standard of living and access to life chances in the former socialist societies, the 1990's have seen a widening gap between poor and rich families (Notburga and Wagner, 1997; Offe, 1997; Columbus, 1998). These trends are likely to affect young people's life chances and their mental and social well-being, because of the major links between developmental potentials and life chances. However, the impact of social inequality during childhood and adolescence, in terms of impairment to health and well-being rather than mortality or morbidity, has received limited attention in cross-national studies of young people. In their recent analysis, Micklewright and Stewart (1999) identified the need for more measurement of child well-being, in order to address this dearth of data.

One cross-national study of young people in West and East Europe and in North America has attempted to measure childhood and adolescent socioeconomic circumstances and investigate their association with health and well-being. This is the Health Behaviour in School-Aged Children: WHO Cross-National Study (HBSC) (Currie et al, 1998; Currie et al, 2000). A description of the study and its methodology is given in the Appendix. It is known that children and adolescents are aware of social inequalities and are able to quite accurately assess the concomitant unequal chances they bring (Burgard, Cheyne and Jahoda, 1989; Duncan, Brooks-Gunn and Klebanov, 1994; Duncan and Brooks-Gunn, 1997). Poverty, as the early adolescent age group experiences it, is likely to have serious consequences not only for life expectancy but also for their health behaviour and health status. This chapter examines the evidence for this assertion using data from the 1997/98 HBSC cross-national survey.

The conceptual framework taken in the chapter has economic 'well-being' conceptualised as a predictor of child health and well-being, with these latter being measured with a number of psychosocial health indicators self-reported by children. These include, for example, reported health, reported happiness, reported symptoms, reported self-confidence and helplessness. In some of the analyses, health behaviours, including smoking, alcohol use, physical activity and nutrition are also considered as health 'outcomes', as explained later. This framework reflects that of the HBSC study as a whole (Currie et al, 1998; Currie et al, 2000) where a socialisation perspective is taken. This approach views children's health, including physical, mental and social well-being, and not just absence of death and disease, as being determined by the social, economic, environmental and psychological contexts in which they live, as well as by individual characteristics. The conceptual framework varies from that of some of the book authors such as Micklewright and Stewart (1999) who consider economic well-being as a measure, per se, of child well-being, with the use of three indicators, child poverty, worklessness in households and unemployment among 20- to 24-year-olds. Although the analysis in this chapter merely examines the statistical associations between indicators of family affluence and deprivation and child health and well-being, it nevertheless conceptualises the relationship as predictive. The data however, being cross-sectional in nature, do not lend themselves to a predictive analytic model.

Measurement of socioeconomic status among adolescents

The measurement of socioeconomic status (SES) of adolescents presents both conceptual and methodological difficulties (Currie et al, 1997) and perhaps for this reason it is omitted from some important surveys of young people (for example, Thomas et al, 1993). Klerman (1993) asserts that the link between economic status and adolescent health is difficult to establish due to significant limitations of existing databases derived from youth surveys. These surveys seldom request economic information from adolescents directly because "few know the income of their parents and some are even uncertain of their parents' occupations" (Klerman, 1993). HBSC research confirms this, with up to 25% of respondents giving responses to the question on paternal and maternal occupation that are unclassifiable (Currie et al, 1997). This highlights the need for other measures of adolescent SES, in addition to occupationally based ones, to be developed.

Given the limitations of parental occupational status as an adequate or useful socioeconomic indicator in self-completed questionnaires to school children, the HBSC group decided to develop additional, non-occupationally based indicators to construct an objective Family Affluence Scale (FAS) (Currie et al, 1998) (see Appendix) which could be utilised cross-nationally. In addition to the objective Family Affluence measure, a measure of subjective family affluence was also used in order to tap into young people's perceptions of their own socioeconomic circumstances (see Appendix).

Findings from the 1997/98 HBSC cross-national survey

Data are presented on the majority of the countries that participated in the 1997/98 survey with the exception of the Czech Republic, French-speaking Belgium, Greenland and Israel which were omitted for technical reasons at this stage of the analysis. Country samples by age group (11-year-olds, 13-year-olds and 15-year-olds) are detailed in Table 14.1. Details of the socioeconomic, health and well-being measures examined are given in the Appendix.

Table 14.1: Country samples by age group

Age group		11 years	13 years	15 years	Total
Country	Austria	1,422	1,518	1,376	4,316
	Belgium – Fl[a]	1,730	1,535	1,559	4,824
	Canada	1,856	2,308	2,403	6,567
	Denmark	1,713	1,807	1,546	5,066
	England	2,279	2,222	1,872	6,373
	Estonia	478	832	587	1,897
	Finland	1,691	1,628	1,545	4,864
	France	1,467	1,421	1,245	4,133
	Germany[b]	1,580	1,613	1,599	4,792
	Greece	1,662	1,315	1,322	4,299
	Hungary	1,435	1,356	818	3,609
	Latvia	1,311	1,199	1,265	3,775
	Lithuania	1,566	1,512	1,435	4,513
	N Ireland	1,068	1,197	1,081	3,346
	Norway	1,733	1,623	1,670	5,026
	Poland	1,627	1,598	1,636	4,861
	Portugal	1,217	1,259	1,245	3,721
	Rep of Ireland	1,495	1,442	1,457	4,394
	Russia[c]	1,308	1,367	1,322	3,997
	Scotland	2,092	1,813	1,727	5,632
	Slovak Rep	1,403	1,543	843	3,789
	Sweden	1,294	1,357	1,151	3,802
	Switzerland	1,668	2,020	1,832	5,520
	US	1,558	1,803	1,808	5,169
	Wales	1,539	1,571	1,427	4,537

[a] Flemmish speaking Belgium

[b] Germany represented by one region only

[c] Russia represented by one region only

Source: Data from the Health Behaviour in School-Aged Children: WHO Cross-National Survey conducted in 1997/98

Between country variations in family affluence

Countries were compared on the basis of the objective measure of family wealth, the FAS, with Table 14.2 presenting countries ranked on the basis of the percentage of 11, 13 and 15-year-olds who are classified in the lowest category of family affluence. Countries in Eastern Europe, the

Table 14.2: Percentage of sample scoring low on Family Affluence Scale by age group and country

	11 year old sample		13 year old sample		15 year old sample	
Rank	**Country**	% low FAS	**Country**	% low FAS	**Country**	% low FAS
1	Russia	52.5	Russia	55.4	Russia	62.2
2	Latvia	45.3	Latvia	49.8	Latvia	54.5
3	Hungary	42.2	Hungary	43.4	Hungary	50.4
4	Slovak Rep	35.7	Slovak Rep	38.0	Slovak Rep	42.5
5	Lithuania	35.3	Lithuania	37.4	Poland	40.8
6	Poland	35.0	Poland	33.1	Lithuania	39.0
7	Rep Ireland	26.4	Rep Ireland	25.8	Rep Ireland	31.8
8	Scotland	26.3	Portugal	23.2	N Ireland	26.5
9	Greece	22.5	N Ireland	22.5	Portugal	25.3
11	*Finland*[a]	*22.4*	*Scotland*[a]	*21.7*	Scotland	23.9
11	*Portugal*[a]	*22.4*	*Greece*[a]	*21.7*	Greece	23.8
12	N Ireland	20.9	England	20.9	England	23.7
13	England	20.0	*Wales*[a]	*20.7*	Fl Belgium	22.4
14	Fl Belgium	19.9	*Fl Belgium*[a]	*20.7*	Finland	22.3
15	Denmark	19.6	Finland	*19.0*	Denmark	22.0
16	Wales	18.4	Austria	18.8	Wales	20.7
17	Austria	18.1	Denmark	18.3	Austria	18.7
18	Germany	17.1	Germany	16.6	Switzerland	18.6
19	Sweden	12.9	Canada	14.7	Germany	16.6
20	Switzerland	12.5	Switzerland	13.6	Canada	15.4
21	Canada	11.0	Sweden	12.2	Sweden	14.2
22	US	10.9	France	12.1	France	12.1
23	France	9.8	US	11.9	US	11.0
24	Norway	6.0	Norway	5.5	Norway	7.8

[a] Italicised countries hold joint ranks
Source: Data from the Health Behaviour in School-Aged Children: WHO Cross-National Survey conducted in 1997/98

NIS Russia, and five CEE countries (Latvia, Hungary, Slovak Republic, Poland and Lithuania) hold the first six positions. All have more than 30% of the population in the lowest FAS category; three (Russia, Latvia and Hungary), have over 40% in this category. At the bottom of the table with 15% or less of the population in this category, in any age group, are Norway, France, the US, Sweden, Canada and Switzerland. The observation that countries thus rank in this expected fashion gives confidence that

Table 14.3: Spearman rank correlation coefficients between country scores on low family affluence and health and well-being measures

Low FAS **Correlated with**	Not healthy (n=24)	Not happy (n=24)	Daily symptoms
11-year sample	0.62[a]	0.56[a]	NS
13-year sample	0.62[a]	0.65[a]	0.40[b]
15-year sample	0.46[b]	0.61[a]	NS

[a] correlation is significant at the 0.01 level (2-tailed)

[b] correlation is significant at the 0.05 level (2-tailed)

Source: Data from the Health Behaviour in School-Aged Children: WHO Cross-National Survey conducted in 1997/98

the FAS is a valid indicator of children's material circumstances, as reported by children themselves.

In order to determine how consistently countries were ranked, according to the proportion of children living in low affluence families in each age group, Spearman rank correlations were calculated between rankings at 11 and 13 years, and between rankings at 13 and 15 years. The correlations were 0.96 ($p<0.01$); and 0.99 ($p<0.01$), respectively, indicating very high levels of stability of ranking of countries across the three age groups. Again this finding lends credibility to the FAS as a valid indicator of children's material circumstances and supports its use in cross-national surveys of children, where children themselves are reporting on their life circumstances.

Socioeconomic circumstances and child health and well-being

In order to examine the inter-relations between low family affluence and child health and well-being, within each age sample, (Spearman rank) correlations between country ranking on low affluence and health and well-being indicators were conducted. The indicators chosen for these analyses were reported health, reported happiness and experience of daily symptoms (see Appendix). Correlations were conducted for each age group separately and the Spearman coefficients are presented in Table 14.3.

In all three age groups there are highly significant correlations between country rankings on the proportion of children scoring low on family affluence and country rankings on poor reported health ('not very healthy') and poor reported happiness ('not happy'). The picture with daily symptoms is less consistent with only the 13-year-old age group showing a significant correlation with family affluence.

From these exploratory analyses, it appears that countries, which have higher proportions of adolescents living in conditions of low family affluence, also have a higher proportion reporting poor subjective health and well-being. Interpretation of these findings must take into account other factors that may impinge on the health and happiness of children living in different countries in the study, and a causal relationship cannot be inferred from this analysis. Nevertheless, this may be one of the first cross-national studies of children to find an association between the young people's self-reported material circumstances and their reported health and well-being, and the findings warrant attention and further investigation and research.

Socioeconomic circumstances and child well-being within countries

Having established that there are significant correlations between countries in children's socioeconomic circumstances and their reported health and well-being, this section will explore the association between family affluence and various health and health behaviour measures within countries by examining evidence from an analysis of the 1997/98 HBSC survey data reported in Mullan and Currie (2000). Tables 14.4 to14.7 are adapted from their publication, which is a chapter in the recently published WHO report of the International Survey (Currie et al, 2000).

The analysis selects 11 countries from across Europe, and the US, to examine the strength of associations between the objective measure of family material circumstances, the FAS, and a range of health and well-being indicators and health behaviours. It also examines associations between children's perceived family wealth and the same range of health and well-being indicators. Data from the 15-year-old age group only are presented, since certain health behaviours, such as smoking and drinking, are not very prevalent in the younger age groups. Tables 14.4 to 14.7 have been constructed to shift attention away from the size and statistical significance of the correlations between the variables and towards the patterning and consistency of their relationships. In general, correlations are small but within acceptable ranges for this type of data (Mullan and Currie, 2000).

Table 14.4: Correlations between selected health/risk behaviours and family affluence (FAS), by country[a]

	Smoking	Been drunk	Exercise	Eat fruit
Austria			0.05-0.1	
Denmark	0.05-0.1		0.101-0.199	
Germany[b]	0.05-0.1		0.05-0.1	0.05-0.1
Hungary			0.101-0.199	0.101-0.199
Latvia		X (0.05-0.1)	0.101-0.199	0.101-0.199
Norway				≥0.201
Portugal	X (0.05-0.1)	X (0.05-0.1)	0.101-0.199	0.05-0.1
Russia[c]	X (0.05-0.1)	X (0.05-0.1)	0.05-0.1	
Scotland		X (0.05-0.1)	0.05-0.1	0.05-0.1
US			0.05-0.1	0.05-0.1
Wales		X (0.05-0.1)	0.101-0.199	0.05-0.1

X = increased affluence significantly associated with an undesirable outcome.

Key

not significant (blank) | 0.05-0.1 | 0.101-0.199 | ≥0.201

Note: Increased affluence significantly associated with a desirable outcome.

[a] adapted from Mullan and Currie (2000)

[b] Germany represented by one region only.

[c] Russia represented by one region only.

Source: Data from the Health Behaviour in School-Aged Children: WHO Cross-National Survey conducted in 1997/98

Family affluence and well-being within countries

Table 14.4 shows the strength of the relationships between family affluence and the following health behaviours: frequency of smoking, lifetime frequency of drunkenness, frequency of fruit consumption and regular vigorous exercise. In the majority of countries higher levels of family affluence are associated with positive health behaviours including more frequent vigorous exercise and fruit consumption. In contrast, the health risk behaviours, smoking and drinking (being drunk) either display no relationship with family affluence, or an increased incidence with increasing family affluence. Thus children from wealthier families appear to engage in more health-enhancing activities as represented by taking regular physical activity and frequent fruit eating. Smoking and drinking (as measured here) among 15-year-olds are not subject to consistent

Table 14.5: Correlations between subjective health well-being indicators and family affluence (FAS) by country[a]

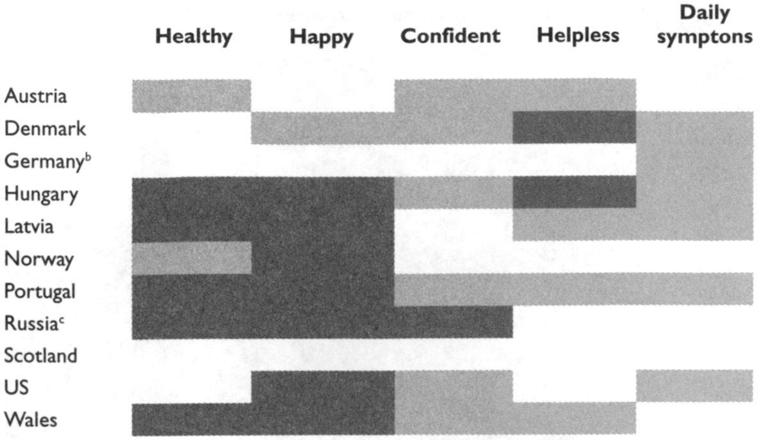

	Healthy	Happy	Confident	Helpless	Daily symptons
Austria	0.05-0.1		0.05-0.1	0.05-0.1	
Denmark		0.05-0.1	0.05-0.1	0.101-0.199	0.05-0.1
Germany[b]					0.05-0.1
Hungary	0.101-0.199	0.101-0.199	0.05-0.1	0.101-0.199	0.05-0.1
Latvia	0.101-0.199	0.101-0.199		0.05-0.1	0.05-0.1
Norway	0.05-0.1	0.101-0.199			
Portugal	0.101-0.199	0.101-0.199	0.05-0.1	0.05-0.1	0.05-0.1
Russia[c]	0.101-0.199	0.101-0.199	0.101-0.199		
Scotland					
US		0.101-0.199	0.05-0.1		0.05-0.1
Wales	0.101-0.199	0.101-0.199	0.05-0.1	0.05-0.1	

X = increased affluence significantly associated with an undesirable outcome.

Key

[ ] – not significant 0.05-0.1 0.101-0.199 ≥0.201

Note: Increased affluence significantly associated with a desirable outcome.

[a] adapted from Mullan and Currie (2000).

[c] Russia represented by one region only.

[b] Germany represented by one region only.

Source: Data from the Health Behaviour in School-Aged Children: WHO Cross-National Survey conducted in 1997/98

patterning according to family affluence. Other cultural, social and psychological factors clearly have a more significant role than material wealth of the family in determining these behaviours.

Table 14.5 presents the strength of associations between family affluence and a range of health and well-being indicators: reported health, reported happiness, self-confidence, perceived helplessness and daily symptoms. In the majority of countries, increased family affluence is associated with feeling healthy, happy and self-confident; while greater incidence of daily symptoms of some description, and feelings of helplessness are associated with lower family affluence in six and five countries respectively.

Table 14.6: Correlations between health/risk behaviours and perceived family wealth, by country[a]

	Smoking	Been drunk	Exercise	Eat fruit
Austria			0.101-0.199	
Denmark			0.101-0.199	
Germany[b]			0.05-0.1	
Hungary	X (0.05-0.1)	X (0.101-0.199)		0.101-0.199
Latvia	X (0.05-0.1)	X (0.05-0.1)	0.101-0.199	≥0.201
Norway				0.05-0.1
Portugal	X (0.101-0.199)	X (0.05-0.1)	0.05-0.1	0.101-0.199
Russia[c]			0.05-0.1	≥0.201
Scotland			0.05-0.1	0.101-0.199
US			0.05-0.1	0.05-0.1
Wales			0.05-0.1	0.05-0.1

X = increased affluence significantly associated with an undesirable outcome.

Key

Note: Increased affluence significantly associated with a desirable outcome.

[a] adapted from Mullan and Currie (2000).

[b] Germany represented by one region only.

[c] Russia represented by one region only.

Source: Data from the Health Behaviour in School-Aged Children: WHO Cross-National Survey conducted in 1997/98

Perceived (subjective) family wealth and well-being within countries

Examination of the correlations in Table 14.6 between perceived family wealth and health behaviours shows that for both positive and negative health behaviours, the patterns are similar to those displayed for the FAS (Table 14.4). Far more consistent patterns across countries are found in the associations between perceived family wealth and measures of reported health and well-being (Table 14.7). Thus, in all countries, Table 14.7 shows that positive perception of family wealth is associated with perceived happiness and feelings of confidence, and is negatively associated with feelings of helplessness. All but one or two countries exhibit the same patterns with respect to perceived health and experience of symptoms.

Table 14.7: Correlations between health/risk behaviours, well-being and perceived family wealth, by country[a]

X = increased affluence significantly associated with an undesirable outcome.

Key

Note: Increased affluence significantly associated with a desirable outcome.

[a] adapted from Mullan and Currie (2000).

[c] Russia represented by one region only.

[b] Germany represented by one region only.

Source: Data from the Health Behaviour in School-Aged Children: WHO Cross-National Survey conducted in 1997/98

Discussion

Country rankings on socioeconomic circumstances and health and well-being

The finding that countries rank according to an expected pattern on low family affluence, that is CEE countries ranking high and west European countries and the US ranking low, gives credence to young people's ability to accurately report their material and social circumstances. In turn, poor subjective well-being was found to be ranked very similarly, and the correspondence between the two measures was highly significant. Also significantly correlated, but to a lesser degree, was poor subjective health. These findings suggest that the sectors of the adolescent population living in materially and socially deprived circumstances (compared to other children their age) are more likely to suffer from poorer well-being and health, and this will account for larger proportions of the adolescent population in the CEE countries.

Patterns of association between socioeconomic indicators and health and well-being within countries

Results indicate that health behaviour and well-being indicators do vary according to socioeconomic circumstances so that those young people from wealthier families engage in more health enhancing activities and have better levels of well-being than their less well-off counterparts. The health and well-being indicators are most consistently related to objective and subjective measures of family wealth. Thus, in all countries, subjective happiness and feeling confident and not feeling helpless and, in the vast majority of countries, perceived health and infrequent experience of symptoms, were all associated with greater affluence.

Smoking and drinking patterns among 15-year-olds are not subject to consistent patterning by socioeconomic circumstances as measured. In contrast, there is evidence of a moderately consistent patterning of physical activity and fruit consumption – both of these behaviours confer health-promoting benefits in the short and longer term. Taking part in sport and other physical activities and eating fruit both have family cost implications in many countries which may explain their patterning by family affluence. From these preliminary results it would appear that greater wealth is associated with greater life chances.

Conclusions

Micklewright and Stewart (1999) have identified an urgent need for more data allowing the monitoring of children's well-being. The HBSC data present the opportunity to describe children's experience of health in a large number of countries from a comparative base since the data are collected with a common research instrument. The data also provide the opportunity to examine the relationship between health and well-being and both objective and subjective measures of family affluence. The research shows that countries in which a relatively high proportion of children experience low material family affluence corresponds powerfully to the countries where high levels of poor self-reported health and happiness exist. Patterns of association within countries are visible, although less dramatic. The most evident associations are between perceived family wealth and perceived health and psychosocial health, including confidence and helplessness.

Clearly these analyses only represent a beginning in utilisation of data collected from children about their own life experiences to understand the relationships between life socioeconomic circumstances and well-being. This line of research will continue with the next HBSC cross-national survey in 2001/2 when a wider range of indicators of positive health and indicators of social capital will be included, in addition to the current measures of socioeconomic circumstances, health and well-being.

Acknowledgments

The 1997/98 HBSC cross-national study was coordinated by Candace Currie, HBSC International Coordinator RUHBC, Medical School, University of Edinburgh. The Research Unit in Health and Behavioural Change (RUHBC) is funded by the Chief Scientist Office of the Scottish Executive Health Department (SEHD) and the Health Education Board for Scotland (HEBS). However, the opinions expressed in this paper are those of the author, not of SEHD or HEBS. The Data Bank Manager was Bente Wold, the Research Centre for Health Promotion, University of Bergen, Norway. The World Health Organization – Regional Office for Europe, has adopted the project as a WHO collaborative study. Erio Ziglio and Vivian Rasmussen were the WHO representatives on the HBSC Assembly at the time of the 1997/98 survey. I would like to acknowledge the principal investigators and other country representatives in the WHO-HBSC research group for the 1997/98 survey.

References

Atkinson, A.B., Rainwater, L. and Smeeding, T.M. (1995) 'Income distribution in OECD countries', Social Policy Studies No 18, OECD.

Burgard, P., Cheyne, W.M. and Jahoda, G. (1989) 'Children's representation of economic inequality: a replication', *British Journal of Developmental Psychology*, vol 7, pp 275-87.

Columbus, F.H. (1998) *Central and Eastern Europe in transition*, Commack: Nova Science Publishers.

Currie, C.E., Elton. R.A., Todd. J. and Platt, S. (1997) 'Indicators of socioeconomic status for adolescents: the WHO Health Behaviour in School-aged Children Survey', *Health Education Research*, vol 12, pp 385-97.

Currie, C. et al (1998) *Health behaviour in school-aged children: A WHO cross-national survey (HBSC): Research protocol for the 1997/98 survey*, Research Unit in Health and Behavioural Change, Edinburgh: University of Edinburgh.

Currie, C., Hurrelmann, K., Settertobulte, W., Smith, R. and Todd, J. (eds) (2000) *Health and health behaviour among young people*, WHO Policy Series: Health Policy for Children and Adolescents, Issue 1, Copenhagen: WHO.

Duncan, G.J., Brooks-Gunn, J. and Klebanov, P.K. (1994) 'Economic deprivation and early childhood development', *Child Development*, vol 65, pp 296-319.

Duncan, G.J. and Brooks-Gunn, J. (eds) (1997) *Consequences of growing up poor*, New York, NY: Russell Sage.

Klerman, L.V. (1993) 'The influence of economic factors on health-related behaviours of adolescents', in S.G. Millstein, A.C. Petersen and E.O. Nightingale (eds) *Promoting the health of adolescents: New dimensions for the twenty-first century*, Oxford: Oxford University Press.

Micklewright, J. and Stewart, K. (1999) 'Is child welfare converging in the European Union?', Innocenti Occasional Papers Economic and Social Policy Series No 69, Florence: UNICEF International Child Development Centre.

Mullan, E. and Currie, C. (2000) 'Socio-economic inequalities in adolescent health', in C. Currie, K. Hurrelmann, W. Settertobulte, R. Smith and J. Todd (eds) *Health and health behaviour among young people*, WHO Policy Series: Health Policy for Children and Adolescents: Issue 1, Copenhagen: WHO.

Notburga, O. and Wagner, G.G. (eds) (1997) *Income inequality and poverty in eastern and western Europe*, Heidelberg: Physica-Verlag.

Offe, C. (1997) *Varieties of transition: The East European and East German experience*, Cambridge: MIT Press.

Thomas, M., Holroyd, S. and Goddard, E. (1993) *Smoking among secondary schoolchildren in 1992*, London: HMSO.

Wold, B., Aaro, L.E. and Smith, C. (1994) *Health behaviour of school-aged children: A WHO cross-national survey (HBSC) research protocol for the 1993-94 study*, Bergen: University of Bergen.

Appendix

The HBSC Study

The Health Behaviour in School-Aged Children (HBSC) Study is a cross-national research study conducted in collaboration with the European Regional Office of the World Health Organisation (WHO). It was initiated in 1983 by researchers from Finland, England and Norway, and since then the study has grown to 30 member countries. Although the study originated in Europe, there has been collaboration with Canada since early in the study's development and, more recently, with the US; and both these countries are now full members. The growing interest in the study worldwide has also resulted in satellite HBSC surveys being conducted independently in Australia, South East Asia and the Middle East. All of the teams conducting HBSC outside the European based study are in communication with the International Coordination Centre in Edinburgh.

The HBSC research study aims to gain new insight into, and increase our understanding of, health behaviours, health and well-being and their social context in young people in the early adolescent years (11-15). As a WHO collaborative project, a key objective is to use the research findings to inform and influence health policy, and in particular health promotion and health education policy, programmes and practice aimed at school-aged children at both national and international levels (Currie and Watson, 1998).

The first survey, conducted in 1983/84, was carried out in four countries (Austria, England, Finland and Norway), and since 1985/86 surveys have been conducted at four-year intervals in the growing number of member countries. In the 1997/98 survey, 26 European countries: Austria, Flemish and French speaking Belgium, Czech Republic, Denmark, England, Estonia, Finland, France, Germany, Greece, Greenland, Hungary, Israel, Latvia, Lithuania, Northern Ireland, Norway, Poland, Portugal, Republic of Ireland, Russia, Scotland, Slovak Republic, Sweden, Switzerland and Wales; and Canada and the US participated. The International Coordinator of the 1997/8 Survey was Dr Candace Currie, University of Edinburgh, and the Data Bank Manager was Dr Bente Wold, University of Bergen.

Description of the HBSC survey

An international research protocol is produced by the international research group for each survey and is published by the International Coordination Centre (for example, Wold et al, 1994; Currie et al, 1998). The protocol includes scientific rationale; details of the survey method, including sampling and survey administration procedures; questionnaire design and codebook. The protocol is only available to HBSC members until one year after the international survey has been completed in all countries. Thereafter countries interested in using the questionnaire may apply for the use of the protocol.

Survey method

Full details of the survey method are published in the International HBSC Research Protocol for the 1997/98 Survey (Currie et al, 1998). A summary is presented here.

The target population

The specific populations selected for sampling in the 1997-98 survey include those in-school youth aged 11, 13 and 15; that is, in their 12th, 14th and 16th years.

Although a national sample is prefered, it is quite acceptable to conduct a study in only one region of a country as long as it is clearly understood that the findings are not representative of the entire country. If it is decided to identify a region within a country for the study, the region should have a population of at least one million, and should constitute a meaningful administrative unit from the point of view of health promotion among adolescents.

Data collection

The data are gathered through a school-based survey questionnaire completed anonymously and confidentially by pupils in the classroom under exam conditions. Either a member of the national research team or an instructed teacher administers the questionnaire. Each country is responsible for their own data collection. Data from all member countries are compiled in an international data file by the elected Data Bank Manager, currently at the University of Bergen, Norway.

Recommended sample size

The sampling technique used is 'cluster sampling' where the cluster is the school class. While the procedure is not as precise as simple random sampling, it is efficient administratively and can be as precise as random sampling if the sample size is increased accordingly. However, it demands that school classes are randomly sampled. The recommended minimum sample size for each of the three age groups is 1,550 students.

The questionnaire

HBSC collects data from young people on a wide range of health behaviours and health indicators, factors that may influence their development as individuals and prevalence in the population. These 'predictors' are primarily characteristics of the children themselves, such as their psychological attributes and personal circumstances, including objective measures of their socioeconomic status; their perceived social environment, such as their family relationships, peer group associations, school climate and perceived (subjective) socioeconomic circumstances. The health behaviours measured include smoking, alcohol use, eating patterns and physical activity. The health and well-being indicators include subjective assessment of general health and happiness; experience of symptoms; psychosocial adjustment including perceived self-confidence, loneliness, and helplessness.

The questionnaire consists of a mandatory set of questions on demographic characteristics, key health behaviours and health indicators, and social context variables relating to family life, peer relationships and life at school, these being considered to be important social domains for the adolescent. These questions have been used in consecutive surveys, thus forming a core of questions on which cross-country comparisons can be made and trends over time can be examined. In addition, there are optional questions on focus areas which countries can use if they wish to study a particular issue in depth. Groups of countries collaborate on the development of these focus areas and they are then able to work together on data analysis and publication relating to them. Each country has the further possibility of adding its own national questions on issues of particular academic interest or national public health concern.

Measures of socioeconomic status, health and well-being

Family Affluence Scale (FAS)

This measure comprised a composite score of number of family cars (or vans), the child having its own unshared bedroom, and number of holidays in the past 12 months. After variable construction, the values were recoded to give three categories of FAS, low, middle and high (Currie et al, 1998; Currie et al, 2000).

Subjective family wealth

This measure was scored according to young people's responses to the question: 'How well off (wealthy) is your family?' with a five-point response scale from very well-off to not at all well-off.

Subjective health and well-being

Two simple indicators of general health and well-being have been used consistently over successive HBSC surveys. These are:

> **'How healthy do you think you are**?' Very healthy/quite healthy/not very healthy.
> **'In general how do you feel about your life at present**?' I feel very happy/ I feel quite happy/ I don't feel very happy/ I'm not happy at all.
> Symptoms: 'In the last 6 months: how often have you had the following – headache, stomach ache, back ache; feeling low, irritable/bad tempered, feeling nervous, have difficulties getting to sleep, feel dizzy. About every day/more than once a week/about every month/rarely or never?'

PART 4

Child and family policies

Introduction

Throughout the 20th century welfare state programmes have tried to alleviate poverty and provide support to families with children. In some countries these programmes have proved to be very successful, while in other countries welfare state programmes were deemed to be aggravating poverty. Part 1 of this volume analyses the impact and trends of tax and transfer programmes for children and families in the 1990s and takes a closer look at the effects of recent policy reforms on children's well-being. In the first chapter Howard Oxley, Thai-Thanh Dang, Michael F. Förster and Michele Pellizzari try to establish the role played by structural changes in household/employment relations and the direct impact of public policy via tax and transfer programmes on child poverty trends in industrialised nations.

Their results reveal no generalised trend in child poverty: some countries recorded significant increases while others – including high poverty countries – included decreases. In the majority of countries, child poverty remained stable throughout the past ten years. Changes in poverty rates were little affected by the shifts in the household structure defined by family type and work status. Thus, where poverty has increased it originated within individual household types (pure poverty effect). Non-working households, which largely depend on transfer income, reveal divergent trends in income transfer policies across countries. Oxley, Dang, Förster and Pellizzari find a widespread increase in poverty before taxes and transfers (for a subset of these countries). This increase was generally more than compensated by increased effectiveness of the tax and transfer system. Thus, income transfer and tax policies appeared to be more effective in reducing poverty at the end of the period than at the beginning. Over this period there may have been some switching from transfers to tax-related benefits for children.

As regards policies, Oxley et al note that poverty is highest among non-working households in all countries, suggesting that employment is a key channel for reducing poverty. However, as large shares of children are living in households with at least one worker, the problems of the working poor also need to be considered. In this context, the authors note that increased spending on children is likely to have a major impact on overall poverty since 60% of poor households are households with children. A further analysis of child policies across countries with poverty data before and after taxes and transfers suggest some trade-off between targeting to low-income groups and overall spending on child-related policies across countries. While the data used for the analysis were fragile, countries that target more are more effective in reducing poverty per dollar spent. However, these countries also tend to spend less on child policies so that the overall impact on poverty or effectiveness is reduced. Thus, countries that target more (which in practice often have high poverty rates) may need to increase spending if they are to make further headway in reducing child poverty. In contrast, countries that have already achieved low levels of poverty through high levels of spending for programmes aimed at all children may achieve further gains most effectively via increased targeting.

Herwig Immervoll, Holly Sutherland and Klaas de Vos explore the role of child benefits for the alleviation of child poverty within the European Union (EU). Their study examines the impact of national child benefits on the national income distribution and poverty estimates, and explores the effects of introducing each national system into the other country. The results are derived from the European Community Household Panel and the Euromod simulation model. Based on these results, Immervoll, Sutherland and de Vos distinguish three country groups. In a first group of countries family benefits are generous, but even without them incomes are sufficient to protect the large majority of children from poverty (Denmark, Luxembourg). In a second group, family benefits are relatively small and appear to have little effect on poverty (Spain, Italy, Greece, Portugal and Ireland). In a third group, family benefits appear to have a significant effect on the protection of children from poverty (United Kingdom, Belgium, Austria, France and the Netherlands).

Immervoll et al have also used microsimulation techniques to examine the extent to which differences in child benefits explain differences in poverty levels between the Netherlands and the UK, two countries that belong to the third group of countries. They also explored the effect of 'swapping' child benefit systems between the two countries. They find that the Dutch system is in transition and that the 'old' system, which depends on both the number and the age of children in a family, is clearly more generous and more effective in reducing poverty than the new system, which depends on age alone. However, the new system appears to be more efficient at reducing poverty. The 'old' Dutch system seems also the most effective and efficient system for child poverty reduction when applied to the UK, even when controlling for the amount spent on benefit.

Furthermore, the authors clearly illustrate the potential that the Euromod simulation model offers to researchers and policy analysts. Although static microsimulation models exist in most member states of the EU and the rest of the Organisation for Economic Co-operation and Development (OECD), Immervoll, Sutherland and de Vos argue that a model which operates at the European level is needed to explore the effects of benefits in a comparable manner in different countries as well as on European child poverty. Euromod is such a model. It provides a Europe-wide perspective on social and fiscal policies that are implemented at European, national or regional level. It is also designed to examine, within a consistent comparative framework, the impact of national policies on national populations or the differential impact of coordinated European policy on individual member states. In the near future, Euromod will make it possible to draw common European poverty lines, construct a common income distribution and generally consider the European population across national boundaries. The simulation of various levels of a common universal benefit for children (or a children's 'Citizen's Income') to replace existing cash benefits and tax expenditures would allow researchers to assess national systems against a set of common benchmarks.

Marcia K. Meyers, Janet C. Gornick, Laura R. Peck and Amanda J. Lockshin discuss a different level of policy intervention: the variation in public policies that supported children in the US as of 1994. The chapter proposes a new approach to understanding how state-level policies may affect childhood poverty in the US, referring to the experience of cross-national research and the construction of welfare state typologies. Meyers et al report that there is substantial variation in policies that support children and their families at the sub-national level in the US. There is considerable variation not only in the dimension of benefit adequacy, but also in the policy structure dimensions; not only in programmes managed principally at the state level, but also on some dimensions of programmes, such as Food Stamps, which are primarily federal. The authors characterise state-level policies in terms of adequacy, inclusion, and commitment for 11 different programmes. In state clusters with high need, they report that child poverty rates varied from 29%, in states providing minimal support, to 20% in states that provided generous support. In states with low need, Meyers et al find that child poverty rates varied from 17% when a conservative approach to support is provided, to 15% where integrated support is provided. Furthermore, they find that configurations of family support packages are only weakly linked to underlying need or demand and that the expansiveness of the packages are associated with lower levels of poverty in states with high or in states with low levels of need.

Cristina Solera analyses the anti-poverty effectiveness of three different welfare states – Italy, Sweden and the UK – by focusing on both income transfers and policies supporting maternal employment, using data from the Luxembourg Income Study (LIS). This study shows that mothers' earnings are very important for families in order to maintain an adequate standard of living. Solera finds that the primary reason for Sweden's low child poverty rates is the integration of women into the labour force, regardless of whether or not they are married or have children. In part, this is the result of policies that stress the importance of a (continued) attachment to the labour market, including good parental leave programmes and a comprehensive system of childcare. Solera concludes that "policies aimed at facilitating the labour market participation of mothers should be regarded as a crucial component of an effective anti-poverty package".

James Kunz, Patrick Villeneuve and Irwin Garfinkel's study is a cross-national analysis of child support provisions in a number of OECD countries also based on the LIS data. Child support is a vital source of income for the single-parent households, a household type that faces particularly high poverty risks throughout the industrialised world. Several OECD countries have introduced new measures aimed at increasing the number and level of private child support payments during the 1990s. Kunz, Villenueve and Garfinkel try to establish whether these attempts have succeeded. They examine the levels and trends of child support payments in seven OECD countries by analysing information obtained from the LIS database variables on child support and alimony received from absent parents.

They find a steady increase of child support receipt among the households eligible for it in Australia between 1981 and 1994 while spousal alimony support payments remained constant. In Belgium, the percentage receiving child support increased considerably in the period 1985-1992, while payments among all those eligible increased slightly and the average share of child support in net income decreased. The results for Denmark and Finland were somewhat more stable, although all percentages declined slightly in Denmark between 1987 and 1992. The situation in the Netherlands did not vary between 1983 and 1987 but then changed dramatically by 1991. Kunz et al observe a large increase in the percentage of those receiving child support in 1991, while the relative level of payments among those receiving child support dropped dramatically. Efforts in the UK seem to have failed. The proportion of single-parent families receiving child support has declined in the period 1979-1995, while payments declined relative to the poverty line. Reform efforts in the US aimed at improving the collection of child support also seem to have failed, as both the proportion of households receiving child support and payment levels dropped between 1979 and 1994.

However, the authors suggest that, at least in the US, the changed composition of those eligible for child support might have influenced the success of the new collection effort. In the past, child support enforcement efforts in the US were successful among the never married mothers. These numbers of never married mothers increased and thus, Kunz et al suggest that the success of recent efforts is negatively influenced by the fact that these efforts are 'swimming upstream'. They conclude that the situation in the US would very likely be worse without those new efforts.

Sheila B. Kamerman and Alfred J. Kahn, in the broadest policy chapter in the volume, investigate the trend in public investment in child and family benefits and services during the 1990s, a period marked by growing social expenditure constraints in most countries. They report that public expenditure/investment in child and family policies in the advanced industrialised countries has not kept up with expenditures on pensions and health and, therefore has declined as a proportion of GDP and social expenditures since the 1950's. Nonetheless, child and family benefits have been protected against budget cuts during the last decade in some nations, and expenditures on children even increased in the late 1990s. Family allowances have been sustained or raised, parental leaves have been extended where they existed and even newly introduced in a few countries, while childcare services have continued to increase in supply. These are hopeful signs in an era of population ageing and increased pressure on social retirement budgets.

Note

[1] Also Bradbury and Jäntti in Chapter One show that levels of market income in the households of the most disadvantaged children vary considerably across countries and according to the authors market incomes play a larger role than state transfers in accounting for cross-national diversity of child poverty rates.

FIFTEEN

Income inequalities and poverty among children and households with children in selected OECD countries

Howard Oxley, Thai-Thanh Dang, Michael F. Förster and Michele Pellizzari

Introduction

How did the economic situation of children develop across 17 Organisation for Economic and Co-operation and Development (OECD) countries over the last decade? This chapter:

- reviews changes in average incomes, the distribution of incomes and poverty of children;
- suggests possible factors underlying these changes;
- analyses the response of the tax/transfer system to changes in market income across countries and over time.

After a short description of the data, the first substantive part of the chapter explores whether the economic situation of children has deteriorated overall. Changes to the overall income distribution of children are then analysed using various distribution indices. This is complemented by an analysis of poverty indicators to assess developments towards the bottom of the distribution. In each case, the possible effect of changing population structures of different household types is examined. The second part of the chapter analyses the impact of income taxes and public transfers on low incomes among children. The chapter concludes with implications of the results for policy.

Sources and data

Data

This study uses a common approach to analyse national data on the distribution of household income in selected years. Data were collected on the basis of a questionnaire completed by national authorities or experts from 17 OECD member countries who drew on the country survey or tax files most appropriate for comparisons over time[1]. The analysis is limited to the decade between the mid-1980s and mid-1990s.

There is somewhat less cross-country comparability in these data than with the Luxembourg Income Study (LIS) data, although a number of problems, described in Burniaux et al, 1998 and Oxley et al, 1999, are common to both. Such problems are almost certainly less significant for comparisons over time. Even so;

- Available years were not always at the same cyclical position and results can be sensitive to the end points chosen.
- These samples may not always accurately reflect changes over time at the extremes of the distribution in some countries.
- Under-reporting or other measurement problems may not remain constant over time[2].

This highlights the need for caution in interpreting these results[3].

The income concept

The key concept for measuring the distribution of income and degree of poverty is *equivalent household disposable income* per individual. The income of all members of the household is combined and then divided by the square-root of the number of individuals in the household[4], to allow for differences in household size and for the existence of household 'economies of scale' in consumption[5]. On the assumption that households generally pool income, equivalent household disposable income is attributed to each individual in the household including children. Data are presented for household market income and disposable income (market income plus income transfers received from general government less income taxes paid).

Some issues of definition

Children are defined as all individuals below 18 years of age. To study the effects of changing family/employment structure of households where children live, five different types are distinguished: single-adult households, working and non-working; and, two-or-more-adult households with no worker, one worker and two or more workers[6]. Where it was not possible to break children down into these five categories, the breakdown was made at the household level (ie children plus the adults living in households with children). In practice, individuals broken down at the household level tend to have higher average incomes and lower poverty rates than children taken separately; but results in terms of changes are broadly the same in the two cases[7].

It should also be noted that lone-parent households only include households with one adult and a child less than 18 years old. Thus, a woman or man living alone with her or his child aged 18 or over would be classed as a two-adult household[8]. This narrow definition may explain some of the differences in results with national studies. Finally, not all countries used the concept of households. For countries where tax data were used, it was the tax unit. This has implications for average household size across countries.

Comparisons are generally made with the total population including those of retirement age. However, where comparisons were made related to employment issues, the working age population was used (the total population less those individuals living in households with a head aged 65 and above).

Comparisons of the incomes of children relative to other income groups should be treated with caution. Their relative positions depend on the choice of equivalence scale, composition effects (changing shares of children living in specific family types) and relative importance of transfers and taxes going to and coming from other groups (particularly for the retired who are taking up an increasing share of overall transfers in many countries)[9].

The economic well-being of children

The importance of children in the population

In all countries under review, the proportion of children in the total population declined, on average by some two to three percentage points, except for Germany, Sweden, the United Kingdom and the United States where this share was kept more or less constant. Therefore, average household size has been falling for the past ten years and in particular in some of the Nordic and Continental European countries.

The family/employment structure of children has evolved as well. Common patterns across countries are[10]:

- The share of children living in lone-parent households has increased in all countries, except Greece. In the most recent years, they have made up on average 11% of all children.
- Those living in non-worker households have risen as well. In the most recent period around 7.5% of all children live in such households. On average, more than half of these children belong to lone-parent households (not working), although this occurs only in 10 of the 15 countries. This pattern has not, however, become more accentuated over time.
- The proportion of children living in two-adult, one-worker households decreased over the ten years, except Turkey. Just one third of children, on average, live in this 'traditional' family context.

Has the economic well-being of children deteriorated?

The development of child incomes and poverty has to be analysed against the demographic background of a general ageing of society. A first issue is whether the average economic situation - as measured by average equivalent disposable income of children - has improved or deteriorated over time. Changes in disposable income (Table 15.1, column 1) show that in real terms child incomes have generally risen. However, when comparing average income of children relative to the working-age population (Table 15.1, column 4), there were declines in 9 of the 14 countries[11].

In order to explore the contribution of the changing family/employment environment of children on the development of their relative incomes, Table 15.2 assesses such impacts using a shift-share analysis. The second column shows the percentage point changes of the incomes of children relative to those of the working-age population. The fourth column disaggregates this change into: (a) that part due to changes in household structure (structural effect) and, (b) that part arising from changes in household income when holding household structure constant

Table 15.1: Trends in the disposable income of children: mid-1980s to the mid-1990s

	Children	Working-age population	Children	
	Average income[a] in real terms		Relative income[b]	
	(per cent changes)	(per cent changes)	(levels[c])	(percentage point changes[d])
Australia, 1984-94	–4.9	-3.0	91.6	1.8
Belgium, 1983-95	..	..	..	..
Canada, 1985-95	–2.2	–1.2	88.9	–0.9
Denmark, 1983-94	7.9	11.0	98.5	–3.3
Finland, 1986-95	55.3	52.2	99.9	–0.3
France, 1984-94	10.4	10.9	95.9	0.2
Germany, 1984-94	16.9	18.5	92.3	–3.1
Greece, 1988-94	5.7	0.8	101.5	6.4
Hungary, 1991-97	..	..	..	..
Italy, 1984-93	5.7	7.1	89.4	–2.7
Mexico, 1989-94	19.9	13.4	85.4	–1.7
Netherlands, 1984-95	18.6	19.3	92.6	2.1
Norway, 1986-95	5.0	4.3	96.8	–2.5
Sweden, 1983-95	7.8	9.3	97.4	–3.4
Turkey, 1987-94	0.0	4.4	90.5	–4.2
UK, 1985-95	16.8	22.8	88.4	–3.2
US, 1985-95	8.4	6.6	86.8	1.9
OECD average (15)	12.2	12.3	93.2	–0.6

[a] Average income is the weighted average of income by family work type for children and individuals in the working-age population respectively.

[b] Relative income of children is the ratio of the average income of children to the average income of the working-age population.

[c] Levels are shown at the end of the period.

[d] In calculating changes over time, the population structure of the working-age population was kept constant.

Source: OECD

(income effect). In the remaining columns, these effects are broken down by household type. Three main results emerge from this table:

Table 15.2: Trends in relative income of children: shift-share analysis

(Changes in percentage points)	Total change	Decomposition of the change[a]	For all household types	By family/work types				
				Single parent		Two parents		
				Not working	Working	No worker	One worker	Two workers
Australia, 1984-94	1.8	Structural effect	–0.4	0.8	0.8	0.6	–4.6	2.0
		Income effect	2.2	0.5	0.2	0.6	0.4	0.5
Canada, 1985-95	–0.9	Structural effect	–0.4	0.4	1.3	0.4	–4.5	1.9
		Income effect	–0.5	0.4	0.3	0.1	–1.0	–0.3
Belgium, 1983-95	..	Structural effect	..	..	..	..	..	..
		Income effect	..	..	..	..	..	..
Denmark, 1983-94	–3.3	Structural effect	–1.9	0.8	1.2	1.0	–2.1	–2.7
		Income effect	–1.5	0.1	–0.3	0.1	0.4	–1.9
Finland, 1986-95	–0.3	Structural effect	–0.1	1.0	0.6	0.7	–3.3	0.9
		Income effect	–0.2	0.0	0.3	–0.1	0.1	–0.5
France, 1984-94	0.2	Structural effect	1.1	0.3	0.2	0.5	–5.8	5.9
		Income effect	–0.9	0.0	–0.5	–0.1	1.0	–1.4
Germany, 1984-94	–3.1	Structural effect	–1.8	0.4	1.6	0.2	–0.7	-3.3
		Income effect	–1.3	0.0	0.1	–0.6	–0.6	–0.2
Greece, 1988-94	6.4	Structural effect	4.4	–1.2	–0.7	–1.0	–6.2	13.4
		Income effect	2.0	0.8	0.1	0.6	1.3	–0.7
Hungary, 1991-97	..	Structural effect	..	..	..	..	..	..
		Income effect	..	..	..	..	..	..
Italy, 1984-93	–2.7	Structural effect	–1.5	0.4	0.4	0.8	–4.0	0.9
		Income effect	–1.2	0.1	0.0	–0.1	–4.0	2.7
Mexico, 1989-94	–1.7	Structural effect	0.5	0.2	2.3	0.4	–7.2	4.8
		Income effect	–2.1	0.0	–0.4	–1.1	1.4	–2.0
Netherlands, 1984-95	2.1	Structural effect	3.4	1.3	1.5	–0.3	–19.5	20.4
		Income effect	–1.3	–0.3	–0.1	–0.6	–1.2	1.0

Table 15.2: contd.../

(Changes in percentage points)	Total change	Decomposition of the change[a]	For all household types	By family/work types				
				Single parent		Two parents		
				Not working	Working	No worker	One worker	Two workers
Norway, 1986-95	–2.5	Structural effect	–0.8	1.3	2.1	1.0	–8.2	3.0
		Income effect	–1.8	0.6	–0.2	–0.1	–0.6	–1.3
Sweden, 1983-95	–3.4	Structural effect	–1.8	0.8	2.6	1.2	–3.0	–3.5
		Income effect	–1.6	–0.1	–0.7	0.1	–0.5	–0.4
Turkey, 1987-94	–4.2	Structural effect	–0.7	0.2	0.5	0.5	4.7	–6.6
		Income effect	–3.5	0.0	–0.3	–0.5	0.3	–2.9
UK, 1985-95	–3.2	Structural effect	0.1	2.2	2.1	–1.7	–6.4	3.8
		Income effect	–3.3	–0.3	–0.6	0.3	–2.2	–0.4
US, 1985-95	1.9	Structural effect	1.0	–0.2	1.2	–0.2	–2.7	2.9
		Income effect	0.9	–0.1	0.3	0.0	–0.8	1.5

[a] Changes due to income and structural effects are both additive across groups. The income effect already neutralises composition effects due to change in the population structure by family/work types as shown in Table 15.1. Therefore, the structural effect only captures changing structure of children across household types. Note that, the structural effect for one group cannot be interpreted independently of the other groups. For instance, a positive (or negative) value indicates whether the share of children in each group has increased (or declined) over the period. However, similar changes in shares would lead to different magnitudes in structural effects reflecting, say, a higher positive impact on child average income arising from more children living in above-average income groups than those living in below-average income groups. Values for individual groups only show which groups have had a stronger impact on the changes and not their marginal contribution.

Source: OECD

- For most countries, the increased share of children living in lower income household types – eg lone-parent and/or non-working households – has led to a faster fall or slower rise in the relative incomes of children. In some countries, the rising share of children in two-worker households appears to have more than offset this negative effect (France, Greece, the Netherlands and the US).
- The pure income effect was negative in most countries indicating that, if the household structure of children had remained unchanged, children's income would have fallen but by less.
- The main source of this decline in avarage incomes of children (pure income effect) appears to have mainly originated in working households with higher than average incomes.

Has the income of children become more unequally distributed?

A second issue concerns the recent developments in income distribution and inequality. Table 15.3 shows three widely used measures of the distribution of incomes of children - the Gini coefficient, the Mean Log Deviation index (MLD) and the Squared Coefficient ofVariation (SCV)[12] and compares these indicators and their trends to those of the entire population.

In general, there has been growing inequality of child incomes (except in Australia, Canada and Denmark, where they narrowed, and in Hungary and the US, where they remained broadly stable). However, when comparing these to the developments at the level of the entire population, inequalities among children tend to be less pronounced and grew slower or decreased faster in Australia, Finland, Denmark (MLD excepted), Hungary, Norway and Sweden.

However, changes in aggregate inequality of child incomes can arise from compositional effects (shifts in the share of children belonging to various household types) or because the distribution of income within and between family types has changed. Table 15.4 provides a commonly used decomposition of the MLD drawing on its 'additive' nature to assess the relative importance of these three effects (see Oxley et al, 1999 for methodology):

- A 'structural' effect: that part of the change in the MLD arising from population shifts between family/employment household types holding everything else unchanged[13].

Table 15.3: Indicators of inequality of the incomes of children

(Changes in absolute difference)	Children[a]			Relative to the entire population[b]		
	Gini	**MLD**	**SCV**	**Gini**	**MLD**	**SCV**
Australia, 1994	**26.4**	**11.5**	**24.0**	**86.6**	**63.5**	**64.8**
Changes, 1984-94	-1.6	-1.5	-2.6	-0.9	-2.0	-3.8
Belgium, 1995	**24.1**	**9.5**	**20.9**	**88.9**	**68.0**	**50.3**
Changes, 1983-95	..	..	..	..	..	..
Canada, 1995	**26.5**	**11.6**	**23.9**	**92.9**	**79.8**	**60.3**
Changes, 1985-95	-0.4	-0.7	-0.4	0.0	0.3	-1.1
Denmark, 1994	**18.0**	**5.4**	**10.6**	**82.7**	**60.9**	**46.1**
Changes, 1983-94	-1.5	-0.9	-1.8	-0.4	0.5	-2.2
Finland, 1995	**18.9**	**5.7**	**12.2**	**82.9**	**63.5**	**50.3**
Changes, 1986-95	1.0	0.6	1.7	-1.1	-0.6	-6.1
France, 1994	**25.7**	**10.8**	**23.7**	**92.2**	**80.9**	**58.7**
Changes, 1984-94	0.8	0.6	2.0	0.5	1.4	-4.8
Germany, 1994	**26.9**	**11.9**	**25.0**	**95.7**	**88.0**	**77.2**
Changes, 1984-94	3.0	2.5	5.0	1.4	1.0	7.2
Greece, 1994	**31.5**	**16.7**	**35.4**	**93.8**	**83.9**	**62.5**
Changes, 1988-94	0.8	0.8	1.6	0.8	1.1	0.5
Hungary, 1997	**27.4**	**12.2**	**26.9**	**79.4**	**51.4**	**46.1**
Changes, 1991-97	0.5	-0.1	1.0	-3.4	-6.8	-17.1
Italy, 1993	**34.5**	**20.5**	**42.9**	**100.0**	**86.4**	**73.4**
Changes, 1984-93	6.3	7.3	15.5	2.5	0.6	-2.6
Mexico, 1994	**49.4**	**43.4**	**118.9**	**93.9**	**86.3**	**41.7**
Changes, 1989-94	2.6	4.4	17.6	0.2	0.7	..
Netherlands, 1995	**23.2**	**8.8**	**18.2**	**91.2**	**74.2**	**72.7**
Changes, 1984-95	2.4	1.9	2.9	0.3	-0.4	0.5
Norway, 1995	**21.0**	**7.3**	**15.4**	**81.9**	**55.6**	**50.5**
Changes, 1986-95	1.0	0.9	1.8	-1.2	-2.2	-0.5
Sweden, 1995	**18.0**	**5.4**	**10.8**	**78.5**	**48.9**	**50.0**
Changes, 1983-95	0.5	0.3	0.5	-0.9	-1.7	-7.5
Turkey, 1994	**46.1**	**36.1**	**107.8**	**93.8**	..	..
Changes, 1987-94	4.4	6.9	31.8	-1.2	..	..
UK, 1995	**30.8**	**15.2**	**34.5**	**95.0**	**86.5**	**68.0**
Changes, 1985-95	4.3	4.1	9.7	1.4	0.9	-3.8
US, 1995	**33.7**	**19.8**	**38.7**	**98.0**	**90.2**	**87.7**
Changes, 1985-95	0.4	0.2	1.4	0.0	-0.3	0.2
OECD average (17)	**28.4**	**14.8**	**34.7**	**89.8**	**73.0**	**60.0**

[a] Inequality indicators are estimated on the basis of decile distributions.

[b] Ratio of inequality indicators of children to the entire population multiplied by 100. For Australia, the number indicates that the level of the Gini coefficient for children is 86.6% of the Gini for the entire population.

Source: OECD

- A 'within-group' effect: that part attributed to a widening or narrowing in the dispersion of incomes within individual family/work status groups.
- A 'between-group' effect: that part of the change in the MLD associated with a widening or narrowing in the average income between the various groups.

The left-hand panel of Table 15.4 presents the MLD indices for all households with children and those for different family/work status types. The widest distribution of incomes appears to be concentrated among non-working households and in single-earner multi-adult households.

The right hand panel indicates the decomposition of MLD into the three components. Although these results should be interpreted cautiously[14], they suggest that a widening (or narrowing) in the distribution within individual groups ('within-group' effect) appears to have been the most important factor driving the changed MLD (both up and down) in virtually all countries. There is wide diversity across countries in the 'structural' effect relating to the changing family and employment structure. Further decompositions (see Oxley et al, forthcoming) indicated that the major source of the overall change in the MLD comes from the 'within-group' effect in one-and two-worker, two-adult households, possibly reflecting widening wage rate distributions (OECD, 1993, 1996). In some countries, the growing weight of two-earner households has tended to narrow overall inequality, as this group has the narrowest distribution.

Child poverty and the impact of the tax and transfer system

Have children become poorer?

A past OECD study covering 13 countries found that in the mid- to late-1980s children's poverty rates were, in general, lower than overall poverty rates, except in Northern America (Förster, 1994). In this study, the results for mid-1990s show that the situation worsened – child poverty rates now exceed overall rates in 10 of the 17 countries studied (Table 15.5)[15].

Table 15.4: MLD decomposition by family type and work status

(% and changes in percentage points)	Households with children	Family type and work status: Single parent: Not working	Single parent: Working	Two parents: No worker	Two parents: One worker	Two parents: Two workers	MLD decomposition[a]: Total	Within group	Between group	Structural effect
Australia, 1994	14.9	3.0	9.2	8.6	10.9	12.2				
Changes, 1984-94	**-0.7**	-3.0	2.2	3.7	1.2	-1.5	**-0.7**	-0.2	-1.2	0.6
Belgium, 1995	9.8	15.6	8.3	5.1	10.6	5.6				
Changes, 1983-95	**..**	..	..	..	..	..	**..**	..	..	..
Canada, 1995	13.0	10.7	11.9	17.3	10.4	9.0				
Changes, 1985-95	**-0.8**	-2.7	-5.2	-9.0	-0.6	-0.5	**-0.8**	-1.0	-0.8	1.0
Denmark, 1994	5.8	4.6	3.6	4.9	6.5	3.7				
Changes, 1983-94	**-1.2**	-14.2	-2.1	-12.9	-1.3	-0.9	**-1.2**	-1.5	-0.4	0.7
Finland, 1995	6.4	4.4	5.2	2.5	3.8	5.9				
Changes, 1986-95	**0.7**	2.9	-0.6	-1.3	-2.6	1.0	**0.7**	0.6	0.0	0.1
France, 1994	11.2	8.8	7.7	6.0	10.8	8.5				
Changes, 1984-94	**-0.8**	1.4	1.9	-7.7	0.8	-1.4	**-0.8**	-0.7	-0.1	-0.1
Germany, 1994	12.5	8.2	21.0	9.7	8.8	9.3				
Changes, 1984-94	**1.5**	0.7	12.5	1.8	1.0	-1.3	**1.5**	0.4	0.5	0.6
Greece, 1994	17.9	28.5	14.2	31.5	17.1	14.3				
Changes, 1988-94	**0.6**	9.6	-2.4	12.1	0.8	2.0	**0.6**	1.7	-0.2	-0.9
Hungary, 1997	..	..	..	..	..	..	..	..	..	..
Changes, 1991-97	**..**	..	..	..	..	..	**..**	..	..	..
Italy, 1993	26.1	51.9	14.5	76.8	19.5	15.0				
Changes, 1984-93	**10.7**	-39.4	6.2	8.3	5.3	6.1	**10.7**	5.5	1.4	3.8
Mexico, 1994	46.1	78.6	41.3	45.6	53.2	37.6				
Changes, 1989-94	**4.7**	61.2	9.8	-7.8	4.8	7.0	**4.7**	5.7	0.7	-1.7

Table 15.4: contd.../

(% and changes in percentage points)	Households with children	Family type and work status					MLD decomposition[a]			
		Single parent		Two parents						
		Not working	Working	No worker	One worker	Two workers	Total	Within group	Between group	Structural effect
Netherlands, 1995	9.7	5.9	12.3	7.6	7.4	6.6				
Changes, 1984-95	**1.5**	0.9	1.9	-3.0	0.1	0.9	**1.5**	0.4	0.5	0.7
Norway, 1995	9.2	24.1	4.8	16.0	8.8	4.8				
Changes, 1986-95	**1.4**	16.3	0.3	-9.3	2.0	-0.2	**1.4**	0.9	-0.4	0.9
Sweden, 1995	6.0	6.9	3.8	9.2	5.1	4.3				
Changes, 1983-95	**-0.3**	..	0.0	..	-0.2	0.4	**-0.3**	-2.2	0.1	1.8
Turkey, 1994	..	..	..	..	.	..	..	..	..	..
Changes, 1987-94	**..**	..	..	..	.	..	**..**	..	..	..
UK, 1995	15.8	5.9	10.3	8.7	15.1	11.2				
Changes, 1985-95	**3.0**	2.1	1.4	5.3	2.3	2.4	**3.0**	2.4	0.5	0.0
US, 1995	20.9	16.8	20.9	21.8	23.7	13.0				
Changes, 1985-95	**0.1**	-0.6	-0.1	7.3	2.7	-0.8	**0.1**	0.2	0.3	-0.4

[a] For detailed description of approach see Oxley et al (1999).

Source: OECD

Cross-country comparisons in level terms

Child poverty rates (defined as 50% of medium equivalent income) show considerable cross-country differences, varying from less than 4% in the Nordic countries and Belgium to more than 20% in Anglo-Saxon and Southern European countries. These do not appear to reflect variation in the family/employment structure of children: for example, higher poverty rates might be expected in countries with a larger share of lone-parent households. Indeed, child poverty rates recalculated using common weights for all countries for each of the family/employment groups (Table 15.5, Column 3) show only small differences – 1 percentage point or less except for the UK. Therefore, cross-country variations in the poverty risks are primarily to be found within each family group. A comparison of poverty risks by household types shows some common features:

- Non-working households have the highest risk of poverty and this group shows the widest cross-country differences of the various household types (Table 15.5, columns 5 and 7). This result suggests widely differing levels of institutional support across countries. In only half of the countries, non-working two-adult households do significantly better than non-working lone-parent households.
- Poverty rates fall sharply in all countries when moving from no-worker to one-worker households even though, once again, lone parents are generally worse off than two-adult households. While this demonstrates the importance of employment, poverty rates vary from over 30% in the US to under 5% for most Nordic countries for single-earner households. This sheds some light on the large differences at the level of market incomes across countries, reflecting differences in job qualification or part-time work of parents. But government support for children – including services such as childcare for working parents – also explains a considerable portion of these differences. Some of these issues will be considered in the next section.

Table 15.5: Poverty rates for children, households with children and by household type

			Households with children[a]		Single parent		Two parents		
(% and changes in percentage points)	Children	Entire population	Un-weighted	Re-weighted	Not working	Working	No worker	One worker	Two workers
Australia, 1994	**10.9**	**9.3**	**9.4**	**8.0**	**42.1**	**9.3**	**18.3**	**8.9**	**5.0**
Changes, 1984-94	–4.6	–2.9	–4.0	–2.9	–37.9	2.0	–46.5	0.3	–0.6
Belgium, 1995	**4.1**	**7.8**	**3.3**	**3.1**	**22.8**	**11.4**	**16.1**	**2.8**	**0.6**
Changes, 1983-95	..	..	..	..	..	..	..	..	..
Canada, 1995	**14.2**	**10.3**	**12.5**	**13.8**	**72.5**	**26.5**	**73.5**	**18.1**	**3.7**
Changes, 1985-95	–1.6	–1.3	–0.9	–2.1	–16.9	–9.8	–10.4	0.0	–1.2
Denmark, 1994	**3.4**	**4.7**	**2.6**	**3.1**	**34.2**	**10.0**	**6.0**	**3.6**	**0.4**
Changes, 1983-94	–1.2	–2.5	–1.1	–2.9	–19.1	–3.2	–19.8	–3.9	–0.6
Finland, 1995	**2.1**	**4.9**	**1.9**	**2.5**	**9.9**	**3.0**	**3.6**	**3.5**	**1.5**
Changes, 1986-95	–0.8	–0.2	–0.5	–0.6	9.9	–4.7	1.2	–1.8	–0.3
France, 1994	**7.1**	**7.5**	**6.7**	**6.8**	**45.1**	**13.3**	**37.5**	**7.3**	**2.1**
Changes, 1984-94	0.5	–0.5	0.5	0.4	5.3	9.7	–0.5	1.2	–1.1
Germany, 1994	**10.6**	**9.4**	**8.4**	**7.7**	**61.8**	**32.5**	**44.8**	**5.6**	**1.3**
Changes, 1984-94	4.5	3.0	3.4	1.7	–12.7	20.8	18.6	2.2	–0.7
Greece, 1994	**12.3**	**13.9**	**11.1**	**10.2**	**36.8**	**16.3**	**22.0**	**15.1**	**5.0**
Changes, 1988-94	–0.3	0.4	–0.2	1.4	7.2	2.1	–4.0	1.1	1.5
Hungary, 1997	**9.7**	**7.3**	**9.4**	..	..	..	..	..	..
Changes, 1991-97	1.7	–1.3	2.4	..	..	..	..	..	..
Italy, 1993	**18.8**	**14.2**	**17.0**	**16.0**	**78.7**	**24.9**	**69.8**	**21.2**	**6.1**
Changes, 1984-93	7.3	3.9	6.7	4.1	–6.8	3.9	–4.1	6.1	4.1

Table 15.5: contd.../

			Households with children[a]		Single parent		Two parents		
(% and changes in percentage points)	Children	Entire population	Un-weighted	Re-weighted	Not working	Working	No worker	One worker	Two workers
Mexico, 1994	**26.2**	**21.9**	**23.0**	**22.3**	**31.0**	**27.2**	**41.5**	**27.2**	**17.6**
Changes, 1989-94	1.4	0.7	–2.4	0.2	22.4	10.0	15.0	–3.9	–0.8
Netherlands, 1995	**9.1**	**6.3**	**7.6**	**6.1**	**41.3**	**17.0**	**51.4**	**4.7**	**1.2**
Changes, 1984-95	5.8	3.2	4.6	3.5	25.4	6.9	36.9	2.4	0.5
Norway, 1995	**4.4**	**8.0**	**3.6**	**3.4**	**29.6**	**4.6**	**30.6**	**3.9**	**0.1**
Changes, 1986-95	0.5	1.1	0.5	–0.4	–17.8	0.0	–3.8	0.8	0.0
Sweden, 1995	**2.7**	**6.4**	**2.5**	**3.5**	**24.2**	**3.8**	**9.5**	**6.0**	**0.8**
Changes, 1983-95	-0.3	0.5	–0.9	–1.3	–21.5	–7.1	–18.3	1.6	–0.2
Turkey, 1994	**19.7**	**16.2**	**16.6**	**17.2**	**39.9**	**16.3**	**40.0**	**17.8**	**14.4**
Changes, 1987-94	–0.7	–0.2	–0.8	0.0	6.0	11.7	5.4	–5.9	1.2
UK, 1995	**18.6**	**11.9**	**15.6**	**13.0**	**69.4**	**26.3**	**50.1**	**19.3**	**3.3**
Changes, 1985-95	8.2	4.4	6.9	6.2	23.8	12.6	–6.2	12.8	2.0
US, 1995	**23.2**	**17.1**	**19.4**	**21.1**	**93.4**	**38.6**	**82.2**	**30.5**	**7.3**
Changes, 1985-95	–2.7	–1.2	–2.2	–0.9	–0.3	–6.3	–3.0	2.9	–2.2
OECD average (16)	**11.7**	**10.6**	**10.1**	**9.9**	**45.8**	**17.6**	**37.3**	**12.2**	**4.4**

[a] Poverty rates of households with children were recalculated using poverty rate for each of the five household groups reweighted by a common population structure based on the average of all countries.

Source: OECD

Another important dimension concerns the family/work structure of the poor – ie what share of the total poor belong to each group (Table 15.6). The data suggest the following patterns.

- Households with children made up around 60%, on average, of the total poor in working-age households. The lowest shares of poor families are found in Nordic countries and Belgium, and the largest shares in Anglo-Saxon and Southern European countries (column 1). This suggests that targeting child poverty is likely to be an effective way of targeting poverty among the overall working-age population in many OECD countries.
- Among households with children, more than 60%, on average, live in working households with at least one earner – including countries with both high and low child poverty (column 2). Thus, policies aiming at reducing poverty among children need to be concerned about working households and in some countries single-earner households.
- Non-working households with children only account, on average, for one third of the poor in households with children and around half of these are lone-parents. However, this is a more important issue for Germany, the Netherlands, Norway (although child poverty is among the lowest) and the UK (non-working lone parents in particular).

Poverty developments over time

A number of recent comparative and national studies put forward the hypothesis of a growing 'childrenisation' of poverty – ie that both risks of children falling poor and the share of children among the poor has been increasing (Forssén, 1998). The results presented in Table 15.5 suggest there are few clear trends in child poverty across countries over the last ten-year period (columns 1 and 2). Child poverty rates increased in 8 of the 16 countries and particularly in Germany, Italy, the Netherlands and the UK. At the same time, a number of countries with high (two-digit) child poverty rates experienced some decline (Australia, Canada, Greece, Turkey and the US). As regards specific household groups, poverty rose in most countries in single-earner households (both lone and two parents) particularly in countries with large increases in the overall child poverty rate.

Table 15.6: Structure of poverty for households with children

(Changes in percentage point difference)	Total[a]	More than one earner	Single parent			Two parents		
			Non-working	Not working	Working	No worker	One worker	Two workers
Australia, 1994	**66.1**	**60.3**	**39.7**	**24.8**	**4.7**	**14.9**	**27.5**	**28.1**
Changes, 1984-94	–16.6	14.4	–14.4	0.0	2.8	–14.5	4.5	7.1
Belgium, 1995	**30.3**	**73.4**	**26.6**	**11.3**	**35.8**	**15.3**	**28.6**	**9.0**
Changes, 1983-95	..	..	..	..	..	..	..	..
Canada, 1995	**64.9**	**60.9**	**39.1**	**20.8**	**12.7**	**18.3**	**28.2**	**20.0**
Changes, 1985-95	–6.1	–8.3	8.3	3.0	0.9	5.3	–5.0	–4.2
Denmark, 1994	**36.6**	**58.0**	**42.0**	**36.8**	**31.2**	**5.3**	**14.6**	**12.2**
Changes, 1983-94	–12.9	–13.5	13.5	14.3	7.2	–0.8	–11.1	–9.7
Finland, 1995	**25.4**	**86.3**	**13.7**	**11.5**	**12.9**	**2.2**	**8.9**	**64.5**
Changes, 1986-95	–9.0	–13.5	13.5	11.5	–6.7	2.0	-9.0	2.1
France, 1994	**61.9**	**61.7**	**38.3**	**11.6**	**8.1**	**26.7**	**36.3**	**17.3**
Changes, 1984-94	–2.9	–5.1	5.1	3.3	5.9	1.8	–2.1	–8.9
Germany, 1994	**48.1**	**52.8**	**47.2**	**20.5**	**14.4**	**26.7**	**32.2**	**6.2**
Changes, 1984-94	–1.4	–2.1	2.1	–1.0	9.7	3.1	–1.3	–10.6
Greece, 1994	**62.2**	**90.3**	**9.7**	**3.5**	**2.2**	**6.2**	**68.4**	**19.7**
Changes, 1988-94	–4.9	5.5	–5.5	–1.5	–0.2	–4.0	–3.5	9.2
Hungary, 1997	**70.1**	..	..	..	..	..	..	..
Changes, 1991-97	2.6	..	..	..	..	..	..	..
Italy, 1993	**72.7**	**78.2**	**21.8**	**4.8**	**2.1**	**17.0**	**59.8**	**16.3**
Changes, 1984-93	2.9	–10.5	10.5	3.2	0.0	7.2	–18.2	7.7

Table 15.6: contd.../

(Changes in percentage point difference)	Total[1]	More than one earner	Single parent			Two parents		
			Non-working	Not working	Working	No worker	One worker	Two workers
Mexico, 1994	**97.9**	**94.7**	**5.3**	**0.5**	**3.3**	**4.8**	**54.5**	**37.0**
Changes, 1989-94	0.2	–3.0	3.0	0.4	2.9	2.6	–11.8	5.9
Netherlands, 1995	**59.0**	**35.5**	**64.5**	**29.4**	**6.3**	**35.1**	**20.8**	**8.4**
Changes, 1984-95	4.3	–18.5	18.5	11.5	2.5	7.0	–21.0	0.0
Norway, 1995	**37.6**	**35.2**	**64.8**	**42.7**	**10.4**	**22.1**	**23.1**	**1.7**
Changes, 1986-95	–10.0	–5.6	5.6	–5.9	2.1	11.5	–7.5	–0.2
Sweden, 1995	**18.5**	**67.2**	**32.8**	**22.7**	**23.0**	**10.1**	**20.9**	**23.3**
Changes, 1983-95	–13.3	–10.8	10.8	7.0	–18.6	3.8	5.9	1.9
Turkey, 1994	**93.0**	**92.1**	**7.9**	**0.6**	**0.2**	**7.3**	**44.2**	**47.7**
Changes, 1987-94	–2.2	–3.7	3.7	0.6	0.2	3.2	–5.2	1.3
UK, 1995	**82.6**	**53.5**	**46.5**	**33.4**	**11.2**	**13.1**	**30.1**	**12.3**
Changes, 1985-95	2.2	15.7	–15.7	14.4	4.6	–30.1	6.9	4.2
US, 1995	**76.4**	**74.9**	**25.1**	**15.8**	**17.6**	**9.3**	**33.3**	**24.1**
Changes, 1985-95	–3.1	1.6	–1.6	–0.5	2.5	–1.1	1.9	–2.9
OECD average (16)	**58.3**	**67.2**	**32.8**	**18.2**	**12.3**	**14.7**	**33.2**	**21.7**

[a] % of total working-age poor (individuals in households with and without children).

Source: OECD

The absence of a general worsening of the situation for children is confirmed by examining 'poverty representation indices' for children and households with children in Table 15.7. The 'representation index' is defined as the share of the poor in a specific population group divided by its population share. For example, non-working couples and single-parent households are, on average, over-represented by four to five times in the poor population relative to the entire population. The only two countries in which the representation index increased significantly were Hungary and the Netherlands; in all other countries it remained broadly stable. Representation indices for non-employed decreased in the last ten-year period in a majority of countries.

Table 15.8 uses the same shift-share analysis as in Table 15.2 to isolate the underlying change in poverty from the effects of changing structure of poverty across the same five groups. The 'structural effect' is shown in the second row for each country, while the third row indicates by how much poverty risks would have changed if the population structure had remained unchanged ('pure' poverty effect). In virtually all countries the 'structural effect' was positive but small and confirms the results found earlier on the weak role of family structure on cross-country differences in child poverty. Therefore, the major driving factor appears to be the 'pure' poverty component, that is, the change in poverty risks within family/working groups. Where poverty risks increased significantly, this mainly occurs among households with two parents and a single breadwinner (France, Germany, Greece and, particularly, in Italy, the Netherlands and the UK).

Child poverty and pre- and post-taxes and transfers

This section reviews the impact of the tax and transfer system on child poverty rates. The number of countries is reduced to 12 and in some cases as few as ten due to data limitations.

Judging the impact of government tax and spending policies on poverty rates should take account of the 'starting point' – ie the rate of poverty before tax and transfers. Table 15.9 shows poverty rates pre- and post-taxes and transfers and the percentage point difference between them. The changes over time in percentage points are shown in the second line for each country. On average across the 12 countries, the poverty rate of children was reduced by about half (from around 21% and around 11% after taxes and transfers). The data also suggest that the tax and transfer

Table 15.7: Poverty representation indices[a]

			Single parent		Two parents		
(Per cent ratio and changes in percentage point difference)	Children	Households with children	Not working	Working	No worker	One worker	Two workers
Australia, 1994	**1.17**	**0.86**	**4.52**	**0.99**	**1.97**	**0.95**	**0.54**
Changes, 1984-94	–0.10	–0.03	–2.03	0.40	–3.34	0.25	0.08
Belgium, 1995	**0.53**	**0.40**	**2.94**	**1.47**	**2.07**	**0.36**	**0.08**
Changes, 1983-95	..	..	..	..	..	..	..
Canada, 1995	**1.38**	**1.34**	**7.07**	**2.58**	**7.16**	**1.76**	**0.36**
Changes, 1985-95	0.02	–0.03	–0.65	–0.55	–0.08	0.20	–0.06
Denmark, 1994	**0.74**	**0.67**	**7.35**	**2.15**	**1.30**	**0.77**	**0.09**
Changes, 1983-94	0.09	–0.18	–0.14	0.30	–2.33	–0.28	–0.06
Finland, 1995	**0.42**	**0.50**	**2.03**	**0.62**	**0.72**	**0.71**	**0.30**
Changes, 1986-95	–0.13	–0.11	2.03	–0.90	0.25	–0.32	–0.05
France, 1994	**0.95**	**0.91**	**6.05**	**1.79**	**5.03**	**0.98**	**0.28**
Changes, 1984-94	0.12	0.11	1.04	1.33	0.25	0.22	–0.12
Germany, 1994	**1.13**	**0.82**	**6.57**	**3.46**	**4.77**	**0.60**	**0.14**
Changes, 1984-94	0.17	–0.11	–5.07	1.63	0.67	0.06	–0.17
Greece, 1994	**0.89**	**0.73**	**2.66**	**1.17**	**1.59**	**1.09**	**0.36**
Changes, 1988-94	–0.05	0.08	0.45	0.12	–0.35	0.04	0.10
Hungary, 1997	**1.33**	**1.23**	..	..	..	..	..
Changes, 1991-97	0.40	0.21	..	..	..	..	..
Italy, 1993	**1.32**	**1.13**	**5.53**	**1.75**	**4.91**	**1.49**	**0.43**
Changes, 1984-93	0.21	–0.03	–2.77	–0.29	–2.27	0.03	0.23

Table 15.7: contd.../

(Per cent ratio and changes in percentage point difference)	Children	Households with children	Single parent		Two parents		
			Not working	Working	No worker	One worker	Two workers
Mexico, 1994	**1.20**	**1.02**	**1.41**	**1.24**	**1.90**	**1.24**	**0.80**
Changes, 1989-94	0.03	–0.02	1.01	0.43	0.65	–0.22	–0.06
Netherlands, 1995	**1.44**	**0.97**	**6.56**	**2.70**	**8.16**	**0.75**	**0.19**
Changes, 1984-95	0.38	0.11	1.43	–0.56	3.48	0.00	–0.04
Norway, 1995	**0.55**	**0.43**	**3.70**	**0.58**	**3.83**	**0.49**	**0.01**
Changes, 1986-95	–0.02	–0.13	–3.17	–0.09	–1.16	0.04	0.00
Sweden, 1995	**0.42**	**0.55**	**3.78**	**0.59**	**1.49**	**0.94**	**0.13**
Changes, 1983-95	–0.08	–0.26	–3.91	–1.24	–3.19	0.20	–0.04
Turkey, 1994	**1.22**	**1.06**	**2.47**	**1.01**	**2.48**	**1.10**	**0.89**
Changes, 1987-94	–0.02	0.02	0.40	0.73	0.37	–0.35	0.09
UK, 1995	**1.56**	**1.09**	**5.82**	**2.21**	**4.20**	**1.62**	**0.28**
Changes, 1985-95	0.18	0.19	–0.21	0.40	–3.23	0.76	0.11
US, 1995	**1.36**	**1.24**	**5.48**	**2.26**	**4.82**	**1.79**	**0.43**
Changes, 1985-95	–0.05	0.03	0.35	–0.19	0.16	0.28	–0.09
OECD average (17)	**1.04**	**0.86**	**4.62**	**1.66**	**3.53**	**1.04**	**0.33**

[a] Share of the poor in a specific population group (i) divided by the population share ie ($poor_i$/poor of working age) (pop_i/pop of working age). This can be rewritten as the ratio of poverty rates ($poor_i/pop_i$) / (poor of working age) / (pop of working age). $Poor_i$ is the number of poor belonging to group i and pop is population.

Source: OECD

systems have had to confront a worsening poverty situation for children before taxes and transfers. With pre-tax-and-transfer poverty rising and after-tax-and-transfer poverty falling (or increasing by less), tax and transfer systems have become more effective in dealing with poverty over time. However, changes at the level of market income may also reflect behavioural responses to more generous tax/transfer systems.

Cross-country comparisons in the tax and transfer system

To explore the links between country tax and transfer systems and their performances in reducing child poverty rates, the data are analysed around the following three concepts. The first is '*effectiveness*' (or outcomes) defined as the percentage point reduction in poverty pre-tax and transfers relative to post-tax and transfers (see Table 15.9).

The second is 'effort' – ie the amount of resources a government lays out for children. This is measured as *total transfers* received by all children as a share of their disposable income (Table 15.10, column 2)[16]. 'Effort' is likely to have an important impact on outcomes.

Finally, '*efficiency*' – the ratio of effectiveness' to 'effort' (ie the reduction in poverty for one percentage point rise in the cost) (Table 10, column 3). Countries that get a bigger 'bang for their buck' show up with a higher value.

Thus:

'Effectiveness' = 'Effort' * 'Efficiency'

A key factor affecting efficiency in poverty reduction is the degree of targeting. For equal effort, countries that target more on low-income groups or on children will be more efficient in achieving poverty reductions. (But conversely, countries that target more may also reduce the overall degree of spending.) The best available measure of targeting on low-income groups is the share of total 'direct' child-related transfers going to the bottom decile (column 5). This variable suffers from the fact that 'indirect' transfers (eg unemployment, disability benefits etc.) received by households with children are not taken into account[17]. The degree of targeting on children is measured by the share of 'direct' child-related benefits in total transfers received by children (column 4)[18]. Column 4 shows the relatively small size of 'direct' transfers. However, they may be important in bringing families with children out of poverty because, in general, they are related to family size and, thus, may help compensate for the impact of larger household size on equivalent household income[19].

Table 15.8: The impact of poverty patterns on poverty rates[a]: shift-share analysis

(Changes in percentage difference)	Total change	Single parent		Two parents		
		Not working	Working	No worker	One worker	Two workers
Australia, 1984-94	**–4.0**	**-1.0**	**0.2**	**–2.5**	**–0.5**	**-0.2**
Structural effect	**1.2**	0.9	0.1	0.7	–0.6	0.1
Pure effect	**–5.2**	-1.8	0.1	–3.2	0.1	-0.3
Belgium, 1995	..	..	..	..	..	..
Canada, 1995	**–0.9**	**0.2**	**0.0**	**0.5**	**–0.9**	**–0.7**
Structural effect	**1.2**	0.7	0.5	0.8	–0.9	0.1
Pure effect	**–2.1**	–0.5	–0.5	–0.3	0.0	–0.8
Denmark, 1994	**–1.1**	**0.1**	**–0.1**	**–0.1**	**–0.6**	**–0.5**
Structural effect	**0.8**	0.5	0.2	0.2	–0.1	0.0
Pure effect	**–1.9**	–0.4	–0.2	–0.3	–0.4	–0.5
Finland, 1995	**–0.5**	**0.2**	**–0.2**	**0.0**	**–0.3**	**–0.3**
Structural effect	**0.1**	0.1	0.1	0.0	–0.1	0.0
Pure effect	**–0.6**	0.1	–0.3	0.0	–0.1	–0.3
France, 1994	**0.5**	**0.3**	**0.4**	**0.2**	**0.1**	**–0.5**
Structural effect	**0.2**	0.2	0.0	0.3	–0.4	0.1
Pure effect	**0.3**	0.1	0.4	0.0	0.5	–0.6
Germany, 1994	**3.4**	**0.6**	**1.0**	**1.1**	**1.0**	**–0.3**
Structural effect	**1.4**	0.9	0.4	0.2	–0.1	0.0
Pure effect	**2.0**	–0.3	0.6	0.9	1.1	–0.3
Greece, 1994	**–0.2**	**–0.2**	**0.0**	**–0.5**	**–0.5**	**1.0**
Structural effect	**–1.3**	–0.3	–0.1	–0.3	–1.1	0.4
Pure effect						
Hungary, 1997	..	..	..	..	..	..

Table 15.8: contd.../

(Changes in percentage difference)	Total change	Single parent		Two parents		
		Not working	Working	No worker	One worker	Two workers
Italy, 1993	**6.7**	**0.7**	**0.1**	**1.9**	**2.2**	**1.9**
Structural effect	**1.9**	0.7	0.1	2.0	–0.9	0.0
Pure effect	**4.8**	0.0	0.0	–0.1	3.1	1.8
Mexico, 1994	**–2.4**	**0.1**	**0.7**	**0.5**	**–4.3**	**0.6**
Structural effect	**–0.7**	0.0	0.5	0.2	–2.4	0.9
Pure effect	**–1.7**	0.1	0.2	0.4	–1.9	–0.3
Netherlands, 1995	**4.6**	**1.7**	**0.4**	**1.8**	**0.3**	**0.4**
Structural effect	**0.1**	0.6	0.2	–0.2	–0.7	0.2
Pure effect	**4.5**	1.1	0.1	2.0	1.1	0.2
Norway, 1995	**0.5**	**0.0**	**0.1**	**0.5**	**–0.1**	**0.0**
Structural effect	**1.1**	0.8	0.1	0.5	–0.3	0.0
Pure effect	**–0.6**	–0.8	0.0	–0.1	0.2	0.0
Sweden, 1995	**–0.9**	**0.0**	**–0.8**	**0.0**	**0.0**	**–0.1**
Structural effect	**0.8**	0.4	0.2	0.4	–0.1	0.0
Pure effect	**–1.7**	–0.4	–1.0	–0.3	0.2	–0.1
Turkey, 1994	**–0.8**	**0.1**	**0.0**	**0.5**	**–1.2**	**–0.2**
Structural effect	**0.6**	0.1	0.0	0.4	1.1	–0.9
Pure effect	**–1.4**	0.0	0.0	0.1	–2.3	0.7
UK, 1995	**6.9**	**3.6**	**1.2**	**–1.7**	**2.7**	**1.2**
Structural effect	**0.5**	2.2	0.5	–1.4	–0.9	0.1
Pure effect	**6.3**	1.3	0.7	–0.3	3.5	1.1
US, 1995	**–2.2**	**–0.5**	**0.2**	**–0.4**	**–0.3**	**–1.1**
Structural effect	**–0.9**	–0.4	0.7	–0.4	–1.0	0.2
Pure effect	**–1.3**	0.0	–0.5	–0.1	0.7	–1.4

[a] See Table 15.2 for method.

Source: OECD

Table 15.9: Poverty rates for children pre- and post-tax and transfer

(Per cent and changes in percentage points)	Poverty rates		
	Post-tax and transfer	Pre-tax and transfer	Reduction
Australia, 1994	**10.9**	**29.9**	**19.0**
Changes, 1984-94	–4.6	9.3	13.9
Belgium, 1995	**4.1**	**14.9**	**10.8**
Changes, 1984-94	..	..	..
Canada, 1995	**14.2**	**22.7**	**8.5**
Changes, 1984-94	–1.6	2.1	3.6
Denmark, 1994	**3.4**	**15.4**	**12.0**
Changes, 1984-94	–1.2	5.4	6.6
Finland, 1995	**2.1**	**17.3**	**15.3**
Changes, 1984-94	–0.8	8.0	8.8
France, 1994	**7.1**	**26.0**	**18.9**
Changes, 1984-94	0.5	1.1	0.7
Germany, 1994	**10.6**	**12.5**	**1.9**
Changes, 1984-94	4.5	2.2	–2.3
Greece, 1994	**..**	**..**	**..**
Changes, 1988-94	..	..	..
Hungary, 1997	**..**	**..**	**..**
Changes, 1987-97	..	..	..
Italy, 1993	**18.8**	**18.0**	**–0.9**
Changes, 1984-94	7.3	7.2	–0.1
Mexico, 1994	**..**	**..**	**..**
Changes, 1989-94	..	..	..
Netherlands, 1995	**9.1**	**17.9**	**8.8**
Changes, 1984-94	5.8	2.5	–3.3
Norway, 1995	**4.4**	**13.3**	**8.9**
Changes, 1984-94	0.5	4.5	4.0
Sweden, 1995	**2.7**	**21.7**	**19.0**
Changes, 1984-94	–0.3	8.4	8.7
Turkey, 1994	**..**	**..**	**..**
Changes, 1987-94	..	..	..
UK, 1995	**18.6**	**32.8**	**14.1**
Changes, 1984-94	8.2	8.9	0.8
US, 1995	**23.2**	**29.2**	**6.0**
Changes, 1984-94	–2.7	0.3	2.9
OECD average (13)	**9.9**	**20.9**	**10.9**

Source: OECD

While these relationships have been formalised in the two equations presented below, they should be seen as largely 'descriptive', all the more so as they only explain a little more than half of the overall variance between countries in 'effectiveness'. While the coefficients are significant[20], not much weight should be placed on their size given the quality of the data and the size of the sample. They suggest the following story.

$$[1]\ LN(Effort) = 3.00^{**} - 0.44^{**}\ LN(Target) + 0.36^{*}\ LN(Poverty) \qquad R2 = 0.49$$

$$[2]\ LN(Efficiency) = 2.31^{**} + 0.23^{**}\ LN(Target) + 0.34^{**}\ LN(Share) \qquad R2 = 0.60$$

First, as suggested above, 'effort' (equation 1) depends on the degree of poverty to start with (Poverty) and the degree of targeting on lower income groups (Target). The positive coefficient on the first variable indicates that countries with greater poverty before tax and transfers spend more. However, the negative coefficient on targeting points to the fact that those which target more tend to spend less. Second, the indicator of 'efficiency' (equation 2) is a positive function of targeting on low-income groups and on children. In particular, increasing the share of transfers in the form of child benefits may make income transfer systems more effective in reducing poverty.

However, when the two equations are substituted back into the identity defining 'effectiveness', the two coefficients for targeting largely cancel out. (The coefficient on Target becomes insignificant when the reduced form for 'effectiveness' is estimated.) In other words, countries with higher 'efficiency' due to targeting have traded a good part of this away by reducing 'effort'. A corollary might be that countries with highly targeted systems (eg the US and Australia) may need to increase spending in this area if they are to make progress in reducing child poverty. Conversely, countries with high degrees of 'effort' and low levels of poverty may find that increased targeting at the margin provides a more efficient way of dealing with 'hard-core' poverty.

Changes in the tax and transfer response over time

These results were not fully confirmed when the variables were expressed in change form, possibly reflecting data quality and statistical noise. It nonetheless appears that changes in 'effectiveness' are related to the changes

Table 15.10: Share of child-related and other transfers going to children

	[1]	[2]	[3]	[4]	[5]
	Effectiveness	'Effort'	Efficiency		
(% and changes in pecentage points)		Transfers % of disposable income	Poverty reduction by % of TR [1]/[2]*100	'Direct' child-related transfers as share of total transfers	'Direct' child -related transfers in the bottom decile/ quintile of the population
Australia, 1994	**19.0**	**17.5**	**108.6**	**32.6**	**23.4**
Changes, 1984-94	13.9	5.3	66.8	6.9	9.0
Belgium, 1995	**10.8**	**18.4**	**58.8**	**72.2**	**5.1**
Changes, 1984-94	..	..	..	..	5.1
Canada, 1995	**8.5**	**19.6**	**43.4**	**13.5**	**18.9**
Changes, 1984-94	3.6	4.9	10.3	–12.9	3.8
Denmark, 1994	**12.0**	**24.9**	**48.0**	**32.9**	**10.2**
Changes, 1984-94	6.6	9.9	12.2	15.0	–2.7
Finland, 1995	**15.3**	**26.8**	**56.9**	**52.6**	**3.1**
Changes, 1984-94	8.8	12.9	10.2	–10.9	–5.2
France, 1994	**18.9**	**17.4**	**108.7**	**105.4**	**26.2**
Changes, 1984-94	0.7	0.4	1.4	–3.4	2.0
Germany, 1994	**1.9**	**8.3**	**22.9**	**..**	**..**
Changes, 1984-94	–2.3	–1.1	–21.8	..	..
Greece, 1994	**..**	**..**	**..**	**..**	**6.0**
Changes, 1984-94	..	..	..	..	0.1

Table 15.10: contd.../

	[1]	[2]	[3]	[4]	[5]
	Effectiveness	'Effort'	Efficiency		
(% and changes in pecentage points)		Transfers % of disposable income	Poverty reduction by % of TR [1]/[2]*100	'Direct' child-related transfers as share of total transfers	'Direct' child -related transfers in the bottom decile/ quintile of the population
Hungary, 1997	**..**	**..**	**..**	**..**	**..**
Changes, 1987-97	..	..	..	..	..
Italy, 1993	**–0.9**	**6.8**	**–13.0**	**..**	**..**
Changes, 1984-94	–0.1	0.7	–0.5	..	..
Mexico, 1994	**..**	**..**	**–**	**..**	**..**
Changes, 1989-94	..	..	–	..	..
Netherlands, 1995	**8.8**	**18.0**	**48.9**	**31.6**	**12.2**
Changes, 1984-94	–3.3	–2.9	–9.0	–10.1	–4.6
Norway, 1995	**8.9**	**13.9**	**63.9**	**69.9**	**17.1**
Changes, 1984-94	4.0	3.2	18.0	–6.2	12.3
Sweden, 1995	**19.0**	**34.0**	**55.9**	**44.8**	**4.1**
Changes, 1984-94	8.7	10.8	11.4	–4.5	–0.6
Turkey, 1994	**..**	**..**	**..**	**..**	**..**
Changes, 1987-94	..	..	..	..	..

Table 15.10: contd.../

	[1]	[2]	[3]	[4]	[5]
	Effectiveness	'Effort'	Efficiency		
(% and changes in pecentage points)		Transfers % of disposable income	Poverty reduction by % of TR [1]/[2]*100	'Direct' child-related transfers as share of total transfers	'Direct' child -related transfers in the bottom decile/ quintile of the population
UK, 1995	**14.1**	**30.4**	**46.5**	**34.5**	**17.3**
Changes, 1984-94	0.8	4.4	-4.8	–5.9	1.1
US, 1995	**6.0**	**8.0**	**74.6**	**25.0**	**57.3**
Changes, 1984-94	2.9	1.4	28.6	13.3	–10.2
OECD average (13)	**10.9**	**18.8**	**55.7**	**46.8**	**16.7**

Note: 'Effectiveness' is drawn from the last column of Table 10. 'Effort' is total transfers received by households with children as a share of their average household disposable income. 'Efficiency' is 'Effectiveness' divided by 'Effort'. The variable for targeting children is the share of "direct" transfers to children as a share of total transfers received by households with children. Total 'direct' transfers to children were calculated by multiplying the average child and family related benefit received by all individuals by the number of individuals in households with children (see footnote 16 in the text for definition of 'direct' transfers). This value was then divided by the total transfers received by all households with children. The targeting low income groups is the share of total 'direct' child related transfers which are received by the bottom decile (bottom quintile for the US). The bottom decile/quintile roughly corresponds to the population of the poor in most of the countries covered here.

in total spending (Equation 3). A number of other variables were introduced but only the change in the contribution of taxes to disposable income in the lowest decile proved significant. In this context, there may have been some switching from transfers towards tax-related benefits for children. Additional data show that, in a significant number of countries, there has been an increasing role for taxes in the support given to low-income working-age households. At the same time, it would appear that, for most countries, the share of family benefits in total benefits has been falling (Table 15.10). On the basis of the results from the cross-country analysis of levels, this might suggest that programmes are becoming less efficient in reducing child poverty.

[3] $\triangle\ Effectiveness = 0.03 + 0.88^{**} \triangle\ Effort - 0.26^{**} \triangle\ Tax_{bottom\ decile}$
$R^2 = 0.77$

Some tentative conclusions

This chapter has aimed at fleshing out what we know about the economic situation of children. While the results need to be interpreted cautiously, the material presented here suggests the following broad lessons:

- Some country groupings continue to do better than others: the Nordic countries and Belgium appear to have maintained their good performance, particularly as regards child poverty, albeit with increases in some. The situation is less sanguine among the Anglo-Saxon countries and certain southern European countries, including Italy although there were improvements among certain of these countries over time.
- No widespread and significant deterioration in the average well-being of children was found (either in absolute terms or relative to total population) despite quite different demographic, labour market and institutional developments among the sample of countries. A few countries excepted, declines in income were not large and changes in the structure of households by work and family type often played a significant role in explaining these changes. Relative to the working age population, the declines in average incomes of children may have been somewhat more marked at the level of market income.
- An examination of three inequality indicators pointed to some widening in the distribution of child incomes. The MLD decomposition suggests that groups with the highest average income and the narrowest within-group distribution were the main source of this change. The widening

did not generally appear to be related to developments within the group of unemployed or of lone-parents or from a widening in average incomes between groups.

- While there are considerable cross-country differences in poverty rates, this does not reflect differences in family structures of children across countries but in the poverty risks for each of the family/working groups.
- Comparison of poverty rates across households by family type and work status indicates markedly lower poverty rates in working households and, particularly, two-earner households. Thus, getting households into employment is an important first step in reducing poverty.
- Aside from the Nordic countries, where child poverty is generally low, 60% of the poor of working age belong to households with children and 40% belong to households with children with at least one worker. This raises two points:
- Since the overlap between poor households and poor households with children is large, fighting child poverty is likely to have a significant impact on overall poverty among the working-age population in most countries.
- The phenomenon of the 'working poor' is not just a North American phenomenon. Anti-poverty policies also need to focus on the working households and not just on the unemployed and lone parents. Single earner households may also require increased attention in some countries.
- There is no evidence of widespread and significant increases in child poverty or growing 'childrenisation' of poverty. In this context, four results should be highlighted:
- There appears to have been a rise in poverty on a pre-tax and transfer basis, compensated by increased 'effectiveness' of the tax and transfer system.
- Increasing shares of non-working and lone-parent households have had a positive effect on poverty rates. But the majority of the changes over time appeared to reflect country policies regarding the support for specific household types.
- While the risk of falling poor is higher among the non-working and lone-parent households, two-adult single-earner households with children tended to show the most widespread increases in poverty rates across countries.
- Finally, looking across countries, there appears to be some trade-off between spending and the degree of targeting. Further, in reducing

child poverty, child benefits may be a means of increasing programme efficiency. Over time, countries may be giving a more important anti-poverty role to taxes.

In conclusion, it remains true that the best way of reducing poverty is to increase employment - and this would certainly wind back some of the deterioration in both incomes and poverty at the level of market income. But many countries also need to pay greater attention to the problems of the working poor and the single-earner households in particular. Indeed, as Esping-Andersen has argued at a recent OECD conference, the two-earner household may be the best model for ensuring that the risks of poverty are minimised.

Second, if child poverty is the objective, then governments may need to focus more resources on child-related benefits, which may help compensate for the effects of household size. Given the importance of poor households with children in the total poor of working age, this would also serve to reduce overall poverty among working-age families.

Finally, while countries that target are more efficient, countries need to ensure that the level of 'effort' is sustained to make sufficient progress in lowering poverty. On this basis, certain countries with high targeting may need to consider increases in overall anti-poverty spending. Such recommendations for greater spending need to be qualified by the following:

- Income support policies should not substitute for strong employment policies but should support such policies. Sweden's success in limiting child poverty has been partly the result of high levels of employment among lone parents, supported by family transfers as well as in-kind provisions (eg childcare facilities).
- Finally, it would be better if pre-tax and transfer poverty were reduced, and in this context, increasing earnings capacity of low-income groups is an important ingredient in success.

Notes

[1] In practice, some country responses lacked full details and in most cases the maximum number of countries is 15; In some tables, they were reduced to as few as ten. The specific years chosen differed across countries – in most cases reflecting data availability. Results for the UK were based on preliminary data.

[2] Breaks in the data occurred for the Netherlands and Sweden, and only partial corrections were possible. The widening in the income distribution over time may be overstated for Italy, because of improvements in the measurement of low-income households in the early 1990s. Finally, a shift of certain pension arrangements from the public to the private sector may distort some data series at a disaggregated level in Finland.

[3] The size of the changes over time for individual components and groups for some countries also suggest that there may be inconsistencies in data sets which have not been accounted for.

[4] That is, an equivalence scale elasticity of 0.5.

[5] See Atkinson et al (1995) for some justification for using this equivalence scale.

[6] This is referred to as two-adult households in the text.

[7] The higher average income and lower poverty rate among *households with children* reflects the fact that two-adult households have, on average, higher incomes than single-adult households and weigh more heavily in the total for this grouping. When comparing *households with children* and *children*, the share of individuals in two-adult households in the total will be greater (in general) in the former because they contain more adult members relative to single-adult households (particularly as two-adult households refers to two *or more* adult households).

[8] This choice reflects the interest in the work status of the household. A child over 18 is considered as a potential worker who can contribute to household income irrespective of whether the individual is the son or daughter of the parent or not.

[9] In those countries where the income from retirement is dominated by transfers from general government (eg most continental European countries), the ratio of incomes pre- to post-tax for the elderly (relative to the average) is very high. The corresponding ratio for other groups including children is correspondingly lower (eg compare France and Germany and Italy with the US).

[10] See Oxley, Dang, Förster and Pellizzari (forthcoming) for detailed results.

[11] Average income of the total population (the denominator) was corrected for changing population structure.

[12] The Gini coefficient is more sensitive to changes towards the middle of the distribution while the SCV and the MLD give greater weight to changes at the top and the bottom of the distribution, respectively.

[13] For example, structural effects indicate the change due to a shift of individuals away from household types with a wider dispersion of income (or average incomes far from the mean) into groups with a narrower dispersion (or with average incomes closer to the mean).

[14] Three caveats should be taken into account when considering these results. First, the MLD index is more sensitive to changes at the bottom of the distribution than at the top. Second, this analysis uses data on households with children rather than children alone. Thus, within each group the distribution of all individuals may differ from the distribution of children. Finally, inequality indices have been estimated on the basis of the deciles rather than the underlying data.

[15] This is sensitive to the equivalence scale used.

[16] Alternatively, this could be measured by net taxes and transfers going to children. Taxes tend to be more concentrated among higher income groups, leaving transfers as the main instrument for tackling poverty. This is less the case for countries with narrow market income distributions (where taxes at the bottom can be important). Transfers may overstate the degree of 'effort' in countries where they are taxed as income because they need to the 'grossed-up' by the value of the tax to get the same net of tax effect. In the event, results using net taxes and transfers were weaker.

[17] Total transfers received by children is composed of: (a) 'direct' transfers – child and family benefits plus other income transfers directed to lone parents which are only received by households with children; and, (b) 'indirect' transfers – those received on the basis of status of the parents (unemployed, disabled etc) as well as housing benefits and social assistance.

[18] Data for France are suspect.

[19] In contrast, indirect transfers (eg unemployment benefits) are often not related to household size. However, the nature of child-related transfers varies considerably across countries: ranging from exclusively income tested benefits in the US to mainly flat rate child benefits in a number of European countries. This means

that the impact of 'direct' child benefits on poverty can be very different from one country to another.

[20] ★ (★★) is significant at the 10% (5%) confidence level.

References

Atkinson, A., Smeeding, T. and Rainwater, L. (1995) *Income distribution in OECD countries*, OECD Social Policy Studies No 18, Paris: OECD.

Burniaux, J.M., Dang, T.T., Fore, D., Förster, M., Mira D'ercole, M. and Oxley, H. (1998) *Income distribution and poverty in selected OECD countries*, Economics Department Working Paper No 189, OECD March.

Forssén, K. (1998) *Child poverty and family policy in OECD countries*, Luxembourg Income Study Working Paper 178, Luxembourg: LIS.

Förster, M. (1994) *The effects of net transfers on low incomes among non-elderly families*, OECD Economic Studies No 22, pp 181-221.

OECD (1993) *Employment Outlook July 1993*, Paris: OECD.

OECD (1996) *Employment Outlook July 1996*, Paris: OECD.

Oxley, H., Burniaux J.M., Dang, T.T. and Mira D'ercole, M. (1999) 'Income distribution and poverty in 13 OECD countries', OECD Economic Studies No 29, pp 55-94, Paris: OECD.

Oxley, H., Dang T.T., Förster M. and Pellizzari, M. (forthcoming) *Trends in income distribution and poverty of children in OECD countries*, Economics Department Working Paper, Paris: OECD.

SIXTEEN

Reducing child poverty in the European Union: the role of child benefits[1]

Herwig Immervoll, Holly Sutherland and Klaas de Vos

Introduction and summary

This chapter explores the role of child benefits in protecting European children from financial poverty. By 'child benefits' we mean regular cash payments made to parents or other carers on behalf of children who are dependent on them. These benefits can take many forms. They may be taxable or non-taxable, income-and/or wealth-tested or universal, contributory or non-contributory. They may vary by the age or parity of the child, or be the same value for all children. The simplest benefit – a universal unconditional flat-rate benefit for all children – can be seen as having many functions in addition to reducing the rate of child poverty (Brown, 1988). For example, it performs a similar role to child tax allowances in contributing to horizontal equity in the net taxation of families of different types. It helps secure some degree of lifetime re-distribution by enhancing family incomes during a period of additional need. It has the potential to redistribute resources towards mothers, which is likely to improve the welfare of their children (Lundberg et al, 1997).

A particular design of benefit will reflect the balance of priorities given to each objective. A benefit that is means tested can be seen as prioritising short-term income maintenance with a lesser regard for the possible adverse consequences of this form of targeting. These include negative effects on work incentives, a reduction in horizontal equity at higher income levels, inequities introduced due to the stigma associated with means testing, and the 'unfairness' of high effective marginal tax rates (see

Atkinson, 1998a). In this chapter we consider the poverty reduction properties of child benefits at the same time as recognising their other functions. Thus we choose not to explore poverty reduction through policy measures that rely on targeting by income (ie by means testing) but instead seek other ways of using cash benefits to target children living on low incomes.

We consider the children of the European Union (EU). They are of interest as a single group for two reasons. First, although social policy co-ordination in Europe has not yet reached the stage of common benefits across countries, comparisons with other EU countries are a major influence on national policy development. Furthermore, convergence of macroeconomic policy and the constraints imposed by the Stability and Growth Pact of 1997 *do* have effects at the micro-level on the living standards and incomes of families with children (Atkinson, 1998b). These effects themselves are unlikely to be common across countries, not least because of varying national responses to the need for adjustments. However, the very combination of policy formulation at the European level with differential national response to its effects motivates the need for a Europe-wide analysis.

The second reason is that, although by global standards the countries of Western Europe are rich, there remains considerable variation among them in average disposable income. Drawing a single European poverty line – and the great dispersion in national poverty rates that this implies – helps to keep the very different absolute standards of income within our view. Even so, we find that there are poor children in the richest countries, suggesting that child poverty is an issue that is rightly considered in European as well as in national terms with, perhaps, scope for a co-ordinated European solution.

Section 2 of the chapter establishes the scale of the problem by using household microdata for 15 countries to count the proportion of children living in households with incomes below a European poverty line. We make an initial attempt to assess the role of existing family benefits in preventing child poverty. This analysis is based on a simple calculation using the European Community Household Panel (ECHP) of the effect on household incomes of the removal of family benefits. The limitations of this approach are spelled out in section 3, which goes on to describe a Europe-wide microsimulation model, EUROMOD, which has been built specifically to overcome these problems. In section 4 we present preliminary results from EUROMOD for two countries – the Netherlands and the UK – to illustrate the capabilities of EUROMOD. We examine the impacts of national child benefits on the national income distributions and estimates of poverty, and explore the effects of introducing each national system into the other country.

European poverty and the role of family related benefits

As a first step, we seek to establish the incidence of financial poverty among European children under existing social policies. There are many approaches to this task. Here, since we focus on Europe as a whole, we draw a European poverty line. Because the calculations are for illustrative purposes only, we confine ourselves to a particular set of assumptions and one data source for each country. Microdata for 13 countries are drawn from the second wave of the ECHP, using the User Data Base (UDB) for Wave 2. Sweden has no ECHP and Finland did not join until Wave 3. For these two countries microdata are drawn from the respective national income distribution statistics, which in both cases are based on a combination of register and survey data. We calculate the numbers of people and numbers of children living in households with equivalised income below proportions of the EU15 mean. In doing this we implicitly assume that if household income falls below the poverty line, then all the individuals within the household are poor to the same extent.

Our choice of the mean as the central measure of income (rather than the median, which is now favoured by Eurostat[2]) is designed to minimise the effort involved in integrating information for Finland and Sweden[3]. Household incomes are measured after taxes and benefits, on an annual basis for 1994 and are converted to a common currency using 1994 Purchasing Power Parity (PPP) adjusted exchange rates. They are equivalised using the modified Organisation for Economic Co-operation and Development (OECD) scale[4]. In calculating the means and performing the head-count calculations, each household is weighted by the number of people in it. The EU15 mean is calculated by weighting the national means by the national population and dividing by the EU15 population. For more information, see Immervoll et al (1999). The EU15 mean is 12,102 PPP-adjusted ECU per equivalent person per year. National means as proportions of the EU15 mean shown in the first column of Table 16.1 range from 0.6 (Portugal) to 1.8 (Luxembourg)[5].

The second and third columns of Table 16.1 show the head-count ratios using 50% of the EU15 mean as the poverty line, for Europeans of all ages and for children aged under 16. Clearly many people aged over

16 are rightly considered children. However, we are safe in assuming that all people aged under 16 are dependent children, and for comparability reasons we adopt this narrow definition[6]. We can make the following observations:

- There is great variation in head-counts across countries, due not only to differences in within-country inequality but also to differences in mean income between countries. Focusing on all ages, we can see that five countries have proportions that are very low: less than half of the all-EU figure of 18% (Luxembourg, Denmark, Finland, the Netherlands and Sweden). A further five countries have proportions lower than the EU average (France, Belgium, Austria, Germany and the UK). The remaining five vary from 50% larger than the all-EU figure (Italy and Ireland) to double the EU figure (Spain and Greece), with the highest proportion (47% of the population) in Portugal.
- At the European level the poverty rate is somewhat higher for children (21%) than for the population as a whole (18%); children are more likely than adults to live in poor households.
- Comparing across countries we see that this is not uniformly the case. This is illustrated in Figure 16.1, which shows the relationship between all-person poverty and child poverty. Countries above the 45° line have child poverty rates lower than adult rates and those below the line have child rates that exceed adult rates. In many of the countries with low poverty rates, children are *less* likely to be poor. This is particularly the case in Denmark, Finland, Luxembourg and Sweden. In contrast, Greece – with the second highest poverty rate – also has a lower rate of child poverty than adult poverty. On the other hand (in descending order of overall poverty rates) children in Portugal, Spain, Ireland, Italy and the UK are *more* likely than adults to be poor. It is possible that these observations are due to the use of the (modified) OECD equivalence scale, which differentiates between the relative needs of younger children (those aged under 14) and others. However, the use of an alternative scale that does not take account of age (square root of household size) produces an *identical* pattern of countries with lower and higher chances of child poverty relative to adult poverty[7].

We now explore the extent to which explanations for differences across countries in head-count ratios for children (and in the relative ratios for children compared to adults) lie in international differences in family benefits.

Table 16.1: Poverty rates and the role of family related benefits (FBEN) in reducing the percentage of children in poor households in 1994

		% in households below poverty line[a]					
		with FBEN		without FBEN			
Country	Mean[b]	All ages	Age <16	Age <16	% point difference	% increase in poor	FBEN as % of income
Germany[c]	13,855	10.7	13.8				
Denmark	13,923	4.2	3.1	7.5	4.4	141.9	4.4
Netherlands	12482	7.8	9.2	15.9	6.7	72.8	3.0
Belgium	13,733	10.6	11.0	21.0	10.0	90.9	6.6
Luxembourg	22,261	3.3	2.5	6.3	3.8	152.0	5.1
France	13,365	10.4	11.4	22.6	11.2	98.2	4.1
UK	13314	15.7	22.2	32.4	10.2	45.9	3.6
Ireland	11,301	27.8	35.1	39.9	4.8	13.7	3.2
Italy	9,905	26.6	30.6	31.8	1.2	3.9	0.4
Greece	8,401	38.9	35.0	36.2	1.2	3.4	0.5
Spain	8,961	34.9	38.3	38.5	0.2	0.5	0.2
Portugal	7,668	46.9	51.7	53.8	2.1	4.1	1.7
Austria	13,659	10.7	14.3	26.1	11.8	82.5	6.2
Sweden	12,128	8.4	5.1				
Finland	11,872	4.2	2.3				
EU12[d]					6.7		
EU15	12,102[e]	18.0	20.6				

[a] 50% of EU15 mean income.

[b] In ECU per year (using PPP-adjusted exchange rates), equivalised using the modified OECD scale, weighted by household size.

[c] Family-related benefits are not available separately for Germany in the ECHP UDB.

[d] EU15 less Germany, Sweden and Finland.

[e] EU15 mean calculated by weighting national means by national populations.

Sources: Own calculations for EU13 from the 2nd wave of the ECHP; for Finland and Sweden the figures are calculated from 1994 Income Distribution statistics

Figure 16.1: Rates of child poverty by all person poverty rates

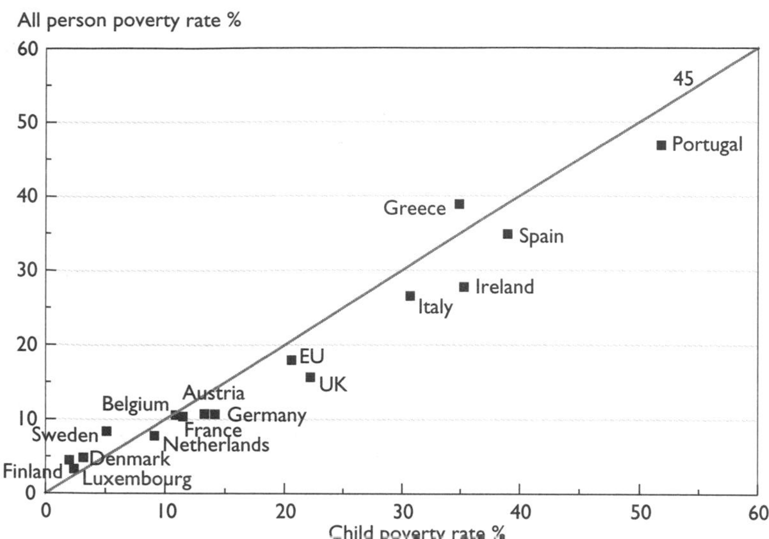

Source: Table 16.1, using as poverty cut-off 50% of EU15 mean income; children aged <16

The ECHP UDB provides – for just 12 countries – a variable 'family-related benefit', which as well as child benefit includes maternity benefit and benefits for carers of disabled dependants[8]. The final column of Table 16.1 shows the proportion of total household disposable income that is made up of these benefits (for all households). It varies from 6.6% in Belgium to 0.2% in Spain. In order to investigate its importance to households with children below the European poverty line, we carry out a rudimentary simulation. We set the value of family-related benefits to zero and re-count the number of children who are in households below the poverty line. For simplicity, we do not re-calculate the poverty line, but leave it fixed. Implicitly, we assume no behavioural adjustments (such as changes in wages or working hours) following this reduction in benefit income. Table 16.1 reports the new head-count ratio for children (labelled 'without FBEN'). It also shows the absolute (percentage point) increase in child poverty and the percentage increase in the proportion of poor children. The European (EU12) rate of child poverty increases by 7%. We can identify three groups of countries:

- Denmark and Luxembourg[9]: child poverty rates are relatively low, with or without family-related benefits. Although the benefits are relatively generous, removing them causes poverty rates to rise by a small absolute amount. However, the percentage increase in the number of poor children is very large.
- Spain, Italy, Greece, Portugal and Ireland: child poverty rates start high but are little affected by the removal of benefits. This is because, with the exception of Ireland, the size of the benefit is small, combined with the fact that the European poverty lines are high in relation to the incomes of households with children in these countries. Benefits would have to be very large to have a significant effect on poverty measured in this way.
- UK, Belgium, Austria, France and the Netherlands[10]: family-related benefits are relatively large in size and are also relatively successful at protecting children from poverty. On removing the benefits, poverty rates rise significantly both in absolute and proportional terms.

Clearly, family benefits have a major role to play in child poverty prevention in Europe. Here, we consider ways in which this role might be improved for each of these groups. In group 1 incomes are already relatively high, meaning that only a small minority of children are below the European poverty line. However, it remains the case that children in the poorest households in these countries are well protected by family benefits. For example, in Denmark, the child poverty rate would rise from 3.1% to 7.5% if family benefits were removed. Children in both countries are already less likely than the population as a whole to be poor. In these countries it would be interesting to explore ways in which benefits for children could be designed to raise the incomes of the small minority who are poor by European standards.

In group 2 countries, relatively low average incomes mean that the generally low benefits cannot bring households with children up to the European poverty line. In these cases it would be interesting to explore the effects of more substantial family benefits on child poverty rates. Need a new benefit be large and expensive to reduce the numbers of children in poverty, or could benefits of modest cost be designed to target particularly on groups vulnerable to poverty?

The third group consists of countries that appear to have family benefits that are relatively successful at reducing child poverty. However, in all these countries, child poverty rates are higher than for the population as a whole. Are there improvements in the design of benefits that could assist in the rather modest target of making child poverty rates no higher than the rates for the whole population? Are there features of particular national systems that other countries could learn from? We note that the six countries in this group (including Germany) have relatively similar PPP-adjusted mean household incomes. With the exception of the UK they also have relatively similar child poverty rates. The UK has a much higher rate (22% compared with between 9% and 14% for the other countries). This is significantly higher than the rate for the UK population as a whole. Can this be explained by inadequacies in the system of UK family benefits? Are there other types of benefit that would reduce the UK's contribution to the European rate of child poverty?

Policy simulation

The figures shown in Table 16.1 have some important limitations in terms of their ability to provide answers to the questions raised in the previous section.

First, we need to be clear about the policy instruments on which we wish to focus. This chapter is about the role of child benefits, rather than family benefits in general. With this narrow focus, we need to be able to distinguish child benefits from the wider category of benefits for which information is available in the ECHP.

Second, even with a single type of benefit as our subject, there are many parameters of the system to consider. Child benefits may vary in many respects as well as their magnitude. The benefits may be taxable or non-taxable, income- or wealth-tested or universal, contributory or non-contributory. They may vary by the age of the child or by the number of children. The definition of an eligible child (or parent) may also vary. To explore how well the benefits perform, from the perspective of poverty reduction or any other function we consider important, we need to be able to focus on particular aspects of their design. In the case of the rudimentary simulation in the previous section, the calculations could not provide a full answer to the question "what if we abolished family benefits across Europe?" because it could not capture the *interactions* between family benefits and other parts of tax-benefit systems. In some countries poorer families would be protected from a fall in income by social assistance schemes. Specific income-tested benefits such as housing benefits may perform a similar role. In practice, in these cases poverty would not increase to the extent shown in Table 16.1. In these countries the operation of child benefits is difficult to separate from the benefit system as a whole. Furthermore, in some countries some child benefits or other family benefits are taxable. Removing the benefits would decrease tax liability. This effect is also not captured in the illustrative calculations in Table 16.1.

In order to isolate the impact of a particular policy, to focus on detailed aspects of policy design, or to explore the implications for microlevel incomes of specific policy changes, a microsimulation model is required. Static microsimulation (or 'tax-benefit') models offer distinct 'levers to pull' and 'buttons to push' so that simulated changes translate directly into changes to actual policy rules that governments can make.

The term 'static' might suggest that such models are inferior to models described as 'dynamic'. However, in this context, a static model is exactly what is needed. Static models allow us to hold constant many variables so that we can focus on the aspects of interest. Specifically, they allow us to separate the direct effects of tax and social security policy on incomes from all the underlying influences on income and from the other characteristics and behavioural patterns of a specific population. So we can 'borrow' policy – or parts of it – from one country and apply it to another country's population. This technique has been used by Atkinson et al (1988) to apply the British tax system to the French population, by de Lathouwer (1996) to compare unemployment schemes for Belgium and the Netherlands, by O'Donoghue and Sutherland (1998) to apply stylised versions of European systems of the taxation of couples to the UK population, and by Redmond (1999) to explore the effects of introducing a UK-style system of means-tested benefits in Hungary.

Static microsimulation models exist in most countries of the EU and the rest of the OECD[11]. However, to explore the effects of benefits in a comparable manner in different countries as well as on European child poverty, we need a model that operates at the European level. EUROMOD is such a model. It provides us with a Europe-wide perspective on social and fiscal policies that are implemented at European, national or regional level. It is also designed to examine, within a consistent comparative framework, the impact of national policies on national populations or the differential impact of coordinated European policy on individual Member states. See Immervoll et al (1999) for more details.

To illustrate the potential that EUROMOD offers in answering questions about the effects of child benefits on child poverty across Europe, we use a preliminary version of EUROMOD for two countries – the Netherlands and the UK. Microdata for the Netherlands are from the 1996 wave of the Socio-Economic Panel (SEP). Households with large amounts of missing information are excluded, bringing the sample to 4,568 households. For the UK we use the 1995/6 Family Expenditure Survey. No observations are excluded since the sample contains no households with significant missing information. There are 6,797 UK households. In each case, the samples are weighted to adjust for non-response bias and to bring the results up to population levels. The simulations are based on the systems of tax and benefit rules current in June 1998, and the income variables in the microdata are updated using the consumer price index (NL) and the retail price index (UK).

One of the advantages of an integrated European tax-benefit model is that consistent income concepts can be used in each country. For the current exercise we use the following definition of household disposable income: wage and salary income (including sick pay paid by government), *plus* self-employment income, *plus* property income (rent, dividends, interest), *plus* other cash market income and occupational pension income (regular private transfers, alimony and child maintenance), *plus* cash benefit payments (social insurance, disability, universal and social assistance benefits, including state pension payments), *minus* direct taxes and social insurance contributions[12].

Given the limitations of the underlying data, not all the relevant components of the respective tax-benefit systems lend themselves to simulation. We simulate income taxes, social insurance contributions, child benefits and other family benefits, and income-tested benefits. In computing income, components that are not simulated in the model are taken directly from the data (ie it is assumed that they are unaffected by the policy reform). In particular, this is the case for contribution-based payments such as unemployment benefits or contributory pensions. More detail on the specific instruments that have been simulated is provided in Immervoll et al (2000).

Household incomes have been equivalised using the modified OECD equivalence scale. In this exercise we use national poverty lines defined as 60% of median equivalised household disposable income, with each household weighted by its size[13]. In exploring the effects of policy changes on the incomes of households with children, we use two alternative definitions of a child. The first is all people aged less than 14 (as in the OECD equivalence scale). The second is the definition of a child used in UK policy: all people aged under 16, plus those aged under 19 who are in full-time secondary education, not married and not a parent themselves. In comparing across countries, monetary amounts have been converted using PPPs[14].

Table 16.2: Populations and baseline scenario (1998): poverty lines and head-counts, the Netherlands and the UK

	Netherlands	UK
Population (thousands)[a]	15,120	57,440
60% median, per month[b]	NFL 1,487(£487)	£443 (NFL 1,351)
% below poverty line		
All	12.6	20.4
Children <14	12.7	29.5
'UK' children	13.6	28.0
Number below poverty line (000s)[a]		
All	1,910	11,740
Children <14	370	3,160
'UK' children	500	3,710

[a] As implied by weights in data.

[b] All amounts are in 1998 currency; conversions use PPP exchange rate.

Source: EUROMOD

Figure 16.2: Cumulative proportions of children (UK definition) by decile group of equivalised household income

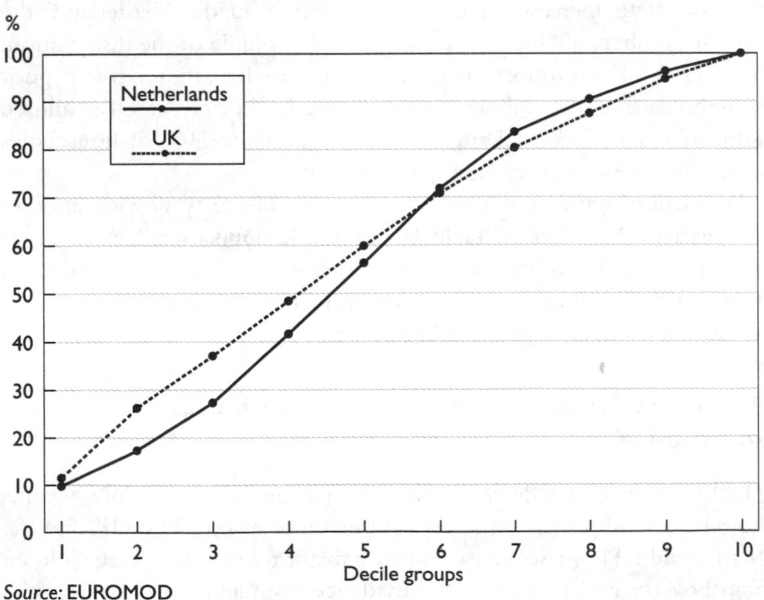

Source: EUROMOD

Table 16.2 shows the poverty lines for the two countries, based on 1998 policy simulated for the 1995 (UK) or 1996 (Netherlands) populations with updated incomes. The cut-off is some 10% higher in the Netherlands than the UK, on the basis of the PPP comparison. This is the reverse of the ranking given by the mean of ECHP incomes for an earlier year, shown in Table 16.1. Table 16.2 shows the percentages of all people and of children (under both definitions) who are living in households with equivalised incomes below the national lines. In spite of the higher poverty cut-off in the Netherlands, the all-person head-count is much lower: 12.6% compared to 20.4% in the UK. We also see that poverty among children in the UK is higher if one adopts the OECD child definition (age<14) as opposed to the one used in the UK tax-benefit system (which includes many 14-18-year-olds), indicating that child poverty is more concentrated among younger children. The opposite is true for the Netherlands, where the poverty rate for older children excluded from the OECD definition but included in the UK definition is 17.0%, substantially higher than the rate for younger children (12.7% for OECD children).

This is confirmed by Figure 16.2, showing the cumulative position of children (UK definition) in the national household income distributions in the two countries. In the UK, the number of children generally decreases with increasing income. In contrast, in the Netherlands the highest numbers of children are found in the middle of the distribution. A much higher proportion of UK children live in relatively poor households than do children in the Netherlands; 37% of UK children compared with 27% of Dutch children are in the 30% of households with the lowest incomes on a national basis.

Population figures and absolute numbers in poverty provide another perspective. As shown in Table 16.2, the UK population is nearly four times the size that of the Netherlands. However, there are 8.5 times as many 'OECD children' and 7.4 times as many 'UK children' in poverty in the UK compared with the Netherlands.

A case study: child benefits in the Netherlands and the UK

The ECHP evidence described in section 2 suggests that family benefits are relatively important to household incomes in both the UK and the Netherlands. They also appear to play a major role in protecting children from poverty in both countries. Evidence from administrative statistics suggests that child benefit itself is a similar proportion of GDP in both countries. In the UK in 1996/7 child benefit was 0.88% of GDP and 7.2% of all government spending on social security benefits, and in the Netherlands child benefit amounted to 0.90% of GDP in 1997, or 5% of total benefit payments[15].

The 1998 systems of child benefit and child support in the Netherlands and the UK were structurally similar in some respects and different in others, as summarised below[16].

Similarities:

- Child benefit is not income or wealth tested.
- Child benefit is non-contributory and not work-tested.
- No income tax or contributions are payable on child benefit.
- There are no child-related income tax allowances/credits, except for lone parents.

Differences:

- Child benefit payments increase with the number of children in the family ('parity') in the old Netherlands system, which is in the process of phased change. There is no variation with parity in the new system. In the UK system, the benefit *decreases* in value per child with the number of children (the amount for the eldest or only child is 23% more than for other children).
- Child benefit payments vary by the age of the child in the Netherlands, not in the UK.
- The definition of a child is slightly different. It includes most 16-17 year-olds in the Netherlands (subject to a child's income limit, employment and education status, and disability conditions). In the UK it excludes a more extensive group of 16-17-year-olds but includes some 18-year-olds.
- Child benefit is not included as income in the assessment of income for social assistance in the Netherlands. There are no specific additions to social assistance rates (except for lone parents and young parents). In the UK, child benefit is included in social assistance income assessments, and there are specific child additions to social assistance payments.

There are other significant differences between the systems of cash child support for low-income families in the two countries – notably in the UK the in-work benefit for parents on low earnings, Family Credit. However, we maintain our focus on the role of child benefit and evaluate a series of scenarios with the aim of exploring the impact of the national systems of child benefit. In each country we start by abolishing the existing child benefit. The motivation is not to evaluate this scenario as a realistic reform option. Rather, by comparing the existing scenario with one where no child benefits are available, it is possible to assess what difference the existing child benefit makes in terms of incomes. We then 'swap systems' and explore the effect of the UK system in the Netherlands and vice versa. However, three factors complicate the exercise. First, both countries operate additional instruments targeted on lone parents. For reasons of clarity we hold these constant and do not explore changes to them.

Second, and as mentioned above, child benefit is integrated differently into the two systems. In the Netherlands, it is not included in income assessments for social assistance, whereas in the UK (Income Support) it is included. Therefore we carry out two versions of 'abolition' for the UK. In the first, child benefit is abolished, but Income Support entitlements are allowed to rise to take its place. In the second, Income Support child payments are reduced by the value of child benefit so that we can evaluate the effect of the universal child payment on all households with children.

The third complication is that policy in both countries is in a transitional phase. In the Netherlands the 1998 scheme is partway between an 'old' scheme, where child benefit payments depended on the age and number of children, and a 'new' scheme that depends on age only and is being phased in so that it will apply to all children by the year 2011. In the UK lone-parent benefits are not paid to new lone parents (or new claimants), but are retained for 'old' claimants. Throughout, our simulations for the UK assume that all lone parents are 'old'. For the Netherlands, the baseline is the actual 1998 hybrid system, but we explore the effects of moving to both the 'old' and the 'new' system in two scenarios. We simulate six scenarios for the Netherlands and five for the UK, as follows:

Scenarios simulated for the Netherlands

NL 1998 – *Base-line scenario:* System of rules current in June 1998.

NL noCB – *Abolish child benefit:* Same as NL 1998 but child benefit amounts reduced to zero.

NL newCB – *New child benefit:* The current child benefit is replaced by the 'new' rules in which the benefit depends only on the age of children, not their parity.

NL oldCB – *Old child benefit:* The current child benefit is replaced by the 'old' rules that are more strongly dependent on parity.

NL UKCB – *UK child benefit:* the current child benefit is replaced by the current UK child benefit. We adopt the UK rules with respect to both the child benefit amounts (except for the UK lone parent additional amount) and eligibility conditions (the child definition). Child benefit is *not* counted as 'means' for social assistance. Using PPP exchange rates the child benefit for one child aged 5 would rise from 314.66 to 454.90 NFL per quarter. For a family with three children all aged between 6 and 9 it would fall from 1372.86 to 1193.86 NFL.

NL UKCBadj – *Revenue neutral UK child benefit:* Same as NL UKCB but instead of paying the same amounts – in PPP terms – as in the UK, all amounts have been increased by about 8% to match the overall cost of the NL 1998 scenario.

Scenarios simulated for the UK

UK 1998 – *Base-line scenario:* System of rules current in June 1998.

UK noCB1 – *Abolish child benefit:* Same as UK 1998 but child benefit amounts are set to zero (the additional amount for lone parents is left unchanged).

UK noCB2 – *Abolish child benefit and reduce Income Support accordingly:* Same as 'UK noCB1' but the child related Income Support amounts are also reduced accordingly. This has the effect that for families on Income Support, the abolition of child benefit is no longer offset by higher Income Support payments.

UK NLCB – *Netherlands child benefit:* Same as UK 1998, except child benefit is replaced by the 'old' Netherlands child benefit. We adopt the

Dutch rules with respect to both the child benefit amounts and eligibility conditions (the child definition). Child benefit is *not* included in the means test for Income Support. Using PPP exchange rates the child benefit for one child aged 5 would fall from £11.45 to £7.92 per week. For a family of three children all aged between 6 and 9, it would rise from £30.05 to £34.56.

UK NLCBadj – *Revenue neutral Netherlands child benefit:* Same as UK NLCB, but instead of paying the same amounts – in PPP terms – as in the Netherlands, all amounts have been reduced by around 32% to match the overall cost of the UK 1998 scenario.

Results

Table 16.3 shows the monthly cost of each of the scenarios in national currency. Our simulation results for the existing systems compare well in cost terms with administrative statistics from each country[17]. In the Netherlands, the new system is substantially less generous than the old, with the actual 1998 system coming in between. The UK system of child benefit is slightly less generous than the corresponding 1998 Netherlands system but more generous than the new Netherlands system that is being phased in. In the UK, the old Netherlands system is very much more generous than the existing UK system, costing around 30% more.

Figure 16.3 shows the effect of moving from the baseline scenario to the alternatives in terms of the percentage change in household income across the national (all household) distributions of income[18]. The distributional effects of the 'noCB' scenarios illustrate the importance of child benefits to family incomes, particularly at the bottom but also in the middle of the distributions in both countries. For the UK the difference between the 'noCB1' and 'noCB2' scenarios shows the extent of dependence on Income Support by families with children in the bottom half of the distribution; around a quarter of the cost of child benefit for all children is made up of payments to families in receipt of Income Support.

Comparing the distributional effects of the 1998 system and the old and new systems in the Netherlands (Figure 16.3a) shows that the current system is partway between the old and the new in its distributional effect as well as its cost. For the Netherlands, Figure16.3a does not indicate any significant distributional effect of introducing the revenue neutral UK

Table 16.3: Child benefit scenarios: revenue effects and poverty headcounts

	Cost per month	All persons	Children (aged <14)	Children (UK defn.)
Poverty headcounts (%)				
Netherlands	*million NFL*			
1998	547	12.6	12.7	13.6
NoCB	0	15.6	19.%	20.2
NewCB	486	12.7	13.0	13.9
OldCB	621	12.2	11.7	12.6
UKCBadj[a]	547	12.7	12.7	13.9
UK	*million £*			
1998	603	20.4	29.5	28.0
NoCB2[b]	0	23.3	37.0	35.0
NLCB	786	19.2	25.8	24.5
NLCBadj	603	20.3	28.9	27.4
Decrease in the number of poor persons per £1,000 per month spent on benefit[c]				
Netherlands				
1998		2.5	1.1	1.4
NewCB		2.7	1.2	1.5
OldCB		2.5	1.1	1.4
UKCBadj		2.4	1.1	1.3
UK				
1998		2.7	1.3	1.5
NLCB		3.0	1.5	1.8
NLCBadj		2.9	1.4	1.7

[a] The UK system, without scaling for revenue-neutrality costs 507 million NFL per month.

[b] The cost of continuing to pay the amount of child benefit to families on Income Support (NoCB1) is £163 million per month.

[c] Using a PPP-adjusted exchange rate of 3.0514 NFL/£.

Source: EUROMOD

system of child benefit. The actual, less generous, UK system results in small losses in the bottom half of the distribution, but these are no greater than the losses that occur under the new Netherlands system. In the UK, however, the introduction of the old Netherlands system would bring significant percentage increases in income, particularly to the bottom quintile (Figure 16.3b). This is to a large extent due to the greater generosity of the Netherlands system. However, even after controlling

Figure 16.3: Percentage change in equivalent household income compared with 1998 scenario (all households)

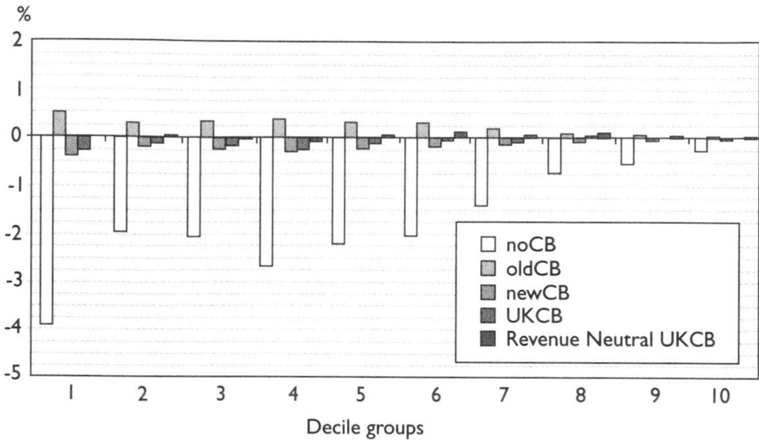

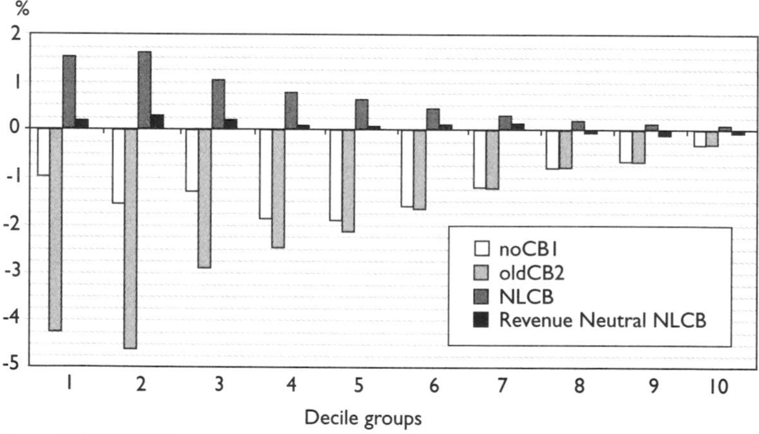

Source: EUROMOD

for the higher cost of the Netherlands system of child benefit, the Netherlands structure of benefit still distributes more to lower income UK households than does the present UK structure.

It is important to note, however, that not everybody would gain from the introduction of the 'old' Netherlands child benefit in the UK. Figure

16.4b shows the number of persons and children gaining (positive values) and losing (negative values) as a result of the revenue neutral reform[19]. Families that are less well off under the 'old' Netherlands child benefit include those with only one child. In addition, some 18-year-olds are still eligible under the UK system, while in the Netherlands persons aged over 17 do not count as children. However, even though there would be children in households worse off after the reform, those gaining from switching to the revenue neutral Netherlands benefit would clearly outnumber the losers. This is true especially for children in the lower income groups. The opposite holds for the Netherlands (Figure 16.4a); the introduction of a revenue neutral UK child benefit in the Netherlands would result in more losers (52%) than gainers (39%) among children in the bottom 40% of the income distribution.

We now turn to the effect of the alternative scenarios on estimates of poverty. We have drawn the poverty lines using the baseline scenarios – the existing 1998 systems. The top part of Table 16.3 shows the poverty rates for the Netherlands and the UK for all persons and for children (using both definitions) under each scenario[20]. The rates, unsurprisingly, are related inversely to the cost of the respective schemes. The most expensive scheme in either country is the 'old' Netherlands scheme, and this is also the most effective in reducing child poverty (and poverty overall). A comparison of schemes that cost the same shows that while the old Netherlands structure is more effective at poverty reduction in the UK than the current UK system, the current Netherlands system remains (somewhat) more effective than the UK structure in the Netherlands.

The lower part of Table 16.3 shows the effects in terms of the absolute reduction in poverty headcounts per unit spending on benefit. We use this measure as one possible indicator for the 'efficiency' of benefits in terms of poverty reduction. For the Netherlands we find that the new scheme is generally the most efficient at reducing poverty, as well as being the cheapest. For the UK, the 'old' Netherlands system is more efficient in terms of child poverty reduction than the current UK child benefit. For each unit of spending, the 'old' Netherlands system removes 15% more children (UK definition) from poverty than does the current UK system (1.77 compared with 1.54 – shown rounded in the table). This effect is reduced but not removed by scaling down the Netherlands system so that it costs the same as the UK system. UK child poverty is reduced by 10% more per unit of spending (1.69 compared with 1.54) even though the schemes cost the same.

Figure 16.4: Gainers and losers from revenue-neutral reforms (000s)

a) Netherlands: UK child benefit compared with NL 1998 scenario

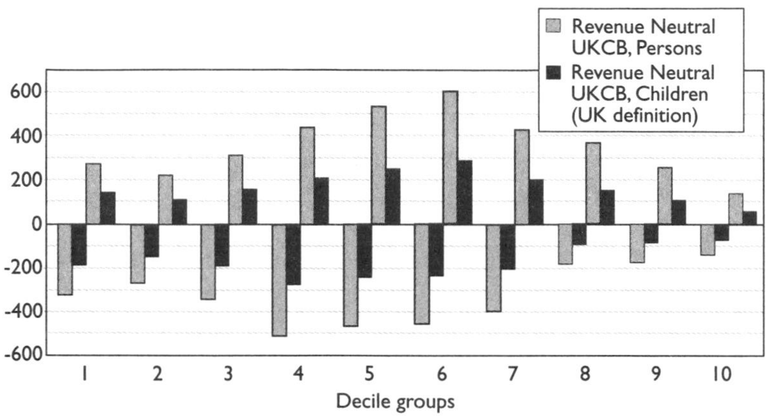

b) UK: NL child benefit (old) compared with UK 1998 scenario

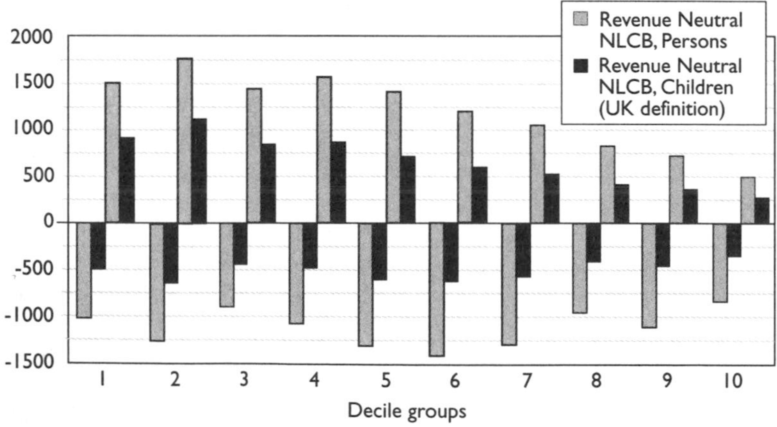

Source: EUROMOD

Comparing the results across countries we find that child benefit generally appears to be more effective at poverty reduction in the UK than in the Netherlands. For example, without child benefit the proportion of Dutch children (using the UK child definition) counted as poor would be 20.2%. This falls 7.6 percentage points to 12.6% with the 'old' Netherlands child benefit. In the UK, 35% of children are counted as poor under the 'no CB' scenario, and this falls by 10.5 percentage points to 24.5% with the introduction of the Netherlands 'old CB'. However, this is mainly a result of the fact that children are more concentrated in lower income households in the UK. Reductions in poverty rates in *percentage* terms are actually higher in the Netherlands than they are in the UK: 38% and 30% respectively in the above example.

Concluding comments

We have seen that family benefits in general and child benefits in particular vary in their importance to household incomes and in the prevention of child poverty across Europe. In some countries family benefits are generous, but even without them incomes are sufficient to protect the large majority of children from poverty. In a second group, family benefits are relatively small and have little effect on poverty. In a third group, family benefits appear to have a significant effect on the protection of children from poverty. The UK and the Netherlands are both members of this third group, and we have used microsimulation techniques to examine the extent to which differences in child benefits explain the very different level of child poverty in the two countries. We also have explored the effect of 'swapping' child benefit systems between the two countries. We find the following:

- The Netherlands system is in transition. The 'old' system, which depends on the number of children as well as the age of the child, is both more generous overall and more effective at reducing poverty than the 'new' system, which depends on age alone. However, per unit of spending the new system is generally the most efficient at reducing poverty.
- In the UK, the 'old' Netherlands system is also the most effective for child poverty reduction in the UK. Even when controlling for the amount spent on benefit, a system that pays more to older children and larger families appears to be the most efficient in reducing poverty rates in the UK.
- Most crucially, we have focused on child benefits (and reforms) that do not involve income, or means, testing. We have shown that the poverty reduction properties of universal child benefits may be improved without compromising the other functions of these benefits.

Clearly, there is scope to take this type of analysis further. It would be interesting to explore the financing of more expensive schemes (through income tax or other means) as an alternative to the scaling down of the benefits. Also, experiments with the variation of benefits by age and family size could be extended outside the scope of existing (or past or projected) policy.

We have used a case study of just two countries with quite similar child benefit systems. A EU15 version of EUROMOD will allow us to compare countries with more diverse systems. EUROMOD also offers us the possibility to carry out similar analyses for larger sub-groups of countries and for the whole EU. As discussed above, it will enable us to draw common European poverty lines, to construct a common income distribution and generally to consider the European population across national boundaries[21]. Simulation of various levels of a common universal benefit for children (or a children's 'Citizen's Income') to replace existing cash benefits and tax expenditures would allow us to assess national systems against a set of common benchmarks.

Our example shows that using microsimulation to seek improvements in policy design across national boundaries can be a quite fruitful exercise. Further work would be needed to draw firm conclusions about the beneficial effects on child poverty in the UK of child benefits that depend on the age of the child and on the number of children. However, we believe that this preliminary output from EUROMOD is the first of many microsimulation exercises to provide valuable pointers for the direction of social policies.

Notes

[1] Immervoll and Sutherland are Research Associate and Director respectively of the Microsimulation Unit in the Department of Applied Economics at the University of Cambridge; de Vos is Senior Researcher at CentER Applied Research, Tilburg. This chapter was written as part of the EUROMOD project, financed by *Targeted Socio-Economic Research* programme of the European Commission (CT97-3060). A longer version is available as Immervoll, Sutherland and de Vos (2000).

We are grateful for access to microdata from the European Community Household Panel (ECHP) 1995 (second wave) made available by Eurostat, the Socio-Economic Panel Survey (SEP) made available by Statistics Netherlands through the mediation of the Netherlands Organisation for Scientific Research-Scientific Statistical Agency, and the UK Family Expenditure Survey (FES), which have been made available by the Office for National Statistics (ONS) through the Data Archive. Material from the FES is Crown Copyright and is used by permission. Neither the ONS nor the Data Archive bear any responsibility for the analysis or interpretation of the data reported here. An equivalent disclaimer applies to the other data sources and their respective providers. We are grateful to Lavinia Mitton for research assistance, to Cathal O'Donoghue for modelling support and advice, and to Tony Atkinson, Fran Bennett and participants at the conference on *Child well-being in rich and transition countries* in Luxembourg for helpful comments. The authors alone are responsible for any errors, as well as the views presented in this chapter.

[2] Eurostat's Statistical Programme Committee agreed the recommendations of the Task Force on Social Exclusion and Poverty Statistics in November 1998. See Eurostat document CPS 98/3/12.

[3] We are very grateful to the EUROMOD project participants from Finland (Esko Mustonen and Heikki Viitamäki) and Sweden (Bengt Eklind) for taking part in the two-stage process to include their countries in the calculations. First, they provided estimates of mean income and population for their countries. In the second stage they calculated the numbers in Finland and Sweden below the EU15 poverty line. Note that the equivalent procedure to integrate Swedish and Finnish headcounts based on *median* incomes would have been much more elaborate.

[4] Single = 1; additional adults (aged >13) = 0.5; children (aged < 14) = 0.3.

[5] It is worth noting that the national means that we have calculated are close, but not identical, to those calculated by Eurostat using the same data source (1999, Table C1.2).

[6] It remains the case that the definition of a dependent child is an important issue for social policy and for its evaluation. There are large differences across European countries in circumstances in which, and the extent to which, older children may be treated as dependent on their parents. For example, people aged up to 30 may be treated as children in Spain, but with the exception of disabled dependants, all people aged 19 and over are considered independent of their parents in the UK. See Millar and Warman (1996) and O'Donoghue and Sutherland (1998, Appendix 2), for more information.

[7] These calculations were done only for countries for which we have ECHP data: not Finland and Sweden.

[8] ECHP UDB variable HI133. This variable is not available for Germany.

[9] It is likely that Sweden and Finland also belong to this group.

[10] It is likely that Germany also belongs to this group.

[11] See Sutherland (1998) for a five country review.

[12] As defined in Atkinson, Rainwater and Smeeding (1995), Table 2.1. Components that are not part of our output income concept include imputed rent from owner occupation, the value of home production, other non-cash incomes, unrealised capital gains or losses, the value of credit or loans (repayments and interest payments are not deducted) and irregular lump sum incomes (regular bonuses are included). Employer contributions are neither added nor deducted. Forms of 'committed expenditure' such as housing costs, child maintenance, alimony payments, etc are not deducted.

[13] As recommended by the Eurostat Task Force on Social Exclusion and Poverty Statistics.

[14] The 1995 household sector PPP is carried forward to June 1998 using the changes in the Harmonised Consumer Price Index of both countries (the resulting 1998 PPP exchange rate is 3.0514 NFL/GBP). The 1995 PPP was taken from Eurostat (1999, p 36).

[15] Office for National Statistics (1998, Table 3.5) and Statistics Netherlands (1998, Table S 60.8). The Netherlands and UK definitions of total benefits may not be comparable.

[16] More detail is provided in Immervoll et al (2000).

[17] The actual figures in monthly terms are 'at least' NFL 543m for the Netherlands (Sociale Verzekeringsbank (1999)) and £607m for the UK (Department of Social Security, 1999, Table 1). These compare with simulated values of NFL 547m and £603m respectively.

[18] In these distributions, households are counted once and are not weighted by household size.

[19] Here 'losers' are persons living in a household whose equivalised household income decreases by at least £1 per month. 'Gainers' are those who are in households that gain at least £1 per month.

[20] All the results reported in this chapter are derived from survey data and are subject to sampling error. However, as shown by Pudney and Sutherland (1994), the statistical reliability of simulated changes in poverty head-counts may be particularly problematic. Our reporting of simulation results should not be taken to suggest that they are statistically significant. It is also worth noting that these measures of poverty reduction could be quite sensitive to choice of equivalence scale. The modified OECD equivalence scale is based on the age and number of persons living in the household. The performance of the different benefits could appear to be quite different if alternative criteria for equivalising incomes were adopted.

[21] In the present chapter we have refrained from exploring the effect of child benefits on EU2 (UK and the Netherlands combined) since this group would be dominated by the UK.

References

Atkinson, A.B. (1998a) *Poverty in Europe*, Oxford: Blackwell.

Atkinson, A.B. (1998b) *EMU, macroeconomics and children*, Innocenti Occasional Papers, Economic and Social Policy Series no 68, Florence: UNICEF International Child Development Centre.

Atkinson, A.B., Bourguignon, F. and Chiappori, P.A. (1988) 'What do we learn about tax reform from international comparisons? France and Britain', *European Economic Review*, vol 32, pp 343-52.

Atkinson, A.B., Rainwater, L. and Smeeding, T. (1995) *Income distribution in OECD countries: Evidence from the Luxembourg Income Study*, Paris: OECD.

Brown, J.C. (1988) *Child Benefit: Investing in the future*, London: Child Poverty Action Group.

Department of Social Security (1999) Social Security Departmental Report, Available on http://www.dss.gov.uk/hq/dssreport/tables/table-1.htm.

Eurostat (1999) *European Community Household Panel (ECHP): Selected indicators from the 1995 wave*, Luxembourg: Office for Official Publications for the European Communities.

Immervoll, H., O'Donoghue, C. and Sutherland, H. (1999) *An introduction to EUROMOD*, EUROMOD Working Paper No 0/99, Cambridge: Department of Applied Economics, University of Cambridge.

Immervoll, H., Sutherland, H. and de Vos, K. (2000) *Child poverty and child benefits in the European Union*, EUROMOD Working Paper No 1/00, Cambridge: Department of Applied Economics, University of Cambridge.

de Lathouwer, L. (1996) 'Microsimulation in comparative social policy analysis: a case study of unemployment schemes for Belgium and the Netherlands', in A. Harding (ed) *Microsimulation and public policy*, Amsterdam: North Holland.

Lundberg, S.J., Pollak, R.A. and Wales, T.J. (1997) 'Do husbands and wives pool their resources? Evidence from the UK Child Benefit', *Journal of Human Resources*, vol 32, no 3, pp 462-80.

Millar, J. and Warman, A. (1996) *Family obligations in Europe*, London: Family Policy Studies Centre.

O'Donoghue, C. and Sutherland, H. (1998) *Accounting for the family: the treatment of marriage and children in European income tax systems*, Innocenti Occasional Papers, Economic and Social Policy Series no 65, Florence: UNICEF International Child Development Centre.

Office for National Statistics (1998) *Annual Abstract of Statistics,* No 134, London: The Stationery Office.

Pudney, S. and Sutherland, H. (1994) 'How reliable are microsimulation results? An analysis of the role of sampling error in a UK tax-benefit model', *Journal of Public Economics*, vol 53, pp 327-65.

Redmond, G. (1999) 'Incomes, incentives and the growth of means-testing in Hungary', *Fiscal Studies*, vol 20, no 1, pp 77-99.

Sociale Verzekeringsbank (1999) 'Child Benefit', Available on http://www.svb.org.

Statistics Netherlands (1998) *National accounts of the Netherlands 1997*, The Hague: Sdu Publishers.

Sutherland, H. (1998) 'Les modèles statiques de microsimulation en Europe dans les années 90' *Économie et Statistique*, vol 315, no 5, pp 35-50.

SEVENTEEN

Public policies that support families with young children: variation across US states

Marcia K. Meyers, Janet C. Gornick, Laura R. Peck and Amanda J. Lockshin

Introduction

One in four children under the age of six in the United States lives in poverty. Although child poverty is high nationwide, there is substantial cross-state variation. In the mid-1990s, for example, the percentage of poor children under age six varied from 11% in Utah to 44% in the District of Columbia (Bennett and Li, 1998). Across the states infant mortality ranged from 5 to 18 deaths per 1,000 live births; high school dropout rates ranged from 3% to 13%; and violent deaths ranged from 19 to 456 per 100,000 teenagers (Annie E. Casey Foundation, 1998).

Such variation suggests that state-level factors, including government policies, influence children's lives. Extensive comparative research examines variation in social policy across industrialised countries, including the US. The impact of policy variation *within* the US has received much less attention. Scholars who do consider state variation typically focus on a single policy variable (such as AFDC benefit levels) and therefore fail to explore variation in how states' packages of programmes – cash and non-cash, transfers and services, targeted and universal – affect families and children.

In this chapter we propose a new approach to understanding how state-level policies may affect childhood poverty in the US. We begin by identifying opportunities for public intervention. Using this framework, we identify characteristics of certain government programmes that we would expect to influence families' resources. Using state-level measures, we employ cluster analysis to identify five groups of states with similar policy packages as of 1994. We then describe the policy packages and examine variation in child poverty rates across the resulting clusters.

The comparative approach we use draws on several lessons from cross-national comparative welfare state scholarship. First, we explicitly characterise and compare policies in and across the US states. Second, we include multidimensional policy variables that go beyond public expenditures. We combine traditional quantitative measures (eg spending per recipient) and qualitative elements (eg programme rules) to capture the magnitude of public investment along with policy 'architecture'. We consider multiple sets of policies, or 'policy packages' by analysing 11 programme areas and three important characteristics of each. Finally, we draw on cross-national scholarship about welfare regimes as a model for studying state variation in the US.

Background

A substantial empirical literature supports the commonsense notion that resources are important to children's immediate life circumstances and long-term prospects. Recent work has demonstrated, for example, not only greater levels of material hardship among poor children (Federman et al, 1996) but also deficits in cognitive abilities (Smith et al, 1997), mental health (McLoyd and Wilson, 1991), physical health and disabilities (McNeil, 1993; Newacheck et al, 1994) and behaviour and learning abilities (Zill et al, 1994). Evidence shows that children who grow up in poor families fare poorly in adulthood as well, with lower educational attainment, earlier childbearing, and lower earnings (Haveman and Wolfe, 1995; Lichter, 1997).

The public policy challenge

The central role of resources in children's well-being raises a particularly vexing social policy challenge; while families with children are among those most in need of resources to support dependent family members, they are also among those least likely to have these resources, for several reasons. In market-based, industrialised economies, the primary source of income for all households is market earnings, but children consume, not contribute to, their family's economic resources. At the same time, children make employment more costly for parents because either a potential earner must remain out of the labour force to care for the child or the family must purchase substitute care. By one recent estimate, raising a child costs a family at least $8,775 annually in direct expenditures and forgone adult earnings (Haveman and Wolfe, 1995).

Other factors reduce resources for some families. Poor children are more likely to live in families headed by younger parents who have accumulated less human capital and command lower market wages than older workers. Single parenthood, divorce and/or non-payment of child support constrain the resources of many families. Families' disposable resources can also be limited by exceptional expenditure needs. Families with seriously ill children, for example, spend as much as 15% of their income on direct costs associated with these children, and care for a disabled child has been found to reduce mothers' earning capacity by as much as 24% (Jacobs and McDermott, 1989; Wolfe and Hill, 1995).

Families' ability to accumulate resources also varies for systemic reasons largely outside their control. Some parents face labour market conditions that put employment and earnings at risk (Blank, 1997). Resources also vary because social factors – including gender differences in caregiving responsibilities, and gender and racial discrimination – affect individuals' opportunities and earnings. The impact of childrearing responsibilities on mother's labour market experiences is particularly relevant. Among mothers in the US, for example, employment is 22 percentage points lower among those with young children than among those whose children are older (Gornick et al, 1998). Women also pay a penalty in wages when they become mothers, beyond what can be explained by measurable productivity-related factors (Korenman and Neumark, 1989; Waldfogel, 1997).

Policy packages and comparative research

The central role of family resources in child well-being, and the variety of factors that can limit families' resources, point to opportunities for public intervention. Public policies that directly address resource constraints arising from the presence of children and from systemic and individual factors hold promise for reducing economic hardship in the short term and improving children's well-being in the long term. Other government policies that shape underlying economic or social conditions (eg national or sub-national economic development and trade policies) may indirectly influence families' economic resources as well, although their overarching goals are broader.

Although the appropriate boundaries for government intervention into private markets and families continue to inspire political debate, there is consensus across the industrialised countries that governments should intervene to reduce hardship and deprivation among those in need (George and Wilding, 1985). There is much less consensus, however, about *how* government should intervene. Disagreements about the role of government are particularly sharp in the US and are rife with racial and ethnic cleavages (Quadagno, 1994). These ideological differences, coupled with the decentralised, federalist structure of US policy making, have produced enormous variation in social policy across the states. With the ongoing devolution of public assistance to the states, codified in the 1996 Personal Responsibility Act, state-to-state variation is increasing.

State variation in social policy provides fruitful ground for research. Substantial cross-national comparative research examines policy variation and outcomes across the industrialised welfare states. In contrast, there is relatively little comparative scholarship on social policy variation across the US states. Plotnick observed that "analyses of inter-state poverty and anti-poverty policies are scarce" (1989, p 21); ten years later, this is still largely true. State policy data are now available, but theoretical or methodological work comparable to cross-national comparative scholarship lags.

The observation that cross-state comparative research is under-developed does not imply that researchers have not made use of state-level variation. Those studying public supports to families with children have used cross-state variation, typically in cash public assistance grants, to study the effects of transfers on outcomes such as teen pregnancy, labour market attachment and educational attainment (Mayer, 1997). Others have examined the relationship between state benefits and poverty-related outcomes, including post-transfer poverty rates and gaps, and various measures of poverty reduction (Schram et al, 1988; Plotnick, 1989; Butler, 1996). However, Ragin's characterisation of the comparative method suggests that most of these studies are not fundamentally comparative because they treat policy output (benefit levels) as an explanatory variable without attempting to "compare cases to each other" (1987, p 59). These studies rarely provide detailed information about policy structures or features at the state level and have been limited by their inclusion of a single or small number of policy variables.

Our aim is to begin to fill this gap in the US cross-state literature, with a particular emphasis on the package of policies that enhance families' resources. Cross-state comparative research is especially timely in the wake of the 1996 welfare reform that abolished the federal entitlement to cash assistance and shifted even more responsibility to the states.

A typology of policy packages

Our comparative study begins with a typology of dimensions of the family support policy package, considering both variation in policy mechanisms and variation in characteristics that should increase policy effectiveness.

Policy mechanisms

At least three types of government assistance hold promise for improving poor children's lives by increasing resources available to their families. The top portion of Figure 17.1 illustrates the relationship of these broad categories to their goals and provides examples of relevant programmes.

Cash and near-cash transfers. Government policies can *increase family resources* directly through categorical transfers designed to offset extra costs associated specifically with the care of children, for example by providing child allowances. Alternately, policies can offset income deficits related to individual characteristics such as family composition (eg lone-parent allowances), limited earning capacity (eg wage supplements), or temporary separations from employment (eg maternity benefits or unemployment insurance). While most policies involve public redistribution of resources, government can also promote private transfers. To support families with children, for example, public child support enforcement policies help ensure private transfer of resources from absent to custodial parents.

Tax policies. Tax policies are also an important tool to enhance family resources. State tax systems embody government choices about who will be taxed and how heavily, through both tax rates and the form of taxation. Sales taxes, for instance, fall more heavily on households with lower incomes and higher proportions of non-elective expenses and so penalise families with children. In income tax policy, exemptions, deductions and credits based on factors such as the presence of children, earnings levels, and childcare expenses will disproportionately benefit families with children by reducing their tax burden. Tax credits, if refundable, can increase families' resources even more directly.

Non-cash transfers and services. Non-cash benefits can increase families' resources through several means. One role of non-cash transfers or services

Figure 17.1: Typology of policy packages: policy mechanisms and policy characteristics

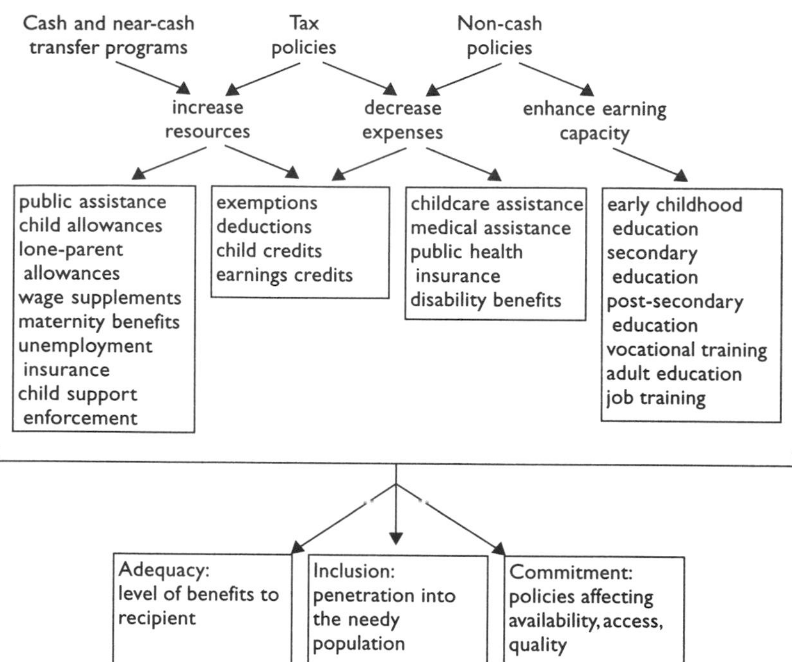

is to *reduce expenses*. Public health insurance or care reduces the financial burden of medical care; childcare assistance reduces the cost of non-parental care for children; disability benefits offset extra medical and related expenses. Non-cash transfers or services may also increase family resources by *enhancing parents' earning capacity*. Some public services aim to change parental characteristics in order to increase parents' ability to earn. These include public programmes for early education, secondary and post-secondary education and vocational training, all of which are assumed to contribute to human capital and earning potential. Specialised services for disadvantaged adults, such as adult basic education or job clubs, are designed to reduce educational or motivational deficits that may constrain earning capacity. At a point in time, early education programmes may have an immediate impact on families' resources by reducing the cost of substitute care for employed parents. Other human capital enhancing programmes may have a lagged effect, increasing future earning capacity.

Policy characteristics

Not only *what* government provides but also *how* it provides benefits has implications for families' economic well-being. Benefit eligibility may be defined narrowly or widely, influencing the proportion of the population that qualifies for assistance. Benefit levels and service packages may be stingy or generous, affecting both the level of assistance and the probability that eligible individuals will seek assistance. Programme administrators may engage in active outreach efforts to encourage participation or create organisational hurdles to discourage it. The bottom portion of Figure 17.1 presents three characteristics of particular interest.

Adequacy concerns the level of benefits that participants receive. Among social insurance programmes, adequacy usually means the level of income replacement for those separated from employment by sickness, old age, childbirth or other conditions. Among social assistance or welfare programmes, adequacy is more typically an absolute value in relation to a minimum standard of living (eg relative to the US poverty line). When benefits are provided as tax relief or non-cash services, adequacy is more difficult to measure because the service is likely to be valued differently, depending on the measure. The measure might be the per recipient cost to government to provide the relief or in-kind benefit, the cost of a similar service obtained through private markets, or the actual value to the recipient. Whatever the measure, the adequacy of benefits will depend on the interaction of programme rules with characteristics of participants, such as family size, prior earnings and actual duration of receipt.

Inclusion concerns the penetration of benefits into the potentially eligible population. It measures the extent of government assistance within the population and the level of security available to vulnerable populations. Actual inclusion will reflect the interaction of government policies, including rules and restrictions on entry and exit, the size of the potentially eligible population and the behavioural response of eligible persons (ie take-up rates). Factors in the local administration of programmes – from the convenience of the local offices to the quality of the interaction between staff and applicants – also affect programme participation by encouraging (or discouraging) take-up among those eligible.

Commitment reflects government choices about the range and quality of assistance. Before adopting rules about benefit levels and eligibility, governments must first elect whether or not to provide benefits at all. In addition, in many programme areas governments decide about the quantity and quality of services to provide, the behavioural or other obligations to impose on participants, and the conditions under which benefits may be forfeited or terminated. These choices affect both benefit adequacy and programme inclusiveness; they also provide important, additional information about states' commitment to increasing the availability, accessibility and quality of programmes.

Data, measurement and analytic methods

Our study of US family support policy capitalises on cross-state variation in the types and characteristics of programmes offered and in commitment to support families via these mechanisms. We use multiple sources of data to measure this variation and then standardise our measures to provide comparable units. Finally, we use cluster analysis to reveal patterns, or state clusters, in the state-to-state variation.

Data selection

We select measures based on our typology, above, and on several theoretical and practical criteria. First, we select programmes and policies that we expect to affect families' resources by increasing income, by decreasing non-elective expenses, or by increasing earnings or earnings potential. Because of the cross-sectional nature of the study, we include only those human capital programmes designed to have immediate effects on the employment or earnings of disadvantaged workers and not other programmes, such as higher education, that have longer-term implications for parents' earnings. Because we are interested in family-level assistance, we do not include a variety of demand-side labour market and economic development policies that may also contribute to parents' earnings by improving employment opportunities.

Second, we select programmes that have a significant *public* component. In most cases, we consider programmes that are fully public, in both financing and delivery. We do not include policies and services that are controlled largely through private mechanisms, such as fringe benefit packages and private childcare.

Third, we concentrate on policies that vary across the states. Some purely federal programmes, such as the Survivors Insurance component of Old Age, Survivors and Disability Insurance, may benefit families with children, but we do not expect to observe substantial variation in these programmes at the state level. We do include programmes, such as Food Stamps and the Supplementary Security Income (SSI) programme, for which the bulk of policy is determined at the federal level but state-level administration has been found to introduce sub-national variation. We also include programmes, such as the Aid to Families with Dependent Children (AFDC) now Temporary Assistance for Needy Families public assistance programme, that are federal-state partnerships in which states dominate policy choices. Still others, such as pre-school, represent state initiatives. In some states, many of these also have substantial sub-state variation. We do not include, however, programmes such as General Assistance or child welfare programmes that are primarily controlled at the local level.

Finally, we concentrate on programmes and policy characteristics for which there are reliable, comparable data across the states in 1994. Some programmes, such as AFDC, have since been substantially or wholly replaced by other programmes. Others, such as Medicaid, have been supplemented in important ways. We expect this analysis to paint an initial portrait of state-level social policy variation and to serve as a baseline for assessing the future direction and impact of these changes.

Data collection, measurement and standardisation

To analyse similarities and differences in the package of policies that states provided in 1994, we created a data set of policy variables across 11 programmatic areas: public assistance (AFDC), childcare (Title IV-A and Child Care and Development Block Grant), child support (enforcement), food assistance (Food Stamps), health insurance (Medicaid), vocational training (JTPA), remedial training (JOBS), early childhood education (state-initiated pre-school), disability assistance (SSI), tax policy (tax deductions, exemptions, credits), and unemployment compensation (Unemployment Insurance).

Administrative data on programme characteristics come from a variety of published sources[1], including the Urban Institute's *New Federalism State Database*, the *Overview of Entitlement Programs (Green Book)* published by the US House of Representatives, and reports and databases available from the US Department of Health and Human Services. Data on policy characteristics come from other public sources including, among many others, the National Governors' Association, the Children's Defense Fund, and the Center on Budget and Policy Priorities. Additional data on states' economic, fiscal, and demographic characteristics come from the Urban Institute and the US Department of Commerce's Bureau of Economic Analysis. Population figures (used principally as denominators in measures of inclusion) and poverty measures were calculated using Current Population Survey data[2]. Data were originally collected on all 50 states and the District of Columbia. Three were excluded from our final analyses due to missing data (District of Columbia) and extreme values (Alaska and Hawaii).

For each of the 11 programme areas, we construct three measures for each of the 48 states. The first set of measures provides an indicator of *adequacy*, or the generosity of benefits received by programme participants. In most programme areas, we calculate adequacy by dividing total annual spending (federal and/or state as appropriate) by the average or total caseload. A common problem in the comparison of the cash value of social welfare benefits is the potential non-comparability of benefits across geographic regions that vary in the cost of living. We partially adjust for differences in cost of living by reporting selected adequacy measures using a state-level cost of living adjustment based on housing costs.

Second, we measure *inclusion*, the extent to which benefits appear to reach needy populations. For these measures we calculate the ratio of the number of actual recipients to the number of potentially needy individuals (or families) or, when possible, to the number of eligible individuals. For most means-tested programmes, the denominator for the inclusion variable is the number of individuals (or families) with pre-transfer incomes below poverty, ie the poverty population *before* considering government cash aid. Note that for some programmes this will provide an *indicator of those served relative to those who may be in need*, not the share of the technically eligible population that is served.

The third set of measures captures *state commitment* in the form of specific policy choices that affect the availability, the accessibility, or the extent of government assistance for families. To operationalise this set of measures, we create commitment scores for nine of the 11 programmes[3]. We identify key policy choices for each programme area and code them to reflect the level of state commitment to helping families secure and retain resources. For example, the AFDC commitment variable is comprised of rules that affect families' ability to obtain and retain benefits and the extent of those benefits: whether the state had a time limit, family cap, or sanctions for programme non-compliance, whether the state had increased earnings disregards, the number of other behaviour-dictating policies adopted by the state, and the maximum benefit for a family of three. In the area of tax policy, to take another example, the state commitment variables measure the impact of tax rules on the poor: the progressivity of the state income tax rates, whether the state had an earned income tax credit, the structure and burden of the state sales tax, and the ratio of federal Earned Income Tax Credit (EITC) recipients to the number of poor, working-aged adults in the state.

The resulting 31 dimensions of policy effort were initially measured in noncomparable units. In order to use these raw variables in our analysis, we transformed the underlying data (to minimise skew) and converted them to comparable units (z-scores).

Cluster analysis

We have argued that no single programme captures the full extent of public support for families, and that no single dimension of policy variation adequately reflects either state policy choices or families' access to support programmes. By measuring multiple elements of policy variation across multiple programmes, we hope to improve the richness, precision and validity of our results. At the same time, such measurement creates a bewildering number of dimensions on which states may be compared. To make sense of this information and take advantage of cross-state variation, we use cluster analysis methods to discover groups of states that appear similar after considering all available data.

Cluster analysis is a "multivariate statistical procedure that starts with a data set containing information about a sample of entities and attempts to reorganize these entities into relatively homogenous groups" (Aldenderfer and Blashfield, 1984, p 7). Cluster analysis has the advantage of providing a parsimonious reduction of complex data, using information on multiple dimensions. Since the cluster method groups observations on the basis of variation across these multiple dimensions simultaneously, the result is automatically weighted to reflect those dimensions in which variation is greatest (UK Department of the Environment, 1995).

Findings

Variation in state policies that support families with children

Table 17.1 illustrates enormous variation in family support policies across the states.

Adequacy. Across the states, average expenditures per participant varied greatly by programme and, more importantly, within programmes. Variation in benefit adequacy was lowest in those programmes – SSI and Food Stamps – that are largely controlled by federal rules. In the federal-

Table 17.1: Variable statistics

	Mean	Standard deviation	Minimum	Maximum
Adequacy: ratio of annualised expenditures to participants				
AFDC	$3,714	$1,211	$1,436	$6,397
Childcare	531	294	73	1,359
Child support	465	122	203	719
Food stamps	1,991	172	1,550	2,316
JOBS	2,176	219	166	8,066
JTPA	4,388	1,207	1,633	7,455
Medicaid	1,059	274	236	1,972
Pre-school	1,350	1,579	0	5,435
SSI	4,940	296	4,531	5,870
Taxes[a]	35	160	-596	307
UI	2,484	743	1,485	4,410
Inclusion: ratio of program participants to potentially needy				
AFDC	57.9%	16.3%	23.8%	92.8%
Childcare	9.4	4.3	2.6	21.5
Child support	30.2	12.6	9.9	66.8
Food stamps	82.8	13.4	51.5	119.4
JOBS	10.7	6.5	2.9	32.7
JTPA	1.3	0.6	0.6	3.6
Medicaid	77.1	16.6	39.7	131.3
Pre-school	7.2	4.7	1.0	19.9
SSI	4.3	1.3	1.9	7.9
UI	33.1	10.0	18.0	56.0
Commitment: index of state policy choices[b]				
AFDC (6)	3.31	0.56	1.70	4.88
Childcare (6)	2.52	0.79	1.11	4.20
Child support (2)	0.92	0.35	0.23	1.74
JOBS (2)	1.41	0.41	0.25	2.35
Medicaid (4)	0.87	0.48	0.01	1.63
Pre-school (2)	2.61	1.35	0.00	4.00
SSI (4)	2.89	0.88	1.06	4.73
Taxes (6)	1.95	0.73	0.28	3.72
UI (5)				

Notes:

[a] The values in this exhibit refer to the amount in taxes that a one-parent family of three pays at the poverty line. Tax inclusion (not shown in middle panel above) is the threshold at which a family starts to pay income tax. This relates to the other programmes' inclusion measures in that it indicates the extent to which a state excludes poor families from paying taxes, or, inversely, how much of the population is 'included' as non-income-taxed. Among the 40 states with an income tax, the lowest threshold was $3,000 and the highest $22,600. The mean threshold was $11,433 and the standard deviation $4,910.

[b] The number in parentheses following each programme represents the number of components (maximum points) that comprise each commitment score.

state partnership programmes, where states have more control over policy rules, annual benefits expenditures per participant differed by as much as $4,931 (for AFDC) to $1,736 (for Medicaid) between the highest- and lowest-spending states. In the areas of childcare and pre-school, modest average expenditures at the national level mask huge variations at the state level. In pre-school provision, states ranged from over $5,000 per enrolled child to zero (in states with no state-initiated pre-school programmes); in childcare, states spent from $73 to $1,359 per poor child under age six.

Inclusion. Variation across states was even more dramatic on measures of inclusion. Unlike expenditure levels, inclusion varied widely even for the federally managed programmes, suggesting large differences in programme administration at the state level. In the least inclusive states, for example, the ratio of children receiving Medicaid to those in pre-transfer poor families was only 40%. The ratio of families with children receiving Food Stamps to pre-transfer poor families with children was barely one half, and the ratio of AFDC recipients to pre-transfer poor families was about one quarter. In contrast, in the most inclusive states the ratio of participants to the pre-transfer poor was 100% or more in Food Stamps and Medicaid. In early care for children, the ratio of children served to all children potentially in need ranged from as low as 1% to as high as 20%. Unemployment Insurance was nearly as variable, with a ratio of recipients to the unemployed that varied from 18% to 56%. Variation was also high for the JOBS programme, in which states enrolled as few as 14% to as many as 33% of AFDC recipients.

Commitment. Commitment indices are comparable in capturing effort, but each is unique with respect to the specific state choices it includes. For the Medicaid programme, for instance, measures of state commitment reflect state choices about both whom they would serve and the types of services they would provide. In the lowest scoring state, all children under age six in families up to 133% of the poverty line were eligible for Medicaid. This state offered only 15 optional Medicaid services, the least of any state. Regarding two of the most important optional services, this state did not offer dental services at all, and it offered prescription drug assistance to restricted populations only. The highest scoring state elected to provide 27 of the optional Medicaid services (including both dental and prescription drug services, though with restrictions). Eligibility thresholds helped place this state above all others; children under age six were eligible for Medicaid up to 225% of the poverty line in 1994.

In the area of tax policy, to take a second example, our measures of state commitment relate to the progressivity of the state tax structure. In the least supportive state, there was no income tax and therefore also no earned income credit to support working families with children. This may help explain why the ratio of federal EITC recipients to poor working-aged adults (75%) was below the national average (77%). In place of an income tax, which can be designed to exempt lower earners, this state relied on a 6% sales tax and had the second highest sales tax burden, consuming an estimated 11.2% of the incomes of families in the lowest quintile. In contrast, the state that scored as most supportive had a progressive income tax code, one in which multiple rates increased with income and one in which people at the poverty line paid little. Although it did not offer a state EITC in 1994, the ratio of federal EITC claimants to poor working-aged adults was more than 90%. Importantly, this state had no sales tax. The other four states that scored especially high are characterised by progressive income tax structures and no sales tax on food; three of them also offered state EITCs, two of which were refundable.

State policy clusters

While multiple measures capture the complexity of the family support package, it is difficult to discern patterns across so many dimensions. In Figure 17.2 we present the results of a cluster analysis that uses the state-level variation in the 31 policy dimensions to group the states into five clusters. Clusters in which the states' mean score is 0.4 or more of a standard deviation *above* the average for *all* states are coded as having a 'high' score. Clusters in which states' mean score is 0.4 or more of a standard deviation *below* the average for *all* states are coded as 'low' performers. At this cut-off point, given a normal distribution, we would expect the high and low tails each to capture about one third of all observations. Since cluster analysis sorts observations (states) on the basis of variation in measures (policy dimensions), the actual distribution – and proportion of clusters coded as low, average or high – varies for each dimension (programme and characteristic).

Variation is clearly evident across the five clusters in terms of policy mechanisms (cash versus non-cash), policy characteristics (adequacy, inclusion, commitment), and policy emphases (eg traditional public assistance versus employment-related programmes).

Minimal support. States in cluster 1 (Alabama, Arkansas, Kentucky, Louisiana, Mississippi, South Carolina, Tennessee, Texas, West Virginia)

Table 17.2: State policy clusters

Cluster	Programme area	Food stamps	SSI	AFDC	UI	Child support	Taxes	Medicaid	Child care	Pre-school	JTPA	JOBS
	Adequacy			L	L				L			H
1	Inclusion		H	L	L				L			L
	Commitment		L	L	L	L	L	L	L			
	Adequacy				L							
2	Inclusion	H			L	L					L	L
	Commitment			L	L			L		H		L
	Adequacy		L		L				L	L		L
3	Inclusion	L		L	L			L		L		H
	Commitment			H								H
	Adequacy	L	H	H	H							
4	Inclusion			H	H							
	Commitment		H		H							
	Adequacy	L	H	H	H		H		H		L	
5	Inclusion	H		H		H				H	H	
	Commitment		H		H		H	H		H		H

H — High = +0.4 stdev
Average = +/– lt 0.4 stdev
L — Low = –0.4 stdev
Not applicable

1 = Minimal support: AL, AR, KY, LA, MS, SC, TN, TX, WV
2 = Limited support: AZ, DE, FL, GA, MO, NC, NM, NV, OK, VA
3 = Conservative support: ID, IN, KS, MT, ND, NE, SD, UT, WY
4 = Generous support: CA, CO, CT, IA, IL, MA, ME, MI, NY, OR, PA, RI, WA
5 = Integrated support: MD, MN, NH, NJ, OH, VT, WI

Source: From authors' analysis

are below the national average on nearly one half of our policy dimensions. The mean score for these states is below our cut-off point on all dimensions of AFDC, on all dimensions of Unemployment Insurance, and on all dimensions of childcare. Notably, Cluster 1 is low on seven of the nine measures of state commitment. The nine states in this cluster provide the minimum in public support to families in terms of both benefit adequacy and inclusion. This pattern holds true across cash and non-cash programmes and across programmes that provide traditional public assistance as well as those that are more employment-related. Not surprisingly, these states are also characterised by restrictive policy choices that impose many eligibility requirements and provide a relatively small array of benefits.

Limited support. The ten states in Cluster 2 (Arizona, Delaware, Florida, Georgia, Missouri, North Carolina, New Mexico, Nevada, Oklahoma, Virginia) have low scores on about one third of the policy dimensions. Lower scores are concentrated in policy areas related to employment and non-welfare forms of economic security, including Unemployment Insurance, child support enforcement, JTPA and JOBS. The exception to this pattern is in the area of early care for children (childcare and pre-school), in which the states have scores at or above the national average. The states in this cluster are not, on average, exceptionally low in benefit adequacy, but they have low inclusion scores in four of the 11 programmes and low state commitment scores in another four. The states in this cluster provide at least a minimal safety net for families, particularly in terms of benefit adequacy and care for children, but they do little more than the minimum to extend benefits to needy families or to adopt policies that improve the quality or availability of support.

Conservative support. The nine states in Cluster 3 (Idaho, Indiana, Kansas, Montana, North Dakota, Nebraska, South Dakota, Utah, Wyoming) also score below the national average on about one third of the dimensions. In this cluster, low and average scores are spread evenly across the cash and non-cash programmes and across programmes that use traditional public assistance and those that use employment-related approaches. The concentration of low scores in care for children – in childcare, pre-school and Medicaid – is notable. In contrast, the states in this cluster have average or even above average scores on programmes that encourage private family responsibility for economic well-being – child support enforcement, JTPA and JOBS in particular. In general, the states in this cluster have low average scores primarily on benefit adequacy and inclusion; scores are near average on most areas of state commitment, with two above our cut-off. Cluster 3 therefore appears to provide conservative support; it falls below the national average in many areas of cash assistance and slightly above average in the programmes that encourage or enforce self-reliance.

Generous support. The 13 states in Cluster 4 (California, Colorado, Connecticut, Iowa, Illinois, Massachusetts, Maine, Michigan, New York, Oregon, Pennsylvania, Rhode Island, Washington) have high average scores on about one third of the policy dimensions and a low average score on only one. High scores in this cluster are especially evident in the cash assistance programmes, including SSI, AFDC and Unemployment Insurance. Scores above the national average are also concentrated in the dimension of benefit adequacy. Given high benefit levels and extensive cash assistance, these states are characterised as providing generous family support within the traditional cash transfer approaches, with less expansive support evident in the non-cash and employment-related arenas.

Integrated support. Finally, the seven states in Cluster 5 (Maryland, Minnesota, New Hampshire, New Jersey, Ohio, Vermont, Wisconsin) provide the most extensive support to families. Policies in these states are highly supportive in nearly all the programme areas: cash transfers and non-cash services, traditional public assistance programmes and employment-related policies. Higher than average scores are particularly evident in programme participation, none of the cluster's average inclusion scores is lower than the national average, and scores are higher than average in five of the eleven programme areas. Notably, the states in this cluster had scores well above the national mean on six of nine state commitment measures, suggesting that they were more likely than other states to have taken active steps to expand or enhance support for families. Although Cluster 5 states do not offer the highest benefits, they do the most overall to assist families in terms of public assistance and non-welfare support.

The family support package

Our analyses demonstrate that states vary widely in the extent and nature of support that they provide to families. To show in more concrete terms what state differences mean to families, Table 17.2 illustrates the average benefit package provided as of 1994 in each of the five clusters. Because benefits measured in dollars correspond to varying levels of purchasing power across the states, we also report mean benefit levels adjusted for the cost of housing, a major expenditure in most household budgets.

A poor family of three living in a state in the *Minimal support* cluster received an average of $1,991 per year in AFDC benefits. The ratio of AFDC recipients to poor families was 42%, and the ratio of children receiving Medicaid to poor children averaged 70%. Child support collections were made on behalf of 25% of one-parent families. Among families receiving AFDC, about 8% were in the JOBS programme. The ratio of Unemployment Insurance recipients to the unemployed was just over one quarter, and the average benefit was $1,957. Families with $13,011 in income began paying state income taxes, and for a family with income at the poverty line, taxes averaged $97.

For a similar family living in a state in the *Limited support* cluster, both the levels of AFDC benefits and the availability of those benefits were much higher. The ratio of AFDC recipients to poor families was nearly 60% and annual benefits were $3,284. The ratio of Medicaid recipients to poor children was over 80%. In other programme areas, such as Unemployment Insurance and child support, the policy package for these families was as meagre as that provided in the *Minimal support* cluster.

A different package of support was available to families in the *Conservative support* cluster. Rates of inclusion were not substantially different from those in the *Minimal support* cluster, although families received a higher AFDC benefit of $3,623 per year. Differences were more striking in programmes promoting family responsibility. Of families receiving AFDC, nearly 20% were enrolled in JOBS – a rate nearly double that of any other cluster. States collected child support, on average, for 32% of single-parent families. Families began paying taxes on incomes at $13,823, and a family with a poverty-line income paid, on average, about one half the taxes ($53) paid by a family with similar income in the *Minimal support* cluster.

The states in the *Generous support* cluster exhibited a very different pattern. Benefits per recipient in several programmes, including AFDC, Medicaid and Unemployment Insurance, were higher than in any of the other four clusters; measures of inclusion were generally high as well. On some measures, however – such as JOBS enrolment and tax relief for poor families – these states did not distinguish themselves as providing more integrated support than those in the *Conservative support* cluster.

Support was greatest in the *Integrated support* cluster. The ratio of families receiving AFDC to poor families was over 70%, and average benefits were $4,678 annually. The ratio of children covered by Medicaid to poor children was particularly high at 86%. States collected child support on behalf of over 40% of single-parent families. Notably, families with incomes up to $15,900 paid no state income taxes. In this cluster's average state, a

Table 17.4: Selected elements of policy package, by cluster

	Minimal	Limited	Conser-vative	Generous	Integrated	Overall
AFDC adequacy	$1,991	$3,284	$3,623	$4,781	$4,678	$3,714
COL-adjusted	*2,144*	*3,331*	*3,902*	*4,648*	*4,471*	*3,739*
AFDC Inclusion	41.5%	59.4%	44.1%	70.1%	71.1%	58.0%
Medicaid Inclusion	69.6%	83.3%	69.2%	78.2%	86.2%	77.1%
Child Support Inclusion	25.4%	23.6%	32.6%	30.4%	42.5%	30.2%
UI adequacy	$1,957	$2,152	$2,117	$3,134	$2,899	$2,484
COL-adjusted	*2,113*	*2,177*	*2,279*	*3,071*	*2,707*	*2,504*
UI inclusion	28.2%	26.8%	29.6%	41.9%	36.3%	33.1%
JOBS inclusion	7.6%	5.9%	19.2%	10.6%	10.7%	10.7%
Tax threshold	$13,011	$12,810	$13,456	$13,823	$15,900	$13,694
COL-adjusted	*14,098*	*13,123*	*14,484*	*13,145*	*15,382*	*13,896*
Taxes at poverty	$97	$67	$53	$56	–$153	$35
COL-adjusted	*107*	*67*	*55*	*60*	*–150*	*39*

Source: From authors' analysis

family with income at the poverty line paid no income taxes but instead *received a tax credit* of $153.

For each of the adequacy measures reported in Table 17.2, we include our estimate of the mean after adjusting for differences in housing costs at the state level. This cost of living adjustment equalises benefit levels slightly, but variation across the clusters remains very large even after considering variation in state-level purchasing power.

Variation in poverty relative to need

The state clusters identified through our analyses are unambiguously associated with different levels of support. While our five state clusters are constructed on the basis of variation in policy, it is likely that these clusters also vary systematically in ways that could be correlated with the policy indicators. If so, our cluster analysis may pick up some of the variation in related but unmeasured background characteristics. For example, states with more low-income families or a higher cost of living may be forced to provide more extensive social programmes; states with greater fiscal resources may be better positioned to provide these programmes. Initial analysis shows, however, that the variation across

Figure 17.3: Child poverty rates by need and policy support

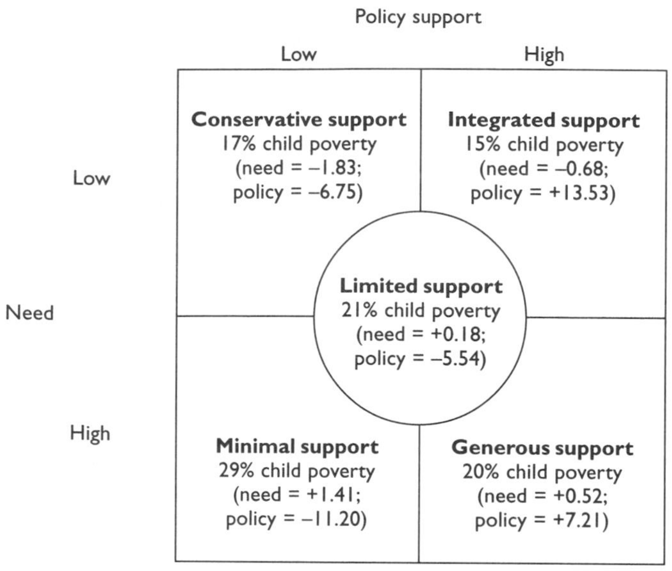

Note: Scores for need and policy support are z-scores of summary indices.
Source: From authors' analysis

clusters is larger than can be accounted for by variation in states' background traits. Future analysis will explore in more depth the relationships between policy, economic conditions and poverty-related outcomes.

Figure 17.3 begins such analysis by exploring the relationship between underlying need, policy supportiveness and child poverty by cluster membership. The measure of need reflects the unemployment rate and the proportion of one-parent families (standardised as z-scores and added). State policy support is measured as the sum of the 31 policy dimensions. This comparison is limited in that variation in the official child poverty rate (based on post-transfer cash income) does not reflect variation in policies – such as childcare and taxes – that affect family resources in other ways. The policy supportiveness measure also is limited because it reduces multiple dimensions of policy to a single, linear dimension.

Despite these limitations, the results are provocative. They suggest a consistent story about the link between policy and poverty. Clusters fall into each of the four quadrants of this graphic, representing all possible combinations of high and low support with high and low need. The least advantageous combination is observed in the cluster we have labelled *Minimal support*. This cluster includes the states that had the highest average levels of unemployment and one-parent families, and the states that provided the lowest level of support to families. These states had an average child poverty rate of 29%, the highest rate observed across the five clusters.

A different combination characterises the states in the *Generous support* cluster. The states in this cluster also had average levels of need that were above the national average, but government support was also well above the national average. For states in this cluster, average child poverty was 20%, that is 9 percentage points lower than in states providing only *Minimal support*.

States in the *Conservative support* cluster had average need levels well below the national average; policy support was also low. It is impossible to know from these cross-sectional data how the configuration of the family support package, with relatively low levels of support with an emphasis on family responsibility, relates to the background conditions. In the short-term, we can observe that the combination of the lowest level of need with *Conservative support* is associated with a relatively low 17% rate of child poverty.

Finally, the combination observed for states providing *Integrated support* provides less ambiguous evidence that states can and do adopt policies that may improve economic security for families, even when underlying background conditions are relatively advantageous. Like those in the *Conservative support* cluster, states in the *Integrated support* group had levels of need below the national average. Although need was low, these states adopted the most expansive family support policies in the country. The combination of lower than average need and higher than average support meant that only 15% of children in these states were poor.

Summary and discussion

Cross-national social welfare studies have often characterised the US as a laggard in the development of policies that support children and their families. This cross-state comparative study reveals that, within the US, there is substantial variation in these policies at the sub-national level. Variation is extreme not only on the most obvious dimensions of benefit adequacy, but also on more subtle dimensions of policy structure, not only in programmes managed principally at the state level, but also on some dimensions of programmes, such as Food Stamps, that are primarily federal.

Rather than reducing this variation to a simple measure of how much states spend, we have characterised state-level policies in terms of adequacy, inclusion and commitment on eleven different programmes, each of which can support families by increasing income, reducing expenditures, or improving earning capacity. Together, these dimensions form a package that may influence families' economic well-being.

This multidimensional approach helps reveal the enormous variation and underlying patterns in state-level policy. We describe these patterns in terms of clusters of states that have similar configurations of the policy package. When we array the clusters relative to the level of the underlying problems (need) and the expansiveness of solutions (policy), there is at least initial evidence that the configuration of the policy package is related to child poverty. In the state clusters that had the highest level of need, child poverty rates varied from 29% in those states providing *Minimal support*, to 20% in states that provided *Generous support*. In the state clusters that had lower levels of need, poverty varied from 17% for states in the *Conservative support* cluster to 15% for states that provided *Integrated support*. We draw two tentative conclusions from this result: first, that the configuration of the family support package is only weakly linked to underlying need or demand; and second, that the expansiveness of this package is associated with lower levels of poverty in clusters of states with both high and low levels of need.

This analysis suggests directions for future research. Our portrait of family policy packages in the US states is painted as of 1994. Since that time, states have assumed even greater responsibility for social welfare policies, and many programmes have changed in meaningful ways. We hope to extend our comparative study of state policies by considering change over time.

The current analysis also relies on the official federal poverty rate as an outcome indicator. In addition to measurement-related problems, this poverty measure imposes an artificial cut-off point that obscures both the depth of poverty, for those below the line, and the economic insecurity of those just above it. As an indicator of the adequacy of a package of family support policies, the poverty measure also fails to capture important benefits, such as childcare, which increase families' net resources by reducing their child-related expenditures. In future analyses we will use alternative measures of poverty and economic well-being.

Finally, and most fundamentally, our reliance on cross-sectional and state-level data to measure policy variation and economic outcomes limits our ability to establish the causal links among economic, demographic and policy factors. Although there is suggestive evidence in this study that state policies matter, it is far from conclusive. Without better controls for other factors contributing to child poverty, we are unable to isolate the impact of policy or to estimate the magnitude of its effects. We expect to return to these questions in future analyses that use policy variation in multivariate and multi-level models.

Though tentative, the conclusions from this study are optimistic. Inequality in family resources may be inevitable and, in the opinion of some observers, a desirable aspect of modern capitalism. As a growing body of child development research reminds us, however, substantial resource constraints damage children's short- and long-term well-being. While we tolerate some level of inequality, there is no compelling defence for levels of resource inadequacy that force parents to make compromises that harm their children. Cross-state variation suggests that states have the opportunity to adopt policies that may improve children's lives.

Notes

[1] Meyers, Gornick, Peck and Lockshin (1999) provide complete detail on data sources, measurement and methodology.

[2] To obtain sufficient samples at the state level, weighted averages were calculated using the CPS data for the years 1993 to 1995. The authors acknowledge the valuable assistance of Jiali Li and Neil Bennett at the National Center for Children in Poverty for generating state-level population estimates from the CPS for this project.

[3] Two programmes (Food Stamps and JTPA) lack the commitment measures because the policy triggers are predominantly federal, not state.

References

Aldenderfer, M.S., and Blashfield, R.K. (1984) *Cluster analysis*, Beverly Hills, CA: Sage Publications.

Annie E. Casey Foundation (1998) *Kids count data book: State profiles of child well-being*, Baltimore, MD: Annie E. Casey Foundation.

Bennett, N.G., and Li, J. 1998. 'Young child poverty in the States: wide variation and significant change', New York, NY: National Center for Children in Poverty.

Blank, R. (1997) *It takes a nation: A new agenda for fighting poverty*, New York, NY: Russell Sage Foundation; Princeton, NJ: Princeton University Press.

Butler, A.C. (1996) 'The effect of welfare benefit levels on poverty among single-parent families', *Social Problems*, vol 43, no 1, pp 94-114.

Federman, M., Garner, T.I., Short, K., Boman Cutter, W., Kiely, J., Levine, D., McGough, D. and McMillen, M. (1996) 'What does it mean to be poor in America?', *Monthly Labor Review*, May, pp 3-17.

George, V. and Wilding, P. (1985) *Ideology and social welfare*, London: Routledge and Kegan Paul.

Gornick, J.C., Meyers, M.K. and Ross, K.E. (1998) 'Public policies and the employment of mothers: a cross-national study', *Social Science Quarterly*, vol 79, no 1, pp 35-54.

Haveman, R. and Wolfe, B. (1995) 'The determinants of children's attainments: a review of methods and findings', *Journal of Economic Literature*, vol 33, pp 1829-78.

Jacobs, P. and McDermott, S. (1989) 'Family caregiver costs of chronically ill and handicapped children: method and literature review', *Public Health Reports*, vol 104, no 2, pp 158-63.

Korenman, S., and Neumark, D. (1989) 'Marriage, motherhood, and wages', *The Journal of Human Resources*, vol 27, pp 233-57.

Lichter, D. (1997) 'Poverty and inequality among children', *Annual Review of Sociology*, vol 23, pp 121-45.

Mayer, S. (1997) *What money can't buy: Family income and children's life chances*, Cambridge, MA: Harvard University Press.

McLoyd, V.C. and Wilson, L. (1991) 'The strain of living poor: parenting, social support, and child mental health', in A.C. Houston (ed) *Children in poverty*, pp 105-35, Cambridge, MA: Cambridge University Press.

McNeil, J. (1993). 'Americans with disabilities 1991-92', *Current Population Reports*, P70-33.

Meyers, M.K., Gornick, J.C., Peck, L.R. and Lockshin, A.J. (1999) *Public policies that support families with young children: Variation across the US States*, New York, NY: Columbia University.

Newacheck, P., Jameson, W. and Halfon, N. (1994) 'Health status and income: the impact of poverty on child health', *Journal of School Health*, vol 64, pp 229-33.

Plotnick, R. (1989) 'How much poverty is reduced by state income transfers?', *Monthly Labor Review*, vol 112, pp 21-26.

Quadagno, J.S. (1994) *The color of welfare: How racism undermined the war on poverty*, New York, NY: Oxford University Press.

Ragin, C. (1987) *The comparative method: Moving beyond qualitative and quantitative strategies*, Berkeley, CA: University of California Press.

Schram, S.F., Turbett, J.P. and Wilken, P.H. (1988) 'Child poverty and welfare benefits: a reassessment with state data of the claim that American welfare breeds dependence', *The American Journal of Economics and Sociology*, vol 47, pp 409-22.

Smith, J.R., Brooks-Gunn, J. and Klebanov, P.K. (1997) 'Consequences of living in poverty for young children's cognitive and verbal ability and early school achievement', in G.J. Duncan and J. Brooks-Gunn (eds) *Consequences of growing up poor*, New York, NY: Russell Sage Foundation.

UK Department of the Environment (1995) *1991 Deprivation Index: A review of approaches and a matrix of results*, London: The Stationery Office.

Waldfogel, J. (1997) 'The effect of children on women's wages', *American Sociological Review*, vol 62, pp 209-17.

Wolfe, B.L. and Hill, S.C. (1995) 'The effect of health on the work effort of single working mothers', *The Journal of Human Resources*, vol 30, p 1, pp 42-62.

Zill, N., Moore, K.A., Smith, E.W., Steif, T. and Coiro, M.J. (1994) *Circumstances and development of children in welfare families: A profile based on national survey data*, Washington, DC: Child Trends.

EIGHTEEN

Income transfers and support for mothers' employment: the link to family poverty risks[1]

Cristina Solera

Introduction

Over the last decades major economic and sociodemographic changes have shaken the Fordist order, creating new risks and new needs. On the sociodemographic side, the increase in women's participation in the labour market, together with the rise of divorces and out-of-wedlock births has made the 'male breadwinner family' no longer pre-eminent. On the economic side, the emergence of skill-intensive technological change and deindustrialisation have reduced the demand for lower-skilled workers, contributing to an increase in structural unemployment and in inequality in the distribution of wages and earnings (Danziger et al, 1995; OECD, 1994, 1995). In other words, the ability of the male breadwinner to maintain the whole family has been weakened. As a consequence of these changes, the risk of poverty has increasingly threatened the working-age population, and in turn, children. Particularly vulnerable are children living in families headed by single mothers and those headed by two adults with limited job skills (Palmer et al, 1988; McFate et al, 1995).

Despite the fact that these economic and demographic changes have affected in a similar way all advanced countries, leading to a common set of risks, poverty among two-parent and one-parent families varies considerably. This variation raises questions about the role of public policies, particularly of social sciences. How have the different countries respponded to these new family poverty risks in the area of social policy? Which dimensions and types of social policy are more effective in facing these risks? In the political and scientific debate the attention has been traditionally placed on income transfers. As Gornick et al point out (1997), much less appreciated is the anti-poverty role of policies that support mothers' employment. Yet, evidence shows that the well-being of families is strongly connected with the position of mothers in the labour market. Everywhere two-earner couples with children and one-parent working families are less likely to be poor compared to single-earner couples and lone mothers on social assistance (Förster, 1994). Indeed mothers' earnings are an important shelter from poverty. First, given the rise in unemployment and the rising inequality in earnings' distribution, mothers' earnings have become relevant in case of fathers' unemployment or low wages[2]. Second, mothers' earnings are extremely important as 'divorce insurance'. The post-divorce poverty risk for women and children depends largely on their previous economic dependence on husbands (Sörensen, 1994). Because of the prevalent gender division of labour and responsibilities within the marriage, in the absence of suitable out-of-home childcare options, a mother may choose not to work or to work in a more flexible but less protected sector (as in the informal sector in Spain and Italy or part-time jobs in private services in the UK). The longer the time spent by mothers outside the labour market or in 'weak' sectors, the more difficult it is for them to enter it or to find better jobs. Indeed, low labour-market attachment and commitment cause human capital depreciation. Hence, mothers who after divorce wish or need to work or improve their position are constrained by their past investment in marriage. Moreover, becoming the only adult in the family, their chances in the labour market are constrained by their present need to balance work and caring responsibilities.

Following the suggestion of Gornick et al (1997) in this chapter I analyse the anti-poverty effectiveness of different welfare states by focusing on both income transfers and social policies supporting maternal employment. Specifically, I compare three countries belonging to distinct welfare regimes: Sweden, the prototype of the universal social democratic model; Italy, with its conservative and familial welfare state, and the liberal UK (Esping-Andersen, 1990, 1999; Forssén, 1998; Sainsbury, 1994). The analysis refers to the situation in the early 1990s, as do my empirical data.

Method and data

The data

The analysis employs cross-sectional data from the Luxembourg Income Study (LIS) database. The LIS database consists of a set of national household surveys that include similar social and economic indicators from a number of industrial nations. Although the various national data sets are not strictly and completely comparable, they do allow for reliable cross-national research on economic well-being (Buhmann et al, 1988; Smeeding et al, 1990). In this work I employ the LIS data for Italy, UK and Sweden that refer to the early 1990s. More precisely, data for the UK are from the 1991 Family Expenditure Survey; data for Sweden are from the 1992 Swedish Income Distribution Survey; data for Italy are from the 1991 Bank of Italy Survey of Household Incomes and Wealth. Because of lack of information on important public transfers, I have integrated the original LIS data for Italy with a microsimulation model of Italian personal income taxes, social security contributions and family allowances (ITAXMOD), worked out at the Instituto di Studi per la Programmazione Econmica (ISPE) (see Di Biase et al, 1995). In this way, it is also possible to produce a meaningful estimate of the anti-poverty effectiveness of Italy's income transfer system[3].

Defining an anti-poverty 'family benefit package'

Income transfers

As widely documented (see Mitchell, 1991; Rainwater and Smeeding, 1995), income transfers play an important role in reducing market-based poverty. There are four mechanisms by which the state can allocate income to individuals or households (Atkinson, 1989). The first is the universal or contingency benefit allocated to all citizens within a certain social category, regardless of employment status or income. Second, there is social insurance, where the benefit is related to the employment status and the contributions paid. The third comprises social assistance that is means-tested, or income-related benefits. The fourth is the indirect transfer through the tax system. In this study all income transfer types are taken into account[4]. Indeed, families with children may qualify for benefits in different ways: either as a right of parenthood (child benefit), due to employment status and previous contribution (eg unemployment benefit

Table 18.1: Income transfer programmes for families with children in Italy, the UK and Sweden (early 1990s)

	Italy	UK	Sweden
Universal programmes	Tax credit for children	Child benefit One-parent benefit	Child benefit Advance maintenance payment
Social insurance programmes	Earnings complement (CIG) Mobility allowance Unemployment benefit	Unemployment benefit	Unemployment insurance and cash labour market assistance
Social Assistance[a]			
General	Vital minimum at local level	Income support	Socialbidrag
Categorical	Family allowances	Family credit	
Housing assistance		Housing benefit	Housing benefit

[a] The means-tested programmes are subdivided in three subgroups following Gough et al (1997).
Source: Bradshaw et al (1996a, 1996b); European Obsevatory on National Family Policies (1992); MISSOC (1991)

and parental leave), or because they are otherwise destitute ('safety net' programmes). Table 18.1 presents programmes relevant to families with children in Italy, the UK and Sweden according to the above distinctions. A brief description of the programmes will be provided in the next section. As already mentioned, this account refers to the situation in 1991-92, as do the empirical data.

Policies supporting maternal employment

Earnings may not be sufficient to ensure a non-poverty standard of living for many children, not only in one-earner families but even in two-earner couples, particularly when the parents are young and with little human capital (Danziger et al, 1995). Public cash transfers are, thus, necessary to supplement market incomes. The public support of childcare costs is also very important. Indeed, childcare costs play a crucial role in two ways. First, the lower the cost of children, the higher the final family income (that is, the lower the risk of poverty). Second, the cost and availability of childcare influence maternal labour supply. Particularly in the case of pre-school children and of low paid mothers, the net return from work may be low or even negative once childcare and work related costs are taken into account[5] (Gornick et al, 1997). This is especially the case for single mothers when, if childcare services are expensive and if the father fails to provide cash and/or in-kind support and the state does not intervene to compensate this failure, working may not pay off (Danziger et al, 1995; Hauser and Fisher, 1990; Saraceno, 1996a; Zanatta, 1996).

The relationship between maternal employment and childcare policies is not linear. Indeed, many factors affect levels of women's employment, such as the gender culture, the general economic condition and the occupational structure. Yet, many studies show that having more affordable childcare increases maternal labour supply (Esping Andersen, 1999; Fagnani, 1996; Gustafsson, 1995b; Leibowitz et al, 1992). Therefore, it reduces poverty risk for families with children. Other policies also influence maternal labour supply, most importantly: (a) parental leave and work-time flexibility for parents[6]; (b) income transfers rules, especially those that determine benefit reductions associated with individual or family income (the 'poverty trap' problem); (c) marginal tax rates and the tax treatment of spouses; (d) public policies that encourage part-time work, for example through the adoption of worker protection or through substantial demand for part-time workers in public employment (Gornick et al, 1997). In this chapter the focus is on social policies, thus (c) and (d) have been excluded from the analysis. Moreover, attention is placed on the support for the employment of mothers with pre-school children[7].

Measuring poverty and welfare state effectiveness

There are various approaches to measuring poverty. Here I define as 'poor' a household in which the income is less than 50% of the median adjusted household income of non-elderly households in the country of residence[8]. Incomes are adjusted for family size by using an equivalence elasticity of 0.55[9]. As an indicator of poverty I use income because the concern is for the capacities of families to participate in the mainstream of their society rather then on their actual spending behaviour (Förster, 1993). Since I focus on the anti-poverty effectiveness of social policies, I use two income measures. *Market, or pre-transfer*[10] *income*, includes all forms of earnings (wages, salaries and self-employment income) plus capital income, occupational pension benefits, and private transfers such as child support. *Post-transfer income* is the *disposable income* of the family and includes all forms of regular cash and near cash income (family allowances, unemployment compensation, etc) net of direct taxes (income and payroll taxes). Hence, the difference between 'pre-transfer income' and 'post-transfer' household income is attributed to government policies. More precisely, the effectiveness of an income transfer system is measured as the proportional reduction of pre-transfer income, that is (pre-post/pre)[11] (Mitchell, 1991).

The anti-poverty effect of public income transfers

Poverty rates among two-parent and one-parent families vary considerably across Sweden, Italy and the UK (Figure 18.1). In Sweden poverty rates for both types of families are extremely low compared to Italy and the UK. In the UK both two-parent and one-parent families face a relatively high risk of poverty, but the situation is dramatic for one-parent families; 57% of them are poor against 14% of British two-parent families and against 4% and 17% of Swedish and Italian one-parent families, respectively.

What is the impact of tax and direct cash-transfer policies on family poverty?

The Swedish income transfer system is more effective in reducing poverty among families with children; 84% of market-based poor families are lifted out of poverty, leaving an overall post-tax and transfer poverty rate of less than 3%. The anti-poverty effect of transfers is high for both family types, but particularly high for one-parent families with a poverty reduction rate of 88%. The result is that there is nearly no difference in the post-transfer poverty rates of one- and two-parent families (Table 18.2). Why has there been such a 'success' in Sweden? Swedish families with children benefit from various and generous cash benefits, mainly universal, aimed at integrating earnings (cf Table 18.1). *Child allowance*, a cornerstone of the Swedish welfare state, is a non-taxable transfer in respect of all children aged less than 16 years[12], irrespective of income and employment status of the parents. The amount is relatively generous; the one-child allowance is about 6% of the median equivalent disposable income for the country (Solera, 1998). In recognition of the heavier economic burdens of families with several children, since 1982 the government has introduced increments for the third and subsequent children (Sundström, 1991).

Additionally, all single parents with children under 18 years can receive a tax-free *advance maintenance payment* on application if the non-custodial parent fails to pay the maintenance allowance. As many studies point out (Kahn and Kamerman, 1988; Sörensen, 1994), the lack of economic support

Figure 18.1: Poverty rates for families with children, by family type (early 1990s)

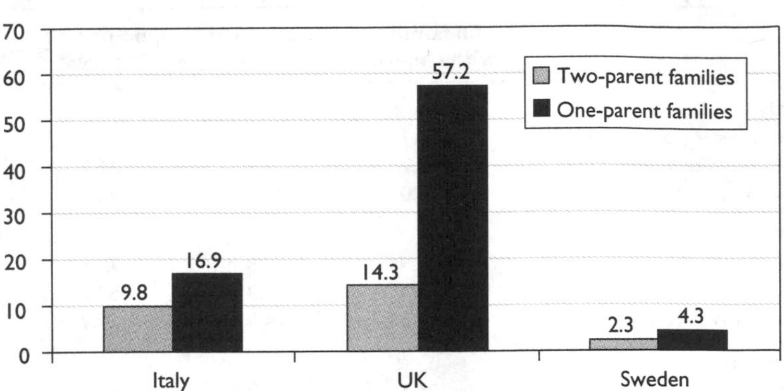

Source: LIS database

from the spouse is a specific risk factor for one-parent families. The Swedish child-support advance system has been explicitly designed to eliminate this risk (Gustafsson, 1995a). Moreover, low-income families with children can obtain a non-taxable monthly *housing allowance*. The size of the allowance depends on family income, number of children and housing costs. Since the income threshold is relatively high, many families with children receive it: 25% of two-parent families and 67% of one-parent families (Solera, 1998). Because the great majority of parents work and can rely on generous universal and social insurance programmes[13], general social assistance plays only a minor role as a temporary source of help (Bradshaw et al, 1996b). However, the minimum income guaranteed is relatively high, around 60% of the national median income (Förster, 1993). This helps to explain the high poverty reduction of the Swedish income transfer system, at the 50% poverty interval but also at the 60% interval (Solera, 1998).

Compared to Sweden, the UK is much less effective in reducing poverty among families with children; only 24% of the pre-transfer poor are lifted out of poverty (Table 18.2). The income transfer system is selective, targeting the most needy, and with a low level of support. Universal transfers and social insurance plans[14] are modest, while means-tested forms of assistance are predominant. The underlying ideology is that, while contributory or taxpayer-financed programmes can place a burden on the economy, create unemployment and discourage work, private provisions can strengthen the economy, enhance incentives to work and

Table 18.2: Income transfer effectiveness for families with children (early 1990s)

	All families with children	Two-parent families[a]	One-parent families[b]
Italy			
Pre-transfer poverty rate	10.1	8.4	22.3
Post-transfer poverty rate	10.7	9.8	16.9
Poverty reduction %	–6.0	–16.0	24.2
UK			
Pre-transfer poverty rate	26.9	16.8	79.3
Post-transfer poverty rate	20.3	14.3	57.2
Poverty reduction %	24.5	14.9	27.9
Sweden			
Pre-transfer poverty rate	17.3	11.9	36.7
Post-transfer poverty rate	2.8	2.3	4.3
Poverty reduction %	83.8	80.7	88.3

[a] Families where there are only two adults married or cohabiting, with one or more children under 18. [b] Families where one adult cares for one or more minor children (under 18) without other adults in the household (older children, parents, etc).

Source: LIS database

boost savings and investment. The government intervenes only as a 'safety net' to guarantee a minimum income, when the family and the market fail. However, the level of social assistance is quite low, around 40% of the national median income[15] (Förster, 1993).

The value of universal *child allowances* and one-parent allowances[16] has been gradually eroded since the 1980s. Hence, families with children can rely on means-tested benefit. The rules for the two main means-tested schemes – Family Credit and Income Support – are representative of the trend that the UK has exhibited from the mid-1970s, moving away from universalism towards targeting and limited support to select groups. *Income Support* is the bottom line of state support for those outside the labour market or employed for not more than 16 hours a week. There are no 'income disregards' for child allowances, maintenance or child alimony received. This means that a single parent on Income Support will not gain any advantages from the payment of child support, designed not to augment lone mothers' and children's resources but as a substitute to public transfer. Moreover, no public responsibility exists to enforce or advance the payment of child support. Since most absent parents are seen as having modest means, the public enforcement of parental support obligations might compel the second family also to claim assistance. The first family will in any case be protected by social security benefits, which are perceived as ensuring as adequate a standard of living as most would receive through private payments (Eekelaar, 1988).

For parents in full-time employment at a low wage, the UK provides another means-tested benefit: *Family Credit*. Its aim is to subsidise low-wage sectors of the economy without broader intervention into wage setting, and it is intended to maintain work incentives and to support families with children. However, since the income thresholds are rather low, married mothers with low earnings potential are economically discouraged to work. In other words, there is the risk of a poverty trap. Indeed, dual-earner couples hardly ever receive Family Credit and, in the early 1990s, constituted only 5% of the households in receipt of it (Scheiwe, 1994). A similar, even more serious, poverty trap exists for single parents on Income Support. By leaving Income Support a mother loses entitlement to free school meals and milk for her child, and to the full coverage of housing costs and interest on mortgage payments. Moreover, if the provision of public childcare services is low – and we will see that it is – she needs to find childcare arrangements for her children and pay for them. As a whole, entering the labour market may not pay off.

Compared to the other two countries, Italy has the least ability to reduce poverty among families with children; the poverty reduction rate is negative for two-parent families and not particularly high for one-parent families. The negative impact means that, in Italy, taxes push more two-parent families into poverty than transfers lift out[17]. In Italy, indeed, income transfer programmes are modest and categorical. A general unemployment compensation scheme does not exist, but there are different ones according to employment status and to the cause of unemployment. Moreover, there is no universal child allowance nor a general national minimum income scheme. Instead we find, on the one hand, means-tested family allowances for households of wageworkers. On the other hand, there are vital minimum programmes granted at the municipality level, but with great variation among regions, and within regions, in terms of the amount and the categories of people who are entitled to benefit from these programmes (Negri and Saraceno, 1996). In particular family allowances, the only existing measure for families with children[18], are inadequate in many ways. First, poor families with children headed by self-employed parents are excluded. Second, allowances are not indexed; from 1988 to 1994 their real value decreased by 38% (Commissione di Indagine sulla Povertà e l'Emarginazione, 1995). In 1991 for poor and near-poor families[19], family allowances were about 5% of the national median equivalent disposable income (Solera, 1998). Third, one-parent families do not receive any supplement, and income thresholds are only slightly higher. Furthermore, as in the UK, the state does not enforce or advance child support, leaving the arrangement and actual payment to the private sphere (family and court). In contrast to Sweden, where nearly all-single parents receive child support payments, in the UK and Italy only 22% are beneficiaries (Solera, 1998). Since the level of support for one- and two-parent families does not differ substantially, the higher poverty reduction observed in Table 18.2 for one-parent families may come as a surprise. The difference is probably due to lower income taxes and to pensions as a principal source of income (invalidity and widow's pension).

Such a weak income support for families with children reflects the familial attitude of the Italian welfare state. Social rights are strictly linked to working status. For those outside the labour market or those not working in the most protected sectors (public sector and large industries) social security is fragile. A conservative family ideology lies behind this. The family is assumed to provide income support to family members outside the labour market. The same ideology, as we will see in the next section, applies also to the caring services. Thus, the traditional family is still the reference point, with the husband as the main income provider (through paid work and, in turn, through his access to social security benefits) and the wife as the main care provider (Saraceno, 1997). However, while these features generally define the corporatist welfare regime (Esping-Andersen, 1990), Italy presents some interesting peculiarities. First, compared to corporatist countries such as France and Germany, in Italy the welfare state not only has an employment based entitlement system and an income transfer bias against social services but also an 'elderly' bias. In Germany and France, although social insurance prevails, universal family allowances and national minimum income schemes also exist. In Italy the income maintenance system is notably lacking for the working age population; 61.5% of the social expenditure is for pensions, against an average of 45.3% in the European Union (Commissione per l'Analisi delle Compatibilità Macroeconomiche della Spesa Sociale, 1997). Second, in Italy, as in Spain and in Portugal, family obligations cross the boundaries of the nuclear family to include a wider range of family members. Hence, the extended family is regarded as a substitute or complement to state provision (Saraceno, 1996a)

Income packages: the role of mother's earnings

With the growing incidence of one-parent families, of unemployment and low wages, the well-being of families is increasingly connected to the position of women in the labour market. In each country when the mother works, the risk of poverty of both one-parent and two-parent families is lower (Tables 18.3 and 18.4).

Table 18.3 shows the income package of one-parent families, that is, how families put together income from different sources: from market activity, from the welfare state and from interpersonal, mainly familial, networks. The analysis of income packages is informative in two ways. At the microlevel, it reveals patterns of institutional dependency. At the macrolevel, it helps describe the role of state, market and family in the distributional system (Bison and Esping-Andersen, 1999).

In Sweden practically all-single parents have earnings. Over 80% of single parents work, most of them full time. Earnings are, therefore, the basis of a one-parent family income package. The welfare state, through social security benefits and advance maintenance payment (here included in the 'Family' component), to a large extent integrates earnings, thus accounting for half of single parents' income package. 'Work and welfare' are clearly fused.

The picture in the UK is the opposite. Paradoxically, in a liberal welfare state the market has a marginal role in the income package of one-parent families, while the state predominates; 68% of their income derives from public transfers. If in Sweden the welfare state is designed to supplement earnings, in the UK it is designed as a substitute. A 'work or welfare' logic shapes the means-tested income transfers rules. Indeed, the entire claim to Income Support is lost if the weekly hours of work exceed 16 and the shift from Income Support to a low-paid job plus Family Credit might not be economically advantageous if childcare costs are high. A parallel substitution logic exists between public and private transfers. Since in the income test, private child maintenance payments are counted in full as income of the mother, such private transfers benefit only those families with an initial level of income higher than the social assistance threshold.

The low incidence of market income in the British package reflects the labour market position of lone parents. Around 60% of lone parents do not work and rely mainly on social assistance, the level of which is, however, very low; 75% are in poverty. Among those who work, 59% are part-time and face a high risk of poverty. In the UK, indeed, a great deal

Table 18.3: Income packages for one-parent families: percentage of disposable income deriving from welfare state, market and family, and poverty rates by lone parents' labour market position (early 1990s)

	Italy	UK	Sweden
Market	68.0	25.0	51.0
Welfare state	18.7	69.0	39.0
Family[a]	13.3	6.0	10.0
Disposable income as % population median	82%	47%	79%
% not-employed	30.6	60.7	16.5
(% poor)	*(40.0)*	*(75.0)*	*(10.6)*
% employed	69.4	39.3	83.5
(% poor)	*(9.2)*	*(28.7)*	*(3.1)*
% employed part-time	na	59.3	35.0
(% poor)		*(48.8)*	*(5.3)*
% employed full time	na	40.7	65.0
(% poor)		*(3.3)*	*(2.3)*

[a] This includes alimony or child support and regular cash private interhousehold transfers.

na = not available

Source: LIS database

of part-time work is confined to low-skilled jobs, with low pay and minimal protection (Burchell et al, 1997). Coupled with scant welfare programmes, part-time employment is likely to be insufficient for single parents trying to escape poverty. Again the UK differs a lot from Sweden, where only 5% of lone parents working part-time are poor (a percentage slightly higher than full-time workers). This is because in Sweden part-time employment implies rather long weekly hours. It gives entitlement to full social benefits, paid vacation and job security, and it is not restricted to unqualified, low-paid jobs (Sundström, 1997). Together with generous and universal public transfers, part-time employment in Sweden often succeeds in protecting families from poverty.

In Italy the welfare state is marginal; only 18% of lone parents' income comes from public transfers. As we have seen, income support programmes are few, mostly categorical and are not generous. Yet, single parents are relatively well off; on average their disposable income is 82% of the non-elderly population median. This is essentially due to the demographic profile of Italian lone parents: mainly well educated with high earnings potential. Indeed in Italy separation and divorce, the principal determinants

Table 18.4: Income packages for two-parent families: percentage of disposable income deriving from welfare state, market and family, and poverty rates by number of earners (early 1990s)

	Italy	UK	Sweden
Market	95.0	83.5	76.3
Welfare state	5.0	16.5	23.7
Disposable income as % population median	92%	90%	107%
%with two earners	44.0	59.0	84.6
(% poor)	*(0.8)*	*(4.0)*	*(1.1)*
% with one earner	54.0	32.0	12.4
(% poor)	*(15.0)*	*(16.6)*	*(5.8)*
% with no earners	2.0	9.0	3.0
(% poor)	*(61.5)*	*(75.6)*	*(22.5)*

Source: LIS database

of lone parenthood[20], are prevalent among middle to upper class women and among those already inside the labour market. This explains to a great extent the higher employment rate of lone mothers compared to married mothers (Table 18.5).

The presence of two adults reduces the risk of not having any earnings or low earnings, due to part-time employment. Indeed, where the mother chooses not to work or, for whatever reason, must stay at home with her children, another adult, the father, can be a full-time earner. Compared to one-parent families, everywhere couples with children are better off and derive most of their income from the market. Yet, differences across countries occur as a consequence of the welfare state role. Relatively speaking, the welfare state is very important in the Swedish income package of two-parent families, less important in the British one and is practically absent in the Italian one (Table 18.4).

Supporting the employment of mothers

As Table 18.5 shows, employment rates for mothers according to the age of their youngest child vary significantly between the three countries. What is the role of social policies in explaining these differences?

Sweden has the highest maternal employment rate, irrespective of family status and child's age. The ability of Swedish women to combine work

Table 18.5: Employment rates of spouse and lone parent, by age of youngest child (early 1990s)

Age youngest child	Italy		UK		Sweden	
	Married mothers	Lone parents	Married mothers	Lone parents	Married mothers	Lone parents
0-3	44.6	(84.3)	44.0	22.0	85.4	80.2
4-5	43.3	(81.2)	65.3	37.4	84.4	80.9
6-18	45.6	67.1	76.0	50.0	91.4	85.2

Notes: Figures in parenthesis indicate estimates deriving from less than 20 units in the sample.

Source: LIS database

Table 18.6: Public provision of childcare

Country	Year	Care as % of children of given age group	
		0-3	3 to school age
Italy	1986	5	>85
UK	1988	<5	35
Sweden	1987	30	80

Source: Gauthier (1996, Table 10.6, p 181)

and parenthood rests on two important programmes: a nation-wide system of public childcare and paid parental leave. Public childcare covers 30% of children under three and 80% of those three to six years old (Table 18.6). Services are generally open from 6.30 am to 6 or 6.30 pm and include several meals. Public childcare is provided in daycare centres or 'in family' through child minders employed by the municipalities. It is heavily subsidised, but parents do pay income-related fees, usually equal to less than 10% of the income of a two-earner family. Single mothers receive preferential treatment in the allocation of limited childcare, and their children are also charged a lower fee than children of nuclear families (Kamerman, 1991; OECD, 1990; Sundström, 1991). Paid parental leave lasts 15 months and, in order to promote gender equality both in the labour market and in the home, either the mother or the father has the right to use it. Twelve months are paid at the same compensation rate of sickness benefits – in most case 90% of current earnings – while the last three months are paid according to a per diem grant. Job security is guaranteed for 18 months. However, if mothers did not have any earnings prior to giving birth, they receive only a low guaranteed amount during their 12 months leave period. Moreover, parents can use child/parental leave until the child is eight years old. This allows parents to 'bank' parental leave in case they need time off when the child starts a new childcare group or begins primary school. Parental insurance can be used to cover a complete leave from work, or can be prorated to permit part-time work by either parent, for full pay, until the year of paid leave is consumed. In addition to these 15 months, parents have the right to: (a) 60 days per child annually in case the child is sick, until the child reaches the age of 12; (b) 10 'daddy days', that is, the right of fathers to take a ten-day leave of absence within sixty days of childbirth; (c) two days per year per child (from the ages of four to 12) for parental participation in daycare and school; (d) the right to part-time work for either or both parents until the child is eight years old. All these parental benefits, with the exception of (d), are payable at 80% of lost income (Gustafsson, 1995b; Sundström, 1991).

The effect of such universal and generous parenting policies, explicitly designed to allow women to combine work and family and, in turn, to achieve full employment and gender equality, is that patterns of women's employment are continuous. The overall employment rate of mothers with pre-schoolers does not differ substantially from the rate of those with older children (Table 18.5)[21]. Rather than exiting the labour market, Swedish women tend to shift to part-time work during the childbearing period[22] (Sundström, 1997). This attachment to the labour force is a key factor in explaining the Swedish low poverty rate among single parents. Through continuous paid work, married mothers gain a certain degree of economic independence that is crucial in protecting them, and their children, from poverty in the event of divorce (Sörensen, 1994).

In contrast to Sweden, the 'young child penalty'[23] in the UK is rather high; mothers with children under three years have employment rates that are about half of those of mothers with school age children (Table 18.5). Indeed, in the UK, women are likely to leave the labour market when they have children and return to paid work, often part-time, after several years of absence, with an adverse effect on their earnings and career progression (Burchell et al, 1997). This is mainly due to inadequate parental leave and childcare policies. British maternity benefits are renowned to be among the lowest in Europe (European Observatory on National Family Policies, 1992). A woman has the right to 18 weeks of paid leave and 29 weeks of unpaid optional leave after childbirth. However, to qualify a woman needs five years of continuous employment with the same employer if she is a part-time worker, and two years if she is a full-time employee. Maternity benefit is paid for six weeks at 90% of salary and 12 weeks at a flat rate of £39.25 in 1990/1. The lower flat rate is available for 18 weeks to women with only six months continuous employment as long as they have paid NI contributions. In parallel, childcare facilities are inadequate, piece-meal, and scarcer than in other EU countries. Only 5% of the under 3s and 35% of children aged three to five are in a publicly funded daycare (Table 18.6). Attendance is mainly on a part-time base and, as is typical of a residual welfare state, children at risk receive priority in the allocation of limited places.

Such scarce public support to caring responsibilities has an unequal impact upon mothers in low-paid jobs as opposed to those with better education and higher incomes, who can afford to pay for private care, and upon lone mothers or married mothers, where the latter can rely on the partner. Indeed, lone mothers in the UK have a very low employment rate compared to married mothers, and compared to women in the other countries. Both demographic and institutional factors explain this. Among lone parents, 38% have never married, the majority are under 30 and with a low educational level[24]. Because of their weak human capital, their chances in the labour market are slim. And the welfare state, through practically non-existent childcare subsides and a weak income support system, does not help.

As far as support for mothers' employment is concerned, Italy lies in a middle position between the extensive Swedish support and the residual British support. Compulsory maternity leave is five months long (two before the delivery and three after) and it is compensated at 80% of the salary. Then the mother or the father have the right to a six months' leave until the child is one year old, at 30% of salary. Moreover, the provision of childcare facilities for children three to five years-old is about 90%. Services are heavily publicly subsidised and are normally open for a full school day (8.30 am to 3.30 or 4.30 pm). On the contrary, the provision of childcare services for the under-3s is very low (Table 18.6) and parents do pay income-relate fees. Thus, after the maternity leave ends and before the child enters pre-primary school, mothers are left without public support. Nevertheless, no 'young child penalty' is observable in the level of maternal employment (Table 18.5). If compared to the UK, where public facilities for the under-3s are equally scarce, this might come as a surprise. One possible explanation could lie in the diffusion and in the cost of private market care. However, private welfare services are rare and expensive in both countries; a full-year place costs 20% (or more) of average two-earner family incomes in Italy, and around 16% in the UK[25]. As Esping-Andersen argues (1999), for both Britain and Italy one might speak of concomitant welfare state and market failure. More lokely, what makes the difference in the maternal employment patterns observed in the two countries is the 'family compensation'; this is very strong in Italy, whereas it is weaker in the UK. Indeed, in Italy the network of relatives plays a crucial role as welfare provider, both offering income and care support. In particular, about two thirds of couples with children and half of lone parents are helped by relatives. If non-working married mothers receive mainly income transfers whereas working married mothers receive mainly help in the form of childcare services, lone parents are helped in both ways (Saraceno, 1998). For Italian single-parent families then, instead of 'welfare state dependency', as in the UK, one might speak of 'extended family dependency'.

Conclusions

Contemporary debates on the family poverty problem underline the importance of adequate social security benefits, mainly through a collective sharing of child cost (child allowances, advance maintenance payments and one-parent allowances) and through general minimum income schemes. Much less appreciated is the anti-poverty role of support for the employment of mothers. Evidently, cash benefits are important. The market alone is insufficient to guarantee welfare. This is so because of unemployment, low wages, or family events (such as a new child or a separation), which could mean that earnings may not be sufficient to provide adequate income. When the State intervenes with generous and universal income transfers – as in Sweden – the poverty risk is greatly reduced. On the contrary, where transfers are mainly selective, on the basis of income or on the basis of employment status, anti-poverty effectiveness is lower. Selective systems on the basis of income – as in the UK – are ineffective because they tend to fix benefits at a low level, in order to encourage the unemployed into the labour market. Yet, in the absence of maternal employment support and other forms of cash help, the British system can create poverty traps. Selective systems on the basis of employment status, such as the Italian one, are ineffective because they tend to reproduce market inequalities.

However, it appears that cash transfers are not the key factor in explaining differences in family poverty across countries. The primary reason for the 'Swedish success' is that women are integrated into the labour force, regardless of whether or not they are married or have children. This is the result of labour market and economic policies that stress full employment. It is also thanks to generous parenting policies, which include not only extensive economic support for families with children but also a comprehensive system of public childcare and a good parental leave programme. The attachment of women to the labour market is particularly important as 'divorce insurance'. Indeed, the Swedish system adequately insures women and children against the risk of after-divorce poverty because a mother already has a job when she gets divorced and she already has daycare for her child. On the contrary, and as confirmation of the significance of mothers' employment, poverty among one-parent families in the UK is dramatically high. This is because the majority of lone parents does not work or work part-time. They rely heavily on social assistance and are forced to use it as an alternative to full-time employment. In Italy, despite negligible public cash benefits, lone parents are relatively well off compared to British lone parents because they are more likely to work. This further underlines the importance of mothers' employment.

Mothers' earnings are therefore very important for families in order to maintain an adequate standard of living. In turn, policies aimed at facilitating the labour market participation of mothers should be regarded as a crucial component of an effective anti-poverty package.

Notes

[1] Many thanks to Gosta Esping-Andersen and Chiara Saraceno for their invaluable comments with regards to this research.

[2] It is important to note that in the majority of advanced countries married couples show a high level of educational and occupational homogamy, that is, an unemployed or low-paid husband is likely to be married with a woman similarly weak on the labour market (Ultee and Luijkx, 1990; Smits et al, 1998). Hence, mothers' earnings might not be a sufficient 'insurance' against fathers' unemployment or low wages, especially in big families. Yet, they are an additional source of income.

[3] I would like to thank Koen Vleminckx for the technical work he did, that is, for having added the microsimulation variables to the 1991 Italian file.

[4] Due to data limitations, in-kind transfers (such as healthcare, housing and education) are not taken into consideration.

[5] The net return to market work is determined not only by the cost and availability of childcare but also by replacement of home work, transportation and related work costs, the logistics of childcare and other activities (eg visits to the doctor, shopping, etc) (Danziger and Jantti, 1995).

[6] The relationship between maternal employment and parental leave policies is more controversial than for childcare. Maternity leave is important because it offers basic income support to new mothers and prevents them from exiting employment following childbirth. However, while childcare services enable mothers to spend more time working, maternity leave enables working mothers to spend more time at home. Some scholars argue that long leave periods may limit certain career-enhancing opportunities. Hence, this limit may have a negative long-term effect on mothers' earnings and, in turn, on their labour supply (Gornick et al, 1997).

[7] As a recent OECD study notes (1990), compulsory schooling does not exhaust the custodial needs of the children of working parents. State school schedules vary across countries according to hours per day, weeks per year, schools vacation, provision of lunch, etc. Nevertheless, all children are covered for at least half a day, without having to pay a lot. However, the variation across countries in the availability and cost of childcare services for pre-school children is bigger.

[8] I define non-elderly households as those headed by a person of less than 55 years.

[9] The resulting equivalence scale assumes moderate economies of scale. A two-person household is assumed to need 1.50 times as much income as one person to maintain a similar standard of living, while a three-person household is assumed to need 1.88 times as much as one person, etc.

[10] With transfers I mean both direct and indirect public transfers, that is both social security transfers and income taxes.

[11] This indicator of effectiveness is based on the assumption that pre-transfer incomes are independent of transfers. But, as widely discussed (O' Higgins et al, 1985; Mitchell, 1991), this is not the case, particularly for those programs that imply a substitution between the market and the state, typically pensions and

means-tested benefits. Given this limit, it has been argued that the poverty reduction indicator should be seen as a measure of welfare state effort more than a good measure of effectiveness. It is also in this sense that it is used in my work.

[12] Also families with children over 16 years who attend high school receive student grants equal to the child allowance until the child leaves high school but not beyond age 20.

[13] The compensation rate for unemployment insurance is 80%, for a period of 300 days. Requirements are not strict: (a) membership of an unemployment-insurance fund for at least one year for employees and two years for self-employed people; (b) 75 days' work over the previous 12 months. For people who are not insured in an unemployment-insurance fund there is a cash labour market assistance flat rate, for 150 days (Swedish National Social Insurance Board 1993, 1994).

[14] For example, unemployment compensation is flat rate, for one year and with severe contributory requirements (MISSOC, 1991).

[15] Indeed, at the 40% poverty interval, the poverty reduction trebles for two-parent families and doubles for one-parent units (Solera, 1998).

[16] One-parent benefit is a supplement to the child allowance rate for the eldest or only dependent child of single parents. Yet, the increment is not generous. Annual child allowances for one-parent families are equal to 5% of the median equivalent disposable income compared to 4% of child allowances for two-parent units (Solera, 1998).

[17] It should be noted that maternity benefits are not included in the transfer income since in the LIS data they cannot be separated from wages. Thus, the anti-poverty effectiveness is underestimated.

[18] Actually Italy provides universal support for the cost of children through tax credit. Yet, the amount is very low and it does not benefit those families at very low income outside the tax net.

[19] Following Smeeding's designation (1991), I define 'near-poor' families as those whose disposable equivalent income is greater than 50% of median equivalent income but less than 62.5% of median equivalent income.

[20] The incidence of out-of-wedlock birth as a determinant of lone parenthood is still very low in Italy. After divorce and separation, widowhood is the second major factor (Zanatta, 1996).

[21] An appropriate analysis of patterns of women's labour market participation in connection with childbearing responsibilities would require longitudinal data. Indeed, cross-sectional data such as the LIS used here, do not allow one to distinguish between cohort, period and age effect. In Table 18.5 mothers of children of the same age at the time of study might themselves be different ages. Also, mothers of children aged 6-18 at the time of study may have behaved differently when their children where young to the mothers with pre-school children at the time of study. These cross-sectional figures give an initial aggregate picture of the prevalent pattern of labour market participation which is largely confirmed by figures based on individual longitudinal data. When analysing the determinants of individual behaviours over time cross-sectional data are extremely weak and longitudinal data need to be used to make any stronger causal inferences (Menard, 1991; Blossfeld and Rohwer, 1995).

[22] As mentioned above, parents have the right to part-time work until the child is eight years old.

[23] This expression was borrowed from Gornick et al's work (1996).

[24] This figure derives from my own calculations, based on LIS data.

[25] The cost of private market care is basically connected to the way a country has responded to the 'cost-disease' problem (Baumol, 1967). Where the tax on labour is high and the wage structure rather egalitarian, the relative cost of labour-intensive personal and social services is high. The result is limited demand. This is the case of most continental economies, including Italy. Where, instead, it is possible to rely on a large pool of low-wage workers, labour intensive market services become affordable. This is the case of the US but, surprisingly, not of British child care services. Britain's deregulation strategy has produced rising income inequalities, but clearly this has not spilled over into childcare costs (Esping-Andersen, 1999).

References

Atkinson, A.B. (1989) *Social insurance and income maintenance*, in A.B. Atkinson (ed) *Poverty and social security*, London: Harvester Wheatsheaf.

Baumol, W. (1967) 'The macroeconomics of unbalanced growth', *American Economic Review*, vol 57, pp 415-26.

Ballestrero, M.V. (1993) 'Maternità', *Digesto*, Torino, UTET, pp 325-51.

Bison, I. and Esping-Andersen, G. (1998) *Unemployment and income packaging in Europe*, Unpublished Paper, Department of Sociology, University of Trento.

Blossfeld, H.P. and Rohwer, G. (1995) *Techniques of event-history modelling: New approaches to causal analysis,* Mahwah: Erlbaum.

Bradshaw, J., Ditch, J., Eardley, I., Gough, I. and Whiteford, P. (1996a) *Social assistance schemes in OECD countries: Volume 1. Synthesis report*, Department of Social Security Research Report 46, London: HMSO.

Bradshaw, J., Ditch, J., Eardley, I., Gough, I. and Whiteford, P. (1996b) *Social assistance schemes in OECD countries: Volume 2. Country report*, Department of Social Security Research Report 47, London: HMSO.

Buhmann, B., Rainwater, L., Schmauss, G. and Smeeding, T. (1988) 'Equivalence scales, well being, inequality and poverty: sensitivity estimated across ten countries using the Luxembourg Income Study (LIS) database', *Review of Income and Wealth,* vol 34, pp 115-42.

Burchell, B.J., Dale, A. and Joshi, H. (1997) 'Part-time work among British women', in H.P. Blossfeld and C. Hakim (eds). *Between equalisation and marginalisation: Women working part-time in Europe and the United States of America*, Oxford: Oxford University Press.

Commissione di Indagine sulla Povertà e sull'Emarginazione (1995) *Verso una Politica di Lotta alla Povertà: L'Assegno per i Figli e il Minimo Vitale*, Roma: Poligrafico e Zecca dello Stato.

Commissione per l'Analisi delle Compatibilità Macroeconomiche della Spesa Sociale (1997) *Relazione Finale*, 28 February.

Danziger, S. and Jantii, M. (1995) *The market economy, welfare state, and the economic well-being of children: evidence from four countries*, Mimeo, University of Michigan, March.

Danziger, S., Smeeding, T.M. and Rainwater, L. (1995) *The western welfare state in the 1990's: Toward a new model of antipoverty policy for families with children*, LIS Working Paper no 128, Luxembourg: Luxembourg Income Study.

Di Biase, R., Di Marco, N., Di Nicola, F. and Proto, G. (1995) 'Itaxmod: a microsimulation model of the Italian Personal Income Tax and of social security contributions', *Documenti di Lavoro*, no 16, Roma: ISPE.

Eekelaar, J. (1988) *England and Wales*, in A.J. Kahn and S.B. Kamerman (eds) *Child support: From debt collection to social policy*, London: Sage Publications.

Esping-Andersen, G. (1990) *The three worlds of welfare capitalism*, Oxford: Polity Press.

Esping-Andersen, G. (1999) *Social foundations of postindustrial economies*, Oxford: Oxford University Press.

European Observatory on National Family Policies (1992) *National family policies in EC-countries in 1991*, Commission of the European Communities.

Fagnani, J. (1996) 'Family policies and working mothers: A comparison of France and West Germany', in M.D. Garcia-Ramon and J. Monk (eds) *Women of the European Union. The politics of work and daily life*, London: Routledge.

Förster, M.F. (1993) *Measurement of low incomes and poverty in a perspective of international comparisons*, OECD Labour Market and Social Policy Occasional Papers, no 14.

Förster, M.F. (1994) *Family poverty and the labour market: an international comparison of labour market participation and working time arrangements based on analysis of microdata from the Luxembourg Income Study*, LIS Working Paper no 114, Luxembourg: Luxembourg Income Study.

Forssén, K. (1998) *Child poverty and family policy in OECD countries*, LIS Working Paper no 178, Luxembourg: Luxembourg Income Study.

Gauthier, A.H. (1996) *A comparative analysis of family policies in industrialised countries*, Oxford: Clarendon Press.

Gornick, J., Meyers, M. and Ross, K. (1996) *Public policies and the employment of mothers: A cross-national study*, LIS Working Paper no 140, Luxembourg: Luxembourg Income Study.

Gornick, J., Meyers, M. and Ross, K. (1997) 'Supporting the employment of mothers: policy variation across fourteen welfare states', *Journal of European Social Policy*, vol 1, pp 45-70.

Gough, I., Bradshaw, J., Ditch, J., Eardley, T. and Whiteford, P. (1997) 'Social assistance in OECD countries', *Journal of European Social Policy*, vol 1, pp 17-43.

Gustafsson, S. (1995a) *Single mothers in Sweden: Why is poverty less severe?*, in K. McFate, R. Lawson and W.J. Wilson (eds) *Poverty, inequality and the future of social policy: Western states in the new world order*, New York, NY: Russel Sage Foundation.

Gustafsson, S. (1995b) *Public policies and women's labour force participation: A comparison of Sweden, Germany and the Netherlands*, in T.P. Schultz (ed). *Investment in women's human capital*, Chicago, IL: University of Chicago Press.

Hauser, R. and Fisher, I. (1990) *Economic well being among one-parent families*, in T. Smeeding, M. O'Higgins and L. Rainwater (eds) *Poverty, inequality and income distribution in comparative perspective*, London: Harvester Wheatsheaf.

Kamerman, S.B. (1991) 'Child care policies and programs: an international overview', *Journal of Social Issues*, vol 47, no 2, pp 179-96.

Kahn, A.J. and Kamerman, S.B. (1988) (eds). *Child support: From debt collection to social policy*, London: Sage Publications.

Leibowitz, A., Klerman, J.A. and Waite, L.J. (1992) 'Employment of new mothers and child care choice: difference by children's age', *Journal of Human Resources*, vol 22, no 1, pp 112-33.

McFate, K., Lawson, R. and Wilson, W.J. (eds) (1995) *Poverty, inequality and the future of social policy: Western states in the new world order*, New York, NY: Russel Sage Foundation.

Menard, S. (1991) *Longitudinal research*, Newbury Park: Sage Publications.

MISSOC (1991) *Social protection in the member states of the community*, Brussels: Commission of the European Communities.

Mitchell, D. (1991) *Income transfers in ten welfare states*, Aldershot: Avebury.

Negri, N. and Saraceno, C. (1996) *Le Politiche Contro la Povertà in Italia*, Bologna: Il Mulino.

O'Higgins, M., Schmaus, G. and Stephenson, G. (1985) *Income distribution and redistribution*, LIS Working Paper no 3. Luxembourg: Luxembourg Income Study.

OECD (1990) 'Child care in OECD countries', in *Employment Outlook 1990*, Chapter Five, Paris: OECD.

OECD (1994) *The jobs study: Facts, analysis and strategy*, Paris: OECD.

OECD (1995) *Employment Outlook*, Paris: OECD.

Palmer, J., Smeeding, T. and Torrey, B.B. (1988) *The vulnerable*, Washington, DC: Urban Institute Press.

Rainwater, L. and Smeeding, T.M. (1995) *Doing poorly: the real income of American children in a comparative perspective*, LIS Working Paper no 127, Luxembourg: Luxembourg Income Study.

Sainsbury, D. (ed) (1994) *Gendering welfare states*, London: Sage Publications.

Saraceno, C. (1996) 'Family change, family policies and the restructuration of welfare', paper for the conference *Beyond 2000: The New Social Policy Agenda*, OECD, Parigi, 12-13 Novembre.

Saraceno, C. (1997) *Le Politiche per la Famiglia*, in M. Barbagli and C. Saraceno (eds) *Lo Stato delle Famiglie in Italia*, Bologna: Il Mulino.

Saraceno, C. (1998) *Mutamenti della Famiglia e Politiche Sociali in Italia*, Bologna: Il Mulino.

Scheiwe, K. (1994) 'Labour market, welfare state, and family institutions: the links to mothers' poverty risks', *Journal of European Social Policy*, vol 4, pp 201-24.

Smeeding, T.M. (1991) *US poverty and the income security policy in a cross national perspective*, LIS Working Paper no 70, Luxembourg: Luxembourg Income Study.

Smeeding, T.M., O'Higgins, M. and Rainwater, L. (eds) (1990) *Poverty, inequality and income distribution in comparative perspective*, London: Harvester Wheatsheaf.

Smits, J., Ultee, W. and Lammers, J. (1998) 'Educational homogamy in 65 countries: an explanation of differences in openness using country-level explanatory variables', *American Sociological Review*, vol 63, pp 264-85.

Solera, C. (1998) *Income transfers and support for mothers' employment: the link to family poverty risks. A comparison between Italy, Sweden and the UK*, LIS Working Paper no 192, Luxembourg: Luxembourg Income Study.

Sörensen, A. (1994) 'Women's economic risk and the economic position of single mothers', *European Sociological Review*, vol 2, pp 173-88.

Sundström, M. (1991) 'Sweden: supporting work, family, and gender equality', in S.B Kamerman and A.J. Kahn (eds) *Child care, parental leave, and the under 3s. Policy innovation in Europe*, New York, NY: Aubourn House.

Sundström, M. (1997) 'Managing work and children: part-time work and the family cycle of Swedish women', in H.P. Blossfeld and C. Hakim (eds) *Between equalisation and marginalisation: Women working part-time in Europe and the United States of America*, Oxford: Oxford University Press.

Swedish National Social Insurance Board (1993) *Social insurance statistics: Facts 1992*, Stockholm: Statistical Division.

Swedish National Social Insurance Board (1994) *Social insurance in Sweden*, Fact Sheets on Sweden, Stockolm.

Ultee, W. and Luijkx, R. (1990) 'Educational heterogamy and father-to-son occupational mobility in 23 industrial nations: general societal openness or compensatory strategies of reproduction', *European Sociological Review*, vol 2, pp 125-49.

Zanatta, A.L. (1996) 'Famiglie con un Solo Genitore e Rischio di Povertà', *Polis*, 1, pp 63-79.

NINETEEN

Child support among selected OECD countries: a comparative analysis

James Kunz, Patrick Villeneuve and Irwin Garfinkel

Introduction

The past 20 years have seen an increase in the percentage of families headed by single parents in virtually all countries of the Organisation for Economic Co-operation and Development (OECD). In the United States, for example, the percentage rose from 22.7 to 27.1 between 1986 and 1996 (OECD, 1999). Over the same period of time, the rate of expansion of government programmes and transfers among OECD countries has declined. Because of these two trends, the collection of private child support has increasingly come to be perceived as a vital source of financial support for single parent families and an important issue in public policy.

Several OECD countries, for example, have established new policies and programmes aimed at increasing the number and level of private child support payments.

Have these attempts succeeded? Have these countries improved their collection of child support over time and in relation to other OECD countries? More generally, how has the collection of private child support evolved in OECD countries over the past two decades? Where do we stand today? In this chapter, we provide preliminary answers to these questions using data from the Luxembourg Income Study (LIS) between the late 1970s and the mid-1990s to examine the levels and trends of child support payments in seven OECD countries. This chapter proceeds as follows. In the next section, we present some background information about child support in general and provide a brief overview of recent changes in child support policies in the countries we examine. Next, we describe the data and methodology used to answer these questions. We then present our results and discuss their implications.

Background

In its broadest sense, child support refers to an income transfer to the caretaker of a child with a non-resident parent (Garfinkel, 1992). Child support can be either public or private. In the US, public child support – financed through the government – is provided through programmes such as the Temporary Assistance to Needy Families and Food Stamps. These programmes are not limited to children with a non-resident parent, but many poor children in single parent families are eligible for them. Private child support is provided by the non-resident parent. The same distinction between public and private child support exists in other countries, although some countries specifically provide benefits, usually in the form of an assured child support benefit, specifically for children in single parent families.

Because of the growth of single parent families, the economic insecurity associated with them, and a growing reluctance to address this economic insecurity through public transfers, several national governments have become increasingly involved in improving private child support collections. These efforts usually address one or more of three goals for improving child support collections: (1) locating and identifying the non-resident parent; (2) increasing payment levels; and (3) increasing the actual payment of child support (Garfinkel, 1992).

In this chapter, we analyse trends in child support collections among seven OECD countries: Australia, Belgium, Denmark, Finland, the Netherlands, the United Kingdom, and the US. Three of these countries – the US, Australia, and the UK – undertook major efforts to improve child support collections either during or just prior to our study period (between the late 1970s and the mid-1990s). Our overview of the countries in our study begins with these three countries.

The US was the first of these countries to enact major child support reform, with the 1975 Child Support Enforcement Amendments. Prior to this time, public enforcement of private child support in the US was almost entirely a state responsibility. These amendments changed this by establishing the federal Office of Child Support Enforcement, requiring all states to establish state offices of child support enforcement, and providing federal reimbursement for about three quarters of each state's enforcement costs (Garfinkel, 1992).

While the 1975 Amendments preceded the years we examine, two other pieces of legislation were adopted during the study period – the 1984 Amendments and the 1988 Family Support Act. Both of these addressed the three goals of improving child support. To improve the identification of the non-resident parent, the 1984 Amendments allowed parenthood (typically paternity) to be established until the child's eighteenth birthday and encouraged states to develop administrative or bureaucratic processes to replace judicial processes. To increase awards, the Amendments required states to adopt numeric child support guidelines. To improve the actual payment of support, states were now also required to withhold child support obligations from wages and other income sources if the non-resident parent was one month delinquent (Garfinkel, 1992).

The 1988 Family Support Act also addressed all three of the goals mentioned above. It contained three provisions to improve the identification of the non-resident parents. The first ordered states to increase the number of cases in which they established paternity. The second required states to obtain the social security number of both parents in conjunction with issuing birth certificates. The third required all parties in a judicial proceeding to take a genetic blood test upon request of any part. To increase the amounts awarded, the Family Support Act made the guidelines that had been established through the 1984 Amendments the presumptive child support award. Finally, to increase the actual payment of support, the Family Support Act strengthened the 1984 Amendments by requiring income withholding at the outset for all orders established after 1994 and by providing financial incentives for states to collect support from non-resident parents living in a different state (Garfinkel, 1992).

In Australia, efforts to improve child support collections did not begin until the late 1980s. Until that point, the payment of child support in Australia was characterised as "a voluntary act exercised by relatively few" (Harrison et al, 1987). In the mid-1980s, a Parliamentary Joint Select Committee recommended the introduction of a scheme involving the collection of maintenance on behalf of resident parents with proceeds paid into general revenue, but that scheme was never implemented (Millar and Whiteford, 1993). Instead, the government established the National Maintenance Inquiry, which ultimately led to a different scheme that more closely resembled the one in force in the US. First, a Child Support Agency was established in June 1988 to collect child support, which would then be paid out to resident parents. Second, an administrative formula was established which governed the level of child support payments established after September 1989.

Great Britain was the last of the three countries to enact child support legislation. Some discussion of improving child support occurred during a general review of social security in the mid-1980s but the real impetus behind reform was a white paper entitled *Children come first* issued in 1989 (Millar and Whiteford, 1993). This paper led to the adoption of the 1991 Child Support Act, which was modelled after the Australian initiative and included two provisions. First, a Child Support Agency was set up within the Department of Social Security to locate non-resident parents and collect child support payments. Second, the agency was required to assess child support payments based on a predetermined formula (Millar and Whiteford, 1993).

In each of these three countries, the last twenty years has seen a change from complete or near-complete non-involvement of the central government to the establishment of agencies that participate in many aspects of the private child support collection. In our remaining four countries, the central governments have had long-standing roles in the collection of private child support. For example, in Denmark, federal provisions for establishing paternity date back to 1960 and when a non-resident parent fails to pay child support or pays it late, there is a long-standing tradition for the government agency to advance payment and attempt to collect it later (Knudsen, 1988). In Finland, single parent families are entitled to child support from the non-resident parent but, in cases of non-payment or non-establishment of paternity, a public child maintenance payment is paid in addition to child allowance (Kahn and Kamerman, 1994). In the Netherlands, a Council for Child Protection manages the collection and disbursement of private child support and is authorised to withhold the income of non-payers (Wiebrens, 1988). While we are not aware, at this point, of major changes regarding child support or related policies in these countries or in Belgium, which would have occurred in the last twenty years, it does not mean that such changes did not occur.

We examine three outcomes among these countries over time: the extent to which households eligible for private child support actually receive it, the amount of child support received and the share of net income represented by child support. These outcomes, of course, can be affected by factors other than child support programmes and policies, such as the earnings of the non-resident parents and the size and composition of eligible households. In addition, the availability of other resources for the family may play a role. For instance, households in countries that provide generous public transfers may be less likely to seek private child support. These factors can vary across countries and across time, so our analysis seeks to examine the first of these outcomes independent of such other factors.

Data and methodology

Data and study variables

The source of data for our analysis is the LIS, a group of data sets containing comparable variables from representative samples of persons and households in a growing number of countries and years. The first wave of data sets, which dates back to 1979 for some countries, provides data from 13 countries. As of mid-1999, in its fourth wave of data gathering, the LIS includes demographic and economic information on the populations of 26 countries.

We would have been interested in examining child support among a larger number of countries but were prevented from doing so largely because of data considerations. The countries selected meet three criteria. First, we wanted to examine the child support situation in comparable industrialised countries, so the countries selected had to be part of the OECD. Second, we selected countries for which the variables needed in the analysis existed in the LIS data or could be derived. Countries such as Norway and Sweden which provide an assured child support benefit unfortunately had to be excluded since their data does not distinguish between the public and private components of child support, an essential distinction when one aims at identifying, as is the case here, the determinants of private child support. Finally, in order to examine the evolution of child support over time, we selected countries for which LIS data existed in at least two waves. The data from seven countries met these three criteria. Table 19.1 presents the years and sample sizes for these seven countries.

Within each of these country/year data sets, we selected non-widow female-headed households (specifically excluding cases where a spouse is present) with at least one child under 18 years old. However, we were not able to ascertain widowhood for at least some of the years for five of the countries. In these cases, we imputed widowhood, based on a procedure available from the authors upon request.

Table 19.1: LIS data sets used and sample size for non-widow female-headed households with children

	Wave I	Wave II	Wave III	Wave IV
Australia				
Year	1981	1985	1989	1994
Sample size	558	265	707	297
Belgium				
Year		1985	1988	1992
Sample size		102	40	81
Denmark				
Year		1987	1992	
Sample size		440	521	
Finland				
Year		1987	1991	
Sample size		1987	1991	
Netherlands				
Year	1983	1987	1991	
Sample size	132	94	101	
UK				
Year	1979	1986	1991	1995
Sample size	240	342	319	436
US				
Year	1979	1986	1991	1994
Sample size	886	749	1,023	4,387

Source: LIS data

In order to allow comparisons of the child support amount across countries and time periods, we created three outcome variables. The first outcome variable measures the amount of child support received in an individual household expressed as a percentage of the relative poverty line specific to this household type, country and year. Following the work of others, the relative poverty line is set to 50% of the median adjusted household income of non-elderly households for each country and year (McFate, Smeeding and Rainwater, 1995). The second outcome variable measures the amount of child support received in an individual household expressed as a percentage of net income received by that household. The third outcome variable, which is used in our regression models, is straightforward; it is a binary variable indicating whether or not any child support was received by the household (1=Yes).

To control for demographic characteristics and the availability of other resources, we use four independent variables in our regression models. Age of the mother is used as a proxy for the non-resident parent's earnings. Both household size (the number of children) and the age of the youngest child are to measure need. The availability of other resources is measured by the *generosity of public transfers,* a variable we created. It is the mean amount of public transfers received by non-widow female-headed households expressed as a percentage of the median net income of two-parent households, according to the country and year. The public transfers included in this calculation are all social insurance and social assistance transfers, which include benefits such as child or family allowances, unemployment compensation and maternity pay for the former and means-tested cash and near-cash benefits for the latter.

Data limitations

The LIS data do not contain some variables that would have been useful in our analysis. For example, earnings of the non-resident parents, which we argue above are an important determinant of child support, are not available for any of the countries. The educational attainment level of resident parents, which might serve as a better proxy than age for the non-resident parents' earnings, is not provided in a way that would allow comparisons of more than a limited number of countries. Another variable that is not widely available is whether the non-resident parent had ever been married, which is unfortunate because never-married parents may differ significantly from those who were separated or divorced.

Another data limitation is the omission of widowhood status in some countries and for some years. Widows are ineligible for child support except in cases where at least one child has a non-resident parent. Including them in our analysis would lead us to underestimate the percentage of eligible households receiving child support and to overlook differences in this percentage between countries and over time that may be due simply to changes in the composition of female-headed households. As noted above, we selected households after imputing widowhood in these cases to minimise this problem, but we have likely misclassified some households, which could possibly be problematic in our analyses.

Finally, we compare the amount of child support across countries and times by using a relative measure in which the denominator is half of the median adjusted household income of non-elderly households for each country and year. While this relative measure is useful because it allows us to make comparisons between countries and to see how child support amounts compare to this relative poverty line, it tells us much less information about whether or not the absolute amount of child support received has changed over time.

Method of analysis

We begin by examining our three outcomes – the percentage of those potentially eligible for child support who actually received it, the amount of child support received as a percentage of the poverty line and the amount of child support as a percentage of net household income – for each country and for each year. We measure the second outcome both among the households which received child support and among all of the households, which were eligible for it. The third outcome is measured among households receiving child support. We use LIS supplied weights in these analyses.

We then employ regression analysis for our first outcome to formally test differences between countries and over time, and to control for other factors that may affect these outcomes. Four regression models are used, each of which examines, through a logistic regression procedure, possible determinants of *whether or not* child support is being paid to non-widow female-headed households with children.

In our first model, only country binomial variables are included, the US being the reference group. In the next model, we add dummies indicating the various waves when the data were collected, with the US 1994 data (wave four) as the reference group. In the third model, our three demographic variables are added, and in the fourth model the variable reflecting generosity of public transfers is included.

Results and discussion

Table 19.2 presents descriptive statistics for our three outcomes. It shows, for example, that the percentage of those potentially eligible for child support in Australia who actually received it has risen over the years from 24.3% in 1981 to 41.0% in 1994. This increase, with a chi-square result of 23.1, is statistically significant at the 1% level. In 1981, the mean child support payment represented 20.5% of the poverty line for those who received it. This is slightly lower than the relative value of 20.8% in 1994. It is somewhat surprising that this percentage has not declined considering the likely changes in the composition of those providing child support. We suspect that a disproportionate number of non-resident parents who pay child support as a result of Australia's enforcement efforts are low-income; since payments from these parents are relatively lower, one would expect to see this outcome decline. When we look at this outcome among all of those eligible to receive child support, the relative value of

Table 19.2: Child support outcomes for non-widow female-headed households with children

		Wave I (1979 -83)	Wave II (1985 -87)	Wave III (1988-92)	Wave IV (1992-95)	Chi-square of % with CS
Australia	Percent receiving CS	24.3	23.8	30.1	41.0	23.1***
	CS as % of poverty line					
	When receiving CS	20.5	19.2	17.5	20.8	
	When eligible for CS	5.0	4.6	5.3	8.5	
	CS as % of net income	17.4	15.6	16.7	17.5	
Belgium	Percent receiving CS		42.2	46.0	62.0	4.8***
	CS as % of poverty line					
	When receiving CS		39.3	43.1	29.1	
	When eligible for CS		16.6	19.8	18.0	
	CS as % of net income		25.7	24.0	16.7	
Denmark	Percent receiving CS		11.1	6.7		5.8*
	CS as % of poverty line					
	When receiving CS		17.6	14.4		
	When eligible for CS		2.0	1.0		
	CS as % of net income		9.3	8.0		
Finland	Percent receiving CS		42.4	45.2		0.1
	CS as % of poverty line					
	When receiving CS		18.2	17.7		
	When eligible for CS		7.7	8.0		
	CS as % of net income		11.3	10.4		
Netherlands	Percent receiving CS	10.2	10.9	29.5		18.0***
	CS as % of poverty line					
	When receiving CS	109.2	97.2	33.2		
	When eligible for CS	11.1	10.6	9.8		
	CS as % of net income	50.7	51.7	20.9		
UK	Percent receiving CS	39.2	36.3	23.9	21.2	38.2***
	CS as % of poverty line					
	When receiving CS	28.4	43.8	33.9	36.5	
	When eligible for CS	11.1	15.9	8.1	7.7	
	CS as % of net income	22.1	27.2	25.9	23.5	
US	Percent receiving CS	32.9	30.9	31.1	32.9	1.2
	CS as % of poverty line					
	When receiving CS	30.2	24.6	27.7	25.4	
	When eligible for CS	10.5	7.6	8.6	8.4	
	CS as % of net income	21.6	17.5	18.1	17.0	

Note: Statistical significance levels: * = 10%; ** = 5%; *** = 1%.
Source: LIS data and authors' analysis of these data

child support has therefore risen, on average, from 5% in 1981 to 8.5% in 1994. The share of net income represented by child support in households receiving it has fluctuated somewhat over the years but was in 1981 and 1994 at almost the same levels with, respectively, 17.4% and 17.5%.

In the UK, the percent receiving child support has declined during the four waves of data collection, from 39.2% to 21.2%. This decrease is statistically significant at the 1% level. Among those receiving child support, payment levels as a percentage of the poverty line have increased. As mentioned above, this change could be due to changes in the composition of those providing child support. However, among the broader group of households eligible for child support, the level of such payments has fallen relative to the poverty line, from 11.1% to 7.7%. For those receiving child support, the share of net income it represented fluctuated over the period examined, but overall it increased slightly with values of 22.1% in 1979 and 23.5% in 1995.

In the US, reform efforts do not seem to have succeeded in raising, overall, either the percentage receiving child support or the payment levels relative to the poverty line. The former has fluctuated around 30% for all four waves of data collection, while the latter, among those eligible for child support, has declined slightly. Among households receiving child support, the share of net income it represented has declined from 21.6% in 1979 to 17% in 1994.

Trends for the remaining four countries are also mixed. In Belgium, the percentage receiving child support was 42.2% in 1985 and 46% in 1988 but jumped to 62% in 1992. This increase is only statistically significant at the 10% level, although this may be due to small sample size. During the same period, the relative measure of payments among all those eligible increased slightly, and the average share of child support in net income decreased. The results for Denmark and Finland were somewhat more stable, though all percentages declined in Denmark between 1987 and 1992. The situation in the Netherlands did not change between 1983 and 1987 but changed dramatically by 1991. For this wave, one can observe a large increase in the percentage of those receiving child support, while the relative level of payments among those receiving child support dropped dramatically. Overall, the relative level of payments among all those eligible decreased only slightly, while the average share of net income represented by child support, for those receiving it, dropped.

Table 19.3 presents the means of the control variables in our sample, using the LIS supplied weights. No sharp demographic trends are apparent in the data, except for a fall in the age of the youngest child in the US,

Table 19.3: Demographic characteristics and availability of public transfers for non-widow female-headed households with children

	Wave I (1979-83)	Wave II (1985-87)	Wave III (1988-92)	Wave IV (1992-95)
Australia				
Age of household head	37.0	35.5	35.4	35.4
Number of children	1.8	1.7	1.8	1.7
Age of youngest child	7.6	7.7	8.1	7.3
Generosity of public transfers	44.0	43.9	24.6	35.9
Belgium				
Age of household head		34.5	34.4	36.4
Number of children		1.5	1.2	1.5
Age of youngest child		7.5	7.9	9.6
Generosity of public transfers		47.3	38.6	33.9
Denmark				
Age of household head		35.1	35.5	
Number of children		1.4	1.4	
Age of youngest child		8.2	8.3	
Generosity of public transfers		57.0	45.0	
Finland				
Age of household head		35.3	37.5	
Number of children		1.4	1.4	
Age of youngest child		8.6	9.2	
Generosity of public transfers		20.3	232.8	
Netherlands				
Age of household head	35.4	35.7	37.9	
Number of children	1.6	1.5	1.6	
Age of youngest child	8.2	7.8	9.0	
Generosity of public transfers	78.9	62.9	54.8	
UK				
Age of household head	38.2	35.7	33.1	33.9
Number of children	1.8	1.7	1.8	1.8
Age of youngest child	8.4	7.6	6.3	6.8
Generosity of public transfers	38.9	49.2	37.5	38.9
US				
Age of household head	37.1	35.3	35.4	35.4
Number of children	2.0	1.9	1.9	1.9
Age of youngest child	10.1	7.4	6.8	7.1
Generosity of public transfers	13.6	11.9	14.6	14.8

Source: LIS data

from 10 years old in 1979 to 7 years old in 1994. Table 19.3 also presents the generosity of public transfers, reinforcing the well-documented finding that public transfers in the US are much less generous than in most other OECD countries.

Table 19.4 shows the results of the logistic regressions with the dependent variable being whether child support was received or not. Model I presents coefficients with a model including only country dummies, with the US as the omitted category. Female-headed households with children in Belgium and Finland are more likely to have received private child support than those in the US, while those in Denmark and the Netherlands are less likely to have received child support. These findings are statistically significant at the 1% level. Differences between the US and Australia, while reflecting the pattern shown in Table 19.2, are barely statistically significant, while female-headed households in the UK are significantly less likely to receive child support. These findings do not seem to be very sensitive to changes in time, as demonstrated by Model II, which includes dummies for the waves of data collection. Neither of these wave dummies is significant, nor does its inclusion change the findings in Model I, except for the dummy variable for Australia, which is no longer statistically significant. In Model III, we add the demographic variables. The age of the youngest child is highly significant, while the number of children is significant at the 10% level. In Model IV we add public transfer generosity, which is not statistically significant. The net inclusion of the demographic and, especially, of the public transfer generosity variables, however, does attenuate the coefficients for the Netherlands and the UK, neither being statistically different from the US in Model IV.

Taken together, these findings suggest mixed results among those countries for which we know about child support reform efforts. Table 19.2 shows for Australia a steady increase of child support receipt among the households eligible for it, even though for the whole period examined the difference between this percentage in Australia and the US is not statistically significant. On the other hand, collection efforts in the US and the UK do not seem to have paid off. One explanation may be weaknesses in policy. In fact, the government in the UK published a report in 1998 that characterised their previous scheme as a failure and introduced a new set of procedures (UK Secretary of State for Social Security, 1998). While child support collection in the US has been viewed more favourably, changes brought about in the 1996 Personal Responsibility and Work Opportunity Act at least implicitly acknowledged a need to strengthen all phases of child support collection.

However, another explanation for the seeming failure of some of these reform efforts could be the changing composition of those eligible for child support. Research has found that, in the US, child support enforcement efforts have been effective among the sub-group needing it

Table 19.4: Determinants of child support receipt among non-widow female-headed households with children: Results from logistic regressions

	Model I	Model II	Model III	Model IV
Australia	–0.095*	–0.084	–0.073	0.052
	(0.057)	(0.061)	(0.061)	(0.130)
Belgium	0.682***	0.686***	0.669***	0.823***
	(0.136)	(0.138)	(0.139)	(0.199)
Denmark	–1.601***	–1.582***	–1.605***	–1.386***
	(0.117)	(0.122)	(0.123)	(0.236)
Finland	0.437***	0.457***	0.395***	0.451***
	(0.095)	(0.101)	(0.102)	(0.114)
Netherlands	–0.811***	–0.802***	–0.811***	–0.506
	(0.148)	(0.151)	(0.151)	(0.318)
UK	–0.157**	–0.152**	–0.130*	0.028
	(0.066)	(0.067)	(0.067)	(0.159)
Wave I (1979-83)		–0.0003	–0.075	–0.060
		(0.062)	(0.063)	(0.064)
Wave II (1985-87)		–0.006	–0.022	–0.012
		(0.062)	(0.063)	(0.063)
Wave III (1988-92)		–0.043	–0.051	–0.075
		(0.057)	(0.057)	(0.062)
Age of mother			–0.003	–0.003
			(0.003)	(0.003)
Number of children			0.037*	0.036*
			(0.021)	(0.021)
Age of youngest child			0.041***	0.041***
			(0.005)	(0.005)
Public transfer Generosity				–0.006
				(0.005)
Constant	–0.745	–0.738	–1.004	–0.918

Notes: Statistical significance levels: * = 10%; ** = 5%; *** = 1%.
The dependent variable = whether received child support [1=yes].
Source: Authors' analysis of LIS data

the most, namely the never married mothers (Garfinkel et al, 1998; Sorensen and Halpern, 1999). The rate of collections though for this group is still lower, and as time has passed more and more of those eligible are never married. Thus, child support enforcement efforts are 'swimming upstream', and the picture would look much worse in the absence of these policy changes.

In at least two of the remaining countries, the findings are somewhat difficult to interpret. Our results show marked increases in the percentage receiving child support in Belgium and the Netherlands. It is not clear to us whether these changes are due to policy enactments or demographic shifts unknown to us or whether they are due simply to the small sample sizes in these countries.

In future work, we intend to account for differences in composition regarding marital status as well as to include information about the resident parents' level of educational attainment, when available, as a proxy for the non-resident parents' earnings capacity. Since this information is not available in a comparable way in all LIS datasets, the number of country/years we can examine will be reduced. We will also further examine the child support policy environments in Belgium and the Netherlands to see whether the observed changes in these countries could plausibly be related to policy changes.

References

Garfinkel, I. (1992) *Assuring child support*, New York, NY: Russell Sage.

Garfinkel, I., Meyer, D. and McLanahan, S. (1998) 'A brief history of child support policies in the Unites States', in I. Garfinkel, S. McLanahan, D. Meyer and J. Seltzer (eds) *Fathers under fire*, New York, NY: Russell Sage, pp 14-31.

Harrison, M., McDonald, P. and Weston, R. (1987) 'Payment of child maintenance in Australia: the current position, research findings, and reform proposals', *International Journal of Law and the Family*, vol 1, April, pp 92-132.

Kahn, A.J. and Kamerman, S.B. (1994) *Social policy and the under-3s: Six country case studies*, Cross-National Studies Research Program, New York, NY: Columbia University School of Social Work.

Knudsen, R. (1988) 'Denmark', in A.J. Kahn and S.B. Kamerman (eds) *Child support: From debt collection to social policy*, Newbury Park, CA: Sage, pp 50-92.

McFate, K., Smeeding, T. and Rainwater, L. (1995) 'Markets and states: poverty trends and transfer system effectiveness in the 1980s', in K. McFate, R.Lawson and W.J. Wilson (eds) *Poverty, inequality and the future of social policy*, New York, NY: Russell Sage, pp 29-66.

Millar, J. and Whiteford, P. (1993) 'Child support in lone-parent families: policies in Australia and the UK', *Policy & Politics*, vol 21, no 1, pp 59-72.

OECD (Organisation for Economic Cooperation and Development) (1999) *A caring world: The new social policy agenda*, Paris: OECD.

Sorensen, E. and Halpern, A. (1999) *Child support enforcement is working better than we think*, New Federalism Paper Series A, No A-31, April, Washington DC: Urban Institute.

United Kingdom Secretary of State for Social Security (1998) *A new contract for welfare: Children's rights and parents' responsibilities*, July.

TWENTY

Child and family policies in an era of social policy retrenchment and restructuring

Sheila B. Kamerman and Alfred J. Kahn

Introduction

We concluded in an earlier study that child and family benefits increased dramatically immediately following World War Two but have not done well in comparison with other social benefits since the 1950s (Kamerman and Kahn, 1997a). Although they continued to grow in real terms, they declined as a portion of overall social expenditures. Moreover, child or family allowances declined as a share of gross wages over time in most countries and as a portion of disposable family income as well. The turning point in public expenditure investment in children was the 1960s, when pension and health benefits expanded and related expenditures began to rise dramatically both as a portion of GDP and as a share of social expenditures. This pattern continued over the next 30 years, while child and family benefits fell further behind. Child and family benefits were not routinely adjusted to reflect rises in the cost of living, while pensions were increasingly linked to wages and often to prices as well, both of which rose significantly in most countries during the intervening years. Nor were they automatically adjusted to reflect rising costs, as was the case with health benefits.

However, despite the generally limited impact of family benefits in reducing poverty, those countries that did put together a diversified and generous package of such benefits (family or child allowances, housing allowances, advanced maintenance benefits, maternity/parenting benefits) were able to reduce child poverty and raise family income. Clearly, to ensure a satisfactory standard of living required jobs and adequate wages, but jobs alone were not necessarily sufficient for assuring an adequate income standard. For many, family-related cash benefits and services were a critical supplement to earnings.

Our final conclusion was that much of the variance in family benefits and services across countries was accounted for by political choice: "countries decide what they want to do and either find the political will to do it or decide that the political effort would be excessive. If the new and growing needs of children and their families in industrialised countries are to be met, this issue of political choice must be underscored ... and ... must be effectively addressed so that political effort may be transformed into political will" (Kamerman and Kahn, 1997a, p 121).

In the 1990s a new call for constrained social welfare spending emerged. This followed the fall of the Berlin Wall, the collapse of the centrally planned socialist economies, the end of the cold war, the expansion of the European Union (EU), emergence of a new global economy and widespread awareness of aging populations and other demographic factors.

The consensus now seems to be that welfare states are changing – or need to change – as a result of contradictory pressures ranging from economic and political need to cut social spending, on the one hand, to demographic and social pressures that lead to increased demand for social protection, making it difficult to cut social expenditures, on the other.

Europe has recently experienced a period of very high and sustained unemployment – and the rates are still high even if on average a little lower now than a few years ago. Social spending has been constrained, and there is concern, in particular, with regard to the cost of pensions, unemployment benefits, fringe benefits, and non-wage labour costs generally. In the midst of all this, those wanting to join the European Monetary Union (EMU) have had to meet very tough criteria regarding debt and inflation. Some people say these developments are all a long-range permanent threat to the welfare state and that generous social policies, which are costly and can create perverse incentives, need to be seen as a thing of the past. While experts appear divided regarding long-range scenarios – and political and union protests in several places have blocked some efforts by government to cut benefits – we do know that the major welfare states have just experienced a period of severe fiscal and budgetary pressures. Many analysts are arguing that the long-range perspective has to be the cutting of social expenditures. We also know that if this occurs, the consequences for children could be especially dire.

It is in this context that we are looking at the question of how child and family benefits and services are faring in this environment. What are the political choices that are being made under these circumstances? Perhaps, by examining what has happened to these benefits and related services in recent years, we can get some sense of the viability of the child and family benefit system under stress. In a broader sense we are exploring an aspect of the welfare state. In its concern with the safety net, taking the rough edges off market processes and enhancing certain values, does the welfare state produce any special dynamics for children and family policy?

We turn first to an overview of government investment in children and their families, and what can be learned from a current look at public social expenditures. We draw on OECD and European System of Integrated Social Protection Statistics (ESSPROS) social expenditure data for a picture that is not fully up to date, but brings us to the mid-to-late 1990s. Following this, we turn to a series of country 'cases', based on government reports, research reports, and interviews with public officials and policy scholars, to bring the picture up to the present. Our question is, what is happening to public investment in child and family benefits and services during this new era of social expenditure constraints, neo-liberal ideology and globalised economies? If they are losing ground, is the loss consistent across countries? Where (in what countries, in which domains) are the major problems emerging? If benefits and services are protected, where and with what rationales? What are the supporting arguments/factors that seem to make a difference?

What the numbers tell us: an overview[1]

An OECD summary of recent trends in social protection in the 1990s (Kalisch et al, 1998) pays attention to family assistance (cash benefits and services) along with pensions and retirement benefits, healthcare, unemployment benefits, long-term care and housing assistance. With regard to family benefits and services, the report notes that some countries raised benefits in the first half of the 1990s, especially for low-income families (often aimed at creating work incentives for those in low-wage work) and some countries targeted their benefits more on such families as a particularly vulnerable group, along with lone-parent families, large families, families with young children, and ethnic and racial minority families. Many countries increased their attention to lone-parent families in particular, often deciding to limit receipt of benefits and encourage labour-force participation by single mothers. Many also tried to improve child maintenance (child support) either by raising the level of expected support from non-custodial parents or establishing or enhancing government support, or strengthening the enforcement of the child support obligations of parents (albeit with limited success). (About half the more industrialised of the OECD countries now provide some form of assured minimum financial support when the non-custodial parent fails to provide such support or provides it at an inadequate level.) Issues with regard to the reconciliation of work and family life have received increasing attention in many countries also, with particular attention being paid to expanding support for early childhood education and care, and to maternity and parental leaves.

Of some interest, the major function of *family benefits* continues to be to supplement wages so as to ensure families with children of an adequate standard of living, while the *family and child services* are increasingly linked to helping reconcile work and family life or facilitating female labour-force participation, along with enhancing child development. Family benefits continue to be largely universal, not income-tested, despite some increase in targeting of benefits. And despite some increase in the use of tax benefits as an instrument of child and family policy, most family benefits are still direct cash benefits. And public expenditures on family cash benefits far surpass expenditures on services in almost all the OECD countries, with the major exceptions being the Scandinavian countries.

As pointed out in a Eurostat report on social protection in the EU, Iceland and Norway (Eurostat, 1999; Whitten, 1999) social spending was not uniform in the 1990s. There was a significant increase from 25.4% of GDP in 1990 to 29% in 1993. Between 1993 and 1995, however, expenditure on social protection declined slightly as a proportion of GDP in the EU (-0.5 percentage points). Between 1993 and 1996 the decline was significant in Sweden (-3.8 percentage points), Finland (-3.3 points, the Netherlands (-2.6 points) and Norway (-2.7 points). Real social spending in these years increased by only about 1% annually for the EU15 (member states only).

Child and family benefits increased slightly as a portion of social expenditures for the whole EU between 1990 and 1996 (from 7.6% to 8%), while in contrast to the earlier pattern, old age and survivors benefits, disability benefits, and sickness benefits experienced declining shares of social spending. (Only unemployment benefit expenditures rose significantly as a portion of social spending, for obvious reasons.)

The nominal value of family benefits increased between 1990 and 1996 in most of the OECD/EU countries, in particular in: Belgium, Denmark,

Germany, Greece, Spain, France, Ireland, Italy, Luxembourg, Austria, Portugal, UK and Iceland – and in the US – but declined slightly in Finland, and more significantly in the Netherlands, Norway and Sweden. Overall, public expenditures for family benefits and services increased in the EU15 between 1993 and 1996 by about 15%. At the same time, family benefits rose only slightly as a portion of social expenditures in the EU15, between 1993 to and 1996, from 7.8% to 8%. However, here too, the pattern was not consistent. They declined in more countries than they increased and peaked in some countries during these years (eg Austria in 1994) while reaching a low point in others (eg Sweden, 1993-94).

Clearly, the picture is evolving. The OECD expenditure data, at the time of this writing, were available only through 1996[2]. For further insights we must look at individual countries.

Some country cases[3]

Now, to the heart of our issue: some recent developments in the child and family policy field in a sample of countries that range in their earlier 'generosity' toward children (Kamerman and Kahn, 1997a) from the Scandinavian countries to Britain and the US, to see how they are currently responding. It is worth noting that the main demographic and social trends in these countries are similar, despite some variations within the group. These trends include: aging populations, declining or low and stable fertility rates, declining rates of marriage, high but stable divorce rates, increased cohabitation, increased lone parenting and out-of-wedlock childbearing, and medium to high rates of female labour force participation.

The Scandinavian countries

The Scandinavian countries, in particular Denmark and Sweden, have long been considered social policy, and child and family policy, leaders in the OECD world. With a stress on universal and comprehensive social policies, the provision of generous social benefits and a goal of gender equity, they have often represented the model to which liberal policy advocates aspire. Social expenditures for children and families, both cash benefits and services combined, constitute the highest proportion of GDP in the OECD countries (about 5% to 6%, the same proportion as public expenditures for education in the US and the average for the OECD countries). The early 1990s provided a serious challenge to this model. Both challenges and the national responses are illustrated below.

Denmark. Denmark began to experience persistently high levels of unemployment in the 1980s, more than a decade before Sweden and Finland. Unemployment rates peaked at 7.6% in the early 1990s but fell to 5.2% by mid-1999, much lower than the OECD average. Danish social expenditures have continued to increase as a percentage of GDP throughout the period, with some decline in the early 1990s but an increase in 1993 and 1994. The Danes have made some reforms in their pension system, cut the duration of unemployment benefits (previously available for several years) and linked work requirements more closely to receipt of unemployment benefits or social assistance. They stress training, education, and an 'active' labour market policy to deal with their unemployment problem (education and training rather than income transfers such as unemployment benefits).

Nonetheless, in the last few years, the Danes have sustained their child and family benefits and even raised them. Support for universalism has continued and even increased. Indeed, Denmark is almost unique in that having moved earlier from universal to somewhat more means tested benefits in the 1980s, it has now returned to a universal approach, convinced of the 'rightness' of this approach for child policy.

Child and family benefits and services account for a much smaller share of GDP than pensions, yet nonetheless constitute a significant share – almost 6% – and the share increased in the 1990s. Despite relatively high rates of children living in lone-parent families – one in five Danish children live with only one parent – the Danish child poverty rate (children living in families with incomes below half the median) is only about 4% in contrast to the comparable US rate of 22% (Rainwater and Smeeding, 1995).

Although childcare is technically a responsibility of municipal governments, funded by a block grant that reflects the number of children, their ages and social conditions, the Danish prime minister announced a few years ago that all children aged one and older, with working parents or parents who are students were guaranteed a place in a subsidised childcare programme. In effect, the Prime Minister announced a standard for all municipalities to follow and, for the most part, they did. As a result, there has been a significant increase in childcare coverage in a country already known for its high rate. In early 1998, coverage rates in out-of-home care covering the full work day, were as follows: 50% of infants under age one (when most mothers are at home on leave), 80% of the one to two-year-olds, and 93% of children aged three to five.

Childcare quality declined somewhat in the early 1990s, albeit from an exceptionally high baseline (lower staff: child ratios, larger groups), but there is beginning a return to earlier standards and conviction that quality matters and should be sustained. Given earlier economic problems, it is understandable that the first priority has been to ensure a full supply of places for all children with employed parents or with special needs. The basic guarantee has been largely met, but there are some shortages in care during irregular or unusual hours (at night, during weekends). Apart from filling these needs, the current intention on the part of the ministry, is to extend coverage to the children of unemployed and at-home parents who wish their children to participate. As essential as childcare/pre-school is if women with young children are to be in the labour force, there is growing conviction that these programmes are important for all children whatever their parents' employment status.

Denmark has a 28-week paid and job protected maternity leave of which two weeks can be used before expected birth. Ten weeks of the post childbirth leave are available to either parent and an additional four weeks can be taken only by fathers. The cash benefit provided while on leave is equal to about 60% of prior wages (up to a maximum), but most employers top this up, so that in effect most working parents receive their full wage while on leave (Moss and Devin, 1999). In addition, a supplementary one-year parental (or childcare) leave was enacted in 1992, paid through the unemployment benefit system at the rate of 60% of the maximum unemployment benefit. The first six months are a guaranteed right and the second has to be in agreement with the employer. Nonetheless, in effect, working parents now have between one–and-a-half and two years paid leave following childbirth.

The government has recently proposed a 'children's policy package' that includes several items for public discussion. These include a proposal that employers must permit workers with school-aged children to take their vacations while their children are on school vacation, that firms should be strongly urged to establish more 'family friendly' policies, and a proposal for more systematic and regular monitoring of the situation of children in Denmark. A Danish government official in mid-1998 commented: "The discussion in Denmark is no longer about what kind of cuts are necessary but which child policy domains are most in need of increased expenditures".

Sweden. Sweden experienced its major economic crisis in the early/

mid-1990s. Economic growth was negative for some years and real GDP fell. Its unemployment rate 'exploded' in the early 1990s reaching a high of more than 8%, four times the rate during the 1980s. The cost of unemployment benefits rose dramatically and the budget deficit 'boomed'. Sweden leads Europe in population aging and has recently announced a reform of its generous old age pensions system. Its child poverty rate rose from 6% in 1990 to 8.5% in 1994 (when the US rate was 22%).

The Swedish economy is now recovering. Sweden's official unemployment rate was about 7.5% in 1998, slightly higher than the OECD average, but this counts beneficiaries of its extensive training and education programmes as employed. Its 'real' unemployment rate would be closer to 10-11%, but it has had a long-standing response to unemployment that includes a stress on 'active' rather than 'passive' labour market policies (education and training programmes rather than unemployment benefits). The Swedes continue to link receipt of social benefits to work, or preparation for work.

During the period of 'hard times' in the mid-1990s, Sweden reduced its child benefit from 750 SK a month (about $100) to 640 (about $80) (the first-ever cut in the nominal value of these benefits). The supplementary benefit provided to larger families with three or four children was reduced for existing large families receiving the benefit, and eliminated for subsequent ones. The child support benefit (guaranteeing a minimal level of support to children in single parent families) was reformed, linking court-ordered support awards to the non-custodial parent's income but eliminating the indexing of the minimum support benefit. The income-tested housing allowance benefit was reduced somewhat and eligibility criteria were more sharply targeted on low-income families. Of particular significance, Sweden reduced the rate at which benefits replaced wages from 90% to a low of 75% for parenting, unemployment and sickness benefits, but the length of time recipients could receive the benefits was not cut.

With regard to services, the supply of childcare was sustained but quality was sacrificed somewhat, although it still compared well internationally. Staff:child ratios declined slightly, group size increased (from 15 to 18 for three to six-year-olds, but lower for one to two-year-olds). Parent fees rose (from 15-20% of operating costs to 25-30% in some municipalities, as compared with about 70% in the US). About 15% of the services were privatised, about half of those now are for-profit, operating largely through contracts with local government.

Despite these cuts, school meals remained free and available to all children during these years, Sweden's universal healthcare was sustained, and expenditures on social assistance and special assistance to refugees were doubled as a share of GDP. Moreover, family benefits, which were increased sharply in the early 1990s, continued to increase until 1995 when modest cuts were imposed, and they began to rise again in 1998.

According to Swedish policy scholars Joachim Palme and Irene Wennemo (1998, p 31), family benefits had been subject to 'temporary retrenchment rather than reform', the cuts were modest and there was no restructuring. Sweden experienced a combination of cuts in transfers (cash benefits), increases in taxes (higher social security contributions), rising unemployment and declining wages. It is this fourfold combination – this quadruple 'whammy' – that hurt children and their families most, not the cuts in benefits and services alone, which were really quite modest. Indeed, policies and programmes for children and their families have clearly been protected.

Within two years, between 1996 and 1998, the Swedish economic situation began to turn around and child and family benefits returned to earlier levels. As of mid-1998 child allowances had returned to their nominal high of a few years before (only slightly below the real high) and are worth about 7.5% of average manufacturing wages. In the spring of 1999, the government proposed an increase in child allowances to 850 SEK per month for the year 2000 and 950 in 2001 (about US $1,425 for the year). The supplementary benefit for larger families was re-instated, benefit replacement rates were increased to 80% of prior wages (from the low of 75%, but not the earlier 90%), and will be raised still further next year. The block grants to municipalities for social services including childcare were close to the high level of the earlier 1990s, the budget was in surplus and the surplus was projected to be even larger for this year.

The Swedish parental leave has been enhanced. In addition to the 18-month paid and job-protected leave for working parents that was established by the end of the 1980s and that can be prorated over a more extended period if desired (one year at 80% of prior wages, three months at a flat rate, and three months unpaid), one month of the leave is now assigned specifically to fathers. Fifty percent of eligible fathers now use the leave, more than in any other country, albeit for much less time than mothers (for about six weeks). In addition to the right of working parents to take paid time off to care for an ill child under age 12, employed grandparents now also have the right to take time off to care for an ill grandchild, if such an arrangement is preferred.

All children of working parents and students are now guaranteed a place in subsidised care from the age of one and the government is increasingly stressing the need to provide access regardless of parental employment status. As in Denmark, the Swedish government is convinced that quality matters and expects to exert more pressure on local governments to ensure a return to the earlier higher quality standards. Centres are held to the same standards of quality, and charge the same fees to parents, regardless of whether they are public, private non-profit or for-profit.

Three Nordic social policy scholars (Lehto, Moss, Rostgaard, forthcoming) have concluded that "The Scandinavian model of social and health services has not weakened significantly during the 1990s. As a matter of fact the model is being accomplished in childcare ... [Any weakening that has occurred] ... seems to be rather marginal in comparison to other trends which indicate that the Scandinavian model is still strong, and it is getting even stronger in the area of childcare."

In short, the Swedish welfare state may be less generous today than a decade ago, but child related benefits and services have been protected (although some Swedes would say 'not enough'). Benefit replacement rates are slightly lower now but nonetheless, at 80% of prior wages, very generous. Child allowances have returned to their nominal highs and with very low inflation are now higher than their earlier real levels. Housing allowances are somewhat reduced and more targeted. Single-parent families have been protected. In looking towards the future, the prime minister announced in his September 14, 1999 statement of government policy that child allowances would be raised again, and he stressed the importance of policies that help men and women reconcile work and family life. In a comparative sense, the Scandinavian model remains extraordinarily generous, especially to children and their families.

Continental European countries

France. Like all the European countries in the 1990s, France has been faced with lower rates of economic growth, high rates of social expenditures, and high and persistent rates of unemployment (about 12% at present and even higher earlier). The government has also been faced with a deficit in its social security system since 1991, and pressure to contain its budget deficit in order to qualify for the EMU. Social expenditures – including education, social services and tax benefits – rose throughout the first half of the 1990s, from 27.7% of GDP in 1990 to 31.2% in 1993 and then declined slightly, to 30.8% by 1996 (the latest figures available). Pensions (old age and survivors) accounted for more than 40% of the expenditures in 1996, health for one third, and family and maternity benefits for almost 9% in 1996, a fairly consistent figure in the 1990s, but down from a high of 10.4% in 1985 and 9.3% in 1990. More than half the expenditures for family benefits are for universal benefits even though there continues to be a trend toward increased targeting.

In 1994, constraints were placed on pensions and healthcare and slowed growth in both of these policy domains. The numbers of the long-term unemployed rose but unemployment benefit expenditures decreased as more of the unemployed exhausted their eligibility for benefits. Yet family benefits increased at an average rate of 11% during the first half of the decade. The basic benefit was increased. The maximum age for family allowances was increased to cover students in higher education, and the allowance paid to parents with school-aged children, provided at the beginning of the school year, was raised substantially. The child rearing allowance for parents with very young children (those under age three) was extended to cover those with two or more children (not three or more as earlier). The numbers of lone mothers benefiting from the means-tested lone parent allowance increased, as did those benefiting from the income-tested housing allowance.

In 1996 some cuts were imposed on the family benefit system, as France prepared to reduce its budget deficit and qualify for the EMU. Family benefits were frozen. The special nine-month allowance provided during pregnancy and the first four months after birth was income-tested. On the other hand, proposals to include family benefits in taxable income and to means test family allowances were rejected. Some changes were made in the income tax system, which favoured high-income families, to make it less generous to such families. The 24 different family allowances including both universal and income tested benefits remain. Pre-school programmes covering all children aged three to five, and half of the two-year-olds in a full-day programme, and childcare services for the under threes, were sustained, but not increased. And, according to an article in *Le Monde* (8 July 1999) reporting on the annual conference of French family organisations, the French government is proposing several modest policy enhancements including continuing efforts to help with the reconciliation of work and family life, ensuring social benefits for those who work part-time, and phasing in an extension of family allowances to youth aged 20-22, if still living at home.

Despite high unemployment rates, severe financial pressures, efforts to reduce the budget deficit, and efforts to move towards more targeting generally including child and family benefits, family benefits remain very important in France and thus far they remain protected.

Austria and Germany. Turning now to Austria and Germany. Since 1990, in addition to the problems facing the other European countries, Germany has been confronted with the problem of adjusting to reunification with East Germany. During the years that followed, unemployment rates rose from about 7-9% in the old Länder or states, and 10-17% in the new. Female labour-force participation rates increased, but female unemployment rates even now remain painfully high – about 15% in the old states and 20% in the new. The high rates in the eastern states are largely due to cuts in childcare services that used to employ women. At the same time, however, child benefit rates were increased from 230 DM to 250, subsequently indexed, and was increased again by another 20 DM per month per child in 2000. A guarantee for a subsidised place in pre-school was introduced for the three to five-year-olds and about 90% are now enrolled, albeit largely in half-day programmes. The child support guarantee for children in single-parent families was modestly improved, and the three-year job-protected parental leave following childbirth was sustained. However, the cash benefit covering the first two years of parental leave continued to decline in real value (it is not index linked and the benefit has not been raised since 1986 when it was first introduced) and is means-tested after the first six months – although at a level that permits most new parents to qualify for it. For each child, women currently receive three years credit towards their pensions, computed at the level of 75% of the average wage; the plan is to raise the credit to 100% of the average wage. Finally, the income tax threshold has been raised to cover the equivalent of the tax-free social assistance benefit level. Overall, although modest, child benefits have been protected in Germany. Those living in the former East Germany experienced some cuts, especially with regard to childcare, but not those in the west. A high official in the Ministry of Family Affairs, Senior Citizens, Women and Youth stressed to us that regardless of the current austerity proposals in Germany, child and family policies will be protected.

Austrian family benefits developed in the 1990s in the context of Austria's efforts at meeting the criteria for joining the EU and, subsequently, the EMU. In 1994-95, Austria carried out an austerity programme in order to qualify for the EMU. Although many experts believe that the cuts that were imposed would have been needed in any case, politicians found it helpful to place the blame on Brussels. The deficit was too high; debt payments were a very large item in the budget and could not continue to rise indefinitely. Two major budget consolidation programmes were established resulting in major cuts in social spending, the first in 1996 and the second in 1997. The first was criticised severely because of its disproportionate impact on low-income families. Although pensions were affected more significantly, in part in response to the obvious demographic problems including the rapid ageing of the population, and unemployment benefits were also cut, children and child policy took a particularly severe hit. Family allowances were reduced by about 100 AS per child per month – a significant decline. The extended parental leave was shortened somewhat and cash birth allowances were largely abolished. Although the family benefit cuts were largely marginal and constituted only a very small portion of total social spending, the public saw these as 'real cuts'. For low-income families, the pain was especially severe. They were hurt both by the cuts in family benefits and the cuts in unemployment benefits.

Public opinion mobilised around preventing further cuts and reversing some of the developments, and the efforts were successful. The cuts were largely reversed, influenced in large part, as well, by a high court decision similar to the German case that ruled that children must be supported by public policy at the same level of adequacy, either through the income tax system or the transfer system. The political compromise between left and right led to a big increase in family allowances, using the device of a refundable tax credit. In addition, the duration of the parental leave was partially restored (the six months that had been cut from the two-year leave was restored, but limited to fathers) and there are proposals to raise the benefit level. There has been a small increase in the supply of childcare places, but a big shortage continues regarding infant and toddler care. A child rearing allowance is now being proposed (similar to the Finnish policy), to pay (at parental option) for in-home care, out-of-home care, or to provide a kind of 'mother's wage' for an at-home mother. Women continue to receive four years' credit towards their old age pension for each child they have. Austrian family allowances remain among the most generous in the EU/OECD countries. The conclusion, according to several Austrian scholars, is that child and family policies are protected now and for the immediate future.

The Anglo-American countries

At the other end of the 'generosity' scale are Britain and the US. We begin with Britain.

Britain. Despite its clear membership in the Anglo-American 'family of nations', its earlier move toward economic liberalism in the Thatcher era, and its stress on means-tested rather than universal benefits, British social policy toward children historically, has been among the most generous in this 'less generous' group (Kamerman and Kahn, 1997a and b). In recent years, following the US pattern, Britain has moved to increase its labour market flexibility, deregulate wages, contain social spending and increase privatisation, and it has reduced its unemployment rate almost to the OECD average.

Recently published evidence from the first sweep of the new European Community Household Panel Survey found that the 1993 British general poverty rate (incomes below 50% of the national median for both individuals and households) was third from the highest out of the European 12, lower only than Portugal and Greece (Bradshaw, 1999a, 1999b). Moreover Britain had the highest child poverty rate of the 12, about 32% as compared with 5% in Denmark, 8% in Sweden and 12% in France. In the second wave (Whitten, 1999), with a higher poverty standard (60% of national median income), Britain still ranked third, now tied with Greece, with only Portugal and Ireland having higher poverty rates in 1994. Its child poverty rate was second highest among the European 15.

Bradbury and Jäntti (1999) found that of the 4 out of 15 EU/OECD countries that had increases in the percentage of children living below the US poverty threshold from 1985 to the mid-1990s, the increase was greatest in UK.

Turning to another database, the LIS survey results for 1985 and 1990, Britain had the third highest poverty rate among the 19 countries, exceeded only by the US and Russia, and it had the highest rate among those countries in which child poverty rates were higher than poverty rates among the elderly.

Under the leadership of Blair and New Labour, there are beginning efforts at reducing the assistance caseload (welfare in US terms) and linking work expectations more closely with benefits. However, despite new encouragements and incentives, there is no equivalent of the US requirement that lone mothers claiming assistance go to work, and there is no time limit on receipt of benefits by lone mothers. Britain has by far the highest rate of social assistance use among the European 15. A minimum wage (a new policy for Britain) was implemented as of 1 April 1999 at a level similar to that of the US minimum wage (£3.60 an hour), with a Low Pay Commission established to monitor its impact and propose recommendations for increases, from time to time. There has been a substantial increase in the basic universal child benefit and the higher benefit for first children, but these are still not indexed. The supplementary lone-parent benefit has been eliminated, and as a result single mothers are worse off now than before. There is a proposal for universal and free pre-school for all four-year-olds (compulsory school begins at age five, and more than half the four-year-olds already attend school or pre-school). The prior British equivalent of the US Earned Income Tax Credit (Family Credit) has been superseded by a more generous Working Families Tax Credit implemented in October 1999. This tax credit also includes a provision for a new childcare tax credit to provide help for working families with moderate incomes. The credit will meet up to 70% of childcare costs (in centres or family daycare providers) up to a maximum of about $160 for a family with one child and $240 a week for those with two or more – far more generous that the US Dependent Care Tax Credit. The child benefit levels under social assistance have been raised. And the government has created a new unit to coordinate policies on social exclusion.

The British government announced in the summer of 1999 that it was increasing maternity and other parental leaves to allow working parents to spend more time with their children. The new British measures that took effect in December 1999 allow biological and adoptive parents to take up to 13 weeks of unpaid leave a year for the first five years of each child's life. Paid maternity leave was increased from 14 to 18 weeks, and women qualified for the benefit more easily. Finally, parents would also be entitled to time off to cope with family emergencies including a child's illness or problems with baby sitters or childcare arrangements. In short, as LSE economist and social policy scholar Howard Glennerster (1997) wrote:

> Distinctively less generous than the Scandinavian or continental European countries, the UK system of welfare is much more dependent on the market and income-tested benefits but keeps its highly developed national minimum safety net and national responsibilities for health and education. It may be called 'a hard core welfare state'. (p 24)

Lone-parent families continue to present a major problem and the long-established policy of supporting lone mothers at home is beginning to change to one of encouraging, if not requiring, that such women take jobs. The big gap in encouraging these women to take jobs, however, is the shortage of affordable (subsidised) childcare, especially for the twos and younger, and that is only beginning to be addressed. The new parental leave policies are clearly a step in the right direction.

The United States (US). The US is well known as a social policy – and child and family policy – laggard (Kamerman and Kahn, 1997a, 1988). Public social expenditures in the US, as a percentage of GDP, are far below the EU countries and most of the more advanced OECD countries, and have been for many years. Even if one includes the voluntary sector and tax expenditures as listed by Adema and Einerhand (1998), the gap may be smaller but the US still lags. Nonetheless, according to the OECD social expenditure database (1998b), family benefits (direct cash expenditures) almost doubled in the first half of the decade. Expenditures on family services rose by more than 50%, and spending on childcare more than tripled. Federal expenditures on children increased also in the years since then, and some states increased their spending on children as well, but firm data are not yet generally and systematically available.

However, in contrast to these other countries, the US has experienced an especially strong economy during the second half of the 1990s, low inflation, a tight labour market and the lowest rate of unemployment currently than at any time in the last 29 years.

During the first half of the 1990s, federal child and family policies expanded significantly. The EITC, (similar to the earlier British Family Credit and the current Working Families Tax Credit), was increased significantly in 1993 and adjusted slightly for family size. Childcare expenditures were increased for children and families receiving social assistance or at risk for receipt, and for compensatory education programmes as well as other early intervention programmes. After a multi-year fight in Congress and rejections by Republican Presidents, the first federal Family and Medical Leave Act (FMLA) was passed and signed into law by President Clinton in 1993, providing for a 12-week job-protected but unpaid parental (family and disability) leave.

At the same time, the debate about the financial viability of the old age pension system and the health insurance programme for the elderly became more intense. And concern about the high and growing budget deficit raised widespread anxiety about public social spending.

A dramatic change in child and family policy occurred in mid-1996 with the enactment of PL 104-193, the Personal Responsibility and Work Opportunities Reconciliation Act. This legislation replaced what had previously been the core US family policy – AFDC – a policy targeted largely on poor single-mother families and providing assistance through matching federal and state grants. Income eligibility and cash benefits varied across the states. With the establishment of a new assistance programme, Temporary Assistance to Needy Families (TANF), assistance policies were devolved still further to the states, a fixed sum of money was provided to each state rather than an amount varying with claimant numbers and caseload size. Eligibility was changed from an entitlement to a time-limited benefit, work was mandated for poor lone mothers with children from three months of age and older, a wide range of sanctions were imposed or permitted, reducing assistance benefits to those who would not abide by the very stringent qualifying rules, and eligibility was constrained, thus restricting access by poor disabled children to more generous benefits and ending eligibility for some poor immigrant children. One result has been a dramatic decline in assistance caseloads from a high of 14 million beneficiaries in 1995 to seven million at present, thereby increasing the potential per capita assistance funds which may be used for direct cash benefits or other child and family-related initiatives.

In addition to establishing the new TANF programme, with what many view as punitive and coercive provisions, several other provisions and related subsequent legislation led to increased public funding for children and families. Included among these are increased federal childcare funds for those families moving from assistance to employment, a new child tax credit benefiting middle class parents primarily, and new legislation substantially increasing funds for child healthcare. Some earlier constraints on immigrants were removed and recently, the President has encouraged states to use unemployment insurance funds as a device for funding a paid FMLA. But at the same time, take-up of the federal in-kind benefit for food, which benefits children in lower-income families, declined significantly and funds for federal child nutrition programmes were cut. Paralleling the cuts in social spending (and some increases in child-specific funding) a budget freeze was imposed on social spending in a further effort at reducing the deficit.

Overall, therefore, despite a far stronger economy than any other of the OECD countries; but with concerns about a budget deficit and a stress on a renewed effort at 're-moralising' social policy, the US picture suggests a mixed story. Public investment in children increased in the first half of the decade. Federal expenditures on social assistance for lone mothers were sustained in the second half of the decade; but eligibility for assistance was curtailed for this group as well as for some poor disabled children, some poor children in immigrant families, and state investments reflect a diverse and mixed picture, too. Some lone mothers leaving assistance for jobs have ended up better off economically than when receiving assistance

(Bravier, 1999; Loprest, 1999, *New York Times*, 1999), but a significant, if not as yet fully known proportion, are worse off even with jobs than they were when receiving assistance. It is alleged, also, that a larger portion of the homeless families are now made up of mothers with children. If or when the economy falters, this group may be in dire straights.

Reports of outcomes now depend heavily on state-level data, and given the diversity of state programmes, it is difficult at this point to obtain a firm picture of impacts. In the guise of concern about the budget deficit, conservatives were able to enact stringent assistance legislation. Yet with a significant budget surplus currently, 'liberals', in the US sense, may advocate for more public spending on education, early childhood programmes and healthcare, along with reforms in the pension and health insurance programmes for the aged. But no action has been implemented as yet, and no clear movement has been made to protect – let alone expand – public investment in children. Moreover, US child poverty rates, although somewhat lower now than earlier in the decade, are far higher than in any other of the advanced industrialised countries, even when in-kind benefits are included.

Why do they protect children?

Child and family benefits, as we have seen, have been favoured in many OECD countries. Why? Rationales for protecting and promoting child policy abound in a variety of national and international platforms. Several of the arguments overlap somewhat.

First, there is a strong *moral argument* for supporting child policies made in almost all the countries. The 46-country Council of Europe's Steering Committee on Social Policy report on *The Crisis of the Welfare State* (1998) begins with a statement of premises including the following:

> The situation of children provides a special rationale for the welfare state. Children do not choose to be born and brought up by poor parents ... If the children cannot be blamed for being poor, the reason why they are found to be in poverty is irrelevant. Whether it is unemployment, sickness, divorce, or simply indolence on the part of their parents, in no case should children be deprived of the opportunity of becoming full citizens. (p 7)

Second, in many countries, there is interest in building social *solidarity*, across generations and classes and strong interest in tempering market forces for the good of the larger society. One consequence is that the children's cause is not associated with a particular party but rather cuts across the political spectrum and generates strong middle class support.

A third argument in several countries is the desire to keep *child poverty* rates low. Extensive research in the US as well as elsewhere has concluded that, as stated in an OECD (1998) report: "The well being of children is drastically reduced by being raised in poverty". (OECD, 1999, p 85; Duncan and Brooks-Gunn, 1997; Chase-Lansdale and Brooks-Gunn, 1995). Wennemo (1994) in her study of the OECD countries from 1950-1985 found that poverty, income inequality and public policies had a greater impact on infant mortality than levels of economic development.

Pronatalism, a fourth rationale, has been a longstanding motivation underlying selected social policies in several countries, certainly at the latent if not manifest level, but it is clearly declining. France has been the leader among those countries expressing pronatal concerns, but French officials now, in contrast with the past, deny any interest in pronatalism.

Fifth, *high female labour-force participation* and the concomitant needs of children whose mothers are working outside of the home, is another factor that cuts across many countries and has been a strong rationale for selected policies, in particular childcare services and maternity and parenting leaves (Kamerman and Kahn, 1981; Esping-Andersen, 1996).

Promoting child well-being as a form of *investment in human capital* is a sixth factor and is discussed in several countries as well. An OECD social policy report (1999) states that early childhood programmes (childcare, pre-school, home visiting) are crucial in establishing a firm basis for further learning and productive adulthood, and especially important for children in disadvantaged families. Some welfare state scholars such as Esping-Andersen (1996, p 264) would argue that human capital investment should take priority even over the goal of egalitarianism, at least for the immediate future.

Still a seventh factor has emerged in recent years in Europe. This is a growing *focus on children per se* rather than the family unit, as targets of social policy, and increased recognition of children as individuals, themselves entitled to rights and to protection regardless of parental status or behaviour. Thus, the Danish sociologist Jens Qvotrup (1994) has argued that "Children are *human beings*, not only 'human becomings'" (p 18). They warrant investment as children, not just for what they may become as adults.

Nor is the European response seen as particularly burdensome. A repeated theme in discussions in several countries is that investment in children is inexpensive, has substantial payoff and is visible. It is easier to improve child policy, given the much lower shares of GDP directed at children as compared with pensions and healthcare.

Conclusions

Public expenditure/investment in child and family policies in the advanced industrialised countries has not kept up with expenditures on pensions and health and, therefore, declined as a portion of GDP and social expenditures generally fairly steadily since the 1950s. Nonetheless, in the 1990s, when many countries deliberately set out to curtail social expenditures, and targeted pension policies especially and, to a lesser extent health, sickness, and unemployment benefits, child and family benefits appear to have been protected. Even where there were some cuts, in some countries in the early or mid 1990s, they have been replaced in more recent years, in part because of widespread public support and in part because they remain only a small part of overall social expenditures. Indeed, the overall trend in child and family expenditures in the EU and the OECD countries has been upward especially in the last half of the 1990s. Family allowances have been sustained or raised. Parental leaves have been extended where they existed and even newly introduced in a few countries. Childcare and Early Childhood Education and Care services have continued to increase in supply. In some countries, the declining birth rate has led to higher per capita benefits, even when total expenditures have not increased or increased only slightly.

The major caveat is that even where benefits have been protected, it is largely nominal benefits that have increased or been sustained. Coupled with this is the increase in lone-mother families in an era in which the family's standard of living increasingly requires two earners and when women's earnings remain, at best, only 75-80% of male earnings.

One other point must be made here. Our focus in this paper has been on child and family cash and in-kind benefits, on the implicit assumption that public investment in children leads to better outcomes. These, however, are not the only significant policies affecting the standard of living and quality of life of children and their families. Micklewright (1998) noted the significance of differential unemployment rates – higher rates in households with children as compared with those with no children – and the need to have such data in order to assess impacts on children. We and others have noted the importance of time as a factor affecting children and their families, especially the constraints on parental time when two parents or a sole parent is in the labour force (Kamerman and Kahn, 1995; Micklewright, 1998). Access to housing is still another important policy. Some would add the need for an entitlement to a minimum income in tough times remains an important issue. The absence of attention to these issues here should not be viewed as suggesting that they are unimportant.

Child and family benefits are low on the agenda in the context of urgent economic, employment and other social policies, but they appear to have been protected at a time when other benefits are under pressure. Certainly, some countries invest more in children than others, but they are likely to be the same countries that invested more in children in earlier years as well. And it is unclear what arguments would lead wealthy but low-investment countries to allocate more. In some countries the moral argument, which can include the anti-poverty issue as well as that of children's rights, is powerful. Where it is not, there is much to be said for the current OECD argument regarding the need to facilitate female labour-force participation in countries with economic restructuring. In the long term, if the goal is to raise the children's cause on the policy agenda, whatever the international or country-specific response to globalisation and its consequences, the human capital concerns in all these countries offer an additional overwhelming and very practical case for adequate investment in our next generations.

Notes

[1] The ESSPROS and OECD data in this section deal only with public expenditures. As W. Adema and M. Einerhand (1998) have recently shown, the addition of tax expenditures and private sector expenditures would add substantially to the totals and significantly reduce the observed gaps among countries. There is no reason to believe that this would affect our child and family policy analysis. Our analysis of developments in the OECD countries is limited to those countries for which there are data for these years, and excludes the most recent additions to the OECD: Czech Republic, Hungary, Poland, Korea and Mexico.

[2] Other analysts, also relying on OECD data, have reported findings similar to ours with regard to family benefits. See in this volume, H. Oxley, Thai-Thanh Dang, M. Forster and M. Pellizzari, 'Income Inequalities and Poverty among Children and Households with Children in Selected OECD Countries: Trends and Determinants'. Subsequent to our reporting, J. C. Gornick and M. Meyers,

looking at 19 countries, found for the mid-1980s to the mid-1990s that whereas spending on family benefits accounted for a smaller share of total social expenditures in most countries, the actual per child and per working mother expenditure grew substantially in most countries, because of the declining fertility rates and concomitant decline in the child population. Growth in spending for paid paternity and parental leave at a time of growth in mothers' employment was particularly steep. 'Cross-National Family Policy Developments During Economic Hard Times', Presented at the Annual Research Conference, Association for Policy Analysis and Management (APPAM), Washington, DC, November 4-5, 1999.

[3] This section is based on several sources: (1) Country reports prepared for the Council of Europe Steering Committee on Social Policy Meeting at Strasbourg, May 5-7,1998 and an integrated report on 'The Crisis of the Welfare State: How to Respect and Guarantee the Social Rights of Individuals whilst Controlling Costs', Draft Final Report of the Coordinated Research Programme in the Social Field 1996/97, April 6, 1998, prepared under the direction of J. Palme, Institute for Social Research, Stockholm, Sweden; (2) Reports from the European Observatory on National Family Policies 1997; (3) OECD Background Documents on 'The New Social Policy Agenda for a Caring World', prepared for the OECD Meeting of the Employment, Labour and Social Affairs, Committee at Ministerial Level on Social Policy, June 23 and 24, 1998 and discussions at OECD in July, 1999; (4) Interviews with government officials in Denmark and Sweden, June/ July, 1998 and in Germany in June, 1999; (5) Interviews at the Danish National Social Research Institute (Niels Ploug, etc) and the Swedish Institute for Social Research (Joachim Palme), June/July, 1998; (6) Interviews in Vienna, June, 1999 with Christoph Badelt, Vice Rector and Professor, University of Vienna, Bernd Marin, Director of the European Centre on Social Welfare Policy and Research, and Helmut Wintersberger, Co-ordinator of the European Family Observatory; (7) Interviews with John Ditch , Professor of Social Policy at the University of York, England, and Coordinator of the European Observatory on National Family Policies, and Jonathan Bradshaw, Professor of Social Policy, University of York, England, and member of the European Observatory; (8) Interviews on July 1999 with Peter Whitten and Eric Marlier at EUROSTAT and various EUROSTAT reports.

References

Adema, W. and Einerhand, M. (1998) *The growing role of private social benefits*, Occasional paper No 32, Paris: OECD.

Bradbury, B. and Jäntti, M. (1999) *Child poverty across industrialized nations*, Unicef Innocenti Occasional Papers, Economic and Social Policy Studies No 71, Florence: UNICEF International Child Development Center.

Bradshaw, J. (1999a) 'Developing poverty measures: research in Europe: defining and measuring poverty', mimeo.

Bradshaw, J. (1999b) 'Prospects for poverty in Britain in the first 25 years of the next century', *Sociology*.

Bravier, R. (1999) 'An early look at the effects of welfare reform', unpublished paper, Washington, DC: Office of Manpower and Budget.

Chase-Lansdale, P.L. and Brooks-Gunn, J. (eds) (1995) *Escape from poverty: What makes a difference for children?*, New York, NY: Cambridge University Press.

Council of Europe (1998) *The crisis of the welfare state*, Strasbourg: Steering Committee on Social Policy.

Duncan, G.J. and Brooks-Gunn, J. (eds) (1997) *The consequences of growing up poor*, New York, NY: Russell Sage Foundation.

Esping-Anderson, G. (ed) (1996) *Welfare states in transition*, Thousand Oaks, CA: Russell Sage.

Eurostat (1999) *Social Protection Expenditures and Receipts 1980-1996*, Luxembourg: Eurostat.

Glennerster, H. (1997) *United Kingdom's social policy: From an old social contract to a new?*, London: London School of Economics.

Kalisch, D.W., Aman, T. and Buchele, L.A. (1998) *Social and health policies in OECD countries: A survey of current programmes and recent developments*, Labour Market and Social Policy Occasional Papers No 33 and Annexe, Paris: OECD.

Kamerman, S.B. and Kahn, A.J. (1981) *Child care, family benefits and working parents*, New York, NY: Columbia University Press.

Kamerman, S.B. and Kahn, A.J. (1988) 'Social policy and children in the United States and Europe', in J.L Palmer et al (eds) *The vulnerable*, Washington, DC: Urban Institute.

Kamerman, S.B. and Kahn, A.J. (1995) *Starting right*, New York, NY: Oxford University Press.

Kamerman, S.B. and Kahn, A.J. (1997a) 'Investing in children: government expenditures for children and their families in western industrialized countries', in A.G. Cornia and S. Danziger (eds) *Child poverty and deprivation in the industrialized countries*, Oxford: Oxford University Press.

Kamerman, S.B. and Kahn, A.J. (eds) (1997b) *Family change and family policies in Great Britain, Canada, New Zealand, and the United States*, Oxford: Oxford University Press.

Lehto, J., Moss, N. and Rostgaard, T. (Forthcoming) 'Universal public care and health care services?', in M. Kautto et al (eds) *Nordic social policy: Changing welfare states*, London: Routledge.

Le Monde, 7 August 1999.

Loprest, P. (1999) *Families who leave welfare: Who are they and how are they doing?*, Assessing the New Federalism Series, Washington, DC: Urban Institute.

Micklewright, J. (1998) *The EMU: Microeconomics and children*, Florence: Innocenti Centre.

Moss, P. and Nevin, F. (eds) (1999) *Parental leaves: Progress of pitfall?*, Netherlands: Interdisciplinary Demographic Institute.

OECD (1998) *Social expenditure data base, 1980-1996*, Paris: OECD.

OECD (1999) *A caring world: The new social policy agenda*, Paris: OECD.

Palme, J. and Wennemo, I. (1998) *Swedish social security in the 1990s: Reform and retrenchment,* Stockholm: The Printing Office of the Cabinet and Ministries.

Qvortrup, J., Bardy, M., Sgritta, G. and Wintersberger, H. (eds) (1994) *Childhood matters: Social theory, practice, and politics*. Brookfield, VT: Ashfield Publishing.

Rainwater, L. and Smeeding, T. (1995) *Doing poorly: The real income of American children in a comparative perspective*, LIS Working Papers No 127, Luxembourg: Luxembourg Income Study.

Talos, E. and Badelt, C. (1999) 'The welfare state between new stimuli and new pressures: Austrian social policy and the EU', *Journal of European Social Policy*, Fall.

The New York Times, 5 August 1999.

Wennemo, I. (1994) *Sharing the costs of children*, Stockholm: Swedish Institute for Social Research.

Whitten, P. (1999) *Living conditions in Europe*, Luxembourg: Eurostat.

What have we learned and where do we go from here?

Koen Vleminckx and Timothy M. Smeeding

"Tackling child poverty is an investment, but it takes a brave politician who is ready to take tough decisions today, for long term returns." (Martin Barnes, Director of the Child Poverty Action Group)

Introduction

The chapters in this volume contain many valuable insights for policy makers and a rich unfinished research agenda for academics and think tanks interested in similar issues. Most of the contributors discuss the policy implications of their findings and formulate some detailed policy suggestions. This section presents an overview of some of the most important findings, policy discussions and research agendas covered. Despite the variety of national differences in economic and policy structures, several policy findings emerge which apply across a wide range of nations and which therefore bear consideration in future attempts to reduce child poverty.

Trends in child poverty and child well-being

Several contributions in this volume reveal a wide range of child poverty rates in countries that are at broadly similar levels of economic development. According to Bradbury and Jäntti relative child poverty rates in the OECD member states varied in the mid-1990s from 3.4% in Finland to 26.3% in the United States (US). Within the European Union (EU), relative child poverty rates ranged from 3.4% in Finland to 21.3% in the United Kingdom (UK). The Nordic countries all had remarkably low levels of relative child poverty, which remained constantly below 5% throughout the 1990s. The Benelux countries and France had slightly higher child poverty rates, but the highest levels of relative child poverty among the continental EU member states were found in Germany, Spain, and, especially, Italy. The relative child poverty rates in these countries had increased during the early 1990s. The highest relative child poverty rate within the EU was found in the UK. This is due to the sharp increases in relative child poverty in the UK during the second half of the 1980s.

As for the transition economies of Central and Eastern European countries, Bradbury and Jäntti report relatively high and increasing relative child poverty rates for both Hungary and Poland during the first half of the 1990s. Yet, the lowest levels of relative child poverty among all the industrialised countries covered by this study are reported for the Czech Republic and Slovakia. However, the highest relative child poverty rate in the entire study was also found in one of the transition economies: Russia.

The Anglophone countries outside Europe are also all high up in the relative child poverty ranking. In Australia the relative child poverty rates increased during the 1990s, while the Canadian rate decreased slightly over the same period. An extremely high relative child poverty rate of 26.3% is reported for the US, which is just a few percentage points below the rate reported for Russia (26.6%). However, the regional differences in relative child poverty rates within the US are as large as those within the EU. This is an important fact, especially since the US recently shifted most of its anti-poverty policy from the federal to the state level.

Rainwater, Smeeding and Coder reveal in this volume, using a 'national' poverty standard, that the relative child poverty rates within the US range from 10.7% in the combined Colorado/Utah/Nevada area to 33.3% in New Mexico.

The range of child poverty rates is slightly compressed when relative child poverty standards are defined and applied for each state, reflecting regional differences in incomes. Based on these 'state' poverty standards, the likelihood that a randomly picked child will live in a poor family ranges from 12.3% in the North-Dakota/South-Dakota area to 25.7% in California. Strikingly the southern states look less poor when state poverty standards are applied and there is clearly more variation within this group of states, often thought to be homogeneous.

Using an absolute poverty definition, based on real standards of living in a country rather than on average income levels, does not make an important difference for the majority of industrialised countries as they remain approximately in the same region in the relative child poverty 'league'. However, there are some important exceptions. Bradbury and Jäntti show that absolute child poverty rates in transition economies such as the Czech Republic and Poland are dramatically higher than the relative child poverty rates in these countries. This clearly reflects the relatively low living standards in these countries, a fact that is ignored in calculations of relative child poverty rates. In Canada and the US absolute child poverty rates are much lower than the relative child poverty rates, reflecting the high living standards in two of the richest countries in the world. However, the relative child poverty rates indicate that an important group of children in both countries are excluded from the normal life of their societies.

The regional disparities in relative poverty rates within the EU have influenced some European governments in their conviction that the EU needs a specific poverty convergence process, which would gradually eliminate these disparities and result in a considerable reduction of poverty rates throughout the Union. Although the EU has different funds and programmes aimed at improving the economic and social cohesion among its member states, new developments aim at introducing clear benchmarks and monitoring programmes.

Poverty benchmarking and the measurement of child poverty and well-being

In recent years several European governments have committed themselves to reduce (child) poverty. In 1997, the Irish Government adopted a National Anti-Poverty Strategy (NAPS), including a global poverty reduction target, which seems to have been successfully implemented. The global poverty reduction target was even modified in 1999 to aim at a greater reduction than initially envisaged. At the same time child poverty has come to be recognised as a major challenge, and Irish policy makers are currently considering various options for improving the situation for families with children. In 1999, the UK government committed itself to end child poverty by 2020 and to reduce it by a quarter by 2004. Although the relatively small falls revealed by the latest statistics are disappointing, significant increases in financial support for children have been made. The Portuguese government made a similar commitment, promising to end child poverty by 2010, while the Irish government recognised that reducing child poverty was a major challenge.

These developments seem to have created the momentum needed to make real progress on a European level. In March 2000, the Lisbon EU

Council called for steps to make "a decisive impact on the eradication of poverty by setting adequate targets" and singled children out as one of the specific groups "for concern". However, the Lisbon Council did not retain the European Commission's proposal to request EU member states to halve child poverty by 2010. Yet, the Lisbon Council set in motion a process that entails great promises for the fight against poverty in Europe. In December 2000, a similar Council organised in Nice decided that the EU member states should implement two-year action plans for combating poverty and social exclusion, similar to the National Action Plans on Employment, which played and continue to play an important role in the improvement of employment policies in Europe. The first National Action Plans on Social Inclusion were submitted to the European Commission by June 2001. In these reports, each government assessed both the level and characteristics of poverty and social exclusion in their country, described the policies they had implemented so far in order to deal with these problems, as well as their aspirations and policies for the future. Several National Action Plans on Social Inclusion submitted in 2001 addressed the issue of poverty and social exclusion among children. The British, Irish and Portuguese governments made child poverty into a key issue, while the Belgian and French governments specifically mentioned children from low-income families as a group of particular concern. Most other governments limited their focus to categories of children that are particularly at risk, such as disabled children and children from minority ethnic groups. The National Action Plans served as a basis for the *Joint Report on Social Inclusion* of the Council and the Commission, submitted to the Laeken Council on 14 December 2001, which was the first policy document on poverty and social exclusion formally endorsed by the EU.

A second major result of the so-called Lisbon process is the development of a common set of EU indicators on poverty and social exclusion. In order to monitor the policies set out in the National Action Plans on Social Inclusion, EU member states had already been invited to develop, at national level, indicators and other monitoring mechanisms capable of measuring progress in regard to each of the specified objectives. In March 2001, the Stockholm Council received a mandate to improve the follow-up in this domain by reaching an agreement on a system of indicators on social inclusion by the end of 2001. The main idea was that these indicators would allow policy makers to better understand the situation in the various member states and to follow important trends. The Social Affairs Council accepted a system of 18 Commonly Agreed Indicators for Social Inclusion and decided that these indicators would be included in the National Action Plans on Social Inclusion and in the *Joint Report on Social Inclusion* starting in 2003.

The system of indicators covers four domains: financial poverty, employment, health and education. Although there is no proposal for commonly agreed indicators on housing, the member states have been requested to use their own indicators to report on adequate housing, housing costs and homelessness in their National Action Plans on Social Inclusion. Although there was broad agreement about the list of concerns to be covered, the portfolio of indicators needed to be balanced. Therefore the Sub-Group on Social Indicators underlined in its proposal the importance of treating them as a whole and not merely a collection of individual indicators. The selected indicators were prioritised by the identification of three separate indicator levels. This was mainly done in order to avoid the loss of transparency by including too many indicators (Atkinson, 2002). 'Level 1' indicators are considered to be lead indicators for the principal dimensions. 'Level 2' indicators are indicators that support these lead indicators and that describe other dimensions of the challenge. 'Level 3' indicators can be selected by the member states and can reflect the specific situation in their country and the importance they give to certain domains. These 'level 3' indicators can provide an opportunity for the development of new indicators and can become a source for future 'level 1' and 'level 2' indicators (Atkinson et al, 2002).

There are no specific indicators on child poverty, although it is suggested to disaggregate the "low income rate after transfers" indicator for various age groups, including those younger than 18. Furthermore, some indicators, such as the one on "early school leavers not in further education or training" and on "persons with low educational attainment" can help governments focus on educational disadvantages related to poverty. Otherwise the issue of child poverty is completely absent from this commonly agreed system of indicators. The Sub-Group on Social Indicators only suggested that "indicators of family distress, such as single parenthood or placements of children, should be considered as valuable additions to the current set of indicators at a later stage". A group of academics consulted by the Belgian presidency during the preparation of the commonly agreed system, also suggested in their report that countries that attach national importance to the reduction of child poverty might consider adding relevant 'level 3' indicators (Atkinson et al, 2002).

Some of the first National Action Plans on Social Inclusion already include indicators on child poverty and well-being. France, Italy, Portugal,

Spain and the UK included a low-income rate for children, and France, Ireland, Italy and the UK referred to the percentage of children in jobless households. The Finnish National Action Plan had included the percentage of children subject to child protection.

As poverty and exclusion of children are to a large extent linked to the poverty and exclusion of their parents, one might question the need for setting up a separate monitoring programme on the subject of poverty and social exclusion among children. The most commonly accepted definitions of poverty and social exclusion, as well as their related indicators, refer to the socioeconomic and cultural status of adults. However, there are some clear arguments to pay particular attention to poverty and social exclusion among children. First of all, children are a group that is particularly vulnerable to poverty and social exclusion. Since they largely depend on adults for their care, many of the causes of poverty and social exclusion are completely beyond the control of children and rarely alterable by children. At the same time they are especially vulnerable to the effects of poverty and social exclusion because their physical, mental, emotional and social capacities are still evolving.

Some of the findings presented in this volume could provide a starting point for the development of specific child poverty benchmarks.

Poverty benchmarking and child poverty

The European Commission defines the poor as "persons, families, and groups of persons whose resources (material, cultural, and social) are so limited as to exclude them from the minimum acceptable way of life in the member state in which they live" (Commission of the European Communities, 1994). This definition is usually implemented by defining a poverty line in terms of income. Most of the contributions in this volume applied a relative standard to define a poverty line, considering persons (adults or children) as being poor when they are living in households with economic resources below a level that is common in the community they are living in. In practice, somebody is defined as being poor when he or she lives in a household with a disposable income, adjusted for the size of the household, that is less than fifty percent of the median disposable income in their country. This is also the method recommended by the European Task Force on Statistics on Social Exclusion and Poverty (Eurostat, 1998), although the Task Force suggests setting the poverty line at sixty percent of the median income in a member state. The use of relative standards to define a poverty line is currently the most common poverty measurement practice, especially in cross-national poverty studies of OECD countries.

An alternative for the relative poverty standards are the 'absolute' or 'fixed real price' poverty standards. These define people as being poor when they are living in a household that is not able to purchase or consume a fixed minimum package of goods in the community they are living in. The US official poverty line is such an absolute poverty measure. It was introduced in the 1960s as part of the Kennedy and Johnson administrations' 'War on Poverty'. It is set in dollars and represents the annual income required to allow a family of a given size to purchase the range of goods and services that are seen as constituting the minimum acceptable way of life in the US. For almost forty years this figure has only been adjusted to reflect changing prices. However, it is currently being reviewed with the goal of developing a more accurate and policy-responsive poverty measure.

In this volume, Bradbury and Jäntti explain how they applied the US official poverty line for a couple with two children to other countries after national currencies had been converted to US dollars by using OECD's Purchasing Power Parities (PPPs). We already mentioned that their results show that the 'absolute' approach does not influence the broad grouping of OECD countries, although there are some important exceptions. Yet, Bradbury and Jäntti are sceptical of the extent to which PPP-adjusted exchange rates correctly reflect the real living standards in these countries. There is currently no absolute child poverty measure that is widely accepted across the industrial world.

Usually the nation is the reference group for defining poverty. However, one of the main points in Rainwater, Smeeding and Coder's contribution is that the question of who is poor could in the future move beyond national borders to groups of nation states, such as the EU, or even to a continental level. The European Commission's Statistical Office (Eurostat) has in the last couple of years published reports on poverty in its member states using both 'national' and 'European' poverty lines. Alternatively, poverty standards could be defined at a regional level. According to Rainwater, Smeeding and Coder, poverty standards should be defined closer to "the social standards that in fact operate when societies define some people as poor", as the evaluations and self-evaluations, which are at the basis of the relative poverty concept, are made in the local community. From this point of view the definition of poverty standards at a state level could be a step in the right direction. However, there are some limitations as one could argue that poverty measures should be defined at the level that is the most relevant for the implementation of anti-povertystrategies, which in most countries remains the national level.

Some contributors have argued that relative income poverty lines are not completely capturing the concept of poverty, because they focus only on the monetary dimension of poverty. A non-monetary deprivation index would reveal the various aspects of living standards and deprivation linked to poverty. The items represented in a deprivation index represent socially perceived necessities that are possessed by most people and reflect basic aspects of current material deprivation. The poverty benchmark adopted by the Irish National Anti-Poverty Strategy (NAPS) focuses on households whose disposable income is situated below the relative income poverty line, while they are also experiencing basic deprivation. Nolan describes in this volume how the use of non-monetary indicators of deprivation can correct the rather partial picture relative poverty rates provide in a situation of rapid growth. As economic growth reached record levels in Ireland during the 1990s, average incomes and the corresponding relative poverty line rose sharply. This resulted in an increase in relative income poverty. When the relative poverty line was combined with a fixed deprivation criterion, this picture changed considerably as the percentage of households falling below the poverty line and experiencing basic deprivation decreased in the period of rapid growth.

Still, both the relative poverty line and the household deprivation indices have some limitations as regards the identification of poor children. Both are designed to measure the extent of deprivation at the level of the household rather than the individual. Both assume the pooling of resources within the household and similar living standards and poverty risk for all household members. Thus, children who are in poverty because of insufficient sharing of resources within the household are not captured by these methods. Nolan suggests that this problem could be corrected by the development of indicators specifically designed to capture deprivation among children, which would allow the combination of relative child poverty measures with specific deprivation indices for children.

In their contribution to this volume, Micklewright and Stewart emphasise the need for a broader and more comprehensive picture of the well-being of children. They prefer a wider view of individual well-being, more similar to that of the United Nations Development Programme's 'Human Development Reports' and the associated 'capability' approach of Amartya Sen. The results presented in their contribution clearly illustrate the importance of a broader approach to child well-being. When they are used to compare the performance of EU and Central and Eastern European countries, they reveal gaps in the achievement of some of the EU member states. Micklewright and Stewart suggest that the EU, which is currently deciding whether some of the Central and Eastern European countries are fit to join, "should also note that the new members may bring important lessons with them and would set, at least in some areas of child welfare, new high standards for the rest of the Union to follow". In our opinion, this also shows that it is important that a broader view is taken when the EU member states decide which poverty benchmarks they will adapt to evaluate the performance of the member states, especially in view of the future membership of the Central and Eastern European countries.

Up to now, we have mainly discussed cross-sectional methods of measuring child poverty and well-being. Yet, new cross-national studies illustrate the importance of measuring the duration of child poverty. Panel surveys such as the Panel Study of Income Dynamics (PSID) and the European Community Household Panel (ECHP) track the same families over time, which allows researchers to establish the proportion of children living in poverty over several consecutive years. Recently some cross-national results on child poverty dynamics were revealed, but unfortunately not in time to allow us to include them in this volume. However, we would like to refer readers to a recent study carried out by the UNICEF Innocenti Research Centre (Bradbury et al, 2000). This study indicates that poverty persists for many children, but also that poverty touches many more children over the years than the standard point-in-time snapshots reveal. It shows that in all six industrialised countries included in the study around six or seven out of every ten children found in the poorest fifth stay poor for at least two years. Between six and nine percent of all children are in the poorest fifth for five consecutive years. In the US and Germany five to six percent were even in the poorest fifth in each of ten consecutive years. It is clear that the perpetuation of poverty year after year for these children gives great cause for concern. Any successful anti-poverty strategy should pay particular attention to the long-term poor. Therefore attempts to study the dynamic aspects of child poverty should be encouraged.

A monitoring process should clearly be based on a range of poverty measures, including relative and absolute, monetary and non-monetary, cross-sectional and dynamic measures. It would be wrong to base a convergence process on one or even one single type of measure. Not only would a monitoring process be more reliable when based on a variety of measures, but this would also provide policy makers with a more complete description of poverty-related problems in their societies. Both the Irish and British governments seem to recognise this, as they are monitoring progress on the basis of a combination of measures, including both absolute and relative poverty measures, as well as direct measures of the living conditions of children.

Focal points for anti-poverty strategies in industrialised countries

Poverty benchmarking is of course but a first step on the road to the successful reduction of child poverty rates. A benchmark says where we want to go, but not how to get there. In order not to lose our way along the road, it is important that we identify the right policy tools needed to reach our goal. Unfortunately it is impossible to identify one single comprehensive anti-poverty policy for children that would be applicable in all industrialised countries. Every country has its own complex institutional traditions, values and environment, which would make any wholesale importation of a set of effective anti-poverty policies from another country. very difficult, if not impossible. However, some of the findings presented in this volume allow us to identify a few focal points for policy makers who are committed to the reduction of child poverty and the improvement of child well-being.

Parental employment, employability and earnings

No doubt, measures aimed at increasing the employment and earnings capacity of parents are key ingredients of any successful policy to reduce child poverty. Several contributions have indicated that there is a close relationship between child poverty and the percentage of households where there is no adult in work. Therefore, the most important step in reducing poverty among children is to ensure that at least one parent is in market employment. Especially the labour market position of mothers should be improved, as mothers' earnings are crucial for maintaining an adequate standard of living of households in a society where the dual-earner model has become prevalent. This is doubly true for single parents where there is only one person to act as both provider and caretaker. In order to optimise parental employment, governments need to increase the job demand for low-skilled workers and improve the employability of mothers.

Promoting employment. In many countries unemployment levels, especially among low-skilled workers, remain high despite improved levels of economic growth. Increasing the job demand for low-skilled workers is therefore an important pre-condition for any anti-poverty policy that aims at increasing the labour-force participation of mothers and workers in general. The European Employment Strategy that has been progressively designed since 1993 has focused on reducing non-wage labour costs, especially for low-skilled low-paid workers, and other measures designed to help groups particularly hit by unemployment. As the macroeconomic climate improved, it recommended exploiting this situation to further reduce taxes and charges on labour, which had been previously constrained by the need to consolidate public budgets, in order to foster a more job-intensive growth. When unemployment rates dropped in several EU member states, the European Employment Strategy started to put more emphasis on improving and updating the skills of workers, job counselling and the removal of various structural obstacles such as unemployment traps. In recent years, European governments have increasingly recognised the need for a more proactive, employment-centred social policy focusing on prevention and the reintegration of unemployment and assistance beneficiaries, including single parents. This can be explained by the need to reduce both supply shortages on the labour market and benefit expenditures, but also as a way to deal with poverty and social exclusion. Nevertheless, it should be clear that despite these measures, many people will remain outside the labour market because they are unable to acquire the necessary skills or because their social and health situation does not allow them to be reintegrated into the labour market. It remains, therefore, important that unemployment and other income-replacement benefit payments remain sufficiently high to prevent families that are not or only partially integrated into the labour market from sliding into poverty.

Parental leave and childcare support. In order to be employed, many parents, especially low-skilled mothers, need state support to facilitate that employment. According to several contributors to this volume, Sweden's low child poverty rates are the result of the integration of women – especially mothers in general and single mothers in particular – into the Swedish labour force. While cultural characteristics have influenced this situation, various contributors underline the importance of a configuration of welfare state policies that traditionally stress the importance of a (continued) attachment to the labour market, including the public provision of childcare and parental leave programmes that allow parents to smoothly re-enter the labour market after a period of caring for their young children.

The development of adequate parental leave programmes and childcare provisions are clearly an important condition for keeping mothers in full-time employment. Davies and Joshi report in this volume that the increased availability of childcare in Britain, as well as maternity leave and more family friendly enterprise policies, have increased the employment continuity of British women around the time of childbirth and thus reduced the indirect cost of children. They report that British women who could afford it increasingly made use of the availability of childcare services. As a result, "the direct cost of childcare is increasingly substituting for the indirect cost caused by self-provisioning" (Davies and Joshi). However, they also find that the direct cost of childcare services still proves to be too high for women with smaller earnings potential, as well as those with middle earnings potential and more than one child. It is one of the main reasons why these women are more likely to stay home to take care of their children.

It is clear that the introduction of comprehensive childcare provisions should be complemented by measures that make it possible for women with lower earnings potential to make use of these services. The greater the cost of childcare services relative to the mother's wage potential, the less likely it is that she will seek full-time employment. This is one of the explanations why employment rates among low-skilled women vary strongly between industrialised nations, while the employment rates among high-skilled women vary less and why the gap between both groups increases when they have to take care of young children (Cantillon et al, 2000). Therefore, it is important to introduce or expand public (support for) childcare services, aimed at reducing the direct cost of these services, as well as subsidies, such as refundable childcare tax-credits, which would (partially) compensate low-income families' expenditures for this type of service.

Many governments seem to have understood this message. In this volume, Kamerman and Kahn indicate that childcare services have continued to increase in supply during the 1990s, and many governments have extended parental leave where it existed and it was even newly introduced in a few countries. Nevertheless, not everybody seems convinced that the provision of adequate and affordable childcare should be the state's responsibility. In the 1998 Employment Guidelines, the European Commission stressed the importance of "an adequate provision of good quality care for children and other dependants in order to support women's entry and continued participation in the labour market" and called for member states to "raise levels of care provision, using the standards of the best performing Member States as a benchmark". Yet, the European Council of Ministers did not retain the proposed benchmark and opted for a much softer approach by stating that "the Member States will strive to raise levels of care provisions where some needs are not met". In 1998, US President Clinton also took an initiative to improve childcare for working families, proposing various measures to make childcare more affordable and to double the number of children receiving childcare subsidies to more than two million by the year 2003. Unfortunately, the US Congress prohibited most elements in the proposal from being turned into legislation.

The problem of low earnings and the working poor. Making families more dependent on market income might not be sufficient to end relative child poverty in a period of increased earnings inequality. Several contributors show that earnings are often not sufficient to protect households with children from poverty and, although children living in two-parent dual-earner families are far less likely to be poor, poverty rates among children living in working single-parent families remain relatively high. In recent years, several countries have introduced or increased minimum wages, but these often remain insufficient to keep households with children out of poverty. Yet, governments are reluctant to further increase the minimum wage levels in their countries because this would risk aggravating the unemployment problem faced by low-skilled workers. Since the expansion of low-wage work might improve the job prospects of less educated workers and make it easier for single-earner households to acquire a second income, we do not necessarily advocate higher minimum wages. It is, however, clear that many governments should do more to support the working poor in cases where wages are not sufficient to ensure a non-poor status for the family.

Supporting families with children

Child-related benefits. Certain governments may need to focus more resources on child-related benefits as a way of raising low-earning families with children from poverty. Although such programmes exist in most OECD countries, there is considerable variation in child-related benefit expenditures. In 1996, countries such as Luxembourg, Ireland, Finland and Denmark spent more than twelve percent of their social protection expenditures on family and child benefits, while Italy, the Netherlands and Spain spent less than five percent. Although total social protection expenditures increased in the EU as a percentage of GDP, the proportion of expenditure on family and child benefits decreased as a percentage of total social expenditure. However, because child populations have fallen in most countries, expenditures on family and child benefits per child still increased.

There is evidence for an increasing role for reduced taxes and refundable tax credits in the support given to low-income working-age households. Many OECD countries offer social tax-breaks and allowances to replace cash benefits, although they tend to be less important in countries with relatively high direct tax levies, such as Denmark, Finland, the Netherlands and Sweden (Adema, 1999). Social tax-breaks are prominent in Belgium, Germany and particularly in the US where the recent increase in their Earned Income Tax Credit (EITC) has made it the largest anti-poverty device for families with children in the otherwise meagre US anti-poverty arsenal. In Germany the value of tax allowances for the cost incurred in raising children alone amounted to almost 0.6% of the German GDP in 1993 (Adema and Einerhand, 1998). Both the Netherlands and the UK have specific tax-breaks for single-parent families and, as mentioned earlier, many countries also use tax credits to compensate expenditures such as childcare services. Yet, such measures often have less effect on the income of families with very low earnings, since their earnings are often too low to fully benefit from such measures. It is therefore important that tax credits for childcare and similar measures aimed at families with low earnings are made refundable. In some cases, it might be useful to pay advances on such tax refunds. In the US, some employers already seem to pay advances on tax refunds to some of their workers, but maybe this is something that should not be left to the discretion of an employer.

Various contributors to this volume describe the importance of child-related cash benefit programmes for reducing child poverty rates. Immervoll et al found that, within the EU, only households with children in Denmark and Luxembourg have sufficiently high-income levels without family benefits to protect them from poverty. However, family benefits proved to be vital for the protection of children from poverty in Austria, Belgium, France, the Netherlands and the UK, while family benefit levels are clearly too low in Ireland, Italy, Greece, Portugal and Spain to have an important effect on poverty rates among households with children. According to Oxley et al the payment of child-related benefits to working households with children is a way to increase both the efficiency and effectiveness of benefit systems. They found that child-related benefits are very effective in reducing poverty rates among children living in single-parent or two-parent households with insufficient earnings. However, the nature of child-related transfers varies considerably across countries: ranging from exclusively income tested benefits in the US to mainly flat-rate child benefits in a number of European countries, which means that the impact of child benefits on poverty can be very different from one country to another. In the case of means-tested child benefits, targeted at the poorest families, there is a clear danger of creating or intensifying unemployment traps, especially for workers with a low earnings potential. The introduction of specific means-tested in-work benefits for low-earning families with children is often thought to be a good way to deal with unemployment traps for low-skilled workers. However, these in-work benefits tend to discourage work effort and the search for better-paid jobs because of the high implicit marginal tax rates. As a result a poverty trap might replace the unemployment trap. Oxley et al also note that countries with higher benefit efficiency due to targeting traded a good part of this away by reducing spending. They observe that "countries with highly targeted systems (eg, the US and Australia) may need to increase spending in this area if they are to make progress in reducing child poverty". As for countries with high degrees of spending and low levels of poverty, they observe that "increased targeting at the margin provides a more efficient way of dealing with 'hard-core' poverty".

The collection of private child support. In the past twenty years the percentage of families headed by single parents increased in virtually all industrialised countries. Although Bradbury and Jäntti show that disparities in the percentage of single parent families do not explain variation in child poverty rates between countries, it remains a fact that children living in single-parent families are more likely to be poor than other children. While some countries provide specific benefits to single parent families, usually in the form of an assured child support benefit, recent efforts to improve the financial situation of these families have concentrated on improving the collection of private child support. Absent parents clearly have the responsibility of continuing to support their children, and this means that they should regularly pay child support as well as frequently contact their children. many embrace their responsibility, but it is clear that many others fail. Therefore enforcement measures are important, although their potential for reducing child poverty is limited as many of the parents who fail to pay child support are more likely to be low earners themselves (Garfinkel et al, 1998).

In this volume, Kunz et al analyse the trends in child support collections among seven OECD countries over the period 1980-95. In this period, several governments started to implement various measures to increase payment levels as well as the actual payment of private child support. Although the results indicate that these efforts might have been successful in Australia, they reveal that similar efforts have proved to be less successful in the UK and the US. In the UK, government experts have come to realise that enforcement measures implemented in the early 1990s had been badly designed. In the US, child support enforcement efforts had been effective among the never-married mothers, who needed it the most. Nevertheless, the rate of collections for this group of never married mothers remained relatively low, while their proportion among those eligible had increased. Thus, Kunz et al conclude that child support enforcement efforts in the US had been 'swimming upstream' and that the quantity and quality of child support payments would probably have been worse without these efforts.

Investment in a socially oriented education policy

In the wake of the 'knowledge society', the promotion of human capital has been established high up on the political agenda. Central to the promotion of human capital is of course the promotion of a socially oriented education policy, which would provide every child regardless of its financial or health situation access to quality education. Although this book does not evaluate education policies, some of the contributions show that such policies could be important in reducing the likelihood of poverty being passed on from generation to generation. Gregg and Machin's findings reveal that educational attainment is an important mechanism underpinning the link between financial distress faced during childhood and the subsequent economic success of individuals. In Germany, however, Büchel et al find a substantial portion of households among the poor who are able to keep educational options open to their children and, in doing so, can offer promising long-term perspectives to their children. Although the authors do not document the German school system, they consider their results to be an indication of Germany's successful socially oriented education policy. Yet, Frick and Wagner find that the children of immigrants in Germany are on a less favourable track than native-born German children. They conclude that there should be additional incentives for children born to immigrants to overcome language disadvantages.

A research agenda for the future

In recent years, economists, sociologists and social policy analysts have accelerated their study of the extent and trends of child poverty and well-being, its consequences for children and the adequacy of public policy in preventing child poverty. The emergence of cross-nationally comparable data on the composition of incomes and household structure (eg the Luxembourg Income Study) and on child outcomes has supported this literature. The various chapters in this volume contain many valuable insights for policy makers, but also identify some items that deserve to be put on the research agendas of academics and think-tanks interested in similar issues.

It seems that efforts by policy makers to implement poverty benchmarks will have to be based on a variety of direct and indirect poverty measures. Researchers could contribute by developing and evaluationg measures that could best serve their purposes. Especially on an international level, more work could be done on absolute poverty measures and direct deprivation measures that could be used in cross-national monitoring processes. Eurostat, the EU statistical agency, has already made some progress in this domain. Furthermore, researchers could contribute by determining which set or combination of measures might be best suited for monitoring processes.

More work is also needed on the multifaceted consequences of child poverty in the long term. Various contributions in this volume have shown that children from poor households are more likely to have low educational achievement, lower wages and health problems in adulthood. However, many factors are at play and it is not always clear if this is due to factors such as low parental education or weak parenting skills often associated with low income but not necessarily caused by it. Research in the UK and the US does seem to confirm that childhood poverty has a genuine impact on a wide range of future events, but the impact is often less severe than expected. However, the total impact when summed across various outcomes could be much larger.

One of the continuing problems researchers face is the lack of data. Very few countries have the data necessary to track children through later life. Many other research themes are also restricted by the limited availability of data. Although new international databases such as the

European Community Household Panel and the World Health Organisation's cross-national 'Health Behaviour in School-Aged Children' Study (HBSC) have recently become available, many researchers still have the need for suitable and accessible data high on their research agenda. No doubt the desire of many governments to monitor the development of poverty in their societies will provide the necessary incentives and means to fulfil at least some of their wishes.

Conclusion

While additional research will undoubtedly be useful to policy makers, the case for the formulation, implementation and improvement of an anti-poverty strategy focused on families with children can already be made. All the contributors to this book underline the need for a comprehensive policy to reduce child poverty rates and improve the well-being of children. The human capital argument provides a strong argument for governments to invest more in the well-being of their children. Child poverty might increase the proportion of poorly qualified persons in the future workforce, which could lead to labour market difficulties and may have detrimental effects on national economies as a whole. We therefore agree with Kamerman and Kahn that the human capital concerns in industrialised countries offer an "overwhelming and very practical case for adequate investment in our next generations".

In recent years, there are encouraging signs of increased public attention for the issue of child poverty and well-being, both in Europe and the US. The renewed commitment in various EU member states to reduce (child) poverty rates has already resulted in clear poverty reductions, while a system of indicators on poverty and social exclusion has been established on an EU level. In the US, child poverty rates have dropped considerably since 1993 and are currently at their lowest level since 1979. Although these results are sometimes seen as a result of the 1996 welfare reform, they are also influenced by a decade-long economic boom. In 2001, the decrease in child poverty rates stagnated while the overall poverty rate increased. Unemployment rates are currently up and, if the current recession lasts, a rise in child poverty rates is again at risk. There are also reports that the number of children estimated to live in extreme poverty has increased since the 1996 welfare reform. Meanwhile in Canada, Campaign 2000 wants to revive the original 1989 all-party House of Commons resolution to end child poverty in Canada by the year 2000, since the aim of the decade-old resolution had not been realised. This should be a warning signal to citizens in other countries that politicians and their policy must be monitored closely in order to verify the realisation of their promises.

Nevertheless, we sincerely hope that more governments will commit themselves to the elimination of child poverty in their countries because of our conviction that it is the fundamental task of any democracy to provide an equal opportunity from birth to every child born under its wings. Especially in the affluent economies of the industrialised world, there are no valid excuses to prevent governments from having a low child poverty rate. The realisation of this goal will merely contribute to the integrity of our democratic values and enrich the cultural and economic fabric of our societies.

Notes

Also from the conference: Bradbury, B., Jenkins, S. and J. Micklewright (2000) 'The dynamics of child poverty in industrialized countries', Innocenti Working Paper 78 (available from www.unicef-icdc.org). This paper is also a chapter in a forthcoming book with the same title and by the same authors, to be published in 2001 by Cambridge University Press.

[1] Although the idea is based on both the 1992 recommendation of the European Commission (92/441/EEC) to adopt minimum income standards to respect human dignity and combat social exclusion, and the 1995 UN Copenhagen Agreement about the desirability of defining and measuring 'absolute' and 'overall' poverty in every country, as a basis for drawing up national plans for the eradication of poverty. Both the declaration and the programme of the UN Copenhagen Agreement was signed by 117 heads of state and 100 European scientists signed a statement to carry this commitment forward.

[2] Soft-law instruments are legally speaking not enforceable. In case the person/ member state does not follow it up, no legal sanction can be taken.

References

Adema, W (1999) *Net social expenditure*, Labour Market and Social Policy Occasional Paper Number 32, Paris: OECD.

Adema, W. and Einerhand, M. (1998) *The growing role of private social benefits*, Labour Market and Social Policy Occasional Paper Number 32, Paris: OECD.

Atkinson, A.B. (1999) 'Macroeconomics and the social dimension', Background paper for the Preparatory Committeee for the Special Session of the UN General Assembly as a follow-up to the Copenhagen World Summit for Social Development (available from www.nuff.ox.ac.uk/users/atkinson/).

Atkinson, A.B. (2000) *A European social agenda: Poverty benchmarking and social transfers*, Euromod Working Paper No EM3/00, (available from www.econ.cam.ac.uk/dae/mu/emod.htm).

Cantillon, B., Ghysels, J., Thirion, A., Mussche, N. and Van Dam, R. (2000) *Emancipatie in twee snelheden: over hoog- en laaggeschoolde vrouwen in 13 OESO-Landen,* CSB Bericht (available from www.ufsia.ac.be/csb/bericht.htm).

Commission of the European Communities (1994) 'The demographic situation of the European Union', Document No. COM(94) 595 final. Luxembourg: Office for Official Publications of the European Communities.

Eurostat (1998) *Recommendations of the Task Force on Statistics on Social Exclusion and Poverty*, Luxembourg: Office for the Official Publications of the European Communities.

Garfinkel, I., Mclanahan, S., Meyer, D. and Selzer, J. (1998) *Fathers under fire*, New York, NY: Russell Sage Foundation.

Rainwater, L. and Smeeding, T.M. (1995) *Doing poorly: The real income of children in a comparative perspective*, LIS Working Paper No 127, Luxembourg Income Study (available from www.lis.ceps.lu).

Vandenbroucke, F. (1999) 'The active welfare state: a European ambition', 'Den Uyl' lecture, Amsterdam.

Index

A

D

E

F

G

H

I

J

K

M

N

O

P

Q

R

S

U

V

W

Y

Z